English Poetry
of the Second World War

English Poetry
of the Second World War

A Biobibliography

Catherine W. Reilly

G. K. HALL & CO.

70 LINCOLN STREET, BOSTON, MASS.

Published 1986 in the United States of America and Canada by
G. K. Hall & Co., 70 Lincoln Street, Boston, Massachusetts 02111,
U.S.A.

Published 1986 by Mansell Publishing Limited
(A subsidiary of the H. W. Wilson Company)
6 All Saints Street, London N1 9RL, England

Library of Congress Cataloging in Publication Data

Reilly, Catherine W.
  English poetry of the Second World War.

  Includes indexes.
  1. English poetry—20th century—Bio-bibliography.
2. World War, 1939–1945—Poetry—Bibliography.
3. English poetry—Commonwealth of Nations authors—
Bio-bibliography. 4. Poets, English—20th century—
Biography. I. Title.
Z2014.P7R45 1986   016.821′91408   85-21650
[PR605.W66]
ISBN 0-8161-8819-X

Printed and bound in Great Britain

Contents

Acknowledgements   vi

Introduction   vii

Bibliographical Notes   xv

Bibliography of Biographical Sources   xxiii

Abbreviations   xxvi

Key to Library Locations   xxviii

Anthologies   1

Index to Anthologies   18

Individual Authors   21

Title Index   365

War poets of other English speaking nations   391

Acknowledgements

I acknowledge, with gratitude, the help of the following while preparing this work: John L. Fuller and R. Julian Roberts; the administrators of the J.C. Maxwell Memorial Fund, for the award of a travel grant; the librarians and staffs of all the libraries visited in the course of my research.

Introduction

War, like love, is a constant theme in poetry. In English literature the terms 'war poet' and 'war poetry' were first applied during the Great War, 1914–1918, and referred particularly to the poetry and verse written by the soldier-poets who served in the trenches of France and Flanders. In actuality the soldier-poets, including those combatants serving in other branches of the armed forces, were in the minority as the vast proportion of poetry and verse written on the theme of the First World War was written by civilians. The bibliography of English poetry of the First World War which was published in 1978 and covers publications issued between 1914 and 1970, lists 2,225 poets, only 417 of whom are known to have served in the armed forces or other uniformed organizations such as the Red Cross.[1] This was the first bibliographical study that attempted to quantify the poetry and verse of the First World War. The results were not unexpected as it was always known that there was a remarkable quantity of poetry and verse, of variable quality, published on the theme of this most terrible war.

Because of the delayed nature of poetry publication it was considered essential to cover items published over a fair period of time after the war in this last study and so also in the present study. It might take a poet several years to gather sufficient material to fill a volume and it could take even longer to secure publication; the work of established poets is constantly being updated by new editions; an 'amateur' poet might wait until late in life to pay for his work to be published by a vanity press.

This present study covers 3,072 separate publications, including eighty-seven anthologies, issued during the years 1939–1980. It identifies 2,679 poets (although some only be pseudonym or initials), 831 of whom are known to have served in the armed forces or other uniformed organizations such as the National Fire Service. One might expect that there would be more poetry published on the theme of the Second World War because of the expansion in the publishing trade during the twenty-one years that separated the wars, and because of the greater number of people personally affected by the war in terms of personal danger. Both men and women were subject to call-up for the

Services or for civilian warwork, and the entire population of the United Kingdom was at risk, to a greater or lesser degree, from enemy action raids. However, the received view appears to be that there were more poets of the First World War. The reverse is now proved and is further reinforced by the fact that this study covers only forty-one years of publications as opposed to the fifty-seven years of publications covered by the First World War study. Another factor to be taken into account is the minimal number of cards and broadsides featuring war poetry published during the Second World War. They are a particular feature in the First World War bibliography and account for a substantial number of poets being listed. The cards, often postcards, are small enough to be carried in the pocket or in a soldier's paybook. Although slight and often trivial items, they were included in the first bibliography because they are typical of the period and are now quite rare.

Of the 831 poets listed here who are known to have been in the uniformed services, 780 are men and 51 are women. Of the 780 men, 373 served in the Army and of these, 30 were killed and 33 taken prisoner of war; 115 served in the Royal Air Force and one in the Air Transport Auxiliary and of these, 21 were killed and four taken prisoner of war; 77 served in the Royal Navy and of these, four were killed and two taken prisoner of war; six served in the Merchant Navy and of these, one was killed; 176 served in an unspecified branch of the armed services and of these, five were taken prisoner of war. A further 32 served in a branch of civil defence, which includes the National Fire Service, Air Raid Precautions and the Home Guard. A few men had served in civil defence before joining the armed services, while Michael Croft served successively in the Royal Air Force and the Royal Navy, and Ian Gomersall served for a short time in the Royal Navy, was discharged on health grounds then joined the Merchant Navy. The latter two are counted here as members of the Service in which they spent most time — Croft in the Royal Navy, Gomersall in the Merchant Navy. Just one civilian became a prisoner of war. Alex Potter, who had served as an infantry officer in the First World War, was on the staff of the *Continental Daily Mail* in France and was interned in Saint-Denis camp for four years.

Of the 51 women, ten served in the Auxiliary Territorial Service, eight in the Women's Auxiliary Air Force, six in the Women's Royal Naval Service, one in the Territorial Army Nursing Service, three in an unspecified branch of the women's services, 13 in the Women's Land Army and the remaining ten in a branch of civil defence, including two in the Women's Voluntary Service.

One hundred and thirty-five of the poets, men and women, wrote poetry and verse on the theme of both World Wars and so are featured in both bibliographies. Eighty-eight of the men saw active service during the First World War, Theodore Stephanides in the Greek Artillery on the Macedonian front from 1917 to 1918. Stephanides also did military service in the Second World War, as did John Blanford, Gilbert Frankau, Herbert Greene, Ian Horobin, William James, Gerard Durani Martineau, Vivian de Sola Pinto and Alexander Wilmot Uloth.

The following list of poets, selected at random, illustrates the wide diversity of non-literary occupations followed: William George Archer, museum keeper; Joan Barton, bookshop owner; Swinfen Bramley-Moore, mechanical engineer; John Cromer Braun, solicitor; George Wallace Briggs, Church of England canon; David Burnett, university librarian; William Henry Charnock, civil engineer; Herbert Corby, civil servant; John Cotton, comprehensive school headmaster; Harry Cross, college servant; Leslie Davison, Methodist minister; Stewart Deas, orchestra conductor; Audrey Field, film censor; George Rostrevor Hamilton, income tax commissioner; Henry Ernest Hardy (Father Andrew), Roman Catholic priest; Richard Harris, actor; Frank Ivor Hauser, drama producer; Adrian Head, circuit judge; Cyril Hodges, industrial manufacturer; Geoffrey Holloway, social worker; George Leslie Lister, further education adviser; James Monahan, Royal Ballet School director; John Normanton, textile worker; Richard Caton Ormerod, diplomat; Frederic James Osborn, town planner; Edith Pickthall, midwife; Enoch Powell, M.P.; Rosamond Praeger, professional artist and illustrator; John Rimington, advertising executive; Ivor Roberts-Jones, sculptor; Patricia Mary St. John, missionary nurse; Frederick Henry Shilcock, inn landlord; David Stafford-Clark, psychiatrist; Ronald B. Wilcock, trade union worker; Arnold Wilkes, banker; Darrell Wilkinson, consultant dermatologist; William Wolff, chartered accountant.

The biographical data, although incomplete in many instances, reveal some interesting facts. Some 513 poets were university-educated. This figure precludes those who received other higher education not leading to a degree, in the professions which now usually require graduate entrance, for example, teaching, librarianship, etc. Of the 513 university students, 222 attended the University of Oxford, 133 attended the University of Cambridge, while the remaining 158 attended various other universities. Two hundred and thirty poets worked in the teaching profession at some time, in universities, polytechnics, colleges and schools.

It will be seen that poetry regarded as good enough for publication is written by many, not just those working in the literary field. Few poets, even those of the highest merit and standing, can make a living out of poetry by sales of their books alone. The 'working poet' or 'full-time poet' is a comparatively recent phenomenon. While publishing his own collections and contributing to magazines and anthologies, he does freelance editing, runs poetry workshops, acts as poetry tutor at residential courses, judges local poetry competitions, travels the country talking about his work, gives poetry readings and may contribute to poetry programmes on radio and television, but it is indisputable that the vast majority of poets depends on other occupations for a livelihood.

The publishing of poetry is a high risk venture in monetary terms. Dominant publishing houses such as Jonathan Cape Ltd, Chatto & Windus Ltd, Faber & Faber Ltd, William Heinemann Ltd, Hutchinson & Co., Oxford University Press, and Sidgwick & Jackson Ltd have always published poetry successfully but perhaps with minimal financial profit on occasions. Once regarded as the poor relation of literature, poetry has experienced a sales boom during the last few years. Matthew Evans, Chairman of Faber & Faber, the leading publishers of poetry, is quoted as saying 'It's phenomenal. We're selling more poetry now than at any time in the last 15 years. The latest Ted Hughes has sold 35,000. Seumas Heaney has sold 25,000 copies so far. The last two years have been a terrific period'.[2]

In recent years, the smaller imprints specializing in poetry, such as the Carcanet Press of Manchester and Harry Chambers of Liskeard, Cornwall, have succeeded in keeping economically viable. This may be due in part to the financial subsidies awarded by the Arts Council of Great Britain and the regional Arts Associations but the history of poetry publication in the middle of the twentieth century is often a sad one of failed companies and lost money. The post-war period saw the demise of the Fortune Press (whose authors had included Gavin Ewart, Roy Fuller, Francis Scarfe, Dylan Thomas and Henry Treece) along with the Falcon Press, Grey Walls Press, Parton Press and others. One publishing venture which lasted only two years, 1951 and 1952, was the Poems in Pamphlet series under the editorship of Erica Marx and published by her Hand and Flower Press at Aldington, Kent. Each pamphlet appeared monthly and was devoted to the work of a writer hitherto not published in book form in England. All were printed in the same attractive format at the Ditchling Press, Sussex, on mould-made rag paper, and could be obtained in single numbers from booksellers at 1*s*. (5p) or by annual subscription at 14*s*. 6*d* (72½p). The series introduced the poetry of Thomas Blackburn, Charles Causley and Michael Hamburger, among others, for the first time in book form.

It is now recognized that there was a wartime increase in the reading of poetry, as there was in every kind of literature. The general popularity of reading was a characteristic of the war, when normal social and family life was severely disrupted. There were long spells of enforced inactivity when people had time to spare, sitting in barracks, in ships at sea, in air raid shelters waiting for the 'all clear', and in remote places where nothing momentous was likely to occur. The public libraries were never so busy, and special libraries for servicemen were established by the military authorities. People read anything and everything and it is more than likely that poetry was read by those who had never read it before and would never read it again.

The decision to extend the coverage of this biobibliography to the largest possible time span of publication has been justified. Only 1,040 items (48 anthologies and 992 individual authors' works) out of the total 3,072 items included were actually published during the war, the remaining 2,032 items (i.e. 66 per cent) being published after the war. To restrict the work to wartime publications only would have resulted in a false assessment of the poetry of the Second World War.

The majority of the publications listed here were published by publishers operating from London but a surprising number of publishers (221) were based elsewhere in the United Kingdom. The history of these provincial publishers of poetry could itself become the subject of a detailed study. The following table gives a breakdown of locations. The list covers private press material but excludes the privately printed and vanity press material. Publishers based in England are listed by county, using the pre-1974 county names, as most items were published before that date. In cases where a publisher changed address, the later location is given. The location of foreign publishers is added to complete the picture:

Bedfordshire, 1
Berkshire, 7
Buckinghamshire, 1
Cambridgeshire, 5
Cheshire, 2
Cornwall, 2
Derbyshire, 4
Devonshire, 4
Durham, 2
Essex, 8
Gloucestershire, 4
Hampshire, 7
Hertfordshire, 7
Kent, 8
Lancashire, 10
Leicestershire, 3
Lincolnshire, 3
Middlesex, 5
Monmouthshire, 2
Norfolk, 1
Northamptonshire, 1
Northumberland, 3
Nottinghamshire, 5
Oxfordshire, 15
Shropshire, 2
Somerset, 6
Staffordshire, 2
Suffolk, 5

Surrey, 5
Sussex, 9
Warwickshire, 5
Westmorland, 1
Wiltshire, 3
Worcestershire, 4
Yorkshire, 15
Guernsey, 2
Jersey, 1
Northern Ireland, 6
Scotland, 30
Wales, 15
Argentina, 1
Australia, 4
Canada, 2
Denmark, 1
Egypt, 1
France, 2
India, 3
Irish Republic, 14
Italy, 2
Japan, 1
Singapore, 1
South Africa, 1
Switzerland, 1
Tunisia, 1
Turkey, 1
United States, 26

The instinct to write verse is common to many people including those with minimum literary talent, and certainly some of the material listed here is of poor literary quality. Vanity publishers, who produce and market books at an author's risk and expense, have always done well with poetry from a business point of view. One such publisher is Arthur H. Stockwell Ltd of Ilfracombe, Devonshire, whose output accounts for 532 of the items. The firm was established in 1898 in the St Paul's area of the City of London and remained there until the premises were bombed in 1940. It should be said that they appear to exercise some degree of editorial control so what they publish is of a reasonable standard. Indeed, they have published the work of such literary figures as R.E.S. Bruce, who edited *Literary Quarterly*, Roland Mathias, who edited *The Anglo-Welsh Review*, Desmond Stewart, one time Assistant Professor of English at the University of Baghdad, and the poet Jon Silkin. Such publishers do provide a service to impatient poets in a field of publishing that is notoriously difficult.

The poorest quality verse is some of that privately published by local newspaper presses and by jobbing printers yet, strangely, this verse is sometimes extremely moving. In wartime the impetus to publish one's verse was often brought about by the death in action of a relative or friend. These verses, often incompetently crafted and mawkish in their sentimentality, arouse the same kind of pity one feels when reading the 'In Memoriam' columns of local newspapers. Bereavement can bestow a certain pathos and dignity on even the most inferior verse. In fairness, it should be stated that not all locally printed material is of poor quality. Presentation items, such as Christmas cards, bearing original verses by established poets were often printed locally.

Literature, especially poetry, that most sensitive of instruments, mirrors the society from which it springs. Even in the more pedestrian verse the social and military historian will find a rich harvest of comment on the war which, as time passes, will assume a greater importance as a record of history. An account of a wartime incident in verse with careful choice of words and language can be more graphic than a longer prose account of the same incident. However, apparent autobiographical clues in the poems must be regarded with a great deal of caution. Poetic licence often results in the transferred voice — poets writing in the imagined role of perhaps a Battle of Britain pilot or a concentration camp victim.

It is disappointing to have found so little poetry and verse written by Channel Islanders who suffered the German occupation. Equally disappointing is the dearth of foreign-printed material written by members of the armed services stationed abroad — pamphlet items such as the leaflets by T.I.F. Armstrong (John Gawsworth) which were printed in Italy and North Africa. Possibly many such items are deposited in regimental museums but it is regrettable that so few are to be found in our national libraries.

It is always difficult to trace poems on a particular theme, unless one can find anthologies that contain poems specifically on that theme. Granger's and other poetry indexes are helpful but, as they have been compiled from a limited number of anthologies, they tend to list only the best known poems by the best known poets. The main volume of Granger, which is the standard work used in most reference libraries, lists 74 poems by 56 authors (one of whom is anonymous) on the theme of the Second World War.[3] As it is an American publication, only the following English poets are represented: W.H. Auden, John Betjeman (two poems), Charles Causley, Keith Douglas, Roy Fuller, David Gascoyne (two poems), John Lehmann, Eiluned Lewis, Roy Macnab, Louis MacNeice (two poems), Herbert Read and Stephen Spender. The supplementary volume adds only two more English poets — A.P. Herbert and

Olga Katzin (Sagittarius) together with another poem by John Betjeman.[4] Clearly, Granger presents a random selection, based as it is on a limited number of anthologies, mainly American. One is, nevertheless, surprised by the absence of poets of such stature as Sidney Keyes, Alun Lewis, F.T. Prince, John Pudney, Henry Reed, Alan Rook, Edith Sitwell and Dylan Thomas.

The anthologies listed in this present work are mainly British publications, so a different picture emerges. The following are the most anthologized poets, the number in brackets after each name denoting the number of anthologies of the total 87 in which their work appears: Roy Fuller (25), Alun Lewis (24), Sidney Keyes (21), Stephen Spender (19), Keith Douglas (18), John Pudney (18), Alan Rook (17), Louis MacNeice (15), Henry Reed (15), W.H. Auden (14), G.S. Fraser (14), Dylan Thomas (14), John Waller (14), Emanuel Litvinoff (13), Henry Treece (13), Cecil Day Lewis (12), Herbert Corby (11), Nicholas Moore (11).

It seems that successive war poetry anthologists tend to perpetuate the original selection of poems chosen by earlier anthologists. A would-be anthologist will already know the names and reputations of the principal war poets. He can turn to the various editions of their works and perhaps make his own selection, after which his most natural source of new material would be the periodicals of the time and the existing collections compiled by other anthologists. As these anthologists will probably already have culled the best material from the periodicals, he will find his choice limited and very little that is new. Even though he may be allowed access to one of the copyright libraries, the sheer quantity of books available is daunting and he would be fortunate indeed to discover worthwhile material on the basis of chance.

This biobibliography, listing some 2,679 poets who have contributed to 2,985 individual listed works and 87 anthologies, gives access to an extremely large number of poems on the theme of the Second World War. Some individual poems are, of course, reproduced in more than one volume but, even so, the total number of war poems involved is likely to be several thousand. Until now nobody has known the extent of the corpus of Second World War poetry. Even an enthusiast of the poetry of the war would be hard-pressed to name 100 war poets. Inevitably, much good poetry has been overlooked. Outstanding literary merit is usually recognized immediately by critics and reading public alike, which means that the major poets are already well known and valued, as are some lesser poets also. The rest are consigned to obscurity on library shelves unless 'rediscovered' by the vagaries of chance. Only the kind of exhaustive bibliographical research that has resulted in this present study, involving as it does the systematic examination of the actual books, can reveal exactly what has been published over the years. Using this work it has been possible for the bibliographer to follow a special interest by editing an anthology of women's poetry and verse of the Second World War, consisting largely of little-known material.[5]

The themes of the poems and verses of the Second World War are as wide-ranging and divergent as the war itself. The main incidents of the war in all its phases are well-recorded, for example Dunkirk, the Battle of Britain, El Alamein, Monte Cassino, the Battle of the Atlantic, Stalingrad, Burma, D-Day, Arnhem and many others. The poems concerned with the bombing of civilian populations are legion: most frequently found are poems on the bombing of London and other British cities, and on the atomic bombs dropped on Hiroshima and Nagasaki. The groups of people written about most consistently are evacuees, refugees, concentration camp victims, Nazi stormtroopers, prisoners of war (especially those held by the Japanese) and air pilots. The leading figures of the war (Churchill, Stalin, Roosevelt, Hitler, Mussolini, Montgomery, Mountbatten, Rommel and others) are the subject of many poems. The war is depicted in all its theatres, at sea, in the air and on the ground.

Throughout the war, servicemen were drafted overseas to British bases in exotic countries like India and Egypt, where the sights, sounds and smells of the alien cultures affected all of them in some measure. The poets among them were soon stimulated by the strangeness of the atmosphere in these places, despite the burden of heat, flies and monsoon rains. A new kind of war poetry emerged. The poets wrote of the fighting, the waiting, the boredom and the routines of military life but they also described the foreign lands where they were stationed in vivid and imaginative language. Much of the poetry inspired by the war deals with personal involvement, the sense of loss or longing, or it describes the emotions felt during a time of action. The incidents of war did not make the poetry; the poetry was made by the poets' honest responses. The work of the major poets is characterized by a cool control and economy of language which suggests that the poets of the Second World War were more worldly-wise, sophisticated and far less idealistic than their counterparts in that earlier war.

The poetry of the Second World War has not yet attracted as much literary and critical attention as that of the First World War but it is a popular misconception that the poetry of the second war is inferior to that of the first. A more accurate assessment would be that the First World War produced some outstanding poetry by a relatively small number of poets, while the Second World War produced a great deal more good poetry. More academic attention focused on these later poets would surely reap a rich reward.

Notes

1. Catherine W. Reilly, *English Poetry of the First World War: a bibliography*. London, George Prior Publishers, 1978, p. xix.
2. Hunter Davies, 'Heavyweight Champions'. *The Sunday Times*, 7 Feb. 1982, p. 13, column 4.
3. *Granger's Index to Poetry*. 6th ed. completely revised and enlarged. Edited by William James Smith. New York, Columbia University Press, 1973. pp. 2220–1.
4. *Granger's Index to Poetry, 1970–1977*. Edited by William James Smith. New York, Columbia University Press, 1978. p. 634.
5. Catherine W. Reilly, ed. *Chaos of the Night: Women's Poetry and Verse of the Second World War*. London, Virago Press, 1984.

Bibliographical Notes

Scope

This biobibliography lists works containing poetry and verse on the theme of the Second World War, 1939–1945, written by English poets (i.e. poets of England, Ireland, Scotland and Wales) both servicemen and civilians, and published during the years 1939–1980. The work of foreign nationals writing in English is included if they served in the British armed forces or if they had some other particular connection with the United Kingdom. Many American and Commonwealth poets had settled in Britain even before the war and so have a place in this biobibliography. Poets of the Irish Republic, a neutral nation in the war, are featured here by virtue of having written about the war, so identifying themselves with it. Indeed, many Irish-born poets retained strong family and cultural links with the United Kingdom long after the founding of the Republic.

The bibliographical research for this study has been carried out at the Bodleian Library, University of Oxford, at the British Library, London, at the Imperial War Museum, London, at Birmingham Central Library, the repository of a unique and important war poetry collection, and at Manchester Central Library, which is especially rich in twentieth century poetry. The research has involved the close examination of several thousand volumes of poetry and verse published from the outbreak of war in September 1939 to the end of 1980, a span of more than forty-one years. The scope is confined to printed material in the form of book, pamphlet, card, or broadside. The British Library printed catalogue attempts to categorize each volume of poetry as either 'poems' or 'verses', a difficult distinction to make in many cases. Here the generic term 'poem' is used throughout.

Many war poems were first published in newspapers and other periodicals, indeed some were only ever published in this form. Periodicals are excluded here, apart from certain annually published anthologies, as in practice the vast majority of periodical publications (either the original copies or microfilmed copies) can be examined at the British Library at Colindale and at the largest university and public libraries. Given the comparative ease of access to periodical publications, which are usually bound in volumes with adequate indexes, this study concentrates instead on those items on the shelves of library stacks, away from public view and only accessible when the name of an author is known.

Arrangement

The biobibliography is in two main parts: Anthologies, followed by an index of compilers, editors, illustrators and writers of forewords, introductions and prefaces; and Individual Authors, followed by a title index.

The symbol in capital letters at the end of each entry in both parts denotes the particular library where the item has been seen but by no means implies that this is the only library holding a copy. *See* Key to Library Locations for a complete list of symbols used.

A version of a standard library catalogue entry is used, the data given being sufficient to identify any item easily. The information in each entry is given in the following sequence: title, sub-title; editor, compiler, etc.; edition if other than the first; place of publication if other than London; publisher, or printer in the absence of a publisher's name; date of publication; pagination; illustrations; series; annotations.

The system of alphabetization used throughout is 'word by word' or 'nothing before something'. For filing purposes the definite or indefinite article at the beginning of a title is ignored. Surnames with the prefix 'Saint' are filed in one single sequence, no matter whether the prefix is in the form 'Saint' or 'St'. Scottish surnames with the prefix 'Mac' are filed in one single sequence, no matter whether the prefix is in the form 'Mac' or 'Mc'.

The place of publication is London unless otherwise stated. The form of publisher's name given on the front of the title-page is preferred although this can be inconsistent and vary from book to book. For the sake of brevity in company names the following abbreviations are employed: '&' replaces 'and'; 'Co.' replaces 'Company'; 'Ltd' replaces 'Limited'. The definite article is omitted where it precedes the name of a publishing house, (e.g. Fortune Press not The Fortune Press).

When the date of publication is not printed inside the book, the supposed publication date is given, in square brackets, from allusions in the text or from outside sources such as bibliographies and library catalogues. If there is some doubt about the supposed date this is indicated by a question mark, (e.g. [1943?]).

The number of pages in single volume works is given in Arabic numerals, counting the colophon page, if any. Preliminary matter is usually separately paged by means of Roman numerals. The pagination is thus recorded, (e.g. xvi, 92 pp.). Unnumbered pages are given in square brackets with certain exceptions: when there are blank pages between the preliminary matter and the text, these pages are counted in the pagination of the preliminary matter; when the final page of text, sometimes a colophon page, is unnumbered as is often the case, it is counted in the pagination of the text.

When a book belongs to a series, the name of the series is given in curved brackets at the end of the entry, followed by the serial number, if any, e.g. (Penguin poets, D100).

Anthologies

This is necessarily a selective list. Every anthology covering twentieth century poetry from 1939 onwards includes at least one or two examples of Second World War poetry.

Each of the 87 anthologies included here has been selected for one or more of the following reasons: it covers Second World War poetry exclusively, often bringing together poems by members of a particular branch of the uniformed services; it contains a section of Second World War poetry, often distinctively titled; it covers war poetry of all periods including that of the Second World War; it was published during or soon after the Second World War and so contains a preponderance of Second World War poetry; it contains relevant contributions by poets not represented elsewhere; it represents the Second World War poetry of a local element, (e.g. 54. POETRY FROM OXFORD IN WARTIME), of a regional element, (e.g. 2. An ANTHOLOGY OF CONTEMPORARY NORTHERN POETRY), or of a particular group of people, (e.g. 20. FOR YOUR TOMORROW: an anthology of poetry written by young men from English public schools who fell in the World War, 1939–1945).

Anthologies containing both poetry and prose are included only when the poetry contribution is substantial and/or significant. Omitted are the volumes of consolatory verse specifically designed to comfort those bereaved by the war. This verse was usually of a religious or spiritual nature and made no mention of the war. Also omitted are the volumes of patriotic verse consisting of poetry taken from other periods and other wars.

Entries in this section are arranged in alphabetical order of title, capitalized, and are numbered consecutively. Appended is an index containing the names of compilers, editors, illustrators, writers of forewords, introductions and prefaces who feature in the entries. These names are arranged in alphabetical order and are followed by the anthology number(s) to which they refer.

Contributors to each anthology are listed in alphabetical order of surname after the main entry. The names of American and Commonwealth poets who are represented in some of these anthologies are omitted, only English poets and those few American and Commonwealth poets who come within the purview of this study being listed. Only initials of forenames are given here but full names, where ascertained, are given in the Individual Authors sections, in which all contributors to the anthologies are listed.

Individual Authors

This is a single alphabetical sequence in author order, then title order of individual works. followed by a 'see also' reference to the serial number(s) of the specific anthology or anthologies from the Anthologies section in which a poet's work is represented. The latter gives a fair indication of the popularity of a particular poet, or at least the popularity of a particular poet with anthologists. Some poets are only represented in the anthologies and in these cases a 'see' reference is made to the appropriate anthologies. Anonymous works are listed under title. Works in more than one volume are given separate entries when the individual volumes have distinctive titles.

The amount of war poetry in each item varies considerably. Each work listed is either a single war poem or is a volume of poems containing at least one example of war poetry. The sub-title '[poems]' is used where the title of a collection *is not* the title of a specific poem, while the phrase '[and other poems]' is used where the title *is* that of a specific poem. When these devices are not used the implication is that the work consists of only one poem (long or short) bearing that title.

Occasionally the work of two or more poets is contained in the same volume. If each poet represented in the volume has contributed war poetry then the same volume is listed under each poet's name. More often than not it is found that the poets have not collaborated in their work so this fact is indicated by the phrase 'Not joint authorship' as an annotation after each entry.

American editions of the work of important poets such as W.H. Auden and Edith Sitwell are to be found in the British Library and the Bodleian Library, Oxford. These editions are included here, even though they may be re-issues or sheets from British editions bound with American publishers' title-pages. Often the American edition may precede the British but in either case it is useful to know that both editions are available.

Nowadays poetry is often published simultaneously in hardback and paperback format, identical in every aspect apart from the binding. In these circumstances only one entry is made. When the paperback edition is published at a later date this later date is incorporated in the book, thus making it technically a new edition, and so a separate entry is made.

Authors' names are given in their most complete form as found in the bibliographical sources consulted, followed by any pseudonyms or other forms of names used. Cross references are given from all alternative forms of name to the form of name selected here, the author's real name being preferred. When the name given on a title-page is other than an author's real name, then the pseudonym is repeated in the entry, (e.g. GRIEVE, Christopher Murray, (Hugh MacDiarmid, pseud.) *The battle continues*; by Hugh MacDiarmid). Every pseudonym is placed alphabetically in sequence and is followed by a cross reference to the author's real name, (e.g. MacDIARMID, Hugh, pseud. *see* GRIEVE, Christopher Murray, (Hugh MacDiarmid, pseud.)).

Noblemen are listed under their family name with a cross reference from their title, no matter which form of name appears on the title-page, e.g. GUINNESS, Bryan, Lord Moyne (author writes as Bryan Guinness); and PLUNKETT, Edward John Moreton Drax, Lord Dunsany (author wrote as Lord Dunsany).

Married women are listed under either their maiden name or their married name, depending on which form of name was used most consistently in their publications, with appropriate cross references given.

Double-barrelled hyphenated names, (e.g. CRAWSHAY-WILLIAMS, Eliot) are listed under the first part of the name with a cross reference from the second part. Double-barrelled names without a hyphen, (e.g. DAY LEWIS, Cecil) are also listed under the first part of the name with a cross reference from the second part.

Brief biographical notes, where ascertained, on each poet are featured in curved brackets immediately after the poet's name. The data come from the standard biographical and reference works listed in the Bibliography of Biographical Sources and also from the anthologies and poetical works that constitute this biobibliography. In addition, many professional directories were consulted on a quick reference basis when there was reason to believe that a poet belonged to a particular non-literary profession. A foreword or introduction can often provide good and reliable information about an author, as can a book jacket. Book jackets, although they carry the publisher's blurb which is aimed at promotion of sales and is often fanciful, nevertheless usually present some indisputable facts about an author. From a bibliographer's point of view, it is perhaps unfortunate that in our learned libraries the practice is to remove the book jacket before the book is put into stock, thus depriving the researcher of what is essentially an integral part of the book as issued by the publisher.

After the initial bibliographical search had been completed, the printed catalogues of the Bodleian Library and the British Library were checked under the poets' names. This revealed many details not found in the books, such as an author's forename(s) in full, the real name of a pseudonymous author, the place of publication, the date of publication, etc. It was thus possible to benefit from the detailed research hitherto undertaken by the cataloguers at these two libraries in the course of their duties. The following example is typical of the kind of confusion that can arise over the form of an author's name in different works: H. N. Forbes on the title-page of a Shakespeare Head Press book in 1941; Henry N. Forbes on the title-page of a British Authors' Press book in 1945; Henry Forbes on the title-page of a Fortune Press book in 1949.

Occasionally there is a difference in the supposed date of publication chosen by the British Library and the Bodleian Library, in which case the British Library date is preferred. The British Library printed catalogue also revealed the existence of some items not found in the stock of the Bodleian Library or any other library visited. Although extremely time-consuming, the checking proved to be a vital exercise as it enabled this study to be linked with the holdings of our two most important national and copyright libraries.

The lives of the famous are well documented and it was necessary only to select the salient points for inclusion in the biographical notes, war service being of paramount importance. Details of organizations to which a poet belonged, such as a school, university or employing company, are particularly useful in the case of the less famous, as organizations keep records which can be consulted should one wish to investigate further. The place where an author was born, or where he lived, is given when known. The local history departments of our public libraries are usually assiduous in maintaining records of local authors, and parish records are available for consultation, either in the parish church or at the appropriate County Record Office. The phrase 'Of London' denotes that an author lived in London at some time.

It was impossible to find the date of death of many minor authors, even those authors who feature in biographical directories. Editors of biographical directories usually obtain their information direct from the author. The information is no longer included in a directory after an author's death, several years may elapse between editions, and no obituary list is made. The annual publication *Who's Who* is perhaps unique in including a list of deaths notified since the previous issue.

No biographical details could be found on 679 of the poets listed, just over 25 per cent of the total. Of these, 59 are represented only in those anthologies which do not include biographical notes, 23 were published by the Fortune Press and 24 by the Mitre Press (both firms now defunct), 37 by Outposts Publications, 377 by the vanity publishers Arthur H. Stockwell Ltd, and the remainder by a wide variety of other publishers. Publishers rightly regard personal information about their authors as confidential, as letters to both Outposts Publications and Arthur H. Stockwell Ltd revealed, but both companies were willing to pass on letters of enquiry to their clients at the last known addresses. It would have been interesting to have pursued such an exercise but hard to justify in terms of time and money in this instance. It is perhaps doubtful that many publishers would have retained records going back forty years in some cases.

All titles are those of first editions unless otherwise stated. The statement of other editions than the first follows the title in each entry. The pagination of later 'editions' is often identical to that of the first edition, implying no substantial change in the text. Any difference is usually in the wording of a preface, foreword or introduction. However, as it was rarely possible to examine editions of the same work together and there was no time for full collation, the publisher's statement of edition has been accepted. It seemed useful to describe all 'editions' if only to show the probability that their texts are identical.

When a title-page is missing from the particular copy of a work examined or where there is no proper title-page, as is sometimes the case in privately printed items, the title is taken from the cover of the book and this is indicated by the phrase 'Title from cover' as an annotation. Sometimes the cover bears a sub-title which is not found on the title-page. In such cases this is indicated by the phrase 'Sub-title on cover is . . .'.

Occasionally the title-page actually bears no title, only perhaps the authors' names as in the case of the Penguin Modern Poets series, nor does a title appear elsewhere in the volume. If this is the case the phrase 'Selected poems' is used and is placed within square brackets. Square brackets are also used to enclose a title which does not appear on the title-page (recto or verso).

On the occasions when two publishing houses have collaborated in the publication of a book, the names of both publishers are given in the entry, separated by a semi-colon, (e.g. Anvil Press Poetry; Routledge & Kegan Paul).

Many works were not handled by commercial publishers but were privately printed. When a publisher's name does not appear inside the book, the implication usually is that the book has been privately printed for the author, or another private individual, at his own expense. In these cases, when the printer's name appears anywhere in the book, it is included as part of the entry in lieu of a publisher and is prefixed by the word 'Printed', (e.g. Printed Liverpool: C. Tinling & Co., Ltd). This information is particularly useful as it often denotes the area where a poet lived. More often than not he would be inclined to use a local printer, especially in wartime.

Privately printed books in this sense should not be confused with books that emanate from private presses. A private press is usually a small establishment using hand presses or small letterpress machines, producing well-printed books often on hand-made paper and often in limited editions. The owner prints solely what he chooses, often his own work or the work of a particular circle of friends, or perhaps some other work (usually previously printed) that he finds attractive. The phrase 'Privately printed' is often found on the title-page of a book in either category where no publisher's or printer's name appears anywhere in the book. 'Privately printed' is placed within square brackets when the phrase does not appear in the book.

The annotations to the entries give supplemental information of many kinds, gleaned from the books themselves in some cases. An annotation is placed within single inverted commas if it reproduced verbatim from the book concerned and/or if it is not in the wording or style which the bibliographer would ideally have chosen. The following examples represent the kind of annotation most commonly encountered:

a. Title from cover.
b. Cover-title is *A Reverie in Verse*. [In this case the cover-title differs from the title printed on the title-page]
c. A broadside [or card]. [These terms describe items consisting of a single leaf printed on one side only]
d. Printed for private circulation.
e. Printed on one side of leaf only.
f. In Scots dialect.
g. Parallel English and French texts.
h. Reprinted from *The Essex Review*.
i. A limited ed. of 200 numbered copies.
j. Written in Oflag VII in the autumn of 1941.

k. All proceeds in aid of the Mayor of Chester's War Relief Fund.

l. Dedicated 'to my mother and father, living under the German occupation in Jersey'.

Title Index

Title entries are given for all works having distinctive titles by individual poets and for anonymous works.

War Poets of other English Speaking Nations

This is a list of Commonwealth and North American poets encountered in the course of the research. The names are arranged alphabetically, with entries under pseudonyms as well as real names, and prefixed by abbreviation for nationality.

Bibliography of Biographical Sources

Atkinson, Frank. *Dictionary of Literary Pseudonyms: a Selection of Popular Modern Writers in English*. 3rd ed. London: Clive Bingley, 1982.

The Author's and Writer's Who's Who and Reference Guide, 1935–36. London: Shaw Publishing Co., [1935].

The Author's and Writer's Who's Who, 1948–49. 1st post war ed. London: Shaw Publishing Co., [1948].

The Author's and Writer's Who's Who. 2nd–6th eds. London: Burke's Peerage Ltd., 1935–71.

Boylan, Henry. *A Dictionary of Irish Biography*. Dublin: Gill & Macmillan, 1978.

Contemporary Authors: a Bio-Bibliographical Guide to Current Writers in Fiction, General Nonfiction, Poetry, Journalism, Drama, Motion Pictures, Television, and Other Fields. [Multi-volumed, multi-sequenced]. Detroit, Michigan: Gale Research Co., 1962–78.

Crone, John S. *A Concise Dictionary of Irish Biography*. Revised and enlarged ed. Dublin: Talbot Press, 1937.

The Dictionary of National Biography, 1922–1930. Edited by J.R.H. Weaver. Oxford University Press, 1937.

The Dictionary of National Biography, 1931–1940. Edited by L.G. Wickham Legg. Oxford University Press, 1949.

The Dictionary of National Biography, 1941–1950. Edited by L.G. Wickham Legg and E.T. Williams. Oxford University Press, 1959.

The Dictionary of National Biography, 1951–1960. Edited by E.T. Williams and Helen M. Palmer. Oxford University Press, 1971.

The Dictionary of National Biography, 1961–1970. Edited by E.T. Williams. Oxford University Press, 1981.

Halkett, Samuel, and John Laing. *Dictionary of Anonymous and Pseudonymous English Literature*. New and enlarged ed. by James Kennedy, W.A. Smith and A.F. Johnson. Vol. 7, *Index and Second Supplement*. London: Oliver & Boyd, 1934.

———. *Dictionary of Anonymous and Pseudonymous English Literature*. Vol. 8,

1900–1950; by Dennis E. Rhodes and Anna E.C. Simoni. London: Oliver & Boyd, 1956.

Handley-Taylor, Geoffrey, ed. *Authors of Wales Today: Being a Checklist of Authors Born in Wales Together with Brief Particulars of Authors Born Elsewhere Who Are Currently Working or Residing in Wales. . .* London: Eddison Press, 1972.

————. *Lancashire Authors Today: Being a Checklist of Authors Born in Lancashire Together with Brief Particulars of Authors Born Elsewhere Who Are Currently Working or Residing in the County Palatine.* London: County Authors Today, 1971.

————. *Yorkshire Authors Today: Being a Checklist of Authors Born in Yorkshire Together with Brief Particulars of Authors Born Elsewhere Who Are Currently Working or Residing in the County. . .* London: Eddison Press, 1972.

The International Who's Who in Poetry. 2 vols. Edited by Geoffrey Handley-Taylor. London: Cornbrook Tower Press, 1958.

International Who's Who in Poetry. 2nd ed., 1970/1971. Edited by Ernest Kay. Cambridge: International Biographical Centre, 1970.

International Who's Who in Poetry. 3rd ed., 1972/1973. Edited by Ernest Kay. Cambridge: International Biographical Centre, 1972.

International Who's Who in Poetry. 4th ed., 1974/1975. Edited by Ernest Kay. Cambridge: International Biographical Centre, 1974.

International Who's Who in Poetry. 5th ed., 1977/1978. Edited by Ernest Kay. Cambridge: International Biographical Centre, 1977.

Kirkpatrick, D. L., ed. *Twentieth-Century Children's Writers.* London: Macmillan Press Ltd, 1978.

Kunitz, Stanley J., and Howard Haycraft, eds. *Twentieth Century Authors: a Biographical Dictionary of Modern Literature.* New York: H.W. Wilson Co., 1942.

————. *Twentieth Century Authors: a Biographical Dictionary of Modern Literature. First Supplement.* New York: H.W. Wilson Co., 1955.

Murphy, Rosalie, and James Vinson, eds. *Contemporary Poets of the English Language.* Chicago & London: St James Press, 1970.

The Poetry Review, and The Poetry Review Supplement. (Bi-monthly). Vol. XXVI, Jan.–Feb. 1935 — Vol. LI, Nov.–Dec. 1960. [Contains Poetry Society members' and correspondents' addresses].

Reilly, Catherine W. *English Poetry of the First World War: a Bibliography.* London: George Prior Publishers; New York: St Martin's Press. 1978.

Roberts, Frank C., comp. *Obituaries from The Times 1951–1960.* London: Newspaper Archive Developments Ltd, 1979.

————. *Obituaries from The Times 1961–1970.* London: Newspaper Archive Developments Ltd, 1975.

————. *Obituaries from The Times 1971–1975.* London: Newspaper Archive Developments Ltd, 1978.

Vinson, James, ed. *Contemporary Dramatists.* London: St James Press; New York: St Martin's Press, 1973.

Vinson, James, and D.L. Kirkpatrick, eds. *Contemporary Dramatists.* 2nd ed. London: St James Press; New York: St Martin's Press, 1977.

Vinson, James, ed. *Contemporary Novelists*. London: St James Press; New York: St Martin's Press, 1972.

Vinson, James, and D.L. Kirkpatrick, eds. *Contemporary Novelists*. 2nd ed. London: St James Press; New York: St Martin's Press, 1976.

Who's Who 1981: an Annual Biographical Dictionary. London: Adam & Charles Black, [1981].

Who's Who 1982: an Annual Biographical Dictionary. London: Adam & Charles Black, [1982].

Who Was Who: a Cumulated Index, 1897–1980. London: Adam & Charles Black, 1981.

Who Was Who, Vol. III, 1929–1940. London: Adam & Charles Black, 1941.

Who Was Who, Vol. IV, 1941–1950. London: Adam & Charles Black, 1951.

Who Was Who, Vol. V, 1951–1960. London: Adam & Charles Black, 1961.

Who Was Who, Vol. VI, 1961–1970. London: Adam & Charles Black, 1971.

Who Was Who, Vol. VII, 1971–1980. London: Adam & Charles Black, 1981.

The Writers Directory 1982–84. Byfleet, Surrey: Macmillan Publishers Ltd, 1981.

Abbreviations

A.D.C.	Aide-de-Camp
anon.	anonymous
b.	born
B.A.	Bachelor of Arts
B.B.C.	British Broadcasting Corporation
Co.	Company
col.	coloured
D.F.C.	Distinguished Flying Cross
D.S.C.	Distinguished Service Cross
ed./eds	edition/s
facsim.	facsimile/s
G.H.Q.	General Headquarters
G.P.O.	General Post Office
H.M.	His (Her) Majesty's
H.M.S.	His (Her) Majesty's Ship
H.Q.	Headquarters
Hon.	Honourable
il.	illustrated, illustration/s
J.P.	Justice of the Peace
Ltd	Limited
M.B.E.	Member of the Order of the British Empire
M.C.	Military Cross
M.M.	Military Medal
M.P.	Member of Parliament
MSS	manuscripts
O.B.E.	Officer Order of the British Empire
por.	portrait
pp.	pages
pseud.	pseudonym
Q.C.	Queen's Counsel
St	Saint

vol./vols	volume/s
Y.M.C.A.	Young Men's Christian Association
Y.W.C.A.	Young Women's Christian Association

Key to Library Locations

BL	British Library, London
BPL	Birmingham Public Libraries (Central Library)
GGA	Guille-Alles Library, Guernsey
IWM	Imperial War Museum, London
MPL	Manchester Public Libraries (Central Library)
OXB	Bodleian Library, Oxford
CWR	Bibliographer's copy

Anthologies

1. **AIR FORCE POETRY**. Edited by John Pudney and Henry Treece. John Lane the Bodley Head, 1944. 90 pp.

H.E. Bates, J. Bayliss, D. Bourne, R.P. Brett, N. Brick, O.C. Chave, T. Corsellis, E.D. Cox, J.C.M. Gibb, R.F.W. Grindal, C. Hamblett, I. Hargrave, P. Hellings, T.R. Hodgson, A.A. Levy, G. Parsons, H. Popham, H.G. Porteus, J. Pudney, A. Richardson, C.R. Sanderson, M. Savage, B.M. Soper, G. Stewart, C.W. Swiny, R. Tong, H. Treece, V. Watkins, R. Wilcox, T.R. Woods, F. Youngstar.   OXB

2. **An ANTHOLOGY OF CONTEMPORARY NORTHERN POETRY: a collection of poems by northern English poets**. Edited by Howard Sergeant. With an introduction by Thomas Moult. George C. Harrap & Co. Ltd. 1947. 154 pp.

W. Addison, A.V. Bowen, L. Bowes Lyon, P. Dehn, R. Fuller, O. Marron, T. Moult, H. Read, A. Rook, H. Sergeant, S. Snaith, E. Thompson, R.C. Trevelyan, J.R. Webb.   MPL

3. **An ANTHOLOGY OF MODERN VERSE, 1940–1960**. Chosen and with an introduction by Elizabeth Jennings. Methuen & Co. Ltd. 1961. 299 pp. (The anthologies of modern verse).

C. Causley, K. Douglas, L. Durrell, R. Fuller, S. Keyes, J. Lehmann, A. Lewis, H. Reed, W.R. Rodgers, E. Sitwell, B. Spencer, D. Thomas, T. Tiller, J. Wain.   BL

4. **An ANTHOLOGY OF WAR POETRY**. Compiled by Julian Symons. Harmondsworth, Middlesex: Penguin Books. [1942]. 189 pp. (Pelican books, A. 98).

Section *The World War (1939–   )*: W.H. Auden, R. Fuller, G. Grigson, L. MacNeice, A. Ridler, F. Scarfe, S. Spender, J. Symons, R. Todd.   OXB

5. **BACKWATER: Oflag IX A/H Lower Camp**. Edited by D. Guy Adams. Frederick Muller Ltd. 1944. 29 pp.

Poetry, prose and water colours by prisoners of war.

D.G. Adams, E.G.C. Beckwith, R.C.S. MacGill, D.R. Oakley-Hill, D.H.C. Read, J.F. Stewart-Phillips.   OXB

6. **The BEST POEMS OF 1940**. Selected by Thomas Moult and decorated by Elizabeth Montgomery. Jonathan Cape Ltd. 1940. 128 pp.

F.C. Ball, L. Binyon, F.C. Bond, R. Furse, S. Lynd, H.B. Mallalieu, E.J.M.D. Plunkett, R. Reynolds, S. Sassoon.   OXB

7. **The BEST POEMS OF 1941**. Selected by Thomas Moult. Jonathan Cape Ltd. 1942. 128 pp.

J.R. Anderson, H. Asquith, R. Church, J.C. Hall, L. Lee, A. Lewis, A.A. Milne, H. Palmer, D.L. Sayers, W. Soutar, S. Spender, E. Thompson, R.G. Vansittart, J. Walker.   OXB

8. **The BEST POEMS OF 1942**. Selected by Thomas Moult. Jonathan Cape. 1943. 112 pp.

J. Buxton, R. Church, M. English, R. Fuller, N. Moore, V. Sackville-West, E. Shanks, W. Soutar, S. Spender.   OXB

9. **The BEST POEMS OF 1943**. Selected by Thomas Moult. Jonathan Cape. 1944. 127 pp.

T. Boggs, B.R. Gibbs, D. Gibson, W.W. Gibson, A. Lewis, P. MacDonogh, N. Moore, H. Palmer, S. Sassoon, W. Soutar, R. Spender, S. Stafford.
                                                                OXB

10. **BILLY THE KID: an anthology of tough verse**. Edited by Michael Baldwin. Hutchinson Educational. 1963. 176 pp.

Section *War war war*: J. Bronowski, C. Causley, C. Day Lewis, K. Douglas, R. Fuller, L. MacNeice, J. Pudney, A. Ross, S. Spender, B. Warr.   OXB

11. **BUGLE BLAST: an anthology from the Services**. Edited by Jack Aistrop and Reginald Moore. George Allen & Unwin Ltd. 1943. 160 pp.

Poetry and prose.

J. Brooke, S. Keyes, L. Little, N. McCallum, J. Pudney, K. Rhys, A. Rook, W.F.M. Stewart, H. Treece.   OXB

12. **BUGLE BLAST: an anthology from the Services**. Second series. Edited by Jack Aistrop and Reginald Moore. George Allen & Unwin. 1944. 184 pp.

Poetry and prose.

W. Andrewes, T.I.F. Armstrong, J. Brooke, H. Corby, N.K. Cruickshank, L. Eveleigh, L. Little, P.J. Little, P. Scott.   OXB

13. **BUGLE BLAST: an anthology from the Services**. Third series. Edited by Jack Aistrop and Reginald Moore. George Allen & Unwin. 1945. 206 pp.
    Poetry and prose.
    W. Andrewes, J. Braddock, H. Manning, F. Newbold, L. Norris, G.A. Wagner.   OXB

14. **BUGLE BLAST: an anthology**. Fourth series. Edited by Jack Aistrop and Reginald Moore. George Allen & Unwin Ltd. 1947. 200 pp.
    Poetry and prose.
    Poetry supplement: J. Brooke, R. Goodman, A. Rook, S.D. Tremayne.   OXB

15. **COMPONENTS OF THE SCENE: stories, poems, and essays of the Second World War**. Introduced and edited by Ronald Blythe. Harmondsworth, Middlesex: Penguin books. 1966. 398 pp. (Penguin original).
    W.H. Auden, G. Barker, R. Campbell, H. Corby, T. Corsellis, R.N. Currey, C. Day Lewis, P. Dehn, K. Douglas, W. Empson, R. Fuller, D. Gascoyne, R. Graves, R. Heppenstall, S. Keyes, A. Lewis, L. MacNeice, M. Peake, F.T. Prince, J. Pudney, K. Raine, H. Reed, W.R. Rodgers, A. Rook, F. Scarfe, E.J. Scovell, E. Sitwell, S. Spender, D. Thomas, T. Tiller, H. Treece, W.J.Turner.
                                                                          OXB

16. **CONTEMPORARY POETS: an anthology of modern poetry**. Edited by Helen Godfrey-Bartram. Senate Books Ltd. [1966]. [iv], 112 pp.
    G.M. Blacker, A.V. Buck, F.E. Copeland, V. Cotton, C.A. Foote, E.R.H. Gwynne, D. Hammond, D.J. May, E. Meaking, A.M. Mitchell, D. Murray, A. Ziolkowska.   OXB

17. **ENGLISH POETRY. Book 5. Modern verse**. [Edited by] W.M. Smyth. Edward Arnold. 1971. viii, 130 pp. (A course in English).
    C. Causley, R.N. Currey, C. Day Lewis, K. Douglas, J. Jarmain, L. MacNeice, J.S. Manifold, J. Pudney, H. Reed, A. Ridler, J. Wain.   OXB

18. **FLASH POINT: an anthology of modern poetry.** Compiled by Robert Shaw. With an introduction by Jon Silkin. Leeds: E.J. Arnold & Son Ltd. 1964. 256 pp.
    W.H. Auden, G. Barker, K. Douglas, T.S. Eliot, R. Fuller, S. Keyes, J. Kirkup, E. Litvinoff, C. Middleton, N. Nicholson, S. Spender.   MPL

19. **FOR THOSE WHO ARE ALIVE: an anthology of new verse**. Edited by Howard Sergeant. Fortune Press. [1946]. 76 pp.
    L. Adeane, C. Hodges, F. King, P. Ledward, E. Litvinoff, S. Read, S. Stafford, R.B. Wright.   OXB

20. **FOR YOUR TOMORROW: an anthology of poetry written by young**

3

men from English public schools who fell in the World War, 1939–1945. Oxford University Press. 1950. xii, 104 pp.

D. Allison, C. Bailey, A.D. Bass, J.F. Boughey, D. Bourne, M. Chenevix Trench, F.R. Dunton, K. Foottit, R. Joly, D.R.G. Jones, S. Keyes, J.D. Maclure, M. Macnaughton-Smith, H.N.T. Medrington, I.O. Meikle, T.A. Mellows, D. Raikes, F. Thompson, A. Tod, J. Wilson.   OXB

21. **A GIRDLE OF SONG: by poets of England, Scotland, Wales, Northern Ireland, Eire, Canada, Australia, New Zealand, India, South Africa and Rhodesia**. Edited by Edith M. Fry. British Authors' Press. [1944]. 160 pp.

P. Braithwaite, V. Brittain, E. Collins, R. Greacen, C. Hassall, P. Huthwaite, R. Pitter, A. Row, V. Sackville-West, R. Shuttleworth, J.S. Starkey.   OXB

22. **The GREENWOOD ANTHOLOGY OF NEW VERSE**. Compiled by Herbert Palmer. Frederick Muller Ltd. 1948. xii, 92 pp.

Section *The war and its impacts*: E.W. Barker, F. Batchelor, R.E. Boulton, E. Clark, C.M. Covell, E. Davey-Collins, H.N. Forbes, J.A. Gaved, D. Gibson, W.W. Gibson, M. Horne, W. Jarman, G.R. Jones, P. Lyth, I. Maclaughlin, H.W. Moore, E. Norton, E.E. Tree, I.P. Turner, E. Walter, J. Way, M. White.   OXB

23. **HANDS TO ACTION STATIONS!: naval poetry and verse from World War Two**. Chosen by John Winton. Illustrated by Captain Jack Broome, DSC, RN. Denbigh: Bluejacket Books, 1980. 143 pp. il.

J.K. Annand, W.R. Bailley, R. Bawcutt, M. Bowden, J.E. Broome, A. Bulley, J. Bush, G.C., T.A. Carey, P. Cree, D. Davie, R. Davies, K.R.E. Dobbs A.I. Doloughan, O. FitzRoy, R. Fuller, R. Furse, B.D. Gallie, H.J. Galsworthy, D.S. Goodbrand, R. Goodman, K. Greenwell, A.J. Grimwade, R. Halliday, N. Hampson, J.A.B. Harrisson, A.P. Herbert, Horsebox, pseud., R.C.M. Howard, R.J. Hunter, W. James, T.G. Longdon-Griffiths, G. Marler, K. Mason, R. Michell, J.H. Millard, J. Moore, G. Morgan, H. Popham, J. Pudney, D.M. Radcliffe, J. Richardson, L.G. Roberts, W.E. Roberts, A. Ross, K.M. Salmon, D.L. Simpson, F. Smewin, J.M. Snelgar, G. Stewart, M.C. Stopes, J.F.T., M. Thwaites, G.H. Vallins, H. Wake, L.J. Wallace, B.J. Waterton, J. Wedge, D. Wherry, J. Whitehouse, P. Woodhouse, R.B. Wright, Yvette, pseud., and thirteen anon.   MPL

24. **HOME IS THE SOLDIER: an anthology of poems**; by Robin Benn [and others]. Fortune Press. 1947. 32 pp.

R. Benn, R.D. Birch, D.B. Reade, P. Savage, R. Shuckburgh.   OXB

25. **I BURN FOR ENGLAND: an anthology of the poetry of World War II**. Selected and introduced by Charles Hamblett. Leslie Frewin. [1966]. 403 pp.

L. Adeane, D. Allison, K. Allott, B. Allwood, K. Amis, T.I.F. Armstrong,

W.H. Auden, A. Bailey, P. Baker, G. Barker, O.M. Barres, J. Bate, H.E. Bates, J. Bayliss, D. Bourne, M. Bowden, J.C. Braun, N. Brick, R.L. Chaloner, O.C. Chave, S. Churchill, W. Clapham, J. Coldwell, A. Comfort, H. Corby, T. Corsellis, E.D. Cox, C. Day Lewis, P. Dehn, P.De Wye, M.J. Disney, K. Douglas, L. Durrell, K. Etheridge, G. Ewart, G.E. Evans, J. Forsyth, G.S. Fraser, C. Fry, R. Fuller, W. Gardiner, D. Gascoyne, J.C.M. Gibb, R. Greacen, B. Gutteridge, S. Haggard, J.C. Hall, L. Halsey, C. Hamblett, N. Hampson, C. Hassall, F.I. Hauser, D. Hawkins, P. Hellings, J.F. Hendry, C. Hodges, T.R. Hodgson, M. Holloway, S. Keyes, F. King, H.G. Knight, P. Ledward, L. Lee, A.A. Levy, A. Lewis, J.M. Lindsay, L. Little, E. Litvinoff, N. Longhurst, N. McCallum, A. McDonald, R. McFadden, L. MacNeice, H.B. Mallalieu, J.S. Manifold, N. Moore, N.T. Morris, M.J. Moynihan, N. Nicholson, H.V.S. Page, G. Parsons, J. Pauker, M. Peake, F. Petheram, L. Phillips, H. Popham, H.G. Porteus, J. Prichard, R. Pride, F.T. Prince, J. Pudney, S. Rayne, H. Read, S. Read, H. Reed, K. Rhys, A. Richardson, A. Ridler, L. Roberts, A. Rook, A. Ross, C.R. Sanderson, D.S. Savage, M. Savage, F. Scarfe, H. Scott, T. Scott, G. Scurfield, J. Segal, H. Sergeant, J.B. Sidgwick, A.E. Simmonds, A. Sinclair, S. Spender, S. Stafford, D. Stanford, G. Stewart, J.B. Stocks, J. Sully, G. Swaine, C.W. Swiny, J. Symons, M.J. Tambimuttu, D. Thomas, T. Tiller, R. Todd, R. Tong, H. Treece, J. Waller, B. Warr, V. Watkins, N. Watson, J. Wedge, L. Whistler, R. Wilcox, G. Woodcock, R.B. Wright, C.K. Young, F. Youngstar, and one anon. **OXB**

26. **INTRODUCING MODERN POETRY: an anthology**. Compiled by W.G. Bebbington. Revised ed. Faber & Faber. 1957. 146 pp.
    W.H. Auden, G. Barker, C. Day Lewis, P. Dehn, C. Dyment, D.J. Enright, R. Fuller, D. Gascoyne, S. Keyes, L. Lee, A. Lewis, L. MacNeice, E. Sitwell, S. Spender, D. Thomas. **OXB**

27. **LITTLE ANTHOLOGY: the first girl writers in battledress**. Edited by Peter Ratazzi. Printed Slough: Kenion Press. [1944]. 36 pp. (Khaki and blue books).
    Title from cover.
    H.D. Bird, M. Francis, P. Ledward, B. Wildgosse. **OXB**

28. **LITTLE REVIEWS ANTHOLOGY**. Edited by Denys Val Baker. George Allen & Unwin. [1943]. 224 pp.
    H. Arundel, I. Fletcher, J.C. Hall, L. Lee, A. Lewis, R. McFadden, W.R. Rodgers, A. Rook, F. Scarfe, I. Serraillier, D. Thomas, V. Turner, G. Woodcock. **OXB**

29. **LYRA: an anthology of new lyric**. Edited by Alex Comfort and Robert Greacen. Billericay, Essex: Grey Walls Press. 1942. 71 pp.
    J. Bayliss, A. Comfort, C. Dyment, G.S. Fraser, R. Greacen, E. Litvinoff, R.

McFadden, N. Moore, A. Ridler, F. Scarfe, I. Serraillier, M.J. Tambimuttu.
OXB

30. **The MARTIAL MUSE: seven centuries of war poetry**. Selected and
edited by Alan Bold, with an introduction and notes. Wheaton. 1976. 227 pp.
(Wheaton studies in literature).
W.H. Auden, G. Barker, R. Campbell, C. Day Lewis, K. Douglas, C.M.
Grieve, T. Gunn, S. Keyes, A. Lewis, P. Porter, J. Pudney, H. Read, H. Reed,
E. Sitwell, W. Soutar, D. Thomas.
MPL

31. **MIDDLE EAST ANTHOLOGY**. Edited by John Waller and Erik De
Mauny. Lindsay Drummond. 1946. 170 pp.
Poetry and prose.
T.I.F. Armstrong, E. De Mauny, K. Douglas, L. Durrell, G.S. Fraser, H.
Howarth, J. Jarmain, S. Keyes, J. Pudney, J. Ropes, R.B. Scott, B. Spencer, J.
Waller, D. Wilkinson.
OXB

32. **MODERN WELSH POETRY**. Edited by Keidrych Rhys. Faber & Faber.
1944. 146 pp.
C. Davies, G.E. Evans, W. Griffith, P. Hellings, R. Herring, N. Heseltine,
A.P. Jones, A. Lewis, R. Mathias, H.M. Williams.
MPL

33. **MORE POEMS FROM THE FORCES: a collection of verses by
serving members of the Navy, Army, and Air Force**. Edited by Keidrych
Rhys. George Routledge & Sons Ltd. 1943. 324 pp.
B. Allwood, P. Baker, D. Bourne, M. Bowden, A.V. Bowen, J.C. Braun,
J.F.W. Bryon, R.L. Chaloner, J. Coldwell, H. Corby, T. Corsellis, E.D. Cox,
N.K. Cruickshank, R.N. Currey, K. Douglas, K. Etheridge, D. Evans, G.
Ewart, G.S. Fraser, R. Fuller, S. Haggard, N. Hampson, P. Hellings, J.F.
Hendry, S. Keyes, P. Ledward, A.A. Levy, A. Lewis, J.M. Lindsay, L. Little, E.
Litvinoff, N. McCaig, A. McDonald, H.B. Mallalieu, J.S. Manifold, T.H.
Middleton, M.J. Moynihan, L. Phillips, J. Prichard, F.T. Prince, J. Pudney, H.
Reed, K. Rhys, A. Rook, F. Scarfe, T. Scott, G. Scurfield, J.B. Sidgwick, F.
Smewin, G.E. Smith, J.B. Stocks, G. Swaine, J. Symons, H. Treece, J. Waller,
V. Watkins, N. Watson, J. Wedge, R.B. Wright.
OXB

34. **MORE POETRY FROM OXFORD**. Edited by William Bell. Fortune
Press. 1947. 60 pp.
R. Chapman, A. Curtis, I. Davie, A. Downs, J. Longrigg, J.G. Moir. OXB

35. **MUSE IN EXILE: an anthology from fighting men of South East
Asia**. [Edited by Len Jackson]. [Printed Calcutta: Essco Press]. [1945].
48 pp. il. (SEAC publications).
Reprinted from *SEAC*, the Services daily newspaper of South-East Asia
Command in 1944–45.

D.S.C., G.D. Carter, T.L. Colley, G.W.G. Driscoll, J. Farley, B.A. Ford, J. Foster, Frolik, pseud., C. Grimes, M. Halliwell, E. Hayman, R. Hunter, A.I. John, K., pseud., J.A.K. Lamont, J. Leasor, A.T. Lusk, J.G.M., Marcus, pseud., P.J. Martin, S.N., J.W. Nevill, E.D.P., G.J. Prosser, H.L. Robinson, L.W. Robinson, R.P. Rowson, K. Saville, D.A. Schaverien, R.St E. Spencer, D. Squib, A.A. Steele, A.C. Tarbat, D. Thomas, R.W.F.W., J.O.R.M. Watt, R.B. Wilcock, W.E. Wyatt.   OXB

36. **NEW LYRICAL BALLADS**. [Edited by] Maurice Carpenter, Jack Lindsay, Honor Arundel. Editions Poetry London. 1945. viii, 164 pp.
D. Alexander, H. Arundel, J. Atkins, M. Carpenter, H. Corby, L. Daiken, I. Davies, T. Farnol, A. Lewis, J. Lindsay, J.S. Manifold, D. Martin, G. Matthews, F. Mayo, H. Nicholson, H.W. Owen, J. Pudney, A. Rattenbury, M. Richardson, J. Rowe, F. Scarfe, R. Swingler, M. Whittock.   MPL

37. **NEW POEMS 1944: an anthology of American and British verse, with a selection of poems from the Armed Forces.** Edited by Oscar Williams. New York: Howell, Soskin. [1944]. 330 pp. por.
T. Corsellis, G.S. Fraser, R. Fuller, J.F. Hendry, S. Jennett, S. Keyes, P. Ledward, A. Lewis, L. MacNeice, H.B. Mallalieu, F.T. Prince, H. Reed, K. Rhys, W.R. Rodgers, J. Symons, D. Thomas.   OXB

38. **The NEW TREASURY OF WAR POETRY: poems of the Second World War**. Edited by George Herbert Clarke, with introduction and notes. Boston: Houghton Mifflin Co. [1943]. xxxiv, 285 pp.
L. Aaronson, M.E. Allan, P.S. Allfrey, W. Ashton, P. Baker, R.G. Barnes, L. Binyon, E. Blunden, H. Brown, I. Brown, R. Church, S. Cloete, R.W. Cumberland, D.G. Davies, P. Dickinson, R. Elwes, W.W. Gibson, J.M. Graham, V. Graham, S. Gwynn, J.C. Hall, G.R. Hamilton, A.G. Herbertson, D. Hudson, E. Humphreys, A. Jackson, O. Katzin, E. Litvinoff, F.L. Lucas, G. Malcolm, G.D. Martineau, J. Masefield, E.H.W. Meyerstein, N. Micklem, L. Minster, E. Muir, M. Newton, M. Peake, J. Perrin, G. Phillips, E.J.M.D. Plunkett, F. Prokosch, O.L. Richmond, A.L. Rowse, V. Sackville-West, C. Schiff, H. Spalding, S. Spender, L. Toynbee, R.G. Vansittart, L. Whistler, T.H. White, A. Young.   BL

39. **OASIS: the Middle East anthology of poetry from the Forces**. Cairo: Salamander Productions. [1943]. xx, 65 pp.
J.G. Barker, J.A.K. Boninger, M. Bowden, J.C. Braun, J. Bristow, D. Burnie, L. Challoner, D. Charles, J. Charnock, J.M. Collard, M. Corbally, A.C.J. Davies, S. Day, E. De Mauny, E.P. Dudley, D. Dunhill, G.S. Fraser, A.N. Freedman, H.M. Fridjohn, W.G. Graham, P. Hellings, H. Henderson, N. Hudis, D. Jones, H. Laming, L.K. Lawler, N. Longhurst, T.W. Louch, E. McHale, G. Malcolm, A.W. Marsden, G.C. Norman, G.O. Physick, J.

Rimington, J. Sayer, C.H.O. Scaife, A. Smithies, C. Smithies, T. Stephanides, R.N. Walker, J. Waller, E.A. Walmsley, D. Wilkinson, C.B. Wilson.

OXB

40. **PERSONAL LANDSCAPE: an anthology of exile**. Compiled by Robin Fedden [and others]. Cover design by Roland Pym. Editions Poetry Ltd. 1945. 118 pp.

K. Douglas, L. Durrell, R. Fedden, C.H. Johnston, R. Liddell, O. Manning, H.G. Porteus, B. Spencer, T. Tiller, G. Williams.   **OXB**

41. **POEMS BY CONTEMPORARY WOMEN**. Compiled by Theodora Roscoe and Mary Winter Were. With a foreword by P.H.B. Lyon. Hutchinson & Co. [1944]. 76 pp.

W. Ashton, E.D. Bangay, V. Brittain, S.D. Clark, C. Doyle, M. Edgelow, V.H. Friedlaender, B.R. Gibbs, J. Grenfell, A. Jackson, D. James, C.L. Lanyon, S. Lynd, V. Meynell, M. Newton, R. Pitter, T. Roscoe, M.D. Spender, L.F. Stewart, M.C. Stopes, O.I. Ward, D.C. Watts, M.W. Were.   **OXB**

42. **POEMS FOR FRANCE; written by British poets on France since the war**. Collected by Nancy Cunard with autobiographical notes of the authors. La France Libre. 1944. xii, 95 pp.

V. Ackland, C.A. Alington, T.I.F. Armstrong, H. Arundel, R. Atthill, J. Beeching, O. Blakeston, D. Bourne, A.V. Bowen, F.J. Brown, A.J. Bull, W. Campbell, R. Cecil, R. Church, A. Comfort, M.C. Craven, N. Cunard, I. Davie, D.G. Davies, D. Evans, P. Gardiner, K. Geering, D. Gibson, V.C. Grant, R. Greacen, C.M. Greive, G.R. Hamilton, J.F. Hendry, R. Heppenstall, W.J.F. Hutcheson, A. Jackson, E. Lewis, J. Lindsay, M. Lochhead, D. Lord, F.L. Lucas, J.H.F. McEwen, C. Mackworth, J.S. Manifold, G. Matthews, E.H.W. Meyerstein, E. Milne, N. Moore, T. Moult, F. Mundy-Castle, H. Palmer, W. Plomer, E.J.M.D. Plunkett, P. Potts, T.W. Ramsey, I. Rathbone, H. Read, S. Read, D. Reilly, A. Ross, J. Rowe, V. Sackville-West, D. Shaw, J. Short, H. Spalding, J.C. Squire, M. Stark, S. Steen, E. Thompson, H. Treece, R.G. Vansittart, S.T. Warner, M.W. Were, R.N.D. Wilson, Zodiac, pseud.

OXB

43. **POEMS FROM INDIA; by members of the Forces**. Chosen by R.N. Currey and R.V. Gibson. Oxford University Press, 1946, xx, 167 pp.

B.C. Amiel, J.O. Bartley, E.L. Black, P.R. Boyle, C. Branson, R. Brooke, F.G. Carnell, J.K. Cassels, B.C. Cave-Brown-Cave, G. Cherry, R.N. Currey, M. Edwardes, S. Fenlaugh, J.W.L. Forge, R.A. George, R.V. Gibson, A.J. Gilliver, D. Gray, K.R. Gray, M.G. Greening, J.B. Hawkins, W.A. Hebditch, P. Hulton, F.H. Larr, R. Levy, A. Lewis, R.V. Leyden, J.C.H. Mollison, I. Morton, T.B.P. Owen, S. Piggott, S. Rickard, W.J.F. Ridler, I. Roberts-Jones, J.H. Robertson, R.F.B. Roling, H.B. Shelley, H.L. Shorto, N.H.C. Smith, L.C. Southgate, F.M. Sweeting, G.P. Symes, G.A. Taylor, H.H. Tilley, P.

Tudor-Owen, V. Watkins, K. Watson, A.P. Wavell, P.F. Widdows, R.B. Wilcock. OXB

44. POEMS FROM ITALY: verses written by members of the Eighth Army in Sicily and Italy, July 1943 — March 1944. With a foreword by Lieutenant-General Sir Oliver Leese, Bart., K.C.B., C.B.E., D.S.O., formerly Commander of the Eighth Army, and an introduction by Siegfried Sassoon. George G. Harrap & Co. Ltd. 1945. 92 pp.

Poems submitted in poetry competitions organized by the Army Educational Corps.

T.I.F. Armstrong, W.A. Armstrong, A. Bailey, O.M. Barres, N.A. Brown, F. Clarke, L.E.S. Cotterell, A.W. Crowther, D.L. Dee, P. De Wye, M.J. Disney, A. Dove, K.G. Harvey, L.J. Hatt, F.I. Hauser, J. Henry, W.E. Hutchinson, W.F.M. Hyde, R.G. Jolly, A. Jones, W.E. Jones, H.G. Knight, I. Königsberg, L. Lilenstein, N. Longhurst, S.F. Lott, M.P. McDiarmid, P.B. McGuire, P.H. Marriott, P.S. Millar, C.A. Morris, N.T. Morris, J. Nichol, H.V.S. Page, F. Petheram, E.G. Porter, J. Porter, R. Pride, D. Rossiter, J. Segal, A.E. Simmonds, A. Sinclair, J.P. Stevenson, J. Sully, S.G. Watts, N. Wilkinson, C.B. Wilson. OXB

45. POEMS FROM *NEW WRITING*, 1936–1946. Edited with a foreword by John Lehmann. John Lehmann. 1946. 189 pp.

W.H. Auden, D. Bain, J. Bronowski, J. Brooke, A. Brown, N. Cameron, R.N. Currey, R. Fuller, R. Graves, B. Gutteridge, N. Hampson, J. Heath-Stubbs, H. Henderson, J. Lehmann, A. Lewis, L. Little, L. MacNeice, H.B. Mallalieu, N. Nicholson, F.T. Prince, M.V.B. Riviere, A. Ross, S. Spender, W.F.M. Stewart, D. Witherby. OXB

46. POEMS FROM THE DESERT: verses by members of the Eighth Army. With a foreword by General Sir Bernard Montgomery, K.C.B., D.S.O. George G. Harrap & Co. Ltd. 1944. 46 pp.

S. Abel, E.Y. Barnard, E.J. Barton, N. Boodson, J. Broome, N.A. Brown, I. Celner, L. Challoner, L.E.S. Cotterell, P.J. Flaherty, G. Harker, F.E. Hughes, W.E. Jones, H.G. Knight, G.O. Physick, P.W.R. Russell, D. Seton-Smith, F.Z. Smith, P.A.A. Thomas, F.O. Watkins, M.St J. Wilmoth, and two anon. BL

47. POEMS FROM THE FORCES: a collection of verses by serving members of the Navy, Army, and Air Force. Edited with an introduction by Keidrych Rhys. Preface by Colonel The Rt Hon. Walter Elliot, M.C. George Routledge & Sons Ltd. 1941. xxiv, 140 pp.

P. Baker, A.V. Bowen, J.C. Braun, T. Corsellis, E.D. Cox, G. Ewart, G.S. Fraser, R. Fuller, L. Halsey, C. Hamblett, C. Hassall, J.F. Hendry, R. Heppenstall, A. Lewis, P.J. Little, E. Litvinoff, J.S. Manifold, M. Peake, J.

Prichard, K. Rhys, A. Rook, T. Scott, G. Scurfield, J.B. Sidgwick, J. Waller, J. Wedge, L. Whistler, C.K. Young. OXB

48. **POEMS OF OUR TIME, 1900–1960**. Original ed. chosen by Richard Church and Mildred Bozman. Modern supplement chosen by Dame Edith Sitwell. J.M. Dent & Sons Ltd. 1959. xxxii, 351 pp.

Section *1930–1946*: J. Bayliss, A.V. Bowen, J. Bronowski, W. Burke, N. Cameron, R. Church, A. Comfort, R. Fuller, C. Hassall, S. Keyes, E. Lewis, E. Rhys, E. Sitwell, W. Soutar, S. Spender, L. Whistler. OXB

49. **POEMS OF THE FORCES: the Fortune Forces anthology**. Fortune Press. [1949]. 152 pp.

T.I.F. Armstrong, I. Bancroft, J. Bayliss, F. Berry, C.P. Billot, R.D. Birch, A.V. Bowen, C. Causley, H. Corby, M. Cullwick, I. Davie, E. De Mauny, G. Ewart, B. Gingell, G. Gordon, W.J. Harvey, J. Hawke-Genn, T.B. Hutton, J.D. James, R. Kidwell, E. Litvinoff, R. Macnab, H.B. Mallalieu, D. Nixon, E. Peters, P. Russell, C.R. Sanderson, J.A. Thompson, R. Tong, R.W. Trudgett, J. Walker, J. Waller, J. Weber. IWM

50. **POEMS OF THE LAND ARMY: an anthology of verse by members of the Women's Land Army**. With a foreword by V. Sackville-West. *The Land Girl*. [1945]. 56 pp.

E. Barraud, M. Browne, F.A.H. Burkitt, M. Capes, A. Coats, A. Hewlett, H. Jerrold, J. Moncrieff. MPL

51. **POEMS OF THE WAR YEARS: an anthology**. Compiled by Maurice Wollman. Macmillan. 1948. xxxiv, 275 pp.

L. Aaronson, J.R. Anderson, T.I.F. Armstrong, W.H. Auden, E. Blunden, A.V. Bowen, L. Bowes Lyon, J.C. Braun, J. Campbell, R. Campbell, R. Church, H. Corby, R.N. Currey, C. Day Lewis, K. Douglas, C. Dyment, R. Fuller, D. Gascoyne, W.W. Gibson, J.C. Hall, G.R. Hamilton, P. Hesketh, J. Jarmain, S. Jennett, S. Keyes, A. Lewis, C.S. Lewis, S. Lynd, J. Pudney, T.W. Ramsey, H. Read, W.R. Rodgers, A. Rook, S. Snaith, W. Soutar, S. Spender, H.F. Summers, E. Thompson, H. Treece, G.A. Wagner, J. Walker, J. Waller. OXB

52. **POEMS OF THIS WAR BY YOUNGER POETS**. Edited by Patricia Ledward and Colin Strang. With an introduction by Edmund Blunden. Cambridge at the University Press. 1942. xii, 100 pp.

Reissued by the Falcon Press in 1947 under the title *Retrospect, 1939–1942*.

J. Atkins, P. Baker, P. Byrne, A. Comfort, T. Corsellis, M.M. Crosland, N.K. Cruickshank, J. Curle, C. Dyment, D. Gascoyne, F. Gelder, D. Gibson, R. Greacen, J.C. Hall, I. Hargrave, M. Holloway, W. Jarman, F. King, P. Ledward, E. Litvinoff, N. Moore, K. Neal, N. Nicholson, S. Read, A. Rook, C.

Sansom, M. Savage, P. Scott, I. Seraillier, M. Smith, M.J. Tambimuttu, M. Vaughan-Williams, J. Waller, B. Warr, L. Whistler, E.D. Young.   OXB

53. **POETRY FROM CAMBRIDGE IN WARTIME: a selection of verse by members of the University**. Edited by Geoffrey Moore. Fortune Press. [1946]. 88 pp.

D. Bain, J. Bayliss, J. Braddock, J. Dalglish, G. Ewart, K. Poolman, J.P. Stern, A. Tod.   OXB

54. **POETRY FROM OXFORD IN WARTIME**. Edited by William Bell. Fortune Press. [1945]. 94 pp.

D. Allison, I. Bancroft, B. Hutton, J.D. James, C. Middleton.   OXB

55. **POETRY FROM OXFORD, MICHAELMAS, 1946 – TRINITY, 1948**; written by members of the University resident during that period. Edited by Norman Mawdsley. Fortune Press. 1949. [ii], 70 pp.

D. Dickey, C. Dobb, R. Fox, S. Green, G. Midgley, P.A.T. O'Donnell, D. Styles, D. Williamson.   OXB

56. **POETRY IN WARTIME: an anthology**. Edited by M.J. Tambimuttu. Faber & Faber Ltd. 1942. 192 pp.

K. Allott, W.H. Auden, G. Barker, A. Beecham, B. Chamberlain, R. Church, S. Coates, A. Comfort, H. Corby, C. Day Lewis, L. Durrell, W. Empson, G. Ewart, J. Forsyth, G.S. Fraser, R. Fuller, D. Gascoyne, J.C. Hall, D. Hawkins, J.F. Hendry, S. Keyes, F. King, L. Lee, A. Lewis, N. McCallum, L. MacNeice, N. Moore, N. Nicholson, M. Peake, K. Raine, H. Read, A. Ridler, L. Roberts, W.E. Roberts, W.R. Rodgers, A. Rook, F. Scarfe, T. Scott, S. Spender, J. Symons, D. Thomas, T. Tiller, R. Todd, H. Treece, J. Waller, V. Watkins, G. Woodcock.   BL

57. **POETRY OF THE FORTIES**. Introduced and edited by Robin Skelton. Harmondsworth, Middlesex: Penguin Books. 1968. 269 pp. (Penguin poets, D100).

P. Anderson, W.H. Auden, G. Barker, A. Comfort, D. Cooke, R.N. Currey, C. Day Lewis, P. Dehn, P. Dickinson, K. Douglas, L. Durrell, D.J. Enright, R. Fedden, G.S. Fraser, E. Frost, R. Fuller, D. Gascoyne, K.R. Gray, J. Heath-Stubbs, A. Henderson, J.F. Hendry, J. Jarmain, S. Jennett, S. Keyes, P. Leigh-Fermor, R. Levy, A. Lewis, R. Liddell, E. Litvinoff, N. McCallum, L. MacNeice, J.C.H. Mollison, J. Monahan, M. Peake, F.T. Prince, K. Raine, H. Reed, I. Roberts-Jones, A. Rook, A. Ross, B. Spencer, R. Spender, S. Spender, D. Thomas, F. Thompson, T. Tiller, J. Walker.   MPL

58. **POETRY OF THE 1940s**: an anthology selected and edited by Howard Sergeant. Longman. 1970. xii, 202 pp. (Longman English series).

K. Douglas, R. Fuller, S. Keyes, A. Lewis, E. Muir, N. Nicholson, H. Reed, E. Sitwell, D. Thomas. OXB

59. **The POETRY OF WAR 1939—45**. Edited by Ian Hamilton. Alan Ross Ltd. 1965. x, 173 pp. il., por.

D. Allison, K. Amis, D. Bain, J. Brooke, N. Cameron, R. Campbell, C. Causley, R. Conquest, H. Corby, R.N. Currey, P. Dehn, K. Douglas, G. Ewart, R. Fuller, B. Gutteridge, N. Hampson, H. Henderson, S. Keyes, A. Lewis, H.B. Mallalieu, F.T. Prince, J. Pudney, H. Reed, A. Ross, J. Symons. MPL

60. **POETS IN BATTLEDRESS: a book of war-time verse**; by Robin Benn [and others]. Fortune Press. [1942]. 24 pp.

R. Benn, R.D. Birch, R. Smith, A. White. OXB

61. **POETS NOW IN THE SERVICES. Number One**. Collected and arranged by A.E. Lowy. Favil Press. [1943]. 16 pp.

Title from cover.

R.D. Birch, J.R. Blyth, K.M. Briggs, H. Compton, T. Horsley, S. Knowles, T.H. Middleton, E.C. Peters, D.B. Reade, M. Savage, P. Savage, R. Smith, A. White, C. Woodhouse. OXB

62. **POETS NOW IN THE SERVICES. Number Two**. Edited by A.E. Lowy. Favil Press. [1943]. [16] pp.

Title from cover.

J. Atkins, B. Bain, P. Baker, R.G. Buchanan, F.A.H. Burkitt, M. Delarche, R. Gentry, A.R. Gowland, T. Horsley, J.M. Lindsay, I.S. MacPhail, T.H. Middleton, E.C. Peters, M. Savage, P. Scott, M.O. Vawser, A. White.

OXB

63. **RETURN TO OASIS: war poems and recollections from the Middle East, 1940—1946**. Editors Victor Selwyn: Erik De Mauny, Ian Fletcher, G.S. Fraser, John Waller. Consultants Tambimuttu, John Cromer, with introduction by Lawrence Durrell. Shepheard-Walwyn: Editions Poetry London, for the Salamander Oasis Trust. 1980. xxxiv, 254 pp. il., maps, facsim.

T.I.F. Armstrong, J.G. Barker, R.E. Bee, G. Begg, J.A.K. Boninger, M. Bowden, H.I. Bransom, J.C. Braun, Bray, pseud., J. Bristow, J.E. Brookes, D. Burnie, K. Burrows, C. Carter, G. Crawthorne, I. Celner, L. Challoner, D. Charles, J. Charnock, R.C. Chopping, P.M. Clothier, B. Cole, J.M. Collard, M. Corbally, M. Croft, A.C.J. Davies, S. Day, E. De Mauny, C.P.S. Denham-Young, K. Douglas, E.P. Dudley, D. Dunhill, A. Dunn, T. Eastwood, D. Everett, P.J. Flaherty, I. Fletcher, G.S. Fraser, A.N. Freedman, H.M. Fridjohn, B.D. Gallie, B.D. Garland, E.B. Gill, C. Gimson, E.F. Gosling, W.G. Graham, P. Hellings, H. Henderson, R. Hildgard, W.G. Holloway, P.R. Hopkinson, L. Howe, B. Howroyd, N. Hudis, J. Jarmain, D. Jones, S. Keyes, H. Laming, L.K. Lawler, R.B. Lester, V.J. Locke, N. Longhurst, T.W. Louch,

E. McHale, D. McHarrie, S. Maclean, G. Malcolm, A.W. Marsden, M. Martin, N.T. Morris, P.M. Moulding, V. Musgrave, A.F. Noble, G.C. Norman, J. Nugent, B. O'Byrne, J. Papasian, G. Pearse, G.O. Physick, F. Pike, F.T. Prince, J. Pudney, M.C. Quinn, T.W. Ramsey, J. Rimington, R.M. Roberts, C. Robinson, J. Ropes, A. Samson, P.A. Saunders, J. Sayer, C.H.O. Scaife, T. Skelton, Alan Smithies, Arnold Smithies, C. Smithies, S. Stainthorp, C. Stanley, T. Stephanides, E. Storey, E. Thoms, N.J. Trapnell, J. Walker, R.N. Walker, J. Waller, E.A. Walmsley, J. Warry, V. West, D. Wilkinson, C.B. Wilson and five anon.   MPL

64. **RHYME AND REASON: 34 poems**. Edited by David Martin. Fore Publications. 1944. 32 pp.

M. Carpenter, C.M. Grieve, J. Lindsay, J.S. Manifold, D. Martin, H. Nicholson, J. Pudney, F. Scarfe, R. Swingler, M. Whittock.   OXB

65. **SAILING TO-MORROW'S SEAS: an anthology of new poems**; by [various writers]. Edited by Maurice Lindsay. With an introduction by Tambimuttu. Fortune Press. [1944]. 47 pp.

C. Hamblett, J.F. Hendry, P. Ledward, J.M. Lindsay, E. Litvinoff, N. Moore, F. Scarfe, T. Scott, J. Singer, R. Todd, H. Treece.   OXB

66. **SALAMANDER: a miscellany of poetry**. Edited by Keith Bullen and John Cromer. George Allen & Unwin. 1947. 128 pp. por.

T.I.F. Armstrong, M. Bowden, J.C. Braun, K. Bullen, E. De Mauny, G.S. Fraser, A. Rook, E.J. Simpson, J. Waller.   OXB

67. **SELECTIONS FROM *THE QUILL*: a collection of prose, verse and sketches; by officers prisoner-of-war in Germany, 1940–1945**. Edited by Captain E.G.C. Beckwith, T.D., 8th Bn The Sherwood Foresters. Country Life Ltd. 1947. 264 pp. il., col. il., por.

Cover-title is *The Quill*.

D.G. Adams, T.B., R.G. Bateson, J. Buxton, F.B. Chancellor, R.N. Christie, D.C.L. Holland, H.R. Horne, N.H. Kindersley, E.H. Lynn-Allen, R.C.S. MacGill, A.N.L. Munby, J.E. Pearson, J.F.S. Phillips, A.C. Rawlings, E. Ritchie, M.V.B. Riviere, C.B. Selby-Boothroyd, S.P. Symington, F.B. Topham, A.R.D. Twysden, R.C. Warlow-Harry, G.E.P. Wood.   OXB

68. **SOLDIERS' VERSE**. Verses chosen by Patric Dickinson. With original lithographs by William Scott. Frederick Muller Ltd. [1945]. viii, 119 pp. il. (New excursions into English poetry).

W.H. Auden, R. Campbell, R. Church, C. Day Lewis, P. Dickinson, T.S. Eliot, D. Gascoyne, S. Keyes, A. Lewis, A. Rook, S. Shannon, S. Spender, D. Thomas, U. Vaughan Williams.   MPL

69. **SOME POEMS IN WARTIME**. Diemer & Reynolds Ltd. [1941]. [ii], 22 pp.

R. Fuller, G. Grigson, N. Moore, F. Prokosch, A. Ridler, F. Scarfe, J. Symons, R. Todd, G. Woodcock. IWM

70. **The SPRING ANTHOLOGY 1940: a compilation of representative verse from the world's living poets**. Mitre Press. [1940]. 160 pp.

E.S.C. Anderson, J.B. Anderson, G. Burnett, A.H. Driver, A. Grosch, H.J. Halford, E.V. Hewins, M. Hodgkinson, E. Hutchinson, W.K. Lewis, J. Pomfret, I. Taylor. OXB

71. **The SPRING ANTHOLOGY 1941: a compilation of representative verse from the world's living poets**. Mitre Press. [1942]. 157 pp.

E.S.C. Anderson, J.B. Anderson, M.A. Bowler, G. Burnett, A. Grosch, E.V. Hewins, E. Hutchinson, W.K. Lewis, W. Matthews, P.J. Piggott, D.A.L. Prince, T.G. Reed, S.M. Spink, I. Taylor. OXB

72. **The SPRING ANTHOLOGY 1942: a compilation of representative verse from the world's living poets**. Mitre Press. [1943]. 145 pp.

E.S.C. Anderson, J.B. Anderson, M.A. Bowler, G. Burnett, F. Docherty, E. Gentle, E.V. Hewins, L.A. Lewis, W.K. Lewis, T.G. Reed, M. W. Rome. OXB

73. **The SPRING ANTHOLOGY 1943: a compilation of representative verse from the world's living poets**. Mitre Press. [1944]. 208 pp.

E.S.C. Anderson, J.B. Anderson, J. Bamford, E. Boothby, M.A. Bowler, D.C.F. Cambridge, F. Docherty, W. Ellams, W.G. Fallon, J.V. Francis, P. Friedlich, J. Gray, E. Hainsworth, H.J. Halford, G. Hanson, E.V. Hewins, M. John, E. Johnson, L.A. Lewis, W.K. Lewis, D.P. Lydford, G. Lynch, T. Marshall, B. Platten, J. Regan, D. Rendall, M.W. Rome, S.J. Saddington, B. Simpson, E. Smith, J.W. Snaith, J.R. Tovey, A. Wallace. OXB

74. **The SPRING ANTHOLOGY: a compilation of representative verse from the world's living poets**. Mitre Press. [1944]. 512 pp.

R. Albone, E.S.C. Anderson, I.L. Arnison, C. Atkins, M. Bartholomew, H. Bass, P.W. Bonds, D. Bowes, M.A. Bowler, G. Burgess, J.A. Canham, R. Capes, J.Y. Chadwick, M. Chamberlain, E. Chatfield, J. Clark, R.S. Clark, D. Clements, A. Collinge, B.R. Collins, W. Courcha, R.V. Darnell, J. Davidson, D. Dean, W. Dingwall, I.D. Doddridge, M. Douglas, E. Dutton, R.L. Edgar, L.B. Eggleston, G.S. Ellis, G. Evans, M. Feates, B. Flemhood, R. Fretton, D. Fullerton, R.A.J. Gazzard, E.A. Goffron, M. Grainger, R.W. Grant, E. Hainsworth, F. Hallett, J.R. Hawkes, J. Hawkins, M. Hawkridge, M. Hayward, R. Heald, F.L. Henderson, I. Howe, E.W. Jackson, E. Jay, M.E. John, C.S. Johnson, P.M. Jones, S. Jones, L. King, K. Kirk, V.M. Land, D.M. Lapsley, J.M. Lee, L.A. Lewis, W.K. Lewis, B. Lucas, G. Lynch, A. McHale, J.

MacKinnon, J. McLennan, J. McPherson, J. Macrobert, P.W. Manser, C. Manzie, S. Marks, E. Mason, R.A. Mee, L. Moir, A.H. Moulding, G. Mullen S. Napier, E. Neville, J.P. Nixon, R.W. Offley, A. Paradox, J. Park, L.H. Pearce, O. Peters, A.E.V. Posner, H. Powell, S.G. Print, J. Proctor, J.N. Radford, F. Richards, A. Robbins, B. Rockett, M. Rose, J.C. Ross, W.G. Rowe, N. Sabin, F.E.W. Savill, M. Sharpe, K.E. Shoyer, H.M.R. Sim, J.E. Smith, A. Snowden, A. Sparks, W.F. Spencer, J.O. Spires, F. Stevens, S.R. Stewart, E. Storey, H.W. Stott, B. Sutton, W.A. Taylor, P.A. Thornton, D. Tindall, F. Townsend, J.E. Treadwell, P.M. Tunnard, C.E. Weatherburn, F. Webb, W.E. Wild, P. Williams, G.S.B. Woodham. OXB

75. **The SPRING ANTHOLOGY 1945: a compilation of representative verse from the world's living poets**. Mitre Press. [1946]. 512 pp.

P.A. Alen, E. Anatole, J.B. Anderson, A. Blair, H.H. Blank, D. Boatwright, E. Boothby, L.B. Bradbury, J.A. Canham, P. Chapman, V. Coates, B. Cohen, J. Colledge, A. Collinge, W. Cooke, H.S. Day, G. Dorling, J. Douglas, R. Douglas, J. Eastwood, L.M. Falconer, W. Fell, R. Fergus, B. Flemhood, E. Gentle, J.P. Grant, T.W. Harrison, J.R. Hawkes, M. Hayward, J. Hewitt, J. Hopkinson, J.D. Huddleston, C. Humphries, E. Hyland, L.M. James, G. Jones, B.D. Kemp, C. Kendrick, E.M. Langford, W.K. Lewis, L. Lowe, D.P. Lydford, E. Lytton, J.F. McCarthy, A. McCaw, I. Marshall, G.J. Mason, W. Matthews, W.R. Merrill, M.R. Milner, G.L. Naylor, J.E. Negus, J.R. Neville, J. Park, G. Parry, L.H. Pearce, L. Read, J. Rogerson, M.L. Sawdon, G. Shaw, P.E. Shorter, S.F. Snell, J.R. Stephinson, H. Strand, H. Syddall, H. Trevelyan-Thomson, M.R. Turner, H. Turvey, J.M. Varcoe, D. Vickers, R.D. Walsh, R. Wardell, O. Watkins, A. Weinstein, R. West-Skinn, G. Wetton, K. White, E. Williams, P.C. Williams. OXB

76. **The TERRIBLE RAIN: the war poets 1939–1945**: an anthology selected and arranged, with an introduction and notes, by Brian Gardner. [New ed.]. Eyre Methuen Ltd. 1978. xxvi, 227 pp.

D. Allison, K. Allott, B. Allwood, W. Andrewes, J. Arlott, T.I.F. Armstrong, W.H. Auden, B. Bain, D. Bain, P. Baker, G. Barker, M. Barsley, J. Bayliss, D. Bourne, C. Branson, J. Bronowski, J. Brooke, A. Bryceson, J. Buxton, N. Cameron, R. Campbell, J.K. Cassels, C. Causley, R.L. Chaloner, R. Conquest, H. Corby, T. Corsellis, R.N. Currey, C. Day Lewis, P. Dehn, P. Dickinson, K. Douglas, G. Ewart, J. Farrar, K. Foottit, G.S. Fraser, D. Gascoyne, B. Gutteridge, S. Haggard, C. Hamblett, M. Hamburger, N. Hampson, C. Hassall, D. Hawkins, H. Henderson, R. Heppenstall, T.R. Hodgson, R.C.M. Howard, J. Jarmain, D.L. Jones, D.R.G. Jones, S. Keyes, F. King, P. Ledward, L. Lee, J. Lehmann, R. Levy, A. Lewis, J. Lindsay, J.M. Lindsay, L. Little, E. Litvinoff, L. MacNeice, H.B. Mallalieu, J.S. Manifold, G. Matthews, F. Mayo, K. Neal, H. Nicholson, N. Nicholson, W. Plomer, A. Potter, E. Powell, F.T. Prince, J. Pudney, D. Raikes, T.W. Ramsey, A. Rattenbury, D.B. Reade, H. Reed, K. Rhys, A. Ridler, M.V.B. Riviere, A. Rook, A. Ross, P. Savage, D.L.

Sayers, V. Scannell, F. Scarfe, P. Scott, I. Serraillier, E. Sitwell, M. Skinner, R. Spender, S. Spender, D. Stanford, G. Stewart, W.F.M. Stewart, G. Swaine, G.P. Symes, J. Symons, G.A. Taylor, D. Thomas, F. Thompson, T. Tiller, H.H. Tilley, R. Todd, J.R. Townsend, H. Treece, D. Van Den Bogaerde, G.A. Wagner, J. Walker, J. Waller, J. Wedge, A.N.C. Weir, D. Welch, L.J. Yates.
OXB

77. **THESE YEARS: an anthology of contemporary poetry**. Edited by Howard Sergeant. Leeds: E.J. Arnold & Son Ltd. [1950]. 112 pp.
A.V. Bowen, R. Church, I. Davies, C. Day Lewis, P. Dehn, L. Lee, L. MacNeice, J. Pudney, H. Reed, H. Sergeant. OXB

78. **THIS LIVING STONE: the Grey Walls anthology of new poems**. Edited with an introduction by Wrey Gardiner, and decorations by W. Barrington Pink. Billericay: Grey Walls Press. 1941. 67 pp.
M.E. Allan, R.D. Birch, S. Bryan, A. Comfort, M. Emmett, M. Howorth, P. Ledward, D. Levertov, N. Moore, R. Pearson, E.C. Peters, J. Waller, B. Warr. OXB

79. **TODAY'S NEW POETS: an anthology of contemporary verse**. Resurgam Books. [1944]. [68] pp.
J. Atkins, P. Baker, E. Berridge, A.V. Bowen, M.M. Crosland, C. Dyment, G.S. Fraser, F. Gelder, E. Litvinoff, N. Matthews, N. Moore, L. Norris, A. Rook, H. Treece. IWM

80. **VERSE OF VALOUR: an anthology of shorter war poems of sea, land, air**. Selected and arranged by John L. Hardie. Glasgow: Art and Educational Publishers Ltd. 1943. xvi, 128 pp. il.
C. Anceps, P. Baker, H. Balfour, G. Boshell, E.D. Cox, P. Dickinson, R. Fuller, R. Furse, W.W. Gibson, C.W. Greatorex, G.R. Hamilton, I.C. Henderson, S. Lynd, E. Mannin, G. Nichols, E. Phillpotts, E.J.M.D. Plunkett, A.L. Rowse, C. Sansom, F. Scarfe, J.B. Sidgwick, R. Spender, L.F. Stewart, E.M. Stobart, E. Thompson, R.B. Van Wart, J. Wedge, D. Wellesley, L. Whistler. OXB

81. **VERSES FROM LINCOLN'S INN**. [Edited by Michael Albery and others]. [Privately printed]. [1979?]. [v], 66 pp.
Section *War*: M. Albery, Q. Hogg, I. Warren. IWM

82. **The VOICE OF POETRY (1930–1950): an anthology**. Edited, with a critical introduction, by Hermann Peschmann. Evans Brothers Ltd. 1950. xliv, 249 pp.
W.H. Auden, L. Binyon, R. Bottrall, H. Corby, K. Douglas, W. Empson, I. Fletcher, G.S. Fraser, R. Fuller, D. Gibson, G.R. Hamilton, J. Heath-Stubbs, S. Keyes, N.T. Morris, E. Muir, F.T. Prince, J. Pudney, H. Reed, A. Rook, F.

Scarfe, E. Sitwell, S. Snaith, S. Spender, J. Symons, D. Thomas, H. Treece, S.D. Tremayne, J. Waller, L. Whistler.   OXB

83. **WAR AND THE POET: an anthology of poetry expressing man's attitudes to war from ancient times to the present**. Edited by Richard Eberhart and Selden Rodman. Westport, Connecticut: Greenwood Press. 1945. xlvi, 240 pp.

Part IV: W.H. Auden, G. Barker, T. Corsellis, R. Fuller, A. Lewis, L. MacNeice, J.S. Manifold, E. Sitwell, S. Spender, G. Stewart, D. Thomas.

BL

84. **WAR POEMS FROM *THE SUNDAY TIMES*: a selection from the poetry by various contributors which has appeared in 'The Sunday Times' since the beginning of the war**. Printed for private circulation. 1945. 94 pp.

C.A. Alington, H. Balfour, R.G. Barnes, L. Binyon, J. Buxton, R. Buxton, E. Chilman, R. Church, H.P. Cooke, N. Coward, R. Evans, B.R. Gibbs, W.W. Gibson, P. Hall, G.R. Hamilton, C. Hollis, C. Humphreys, G.H. Johnstone, F.L. Lucas, S. Lynd, J.H.F. McEwen, S. Maiden, H. Palmer, E.J.M.D. Plunkett, I. Procter, E. Raymond, E. Shanks, F. Singleton, J.C. Squire, P. Steegman, E. Talbot, R.G. Vansittart, G.W. Young.   OXB

85. **WAR POETRY: an anthology**. Edited with introduction and commentaries [by] D.L. Jones, Pergamon Press. [1968]. xii, 142 pp. (The Commonwealth and international library. Pergamon Oxford English series).

Section *The Second World War*: B.C. Amiel, C. Causley, L. MacNeice, H. Reed, R. Todd.   OXB

86. **WHERE STEEL WINDS BLOW**. Edited by Robert Cromie. New York: David McKay Co., Inc. 1968. xxx, 192 pp.

K. Barnes, E. Brock, T. Burke, A. Comfort, H. Corke, K. Douglas, D. Gascoyne, K. Gershon, M. Hacker, A.P. Herbert, K. Hopkins, L. MacNeice, H. Reed, H. Treece, J. Wain, H. Wolfe, T. Wright.   OXB

87. **WHILE THEY FOUGHT: an anthology of prose and verse exploring the lives of those who did not fight, but who had to endure the Second World War**. Compiled by Michael Marland and Robin Willcox. With a reading list by Cecilia Gordon and questions for discussion and suggestions for writing by Geoffrey Halson. Longman. 1980. viii, 167 pp. il. (Longman imprint books).

R. Fuller, D. Hawkins, P. Ledward, A. Lewis, E. Muir, N. Nicholson, V. Scannell, S. Spender.   OXB

Index to Anthologies

Compilers, Editors, Illustrators and Writers of Forewords, Introductions, Prefaces

ADAMS, D. Guy 5
AISTROP, Jack 11, 12, 13, 14
ALBERY, Michael 81
ARUNDEL, Honor 36
BAKER, Denys Val 28
BALDWIN, Michael 10
BEBBINGTON, W.G. 26
BECKWITH, E.G.C. 67
BELL, William 34, 54
BLUNDEN, Edmund 52
BLYTHE, Ronald 15
BOLD, Alan 30
BOZMAN, Mildred 48
BROOME, Jack 23
BULLEN, Keith 66
CARPENTER, Maurice 36
CHURCH, Richard 48
CLARKE, George Herbert 38
COMFORT, Alex 29
CROMER, John 63, 66
CROMIE, Robert 86
CUNARD, Nancy 42
CURREY, R.N. 43
DE MAUNY, Erick 31, 63
DICKINSON, Patric 68
DURRELL, Lawrence 63
EBERHART, Richard 83
ELLIOT, Walter 47
FEDDEN, Robin 40

FLETCHER, Ian 63
FRASER, G.S. 63
FRY, Edith M. 21
GARDINER, Wrey 78
GARDNER, Brian 76
GIBSON, R.V. 43
GODFREY-BARTRAM, Helen 16
GORDON, Cecilia 87
GREACEN, Robert 29
HALSON, Geoffrey 87
HAMBLETT, Charles 25
HAMILTON, Ian 59
HARDIE, John L. 80
JACKSON, Len 35
JENNINGS, Elizabeth 3
JONES, D.L. 85
LEDWARD, Patricia 52
LEESE, Oliver 44
LEHMANN, John 45
LINDSAY, Jack 36
LINDSAY, Maurice 65
LOWY, A.E. 61, 62
LYON, P.H.B. 41
MARLAND, Michael 87
MARTIN, David 64
MAWDSLEY, Norman 55
MONTGOMERY, Bernard 46
MONTGOMERY, Elizabeth 6
MOORE, Geoffrey 53

MOORE, Reginald   11, 12, 13, 14
MOULT, Thomas   2, 6, 7, 8, 9
NEW WRITING   45
PALMER, Herbert   22
PESCHMANN, Hermann   82
PINK, W. Barrington   78
PUDNEY, John   1
PYM, Roland   40
The QUILL   67
RATAZZI, Peter   27
RHYS, Keidrych   32, 33, 47
RODMAN, Selden   83
ROSCOE, Theodora   41
SACKVILLE-WEST, V.   50
SASSOON, Seigfried   44
SCOTT, William   68
SELWYN, Victor   63

SERGEANT, Howard   2, 19, 58, 77
SHAW, Robert   18
SILKIN, Jon   18
SITWELL, Edith   48
SKELTON, Robin   57
SMYTH, W.M.   17
STRANG, Colin   52
SUNDAY TIMES   84
SYMONS, Julian   4
TAMBIMUTTU, M.J.   56, 63, 65
TREECE, Henry   1
WALLER, John   31, 63
WERE, Mary Winter   41
WILLCOX, Robin   87
WILLIAMS, Oscar   37
WINTON, John   23
WOLLMAN, Maurice   51

Individual Authors

A.C.T. *see* **TARBAT, Alan C.,** (A.C.T.)

A.M. *see* **M., A.**

A.T. *see* **T., A.**

AARONSON, Lazarus, (Leonard Aaronson, pseud.) (1894–   . Of London)
The homeward journey, and other poems. Christophers. 1946. 64 pp.   BPL
see also   38, 51

AARONSON, Leonard, pseud. *see* **AARONSON, Lazarus**, (Leonard Aaronson, pseud.)

ABBOTT, Claude Colleer (1889–1971. Educated at King Edward VI School, Chelmsford, and Gonville & Caius College, Cambridge. Poet of the First World War. Artists' Rifles Officer Training Corps, 1918. Second-Lieutenant, Irish Guards Special Reserve. Professor of English Language & Literature, Durham University, 1932–54)
Collected poems, 1918–1958. Sidgwick & Jackson. 1963. viii, 168 pp.   MPL
The sand castle, and other poems. Jonathan Cape. 1946. 54 pp.   MPL

ABBOTT, Frank Willis
Songs of London: [poems]. Regency Press. [1962]. 88 pp.   MPL

ABBOTT, Mason (1920–   . Served in the Far East, captured by the Japanese in 1942. Of Kendal, Lake District)
Twicers: [poems]. Walton-on Thames: Outposts Publications. 1980. 12 pp.
OXB

ABBOTT, W.H. (Poet of the First World War)
Twenty-five sonnets. First series. Edwin Trim & Co., Ltd. 1949. 28 pp.

IWM

Twenty-five sonnets. Second series. Edwin Trim & Co. Ltd. 1950. 28 pp.

IWM

ABEL, S. (Corporal. Served with the Eighth Army in the Western Desert) *see* 46

ABRAHAM, Nellie (Poet of the First World War)
Poems for the people. Ilfracombe: Arthur H. Stockwell, Ltd. 1952. 16 pp.

OXB

ABREY, Colin
Poems. Ilfracombe: Arthur H. Stockwell Ltd. 1970. 15 pp.   OXB

ACKERLEY, Joe Randolph (1896–1967. b. Herne Hill, Somerset. Educated at Rossall School and Cambridge University. Assistant, B.B.C. Talks Department, 1928–35. Literary editor of *The Listener*, 1935–59)
Micheldever, and other poems. With an introduction by Francis King and a frontispiece by Don Bachardy. Ian McKelvie. 1972. 29 pp. por.
     A limited ed. of 350 numbered copies.   OXB

ACKLAND, Valentine (1906–69. Educated at Queen's College, London, and in Paris. A close friend of Sylvia Townsend Warner, with whom she published a book of poems in 1933. Served as a Civil Defence clerk in Dorset. Converted to Roman Catholicism in 1946)
Further poems. Beckenham, Kent: Welmont Publishing. [1978]. 71 pp. il. (by Colin Kersey). (Welmont poets).
     Cover illustration of the author is reproduced from an original drawing by Eric Gill.   OXB
The nature of the moment, [*and other poems*]. Chatto & Windus. 1973. 63 pp.
see also 42   BL

ADAMS, Donovan Guy (Lieutenant-Colonel, East Surrey Regiment. Captured at St Valery, France, when commanding the 2nd/6th East Surreys in 1940. Held prisoner of war in Germany until 1945. Novelist, and editor of the anthology *Backwater*, 1944) *see* 5, 67

ADCOCK, Fleur (1934– . b. New Zealand. Spent the war in England, returning to New Zealand with her family in 1947. There she married the poet Alistair Campbell, later divorced. Graduated from Victoria University, Wellington, afterwards training as a librarian. Settled in London in 1963)
The inner harbour, [*and other poems*]. Oxford Univesity Press. 1979. viii, 55 pp.

OXB

The scenic route: [*poems*]. Oxford University Press. 1974. [viii], 43 pp.

OXB

ADDERLEY, Thomas Edward Browne
Limerick pastoral, and other poems. Dublin: Richview Press. 1953. 27 pp.
OXB
Poems by a quasi-rebel. Mitre Press. 1960. 69 pp.
MPL

ADDISON, William (1891–1966. b. Dunfermline. Educated at George Watson's College, Edinburgh, and Edinburgh and Glasgow Universities. Church of Scotland minister, Parish of Ettrick and Buccleuch, 1929–53)
Ettrick verse. Edinburgh: Ettrick Press Ltd. 1949. 72 pp.
Some in Scots dialect.
BL
Napier verse. Printed Selkirk: Walter Thomson. 1960. 32 pp. por.
OXB
see also 2

ADEANE, Louis (Worked in Civil Defence. Imprisoned as a conscientious objector)
The night loves us: thirty-two poems. Fordingbridge, Hampshire: Delphic Press. [1946]. 39 pp.
OXB
see also 19, 25

ADIE, Catherine Scott- *see* **SCOTT-ADIE, Catherine**

AITKENHEAD, Mary Gardner Ure (Of Oldham, Lancashire?)
Songs and verses. Printed Newport, Monmouthshire: R.H. Johns Ltd. 1967. xiv, 117 pp. il. (by the author).
OXB

AKERS, Charles J.H. (Of York)
Thirty-one poems. York: Author. [1946]. [iv], 54 pp.
OXB

ALANE, Bernard (Served in H.M. Forces for five years, at home and in the Far East)
Because no angels came: new poetry. Ilfracombe: Arthur H. Stockwell, Ltd. 1949. 96 pp.
OXB

ALBERY, Michael (1910–75. Educated at Uppingham School, and Exeter College, Oxford. Called to the Bar in 1934. Served in Royal Artillery from outbreak of war until discharged on account of wounds in June 1942. Q.C. and writer on law. Director of Wyndham Theatres Ltd, 1947–62) *see* 81

ALBONE, Ronald (Served in H.M. Forces) *see* 74

ALCESTE, pseud.
"Peace in our time", [*and other poems*]; by "Alceste". Ilfracombe: Arthur H. Stockwell, Ltd. [1944]. 16 pp.
OXB

ALDEN, John (1902–62. b. New York State. Educated at Tonbridge School and Oxford University. Lived in Kent for many years)

The crossways, [and other poems]. Aldington, Kent: Hand and Flower Press. [1951]. 357–388 pp. (Poems in pamphlet, 1951, XII). BL

Kentish rhymes: or, obiter cantiana. With decorations by Stanley Hickson. Printed City of Canterbury School of Art. 1945. viii, 13 pp. il. BL

ALDER, Eric Reginald

Witness the darkness, and other poems. Ilfracombe: Arthur H. Stockwell, Ltd. 1950. 16 pp. OXB

ALEN, P.A. (Served in H.M. Forces) *see* 75

ALEXANDER, Dai *see* 36

ALEXANDER, Elizabeth, pseud. *see* **SLATER, Dora Helen Agnes**, (Elizabeth Alexander, pseud.)

ALINGTON, Cyril Argentine (1872–1955. Educated at Marlborough College, and Trinity College, Oxford. A Doctor of Divinity. Poet of the First World War. Headmaster of Shrewsbury School, 1908–16, and of Eton College, 1916–33. Chaplain to the King, 1921–33. Dean of Durham, 1933–51. One son was killed on active service in the Second World War)

In shabby streets, and other verses. Eton College; Spottiswoode, Ballantyne & Co. Ltd. 1942. 63 pp. MPL
see also 42, 84

ALLAN, Mabel Esther (1915– .b. Wallasey, Cheshire. Educated at private schools. Served in Women's Land Army. Crime writer and children's novelist) *see* 38, 78

ALLEN, Bill *see* **ALLEN, Christopher Edward** (Bill)

ALLEN, Christopher Edward (Bill) (Commissioned in Royal Air Force)
Meditations in verse; by C.E. ('Bill') Allen. Ilfracombe: Arthur H. Stockwell, Ltd. 1954. 16 pp. OXB

ALLEN, Esmond Harcourt Lynn- *see* **LYNN-ALLEN, Esmond Harcourt**

ALLEYNE, E.
Slowly into twilight: [poems]. Ilfracombe: Arthur H. Stockwell, Ltd. [1965]. 16 pp. OXB

ALLFREY, Phyllis Shand (1915– . b. Dominica, West Indies, where her father was Crown Attorney. Returned to England during the war, working for

London County Council as a welfare adviser to the bombed. A founder of the Dominican Labour Party, she was elected M.P. and became a minister of the Federal Government. Editor of the *Dominica Star*. Novelist and poet)

In circles: poems. Printed Raven Press. 1940. 20 pp.

A limited ed. of 300 numbered copies. OXB
see also 38

ALLISON, Drummond (1921–43). b. Caterham, Surrey. Educated at Bishop's Stortford College, and Queen's College, Oxford. A friend of John Heath-Stubbs and Sidney Keyes. Lieutenant, East Surrey Regiment, seconded to West Surrey Regiment as an Intelligence Officer. Served in North Africa and Italy. Killed in the fighting on the Garigliano, 2 December 1943)

The poems of Drummond Allison. Edited by Michael Sharp. Reading: Whiteknights Press. 1978. xviii, 86 pp.

Dedicated to John Heath-Stubbs. A limited ed. of 200 numbered copies. OXB

The yellow night: poems 1940–41—42–43. Portrait and decorations by David Haughton. Fortune Press. 1944. 48 pp. il., por. BPL
see also 20, 25, 54, 59, 76

ALLOTT, Kenneth (1912–73. b. Glamorgan. Educated at King's College, Durham, and St Edmund Hall, Oxford. Assistant editor of *New Verse*, 1938–39. Biographer, poet and critic. Worked as a journalist, schoolmaster, and staff tutor in adult education. Taught at Liverpool University from 1947. General editor of the *Pelican Book of English Prose*)

Collected poems. Foreword by Roy Fuller. Secker & Warburg. 1975. 110 pp. MPL

The ventriloquist's doll, [and other poems]. Cresset Press. [1943], 64 pp. MPL
see also 25, 56, 76

ALLWOOD, Brian (–1944. Worked with Mass Observation before the war. Joined the Royal Air Force in 1941. Sent to North Africa in 1942, mentioned in despatches in June 1943. Killed in Italy on 30 June 1944 and is buried at Caserta)

Now or never, [and other poems]. Resurgam Books. [1944]. 16 pp. (Resurgam younger poets, 10).

Title from cover. OXB
see also 25, 33, 76

ALMEDINGEN, Editha Martha (1898–1971. b. St Petersburg, Russia. Educated at Xenia Nobility School and Petrograd University. Lecturer on English Mediaeval History & Literature at Petrograd University, 1920–22. Came to England in 1923. Lecturer on Russian Literature, Oxford University, 1951. Novelist and poet)

Out of Seir: a poem. John Lane the Bodley Head. 1943. 32 pp. MPL

Poloniae testamentum: a poem. John Lane the Bodley Head. 1942. 94 pp.
A limited ed. of 500 numbered copies.   MPL

ALSTON, Audrey (Of Norfolk?)
Some thoughts: [poems]. Printed Norwich: Rigby Printing Co. Ltd. [1944].
40 pp.   OXB

ALTER EGO, pseud.
Regime already: [poems]; by Alter Ego. Ilfracombe: Arthur H. Stockwell, Ltd.
[1942]. 19 pp.   OXB

AMIEL, Barry Conrad (Lieutenant, Heavy Anti-Aircraft, Royal Artillery.
Served in the Middle East and India. Of London)   *see*   43, 85

AMIS, Kingsley (1922–   . b. London. Educated at City of London School,
and St John's College, Oxford. Lieutenant, Royal Corps of Signals, 1942–45.
Lecturer, University College, Swansea, 1949–61. Fellow of Peterhouse,
Cambridge, 1961–63. Married the novelist Elizabeth Jane Howard, later
divorced. Novelist, poet, playwright, journalist, editor, and writer of short
stories and non-fiction)
Bright November: poems. Fortune Press. [1948]. 32 pp.   MPL
A case of samples: poems 1946—1956. Victor Gollancz Ltd. 1956. 72 pp.
                                                                          OXB
Collected poems, 1944—1979. Hutchinson. 1979. [ii], 154 pp.   OXB
see also   25, 59

AMOS, Stella W.R.
Selected poems (illustrated). Ilfracombe: Arthur H. Stockwell, Ltd. [1948].
16 pp. il.   OXB

AMSTUTZ, Eveline (Brought up in Dorset and educated privately. Poet of the
First World War. Married a Swiss. Lived in St Moritz for nine years, eventually
settling in a large house by the Lake of Zurich)
A book of verse. Zurich: Amstutz, Herdeg & Co. 1943. 85 pp.
A limited ed. of 500 copies.   MPL

ANATOLE, Ephraima (Of London)   *see*   75

ANCEPS, Charles   *see*   80

ANDERSON, Elspeth S.C. (Of Edinburgh)   *see*   70, 71, 72, 73, 74

ANDERSON, Gwyneth
A time to speak, [and other poems]. Aldington, Kent: Hand and Flower Press.
1951. 165–196 pp. (Poems in pamphlet, 1951, VI).   BL

ANDERSON, James B. (Of Ayrshire) *see* 70, 71, 72, 73, 75

ANDERSON, John Redwood (1883–1964. b. Manchester. Educated privately, and for a short time at Trinity College, Oxford. Assistant master at Hymers College, Hull, 1915–43)
Brim of day: [*poems*]. Fortune Press. 1945. 24 pp.　　　　　　**OXB**
see also 7, 51

ANDERSON, Lex (Of Edinburgh)
Grim and gay: poems. Illustrations by James Proudfoot. Edinburgh: Privately printed. 1944. xvi, 279 pp. il.　　　　　　**BPL**

ANDERSON, Mary Désirée (1902–　b. Great Shelford, Cambridgeshire, daughter of Sir Hugh Anderson, Master of Gonville & Caius College, Cambridge. A civilian in London during the early years of the war. Writer on British churches. Married Sr Trenchard Cox)
Bow bells are silent: [*poems*]. Williams & Norgate Ltd. 1943. 32 pp.　　**OXB**

ANDERSON, Patrick (1915–　. b. Ashtead, Surrey. Educated at Sherborne School, Worcester College, Oxford, and Columbia University, New York. Former President of the Oxford Union. Travelled widely in Canada, the United States and the Far East, 1938–52. Involved in poetry activities centred in Montreal in the 1940s. Assistant Professor, McGill University, Montreal, 1948–50. Lecturer, Malaysia University, 1950–52. Lecturer, Dudley Training College, Worcestershire, 1954–57. Appointed to Trent Park College of Education, Hertfordshire, in 1957) *see* 57

ANDREW, Father *see* **HARDY, Henry Ernest** (Father Andrew)

ANDREWES, Walter (1913–　. Educated at Canford School, and Keble College, Oxford. Editor of *Isis*. Literary agent before the war. Served in the Army, going to France in 1939 and returning via Dunkirk. Later became a Staff Captain based in London) *see* 12, 13, 76

ANDREWS, Arthur Westlake (Educated at Charterhouse, and Magdalen College, Oxford. Served in France in the First World War, a Special Constable in the Second. Of St Ives, Cornwall)
Selected poems on West Penwith; and, Reflections. Vol. 1. St Ives: Author. 1957. 60 pp.　　　　　　**OXB**

ANDREWS, Averil
The little monkey, [*and other poems*]. Oxford: Shakespeare Head Press. 1939. [vi], 30 pp.　　　　　　**OXB**
White allegory, and other poems. Printed Lewes: W.E. Baxter, Ltd. [1950]. 23 pp.
　　　　　　OXB

ANGELINA, pseud.
An autobiography in poetry; [by] Angelina. Parkgate nr Southampton: G.A. Bast. 1973. 57 pp.   OXB

ANGOLD, John Penrose (1909–43. A law student before the war. Pilot Officer, Royal Air Force. Killed on active service)
Collected poems. With an introduction by Ronald Duncan. Peter Russell. 1952. 56 pp.
    A limited ed. of 350 numbered copies.   OXB

ANNAND, J.K.   *see*   23

The ANONYMOUS ELEGIES, and other poems. Fortune Press. 1945. 24 pp.   OXB

APTHOMAS, Ifan (1917–   . of Wrexham, North Wales)
Journey to the silverless island: [poems]. Bala: Cromlech Press. [1958]. 20 pp.
                                                                         OXB

ARCHER, Elaine, pseud.
The cycle of the months, and other poems; by "Elaine Archer". Ilfracombe: Arthur H. Stockwell, Ltd. [1942]. 16 pp.   OXB

ARCHER, Jack (Of Leicester)
A short collection of poems. Leicester: Clifton Press Ltd. 1975. 28 pp.
    Title from cover.   OXB

ARCHER, William George (1907–79. Educated at Strand School, and Emmanuel College, Cambridge. Entered Indian Civil Service in 1930. Held a variety of important posts, retiring in 1948. Keeper, Indian Section, Victoria & Albert Museum, 1948–59)
The plains of the sun: poems. Routledge. 1948. xii, 107 pp.   OXB

ARCHIBALD, Ruth
Clarion call: war-time poems. Epworth Press. 1944. 36 pp.   BL

ARIEL, pseud.   *see*   **CHAVE, Owen** (Ariel, pseud.)

ARKELL, Reginald (1882–1959. Educated at Burford Grammar School, Oxfordshire. Trained as a journalist. Poet of the First World War. Author and dramatist, he wrote many revues and musical comedies. Lived at Cricklade, Wiltshire)
Collected green fingers: a present for a good gardener: [poems]. Pictured by Eugène Hastain and Edgar Norfield. Herbert Jenkins. 1956. 255 pp. il.   OXB
Green fingers again: a further present for a good gardener: [poems]. Pictured by Edgar Norfield. Herbert Jenkins Ltd. 1942. 96 pp. il.   IWM

War rumours. Rhymed by Reginald Arkell. Pictured by Edgar Norfield. C. Arthur Pearson Ltd. 1939. 45 pp. il.   BPL

ARLETT, Vera Isabel (1896–   . b. Wolverhampton. Lecturer, playwright, poet, contributor to many periodicals. Received the Medal for Lyric Poetry at Liverpool University, 1931. Of Worthing, Sussex)
Christmas carols and winter poems. Hove, Sussex: Combridges. 1944. 25 pp.
                                                                        OXB

ARLOTT, John (1914–   . b. Basingstoke, Hampshire. Educated at Queen Mary's School. Clerk in a mental hospital, 1930–34. Police Detective Sergeant, 1934–45. B.B.C. Producer, 1945–50. General Instructor, B.B.C. Staff Training School, 1951–53. Cricket commentator and producer of poetry programmes. Wine correspondent and general writer for *The Guardian*. Sports Journalist of 1979, Sports Personality of 1980, Sports Presenter of the Year 1980)
Clausentum: sonnets. Drawings by Michael Ayrton. Jonathan Cape. 1946. 28 pp. il.   MPL
Of period and place: [poems]. Jonathan Cape. 1944. 45 pp.   IWM
see also 76

ARMOUR, Margaret (–1943. b. West Lothian. Educated at George Watson's Ladies College, Edinburgh. Studied and taught German in Munich. Translator from the German of Heinrich Heine. Married W.B. Macdougall in 1895. Lived in Edinburgh)
Singing down the years: selected poems. Edinburgh: Albyn Press. 1954. 75 pp.
                                                                        OXB

ARMSTRONG, Terence Ian Fytton, (John Gawsworth, pseud.) 1912–70. b. Kensington, London. Educated at Merchant Taylors' School. Co-ordinator of the neo-Georgian lyric poetry movement in 1937. Served in the Royal Air Force, 1941–46, as a Sergeant in North Africa, the Middle East and Italy, and as a Flying Officer in India. Elected to the Salamander Society of Poets, Cairo, 1944. Poet, bibliographer and bookman. Editor of *The Literary Digest* and *The Poetry Review*)
The collected poems of John Gawsworth. Sidgwick & Jackson Ltd. 1948. xvi, 143 pp. por.   MPL
De Londres à Carthage: poèmes; [by] Jean Gawsworth. Tunis: Ed. Saliba. [1944?]. 12 pp. por.
    Title from cover. A limited ed. of 110 numbered copies. Parallel English and French texts.   OXB
Deux poèmes de la Tunisie; [by] John Gawsworth. Traduits par Arthur Pellegrin. Printed Italy. 1944. [3] pp.
    Title from cover. Parallel English and French texts.   OXB
Into Europe: ten verses, September–December 1943, for J.H.R. Owen; [by] John Gawsworth. Printed Italy. 1944. [8] pp.

Title from cover. OXB

Legacy to love: selected poems, 1931–1941; by John Gawsworth. Collins. 1943.
80 pp. por. MPL

Marlow Hill: poems; by John Gawsworth. Richards. 1941. 32 pp. OXB

The mind of man: poems; by John Gawsworth. Richards. 1940. 32 pp. il. OXB

Out of Africa: fourteen verses, November 1942–July 1943; [by] John Gawsworth.
Printed Italy. 1944. [8] pp.

Title from cover. OXB

Pensées en Tunisie; [by] John Gawsworth. Traduction de Nancy Cunard.
Printed Italy. 1944. [8] pp.

Title from cover. Parallel French and English texts. OXB

see also 12, 25, 31, 42, 44, 49, 51, 63, 66, 76

ARMSTRONG, W.A. (Lieutenant. Served with the Eighth Army) *see* 44

ARNISON, I.L. (Of Middlesex) *see* 74

ARTHUR, Brendon S. (Of Buckinghamshire?)

Aston Clinton, and other poems. Arthur H. Stockwell, Ltd. [1941]. [24] pp.
OXB

ARUNDEL, Honor (1919–73. b. Llanarmon, Gwynedd. Educated at Hayes
Court, Kent, and Somerville College, Oxford. Called up for work as a fitter in
an engineering factory. Co-editor of the anthology *New Lyrical Ballads*, 1945.
Married Alex McCrindle in 1952. Journalist, critic of film, radio and
theatre) *see* 28, 36, 42

ASHBROOK, John (b. Lancashire, son of a Manchester businessman.
Educated at Manchester Grammar School and Manchester University. An
educational psychologist. Of Manchester)

In the footsteps of the opium eater, [and other poems]. Liskeard: Harry Chambers.
1980. 62 pp. (Peterloo poets). OXB

ASHTON, Winifred, (Clemence Dane, pseud.) (1888–1965. b. Blackheath.
Educated in England, Germany and Switzerland, and at the Slade School of
Art. Novelist, playwright, short story writer. President of the Society of Women
Journalists. Compiled *The Shelter Book* — 'tales, poems, essays, notes and
notions for use in shelters, tubes, basements and cellars in war time', 1940)

Trafalgar Day 1940; by Clemence Dane. William Heinemann Ltd. [1940].
14 pp. MPL

see also 38, 41

ASHTOWN, Lord *see* **TRENCH, Robert Power, Lord Ashtown**

ASHWIN, John (Of Devonshire)
In this our day: [poems]. [Torquay]: Torquay Times & Devonshire Press Ltd. [1944]. 39 pp. IWM

ASKE, Lake (Of West Bridgeford, Nottingham)
The high and the lowly: poems. Fortune Press. 1956. 30 pp. OXB

ASPLEN, Gertrude
Poems old and new, grave and gay. Ilfracombe: Arthur H. Stockwell, Ltd. 1951. 103 pp. OXB

ASQUITH, Hon. Herbert (1881–1947). Eldest surviving son of 1st Earl of Oxford & Asquith. Educated at Winchester College, and Balliol College, Oxford. President of the Oxford Union, 1903. Called to the Bar, 1907. Poet of the First World War. Saw active service in France and Flanders as Captain, Royal Field Artillery. With Sussex Home Guard in 1940, later becoming second in command of a Company)
Youth in the skies, and other poems. Sidgwick & Jackson Ltd. 1940. viii, 97 pp. IWM
see also 7

ATKIN, Leon (Army Chaplain)
If men should ask: poems of war and peace. Cardiff: Western Mail and Echo Ltd. 1947. 71 pp. por. OXB

ATKINS, Charles (Served in H.M. Forces) *see* 74

ATKINS, John (1916– . b. Carshalton, Surrey. Educated at Bristol University. Served in the Home Guard. Lecturer in English at Benghazi University, Libya, 1968–70, and at Lodz University, Poland, 1970–76. Literary critic and novelist. Of Colchester, Essex)
Experience of England: [poems]. Favil Press Ltd. [1943]. 16 pp. (Resurgam younger poets, 8).
    Title from cover. BL
see also 36, 52, 62, 79

ATTFIELD, Hilda M. (b. Durham. Lived in the United States)
Echoes of war, and other verse. Ilfracombe: Arthur H. Stockwell, Ltd. [1943]. 47 pp. OXB

ATTHILL, Robin (1912– . Educated at Stowe School, and Trinity College, Oxford. A schoolmaster from 1935, teaching at Ampleforth College and at Sherborne and Downside Schools. Poet, lecturer on local history and industrial archaeology. Of Bath)
If pity departs, and other poems. Andrew Dakers Ltd. 1947. 64 pp. IWM
see also 42

AUDEN, Wystan Hugh (1907–73. b. York. Educated at Gresham's School, Holt, and Christ Church, Oxford. Taught at Larchfield Academy, Helensburgh, and at the Downs School, Colwall, after leaving Oxford. Leader of the group of left wing poets in the 1930s. Married Erika, daughter of Thomas Mann, in 1935. Served in the Spanish Civil War. Emigrated to the United States early in 1939, eventually becoming an American citizen. His residence there was the subject of a question in the House of Commons on 13 June 1940. Served with the Strategic Bombing Survey of the United States Army. Held teaching appointments at Michigan University, Ann Arbor, 1941–42, at Swarthmore College, Pennsylvania, 1942–45, and at Smith College, Massachusetts, in 1952. Professor of Poetry, Oxford University, 1956–61. Leading poet of the twentieth century, recipient of many literary honours and awards)

Another time: poems. Faber & Faber Ltd. 1940. 125 pp. MPL

Collected poems. Edited by Edward Mendelson. Faber & Faber. 1976. 696 pp. OXB

The collected poetry of W.H. Auden. New York: Random House. [1945]. xiv, 466 pp.

Dedicated to Christopher Isherwood and Chester Kallman. OXB

Collected shorter poems, 1927–1957. Faber & Faber Ltd. 1966. 351 pp. OXB

Collected shorter poems, 1927–1957. Faber & Faber Ltd. 1969. 351 pp. (Faber paper covered editions). OXB

Collected shorter poems, 1930–1944. Faber & Faber Ltd. 1950. 303 pp. MPL

The double man: [poems]. New York: Random House. [1941]. 189 pp.

Includes substantial notes. OXB

The English Auden: poems, essays and dramatic writings, 1927–1939. Edited by Edward Mendelson. Faber & Faber. 1977. xxvi, 469 pp. MPL

New year letter. Faber & Faber. 1941. 188 pp. MPL

Selected poems. Edited by Edward Mendelson. Faber & Faber. 1979. xxii, 314 pp. OXB

A selection: [poems]. With notes and a critical essay by Richard Hoggart. Hutchinson Educational. 1961. 224 pp. (Hutchinson English texts). MPL

see also 4, 15, 18, 25, 26, 30, 45, 51, 56, 57, 68, 76, 82, 83

AULD, Thomas McNeill (Served with the Royal Flying Corps in the First World War. Of Twickenham, Middlesex)

Beyond these voices: [poems]. G.T. Foulis & Co., Ltd. [1954]. 46 pp. OXB

The book of Thomas Rhymer: [poems]. Richmond, Surrey: Richmond and Twickenham Arts Club. 1946. 48 pp. IWM

AUSTIN, Charles

Trapped man, break out!: [poems]. Walton-on-Thames: Outposts Publications. 1975. 36 pp. OXB

AYERS, Rowan (Worked for the B.B.C.)
Aspects in adolescence (being the moods of a young man): [*poems*]. Arthur H. Stockwell Ltd. [1940].˙32 pp.   OXB

AYLING, Alan
The long way round: a selection of poems. Andoversford, Gloucestershire: Whittington Press. [1977]. xii, 56 pp.
    A limited ed. of 200 numbered copies.   OXB

AYLWYN, Alice, pseud.
Many moods: a selection from the verses of Alice Aylwyn. Chaterson Ltd. 1950. xii, 58 pp.   OXB

B., E.H. *see* **BLAKENEY, Edward Henry**, (E.H.B.)

B., M.B. *see* **BOOTH, Madeleine Beatrice**, .(M.B.B.)

B., T. (Prisoner of war in Germany, 1940–45) *see* 67

BAILEY, A. (Corporal. Served with the Eighth Army) *see* 25, 44

BAILEY, A. Henry (Served with the Royal Queen's Regiment in the Western Desert and Italy. Of Portsmouth)
One man's war: poems. Printed Dunfermline: Pandaprint. [1979]. [11] pp.
    Title from cover.   BPL
One man's war: poems. [Portsmouth]: Author. [1980]. [29] pp.
    Printed on one side of leaf only.   OXB

BAILEY, Cameron (1922–44. Educated at St Edward's School, Oxford. Served in the King's Royal Rifle Corps in Normany. Killed in action in August 1944) *see* 20

BAILEY, James Richard Abe (1919– . b. England, brought up in South Africa. Flew with Oxford University Air Squadron pre-war. Served in Fighter Command)
F as in flight: [*poems*]. Eton, Windsor: Shakespeare Head Press. 1961. 71 pp.
    MPL

BAILLEY, W.R. (Chief Stoker, Royal Navy) *see* 23

BAIN, Bruce, (Richard Findlater, pseud.) (1921– . b. London. Served in the Royal Air Force. Journalist, critic and author) *see* 62, 76

BAIN, Donald (1922— . b. Liverpool. Educated at King's College Cambridge. Served in the Royal Artillery and the Gordon Highlanders, invalided out in 1944. Took up an acting career. A contributor to *Penguin New Writing* and co-editor of *Oxford and Cambridge Writing*, 1942)   *see*   45, 53, 59, 76

BAIN, Robert (Poet of the First World War. Writer on Scottish history)
Mice and men: [*poems*]. Glasgow: John Wylie & Co. 1941. 44 pp.   OXB

BAIRACLI-LEVY, Juliette de   *see*   **DE BAIRACLI-LEVY, Juliette**

BAIRD, Alexander (1925–   . b. Liverpool. Educated at Liverpool Institute High School, and Emmanuel College, Cambridge. Served with the Royal Air Force in Italy, Egypt and Iraq. Lecturer in English Literature at Hiroshima University, Japan, 1959–62. Worked for the British Council until 1965, then at Exeter University)
Poems. Chatto & Windus; Hogarth Press. 1963. 48 pp. (Phoenix living poets).
MPL

BAKER, Doris
Poems. Ilfracombe: Arthur H. Stockwell Ltd. 1946. 28 pp.   OXB

BAKER, Edward (1916–   . Of Blackheath, Staffordshire)
Initial effort: 52 poems of war and peace. Fortune Press. 1943. 64 pp.   BPL

BAKER, Peter (1921–66. About to enter Trinity College, Cambridge, when war was declared but instead enlisted in the Royal Artillery. Captain in Intelligence in 1941, returning to field service in 1942. Served in Africa and Italy, being wounded. Captured by the Gestapo. General editor of Resurgam Books. Publisher and M.P.)
"The beggar's lute": 21 poems writen under the impact of war. Favil Press Ltd. [1940]. [6] pp. (Resurgam younger poets, 1).
   Title from cover.   BL
see also   25, 33, 38, 47, 52, 62, 76, 79, 80

BAKER, William Walter
War poems, and others. Ilfracombe: Arthur H. Stockwell, Ltd. 1945. 48 pp.
OXB

BALDWIN, Marjorie (1911–   . At Louvain University, Belgium, in May 1940 on an exchange fellowship in philosophy. One of 1,700 people evacuated on a troopship escorted by two British destroyers and fourteen French planes, finally reaching Dover on 17 May. Member of Camden Poetry Group and an elected member of the Poetry Society of America. Of Horsham, West Sussex)
Poems and translations. Fortune Press. 1961. 48 pp.   MPL

BALDWIN, Michael (1930–   . b. Gravesend. Educated at St Edmund Hall, Oxford. Lecturer at London University and Whitelands College. Novelist, poet, broadcaster, and writer on educational subjects. Editor of the anthology *Billy the Kid*, 1963)

    Buried god: selected poetry. Hodder & Stoughton. 1973. 215 pp.   OXB

BALFOUR, Harold, Lord Balfour of Inchyre (1897– . Joined 60th Rifles in 1914, attached to Royal Flying Corps in 1915 and Royal Air Force in 1918, serving on the western front. Conservative M.P. for Isle of Thanet, 1929–45. Under Secretary of State for Air, 1938–44. Shared responsibility for building up Britain's air strength and played a leading part in the conception of the Commonwealth Air Training scheme) *see*   80, 84

BALL, Arthur
    A place for Tritons, [and other poems]. Printed Headley Brothers Ltd. [1954]. 63 pp.   OXB
    Sea acres: [poems]. Peter Ratazzi. 1947. [ii], 68 pp.   OXB

BALL, F.C. *see* 6

BALL, Richard (1919–)
    Chain, [and other poems]. Ilfracombe: Arthur H. Stockwell Ltd. 1974. 117 pp.
        OXB
    In memory of Dylan Thomas: [poems]. Corsham, Wiltshire: Gazebo Books. 1969. viii, 35 pp.   OXB

BALLANTRAE, Lord *see* **FERGUSSON, Bernard, Lord Ballantrae**

BAMFIELD, John H.
    Verses grave and gay. Printed Bristol: J.W. Arrowsmith Ltd. 1960. [ii], 147 pp.
      Printed for private circulation.   OXB

BAMFORD, James (Served in H.M. Forces)   *see* 73

BANCROFT, Ian (Educated at Oxford University. Served in H.M. Forces) *see* 49, 54

BANGAY, Evelyn D. (Of Chesham, Buckinghamshire. Closely associated with the Poetry Society) *see* 41

BANISTER, Elsie M. (Artist in oils and water colours. Of Ainsdale, near Southport, Lancashire)
    O, sweet oasis: selected poems. Southport: Robert Johnson & Co. Ltd. [1940]. 64 pp.   OXB

BANKS, A.E., (Dede, pseud.)
    Selections from everyday verse; by Dede. Ilfracombe: Arthur H. Stockwell Ltd. 1975. 16 pp.   OXB

BANKS, H. Beadon- *see* **BEADON-BANKS, H.**

BARBER, Lois M.
For such a time as this: poems. Ilfracombe: Arthur H. Stockwell, Ltd. [1943].
16 pp.   OXB

BARKER, Eric Wilson (1905–73. b. Esher, Surrey. Educated at schools in
Surrey and Sussex. Became an American citizen, living at Big Sur, California.
Full-time writer and enthusiastic gardener)
A ring of willows: poems. Preface by Henry Miller. Andre Deutsch. 1961. 39 pp.
Dedicated to John Cowper Powys.   OXB
see also 22

BARKER, George (1913–   . b. Loughton, Essex. Educated at Marlborough
Road School, Chelsea, and polytechnic. Professor of English Literature at
Imperial Tohoku University, Japan, in 1939. Went to the United States,
1940–43, afterwards returning to Britain. Lived in Rome, 1960–65. Arts
Fellow, York University, 1966–67. Visiting Professor, Florida International
University, 1974. Joint winner of the Cholmondeley Award, 1980)
Collected poems, 1930–1955. Faber & Faber. 1957. 245 pp.   MPL
Eros in dogma: [poems]. Faber & Faber. 1944. 61 pp.   OXB
[Selected poems]; [by] George Barker, Martin Bell, Charles Causley.
Harmondsworth, Middlesex: Penguin Books. 1962. 128 pp. (Penguin modern
poets, 3).
Not joint authorship.   BL
The true confessions of George Barker: [poems]. MacGibbon & Kee. 1965. 86 pp.
MPL
see also 15, 18, 25, 26, 30, 56, 57, 76, 83

BARKER, J.G., (J.G. Meddemmen, pseud.) (1917–   . Conscripted into the
Army in 1940, serving in twelve foreign countries including Egypt. Of
London) *see* 39, 63

BARNARD, E.Y. (Lieutenant. Served in the Western Desert with the Eighth
Army) *see* 46

BARNES, Keith (Studied at the Royal Academy of Music. Lived on the
continent and in Berkeley, California. His work has appeared in numerous
magazines and has been broadcast by the B.B.C. and in New York) *see* 86

BARNES, Ronald Gorell, Lord Gorell (1884–1963). Educated at
Winchester College, Harrow School, and Balliol College, Oxford. On editorial
staff of *The Times*, 1910–15. Poet of the First World War. Captain and Adjutant,
7th Battalion, The Rifle Brigade, 1915–16. Major, General Staff, 1917. As
Deputy Director of Staff Duties (Education) at the War Office, he founded the

Royal Army Educational Corps. Under-Secretary of State for Air, 1921–22. Held many and varied public appointments. Company Commander, West Sussex Home Guard, 1940–45. Lived at Arundel)

Wings of the morning, and other new poems of peace and war; by Lord Gorell. John Murray. 1948. viii, 71 pp.   IWM
see also 38, 84

BARNHILL, W.W.

West African rhymes. Ilfracombe: Arthur H. Stockwell, Ltd. 1948. 80 pp.
        OXB

BARNS-GRAHAM, John Wedderburn (Served in the Home Guard)

"Gathered from my years": [*poems*]. Vol. 2. Printed Cupar: J. & G. Innes, Ltd. [1979]. 112 pp.
    Title from cover. [No copy of Vol. 1 traced]   OXB

BARNSLEY, Alan, (Gabriel Fielding, pseud.) (1916– . b. Hexham,

Northumberland, a descendant of the novelist Henry Fielding. Educated at St Edward's School, Oxford, Trinity College, Dublin, and St George's Hospital, London. Served as a Captain in Royal Army Medical Corps, 1943–46. General medical practitioner at Maidstone, Kent, 1954–64. Appointed Professor of English, Washington State University, United States, in 1967)

The frog prince, and other poems. Aldington, Kent: Hand and Flower Press. [1952]. 249–284 pp. (Poems in pamphlet, 1952, IX).   OXB

XXVIII poems; by Gabriel Fielding. Aldington, Kent: Hand and Flower Press. 1955. 37 pp.   OXB

BARRAUD, Enid (Served in the Women's Land Army, Cambridge-

shire) *see* 50

BARRES, O.M. (Volunteer. Served with the Eighth Army) *see* 25, 44

BARRON, Edna

Wanderlust, and other poems. Ilfracombe: Arthur H. Stockwell, Ltd. [1954]. 16 pp.   OXB

BARROWMAN, Jean

Poems. Ilfracombe: Arthur H. Stockwell, Ltd. [1956]. 32 pp.   OXB

BARRY, Alice Frances (1861?–1951. Granddaughter of Sir Charles Barry,

designer of the Houses of Parliament. Died in July 1951, aged 90. Of Worthing, Sussex)

Last poems. Hove: Combridges. 1952. 31 pp.   OXB

BARSLEY, Michael (1913– . Began the war as a conscientious objector but

became disillusioned with pacificism. He was a farm worker in the Midlands then an ambulance driver in London. A full-time writer after the war)

Alice in Wunderground, and other blits [sic] *and pieces:* [*poems*]. Illustrated by the author. John Murray. 1940. 48 pp. il. OXB

Grabberwocky and other flights of fancy: [*poems*]. Illustrated by Osbert Lancaster. John Murray. 1939. 43 pp. il. IWM

see also 76

BARTHOLOMEW, Marie (Of Warwickshire) *see* 74

BARTLETT, Elizabeth (1924– . b. near the Kent coalfields, daughter of an ex-Sergeant in the Army and a house-parlourmaid. Won a scholarship to grammar school, only to be removed at age of fifteen to work in a hypodermic needle factory. Began writing poetry at school and was first published at age of nineteen)

A lifetime of dying: [*poems*]. Liskeard: Harry Chambers. 1979. 64 pp. (Peterloo poets). OXB

BARTLETT, Wilfred H. (1913–48. Served in the Royal Navy. After being invalided out became landlord of the *Rose and Crown*, a country inn at Calverleigh, near Tiverton, Devonshire)

Poems of purpose. Ilfracombe: Arthur H. Stockwell, Ltd. [1943]. 24 pp.
OXB

Soliloquy in summer, [*and other poems*]. Williams & Norgate. 1950. 79 pp.
OXB

The swinging lantern: [*poems*]. Williams & Norgate, Ltd. 1947. 32 pp.
OXB

BARTLEY, J.O. (b. and educated in Ireland. Major, General Staff, serving as Deputy Chief Press Adviser to the Government of India. Writer, journalist, poet and university professor) *see* 43

BARTON, E.J. (Trooper. Served in the Western Desert with the Eighth Army) *see* 46

BARTON, Joan (1908– . b. Bristol. Educated at Colston's Girls School and Bristol University. Illness curtailed her studies and she began her working life as a bookseller. Later employed by the B.B.C. and by the British Council, where she directed a department during the war. In 1947 started the White Horse Bookshop in Marlborough, Wiltshire, in partnership with Barbara Watson. Sold it after twenty years, moving to Salisbury. Reviewer for *New Statesman*)

The mistress, and other poems. Hull, Yorkshire: Sonus Press. [1972]. 64 pp.
OXB

BARTON, Kenneth
Selected poems. Birmingham: Cornish Brothers Ltd. 1944. 56 pp.   OXB

BARTON, Saxon (1892–1957. Educated at Greenbank School, Liverpool, Loretto School, Musselburgh, and Liverpool and Edinburgh Universities. Temporary Surgeon-Lieutenant, Royal Navy, in charge of H.M.S. *Dwarf* in the Cameroons and West Coast of Africa. Became a gynaecological and obstetrical surgeon, holding appointments in Liverpool hospitals)
Songs before sunset: [poems]. Epworth Press. 1943. 76 pp. il.   BPL
Songs by the wayside: [poems]. British Authors' Press. 1944. [vi], 80 pp. il.
   Includes *Lancashire Songs* and *Songs for a Lover*.   OXB

BASS, Anthony David (1921–44. b. London. Educated at University College School, Hampstead. Went up to Wadham College, Oxford, in the autumn of 1939. Served in a Bomb Disposal Squad then joined a Parachute Field Ambulance Unit with which he went to France in the early hours of D-Day. Killed by an enemy shell in August 1944 as he was giving morphia to a wounded man)
Poems. Favil Press. 1946. 24 pp.   IWM
see also   20

BASS, Howard (Of Hampshire)   *see*   74

BATCHELOR, Frank (1901–   . b. London. Educated at John Bright Grammar School, Llandudno, North Wales. Editor of *The Bay*)   *see*   22

BATE, John (Served with the Royal Engineers in a Bomb Disposal Squad)   *see*   25

BATES, Alan
The fatal assonance: poems. Drawings by Marlene Staniforth. Leicester: Campton. [1969]. [51] pp. il.
   Printed on one side of leaf only.   OXB

BATES, Herbert Ernest, (Flying Officer X, pseud.) (1905–74. b. Rushden, Northamptonshire. Educated at Kettering Grammar School. Worked as a provincial journalist and clerk before publishing his first novel at age of twenty. Squadron Leader, Royal Air Force. Celebrated novelist and short story writer. Many of his stories of service life were originally published under the pseud. 'Flying Officer X')   *see*   1, 25

BATES, Rachael (Of Ambleside, Lake District)
Songs from a lake: lyrical verse. Hutchinson & Co., Ltd. 1947. 71 pp.   OXB

BATESON, R.G. (Captain, Royal Army Ordnance Corps. Captured in France in 1940, held prisoner of war in Germany until 1945) *see* 67

BATTCOCK, Marjorie (b. Highgate, London. Educated at The Study, Wimbledon Common, and King's College, London. Librarian, journalist and short story writer)

Casual acquaintance, [and other poems]. Mitre Press. [1964]. 48 pp.   OXB

Chiaroscuro, [and other poems]. Dulwich Village: Outposts Publications. 1960. 12 pp.   MPL

The filigree bridge: [poems]. York: Guild Press. 1956. 16 pp. (Guild poets).   BL

BAUMER, Sybil

Ave vita!, and other verses. Mitre Press. [1958]. 64 pp.   OXB

BAWCUTT, Roy *see* 23

BAYLISS, John (1919– . b. Wotton-under Edge, Gloucestershire. Educated at Latymer Upper School, and St Catharine's College, Cambridge. Literary editor of *Granta.* Flight Lieutenant, Royal Air Force, serving in India. Assistant Principal, Colonial Office, 1946–49. Editor with the publishers Macmillan & Co., 1949–52. With Northern Rhodesia & Nyasaland Publications Bureau in Lusaka, 1952–59)

A romantic miscellany: [poems]; by John Bayliss and Derek Stanford. Fortune Press. 1946. 63 pp.

Not joint authorship.   BPL

Venus in Libra. Walton-on-Thames: Outposts Publications. 1977. 51 pp.   OXB

The white knight, and other poems. Fortune Press. 1944. 48 pp.   OXB

see also 1, 25, 29, 48, 49, 53, 76

BEACALL, Phyllis

Scant harvest: poems written during the years 1929–1949. Fortune Press. [1950]. 44 pp.   IWM

BEADNELL, Mary (Of Skipton, Yorkshire)

Dale's feet, [and other poems]. Walton-on-Thames: Outposts Publications. 1969. 12 pp.   OXB

BEADON-BANKS, H. (Served in the Army in the North West Province of India)

A collection of poems. Printed St. Leonards-on-Sea: King Bros. & Potts, Ltd. [1945]. 24 pp.   OXB

BEALES, Francis E.
Victory poems, and others. Ilfracombe: Arthur H. Stockwell, Ltd. [1944]. 16 pp.
OXB

BEAMES, Peter (1913–41. Joined the Army in 1939. Subaltern, King's Dragoon Guards. Killed in action at Tobruk on 23 November 1941)
The swallow, and other poems. Shrewsbury: Wilding & Son Ltd. [1946]. 39 pp.
OXB

BEATON, Gwen C.
Thoughts and fancies: verse. Ilfracombe: Arthur H. Stockwell, Ltd. [1947]. 16 pp.
OXB

BEATTIE, Pamela (1932– . On editorial board of *Orbis*. Member of the Poets Council and the Poetry Society. A contributor to many periodicals. Of Worcester)
Beyond the minotaur: [*poems*]. Outposts Publications. 1969. 12 pp.
OXB

BECK, R.
For those who died, [*and other poems*]. Edward O. Beck, Ltd. 1946. 30 pp.
A limited ed. of 250 numbered copies.
OXB

BECKER, M. Janet (Of Suffolk ?)
Flowers by post, and other verse. Printed Halesworth, Suffolk: J.S.P. Denny. [1944]. [22] pp.
OXB

BECKWITH, Edward George Chichester (Captain, Sherwood Foresters. Captured with the 8th Battalion in Norway on 4 May 1940, spending the rest of the war in German prison camps. Editor of the anthology *Selections from The Quill*, 1947)
Poems on several occasions. Cheltenham: Thomas Hailing Ltd. [1943]. 46 pp.
BL
see also 5

BEE, pseud. *see* **BOSHELL, Gordon**, (Bee, pseud.)

BEE, Ronald E. (Royal Corps of Signals. Served with 8th Army Signals in Egypt, Sicily, Italy and Austria) *see* 63

BEECHAM, Audrey (1915– . Educated at Wycombe Abbey School, and Somerville College, Oxford. Visited Spain during the summer vacation of 1936, assisting the Catalan anarchists. Engaged in freelance literary work in London, 1938–40, then moved to Oxford, employed by the University in teaching and research, 1940–50. During the war she was active in the Women's Home Defence which was intended to support the Home Guard in the event of a

German invasion. From 1950–80 she continued an academic career at Nottingham University. Retired to Oxford)

The coast of Barbary: [*poems*]. Hamish Hamilton. 1957. x, 66 pp.   MPL

Different weather: poems. Weybrook Press. 1980. 72 pp.   OXB

see also 56

BEECHING, Jack (Served in the Fleet Air Arm as a Petty Officer Radio Mechanic)

Truth is a naked lady: [*poems*]. Sudbury, Suffolk: Myriad Press. 1957. 32 pp. il. (by Paul Rudall).

A limited ed. of 200 numbered copies signed by the author. The second book of the Myriad Press, set and printed by hand.   OXB

see also 42

BEER, Maureen June

'Tween ten and twenty: [*poems*]. Truro, Cornwall: Avon Books. [1967]. [vi], 38 pp.   OXB

BEER, Patricia (1924–   . b. Exmouth, Devonshire. Educated at Exmouth Grammar School, Exeter University, and St Hugh's College, Oxford. Lecturer in English, Padua University, 1947–49, British Institute, Rome, 1949–51, and Goldsmiths' College, London, 1962–68. Married architect John Damien Parsons in 1964. A full-time writer — a poet, novelist and literary critic)

Driving west: poems. Victor Gollancz Ltd. 1975. 46 pp. (Gollancz poets).

      OXB

Just like the resurrection: [*poems*]. Macmillan. 1967. 47 pp.   OXB

Selected poems. Hutchinson. [1979]. 152 pp.   OXB

BEGG, Gordon (Served in the Western Desert)   *see*   63

BEGG, James (Served in the Royal Air Force)

First attempt: [*poems*]. Ilfracombe: Arthur H. Stockwell, Ltd. [1963]. 48 pp.

      OXB

BEIGHTON, John (Writer on Rome)

Sirmio unvisited, and other poems. Magpie Press. 1967. 71 pp.

A limited ed. of 155 numbered copies.   OXB

BELL, Arnold Craig (1911–   . b, Lancaster. Educated at Kingswood School, Bath. Translator from the French of Alexandre Dumas. Of Harrogate, Yorkshire)

Passer-by: twenty-four poems; by Craig Bell. Mitre Press. [1957]. 32 pp.

      OXB

Poems of an agnostic. Walton-on-Thames: Outposts Publications. 1979. 48 pp.

      OXB

BELL, Craig *see* **BELL, Arnold Craig**

BELL, Ian (1913– . b. Radlett, Hertfordshire. Educated at Canford School, and St Peter's Hall, Oxford. Entered the Diplomatic Service, holding posts around the world. Vice-Consul in Valparaiso, 1938, and in Montevideo, 1940. Retired to the Isle of Skye)
The scarlet flower, and other poems. Hollis & Carter. 1947. vi, 58 pp.   OXB

BELL, Leslie E. (Writer on Devon topography)
Coggin's Barrow, [*and other poems*]. Ilfracombe: Arthur H. Stockwell, Ltd. [1945]. 48 pp.   OXB

BELL, Martin (1918— . b. Southampton. Educated at Taunton School, and University College, Southampton. Corporal, eventually Acting Sergeant, Royal Engineers, 1939–46. Spent two years in Lebanon managing a saw-mill for the Army, and two years in Italy. Taught in London schools, 1946–67. Appointed Gregory Fellow in Poetry, Leeds University, 1967)
Collected poems, 1937–1966. Macmillan; New York: St Martin's Press. 1967. xiv, 114 pp.   MPL
[*Selected poems*]; [by] George Barker, Martin Bell, Charles Causley. Harmondsworth, Middlesex: Penguin Books. 1962. 128 pp. (Penguin modern poets, 3).
      Not joint authorship.   BL

BELL, Sydney (Experienced a dive-bombing attack)
Celts, and other poems. With a preface by Sir Hugh S. Roberton. Dublin: Browne & Nolan Ltd. 1946. 111 pp.   OXB

BELL, William (1924–48. b. Belfast. Educated at Merton College, Oxford. Sub-Lieutenant, Royal Naval Volunteer Reserve, serving in the Fleet Air Arm. Killed in a climbing accident on the Matterhorn in August 1948. Editor of the anthologies *Poetry from Oxford in Wartime*, 1945, and *More Poetry from Oxford*, 1947)
Elegies: [*poems*]. Fortune Press. [1945]. 24 pp.   OXB
Mountains beneath the horizon: [*poems*]. Edited with an introduction by John Heath-Stubbs. Faber & Faber Ltd. 1950. 73 pp. por.   OXB

BELLERBY, Frances (1899–1975). b. Bristol of English and Welsh parentage. Attempted verse at the age of four. Educated at Mortimer House, Clifton. Married John R. Bellerby. Lived for many years in Cornwall, then on the edge of Dartmoor in Devon. Novelist and short story writer, her work is mainly concerned with the West Country)
The first-known, and other poems. Enitharmon Press. 1975. 62 pp.   OXB
Plash Mill, [*and other poems*]. Peter Davies. 1946. 64 pp.   IWM
The stuttering water, and other poems. Gillingham, Kent: ARC. [1970]. 19 pp.

A limited ed. of 200 copies of which twenty-five are numbered and signed by the author. BL

BENDER, Gillian Mary
Gethsemane:[*poems*]. Ilfracombe: Arthur H. Stockwell, Ltd. 1973. 54 pp.
OXB

BENJAMIN, Helena
Britain, please answer me, [*and other poems*]. Ilfracombe: Arthur H. Stockwell Ltd. 1971. 15 pp. OXB

BENN, Robin (Commissioned in the Army) *see* 24, 60

BENNETT, Alfred Gordon (1901–62. b. Warrington, Cheshire. Educated at Boteler Grammar School, Warrington, and The Leys School, Cambridge. Pilot Officer in Intelligence, 1941, Flying Officer, 1943–45. Worked in theatre, documentary filming and publishing)
Purple testament: poems through war to peace. Fortune Press. 1950. 92 pp. por.
MPL

BENNETT, E.R.A.V. (Served in the Royal Navy, taking part in the invasion of Sicily)
My maritime moods: a miscellany of original poems. Ilfracombe: Arthur H. Stockwell, Ltd. 1945. 24 pp. OXB

BENNETT, M.A.
Victory and peace, and other poems. Ilfracombe: Arthur H. Stockwell, Ltd. 1948. 16 pp. OXB

BENNETT, Simon Harry (Of Glasgow)
The mysterious universe, and other poems. Hanover Press. 1954. 174 pp. por.
OXB

BENNETT, Vernon Harold (Served in the Army)
Beyond the veil: a new anthology of poems. Fortune Press. 1957. 60 pp. OXB
Broken wings: a soldier's diary: [*poems*]. Fortune Press [1959]. 40 pp. BPL
Portsmouth ho!: [*poems*]. Mitre Press. [1973]. 48 pp. OXB
A veil of darkness: a personal anthology of poems. Fortune Press. 1957. 64 pp.
OXB

BENSON, Bernard J. (Of Guernsey, Channel Islands?)
Songs and snatches: poems of today and yesterday. Mitre Press. [1970]. 75 pp. por.
OXB

BERESFORD, Anne (1930– . b. Redhill, Surrey. Educated at a small private school, then at a convent. Trained at the Central School of Dramatic Art, London. Married poet Michael Hamburger in 1951. Appeared on the stage and broadcast on radio. Taught music and movement. Appointed drama teacher at Wimbledon Girls' High School in 1968)

The curving shore: [*poems*]. Agenda Editions. 1975. 49 pp. il. OXB

The lair: [*poems*]. Rapp & Whiting. 1968. 61 pp. OXB

BERESFORD, Madeline G.

Oddments: [*poems*]. Ilfracombe: Arthur H. Stockwell, Ltd. [1942]. 8 pp.
 OXB

BERINGTON, Olguita Queeny (–1981. Of Malvern, Worcestershire)

Different like a zoo: [*poems*]. Palladium Press. 1949 [i.e. 1950]. 88 pp.

BERNERS, Margaret

More war-time musings: [*poems*]. Ilfracombe: Arthur H. Stockwell, Ltd. 1945. 16 pp. OXB

Wartime musings [*poems*]. Ilfracombe: Arthur H. Stockwell, Ltd. [1945]. 16 pp.
 OXB

BERRIDGE, Elizabeth (1921–   . b. London. Spent the war in London and Wales, starting a family and helping her husband, Reginald Moore, produce literary magazines and anthologies. Novelist, poet, critic and short story writer. Received Best Novel of the Year Award from the *Yorkshire Post* in 1964)

Triad one: short stores by James Gordon, poems by Elizabeth Berridge, a novel by Gwyn Thomas. Edited by Jack Aistrop. Dennis Dobson Ltd. 1946. 194 pp. il. (by Ida Procter). OXB

see also 79

BERRY, Alfred H. (Of Kent?)

Light and shade: a small selection of epic, descriptive and humorous verse. Printed Canterbury: J.A. Jennings, Ltd. 1945. 40 pp. OXB

BERRY, Charles Ackerman (1908–   . b. London. Served in the Merchant Navy, and worked as a freelance journalist. After the war until 1968 was in the Ambulance Service and in Civil Defence. Of Bristol)

Threshold, and other poems. Bristol: Redcliffe Press. 1979. 32 pp. OXB

BERRY, Francis (1915–   . b. Malaya. Educated at Hereford Cathedral School, Dean Close School, and University College, Exeter. Solicitor's articled clerk, 1931. War service, 1939–46. Professor of English at Sheffield University, 1947–70, and at Royal Holloway College, London, 1970–80. Held visiting lectureships in the United States, Jamaica, Malawi and Australia)

Fall of a tower, and other poems. Fortune Press. 1943. 48 pp. OXB

The galloping centaur: poems 1933–1951. Methuen & Co. Ltd. 1952. x, 198 pp.
MPL

Murdock, and other poems. Andrew Dakers Ltd. 1947. 55 pp.   OXB
see also 49

BERTOLLA, Alan (1938–   . b. East London, grew up in Dagenham, Essex)
Acrobat, and other poems. Cover designs and illustrations by the author. Harold Wood, Essex: Tully Potter. [1971]. 28 pp. il.

Published for the Poetry One workshop group in Havering.   OXB

BETHELL, Samuel Leslie
Selected poems; [by] George Every, J.D.C. Pellow, S.L. Bethell. Staples Press Ltd. [1945]. 77 pp.

Not joint authorship. No war poetry by Every.   BL

BETJEMAN, Sir John (1906–84. b. Highgate, London. Educated at Marlborough College, and Magdalen College, Oxford. Served as United Kingdom Press Attaché in Dublin, 1941–43. At Admiralty, London, 1944. Associated with the British Council, 1944–46. Reviewer for the *Daily Herald*. Made many appearances on television, discussing literature, architecture and Victorian England. Recipient of honorary degrees from several universities and of numerous awards and honours for poetry and architectural writings. Appointed Poet Laureate in 1972)
Collected poems. Compiled by The Earl of Birkenhead. Enlarged ed. Introduction by Philip Larkin. Boston: Houghton Mifflin Co. 1971. xliv, 366 pp.   OXB
John Betjeman's collected poems. Compiled and with an introduction by The Earl of Birkenhead. John Murray. 1958. xxviii, 279 pp.   MPL
John Betjeman's collected poems. Compiled and with an introduction by The Earl of Birkenhead. 2nd ed. John Murray. 1962. xxviii, 292 pp.   MPL
John Betjeman's collected poems. Compiled and with an introduction by The Earl of Birkenhead. Enlarged [3rd] ed. John Murray. 1970. xxxii, 366 pp.   MPL
John Betjeman's collected poems. Compiled and with an introduction by The Earl of Birkenhead. Enlarged [3rd] ed. John Murray. 1972. xxxii, 366 pp. (John Murray paperbacks).   OXB
John Betjeman's collected poems. Compiled and with an introduction by The Earl of Birkenhead. 4th ed. John Murray. 1979. xxxii, 427 pp.   OXB
John Betjeman's collected poems. Compiled and with an introduction by The Earl of Birkenhead. 4th ed. John Murray. 1980. xxxii, 427 pp. (John Murray paperbacks).   OXB
New bats in old belfries: poems. John Murray. 1945. vi, 54 pp.   MPL
Selected poems. Chosen with a preface by John Sparrow. John Murray. 1948. xxii, 127 pp.   MPL
Slick but not streamlined: poems and short pieces. Selected, and with an introduction

by W.H. Auden. Garden City, New York: Doubleday & Co., Inc. 1947. 185 pp.

OXB

BEVAN, Jack (b. Blackpool. Educated at Cambridge University. Served in the Royal Artillery for six years in Iceland and Italy. Schoolmaster and college lecturer)

Brief candles: [*poems*]. Dulwich Village: Outposts Publications. 1962. 16 pp.

OXB

Dragon's teeth: [*poems*]. York: Guild Press. 1956. 16 pp. (Guild poets).   BL

My sad Pharaohs: [*poems*]. Routledge & Kegan Paul. 1968. viii, 110 pp.

OXB

BIBBY, Bob

Warchild: a sequence: [*poems*]. Walton-on-Thames: Outposts Publications. 1975. 24 pp.   OXB

BICKLE, Judith Brundrett (b. Lancashire. Educated at Marlborough College, Buxton. Violinist, broadcaster, novelist and poet. Of Bridgwater, Somerset)

Collected poems. With a foreword by Laurence Housman. Mitre Press. [1947]. [ii], 102 pp.   OXB

This is my harvest: [*poems*]. Robert Hale Ltd. 1962. 137 pp.   MPL

BILLINGHAM, Edgar

Midland poems. Birmingham: Cornish Brothers Ltd. 1944. [viii], 48 pp.

IWM

BILLOT, Cecil Philip (Served in H.M. Forces)

The grass grows through: a poem sequence. Fortune Press. 1945. [ii], 18 pp.

IWM

To the city: a poem sequence. With an introduction by Henry Treece. Fortune Press. 1944. 28 pp.   OXB

see also 49

BINDER, B.H.

Random rhymes. Hutchinson & Co. Ltd. 1943. 48 pp.   OXB

BINYON, Laurence (1869–1943. b. Lancaster. Educated at St Paul's School, and Trinity College, Oxford. Newdigate Prizeman, 1890. Poet of the First World War and art historian. Employed at the British Museum from 1893, becoming Keeper of Prints and Drawings in 1932. Professor of Poetry at Harvard University, 1933–34. President of the English Association, 1933–34, and of the English Verse-Speaking Association, 1934–35. Byron Professor at Athens University, 1940, when he lectured for five months on English poets)

The burning of the leaves, and other poems. Macmillan & Co. Ltd. 1944. viii, 18 pp.

OXB

The north star, and other poems. Macmillan & Co. Ltd. 1941. viii, 61 pp.

OXB

see also   6, 38, 82, 84

BIRCH, Clarice A.

Poetic potpourri. Ilfracombe: Arthur H. Stockwell Ltd. 1980. 48 pp.   OXB
Sea and sympathy: [*poems*]. Ilfracombe: Arthur H. Stockwell Ltd. 1979. 16 pp.

OXB

BIRCH, R. Dennis (Commissioned in the Royal Artillery. Of Lichfield, Staffordshire)

Four and twenty: poems of to-day and yesterday. Fortune Press. 1945. 24 pp.

OXB

see also   24, 49, 60, 61, 78

BIRCHAM, Grace

Carnival town, and other poems. Ilfracombe: Arthur H. Stockwell, Ltd. 1955.
24 pp.   OXB

BIRD, Arthur W. (Brother of Kenneth Bird, the artist working under the pseud. of Fougasse and editor of *Punch*)

Just a few lines: verses; by A.W.B. (Arthur Bird). Drawings by Fougasse
(Kenneth Bird). Methuen & Co. Ltd. 1943. 80 pp. il.   OXB

BIRD, H.D. (1920–   . Subaltern, Auxiliary Territorial Service)   *see*   27

BIRD, J.M.

Song of freedom, and other poems. Arthur H. Stockwell Ltd. [1941]. 16 pp.

OXB

BIRNIE, Mary S.

Singing in the fog: a book of verse. Ilfracombe: Arthur H. Stockwell, Ltd. [1942].
[iv], 135 pp.   OXB

BISHOP, John (1931–   . Grew up in South London. Founder of Autolycus Publications)

I from my small corner: [*poems*]. Autolycus Publications. [1973]. 20 pp.
   Title from cover.   OXB

BISHOP, Mary Davidson (1905–57. b. Manitoba, Canada. Spent two years in Oxford. Became a lecturer in English Language at Isleworth Polytechnic)

In heaven's view: a selection of the verse of Mary (Davidson) Bishop. With a foreword
by the Principal, Isleworth Polytechnic. Hounslow: Cedar Press. 1958. xiv,
46 pp. il., por., facsim.
   A limited ed. of 600 numbered copies.   OXB

Prairie summer, and other poems. [2nd ed.]. Minety, Wiltshire: Taylor & Sons. 1977. xiv, 25pp. por.   OXB
   [No copy of lst ed. 1958 traced]

BISHOP, Peter R.
The countryside, and other poems. Ilfracombe: Arthur H. Stockwell, Ltd. 1948. 16 pp.   OXB

BLACK, Edward Loring (1915–   . b. Sutton Coldfield. Educated at Bishop Vesey's Grammar School, and St Catharine's College, Cambridge. A schoolmaster before joining the Royal Air Force. Served in India as a Flight Lieutenant. College administrator and writer on English language and literature) *see* 43

BLACKBURN, Thomas (1916–77. b. Hensingham, Cumberland. Educated at Bromsgrove School and Durham University. Principal Lecturer in English, College of St Mark & St John, Chelsea. Gregory Poetry Fellowship, Leeds University, 1964–66)
The devil's kitchen: [poems]. Chatto & Windus. 1975. 32 pp. (Chatto poets for the young).   OXB
The fourth man: poems. MacGibbon & Kee. 1971. 55 pp.   OXB
In the fire, [and other poems]. Putnam. 1956. 32 pp.   OXB
Selected poems. Hutchinson. 1975. 88 pp.   OXB

BLACKER, Gertrude Mary (Trudy) (1913–   . b. Shipton, Yorkshire. Educated at Queen Anne Grammar School, York. Married a farmer, living at Kirk Hammerton from 1944)
Here in the country's heart: [poems]; [by] Trudy Blacker. Driffield: Ridings Publishing Co. 1968. [36] pp. il. (by Julie Alden).   OXB
see also   16

BLACKER, Trudy   *see*   **BLACKER, Gertrude Mary** (Trudy)

BLAIR, pseud. *see* **BLAIR-FISH, Wallace Wilfrid,** (Blair, pseud.)

BLAIR, Anthony (Of Berkshire)   *see*   75

BLAIR-FISH, Wallace Wilfrid, (Blair, pseud.) (1889–1968. Educated at Pembroke College, Oxford. Journalist on literary staff of *The Sunday Times* and *Sunday Chronicle*, 1908–17. With Ministry of Food, 1917–19. Joint Managing director and publisher of Shakespeare Head Press, Ltd, 1921–22. Director of the Rural Industries Bureau, 1926–27. Secretary of Rotary International Association for Great Britain and Ireland, 1928–37)
Tides and fashions: [poems]; by Blair. Ipswich: Norman Adlard & Co. 1969. xii, 65 pp. por.   OXB

BLAKELOCK, Denys (1901–70. Educated at Aldenham. Actor, writer and poet. Teacher of diction and audition technique at the Royal Academy of Dramatic Art, 1954–62. Broadcast on radio and made numerous appearances on stage, film and television. A close friend of Eleanor Farjeon)

The waters: poems. Dublin: Assisi Press. 1955. [ii], 38 pp.

'For Eleanor Farjeon'. OXB

BLAKEMORE, Trevor (–1953. b. Chislehurst. Educated at Wellington College, and Gonville & Caius College, Cambridge. Poet of the First World War. Organizer of literary clubs and a prominent figure in London literary life. During the Second World War he lived in Bristol, where he conducted the Portfolio Club. Poet and prose writer)

The ballades of Trevor Blakemore. Introduction by Guy Ramsey. Neville Spearman. 1955. 36 pp. por. OXB

Poems. Foreword by Sir Compton Mackenzie. Neville Spearman. 1955. 159 pp. por., facsim. OXB

BLAKENEY, Edward Henry, (E.H.B.) (1869–1955. Educated at Westminster School, and Trinity College, Cambridge. Headmaster of Sandwich Grammar School, 1895–1901, of Borlase's School, Marlow, 1901–04, and of the King's School, Ely, 1904–18. Poet of the First World War. Master at Winchester College, 1918–30. Lecturer in English Literature at Southampton University, 1929–31. Lived in Winchester)

[*Four poems dedicated to the men of the Services*]. Winchester: Author. 1943. 3 pp.

A single sheet folded once to give two leaves, printed by the author at his private press. OXB

Hitler, in 1944. [Winchester]: [Author]. [1944].

A broadside printed by the author at his private press. BL

The last load home: verses written in war-time. Winchester: Author. 1943. [44] pp.

Printed by the author at his private press on handmade paper on one side of leaf only. OXB

Malta to-day; [by] E.H.B. [Winchester]: [Author]. 1942.

A broadside printed by the author at his private press. BL

Now and then: a sheaf of epigrams. Winchester: Author. 1942. [13] pp.

Printed by the author at his private press. OXB

BLAKESTON, Oswell (Author, artist and film specialist. Contributor to various periodicals. Of Wimbledon, London) *see* 42

BLANFORD, John (Flew with the original Royal Air Force in France in 1918. Served with The Buffs as a Major throughout the Second World War. Of Worthing, Sussex)

Poems. Mitre Press. [1954]. 117 pp. IWM

BLANK, H.H. (Of Surrey) *see* 75

BLATHWAYT, William (1882– . Poet of the First World War. Of Batheaston, Somerset)

The great magician: [*poems*]. Sir Isaac Pitman & Sons, Ltd. 1940. 64 pp.
OXB

Through years of stress: [*poems*]. Sir Isaac Pitman & Sons, Ltd. 1948. 62 pp.
OXB

BLUNDEN, Edmund (1896–1974. b. Yalding, Kent. Educated at Christ's Hospital, and Queen's College, Oxford. Major poet of the First World War. Served with the Royal Sussex Regiment in France and Belgium, 1916–19. Awarded the M.C. Professor of English Literature at Tokyo University, 1924–27. Fellow and Tutor, Merton College, Oxford, 1931–43. On staff of Oxford University Senior Training Corps, 1940–44. With United Kingdom Liaison Mission, Tokyo, 1948–50. Appointed Head of English Department at Hong Kong University in 1953. Elected Professor of Poetry at Oxford University in 1966. Awarded Hawthornden Prize, 1922, and Queen's Gold Medal for Poetry, 1956. Lived at Long Melford, Suffolk, latterly)

After the bombing, and other short poems. Macmillan & Co. Ltd. 1949. viii, 52 pp.
MPL

Eleven poems. Cambridge: Golden Head Press. 1965. 21 pp. facsim.
    A limited ed. of 220 copies.
OXB

Poems, 1930–1940. Macmillan & Co. Ltd. 1940. xiv, 264 pp.
OXB

Poems of many years. Collins. 1957. 312 pp.
MPL

Shells by a stream: new poems. Macmillan & Co. Ltd. 1944. viii, 60 pp.
MPL

see also   38, 51

BLUNT, Gregory

Crucified landscape, and other poems. Outposts Publications. 1963. 16 pp.
OXB

BLUNT, Reginald (1857–1944. Educated at Haileybury School, and King's College, London. Worked as a railway engineer, 1879–87. General Superintendent to the Managers of the Stock Exchange, 1902–19. Trustee, Thomas Carlyle's house, 1895. Writer on Chelsea, founding the Chelsea Society in 1927)

Random rhymes. Richards Press Ltd. 1940. x, 92 pp.
OXB

BLYTH, James R. (1925–42). Killed in an accident on 12 October 1942 while serving in the Merchant Navy)

Poems. Foreword by Eva Dobell. Appreciation by William Curran Reedy. Favil Press. 1944. 32 pp.
IWM

see also   61

BOATWRIGHT, D. (Served in H.M. Forces) *see* 75

BODY, Alfred Harris (1900–)
Island legacy: poems. Bickley, Kent: University of London Press Ltd. 1942.
44 pp. MPL

BOGARDE, Dirk, pseud. *see* **VAN DEN BOGAERDE, Derek**, (Dirk
Bogarde, pseud.)

BOGGS, Tom *see* 9

BOLD, Alan (1943– . b. Edinburgh. Educated at Edinburgh University,
Poet, anthologist, critic and painter. Travelled in East Germany,
Czechoslovakia, France, Holland, Italy and Belgium. Worked on the editorial
staff of *Times Educational Supplement*, 1966–67, and as a freelance journalist.
Editor of the anthology *The Martial Muse*, 1976)
A perpetual motion machine: [*poems*]. Chatto & Windus; Hogarth Press. 1969.
64 pp. (Phoenix living poets). OXB
This fine day: [*poems*]. Dunfermline: Borderline Press. 1979. viii, 55 pp. OXB
To find the new: [*poems*]. Chatto & Windus; Hogarth Press. 1967. 64 pp.
(Phoenix living poets). OXB

BOLTON, Deric
Grown over with green-ness: [*poems*]. Walton-on-Thames: Outposts
Publications. 1976. 48 pp. OXB
A view from Ben More, and other poems. Walton-on-Thames: Outposts
Publications. 1972. 44 pp. OXB
The wild uncharted country. Walton-on-Thames: Outposts Publications. 1973.
48 pp. OXB

BOMBARDIER, pseud. *see* **CHALLONER, Louis**, (Bombardier, pseud.)

BOND, Edward (1934– . b. London. Educated at state schools to age of
fourteen. Did national service in the Army. Playwright and director, member of
the Writers Group of the Royal Court Theatre, London. Recipient of several
drama awards)
Theatre poems and songs. Edited by Malcolm Hay and Philip Roberts. Eyre
Methuen. 1978. xii, 147 pp. OXB

BOND, Freda Constance (Writer of children's novels. Of London) *see* 6

BONDS, P.W. (Of Devonshire) *see* 74

BONINGER, James Arthur Kurt (1911– . b. Germany of an English
mother and German father. Educated at Berlin University. Left Germany in

1936 after a skirmish with the Gestapo. Settled in Kenya. Joined the Army in 1941, serving in the Middle East. Demobilized 1946 in Kenya, becoming a Provincial Information Officer. Returned to Britain in 1960 to join the Ministry of Overseas Development. Retired in 1973. Of Sudbury, Suffolk) *see* 39, 63

BOOCOCK, Dorothy Emmie (Had two sons in H.M. Forces)
We three, and other poems. Ilfracombe: Arthur H. Stockwell, Ltd. 1952. 15 pp.
OXB

BOODSON, N. (Sergeant. Served with the Eighth Army in the Western Desert) *see* 46

BOOTH, Madeleine Beatrice, (M.B.B.)
Life is sweet, and other poems; by M.B.B. Ilfracombe: Arthur H. Stockwell, Ltd. 1953. 24 pp.
OXB

BOOTHBY, E. (Of Northumberland. Served in H.M. Forces) *see* 73, 75

BOOTHROYD, C.B. Selby- *see* **SELBY-BOOTHROYD, C.B.**

BORMAN, George
Fortune's wild wheel: [*poems*]. Ilfracombe: Arthur H. Stockwell Ltd. [1942]. 24 pp.
OXB
Hope's harvest: a book of verse. Ilfracombe: Arthur H. Stockwell, Ltd. [1942]. 24 pp.
OXB
Strange days and yet we sing: poems. Arthur H. Stockwell, Ltd. [1941]. 24 pp.
OXB
The tranquil flame: [*poems*]. Ilfracombe: Arthur H. Stockwell, Ltd. [1943]. 24 pp.
OXB

BOSHELL, Gordon, (Bee, pseud.) (1908– . b. Blackburn, Lancashire. Educated at Bradford Technical College. Trained as a journalist. With the B.B.C. in London as scriptwriter then editor, 1940–44. Assistant editor, Reuters Features Service, 1944–45. Features editor on *Daily Mirror* and *Daily Herald*, 1945–51. Served in various parts of the world with the World Health Organisation, 1951–67. Founder-editor of *World Health.* Freelance writer from 1967. Novelist and writer of children's stories)
My country, 'tis of thee: a new war-time commentary in verse by the famous writer and broadcaster. W.H. Allen & Co., Ltd. 1943. 48 pp. (Hurricane books).   BL
My pen my sword: [*poems*]. Hodder & Stoughton. 1941. 92 pp.   OXB
see also 80

BOTTRALL, Ronald (1906– . b. Camborne, Cornwall. Educated at Redruth County School, and Pembroke College, Cambridge. Lector in English, Helsingfors University, Finland, 1929–31. Commonwealth Fund Fellowship,

Princeton University, 1931–33. Professor of English, Raffles College, Singapore, 1933–37. Assistant Director, British Institute, Florence, 1937–38. Secretary, School of Oriental & African Studies, London University, 1939–45. Temporary Administrative Officer at the Air Ministry, 1940, Priority Officer, 1941. Held British Council appointments in Sweden, Italy, Brazil, Greece and Japan, 1941–59. With United Nations Food & Agriculture Organization, 1963–65)

The collected poems of Ronald Bottrall. Sidgwick & Jackson. [1961]. xii, 244 pp.
OXB

Farewell and welcome: poems. Editions Poetry London. 1945. 80 pp.　　OXB
The palisades of fear: poems. Editions Poetry London. 1949. 72 pp. il. (by Franciszka Themerson).　　OXB
Poems 1955–1973. Anvil Press Poetry; Routledge & Kegan Paul. 1974. 158 pp.
OXB
Selected poems. With a preface by Edith Sitwell. Editions Poetry London. 1946. 64 pp.　　OXB
see also　82

BOUCH, Thomas (1882–1963. b. Warwick. Educated at Cheltenham College, and Magdalen College, Oxford. Served in the 10th Hussars, 1904–07 and 1914–15. Major attached to H.Q., Cavalry Corps, British Expeditionary Force. Poet of the First World War. Master of Foxhounds)

Coat of many colours: [poems]. Caravel Press. 1953. xiii, 132 pp.　　OXB

BOUGHEY, John Fletcher (1919–40. b. Caterham, Surrey. Educated at Eton College, and Magdalene College, Cambridge. Lieutenant, Coldstream Guards. Killed in action at sea on 31 August 1940)　*see*　20

BOULTON, Marjorie (1924–　. b. Teddington, Middlesex. Educated at Somerville College, Oxford. Teacher and college principal, becoming a full-time writer. Member of Academy of Esperanto, receiving Esperantist Author of the Year Award, 1958)

Preliminaries: [poems]. Fortune Press. 1949. 36 pp.　　OXB

BOULTON, Rachel E. (Of Winscombe, Somerset, and Taunton, Devon)　*see*　22

BOURNE, David (1921–41. b. Meopham, Kent. Educated at Cranbrook School. Volunteered for the Royal Air Force in December 1939, joined in July 1940 and was commissioned as a fighter pilot in January 1941. He served in the 43rd Brigade and was instrumental in saving his Squadron Leader's life during an air attack. Killed in action on 5 September 1941)

Poems. John Lane the Bodley Head. 1944. 63 pp.　　IWM
see also　1, 20, 25, 33, 42, 76

BOURNE, M.
    Poems. Ilfracombe: Arthur H. Stockwell Ltd. [1944]. 15 pp.   OXB
    Poems. [New ed.]. Ilfracombe: Arthur H. Stockwell, Ltd. [1946]. 16 pp.
                                                 OXB

BOURNE-JONES, Derek (Of Eastbourne, Sussex)
    The pain and the pleasure: [*poems*]. Eastbourne: Downlander Publishing. 1979.
56 pp.   OXB
    Vain words?: poems and verse. Ilfracombe: Arthur H. Stockwell Ltd. 1973.
63 pp.   OXB

BOWDEN, Max (Captain, Royal Artillery. Served in the Middle
East) *see* 23, 25, 33, 39, 63, 66

BOWEN, Arnold Vincent (1901–47. b. Calcutta, India. Educated at La
Martinère School, Calcutta. Came to England in 1922. After some teaching and
acting joined the Army in 1928. Transferred to reserve in 1929. On active
service from August 1939 as a Corporal, Royal Army Medical Corps. Invalided
out in February 1944. Settled in Birkenhead, becoming involved in poetry
readings, lecturing, writing, music and singing)
    Brief matchlight: [*poems*]. Dulwich Village: Outposts Publications. 1958.
12 pp.   OXB
    Lyrics of love and death. With an introduction by Herbert Palmer. Fortune
Press. 1943. 54 pp. por.   IWM
    The poet's hour, [*and other poems*]. Dulwich Village: Outposts Publications.
1957. 12 pp.   OXB
see also 2, 33, 42, 47, 48, 49, 51, 77, 79

BOWEN, John Charles Edward (b. Bombay. Captain in the Indian Army,
serving in the 6th Duke of Connaught's Own Lancers. Scholar of Persian
literature)
    Poems. Frontispiece by Eric Kennington. John Baker. 1968. 61 pp. col. il.
                                            MPL

BOWERS, Robert Hood
    Hitler's war: a series of fourteen poems suggested by the events of the past two years.
[Privately printed]. [1942]. 27 pp.
        Title from cover.   OXB

BOWES, D. (Served in H.M. Forces) *see* 74

BOWES LYON, Lilian (1895–1949. b. Bellingham, Northumberland,
youngest daughter of Hon. Francis Bowes Lyon. A granddaughter of the 13th
Earl of Strathmore and a cousin of Queen Elizabeth the Queen Mother. Poet of
the First World War, serving as a Voluntary Aid Detachment nurse in London

and Oxfordshire. Farmed in Dorset and lived abroad in France, Switzerland, Italy and Greece. In the Second World War helped in the evacuation of children from the East End of London and in rehousing the bombed, working in canteens and shelters. Severely crippled during her last years)

Collected poems. Introduced by C. Day Lewis. Jonathan Cape. 1948. 191 pp. MPL

Evening in Stepney, and other poems. Jonathan Cape. 1943. 23 pp. IWM
A rough walk home, and other poems. Jonathan Cape. 1946. 31 pp. IWM
Tomorrow is a revealing: [*poems*]. Jonathan Cape. 1941. 48 pp. OXB
see also 2, 51

BOWLER, Mabel A. (Of Derbyshire) *see* 71, 72, 73, 74

BOX, William (Poet of the First World War)
Forty poems. Chester & Lang. 1944. [vi], 50 pp. OXB
Forty poems. 3rd ed. Chester & Lang. 1945. [vi], 50 pp. IWM
[No copy of 2nd ed. 1945 traced]

BOYARS, Arthur (1925– . b. London. Educated at University College School, and Wadham College, Oxford. Editor of *Mandrake*, 1946–57, and co-editor of *Oxford Poetry* in 1948. Freelance reviewer of books and music for several periodicals and for the B.B.C. Third Programme)
Poems. Fortune Press. 1944. 32 pp. OXB

BOYD, Edward (Of Scotland)
Night flight, [*and other poems*]. Glasgow: Scoop Books Ltd. 1945. 31 pp. (Modern Scots poets). BPL

BOYLE, Patrick Reginald, Lord Cork and Orrery (1910– . Educated at Harrow School, and the Royal Military College, Sandhurst. Served in the war with Royal Ulster Rifles, Burma Rifles, Cameronians, and the Parachute Regiment. Severely wounded while fighting with the Chindits in Burma. Deputy Speaker, House of Lords, 1973–78. Member, Diocesan Assembly, Russian Orthodox Church in Great Britain) *see* 43

BRACHER, Steven (Served in South-East Asia Command)
The hunting of the hare: "New Forest Beagles will meet: Royal Oak, Fritham": a poem. Williams & Norgate Ltd. 1947. 24 pp.
Written in the British Military Hospital, South Eastern Asia Command, 1945. OXB

BRADBURY, Laurence B. (Served in H.M. Forces) *see* 75

BRADDOCK, Joseph (1902– . b. Streatham, London. Educated at St John's College, Cambridge. Poet, writer and lecturer. Worked for the British Council as a teacher of English on loan to the Polish Depot School, Royal Air Force. Later worked in London as an official of the Lord Mayor's National Air Raid Distress Fund. Of Wadhurst, Sussex)

No stronger than a flower: poems 1935–1960. Robert Hale Ltd. 1960. 48 pp.

IWM

see also   13, 53

BRADFIELD, Joan Bell
The idyll, and other poems. Ilfracombe: Arthur H. Stockwell, Ltd. [1955]. 16 pp.

OXB

BRADLEY, Diana C.
The peace bells, and other poems. Ilfracombe: Arthur H. Stockwell, Ltd. [1942]. 16 pp.

OXB

BRADLEY, Mabel M.
The collected works of Mabel M. Bradley: [poems]. Regency Press. [1978]. 32 pp.

OXB

BRADSHAW, Percy Venner (1877–1965. Educated at Haberdashers' Aske's School, Goldsmiths' College and Birkbeck College, London. Professional artist, illustrator and art teacher. Founder and principal of the Press Art School. Sales and publicity controller, Sun Engineering Co., 1932–46. Writer on practical drawing and illustration)
Marching on: verses. Sketches by Bert Thomas. W.H. Allen & Co., Ltd. 1943. 127 pp. il.

IWM

BRADY, Robert Kilian
Pulp in Bosnia: [poems]. Fortune Press. 1948. 32 pp.

IWM

BRAIN, Russell, Lord Brain (1895–1966. Educated at Mill Hill School, New College, Oxford, and the London Hospital. Disapproving strongly of war, he joined the Friends Ambulance Unit in the First World War. A distinguished physician and neurologist, he received many medical honours. President of the British Association in 1963)
Poems and verses. Printed Cambridge: Rampant Lions Press. [1961]. [vi], 50 pp.

A limited ed. of 100 privately printed copies designed and printed by Will Carter.

OXB

BRAITHWAITE, P.   *see*   21

BRAM   *see*   CROSS, Harry (Bram)

BRAMLEY-MOORE, Swinfen (1883– . M.C. Major, Royal Army Service Corps. A professional mechanical engineer)

Forward to victory, [*and other poems*]. A.R. Mowbray & Co. Ltd. 1941. 48 pp.
OXB

BRAND, M.M.

Thoughts, [*and other poems*]. Ilfracombe: Arthur H. Stockwell, Ltd. 1966. 27 pp.
OXB

BRANSOM, Harold Ian (Brigadier-General. Served in the Middle East. Captured when Royal Artillery Commander, 32nd Army Tank Brigade)

Inferior verse (Part I) February–April, 1942, of fighting men in the Western Desert. Printed Newcastle upon Tyne: Doig Bros. & Co. Ltd. 1942. 32 pp. il., por.
IWM

see also 63

BRANSON, Clive (1907–44. b. India. Educated at Bedford School and the Slade School of Art. Fought in Spain, a member of the British Battalion of the International Brigade. Was captured and spent eight months in a prison camp. A writer and artist, he was an exhibitor at the Royal Academy. Served in India as a Sergeant in the Royal Armoured Corps. Killed in action in the Arakan on 25 February 1944) *see* 43, 76

BRATTON, Frederick (Served in the Royal Army Medical Corps. Of Wallingford, Berkshire)

Dust of war: [*poems*]. Printed Bradford: Jongleur Press. [1947]. [16] pp.
OXB

BRAUN, John Cromer, (John Cromer, pseud.) (1916– . b. Portsmouth. Educated at Portsmouth Grammar School. Joined up in 1940 as a Private in the Hampshire Regiment, posted to Egypt in September 1940 and transferred to Field Security, Cairo. Commissioned 1941 in Intelligence Corps, finally Major in Security Intelligence, Middle East. Co-founder of the Salamander Society with Keith Bullen, and co-editor of the anthology *Salamander*, 1947. A solicitor and a consultant in European and consumer affairs) *see* 25, 33, 39, 47, 51, 63, 66

BRAY, pseud. (Served in the Middle East) *see* 63

BEARLEY, T.

Faith in freedom: [*poems*]. Batley: J.S. Newsome & Son, Ltd. 1941. [ii], 49 pp.
BL

Faith in freedom: [*poems*]. 2nd ed. Oxford: Joseph Vincent. 1942. 64 pp.

A limited ed. of 200 copies printed for private circulation. 'Profits will be devoted to H.R.H. the Duke of Gloucester's Red Cross Fund'.
OXB

BREED, Constance
Sonnets on the fens, and other poems. Fortune Press. 1948. 32 pp.   OXB

BRENNAND, George
Saraband and satyricon: poems and verses, orthodox and heterodox. Kineton: Roundwood Press. 1970. xvi, 235 pp.
    A limited ed. of 250 numbered copies signed by the author.   MPL

BRETT, R.P. (Aircraftman, Royal Air Force) *see* 1

BRICK, Norman (Flight Sergeant, Royal Air Force) *see* 1, 25

BRIDGEMAN, Roger (Of Guernsey, Channel Islands?)
Essays in doggerel: [*poems*]. St Peter Port, Guernsey: Toucan Press. 1968. 36 pp.   OXB

BRIDLE, O.E.
My life of verse: [*poems*]. Printed Regency Press. [1977]. 32 pp.   OXB

BRIDSON, Douglas Geoffrey (1910–80. B.B.C. writer and producer, a distinguished figure in sound broadcasting. Poet and dramatist who worked with Joan Littlewood in her early struggling days. Lived in Highgate, London)
The Christmas child, [*and other poems*]. Falcon Press. 1950. [viii], 240 pp.
    MPL

BRIERLEY, A.R. (Major. Fought in the First World War. of Chester)
A mixed grill of Chester poems. Printed Chester: Phillipson & Golder Ltd. [1945]. 16 pp.
    Title from cover. All proceeds in aid of the Major of Chester's War Relief Fund.   OXB

BRIGGS, George Wallace (1875–1959. Educated at Emmanuel College, Cambridge. Parish appointments at Norwich and Loughborough, then Canon of Leicester, 1927–34. Canon of Worcester, 1934–56, Vice-Dean, 1944–55. Joint editor of *Prayers and Hymns for Use in Schools*)
Songs of faith: [*poems*]. Oxford University Press. 1945. viii, 64 pp.

BRIGGS, K.M. (Served in Women's Auxiliary Air Force) *see* 61

BRINDLEY, Louis H. (Irish)
Poems. Dublin: Cuala Press. 1945. [viii], 135 pp.
    A limited ed. of 100 numbered copies privately printed for the author.
    OXB

BRISTOW, John (Served in the Middle East) *see* 39, 63

BRITTAIN, Vera (1893–1970. b. Newcastle under Lyme, Staffordshire, but spent her childhood in Macclesfield and Buxton. Educated at St Monica's, Kingswood, and Somerville College, Oxford. Abandoned Oxford temporarily to serve as a Voluntary Aid Detachment nurse during the First World War. Her experiences are recorded in *Testament of Youth*, 1933. Poet of the First World War. She lectured at home and abroad as a publicist for feminist and pacifist causes. Married George Catlin. Their daughter is the politician Shirley Williams) *see* 21, 41

BROCK, Edwin (1927– . b. London. Educated at state schools. Served in Royal Navy with the Pacific Fleet. Worked as a journalist, 1947–51, and with the Metropolitan Police, 1951–59. With advertising agencies from 1964, then a freelance writer from 1972. Of Norfolk)

Here . Now . Always. Secker & Warburg. 1977. 153 pp.

An autobiography in prose and verse. OXB

Invisibility is the art of survival: [*poems*]. New York: New Directions Books. 1972. [viii], 88 pp. OXB

The portraits and the poses: [*poems*]. Secker & Warburg. 1973. 63 pp. OXB

[*Selected poems*]; [by] Edwin Brock, Geoffrey Hill, Stevie Smith. Harmondsworth, Middlesex: Penguin Books. 1966. 128 pp. (Penguin modern poets, 8).

Not joint authorship. No war poetry by Smith. MPL

With love from Judas, [*and other poems*]. Lowestoft: Scorpion Press. 1963. 66 pp.

The first twenty-five copies of this ed. are numbered and signed by the author. OXB

see also 86

BROCKLEHURST, William (Of Hull, Yorkshire)

War poems, grave and gay. A. Brown & Sons, Ltd. 1944. viii, 105 pp. por.

OXB

BROCKWAY, James (1916– . b. Birmingham. Educated at the London School of Economics. An executive with Ministry of Labour, 1935–40. Flight Lieutenant, Royal Air Force, 1940–45. Writer and translator)

No summer song: poems. Fortune Press. 1949. [ii], 62 pp. OXB

BRODRIBB, Charles William (1878–1945. b. London. Educated at St Paul's School, and Trinity College, Oxford. Poet of the First World War. Joined editorial staff of *The Times* in 1904, becoming assistant editor and special writer, 1914–45. His special interests were classical scholarship and London antiquities)

Poems. With an introduction by Edmund Blunden. Macmillan & Co. Ltd. 1946. xviii, 102 pp. por. MPL

BRONOWSKI, Jacob (1908–74). Educated at Central Foundation School,

London, and Jesus College, Cambridge. Senior lecturer, Hull University, 1934–42. Seconded to government service in 1942 with Joint Target Group, Washington, and Chiefs of Staff Mission to Japan, 1945. Seconded to United Nations Educational, Scientific & Cultural Organization as Head of Projects, 1948. Employed by the National Coal Board, 1950–64. With the Council for Biology in Human Affairs, as Senior Fellow from 1964 and as Director from 1970. Scientist, mathematician, writer, radio and television broadcaster, and authority on William Blake) *see* 10, 45, 48, 76

BROOK, Florence Foster (Of Beckermonds in Langstrothdale, Yorkshire)
Songs from the dales: [poems]. Printed Ripon: Wakeman Press. [1959]. 24 pp.
Title from cover. OXB

BROOK-BROWNE, Donald
The first miscellany: poems, lyrics and fragments. Manchester: Pyramid Publishing Co. [1952]. 24 pp. MPL

BROOKE, Charles
Moments grim and gay: [poems]. Ilfracombe: Arthur H. Stockwell, Ltd. [1944]. 16 pp. OXB

BROOKE, Jocelyn (1908–66. b. Sandgate, Kent. Educated at Bedales School, and Worcester College, Oxford. Served in the Royal Army Medical Corps in several war theatres including North Africa and Italy. Worked in the wine and the book trades. Lived near Canterbury, Kent)
December spring: poems. John Lane the Bodley Head. 1946. 72 pp. OXB
The elements of death, and other poems. Aldington, Kent: Hand and Flower Press. [1952]. 349–383 pp. (Poems in pamphlet, 1952, XII). OXB
see also 11, 12, 14, 45, 59, 76

BROOKE, Ralph (1918– . Educated at Birmingham University. Called up in 1939. Staff Sergeant, Royal Army Pay Corps. Served in India) *see* 43

BROOKES, J.E. (Private with 2/5 Battalion, Australian Imperial Forces, 1940–45. Of Galhampton, Yeovil, Somerset) *see* 63

BROOME, J. (Private. Served with the Eighth Army in the Western Desert) *see* 46

BROOME, Jack *see* **BROOME, John Egerton** (Jack)

BROOME, John Egerton (Jack) (1901– . b. Seattle, United States. Educated at the Royal Naval Colleges, Osborne and Dartmouth. Captain, Royal Navy. Freelance writer, artist and journalist. Editor of Sketch, 1946–61. Of London)

"Services wrendered" by Sonia Snodgrass, goaded by J.E. Broome: [*poems*]. Sampson
Low, Marston & Co., Ltd. [1946]. 96 pp. il.   IWM
    Services wrendered: [*poems*]; [by] Captain Jack Broome. William Kimber. 1974.
128 pp. il., col. il.   OXB
see also 23

BROWN, Alan C.
The secret river: [*poems*]. Illustrations by Caroline Hutchinson. Fortune Press.
[1954]. [ii], 70 pp. il.   OXB

BROWN, Antony *see* 45

BROWN, C.C.
Mural ditties and Sime Road soliloquies. Illustrated by R.W.E. Harper.
Singapore: Kelly & Walsh Ltd. [1948]. [ii], 26 pp. il.   IWM

BROWN, F.J. (Rejected as unfit for military service in 1939. Worked with a
documentary film unit from 1942) *see* 42

BROWN, Helen McInnes (Scottish)
Poems. Glasgow: Jackson, Son & Co. 1949. 64 pp.
    Printed for private circulation.   OXB

BROWN, Hilton (1890–1961. b. Elgin, Scotland. Educated at Elgin Academy
and St Andrews University. Entered the Indian Civil Service in 1913, serving in
the Madras Presidency until 1934. In 1940 joined the B.B.C. writing staff until
1946. Novelist and travel writer, especially on India) *see* 38

BROWN, Ivor (1891–1974. b. Penang, Malaya. Educated at Cheltenham
College, and Balliol College, Oxford. Author and journalist. London dramatic
critic and leader-writer for *The Manchester Guardian*, 1919–35, subsequently
working for *Sketch*, *Weekend Review* and *Punch*. Editor of *The Observer*, 1942–48.
Chairman of the British Drama League, 1954–65. A governor of the Old Vic
and the Royal Shakespeare Theatre) *see* 38

BROWN, Maurice (Sailed on a tramp steamer in the Atlantic convoys to and
from the United States)
    Twelve poems. Ilfracombe: Arthur H. Stockwell, Ltd. 1946. 16 pp.   OXB

BROWN, N.A. (Sergeant. Served with the Eighth Army in the Western Desert
and Italy) *see* 44, 46

BROWN, Thomas
The collected poems of Thomas Brown. Printed Regency Press. [1976]. 23 pp.
                                                                               OXB

BROWNE, Donald Brook- *see* **BROOK-BROWNE, Donald**

BROWNE, Harry T., (John o' the North, pseud.) (Wrote verses for the *Belfast Telegraph*)
Various verses; by John o' the North. Illustrated by Doris V. Blair. Belfast: Derrick MacCord. 1945. 83 pp. il.   IWM

BROWNE, Marjory (Served in the Women's Timber Corps of the Land Army) *see* 50

BROWNE, Maurice (1881–1955. Educated at Winchester College, and Peterhouse, Cambridge. Actor-manager and dramatist. With Harold Monro co-founder of Samurai Press from which the Poetry Bookshop originated. Founder and director of Chicago Little Theatre, 1912–18. Presented many plays in England and the United States)
In time of war, [and other poems]. Alliance Press Ltd. [1944]. 24 pp.   OXB
Road from Delavan: [poems]. Cyril Edwards. 1947. 43 pp.   OXB

BROWNE-CAVE, Bryan William Cave- *see* **CAVE-BROWNE-CAVE, Bryan William**

BROWNING, George Albert (Of Leicestershire?)
Love triumphant, and other poems. Printed Leicester: R.T. Mould & Co. Ltd. 1955. [vi], 72 pp.   OXB

BROWNJOHN, Alan (1931– . b. London. Educated at Brockley County School, and Merton College, Oxford. Senior lecturer in English, Battersea College of Education. Chairman of the Literature Panel, Greater London Arts Association, 1973–76. Contributor of poems, articles and reviews to leading journals)
The lions' mouths: poems. Macmillan. 1967. x, 54 pp.   MPL
[Selected poems]; [by] Alan Brownjohn, Michael Hamburger, Charles Tomlinson. Harmondsworth, Middlesex: Penguin Books. 1969. 192 pp. (Penguin modern poets, 14).
  Not joint authorship. No war poetry by Hamburger or Tomlinson.
                                                      MPL

BROWNLEE, Hamilton (Of Scotland)
Poetical medley. Ilfracombe: Arthur H. Stockwell Ltd. [1966]. 48 pp.
                                                      OXB

BRUCE, George (1909– . b. Fraserburgh, Aberdeenshire, where his family owned a herring curing firm. Educated at Fraserburgh Academy and Aberdeen University. Taught at Dundee High School, 1933–46. Producer for the B.B.C.

in Aberdeen, 1946–56. Talks producer in Edinburgh, 1956–70. Fellow in Creative Writing at Glasgow University, 1971–73)

The collected poems of George Bruce. Edinburgh at the University Press. [1971]. [xii], 121 pp. OXB

Sea talk, [and other poems]. Glasgow: William Maclellan. [1944]. 36 pp. il. (by T.S. Halliday). (Poetry Scotland series). OXB

Selected poems. Oliver & Boyd. 1947. 23 pp. (Saltire modern poets). OXB

BRUCE, Robert Elton Spencer (1936–71. Educated at Christ's Hospital. Editor of *Literary Quarterly* and *New Chapter*, 1957–58, and of *Woman's Own*, 1968–70. Lived at Caterham, Surrey)

Escape and surrender: poems. Ilfracombe: Arthur H. Stockwell, Ltd. 1955. 16 pp. OXB

BRYAN, Sarah *see* 78

BRYANS, Robert Harbinson, (Robert Harbinson, pseud.) (1928– . b. Belfast. Evacuated as a child in July 1940 to the Erne Valley. Schoolmaster, 1948–52, lecturer with the British Council, 1954–55. Travel writer, poet and novelist. Of Brighton, Sussex)

Songs out of Oriel: [poems]; by Robert Harbinson. BCM-Productions. 1974 144 pp. il. OXB

BRYCESON, Alexander (1919– . Educated at Magdalene College, Cambridge. Served in the Royal Air Force. Shot down over Germany early in 1941, spending four and a half years in a number of prisoner of war camps) *see* 76

BRYNE-THOMAS, Lilian (Of Wales)

Smoke: a collection of poems. Illustrations by C. Ford-Dunn. Newport, Mon.: R.H. Johns, Ltd. 1945. 56 pp. il. OXB

BRYON, J.F.W. (Lance-Bombardier, Royal Artillery) *see* 33

BUCHAN, Hon. William (1916– . Son of John Buchan, Lord Tweedsmuir. Educated at Eton College, and New College, Oxford. Squadron Leader, Royal Air Force. Served in India)

Personal poems. Gerald Duckworth & Co. Ltd. 1952. 38 pp. MPL

BUCHANAN, Frank

Peregrine. Introduction by Ronald Duncan. Rebel Press. 1968. 40 pp. OXB

This watering place: poems. Fortune Press. 1943. 44 pp. OXB

BUCHANAN, Roy Graham (Served in Yorkshire & Lancashire Regiment)

Blackout: [*poems*]. Oxford: Shakespeare Head Press. 1940. 32 pp.   BPL
see also   62

BUCK, A.V.   *see*   16

BUESNEL, Maurice
The tallest tower, [*and other poems*]. Dulwich Village: Outposts Publications. 1961. 12 pp.   OXB

BUIN, Helena F.
The moods of the year, in verse. Ilfracombe: Arthur H. Stockwell, Ltd. [1949]. 16 pp.   OXB

BUIST, Alexander (Scottish poet of the First World War)
The gleam and the dark: poems. Oxford: George Ronald. [1954]. 111 pp.
   OXB
Here no security, [*and other poems*]. Eton, Windsor: Shakespeare Head Press. 1958. [viii], 64 pp.   MPL
Reviresco: [*poems*]. Dunfermline: H.T. Macpherson Ltd. 1961. 67 pp.
   OXB

BULL, Arthur Joseph (b. Lincoln. Educated at Hymers College, Hull, and Magdalen College, Oxford, graduating in English. Taught in a Lancashire grammar school)
Chromatic airs: a selection of verse. Chorley: Chorley Guardian Co., Ltd. 1948. 80 pp.   MPL
Collected poems. Selected and arranged by Howard Sergeant. Walton-on-Thames: Outposts Publications. 1975. 122 pp.   OXB
Drift: poems and sonnets. Aldington, Kent: Hand and Flower Press. [1952]. 57–88 pp. (Poems in pamphlet, 1952, III).   OXB
Selected poems. Chosen and arranged by Howard Sergeant. Outposts Publications. 1966. 80 pp.   MPL
Winter crop: [*poems*]. Dulwich Village: Outposts Publications. 1956. 12 pp.
   OXB
see also   42

BULLEN, Keith (–1946. Educated at Jesus College, Oxford. Headmaster of the English Preparatory School at Gezira, Cairo, where he kept open house for his friends and writers in the Forces. Co-founder of the Salamander Society with John Cromer Braun and co-editor of the anthology *Salamander*, 1947. A scholar of French poetry)   *see*   66

BULLETT, Gerald (1893–1958. Educated at Jesus College, Cambridge. Wrote his first published novel in 1914. Poet of the First World War. Served with the Royal Flying Corps in France. Author of fiction, criticism and numerous contributions to literary journals)

Collected poems. Preface by E.M.W. Tillyard. J.M. Dent & Sons Ltd. 1959. x, 86 pp.   MPL

   Poems. Cambridge at the University Press. 1949. 64 pp.   OXB

   Winter solstice. Cambridge at the University Press. 1943. 14 pp.   IWM

BULLEY, Anne (Served with the Women's Royal Naval Service in Ceylon)

   Selected poems. Kinnesswood, Kinross: Lomond Press. 1980. 16 pp.

      A limited ed. of 300 copies.   OXB

see also   23

BURET, Theobald Purcell-   *see*   **PURCELL-BURET, Theobald**

BURGESS, George (Served in H.M. Forces)   *see*   74

BURKE, Thomas (1886–1945. Married writer Winifred Welles. Writer on London. Of Eltham)   *see*   86

BURKE, Winifred, (Winifred Welles), (Clare Cameron, pseud.) (Née Welles. Brought up in the East End of London. Married writer Thomas Burke. In the war was editor of *The Middle Way*, journal of the Buddhist Society)

   A stranger here: [poems]; by Clare Cameron. Privately printed. 1942. 32 pp.

      A limited ed. of 250 numbered copies.   OXB

see also   48

BURKITT, Frances A. Heneage (Served in the Women's Land Army, West Kent. Of Frant, Sussex)   *see*   50, 62

BURN, Michael (1912– . Educated at Winchester College, and New College, Oxford. Journalist with *The Times*, 1936–39. Lieutenant, 1st Battalion, Queen's Westminsters, King's Royal Rifle Corps, 1939–40. Officer in Independent Companies, Norwegian Campaign, 1940, subsequently Captain, No. 2 Commando. Captured in raid on St Nazaire, 1942, spending three years as a prisoner of war, part of the time in Colditz. Foreign correspondent for *The Times* in Austria, Yugoslavia and Hungary. Novelist, poet and playwright. Of Gwynedd, North Wales)

   The flying castle: [poems]. Illustrated by Richard Macdonald. Rupert Hart-Davis. 1954. 40 pp. il.   OXB

   Open day and night, and other poems. Chatto & Windus; Hogarth Press. 1978. 46 pp. (Phoenix living poets).   OXB

BURNELL, Mary Seton

Pictures in verse. Mitre Press. 1961. 35 pp.   MPL

BURNETT, Beatrix
Sign of the pentagram, [and other poems]. Ilfracombe: Arthur H. Stockwell, Ltd.
1950. 24 pp.   OXB

BURNETT, David (1937– . b. Scotland, brought up in Edinburgh.
Educated at Edinburgh University. University librarian. Author of papers on
professional and scholarly topics)
Jackdaw: [poems]. With engravings by Kirill Sokolov. Edinburgh: Tragara
Press. 1980. 69 pp. il.
    A limited ed. of 150 hand-set copies.   OXB

BURNETT, Grace (Of Wiltshire) *see* 70, 71, 72

BURNIE, Douglas (Served in the Middle East) *see* 39, 63

BURNS, George S. (Served at Dunkirk at age of twenty-one)
A poetical walk: [poems]. Ilfracombe: Arthur H. Stockwell Ltd. 1976. 48 pp
                                                                               OXB

BURNS, Jim (1936– . b. Preston, Lancashire. Educated at local schools.
Served in the Army, 1954–57, partly in Germany. Poet, journalist and
publisher of the little magazine *Move*, 1964–68)
The store of things, [and other poems]. Manchester: Phoenix Pamphlet Poets
Press. 1969. 27 pp.
    A limited ed. of 1,000 copies of which the first fifty copies are numbered,
signed by the author and bound in hard covers.   OXB

BURROWS, Ken (Served in the Middle East from January 1943 to 1947, first
with the 16/5 Lancers in the 6th Armoured Division. Of Alvaston,
Derby) *see* 63

BURROWS, Leo (Staff Sergeant, Royal Electrical and Mechanical Engineers.
Served in the Middle East and Italy)
The Eighth Army epic: the African phase. Gateshead on Tyne: Northumberland
Press Ltd. [1944]. 15 pp.   OXB
The unfinished C.M.F. pot pourri: the Italian phase. Gateshead on Tyne:
Northumberland Press Ltd. [1945]. 19 pp.   OXB

BURTENSHAW, Nan
The wilderness speaks, [and other poems]. Ilfracombe: Arthur H. Stockwell, Ltd.
1974. 20 pp.   OXB

BURTON, Doris (1894– . b. Bishop's Stortford, Essex. Educated privately
and in Switzerland. Writer on Catholicism and contributor to Catholic
magazines. Of London)

The incarnation, and other poems. Ilfracombe: Arthur Stockwell, Ltd. 1946.
48 pp.   OXB

BURY, Adrian (Novelist, poet, writer on painting and art. An Air Raid
Warden in London during the bombing raids)
 Battle with the dark, and other poems. Grant Richards. 1942. 29 pp. OXB
 Eros uncrowned: [poems]. Printed Westminster Press. 1949. 48 pp. OXB

BUSH, John *see* 23

BUSWELL, John
 Wayside thoughts, and other poems. Ilfracombe: Arthur H. Stockwell, Ltd. 1947.
24 pp.   OXB

BUXTON, John (1912– . b. Bramhall, Cheshire. Educated at Malvern
College, and New College, Oxford. Served as Lieutenant, No. 1 Independent
Co., taken prisoner in Norway in 1940 and interned in Oflag VI1 until May
1945. Recipient of an Atlantic Award in 1946. Fellow of New College and
Reader in English Literature, Oxford University. Of Malmesbury, Wiltshire)
 Atropos, and other poems. Macmillan & Co. Ltd. 1946. viii, 48 pp. BPL
 "Such liberty": [poems]. Macmillan & Co. Ltd. 1944. viii, 41 pp.
  Written from a prison camp in Germany. IWM
 Westward. Jonathan Cape. 1942. 44 pp.
  Written in Oflag VII in the autumn of 1941. MPL
see also 8, 67, 76, 84

BUXTON, Rufus, Lord Noel-Buxton (1917–80. Educated at Harrow
School, and Balliol College, Oxford. Invalided out from 163 Officer Cadet
Training Unit (Artists Rifles), 1940. Research assistant, Agricultural
Economics Research Institute, Oxford, 1941–43. Lecturer to the Forces,
1943–45. Producer, B.B.C. North American Service, 1946–48. On editorial
staff of *Farmer's Weekly*, 1950–52) *see* 84

BYRNE, Patrick *see* 52

C., D.S. (Served in South-East Asia Command) *see* 35

C., G. *see* 23

C., J.P.
 Poetic justice: [poems]; by J.P.C. Illustrated by Leslie Starke. Stevens & Sons
Ltd. 1947. xii, 84 pp. il. OXB

CADAXA, Armindo Bonanco Menol (Of Portuguese origin or descent)
 Earthquake at Delphi, [and other poems]. Outposts Publications. 1966. 44 pp.
                                                                OXB

CADDICK, Arthur (1911–   . Educated at Wadham College, Oxford. Writer, tutor for Bar finals and teacher. Won 1st prize for poetry, Six Nations Inter-Celtic Festival, 1949. Founder and Secretary of Guild of Cornish Craftsmen, 1959. Broadcaster on B.B.C. radio and contributor to various periodicals. Of Penzance, Cornwall)

Quiet lutes and laughter: selected poems, grave and gay. Fortune Press. 1955. 40 pp.
OXB

The speech of phantoms: [poems]. Saint Ives: Latin Press. 1951. 16 pp. (Crescendo poetry series, 1).

Title from cover.   OXB

CAMBRIDGE, D.C.F. (Of Middlesex) *see* 73

CAMERON, Clare, pseud. *see* **BURKE, Winifred, (Winifred Welles)**, (Clare Cameron, pseud.)

CAMERON, John Cullen

Poetical works. Ilfracombe: Arthur H. Stockwell Ltd. 1969. 44 pp.   OXB

CAMERON, Norman (1905–53. b. Bombay, India. Educated at Fettes College, and Oriel College, Oxford. An advertising copy-writer with J. Walter Thompson before the war. Served in Intelligence. In 1943 was sent with a political unit to the Eighth Army in Africa and Italy, where he wrote propaganda leaflets to be dropped behind enemy lines. Worked for a time with the occupation forces in Austria)

The collected poems of Norman Cameron, 1905–1953. With an introduction by Robert Graves. Hogarth Press. 1957. 72 pp. por.   OXB

Forgive me, sire, [and other poems]. Fore Publications Ltd. 1950. 24 pp. (Key poets, 10).   BL

Work in hand: [poems]; [by] Alan Hodge, Norman Cameron, Robert Graves. Hogarth Press. 1942. 64 pp.

Not joint authorship.   BL

see also 45, 48, 59, 76

CAMMELL, Charles Richard (Poet of the First World War. Writer on the artist Pietro Annigoni)

XXI poems. Edinburgh: Poseidon Press. 1943. [vi], 29 pp.

A limited ed. of 100 numbered copies signed by the author, printed by H.D.C. Pepler at the Ditchling Press, Sussex, on Batchelor handmade paper.
OXB

XXI poems. Edinburgh: Poseidon Press. 1943. [vi], 29 pp.

A limited ed. of 250 copies, printed by H.D.C. Pepler at the Ditchling Press, Sussex, on Batchelor handmade paper.   OXB

The triumph of beauty, [and other poems]. 6th ed. With 'Scotland's ode to victory', and other poems. Edinburgh: Poseidon Press. 1945. vi, 29 pp.

A limited ed. of 250 numbered copies, printed by H.D.C. Pepler at the Ditchling Press, Sussex, on handmade paper.   OXB
   [Earlier eds published pre-war]

CAMPBELL, Alan (1917–77. Educated at Aldenham School, Ecole des Sciences Politiques, Paris, and Trinity Hall, Cambridge. Commissioned in the Royal Artillery, 1939. Served in France and Belgium until taken prisoner of war in 1940. Q.C. and a Recorder of the Crown Court from 1976. Served on several legal committees)
   Colditz cameo: a collection of verse written by a prisoner of war in Germany, 1940–1945. Ditchling, Sussex: Ditchling Press Ltd. [1954]. 47 pp. por.   BPL

CAMPBELL, Archibald Kenneth (1896–   . b. Yokohama, Japan. Educated at Elizabeth College, Guernsey, and Durham University. Served in the First World War. A clergyman, Canon of St John's, Oban, Argyll. Writer on small boat sailing)
   The banner of Mars, and other poems. Glasgow: William Maclellan. 1951. 51 pp.
                    BL

CAMPBELL, Clare
   London allegiance: poems. Fortune Press. 1953. 48 pp.   IWM

CAMPBELL, Joseph (1879–1944. b. Belfast. One of the poets of the Irish literary renaissance at the beginning of this century. Poet of the First World War. Settled in New York in 1925, founding a School of Irish Studies at Fordham University. Returned to Ireland in 1939)   *see*   51

CAMPBELL, Roy (1901–57. b. Durban, South Africa. Educated at Durban High School. A pre-war poet, he lived in France, Portugal and Spain, where he became known as a bull-fighter and steer-thrower. Saved the Carmelite archives at Toledo while fighting on Franco's side in the Spanish Civil War. Joined the British Army in 1940, serving as a Sergeant in North and East Africa until invalided out in 1944. On the Literary Advisory Board of the B.B.C., 1945–49. Killed in a car crash in Portugal)
   The collected poems of Roy Campbell. Bodley Head. 1949. 297 pp.   OXB
   The collected poems of Roy Campbell. Vol. 2. Bodley Head. 1957. 256 pp.
                    OXB
   Poems of Roy Campbell. Chosen and introduced by Uys Krige. Cape Town: Maskew Miller Ltd. 1960. [vi], 142 pp.   BL
   Selected poetry. Edited by J.M. Lalley. Bodley Head. 1968. 221 pp.   OXB
   Sons of the mistral: [poems]. Faber & Faber. 1941. 80 pp.   OXB
   Talking bronco, [and other poems]. Faber & Faber Ltd. 1946. 91 pp.   BPL
see also   15, 30, 51, 59, 68, 76

CAMPBELL, Wilma, Lady Cawdor (Daughter of Vincent C. Vickers and niece of Sir Archibald Clark Kerr, British Ambassador to Moscow. Wife of the Women's Land Army, North Riding of Yorkshire) *see* 50
Own Cameron Highlanders in France, January–June 1940. An ardent friend of Fighting France) *see* 42

CANHAM, J.A. (Of Norfolk) *see* 74, 75

CANON, Judy
Rest awhile, and other poems. Ilfracombe: Arthur H. Stockwell, Ltd. [1946].
16 pp. OXB

CAPES, Molly (b. London. Educated at Wycombe Abbey School. Served in the Women's Land Army, North Riding of Yorkshire) *see* 50

CAPES, Renalt (Served in H.M. Forces. Biographer of Lord Nelson, Alexander Dumas and others) *see* 74

CAPRON, Clare I. (Of Milford-on-Sea, Hampshire)
Off the prong: [*poems*]. Printed Lymington: King. [1944]. [ii], 40 pp. il.
OXB
On the wing: [*poems*]. Printed Lymington: King. [1942]. [ii], 34 pp. OXB
Our fresh springs: [*poems*]. Printed Lymington: King. 1947 [iv], 43 pp. il.
OXB

CAREY, T.A. (Able Seaman, Royal Navy) *see* 23

CARGNELLI, Renata Letitia (b. Trieste, Italy. Educated in England. Journalist, essayist, translator, lecturer and traveller)
The revolutionary generation, [*and other poems*]. Mitre Press. [1961]. 76 pp.
OXB

CARNELL, Francis George (Educated at Oxford University. Joined the Army in the ranks of the Royal Armoured Corps, becoming a Lieutenant-Colonel in the Army Educational Corps. Served in West Africa, South-East Asia and India) *see* 43

CARPENTER, Maurice, (Miles Carpenter, pseud.) (1911–78. Educated at Birkbeck College, London. Writer and contributor to many periodicals. Co-editor of the anthology *New Lyrical Ballads*, 1945. Of Wootton Bassett, Wiltshire) *see* 36, 64

CARPENTER, Miles, pseud. *see* **CARPENTER, Maurice**, (Miles Carpenter, pseud.)

CARROLL, Richard
The inner voice: poems. Printed Tongeren, Belgium: A. & A. Nys. [1968]. [iv], 53 pp. OXB
The prelude: poems. Printed Antwerpen: Gust. Dirix n.v. 1970. 59 pp.
A limited ed. of 100 copies with fifty numbered and signed by the author OXB

CARSON, Amy Kathleen
A garland of verse: poems. Ilfracombe: Arthur H. Stockwell, Ltd. [1944]. 48 pp. OXB

CARSON, J.
My heart's desire: [*poems*]. Ilfracombe: Arthur H. Stockwell, Ltd. 1946, 32 pp. OXB

CARTER, C. (Served in the Middle East) *see* 63

CARTER, G.D. (Served in South-East Asia Command) *see* 35

CARTLAND, Barbara (Best-selling writer of romantic and historical novels and historical biography. Organized many pageants pre-war in aid of charities. Married twice. Made two lecture tours in Canada, 1940. Honorary Junior Commander, Auxiliary Territorial Service. Lady Welfare Officer and Librarian to all Services in Bedfordshire, 1941–49. County Cadet Officer for St John Ambulance Brigade in Bedfordshire, 1943–47. Freelance writer, lecturer and public speaker. Of Hatfield, Hertfordshire)
Lines on life and love: [*poems*]. Hutchinson. 1972. 48 pp. OXB

CARTLEDGE, Arthur (Served in France)
Light shade: [*poems*]. Ilfracombe: Arthur H. Stockwell Ltd [1968]. 44 pp. OXB

CARY, Joyce (1888–1957. Educated at Clifton College, and Trinity College, Oxford. Studied art in Edinburgh. Served in the Balkan War, 1912–13, in the Montenegrin Battalion and British Red Cross. With the Nigerian Regiment in the Cameroons campaign, 1915–16. Writer of novels, short stories and political philosophy)
Marching soldier. Michael Joseph Ltd. 1945. 28 pp. BPL

CASHMORE, Alfred
We take it singing: [*poems*]. Ilfracombe: Arthur H. Stockwell, Ltd. [1942]. 16 pp. OXB

CASPALL, John Edward (Of Luton)
The doubtful crown, [*and other poems*]. Dulwich Village: Outposts Publications. 1956. 12 pp. OXB

CASSELS, James Kenneth (1909–   . b. Scotland. Educated at Edinburgh University. A teacher, he studied for ordination before the war. Joined the British Expeditionary Force in 1939 and was evacuated from Dunkirk. Gained Parachute 'wings'. Served in South-East Asia Command with the West African Signals. Became a Church of Scotland minister)   *see*   43, 76

CASSIDY, John (b. Lancashire. After service with the East African Army, he graduated from Manchester University. Lecturer in literature and drama)
   An attitude of mind, [*and other poems*]. Hutchinson. 1978. 80 pp.   OXB

CASTLE, Frances Mundy- *see* **MUNDY-CASTLE, Frances**, (Peggy Whitehouse, pseud.)

CAUSLEY, Charles (1917–   . b. Launceston, Cornwall. Educated at Horwell Grammar School, Launceston College and Peterborough Training College. Served on lower deck in Royal Navy, 1940–46, mostly with Communications Branch in the Atlantic, Orkneys and Gibraltar. Teacher, poet and broadcaster. Literary editor, B.B.C. West Region radio, 1953–56. Member of Arts Council Poetry Panel, 1962–66. Visiting Fellow in Poetry, Exeter University, 1973. Recipient of Queen's Gold Medal for Poetry, 1967, and a Cholmondeley Award, 1971. Of Launceston)
   Collected poems, 1951–1975. Macmillan Ltd. 1975. 289 pp.   OXB
   Collected poems, 1951–1975. Paperback ed. Macmillan. 1979. 289 pp.   OXB
   Farewell, Aggie Weston: [*poems*]. Aldington, Kent: Hand and Flower Press. [1951]. 32 pp. (Poems in pamphlet, 1951, I).   BL
   Johnny Alleluia: poems. Rupert Hart-Davis. 1961. 61 pp.   OXB
   [*Selected poems*]; [by] George Barker, Martin Bell, Charles Causley. Harmondsworth, Middlesex: Penguin Books. 1962. 128 pp. (Penguin modern poets, 3).
       Not joint authorship.   BL
   [*Selected poems*]; [by] Charles Causley and Kathleen Raine. Longmans, 1969. [iv], 28 pp. (Longmans' poetry library).
       Not joint authorship. No war poetry by Raine.   OXB
   Survivor's leave: [*poems*]. Aldington, Kent: Hand and Flower Press. [1953]. 46 pp.   OXB
   Union Street: poems. With a preface by Edith Sitwell. Rupert Hart-Davis. 1957. 95 pp.   BL
see also   3, 10, 17, 49, 59, 76, 85

CAVE-BROWN-CAVE, Bryan William (1915–   . Educated at Shrewsbury School, and St Edmund Hall, Oxford. At Oxford he was Secretary of Oxford University Dramatic Society. Entered the Army in 1939. Sent to India in 1942, being posted to New Delhi in 1943 to start broadcasting services for India and South-East Asia Commands)

'To-night is on the mountain': poems 1941–1946. Oxford University Press. 1948. viii, 31 pp. OXB
see also 43

CAWDOR, Lady *see* **CAMPBELL, Wilma, Lady Cawdor**

CAWTHORNE, Graham (Squadron Leader, Royal Air Force. Stationed at 216 Group in the Desert Museum on the Suez Road near Heliopolis, Cairo. Journalist and writer) *see* 63

CECIL, Robert (1913– . Educated at Wellington College, and Gonville & Caius College, Cambridge. Entered the Foreign Service in 1936. Served in Paris, then in London until 1951. Held diplomatic appointments in Copenhagen, Hanover, Bonn and New York, 1953–61. Head of the Cultural Relations Department at the Foreign Office, 1962–67. Reader in Contemporary German History, Reading University, 1968–78. Chairman, Institute for Cultural Research)
Levant, and other poems. Fortune Press. [1940]. 40 pp. OXB
Time, and other poems. Putnam. 1955. 31 pp. OXB
see also 42

CELNER, I. (Lance-Corporal. Served in the Western Desert with the Eighth Army) *see* 46, 63

CHADWICK, Joan Yvonne (Of Yorkshire) *see* 74

CHADWICK, Philip
Dawn music, [*and other poems*]. Brighton: Crabtree Press Ltd. 1946, 62 pp. OXB

CHAIR, Somerset De *see* **DE CHAIR, Somerset**

CHALLONER, H.K., pseud. *see* **MILLS, Janet Melanie Ailsa**, (H.K. Challoner, pseud.)

CHALLONER, Louis, (Bombardier, pseud.) (1911– . b. Blackpool, Lancashire. Served in North Africa with the Eighth Army from Bir Hacheim to Cairo and from Alamein to Cape Bon and Algiers)
Libya, and other poems; by 'Bombardier'. Romford Poetry Centre. [1947?]. 24 pp.
A limited ed. of 200 numberd copies. BPL
see also 39, 46, 63

CHALONER, Robert Laver (1916– . Educated at Jesus College, Oxford. Captain, Royal Artillery. Served in Medium Artillery from Caen to Hamburg. Journalist after the war) *see* 25, 33, 76

CHAMBERLAIN, Brenda (1912– . b. Bangor, North Wales. Educated at the Royal Academy Schools, London. Poet and painter. Helped run the Caseg Press at Llanllechid, Caernarvonshire, in collaboration with her husband John Petts, 1935–42. Lived in Greece for six years and travelled widely in Denmark, France and Germany. Of Allt Glanrafon, Bangor)
The green heart: poems. Oxford University Press. 1958. viii, 76 pp.　　　OXB
see also　56

CHAMBERLAIN, M. (Of Gloucestershire)　*see*　74

CHAMPKIN, Peter (1918– . b. Hong Kong. Educated at Cambridge University. Assistant Secretary of the School Examinations Department at London University, 1951–78. Of Battle, Sussex)
In another room, [*and other poems*]. With a foreword by T.R. Henn. Linden Press. 1959. 60 pp.　　　MPL

CHANCELLOR, F.B. (Lieutenant, The Bays. Captured in France in 1940, held prisoner of war in Germany until 1945)　*see*　67

CHAPIN, Christina (1900– . Schoolgirl poet of the First World War)
Poems, 1929–1941. Oxford: Shakespeare Head Press. 1941. 40 pp.　　　MPL

CHAPMAN, Arthur Edward (Rector of Tiverton, Devon, 1921–45).
Verses (Disjecta fragmenta). Ilfracombe: Arthur H. Stockwell, Ltd. 1946. 79 pp.
　　　OXB

CHAPMAN, John Alexander
War: [*poems*]. [Windsor]: Savile Press. 1951. viii, 64 pp.　　　OXB

CHAPMAN, Peggy (Of Norfolk)　*see*　75

CHAPMAN, Raymond (1924– . b. Cardiff. Educated at Jesus College, Oxford, and King's College, London. University teacher. Of Barnes, London)
Early poems; by Raymond Chapman and J.D. James. Fortune Press. [1946]. 64 pp.
　　Not joint authorship.　　　OXB
Prince of the clouds, and other poems. Fortune Press. 1947. 36 pp.　　　OXB
see also　34

CHARLES, Dudley (Served in the Middle East)　*see*　39, 63

CHARNOCK, Harry　*see*　**CHARNOCK, William Henry**

CHARNOCK, John (Served in the Middle East)　*see*　39, 63

CHARNOCK, William Henry (1902– . Educated at Lancing College, and St John's College, Cambridge. A civil engineer)

Ephemerid, [and other poems]. Printed Brighton: Southern Publishing Co. Ltd. 1950. 48 pp. OXB

Epilogue, [and other poems]; by Harry Charnock. Chesterfield: Guild Press. 1954. 16 pp. (Guild poets). BL

CHATFIELD, Evelyn (Of Hampshire) *see* 74

CHAVE, Owen C., (Ariel, pseud.) (Flight Lieutenant, Royal Air Force. Died on active service)

Winged victory: poems of a Flight Lieutenant; by Ariel. Oxford: Basil Blackwell. 1942. 32 pp. OXB
see also 1, 25

CHENEVIX TRENCH, Maxwell (1921–43. b. Westerham, Kent, Educated at Wellington College, and Gonville & Caius College, Cambridge. Commissioned in the Royal Engineers, 8th Field Squadron, North Africa. Killed while clearing a minefield for the passage of the 6th Armoured Division through the Fondouk Pass on 10 April 1943. Mentioned in despatches)

Dawn passage, [and other poems]. Fortune Press. 1945, 24 pp. por. IWM
see also 20

CHERRILL, Maud (Taught at St Petroc's School, Bude)

Padstow lights: poems. With a memoir by Roger Venables, and a foreword by L.A.G. Strong. Oxford: Scrivener Press. 1949. 127 pp. OXB

CHERRY, Graham (1910– . Educated at St Alban's School and Oxford University. Lieutenant-Colonel, 60th Rifles. Staff Officer with 7th Indian Division, 1942–44. Served in Burma) *see* 43

CHEYNE, N. Gilbert

From my heart to yours: poems. Epworth Press. 1948. 48 pp. OXB

CHILMAN, Eric (1893– . b. Beverley, Yorkshire. Educated at Hull Technical College. Poet of the First World War, serving as a Private in the East Yorkshire Regiment. Journalist and writer on food and wine. Of London)

Sixty lyrics and one. Frederick Muller Ltd. 1945. 64 pp. IWM
see also 84

CHILTON, Henry Herman (1863– . b. Brussels. Educated at Wolverhampton Grammar School and in Milan. Lock manufacturer. J.P. of Willenhall, Staffordshire)

The seeker: a poem. Birmingham: Cornish Brothers Ltd. 1943. [x], 106 pp. OXB

CHOPPING, Ralph C. (Served in the Middle East) *see* 63

CHRISTIE, R.N. (Major, Gordon Highlanders. Captured in France in 1940, held prisoner of war in Germany until 1945) *see* 67

CHRISTIE-MURRAY, Elisabeth (Married the Reverend David Hugh Arthur Christie-Murray. Had one son and three daughters. Lived at Harrow-on-the-Hill, Middlesex)
When soft voices die: selected poems. Harrow-on-the-Hill: David Christie-Murray. 1967. [33] pp.
    Title from cover.   OXB

CHURCH, Richard (1893–1972. b. London. Educated at Dulwich Hamlet School. Poet of the First World War. Spent about twenty-five years in the Civil Service until 1933, coming to loathe bureaucracy. Novelist, poet, critic and freelance literary journalist. Vice-President of the Royal Society of Literature and President of the English Association. Recipient of the Femina Vie Heureuse Prize, 1937, the *Sunday Times* Prize for Literature, 1955, and Foyle's Poetry Prize, 1957)
The collected poems of Richard Church. J.M. Dent & Sons Ltd. 1948. xii, 291 pp.
                                      IWM
The lamp. J.M. Dent & Sons Ltd. 1946. 96 pp.   BPL
The solitary man, and other poems. J.M. Dent & Sons Ltd. 1941. 80 pp.
    A limitd ed. of 900 copies.
Twentieth-century psalter. J.M. Dent & Sons Ltd. 1943. [vi], 74 pp.
                                      MPL
see also   7, 8, 38, 42, 48, 51, 56, 68, 77, 84

CHURCHILL, Sarah (1914–82. Daughter of Sir Winston and Lady Churchill. Dancer and actress, first appearing on stage in 1936. Served in the Women's Royal Air Force as an Aircraftwoman and subsequently as a commissioned officer, 1941–45. Returning to the theatre she concentrated on straight acting, appearing in the West End and touring Britain and the United States. She was married three times, to Vic Oliver (marriage dissolved), to Antony Beauchamp who died in 1957, and to Lord Audley, who died in 1963)
The collected poems of Sarah Churchill. With songs by some of her friends. Leslie Frewin. [1974]. 216 pp. por.   OXB
The empty spaces: poems. Leslie Frewin. [1966]. 96 pp. por.   MPL
The unwanted statue, and other poems. Leslie Frewin. [1969]. 96 pp. por.
                                      MPL
see also   25

CLAPHAM, Walter *see* 25

CLARE, Helen, pseud. *see* **CLARKE, Pauline**, (Helen Clare, pseud.)

CLARIDGE, Joan
    Random reveries: [poems]. Heath Cranton Ltd. 1945. 39 pp.   **OXB**

CLARK, Cumberland (1862– . b. London. Educated at King's College, London, and in Sydney, Australia. Poet of the First World War. Journalist, dramatist, lecturer and writer on Shakespeare. Lived in Bournemouth)
    The British Empire at war: [poems]. Bournemouth: Henbest Publicity Service, Ltd. 1940. 140 pp.   **BL**
    The war poems of a patriot. Printed Bournemouth: Henbest Publicity Service Ltd. 1940. 48 pp.
        Title from cover.   **OXB**
    War songs of the Allies. 2nd ed. Printed Southampton: J.E. Barnes Ltd. 1940. 262 pp.
        Verses and song choruses.   **OXB**
    War songs of the Allies. 3rd ed. Printed Southampton: J.E. Barnes Ltd. 1940. 291 pp. por.
        Verses and song choruses.   **BL**
        [No copy of 1st ed. traced]

CLARK, David Stafford- *see* **STAFFORD-CLARK, David**

CLARK, Eric (1911– . b. Belfast. Educated at Larkfield College, and Queen's University, Belfast. Served in the Royal Corps of Signals, 1940–46. Awarded the Burma Star. Journalist, television scriptwriter, art teacher, and writer of non-fiction for children. Managing editor of The Galleon Press, Belfast, from 1940) *see* 22

CLARK, Gideon (Novelist, dramatist and journalist. Worked for the Press Association, Central News, *The Times*, *Daily Herald* and others. Of Harpenden, Hertfordshire)
    The camp site, [and other poems]. Dulwich Village: Outposts Publications. 1958. 16 pp.   **OXB**
    Time's beauty, [and other poems]. Dulwich Village: Outposts Publications. 1957. 12 pp.   **OXB**

CLARK, Henry William (1869–1948. b. London. Educated at University College School, Hackney Theological College and in Germany. Poet of the First World War. Congregational minister in Greenock and Woking. Headmaster of St George's School, Harpenden, 1919–26, and of St John's School, Broxbourne, 1930–34. Writer on religious topics and of educational textbooks)
    Collected poems, new and old. Williams and Norgate Ltd. 1941. 191 pp.   **MPL**

CLARK, Howard (b. Hull, Yorkshire. Served in the Rifle Brigade)

Dodging the lions and tigers: [*poems*]. Driffield: Ridings Publishing Co. [1973]. [ii], 29 pp.

    Title from cover.   OXB

CLARK, Jacqueline (Of Kent) *see* 74

CLARK, Laurence (1914– . b. Maidstone, Kent. Educated at Peterhouse, Cambridge. Novelist, poet, and writer on economics and politics. Of Rickmansworth, Hertfordshire)
    Thirty-nine preludes: [*poems*]. Villiers Publications. 1953. 47 pp.   IWM

CLARK, Leonard (1905–81. b. St Peter Port, Guernsey. Educated at Monmouth School, and Normal College, Bangor. Held teaching posts in Gloucestershire and South London before being appointed H.M. Inspector of Schools in 1936. Served in Devon Regiment of the Home Guard, 1940–43. Consultant on poetry for Seafarers' Education Service, 1940–54. Member of Literature Panel of the Arts Council, 1965–69)
    The hearing heart: [*poems*]. East Finchley: Enitharmon Press. 1974. 45 pp.
                                               OXB

CLARK, R.R. (Served with the Eighth Army)
    Tatie bread, and other poems. Belfast: Galleon Press. [1946]. 35 pp.   OXB

CLARK, Robert S. (Of London) *see* 74

CLARK, Susan D'Arcy (Writer and composer. All her children served in the war. A member of the Society of Women Journalists. Of Derbyshire) *see* 41

CLARKE, Austin (1896–1974. b. Dublin. Educated at Belvedere College, and University College, Dublin. Lecturer in English at University College, Dublin, 1917–21. Foundation Member of the Irish Academy of Letters, 1932, becoming its President, 1952–54. President, Irish P.E.N., 1939–42 and 1946–49. Chairman of the Dublin Verse Speaking Society and of the Lyric Theatre Company. Writer of novels, poetry and verse-plays, freelance reviewer and broadcaster)
    Collected poems. Edited by Liam Miller. Dublin: Dolmen Press; Oxford University Press. 1974. xvi, 568 pp.   OXB
    Later poems. Dublin: Dolmen Press. 1961. [vi], 96 pp.   OXB

CLARKE, Douglas A. (Of Jersey, Channel Islands. Evacuated to England in 1940)
    Poems. Ilfracombe: Arthur H. Stockwell, Ltd. [1944]. 23 pp.
    Dedicated 'to my mother and father, living under the German occupation in Jersey'.   OXB

CLARKE, Enid G.
The divine caller, and other poems. Ilfracombe: Arthur H. Stockwell Ltd. [1950].
16 pp.   OXB

CLARKE, F. (Battery Quartermaster-Sergeant. Served with the Eighth
Army) *see* 44

CLARKE, F.C. (Served with the Eighth Army in the Western Desert)
The road of time: [*poems*]. Chichester: Janay Publishing Co. 1972. [xii], 150 pp.
                                                                                          OXB

CLARKE, Pauline, (Helen Clare, pseud.) (1921– . b. Kirkby-in-Ashfield,
Nottinghamshire. Educated at Somerville College, Oxford. Writer of children's
stories, winning the Library Association's Carnegie Medal in 1968. Married
Peter Hunter Blair. Of Cambridge)
Poems from Sherwood Forest. Ilfracombe: Arthur H. Stockwell, Ltd. [1959].
24 pp.   OXB

CLARKE, William (1908– . b. London. Sergeant in the Royal Army
Medical Corps, narrowly escaping death at Dunkirk. On the London Poetry
Secretariat list)
Shades of khaki, and other poems. Stockport: Harry Chambers. [1976].
35 pp. por. (Peterloo poets).   OXB

CLEE, John (Of Bristol. Member of the Bristol Savages Artists' Club 'blue
feather' insignia)
Blue feather poems, and other verse. Foreword by Donald Hughes. Bristol:
Burleigh Press. [1960]. 79 pp.   MPL

CLEMENT, Joyce
Silhouette: [*poems*]. Ilfracombe: Arthur H. Stockwell, Ltd. [1953]. 16 pp.
                                                                                          OXB

CLEMENTS, D. (Of London) *see* 74

CLIFTON, Harry (1907– . b. London. Educated at Christ Church, Oxford.
Lived in Galway, Ireland)
Gleams Britain's day. Duckworth. 1942. viii, 257 pp.   IWM

CLOETE, Stuart (1897–1976. b. Paris of British parentage. Educated at
Lancing College. Served as Second-Lieutenant in the King's Own Yorkshire
Light Infantry, 1914–17, and in the Coldstream Guards from 1917 until his
retirement because of wounds in 1925. Farmed in South Africa, 1925–35 and
1949–53. A Trustee of the South African Foundation)

The young men and the old: [*poems*]. Boston, Mass.: Houghton Mifflin Co. 1941. [x], 37 pp.   BL
see also 38

CLOTHIER, P.M. (Served in the Middle East) *see* 63

COATES, Edward Groves
The British Empire, and other poems. Ilfracombe: Arthur H. Stockwell, Ltd. 1954. 14 pp.   OXB

COATES, Irene (Educated at Cambridge University. Contributed to *Granta*)
Poems of change. Fortune Press. [1954]. 52 pp.   OXB

COATES, Stephen (Writer on human psychology)
First poems. Fortune Press. [1943]. 32 pp.   OXB
Second poems. Editions Poetry London. 1947. 51 pp.   OXB
see also 56

COATES, Vera (Of Yorkshire) *see* 75

COATH, Hilda Mary
Selected poems. Regency Press. [1971]. 52 pp. il.   OXB

COATS, Alice (1905–78. b. Birmingham. Educated at Edgbaston High School for Girls, Birmingham College of Art, and the Slade School, University College, London. Served in the Women's Land Army, Warwickshire, 1940–45. Artist and writer on plants. Lived in Handsworth, Birmingham) *see* 50

COBBETT, Daisy Leggett (In Canada in 1940)
Beauty for ashes: [*poems*]. Ilfracombe: Arthur H. Stockwell, Ltd. 1956. 32 pp.
                                                                                   OXB
Oil of joy: [*poems*]. Ilfracombe: Arthur H. Stockwell, Ltd. 1960. 80 pp.
                                                                                   OXB

COBHAM, Rosemary (1912–79. Educated at Lady Margaret Hall, Oxford. Volunteered for the Auxiliary Territorial Service at the time of Dunkirk. A Christian Scientist)
Collected poems. A.E. Callam. 1955. 74 pp.   OXB
Kaleidoscope plus: [*poems*]. Foreword by Lord Gore-Booth. Partnership Editions; Shepheard-Walwyn. [1980]. 159 pp. col. por.

COCHRANE, Adelaide
Sunshine and shadow, [*and other poems*]. Ilfracombe: Arthur H. Stockwell, Ltd. 1957. 16 pp.   OXB

COCKERELL, Clement William (of Truro, Cornwall)
Poems of two worlds. Ilfracombe: Arthur H. Stockwell, Ltd. 1946. 64 pp.
OXB

COCKERILL, Sir George (1867–1957. b. Newquay, Cornwall. Educated at Cheltenham College. Joined 2nd Queen's Regiment in 1888, serving in India and South Africa. Retired in 1910 as Lieutenant-Colonel commanding 7th Fusiliers. In the First World War became Deputy Director of Military Operations & Military Intelligence, and Director of Special Intelligence, 1915–19)
Late harvest: a miscellany of verse. Hutchinson & Co. Ltd. [1946]. 84 pp.
MPL

COCKLAKE, pseud.
"My dog Pip", and other poems; by Cocklake. Ilfracombe: Arthur H. Stockwell, Ltd. 1947. 40 pp.
OXB

COCKS, Ruby Louise (Of Dorset)
More verses from Dorset. Ilfracombe: Arthur H. Stockwell, Ltd. 1946. 16 pp.
OXB
Verses from Dorset. Ilfracombe: Arthur H. Stockwell, Ltd. [1944]. 16 pp.
OXB
Verses from Dorset. [New ed.]. Ilfracombe: Arthur H. Stockwell, Ltd. [1950]. 24 pp.
OXB

COGDON, John George
Fact and fantasy in verse. Regency Press. [1968]. 63 pp.
OXB

COHEN, Betty (Of Cardiganshire)   *see*   75

COLDWELL, James (Lieutenant, Royal Navy)   *see*   25, 33

COLE, B. (Private with the Royal Sussex Regiment at El Alamein. Of Westcliff-on-Sea, Essex)   *see*   63

COLEMAN, E.R. (Of Sussex)
Poems of war-time Sussex. Ilfracombe: Arthur H. Stockwell, Ltd. [1944]. 15 pp.
OXB

COLEMAN, Marion (1898– . Educated at Derby High School and Cheltenham Ladies' College. Studied medicine at the Royal Free Hospital. Worked in general practice in various places including the East End of London and Hull. In 1944 joined the Catholic Committee for Relief Abroad. Worked in a camp near Bari, southern Italy, afterwards with the Save the Children Fund in Germany and Poland. Became qualified in psychological medicine, working in Gloucester and London until retiring in 1975)

Myself is all I have, [*and other poems*]. Walton-on-Thames: Outposts Publications. 1969. 12 pp. OXB

November spell, [*and other poems*]. Walton-on-Thames: Outposts Publications. 1975. 12 pp. OXB

COLLARD, J.M. (Served in the Middle East. An historian. Of Gerrards Cross, Buckinghamshire) *see* 39, 63

COLLEDGE, J. (Of London) *see* 75

COLLEY, T.L. (Served in South-East Asia Command) *see* 35

COLLINGE, Albert (1911– . b. Manchester. Educated at St Brigid's Roman Catholic School, Bradford, Manchester. An engineering worker. Boxed as an amateur in the Manchester area, 1930–33. A member of the Lancashire Authors Association, the Lancashire Dialect Society and the Manchester Writers' Circle) *see* 74, 75

COLLINS, B.R. (Of Sussex) *see* 74

COLLINS, Ellen Edith Hannah, pseud. *see* **REDKNAP, Ellen Edith Hannah**, (Ellen Edith Hannah Collins, pseud.)

COLLINS, Ellodë (Of Bournemouth and London) *see* 21

COLLINS, Evelyn Davey- *see* **DAVEY-COLLINS, Evelyn**

COLLINS, William John Townsend (1868–1952. b. Stratford-on-Avon. Educated at a national school. Worked as a journalist in Stratford-on-Avon, Birmingham, Surrey and South Wales. Lived in Newport, Monmouthshire)

"Pilgrimage", *and other poems*. Newport: R.H. Johns Ltd. 1944. 72 pp. OXB

COLLIS, Harriett

Helpful and comforting poems. Ilfracombe: Arthur H. Stockwell Ltd. [1960]. 48 pp. OXB

COLQUHOUN, Arthur

Songs of the free: [*poems*]. Arthur H. Stockwell Ltd. [1940]. 8 pp. Dedicated to Mr Chamberlain. OXB

COLVILLE, Geraldine (Née FitzGibbon. Translator from the French)

Poems, 1939–1968. Aix-en-Provence: F. Prochaska. [1972]. [vi], 48 pp. por. (by Morton Colville).

A limited ed. of thirty numbered copies printed by hand on an Albion press of 1858.

COMFORT, Alexander (1920– . b. Palmer's Green, London. Educated at Highgate School, Trinity College, Cambridge, and the London Hospital. Refused military service. Co-editor of the anthology *Lyra*, 1942. Poet, novelist, critic, and doctor with a distinguished academic career in medicine, holding important medical appointments in Britain and the United States. President, British Society for Research on Ageing, 1967. Jailed in 1962 with others including Bertrand Russell for organizing a sit-down in Trafalgar Square in protest against the use of nuclear weapons. From 1978 a consultant psychiatrist in Los Angeles)

Elegies. Routledge. 1944. 32 pp. OXB

France, and other poems. Favil Press Ltd. [1941]. [6] pp. ("Resurgam" younger poets, 7).

    Title from cover. BL

The signal to engage: poems. Routledge. 1946. 41 pp. BPL

A wreath for the living: [poems]. Routledge. 1942. 40 pp. BPL

see also 25, 29, 42, 48, 52, 55, 56, 78, 86

COMPTON, Henry (1909– . Sergeant of the Guards. Served in the Intelligence Corps. Poet and writer on communication and industrial and commercial management. Of Banbury, Oxfordshire)

Kindred points: [poems], followed by thirteen sonnets. George Allen & Unwin Ltd. 1951. 62 pp. MPL

see also 61

CONNELL, John, pseud. *see* **ROBERTSON**, John Henry, (John Connell, pseud.)

CONNOR, Gwendolyn Edith (Of Exeter, wife of Mr Tapley-Soper)

Springtime in Devon, and other poems, including, Victors and vanquished. Printed Exeter: A.H. Roberts. 1946. 48 pp. il. OXB

CONQUEST, Robert (1917– . b. Great Malvern, Worcestershire. Educated at Winchester College, and Magdalen College, Oxford. Enlisted in 1939 with the Oxfordshire & Buckinghamshire Light Infantry. Served in Bulgaria and the Ukraine, demobilized as a Captain in 1946. Joined the Diplomatic Service after the war, serving in the Balkans and with the United Nations, 1945–56. Fellow, London School of Economics, 1956–58. Literary editor of the *Spectator*, 1962–63. Held various academic appointments in the United States. Historian, poet, literary critic, science fiction writer, and writer on Russian affairs)

Arias from a love opera, and other poems. Macmillan. 1969. 64 pp. OXB

Forays: [poems]. Chatto & Windus; Hogarth Press. 1979. 48 pp. (Phoenix living poets). OXB

Poems. Macmillan & Co. Ltd. 1955. viii, 66 pp.

'In memory of Maurice Langlois, poet, died in the hands of the secret police of the occupying power'.　　　　　　　　　　　　　　　OXB
see also　59, 76

CONSTANTINE, Pamela (1931–　. Née Page. Educated at Brentwood Grammar School, Essex. Publisher's reader and contributor to many periodicals)

Spring sowing: [poems]. Hodder & Stoughton. 1950. 63 pp.　　　　MPL

COOK, Arthur Malcolm (1883–1964). Educated at Bedford School, and Hertford College, Oxford. Ordained in 1908, Chaplain to H.M. Forces, 1915–16. Held livings in Lincolnshire, becoming Canon of Lincoln. Writer on Lincoln and Lincolnshire. Lived at Boston)

Some Boston ballads. Illustrated by G.M. Brough. Boston, Lincs.: [Author]. [1947]. 20 pp. col. il.

　　Title from cover.　　　　　　　　　　　　　　　　　　　　OXB

COOK, C.C. McNeill

Cobwebs: a book of verse. Ilfracombe: Arthur H. Stockwell, Ltd. [1942]. 16 pp.
　　　　　　　　　　　　　　　　　　　　　　　　　　　　　OXB

COOK, John (1898–　. b. Aberdeen. Educated at Aberdeen University. A school teacher. Of Sutherland)

The Strad, and other poems. Outposts Publications. 1967. 36 pp.　　OXB

COOKE, Dorian (Poet of the Apocalyptic movement. In Egypt during the war)

Fugue for our time, [and other poems]. Fore Publications Ltd. 1950. 22 pp. (Key poets, 6).　　　　　　　　　　　　　　　　　　　　　　　　BL

Fugue for our time, [and other poems]. Denver: Alan Swallow. 1950. 22 pp. (Key poets, 6).

　　Printed at the Blackmore Press, Gillingham, Dorset.　　　　　　BL
see also　57

COOKE, Greville (1894–1982. b. London. Educated at Hamilton House, Ealing, the Royal Academy of Music, and Christ's College, Cambridge. Received theological training at Ridley Hall, Cambridge, ordained in 1918. Poet of the First World War. Held church appointments at Tavistock, Ealing, Cransley, Buxted and St Paul's Cathedral. Canon of Peterborough Cathedral from 1956. Professor, Royal Academy of Music, 1925–59. Writer on religious and musical topics)

Jenny Pluck Pears, and other poems. Haywards Heath, Sussex: Charles Clarke Ltd. [1973]. [x], 72 pp.　　　　　　　　　　　　　　　　　　OXB

COOKE, Harold P. *see* 84

COOKE, William (Of Lancashire) *see* 75

COOKES, Ann R.
Night on the plain, and other poems. Ilfracombe: Arthur H. Stockwell, Ltd. [1943]. 16 pp. OXB

COOPER, Thomas Bruce (D.F.C. Squadron Leader, Royal Air Force. Killed on active service after completing sixty-six operations as a navigator)
Mixed grill verse. Ilfracombe: Arthur H. Stockwell, Ltd. 1945. 24 pp. por.
OXB

COPELAND, Francis E. *see* 16

CORBALLY, Molly (A State Registered Nurse. Enrolled in the Territorial Army Nursing Service. Called up in January 1940. Posted to Egypt for four years service at 19th General Field Hospital, Bitter Lakes, nursing battle casualties. Of Chichester, Sussex) *see* 39, 63

CORBETT, James (b. Australia but came to England as a child, spending most of his life there. Associated with Theatre Workshop)
Gallery: [*poems*]. St Albans: Piccolo Press. [1978]. [ii], 14 pp. il. OXB

CORBETT, John M.
The park, and other poems. Ilfracombe: Arthur H. Stockwell, Ltd. 1946. 16 pp.
OXB

CORBY, Herbert (1911– . b. Bloomsbury, London. Educated at Langdon Hills School, Essex, and Acland Central School, Kentish Town. In the thirties was one of the Neuburg Group which included Dylan Thomas and Pamela Hansford Johnson. Served in the Royal Air Force for five years, as an armourer in a bomber squadron, working on Hampdens and Lancasters, then as an Armaments Instructor. After the war a civil servant at the Foreign Office)
The glitter shops, the girls: [*poems*]. Fortune Press. [1968]. [ii], 94 pp. BL
Hampdens going over: [*poems*]. Editions Poetry London. 1945. 77 pp. il.
OXB
Time in a blue prison, [*and other poems*]. Fortune Press. [1947]. 64 pp. OXB
see also 12, 15, 25, 33, 36, 49, 51, 56, 59, 76, 82

CORK AND ORRERY, Lord *see* **BOYLE, Patrick Reginald, Lord Cork and Orrery**

CORKE, Hilary (1921– . b. Malvern, Worcestershire. Educated at Charterhouse, and Christ Church, Oxford. Married the poet Sylvia Bridges, granddaughter of Robert Bridges. Served in the Royal Artillery, 1941–45.

Lectured for two years at Cairo University and for four years at Edinburgh University. From 1956 a freelance writer and translator)

The early drowned, and other poems. Secker & Warburg. 1961. 84 pp.   OXB
see also   86

CORLETT, A.L.
Poems. Ilfracombe: Arthur H. Stockwell, Ltd. 1946. 32 pp.   OXB

CORNFORD, Frances (1886–1960. Daughter of Sir Francis Darwin. Educated at home. In 1908 married Francis Macdonald Cornford, who became Professor of Ancient Philosophy at Cambridge. One of their sons was John Cornford, poet and Communist activist, who was killed fighting for the Spanish republic in December 1936. Awarded Heinemann Prize for Poetry, 1948, and the Queen's Medal for Poetry, 1959)

Collected poems. Cresset Press. 1954. 117 pp.   OXB
Travelling home, and other poems. Illustrated by Christopher Cornford. Cresset Press. 1948. 48 pp. il.   OXB

CORNISH, Marion (1907–72. Of Sussex?)
Half century's verse. Printed Eastbourne: Strange the Printer Ltd. 1973. 87 pp.   OXB

CORNWALL, Hugh (Of West Norwood, London)
Short poems. Vol. 2. Printed West Norwood: H.E. Cornwall. 1944. [26] pp. il. (by the author).
   Printed for private circulation.   OXB
Short poems. Vol.3. Printed West Norwood: H.E. Cornwall. 1945. [23] pp.
   Printed for private circulation.   OXB
Short poems. Vol. 4. Printed West Norwood: H.E. Cornwall. 1946. [23] pp.
   Printed for private circulation.   OXB
   [The 1st vol. (unnumbered) 1942 contains no war poetry]

CORRIE, Donald (1886–   . Educated at Eton College, and King's College, Cambridge. Awarded M.B.E. in 1919. Deputy Director of Army Education, War Office, 1940–46)

Gleanings of the years: a selection of verses, grave and gay. With a foreword by Sir Shane Leslie. Driffield: Guild Press. 1959. 18 pp.   OXB

CORSELLIS, Timothy (1921–41. Educated at Winchester College. Worked in Air Raid Precautions during the London blitz. Served as a 2nd Officer in the Air Transport Auxiliary. Killed while flying, 1941. A friend of the Royal Air Force poet Nigel Weir, on whose death in action Corsellis wrote his last published poem) *see*   1, 15, 25, 33, 37, 47, 52, 76, 83

COTTERELL, Laurence E.S. (A pre-war Yeoman, a saddle-soldier, horsed cavalryman and then dispatch-rider, 1939–46. Served in the Middle Eastern and European theatres. Publisher, literary adviser and reviewer for national newspapers. His appointments have included Chairmanship of the Poetry Society) *see* 44, 46

COTTINGHAM, Mary (Of Colchester, Essex)
Sun and shade: verses. Colchester: Author. 1962. 20 pp. OXB

COTTON, John (1925– . b. London. Educated at London University. Served as an officer in the Royal Naval Commandos in the Far East. Founder and editor of *Priapus*, a magazine of poetry and art. Editor of *The Private Library* from 1969. Headmaster of a comprehensive school in Hertfordshire from 1963. Of Berkhamstead)
Old movies, and other poems. Chatto & Windus; Hogarth Press. 1971. 48 pp. (Phoenix living poets). OXB

COTTON, Victoria *see* 16

COURCHA, W. (Of London) *see* 74

COURT, Lily (Of Wales)
Lyrics of leisure: [poems]. Penmaenmawr: Venture Press. 1946. [ii], 42 pp. il. OXB

COURTNEY, Joseph Monlas (Poet of the First World War. Served as Captain, Royal Army Medical Corps)
A hundred sonnets. Abingdon: Abbey Press. 1966. [ii], 54 pp. MPL

COVELL, Clarice M. (Of Leeds, Yorkshire) *see* 22

COWARD, Sir Noel (1899–1973. b. Teddington, Middlesex. Educated at Chapel Road School and privately. Made his first appearance on stage in 1910. During the First World War enlisted in the Artists' Rifles, but was discharged for health reasons. Gave many stage performances in London and New York and cabaret in London and Las Vegas. Lyric writer, short story writer, and writer for stage and screen. Latterly lived in Montreux, Switzerland)
Not yet the dodo, and other verses. Heinemann. 1967. viii, 90 pp. OXB
see also 84

COWIE, Donald, (Julian Mountain, pseud.)
London: a satirical poem. Malvern: Tantivy Press. 1945. 55 pp. MPL
The poetical works. Vol. 1. Malvern: Tantivy Press. 1946. 254 pp.
  Cover-title is *The Collected Poetical Works of Donald Cowie*. OXB
The poetical works. Vol. 2. Malvern: Tantivy Press. [1947?]. 256 pp.

Cover-title is *The Collected Poetical Works of Donald Cowie*. OXB
Prose and verse: being a choice from the contemporary work in imaginative writing of Donald Cowie and Julian Mountain. Malvern: Tantivy Press. [1945]. 64 pp.
    A limited ed. of 1,000 copies. OXB

COWIE, W.J., (Deskford Bard, pseud).
Heather mixture: ballads. Glasgow: William Maclellan. 1955. 48 pp. OXB

COX, E. Denyer (Pilot Officer, Royal Air Force. Of Birmingham) *see* 1, 25, 33, 47, 80

COX, Godfrey (1918– . Served in the desert. A member of Derby Writers Guild. Fellow of the International Poetry Society. Of Codnor, Derbyshire)
Out of the muddle: a selection of verse. Ilfracombe: Arthur H. Stockwell, Ltd. 1949. 32 pp. OXB

COX, Morris (Owner of the Gogmagog Press, London)
Poems, 1970–71. Gogmagog Press. 1972. [96] pp. col. il.
    A limited ed. of fifty numbered and signed copies printed at author's private press. BL
War in a cock's egg. Gogmagog Press. 1960. 36 pp. col. il.
    A limited ed. of fifty numbered copies designed, printed and signed by the author at his private press. Dedicated to 'Ray Maddieson, Ambulance Driver, London Civil Defence, friend and co-worker, World War, 1939–1945'.
OXB

CRAIG, Alec (1897– . Educated at St Mary Islington Parochial School and Barnsbury Central School. Poetry organizer of the Contemporary Poetry and Music Circle. Writer on banned books and censorship. Of London)
The aspirin eaters, [and other poems]. Fortune Press. 1943. 28 pp. OXB
The Prometheans, [and other poems]. Fortune Press. 1955. 32 pp. IWM

CRAIG, David (Born after the Second World War)
Latest news: poems. Linocuts by Ken Sprague. Lancaster: Fireweed Ltd. [1977]. 72 pp. il. OXB

CRAIG, Maurice James (1919– . b. Belfast. Educated at an English public school, Magdalene College, Cambridge, and Trinity College, Dublin. Inspector of Ancient Monuments with the Ministry of Works. Writer on Dublin and general writer. Of Dublin and London)
Some way for reason: poems. William Heinemann Ltd. 1948. viii, 61 pp. OXB
Twelve poems. Dublin: Privately printed. 1942. 16 pp.
    A limited ed. of 100 numbered copies. OXB

CRAREY, Elizabeth Dunstan- *see* **DUNSTAN-CRAREY, Elizabeth**

CRAVEN, Mollie Charteris (Worked for the Labour Movement) *see* 42

CRAWFORD, James (A doctor)
"The rhymes of a rambling rhymer": some rhyme and some reason. Ilfracombe: Arthur H. Stockwell, Ltd. 1946. 24 pp.   OXB

CRAWSHAY-WILLIAMS, Eliot (1879–1962. Educated at Eton College, and Trinity College, Oxford. Entered the Army in 1900, serving in England and India. Liberal M.P. for Leicester, 1910–13. Poet of the First World War. Commanded 1st Leicestershire Royal Horse Artillery in Egypt and Sinai, 1915–17. Lieutenant-Colonel attached to H.Q. Northern Command, 1918–20. Chief Civil Defence Officer, 1941–43, Lecturer to H.M. Forces, 1943–45. Chairman, Coed y Mwstwr (Approved) School, 1945–47. Lived at Bridgend, Glamorgan, and latterly near Deal, Kent)
Barrage: a collection of poems. With decorations by Sybil C. Williams. John Long Ltd. [1944]. 55 pp. il.   BPL
Flak: a collection of poems. John Long Ltd. [1944]. 56 pp. il. by (Sybil C. Williams).   OXB

CREAN, Peter
Bones and ashes: poems. Caucasus Press. 1954. 27 pp.   OXB

CREE, Peter *see* 23

CRESSALL, Nora (In London during the air raids)
From the Caribbean to England in verse. Ilfracombe: Arthur H. Stockwell Ltd. 1970. 80 pp.   OXB

CREW, Margaret
Tread lightly here: [poems]. Ilfracombe: Arthur H. Stockwell, Ltd. 1975. 40 pp.   OXB

CROFT, Michael (1922– . b. Oswestry, Shropshire. Educated at Burnage Grammar School, Manchester, and Keble College, Oxford. Served in the Royal Air Force, 1940–41, and in the Royal Navy, 1942–46. After a short career as an actor, taught at Alleyn's School, 1950–55. Founder and Director of the National Youth Theatre) *see* 63

CROMER, John, pseud. *see* **BRAUN, John Cromer**, (John Cromer, pseud.)

CROOME, Pam (1917– . Journalist and columnist. Did advertising work with the London Press Exchange. Worked in the Press Liaison Department, Dutch Foreign Office in London during the war. Housewife and magistrate of Thaxted, Essex. Won International Academy of Poets 1st prize in 1977)

Journey of the years: [poems]. Thaxted: Cromach Press. [1979]. [40]. pp. por.
Sub-title on cover is *A diary of over seventy poems.*   OXB

CROSBIE, Marjorie (b. Wolverhampton. Poet of the First World War.
Freelance writer)
Blue and gold: poems. Birmingham: Cornish Brothers Ltd. 1944. 64 pp.
OXB

CROSLAND, Margaret McQueen (b. Bridgnorth, Shropshire. Educated at
London University. Writer on French literature and translator from the French.
Received Prix Bourgogne, France, 1975. Of Upper Hartfield, Sussex)
Strange Tempe, [and other poems]. Fortune Press. [1946]. 32 pp.   IWM
see also   52, 79

CROSS, Harry ("Bram") (A Servant of Pembroke College, Cambridge)
Poetic reflections of university life at Pembroke College, Cambridge. Cambridge:
Express Printing Co., Ltd. 1951. 39 pp. por.   OXB

CROSSLEY, Sir Kenneth (1877–1957. Educated at Eton College, and
Magdalen College, Oxford. Rowed bow in the Oxford eight. Chairman of
Crossley Motors Ltd, and a director of William Deacon's Bank, Ltd. Travelled
extensively, making shooting expeditions to Ceylon, India, Nepal, America,
South Africa, Canada and elsewhere)
Mere verses. Fortune Press. 1952. 136 pp. il.   MPL

CROWDER, George
Success, and other poems. Ilfracombe: Arthur H. Stockwell, Ltd. [1942]. 20 pp.
OXB

CROWE, Daisy Doreen Darrington
Poems of quality. Ilfracombe: Arthur H. Stockwell, Ltd. 1955. 16 pp.   OXB

CROWE, William Haughton (A doctor. Of Carlingford Lough, Mourne
Mountains)
More verses from Mourne. Dundalk: Dundalgan Press. 1970. vi, 74 pp.   OXB

CROWTHER, A.W. (Lieutenant. Served with the Eighth Army in
Italy) *see* 44

CRUICKSHANK, Norah K. (Non-commissioned officer in the Auxiliary
Territorial Service, attached to the Royal Army Service Corps. German scholar
and translator. Of Sudbury, Suffolk)
In the tower's shadow: [poems]. Oxford University Press. 1948. [viii], 56 pp.
MPL
see also   12, 33, 52

CULLINGFORD, Ada (1908– . b. East Anglia. Studied the violin for ten years. Mental nurse, a member of the Royal Medico-Psychological Association. Of Sutton Scotney, Hampshire)

Collection of poems. Ilfracombe: Arthur H. Stockwell Ltd. 1969. 108 pp.
OXB

Collection of poems. Vol. VII. Ilfracombe: Arthur H. Stockwell Ltd. 1980. 72 pp. por. OXB

[Other vols contain no war poetry]

CULLWICK, Michael (Served in H.M. Forces)

Thoughts and poems. Fortune Press. 1943. 32 pp. OXB
see also 49

CUMBERLAND, Robert W. (A. Training Commander with the Air Raid Warden Service) *see* 38

CUMMINS, Phyllis Deborah (b. London. Translator from the French and Italian. Television playwright)

The defeated: [*poems*]. Macmillan & Co. Ltd. 1947. viii, 64, pp. OXB

CUNARD, Nancy (1896–1965. Daughter of Sir Bache and Lady Emerald Cunard. Poet of the First World War. Settled in Paris in the high café society of the twenties and thirties. At her home in Normandy she founded the Hours Press. Correspondent for the *Manchester Guardian* in the Spanish Civil War. Worked for the Free French in London. Editor of the anthology *Poems for France*, 1944)

Man = ship = tank = gun = plane: a poem. Dorchester: [Author]. [1944]. [41] pp.

A limited ed. of 400 numbered copies. Dedicated to Edward Thompson.
BL

Relève into Maquis. Derby: Grasshopper Press, 1944. [4] pp.

A limited ed. of 250 copies. OXB
see also 42

CUNNINGHAM, A.W. (Served as an infantryman of the Eighth Army in the Western Desert. Later at G.H.Q., 2nd Echelon, Middle East Command, when in the Royal Army Service Corps)

Into the westering sun: poems in peace and war. Ilfracombe: Arthur H. Stockwell Ltd. 1976. 103 pp. OXB

CUNNINGHAM, Sir Charles (1884–1967. Educated at Campbeltown Grammar School, Argyll. With the Indian Police Service, 1904–38. Deputy Controller, Air Raid Precautions, Buckinghamshire, 1939. Inspector of Constabulary, Home Office, 1940–45. One son killed in action, 1940)

The shining sword: epic of an island: [*poems*]. Illustrated by Fay Watson. P.R.M. Publishers Ltd. [1962]. 36 pp. il.   MPL

CUNNINGHAM, David
Collected poems. Mitre Press. [1953]. 95 pp.   MPL

CURLE, Jock   *see*   52

CURLING, Denis James   (1921–42. Sergeant-Pilot, Royal Air Force Voluntary Reserve. Trained at the British Flying Training School, Oklahoma, United States. Killed in action, 1942)
Poetic pilgrimage: poems. Printed Cambridge: W. Heffer & Sons Ltd. 1966. viii, 64 pp. por.
    Privately printed for author's father.   IWM

CURR, Christian
Queen's shores, and other verses. With drawings by Tom Curr. Oliver & Boyd Ltd. 1943. 64 pp. il.   IWM
Queen's shores, and other verses. With drawings by Tom Curr. 2nd ed. Edinburgh: McLagan & Cumming Ltd. 1944. 68 pp. il.   OXB

CURREY, Ralph Nixon   (1907–   . b. South Africa, spending his first thirteen years in the Transvaal and Natal. Educated at Kingswood School, Bath, and Wadham College, Oxford. A schoolmaster before the war. Joined the Army in 1941, serving in the Royal Artillery, then in the Army Educational Corps. Posted to India in 1943, becoming Staff Major. Co-editor of the anthology *Poems from India*, 1946, and author of the critical pamphlet *Poets of the 1939–45 War*, 1960. Head of English, Royal Grammar School, Colchester, Essex, 1946–72)
Indian landscape: a book of descriptive poems. Routledge. 1947. 56 pp.   OXB
This other planet, [*and other poems*]. Routledge. 1945. 50 pp.   IWM
Tiresias, and other poems. Oxford University Press. 1940. xii, 60 pp.   OXB
see also   15, 17, 33, 43, 45, 51, 57, 59, 76

CURTIS, Antony   (1926–   . b. London. Educated at Merton College, Oxford, winning the Chancellor's Essay Prize in 1949. Literary editor. Of London)   *see*   34

CUST, Emmeline Mary   (Nina)   (1867–1955. Daughter of Sir William Welby-Gregory and the Hon. Victoria Stuart-Wortley, formerly maid-of-honour to Queen Victoria. In 1893 married Henry John Cokayne, heir to the barony of Brownlow)
Not all the suns: poems, 1917–1944; by Nina Cust. Nicholson & Watson. 1944. [viii], 51 pp.   OXB

CUST, Nina   *see*   **CUST, Emmeline Mary** (Nina)

93

CUTHBERTSON, David Cunningham (1881–   )
More dream roads: [*poems*]. Stirling: Eneas Mackay. 1941. 71 pp.   OXB
Still more dream roads: [*poems*]. Stirling: Eneas Mackay. 1945. 59 pp.   OXB

CUTTING, Gwendoline M.
Garden of memories: [*poems*]. Ilfracombe: Arthur H. Stockwell Ltd. [1966].
26 pp.   OXB
Hearts of oak: [*poems*]. Ilfracombe: Arthur H. Stockwell Ltd. [1967]. 32 pp.
                                                                      BL
Poems. Ilfracombe: Arthur H. Stockwell Ltd. [1965]. 16 pp.   BL

D.S.C.   *see*   **C., D.S.**

D-DAY. Liverpool: [Privately printed]. 1954. [20] pp.
   A long anon. poem.   BPL

DABB, Kathleen
Nature revealed: [*poems*]. Ilfracombe: Arthur H. Stockwell, Ltd. 1974. 43 pp.
                                                                      OXB

DAIKEN, Leslie (1912–64. b. Dublin. Educated at St Andrew's College,
Wesley College, and Trinity College, Dublin. Features editor at Reuters News
Agency in London. Lecturer on modern language. Executive of the
Linguaphone Institute. Worked on documentary films for the B.B.C. Writer on
children's toys and games)
Signatures of all things: [*poems*]. Hoddesdon: Clock House Press. 1945. [vi],
79 pp.   OXB
see also   36

DALGLISH, J. (Educated at Cambridge University. Sub-Lieutenant, Royal
Naval Volunteer Reserve)   *see*   53

DALMA, pseud. (Of Whitley Bay, Northumberland)
"Thoughts" for quiet moments: [*poems*]; by Dalma. [Whitley Bay]: [Privately
printed]. [1944]. 12 pp.
   Title from cover.   OXB

DALTON, Joan Lily
Morning prayer, and other poems. Ilfracombe: Arthur H. Stockwell, Ltd. 1955.
64 pp.   OXB

DALY, Gwen, (Gwen, pseud.) (Of the West Midlands)
Everyday thoughts and versatile verses; from the pen of Gwen. Regency Press Ltd.
[1980]. 64 pp.   OXB

Rhymes for quiet times; from the pen of Gwen. Regency Press. [1979]. 64 pp.
OXB

DAMPIER, Sir William Cecil (1867–1952. b. London. Educated at Trinity College, Cambridge. Scientist and Fellow of Winchester College, 1917–47. Held many public appointments on scientific and agricultural committees)
East and west: old fashioned rhymes, grave and gay; written by Sir William Cecil Dampier and now brought together for his children and grandchildren. Cambridge: Bowes & Bowes. 1946. [vi], 16 pp.
OXB

DANE, Clemence, pseud. *see* **ASHTON, Winifred**, (Clemence Dane, pseud.)

DANIELLS, Geraldine
Look towards the green, and other poems. Ilfracombe: Arthur H. Stockwell, Ltd. 1953. 24 pp.
OXB

DARBY, Maureen (A child in the war)
Pendulum: [*poems*]. Walton-on-Thames: Outposts Publications. 1975. 24 pp.
OXB

DARBY, Nell May
Faith and fancy: [*poems*]. Mitre Press. [1969]. 39 pp.
OXB

DARE, Simon, pseud. *see* **HUXTABLE, Marjorie**, (Simon Dare, pseud.)

DARK, Jeanne
Days of grace: a booklet of verse. Ilfracombe: Arthur H. Stockwell, Ltd. 1951. 16 pp.
OXB

DARNELL, R.V. (Served in H.M. Forces) *see* 74

DARYUSH, Elizabeth (1887–1977. b. London, daughter of Robert Bridges, the Poet Laureate. Educated by private tuition. Poet of the First World War. Married Ali Akbar Daryush in 1923, living for several years in Persia. Finally settled at Boars Hill, Oxford)
Collected poems. With an introduction by Donald Davie. Manchester: Carcanet New Press. 1976. 198 pp.
OXB

DAVEY, Margaret Robinson
Sunshine and shadow: [*poems*]. Ilfracombe: Arthur H. Stockwell, Ltd. 1955. 28 pp.
OXB

DAVEY-COLLINS, Evelyn (Novelist) *see* 22

DAVID, pseud.
Sonnets and poems; by David. Ilfracombe: Arthur H. Stockwell, Ltd. [1943].
47 pp.   OXB

DAVIDSON, Gwendoline (Of Tulloch, Scotland)
A cure for the blues, and other poems. Ilfracombe: Arthur H. Stockwell, Ltd.
[1943]. 16 pp.   OXB
Fallen leaves: [*poems*]; by Mrs. Davidson of Tulloch. Henley-on-Thames: Higgs
& Co. 1943. 19 pp.   BL
Glimpses in the dark: [*poems*]; by Mrs. Davidson of Tulloch.
Henley-on-Thames: Higgs & Co. 1940. 31 pp.

DAVIDSON, John (Of Glasgow)   *see*   74

DAVIDSON, Maude (Of Onchan, Isle of Man)
Island thoughts, and other poems. Printed Ilfracombe: Arthur H. Stockwell Ltd.
1974. 62 pp.   OXB

DAVIE, Donald (1922– . b. Barnsley, Yorkshire, Educated at Barnsley
Holgate Grammar School, and St Catharine's College, Cambridge. Sub-
Lieutenant, Royal Naval Volunteer Reserve, 1941–46. Poet, critic, anthologist.
Held senior university appointments in Dublin, California, Cambridge,
Cincinnati and Essex. Professor of Humanities, Vanderbilt University,
Tennessee, from 1978)
Brides of reason: [*poems*]. Eynsham, Oxford: Fantasy Press. [1955]. [viii],
41 pp.
     Sub-title on cover is *A selection of poems*.   OXB
Collected poems, 1950–1970. Routledge & Kegan Paul. 1972. xviii, 316 pp.
                                                                          OXB
In the stopping train, and other poems. Manchester: Carcanet. 1977. 55 pp.
                                                                          OXB
Poems. Turret Books. 1969. [23] pp. (Turret booklet second series, 3).
     Printed on one side of leaf only. A limited ed. of 100 numbered copies
signed by the author.   OXB
The shires: poems. Routledge & Kegan Paul. 1974. [64] pp. il.   OXB
see also   23

DAVIE, Ian (1924–   ). Educated at Edinburgh Academy, and St John's
College, Oxford. Captain, Gordon Highlanders, serving in India and Burma.
Head of English, Marlborough College, 1965–68. Schoolmaster and Director of
Theatre, Ampleforth College from 1968. Poet, dramatist, writer on philosophy
and theology. Of Malton, North Yorkshire)
Aviator loquitur, and other poems including A Christmas devotion. Fortune Press.
1943. 44 pp.   IWM
Harvest in hell, [*and other poems*]. Fortune Press. [1946]. 28 pp.

'In memoriam Michael Macnaughton Smith, Sergeant Navigator, R.A.F.V.R., killed in action, June 1944'.   BPL

Piers Prodigal, and other poems. Foreword by Siegfried Sassoon. Harvill Press. 1961. 52 pp.   IWM
see also   34, 42, 49

DAVIES, A.C.J. (Served in the Middle East)   *see*   39, 63

DAVIES, Charles (Of Wales)   *see*   32

DAVIES, Dudley Garnet (Rector of Bletchington Oxfordshire, a country living in the gift of Queen's College, Oxford. Local Head Air Raid Warden, 1939–41. Served in the Home Guard)

Boatrace, and other poems. Oxford: Alden Press. 1971. iv, 61 pp.   OXB
see also   38, 42

DAVIES, G.K.

Poems of every day. Ilfracombe: Arthur H. Stockwell, Ltd. [1943]. 32 pp.
                                                                                                     OXB

DAVIES, Idris, (Garmon, pseud.) (1905–53. b. Rhymney, Monmouthshire. Worked underground as a miner before qualifying as a teacher at Loughborough College and Nottingham University. In the war taught in the London area before returning to teach in South Wales)

Collected poems of Idris Davies. Edited by Islwyn Jenkins. Llandysul: Gomerian Press. 1972. xxxii, 190 pp.   OXB

Jewels and dust: [poems]; by Garmon. Abertridwr: Cymric Federation Press. 1947. 48 pp. il., por.   OXB

Selected poems of Idris Davies. Faber & Faber. 1953. 68 pp.   OXB

Tonypandy, and other poems. Faber & Faber. 1945. 70 pp.   IWM
see also   36, 77

DAVIES, Oliver (Poet of the First World War)

Plain song: [poems]. Staples Press. 1949. 70 pp.   MPL

DAVIES, Richard (Coder, Royal Navy)   *see*   23

DAVIES, Rona

Poetic miscellany. Ilfracombe: Arthur H. Stockwell, Ltd. 1951. 48 pp.
                                                                                                     OXB

DAVIES, William Henry (1871–1940. b. Newport, Monmouthshire. Apprenticed to picture framing. Became a tramp in the United States for six years, making eight or nine trips with cattle to England. Returned and settled in common lodging houses in London. Made several walking tours as a pedlar of lace, pins and needles. Sometimes sang hymns in the street. Became a poet at the age of thirty-four. Poet of the First World War)

The complete poems. Paperback ed. Jonathan Cape. 1967. xxxiv, [2], 23–616 pp. MPL

The complete poems of W.H. Davies. With an introduction by Osbert Sitwell and a foreword by Daniel George. Jonathan Cape. 1963. xxxiv, [2], 23–616 pp.
MPL

The essential W.H. Davies. Selected with an introduction by Brian Waters. Jonathan Cape. 1951. 333 pp.

Poetry and prose. OXB

The poems of W.H. Davies, 1940. Jonathan Cape. 1940. [ii], 525 pp. por.
OXB

DAVISON, Leslie (1906–77. Educated at Bede School, Sunderland. Trained for the Methodist ministry at Victoria Park United Methodist College, Manchester. Held various appointments including South London Mission, 1937–44. An Alderman of Bermondsey, 1940–44, and London County Councillor, 1942–44. General Secretary, Home Mission Department of Methodist Church from 1965)

Ballads of Bermondsey. Illustrations by Ernest Hasseldine. Epworth Press. 1943. 32 pp. il. OXB

DAVRIL-HOLDING, Cynthia (Of English origins but lived in America during the war. An ed. of her poems was published in London in 1922)

Poems, 1936–1945. Los Angeles: Ward Ritchie Press. 1946. x, 112 pp. BL

DAWES, Richard Arthur Aston

On the far side: collected verses, 1928–1950. Ilfracombe: Arthur H. Stockwell, Ltd. [1951]. 44 pp. OXB

DAWNE, Michael

Memory reverie: a book of verse. Ilfracombe: Arthur H. Stockwell, Ltd. [1943]. 40 pp. BPL

DAWSON, Albert Mason Patrick (Of Saltdean, Sussex)

The pageant of man (poems: grave and gay). Headley Brothers. 1943. 100 pp.
MPL

DAWSON, Nancy

Sunshine rays: a booklet of verse. Ilfracombe: Arthur H. Stockwell, Ltd. [1943]. 12 pp. OXB

DAY, April

Sunshine and showers: [poems]. Ilfracombe: Arthur H. Stockwell, Ltd. 1960. 48 pp. OXB

DAY, H.S. (Served in H.M. Forces) *see* 75

DAY, Stella (Served in Women's Royal Air Force in the Middle East. Married S. Sims) *see* 39, 63

DAY LEWIS, Cecil (1904–72. b. near Sligo, Ireland, son of a clergyman. Educated at Sherborne School, and Wadham College, Oxford. Associated with W.H. Auden, Christopher Isherwood, Louis MacNeice and Stephen Spender in the pre-war decade. Taught at schools in Oxford, Helensburgh and Cheltenham before becoming a full-time writer in 1935. Served in the Home Guard in Devon, 1940. Worked in the Ministry of Information, 1941–46, Professor of Poetry, Oxford University, 1951–56, Member of the Arts Council, 1962–68. Appointed Poet Laureate in 1968. Wrote detective novels under pseud. of Nicholas Blake)

Collected poems. Jonathan Cape; Hogarth Press. 1954. 370 pp.   MPL
Collected poems 1954. Jonathan Cape. 1970. 370 pp. (Jonathan Cape paperbacks, 78).   OXB
The gate, and other poems. Jonathan Cape. 1962. 68 pp.   OXB
Poems in wartime. Jonathan Cape. 1940. 19 pp.
    The designs on the cover and title-page reproduced from drawings by John Piper.   OXB
Poems 1943–1947. Jonathan Cape. 1948. 93 pp.   IWM
Poems 1943–1947. 1st American ed. New York: Oxford University Press. 1948. viii, 74 pp.   BL
Poems of C. Day Lewis, 1925–1972. Chosen and with an introduction by Ian Parsons. Jonathan Cape; Hogarth Press. 1977. xviii, 345 pp.   OXB
Requiem for the living, [and other poems]. New York: Harper & Row. [1964]. x, 101 pp.   BL
Selections from his poetry. Selected with an introduction and notes by Patric Dickinson. Chatto & Windus. [1967]. [viii], 88 pp. (The Queen's classics: certificate books).   OXB
Word over all, [and other poems]. Jonathan Cape. 1943. 52 pp.   BPL
see also   10, 15, 17, 25, 26, 30, 51, 56, 57, 68, 76, 77

DAYMOND, Peter
Snatches of verse. Printed Battley Brothers Ltd. [194–]. 28 pp.
    Title from cover.   IWM

DEAN, Dorothy (Of London) *see* 74

DEAS, Stewart (1903–85. b. Edinburgh. Educated at George Watson's College and Edinburgh University. Conductor of Edinburgh Opera Co., 1931–33, music critic *Glasgow Evening Times*, 1934–35, Professor of Music, Capetown University, 1935–38. War service in the Foreign Office and with the B.B.C. at Caversham. Music critic for *The Scotsman* in London, 1939–44. Professor of Music, Sheffield

University, 1948–68. Conductor of various orchestras including Hallé, London Symphony and Royal Philharmonic)

Or something, [and other poems]. Favil Press. 1941. [vi], 30 pp.   OXB

DE BAIRACLI-LEVY, Juliette (b. Manchester. Educated at Withington Girls' High School, Manchester, and Lowther College, North Wales. Studied biology and veterinary medicine at Manchester and Liverpool Universities but never qualified formally. Served in the Forestry Section of the Women's Land Army. Writer, botanist, practical herbalist, and anthologist of gypsy lore. Of Kythera, Greece)

The willow wreath: [poems]. Smyrna, Turkey: De Bairacli-Levy. 1943. 39 pp.   OXB

The yew wreath: [poems]. Ian Allan Ltd. 1947. 48 pp. il.   OXB

DE BARY, Anna Bunston (Novelist and journalist. Poet of the First World War. Of Wimbourne, Dorset)

Collected poems of Anna Bunston De Bary. Mitre Press. [1947]. 236 pp.   OXB

Songs of spiritual conquest: [poems]. Selected from the works of Anna Bunston De Bary by Richard Brome. Bournemouth: W.H. Smith & Son. [1941]. [x], 62 pp.   OXB

DE CHAIR, Somerset (1911– . Son of Governor of New South Wales, Australia. Educated at King's School, Paramatta, and Balliol College, Oxford. Conservative M.P. for South West Norfolk, 1935–45. Parliamentary Private Secretary to Minister of Production, 1942–44. Served with Household Cavalry in Iraq and Syria, being wounded. Connected with United Nations Association, 1947–50. M.P. for South Paddington, 1950–51. Novelist, poet, translator, biographer, and writer on military history)

Collected verse. Regency Press. [1970]. 108 pp. (English lyric poets, vol. IX).   OXB

The millennium, and other poems. Falcon Press. 1949. 63 pp.   MPL

The millennium, and other poems. Falcon Press. 1949. 63 pp.

    A limited ed. of four special numbered copies. This ed. contains the name Carmen on pp. 48 and 54 which is omitted from the public ed.   OXB

DEDE, pseud. *see* **BANKS, A.E.**, (Dede, pseud.)

DEE, D.L. (Sergeant. Served with the Eighth Army)   *see*   44

DEGE, Florence

The peace of God, [and other poems]. Skeffington & Son, Ltd. [1941]. 63 pp.   MPL

DEHN, Paul (1912–76. b. Manchester. Educated at Shrewsbury School, and Brasenose College, Oxford. Served in London Scottish and Intelligence Corps, reaching rank of Major as an instructor with Special Operations Executive. Film critic to London national newspapers, 1936–63. Scriptwriter, poet, librettist and columnist)

The day's alarm: [*poems*]. Hamish Hamilton. 1949. 53 pp.   IWM

The fern on the rock: collected poems, 1935–1965. Hamish Hamilton. 1965. xii, 107 pp.   MPL

Quake, quake, quake: a leaden treasury of English verse. Drawings by Edward Gorey. Hamish Hamilton. 1961. 109 pp. il.   OXB

see also   2, 15, 25, 26, 57, 59, 76, 77

DE HOGHTON, Sir Anthony (1919–78. Educated at Beaumont, and Magdalen College, Oxford. Succeeded to baronetcy in 1958)

24 poems. Fortune Press. [1945]. 24 pp.   OXB

DEIGHTON, George Geoffrey (Self-styled 'South Yorkshire's miner poet')

A salute to Britain in peace or war, [*and other poems*]. Ilfracombe: Arthur H. Stockwell, Ltd. [1966]. 36 pp.   OXB

DE LA MARE, Walter (1873–1956. b. Charlton, Kent. Educated at St Paul's Cathedral Choir School. Followed a career in commerce from 1890 to 1908, thereafter devoting his time to writing. Published poetry, stories, criticism and anthologies. Poet of the First World War. Awarded a Civil List pension for the distinction of his literary work. Recipient of honorary degrees from Oxford, Cambridge, St Andrews, Bristol and London Universities)

The burning-glass, and other poems. Faber & Faber Ltd. 1945. 106 pp.   IWM

The collected poems of Walter De La Mare. Faber & Faber. 1979. 467 pp.
      OXB

The complete poems of Walter De La Mare. Faber & Faber. 1969. xvi, 948 pp.
      BL

Inward companion: poems. Faber & Faber Ltd. 1950. 97 pp.   OXB

Selected poems. Chosen by R.N. Green-Armytage. Faber & Faber Ltd. 1954. 208 pp.   OXB

DELARCHE, Michael (Served in Surrey Wardens' Service. Of South West London) *see* 62

DE MAUNY, Erik (1920– b. London of French and English parentage. Educated at Wellington College, New Zealand, Victoria University of Wellington and London University. Sergeant in No. 2 New Zealand Expeditionary Force, 1940–45, serving in the Middle East, the Pacific and Italy. Co-editor of the anthologies *Middle East Anthology*, 1946, and *Return to Oasis*, 1980. B.B.C. foreign correspondent from 1958) *see* 31, 39, 49, 63, 66

DENEY, Mary du *see* **DU DENEY, Mary**

DENHAM-YOUNG, C.P.S. (Colonel commanding the Signal Regiment of the 51st Highland Division from 1941 in Scotland until 1943 in Tripoli. Of Oxford) *see* 63

DENNIS, Edward James (Of Hull, Yorkshire)
Of a son, and other verses. Hull: Robin Press. [1950]. 48 pp.
A limited ed. of 250 numbered copies printed and published by the author.
OXB

True intent: a few verses. Hull: Author. [1945]. 8 pp.
Title from cover. OXB

DERWENT, Lord *see* **JOHNSTONE, George Harcourt, Lord Derwent**

DESCHAMPS, Marion (b. Suffolk. A nurse during the war. Writer on France, contributing gastronomic and travel articles to numerous journals. Married to a Frenchman living near Limours)
The search of Llanretny, and other poems. Mitre Press. [1970]. 62 pp.   OXB

DESKFORD BARD, pseud. *see* **COWIE, W.J.**, (Deskford Bard, pseud).

DESMOND, Harry (Poet of the First World War, he fought on the Somme. Became a full-time fireman in the Auxiliary Fire Service, Leeds, in the Second World War)
The broken melody, and [*other*] *poems*. Arthur H. Stockwell, Ltd. [1941]. 80 pp. por.   OXB
"Churchill's finest hour": selected poems. Leeds: Artprint. [1965]. [28] pp.
OXB
Golden orchids: [*poems*]. Ilfracombe: Arthur H. Stockwell, Ltd. 1946. 79 pp.
OXB
The sands are sinking on the desert waste, and other poetical works. Ilfracombe: Arthur H. Stockwell, Ltd. [1943]. 216 pp. por.   OXB
The voice of to-morrow, and other poems. Ilfracombe: Arthur H. Stockwell, Ltd. [1942]. 88 pp. por.   OXB

DEVEY, Bessie
The bells of victory, and other poems. Ilfracombe: Arthur H. Stockwell, Ltd. [1944]. 16 pp.   OXB

DEWAR, Hugo (Served in H.M. Forces)
Tea-leaves, dust and ashes: [*poems*]. C. Lahr. [1947]. 16 pp.   BL
Within the thunder: [*poems*]. Porcupine Press Ltd. 1946. 45 pp.
Sub-title on cover is *Poems of a conscript*.   IWM

DE WYE, Paul (Flight Lieutenant, Royal Air Force. Served with the Eighth Army) *see* 25, 44

DICK, Charles (A prisoner of war, held in camps in Poland. Of Morpeth, Northumberland)
The poems of a prisoner of war. Morpeth: Author. [1946]. 43 pp. il. (by the author).   OXB

DICKEY, Daniel (Educated at Exeter College, Oxford)   *see*   55

DICKINSON, Ernest (Of Nottingham)
A Joseph coat: [*poems*]. Nottingham: Author. [1968]. 77–100 pp.
  Title from cover.   OXB

DICKINSON, Patric (1914–   . b. Nasirabad, India. Educated at St Catharine's College, Cambridge, where he was a golf blue. Schoolmaster, 1936–39. Served in Artists' Rifles, 1939–40, invalided out after a severe accident. Editor of the anthology *Soldiers' Verse*, 1945. Married poet and editor Sheila Shannon. Worked for the B.B.C. as producer and poetry editor, 1942–48. Critic, dramatist, poet, translator and broadcaster. Professor of Rhetoric, City University of London, 1964–67. Received Atlantic Award in Literature, 1948, and Cholmondeley Award for Poetry, 1973. Of Rye, Sussex)
More than time, [*and other poems*]. Chatto & Windus; Hogarth Press. 1970. 42 pp. (Phoenix living poets).   OXB
Selected poems. Chatto & Windus. 1968. 132 pp.   MPL
Stone in the midst; and, Poems. Methuen & Co. Ltd. 1948 [xii], 109 pp.
                                                                          MPL
Theseus and the minotaur; and, Poems. Jonathan Cape. 1946. 103 pp.   IWM
The world I see, [*and other poems*]. Chatto & Windus; Hogarth Press. 1960. 48 pp. (Phoenix living poets).   OXB
see also   38, 57, 68, 76, 80

DIGGLE, W. Wrigley
Collection of original verse. Ilfracombe: Arthur H. Stockwell, Ltd. 1946. 16 pp.
                                                                          OXB
Collection of original verse, letters, prose, play. Vol. II. Ilfracombe: Arthur H. Stockwell, Ltd. 1947. 48 pp.   OXB

DINGWALL, W. (Served in H.M. Forces)   *see*   74

DISNEY, M.J. (Lieutenant. Served with the Eighth Army)   *see*   25, 44

DIXEY, Giles (Poet of the First World War. Served with the Royal Air Force in the Western Dessert in the Second World War. Of Oxford)
Fūrin: collected verses. Oxford: B.H. Blackwell, Ltd. 1948. [4], viii, 394 pp.
                                                                          OXB
Hymns without faith: [*poems*]. Oxford: H.G. Dixey. 1946. 16 pp.

A limited ed. of eighty-three numbered copies hand-printed by the author.
OXB

Ourselves a dream: verses. Oxford: H.G. Dixey. 1947. 24 pp.
A limited ed. of eighty-three numbered copies hand-printed by the author.
OXB

Sonnets from Libyan Tripoly. Oxford: H.G. Dixey. 1946. 16 pp.
A limited ed. of eighty-three numbered copies hand-printed by the author.
OXB

Sonnets from the Levant. Oxford: H.G. Dixey. 1946. 16 pp.
A limited ed. of eighty numbered copies hand-printed by the author.
OXB

Sonnets from the Western Desert. Oxford: H.G. Dixey. 1946. 16 pp.
A limited ed. of eighty-three numbered copies hand-printed by the author.
OXB

Sonnets in sand. Oxford: H.G. Dixey. 1946. 16 pp.
A limited ed. of eighty-three numbered copies hand-printed by the author.
OXB

DIXON, Alan (1936–   . b. Liverpool. Of Peterborough)
The upright position: a collection of poems. Woodford Green: Poet & Printer. 1970. 44 pp. OXB

DOBB, Clifford (Educated at St Edmund Hall, Oxford. Served in North Africa) *see* 55

DOBBS, Kildare R.E. (Sub-Lieutenant, Royal Naval Volunteer Reserve) *see* 23

DOBLE, K.
Poems. Ilfracombe: Arthur H. Stockwell, Ltd. [1941]. 24 pp. OXB

DOCHERTY, Frank (Of Edinburgh) *see* 72, 73

DOCHERTY, John, (Jonathan Morgan Jones, pseud.)
A walk round the city and other groans: [poems]. Experienced and written by Jonathan Morgan Jones. Bala: North Wales Bookprint. [1969]. [ii], 70 pp.
OXB

DOCKYARD, M.T. : [poems]. [194–   ]. col. il.
A broadside. IWM

DODD, Arthur Edward (1913–   . b. Stoke-on-Trent, Staffordshire. Educated at London University. Chief Information Officer, British Ceramic Research Association, Stoke-on-Trent, 1938–70. Poet, playwright, and writer on ceramics and archaeology)

Poems from Belmont. Fortune Press. [1955]. 68 pp.   MPL
Words and music: fifty poems. Fortune Press. [1963]. 74 pp.   BL

DODD, Charles
The dawn of peace. Ilfracombe: Arthur H. Stockwell, Ltd. 1946. 15 pp. OXB

DODDRIDGE, I.D. (Served in H.M. Forces) *see* 74

DODSWORTH, Nellie (1904–78). b. Swindon, Yorkshire. Became active in
Sheffield political life during the war, when she worked first in factories then in
government offices. Married three times)
Selected poems. Privately published by Barbara Whitehead. 1979. [vi], 37 pp.
il.   OXB

DOLOUGHAN, A.I. (Able Seaman, Royal Navy. Served on H.M.S.
Urchin) *see* 23

DOLPHIN, May I.E. (Poet of the First World War)
Swords and ploughshares: [poems]. Durham: G. Bailes & Sons. [1947]. 35 pp.
   Dedicated 'to my son, Humphrey, prisoner of war, 1940–45'.

DOMINICK, John
Meditations: [poems]. J.A. Allen & Co. 1950. [19] pp.   OXB

DONALD, A.A.
Burma victory, and other poems. Ilfracombe: Arthur H. Stockwell Ltd. [1947].
71 pp.   IWM

DONALD, Alexandra
Prelude: [poems]. Arthur H. Stockwell, Ltd. [1941]. 16 pp.   OXB

DONALDSON, Celia J.
Orcadian twilight, [and other poems]. Belfast: Quota Press. 1943. 40 pp.
                                                                      OXB

DONOVAN, Jo
A white light from the sea: [poems]. Walton-on-Thames: Outposts Publications.
1977. 20 pp.   OXB

DORLING, Georgina (Of Suffolk) *see* 75

DOUGLAS, Lord Alfred (1870–1945. Son of 8th Marquess of Queensberry.
Educated at Winchester College, and Magdalen College, Oxford. Editor of
Plain English and Plain Speech and its founder. Received into the Catholic Church
in 1911. Lived latterly in Hove, Sussex)
Sonnets. Richards Press Ltd. [1943]. 79 pp.   BL

DOUGLAS, James (Of Northumberland) *see* 75

DOUGLAS, Keith (1920–44. b. Tunbridge Wells. Educated at Christ's Hospital, and Merton College, Oxford, winning his education by scholarship. At Oxford he edited *Cherwell* and became known as a poet of great promise. A Captain in the Tanks Corps, he trained with the Scots Greys, and was posted to Alexandria with the Nottinghamshire (Sherwood Rangers) Yeomanry. Fought in a Crusader tank from Alamein to Tunisia, apart from one spell when wounded by a mine. His book *Alamein to Zem Zem*, 1946, is a classic account of desert warfare. Returned to England to train for D-Day. Arranged for publication of his poetry, writing 'I cannot afford to wait, because of military engagements which may be the end of me'. Killed by enemy artillery near Tilly on 9 June 1944, his third day in Normandy. Mentioned in despatches for going behind enemy lines to get information)

Alamein to Zem Zem. Editions Poetry London. 1946. 142, xvi pp. il., col. il. (by the author).

A prose account of tank warfare in the desert, followed by his poems.

OXB

The collected poems of Keith Douglas. Edited by John Waller and G.S. Fraser. Editions Poetry London. 1951. xxii, 151 pp. por., facsim. BPL

Collected poems. Edited by John Waller, G.S. Fraser and J.C. Hall. With an introduction by Edmund Blunden. Faber & Faber. 1966. 164 pp. por.

BPL

Complete poems. Edited by Desmond Graham. Oxford University Press. 1978. xiv, 145 pp. OXB

Complete poems. Edited by Desmond Graham. [Paperback ed.]. Oxford University Press. 1979. xiv, 145 pp. IWM

Selected poems; by John Hall, Keith Douglas, Norman Nicholson. John Bale & Staples Ltd. 1943. 77 pp. (Modern reading library, 3).

Not joint authorship. BL

Selected poems. Edited with an introduction by Ted Hughes. Faber & Faber. 1964. 63 pp. BPL

see also 3, 10, 15, 17, 18, 25, 30, 31, 33, 40, 51, 57, 58, 59, 63, 76, 82, 86

DOUGLAS, Marion (Writer on Northumbrian tales and legends. Of County Durham) *see* 74

DOUGLAS, Mary (Of Nottingham)

Verse by the way. Printed Nottingham: Walter Barker. [1944]. [ii], 24 pp.

OXB

DOUGLAS, Ronald (Served in H.M. Forces) *see* 75

DOVE, A. (Private. Served with the Eighth Army) *see* 44

DOVER, Cedric (1904–61. b. Calcutta, India. Educated in Calcutta and at Edinburgh University. Contributed poems, essays and reviews to periodicals in India, Burma, Ceylon and America. Had a special interest in race, colour and social problems. Author of *Half-Caste*)

Brown phoenix, [and other poems]. College Press. 1950. 40 pp.   OXB

DOWNAR, Joan

River people, [and other poems]. Hitchin: Mandeville Press. 1976. [11] pp.
                                                                                OXB

DOWNEY, Gertrude

This tremendous lover, and other poems. Ilfracombe: Arthur H. Stockwell Ltd. [1959]. 36 pp.   OXB

DOWNS, Alan (A member of Oxford University between 1944 and 1946) *see* 34

DOYLE, Camilla (Lived in Norwich, her birthplace. A painter as well as a poet, studying at the Slade School and in Paris) *see* 41

DRAPER, Ann Leslie

Salute the Empire in poem and song: [poems]. Ilfracombe: Arthur H. Stockwell, Ltd. [1944]. 16 pp.   OXB
A voice from the past: poems. Ilfracombe: Arthur H. Stockwell, Ltd. [1944]. 16 pp.   OXB

DRINAN, Adam, pseud. *see* **MACLEOD, Joseph Todd Gordon**, (Adam Drinan, pseud.)

DRISCOLL, G.W.G. (Served in South-East Asia Command) *see* 35

DRIVER, A.H. (Of Herefordshire) *see* 70

DRUCE, Louise E.

Moon in cirrus, and other verse. Ilfracombe: Arthur H. Stockwell, Ltd. [1944]. 16 pp.   OXB

DU DENEY, Mary (Poet of the First World War. Of Bridgwater, Somerset)

War poems. Printed St. Ives: James Lanham Ltd. 1944. [12] pp.   OXB

DUDLEY, Edith Spilman (Of Lincolnshire)

A Lincolnshire garland, (and a short miscellany): [poems]. Illustrations by H.D.S. Smith. Coronation year ed. Scunthorpe: W.H. & C.H. Caldicott. 1953. 80 pp. il., por.   OXB
Lyrics of lovely Lincolnshire, (and a short miscellany): [poems]. Revised and

enlarged ed. Illustrations by H.D.S. Smith. Scunthorpe: W.H. & C.H. Caldicott. 1946. 64 pp. il. BL

DUDLEY, Edward Perry (Served in the Middle East. A professional librarian, becoming Chief Librarian, City of London, then Lecturer in Librarianship, North West Polytechnic, London) *see* 39, 63

DU FEU, Frank Thomas (In Jersey, Channel Islands, during the German occupation)
Humorous verse, written during the German occupation of Jersey. [Jersey]: [Privately printed]. [1946]. 32 pp.
Title from cover. OXB

DUGBARTEY, John Laurence N.
Short poems. Ilfracombe: Arthur H. Stockwell, Ltd. 1951. 16 pp. OXB

DUNCAN, Alison Haldane- *see* **HALDANE-DUNCAN, Alison**

DUNCAN, Ronald (1914–82. b. Salisbury, Rhodesia. Educated in Switzerland and at Cambridge University. Travelled extensively, living for a time with Gandhi in India. Friend of T.S. Eliot and Ezra Pound, Edited *Townsman*, 1938–46. Farmed in Devon from 1939. Founded Devon Festival of Arts in 1953 and the English Stage Company, Royal Court Theatre, London, in 1955. Prolific writer and playwright)
Auschwitz. With drawings by Feliks Topolski. Bideford: Rebel Press. 1978. [15] pp. il.
A limited ed. of 100 numbered copies signed by the author and illustrator. The drawings were done in Belsen camp on 28 April 1945. IWM
For the few: [*poems*]. [Welcombe]: Rebel Press. [1977]. 63 pp. OXB
Postcards to Pulcinella: poems. Fortune Press. [1941]. 24 pp. OXB
The solitudes, [*and other poems*]. Faber & Faber. 1960. 59 pp. MPL

DUNHILL, David (1917– . b. London, Trained as journalist. Joined the Royal Air Force as a clerk, being sent to the Western Desert in 1941. Freelance writing led to a posting to *Tripoli Times*. In 1943 worked with Inter-Services Publications Directorate in Cairo, producing *Air Force News, Parade*, etc. Became an announcer with Middle East Forces Broadcasting in 1945, later that year joining the B.B.C. Resigned in 1970 to become a freelance writer and broadcaster. Of Plymouth, Devon) *see* 39, 63

DUNKER, Christine
Drifting leaves: [*poems*]. Walton-on-Thames: Outposts Publications. 1979 24 pp. OXB

DUNKER, Douglas
A fastidious taste: some incongruous inferences: [*poems*]. Walton-on-Thames: Outposts Publications. 1979. 20 pp.   OXB
Through half-closed eyes, [*and other poems*]. Walton-on-Thames: Outposts Publications. 1979. 32 pp.   OXB

DUNKERLEY, William Arthur, (John Oxenham, pseud.) (185-?–1941. b. Manchester. Educated at Old Trafford School and Victoria University, Manchester. Went into business, living for some years in France and the United States. Travelled throughout Europe and Canada, returning home to become a full-time writer of novels and popular verse. Poet of the First World War)
Wide horizons: some selected verse for these times; by John Oxenham. Methuen & Co. Ltd. 1940. [ii], 64 pp.   OXB

DUNKERLEY, William Donald (1908?–40. Lieutenant-Commander, Royal Navy. Lost on active service in August 1940 at age of thirty-two while in command of H.M.S. *Thames*)
Groping poet, [*and other poems*]. Oxford: Shakespeare Head Press. 1941. [viii], 60 pp.   IWM

DUNN, A. (Lance Bombardier, Royal Artillery. Served in the Middle East at Tobruk. Of Bradford, Yorkshire) *see* 63

DUNPHY, P.
Panorama: a book of verse. Ilfracombe: Arthur H. Stockwell, Ltd. [1947]. 16 pp.   OXB

DUNSANY, Lord *see* **PLUNKETT, Edward John Moreton Drax, Lord Dunsany**

DUNSTAN-CRAREY, Elizabeth (1909–73. b. Ashwellthorpe Rectory, Norfolk. In 1926 married a civil engineer in the Colonial Service and travelled widely in East and West Africa)
Various verses. Ilfracombe: Arthur H. Stockwell Ltd. 1974. 77 pp.   OXB

DUNTON, Frederick Ross (1922–44. b. Manchester. Educated at Malvern College, and Christ's College, Cambridge, Flight-Lieutenant, Royal Air Force. Reported missing when piloting a Lancaster in bombing operations against Stettin, Germany, on 29–30 August 1944) *see* 20

DUNTON, Michael
A selection of verse. Ilfracombe: Arthur H. Stockwell Ltd. 1955. 16 pp.   OXB

DUNWORTH, Eira
  Particles of truth: [*poems*]. Ilfracombe: Arthur H. Stockwell, Ltd. 1955. 24 pp.
  OXB

DURNFORD, John (Educated at Sherborne School. Joined the Royal Artillery in September 1939. In action with the Lanarkshire Yeomanry as a Territorial officer from the Siamese frontier to the last days of the battle for Singapore in 1941–42. Held prisoner of war in Siam, 1942–45)
  Immortal diamond: [*poems*]. Ilfracombe: Arthur H. Stockwell Ltd. 1975. 62 pp.
  OXB

DURRELL, Lawrence (1912– . b. Julundur, India. Educated at St Joseph's College, Darjeeling, and St Edmund's School, Canterbury. Foreign Service Press Officer in Athens and Cairo, 1941–44, and Press Attaché in Alexandria, 1944–45. Before becoming a full-time writer in 1957 he held a series of appointments — Director of Public Relations, Dodecanese Islands, Greece; Press Attaché, Belgrade; Director of the British Council Institutes in Kalamata, Greece, and Cordoba, Argentina; Director of Public Relations, Government of Cyprus. A distinguished novelist, poet and general writer)
  Cities, plains and people: poems. Faber & Faber Ltd. 1946. 72 pp.   MPL
  Collected poems. Faber & Faber. 1960. 288 pp.   MPL
  Collected poems. New ed. Faber & Faber. 1968. 327 pp.
    Called 2nd ed. in author's preface.   OXB
  Collected poems 1931–1974. Edited by James A. Brigham. Revised ed. Faber & Faber. 1980. 350 pp.   OXB
  A private country: poems. Faber & Faber Ltd. 1943. 79 pp.   OXB
  Selected poems. Faber & Faber. 1956. 79 pp.   MPL
  Selected poems. New York: Grove Press, Inc. [1956]. 79 pp. (Evergreen books, E–57).   BL
  Selected poems. New York: Grove Press. [1956]. [ii], 79 pp.
    A limited ed. of 100 specially bound, numbered copies.   OXB
  Selected poems, 1935—1963. Faber & Faber. 1964. 95 pp.   MPL
  Selected poems of Lawrence Durrell. Selected and with an introduction by Alan Ross. Faber & Faber. 1977. 96 pp.   OXB
  see also   3, 25, 31, 40, 56, 57

DUTTON, Eric (Served in H.M. Forces)   *see*   74

DU VALLON, Katharine de Jacobi
  This day is mine, [*and other poems*]. Culmstock, Devon: Avon Books. 1965. [47] pp.
    Printed on one side of leaf only.   OXB

DWYER, Les   *see*   **DWYER, Lewis, D.,** (Les Dwyer)

DWYER, Lewis D., (Les Dwyer) (1930– . A boy soldier, regular soldier, mercenary and holder of a variety of other jobs. Lived in Palestine with the Arabs, 1948–50. Served in Korea)

Shadows — of mystic make-believe: [*poems*]; [by] Les Dwyer. Ilfracombe: Arthur H. Stockwell Ltd. 1974. 135 pp. il. OXB

DYMENT, Clifford (1914–71. b. Alfreton, Derbyshire, of Welsh parentage. Educated at Loughborough Grammar School. Freelance literary journalist and critic, 1934–40. Writer of film commentaries, and director of documentary films for the Ministry of Information, British Council, War Office and other official bodies, 1942–48. Received an Atlantic Award in Literature, 1950)

The axe in the wood: poems. J.M. Dent & Sons Ltd. 1944. 48 pp. IWM
Collected poems. Introduction by C. Day Lewis. J.M. Dent & Sons Ltd. 1970. xvi, 110 pp. por. MPL
Poems, 1935–1948. J.M. Dent & Sons Ltd. 1949. 64 pp. IWM
see also 26, 29, 51, 52, 79

E.D.P. *see* **P., E.D.**

E.H.B. *see* **BLAKENEY, Edward Henry**, (E.H.B.)

E.R.G. *see* **LUCIAN**, pseud., (E.R.G.)

EADES, George (Flying Officer, Royal Air Force)

Operation by night. Hodder & Stoughton Ltd. 1942. 43 pp. por. BL
Thy muse hath wings: [*poems*]. Oxford: Pen-In-Hand Publishing Co. Ltd. [1941]. 31 pp.
　'A very limited first edition' — dust-jacket. IWM
Thy muse hath wings: [*poems*]. 2nd ed. Oxford: Pen-In-Hand Publishing Co., Ltd. 1942. 46 pp. OXB

EARLEY, Tom (1911– . b. Mountain Ash, Glamorgan. Educated at Mountain Ash Grammar School, and Trinity College, Carmarthen. A schoolmaster in Maidenhead and London, 1931–45. Taught at St Dunstan's College, London, 1945–71. Member of the Welsh Academy from 1972)

Rebel's progress, [and other poems]. Llandysul: Gomer Press. 1979. 82 pp.
OXB
Welshman in Bloomsbury: [*poems*]. Outposts Publications. 1968. 24 pp.
OXB

EASTON, A. (Miss Easton)

Spring, and other poems. Ilfracombe: Arthur H. Stockwell, Ltd. [1949]. 16 pp.
OXB

EASTWOOD, James (Of Yorkshire. Served in a coal mine as a 'Bevin Boy'. Novelist) *see* 75

EASTWOOD, Thomas (Served in the Middle East)
  Desert wind: poems. Fortune Press. 1947. 48 pp.   IWM
see also 63

EDGAR, R.L. (Of County Durham) *see* 74

EDGELOW, Marguerite (Graduated from London University with a diploma in journalism. Taught art, English and history as a war job. Critic and reviewer. Married Edward Wykeham Edmonds. Of Gerrards Cross and Jordans, Buckinghamshire, and Maidstone, Kent) *see* 41

EDMONDS, Edward Wykeham (1908–   . Educated at Haileybury School, and Keble College, Oxford. Fellow of St Augustine's College, Canterbury, 1933–38. His poems were published in *Oxford Magazine, Time and Tide* and other journals. Married Marguerite Edgelow)
  Versailles summer: [poems]. Williams & Norgate Ltd. 1940. 48 pp.   OXB

EDWARDES, Michael (1923–   . b. Liverpool. Educated at Merchant Taylors' School, and the Sorbonne, Paris. Served with the Royal Corps of Signals in India. Writer on India) *see* 43

EDWARDS, Aerona (Of Radnorshire ?)
  V for victory: 20 poems. Printed Llandrindod Wells: C.C. Hughes. [194-]. 23 pp.   BPL

EDWARDS, Barbara Catherine
  Poems from hospital. Dulwich Village: Outposts Publications. 1962. 12 pp.
                    OXB

EDWARDS, G.A.
  Wye Valley verse. Ilfracombe: Arthur H. Stockwell, Ltd. 1948. 24 pp.   OXB

EDWARDS, Stewart Hylton (1924–   .b. London. Evacuated to Sussex. Studied music at the Guildhall School of Music and Drama. Volunteered at eighteen for the Royal Marines, reaching the rank of Captain. Served in the Commandos and later at sea in the Normandy landings and in the South West Pacific. Fellow of Trinity College, London, and a Wainwright Memorial Scholar)
  A fool of time [and other poems]. William Murray & Sons. 1975. xvi, 76 pp.
                    OXB
  The unborn, [and other poems]. Walton-on-Thames: Outposts Publications. 1979. 36 pp.   OXB

EDWARDS, Will H.
A few simple verses. With illustrations by Margaret Holman. Ilfracombe:
Arthur H. Stockwell, Ltd. 1950. 41 pp. il.   OXB

EGGLESTON, Lilias Blanch (Of Middlesex)   *see*   74

EINSTEIN, Lewis (–1967). Member of the United States Foreign Service,
holding important posts world-wide. In the First World War he succeeded in
getting improved treatment for prisoners of war. Settled in London in 1929. His
house in Cumberland Place was bombed in the Second World War. He moved
to Paris in 1950)
   Scattered verses. Florence: Tipografia Giuntina S.A. 1949. 142 pp.
      A limited ed. of 200 copies printed for private distribution.   OXB
   The winged victory, and other verses. De La More Press. 1941. 51 pp.
      A limited ed. of 100 copies printed for private distribution.   BL

ELDER, Madge (Of Melrose, Scotland)
   A winter garland, 1941–1945: [*poems*]. Galashiels: John McQueen & Son, Ltd.
1947. 31 pp.   OXB

ELIAS, Charles Frederick (Of Cheshire ?)
   Greenfield verses. Printed West Kirby: F. Gould. [1943]. [12] pp.   OXB

ELIOT, Thomas Stearns (1888–1965. b. St Louis, United States. Educated at
Harvard University, the Sorbonne, Paris, and Merton College, Oxford. Lived
in England from 1914, becoming a naturalized Briton in 1927. Playwright, poet,
essayist and one of the most important and formative influences on twentieth
century writing. A director of the publishers Faber & Faber Ltd. Received
many high academic honours, including the Nobel Prize for Literature, 1948)
   Collected poems, 1909–1962. Faber & Faber Ltd. 1963. 240 pp.   OXB
   Collected poems, 1909–1962. [New] ed. Faber & Faber Ltd. 1974. 238 pp.
(Faber paper covered editions).   OXB
   The complete poems and plays, 1909–1950. New York: Harcourt, Brace & Co.
[1952]. viii, 392 pp.   OXB
   The complete poems and plays of T.S. Eliot. Faber & Faber. 1969. 608 pp.
                                                                            OXB
see also   68

ELIZABETH JANE, pseud.
   Clean fingers: a series of deep thoughts in verse; by Elizabeth Jane. Ilfracombe:
Arthur H. Stockwell, Ltd. [1947]. 16 pp.   OXB

ELLAMS, Winifred (Of Staffordshire)   *see*   73

ELLIOTT, Arthur John
Poems. Ilfracombe: Arthur H. Stockwell, Ltd. [1957]. 16 pp.   OXB

ELLIOTT, C.W.
"Storm", and other poems. Ilfracombe: Arthur H. Stockwell, Ltd. 1946. 16 pp
          OXB

ELLIS, G.S. (Served in H.M. Forces) *see* 74

ELLIS, Lilian (Of Northumberland) *see* 74

ELLIS, Randolph
The disasters of war: [poems]. Prints [by] Nicholas Parry. [Market Drayton]:
Tern Press. 1975. 48 pp. il.
     A limited ed. of 100 numbered copies signed by author and artist. OXB

ELLIS, Roger Henry (1910–   . b. Mansfield, Nottinghamshire. Educated at
Sedburgh School, and King's College, Cambridge. Appointed Assistant
Keeper, Public Record Office in 1934, becoming Principal Assistant Keeper in
1956. Served in the Army, 1939–45, becoming a Major with 5th Fusiliers in the
Mediterranean theatre. Monuments, Fine Arts & Archives Officer in Italy and
Germany, 1944–45. Lecturer at University College, London, 1947–57. Sec-
retary, Royal Commission on Historical Manuscripts, 1957–72. President,
Society of Archivists, 1964–73)
Ode on Saint Crispin's Day, 1939–1979. Weybrook Press. 1979. 58 pp.
     Sub-title on cover is *A sequence of verses on the war of 1939–1945 and the years
upon which its shadow has fallen*.   IWM

ELVIN, Harold (1909–   . b. Buckhurst Hill, Essex. Historical novelist, poet,
journalist, and designer of ceramics and furniture. Escaped to Sweden after the
German occupation of Norway in 1940. Received a Tom Gallon Trust Award
for Fiction, 1960–61, and a Winston Churchill Fellowship, 1968–69. Of
Kensington, London)
When she cried on Friday, and other poems. Southern Cross Press Ltd. 1963. [iv],
42 pp.   OXB

ELWES, Sir Richard (1901–68). Educated at The Oratory School, and Christ
Church, Oxford. Commissioned in the Northamptonshire Yeomanry, 1923.
Called to the Bar, 1925. Served in France as Staff Captain, 69th Infantry
Brigade, from October 1939, returning via Dunkirk. Major, July 1940,
Lieutenant-Colonel Assistant Adjutant-General, War Office, 1941–45. Judge of
the High Court of Justice, 1958–66)
First poems. Hodder & Stoughton. 1941. 44 pp. por.
     Dedicated to Anthony Eden.   MPL
see also 38

EMERIC, Pauline (Of London)
I wonder, and other poems. Favil Press. 1942. [vi], 58 pp.   OXB

EMERY, Dorothy
Ebony, and other poems. Ilfracombe: Arthur H. Stockwell, Ltd. 1974. 20 pp.
                                                                              OXB

EMERY, John James (1881– . b. Bengal, India. Served in the Royal
Warwickshire Regiment until discharged on age grounds in October 1941.
Joined 9th Worcestershire Home Guard)
Britain, her Allies and the Axis: [*poems*]. Ilfracombe: Arthur H. Stockwell, Ltd.
[1942?]. 54 pp.   IWM

EMMETT, Mary *see* 78

EMPSON, Sir William (1906–84. b. Howden, Yorkshire. Educated at
Winchester College, and Magdalene College, Cambridge. Professor of English
Literature, Tokyo, 1931–34, and Peking, 1937–39. Chinese editor at the
B.B.C., 1941–46, after a year in the Monitoring Department. Returned to
Peking National University in 1947. Professor of English Literature at Sheffield
University, 1953–71. Literary critic, poet, and writer on language)
Collected poems. Chatto & Windus. 1955. [x], 119 pp.   OXB
Collected poems of William Empson. New York: Harcourt, Brace & Co. [1959]. x,
113 pp.   OXB
The gathering storm: [*poems*]. Faber & Faber Ltd. 1940. 71 pp.   OXB
see also   15, 56, 82

EMSWORTH, Robert
By contrast: verses for young and old. Ilfracombe: Arthur H. Stockwell, Ltd. 1974.
83 pp.   OXB

ENGLAND, Roye
The price: a poem in twenty-one cantos. Abingdon-on-Thames: Abbey Press. 1963.
[viii], 27 pp.   IWM

ENGLEHEART, Francis (1896– . b. Suffolk. Educated at Magdalen
College, Oxford. Enlisted in the Volunteer Corps and served 1916–19. A county
councillor, magistrate and parish councillor, he farmed his own estate. Army
Welfare Officer and Special Constable, 1939–45)
A selection of poetry. Foreword by Sir Francis Meynell. Ipswich: Norman
Adlard & Co. Ltd. 1965. xvi, 71 pp. por.   OXB

ENGLISH, Mary (Of Cobham, Surrey) *see* 8

ENNIS, Julian, pseud. (Publisher's blurb states 'Julian Ennis is the pen name of a man whose work is constantly with young people'. Contributed poems to many periodicals. Some have been recorded by the British Council)

Cold storage: poems; by Julian Ennis. Pergamon Press. 1970. viii, 62 pp. (Pergamon English library: Poets today).　　　　　　　　　　　　MPL

ENRIGHT, Dennis Joseph (1920– . b. Leamington. Educated at Leamington College, and Downing College, Cambridge. Lecturer in English, University of Alexandria, 1947–50. Held senior university appointments in Birmingham, Japan, Berlin, Bangkok, Singapore and Warwick. Co-editor of *Encounter*, 1970–72. Director of the publishers Chatto & Windus. Received Cholmondeley Poetry Award in 1974. Poet, novelist, literary critic, editor, writer on Japan and translator of Japanese verse)

Bread rather than blossoms: poems. Secker & Warburg. 1956. 95 pp.　　OXB

Selected poems. Chatto & Windus. 1968. 96 pp.　　　　　　　　　　OXB

see also　26, 57

ESDAILE, Arundell (1880–1956. Educated at Lancing College, and Magdalene College, Cambridge. Appointed to Department of Printed Books, British Museum in 1903, becoming Secretary, 1926–40. Lecturer in Bibliography, London University School of Librarianship, 1919–39. President of The Library Association, 1939–45)

Autolycus' pack, and other light wares: being essays, addresses and verses. Grafton & Co. 1940. x, 222 pp. por.　　　　　　　　　　　　　　　　　BL

Four poems of the Second World War. Winchester: Mr Blakeney's Private Press. [1945]. [5] pp.

　　Printed on one side of leaf only. Title from cover.　　　　　　　BL

Two [i.e. four] poems of the Second World War. Winchester: Mr Blakeney's Private Press. 1945. 7 pp.

　　Printed on one side of leaf only. Title from cover.　　　　　　　OXB

Wise men from the west, and other poems. Andrew Dakers Ltd. 1949. 84 pp.

　　　　　　　　　　　　　　　　　　　　　　　　　　　　　　MPL

ETHERIDGE, Ken (1911– . Educated at Amman Valley Grammar School, and University College, Cardiff. Served in Royal Air Force. Writer on costume and stage design and writer for radio and stage. Of Ammanford, Carmarthen)

Poems of a decade. Hull: Guild Press. 1958. 16 pp. (Guild poets).　　BL

Songs for courage: [poems]. Printed Llandyssul: Gomerian Press. 1940. 74 pp.

　　　　　　　　　　　　　　　　　　　　　　　　　　　　　　OXB

see also　25, 33

EVANS, D. (Sergeant, Royal Air Force. Served in North Africa)　*see*　42

EVANS, D. Martin

Scenes from life, in verse. Ilfracombe: Arthur H. Stockwell, Ltd. 1946. 20 pp.

　　　　　　　　　　　　　　　　　　　　　　　　　　　　　　OXB

EVANS, David (Private, Bomb Disposal Squad)　*see*　33

EVANS, George Ewart (1909– . b. Abercynon, Glamorgan. Educated at Mountain Ash Grammar School, and University College, Cardiff. Served in the Royal Air Force. Writer of short stories, verse, and radio and film scripts. Visiting Fellow, Essex University, 1973–1978. Of Norwich) *see* 25, 32, 33

EVANS, Gerald (Of Glamorganshire) *see* 74

EVANS, Idrisyn Oliver (1894– . b. Bloemfontein, South Africa. Executive Officer, Ministry of Works & Public Buildings, 1912–62. Poet of the First World War. Lecturer, general writer and expert on flags. Of Tadworth, Surrey)
Sparks from a wayside fire: verses. Printed H.H. Greaves Ltd. 1954. 32 pp.
IWM

EVANS, J.S.L.
Poems. Arthur H. Stockwell, Ltd. [1942]. 10 pp. OXB

EVANS, Ruth *see* 84

EVELEIGH, Laurie (Air Raid Warden in the London blitzes. Volunteered for the Royal Navy in 1941 when he was nineteen. Sailed with the Arctic convoys) *see* 12

EVERETT, Donald (Served in the Middle East, including Cyprus)
A world stretching out: [poems]. Walton-on-Thames: Outposts Publications. 1974. 36 pp. OXB
see also 63

EVOE *see* **KNOX, Edmund Valpy**, (Evoe)

EWART, Gavin (1916– . b. London. Educated at Wellington College, and Christ's College, Cambridge, where he was taught by F.R. Leavis and I.A. Richards. Commissioned in the Royal Artillery, 1940–46, serving in North Africa and Italy. Worked for the British Council, 1946–52. Advertising copywriter, 1952–71, thereafter a freelance writer. Won a Cholmondeley Award in 1971)
The collected Ewart, 1933–1980: poems. Hutchinson. 1980. 412 pp. OXB
The Gavin Ewart show: poems. Trigram Press. 1971. 63 pp. il. (by Michael Foreman). OXB
Londoners: [poems]. Drawings by Colin Spencer. Heinemann. 1964. viii, 56 pp. il. OXB
No fool like an old fool: poems. Victor Gollancz Ltd. 1976. 76 pp. (Gollancz poets). OXB
Two children: poems. Keepsake Press. 1966. [ii], 20 pp.
    A limited ed. of 175 copies signed by the author. OXB
see also 25, 33, 47, 53, 56, 59, 76

EYRE, Frank (Writer on the fire service)
Twenty poems. Richards Press Ltd. [1941]. 36 pp. (Selections from modern poets). OXB

F., V.H.
Flying bombs; [by] V.H.F. [194-].
A card. 'These verses appeared in a London newspaper at the time of the heavy air raids under the title *Air Raid Night*'. IWM

FABER, Sir Geoffrey (1899–1961. Educated at Rugby School, and Christ Church, Oxford. Employed by Oxford University Press, 1913–14. Poet of the First World War. Captain, 8th Battalion, London Regiment (Post Office Rifles). Served in France and Belgium. Estates Bursar of All Souls College, Oxford, 1923–51. Publisher and President, Faber & Faber Ltd. President of Publishers' Association, 1939–41. Chairman of National Book League, 1951–60)
The buried stream: collected poems 1908 to 1940. Faber & Faber Ltd. 1941. 256 pp.
BPL

Twelve years. Privately printed. 1962. 31 pp.
'Begun on the day after the bombardment of London in May 1941, and finished in November 1953'. OXB

FAINLIGHT, Leslie
All are waiting: [*poems*]. Walton-on-Thames: Outposts Publications. 1969. 27 pp. OXB

FALCKE, Derek
"A cow from Jersey", and other verses. Illustrations by Jeanne Groves. Falcke Publicity. [1949]. [28] pp. il. OXB

FALCONER, L.M. (Of Derbyshire) *see* 75

FALLON, W.G. (Served at sea) *see* 73

FARLEY, J. (Sergeant. Served in South-East Asia Command) *see* 35

FARLEY, Richard (Air Gunner, Royal Air Force. Trained in Canada)
Social impressions of an air gunner: [*poems*]. Ilfracombe: Arthur H. Stockwell, Ltd. 1947. 16 pp. OXB

FARNOL, Tom *see* 36

FARRAR, James (1923–44. b. Woodford, Essex. Educated in Sutton, Surrey. At the beginning of the war he worked on a farm in Cornwall, joining the Royal Air Force in 1942. Killed in a Mosquito aircraft on 26 July 1944 while attacking a V-1 flying bomb)

The unreturning spring: being the poems, sketches, stories, and letters of James Farrar. Edited and introduced by Henry Williamson. Williams & Norgate Ltd. 1950. 242 pp. por.   OXB

The unreturning spring: being the collected works of James Farrar. Edited and introduced by Henry Williamson. New ed. Chatto & Windus. 1968. 243 pp. por.

    Poetry and prose.   OXB
see also 76

FARREN, Robert, (Roibeard O'Farachain) (1909– . b. Dublin. Educated at St Patrick's College, Drumcondra, and the National University of Ireland. Playwright and writer in both English and Irish. Appointed Director of the Abbey Theatre, Dublin, in 1940. Deputy Director of Broadcasting at Radio Eireann, Dublin)

Rime, gentlemen, please, [and other poems]. Sheed & Ward, Ltd. 1945. 112 pp.
     OXB

FASSAM, Thomas (1909– . Educated at Chatham House, and King's College, London. Editor of Kentish Times Newpapers, 1930–41. Flight Lieutenant, Royal Air Force, serving in the Middle East. Production editor for Pitman Press, 1947–50. Held other journalistic appointments including editorship of *Industrial Welfare* and *Foreman*. Lectured on English language and literature. Co-founder of the Mediaeval Drama Society)

My tongue is my own: selected poems. Aldington, Kent: Hand and Flower Press. 1950. xiv, 94 pp.   IWM

The shrapnel in the tree: poems 1940–1941. Cobham: Hand and Flower Press. 1945. [iv], 24 pp.

    A limited ed. of 285 numbered copies of which 280 are for sale.   BPL

FATHER ANDREW *see* **HARDY, Henry Ernest**, (Father Andrew)

FAULKNER, R. Cleveland (Of Kent)
"We Kentish men": a collection of poems. Ilfracombe: Arthur H. Stockwell, Ltd. [1948]. 24 pp.   OXB

FEATES, M. (Of London) *see* 74

FEATHER, John Waddington- *see* **WADDINGTON-FEATHER, John**

FEDDEN, Robin (1908—77. b Burford. Oxfordshire. Educated at Clifton College, Magdalene College, Cambridge, and abroad. Worked for the National Trust as Historic Buildings Secretary, 1951–74, and Deputy Director-General, 1968–74. General and travel writer, and co-editor of the anthology *Personal Landscape*, 1945)

The white country, [and other poems]. Turret Books. 1968. 26 pp.

A limited ed. of 150 copies of which the first fifty are numbered and signed by the author.   OXB
see also 40, 57

FEILDEN, F. Ernest (Pioneer in founding the 1st National Service Corps established in Blackburn in 1913 under the auspices of Field-Marshal Lord Roberts. Served in the Royal Army Medical Corps. Afterwards became a general medical practitioner in St Saviours, Guernsey)
Golden gleams, [and other poems]. Printed Guernsey: Wardleys. [1949]. 51 pp.
                                                                                     GGA

The greater war, depicting true and authentic records in doggerel verse. Presented in compliment as a souvenir for all time, none being for sale or profit. Printed Guernsey: Wardleys. [1946]. [ii], 233 pp. por.
'Dedicated to The Rt Hon Winston Churchill'.   IWM
The kaleidoscope of years — of passing years, in poem form. Printed Guernsey: Wardleys. [1949]. [viii], 258 pp. il., col. il., por.

Illustrated by author's black and white and coloured drawings pasted onto pages.   GGA

FEINER, Alfred
Pages from a biography: [poems]. Outposts Publications. 1967. 24 pp.   OXB
Panta re, [and other poems]. Favil Press. 1965. [vi], 41 pp.   OXB
Second harvest: [poems]. Favil Press. [1963]. [viii], 73 pp.   MPL

FEINSTEIN, Elaine (1930– . b. Bootle, Lancashire, brought up in Leicestershire. Educated at Newnham College, Cambridge, later reading for the Bar. On the editorial staff of Cambridge University Press, 1960–62, lecturer in English, Bishop's Stortford Training College, Hertfordshire, 1963–66, Assistant Lecturer in Literature, Essex University, 1967–70. Poet, novelist and short story writer, she translated the poems of Tsvetayeva for Oxford University Press)
The magic apple tree, [and other poems]. Hutchinson. 1971. 60 pp.   MPL

FELIX, Isaiah Anthony (Of Reading, Berkshire)
Poems. Reading: Author. [1975]. 32 pp.   OXB

FELL, James Black
Song of Noel, and other poems. Herbert Jenkins. 1961. 93 pp.   MPL

FELL, W. (Served in H.M. Forces) *see* 75

FELTON, A.W.
Battles long ago, and other poems. Ilfracombe: Arthur H. Stockwell, Ltd. 1976.
80 pp.   OXB

FENLAUGH, Stephen (1924–   Educated at Oxford University and abroad. Lieutenant, Royal Artillery (Field), he served in India)   *see*   43

FENN, Anthony Fourdrinier (Reverend, of St Swithin's Rectory, Bintry, Norfolk. Honorary Chaplain to the Forces)
  War time verses. [Privately printed]. [1941]. 8 pp.
    'All profits will be given to the Red Cross Society'.   BL

FERGUS, R. (Served in H.M. Forces)   *see*   75

FERGUSSON, Bernard, Lord Ballantrae (1911–80. Educated at Eton College, and Royal Military College, Sandhurst. Joined The Black Watch in 1931. A.D.C. to Major-General (later Field-Marshal) Wavell at Aldershot, 1935–37. Served in Palestine in 1937, Instructor at Sandhurst, 1938–39. Served 1939–45 in the Middle East, India and the Wingate expeditions into Burma, being wounded and twice mentioned in despatches. Director of Combined Operations (Military), 1945–46, Assistant Inspector-General, Palestine Police, 1946–47. Governor General of New Zealand, 1962–67. Appointed Chairman of British Council in 1972)
  Hubble-bubble, [and other poems]. Drawings by Charles Gore. Collins. 1978. [viii], 103 pp. il.   OXB
  Lowland soldier: [poems]. Collins. 1945. 64 pp.   BPL

FERMOR, Patrick Leigh- *see* **LEIGH-FERMOR, Patrick**

FERRETT, Mabel (1917–   . b. Leeds, Yorkshire. A teacher, she held various posts in Leeds. Evacuated with Armley Boys' School to Lincoln on 1 September 1939. Worked in Civil Defence and became a fire watcher. Committee member of Yorkshire Poets' Association, Fellow of International Poetry Society, and one of the Pennine Poets. Of Heckmondwike, West Yorkshire)
  The years of the right hand: [poems]. Bakewell: Hub Publications Ltd. [1975]. [iv], 26 pp.   OXB

FERRIS, Marjorie P.
  One year in October, and other poems. Ilfracombe: Arthur H. Stockwell Ltd. 1974. 71 pp.   OXB

FEU, Frank Thomas Du *see* **DU FEU, Frank Thomas**

FFINCH, Michael (1934–   . b. Rochester, Kent. Educated at Repton School, and St Edmund Hall, Oxford. A schoolboy in the war, living at Feltham, Middlesex)
  Selected poems. Kendal: Titus Wilson. 1979. [vi], 63 pp.   OXB

FIDLER, Margaret Sheppard (Writer on cookery. Of Edgbaston, Warwickshire)
Poems of praise. Oxford: A.R. Mowbray & Co. Ltd. 1978. [ii], 56 pp. (Becket publications). OXB

FIELD, Audrey (1910– . b. South Africa and brought to England as an infant. Educated at Lady Margaret Hall, Oxford, and in Geneva. Secretary to Lord Ponsonby when he was Leader of the Opposition in the House of Lords. She trained as a family caseworker and during the war devoted herself chiefly to the billetting and welfare of evacuee children. Joined the British Board of Film Censors in 1948, later promoted an Examiner of Films until retirement in 1973).
Messiah every Christmas: a book of verse. Fortune Press. [1965]. 48 pp.
OXB

FIELDING, Gabriel, pseud. *see* **BARNSLEY, Alan**, (Gabriel Fielding, pseud.)

FINCHER, Norah M.
Mingling, and other poems. Ilfracombe: Arthur H. Stockwell, Ltd. 1972. 16 pp.
OXB

FINDLATER, Richard, pseud. *see* **BAIN, Bruce**, (Richard Findlater, pseud.)

FINLASON, Eric C.
The Statue of Liberty: [poems]. Quality Press. 1942. [ii], 31 pp. OXB

FINLAY, Ann (Of Edinburgh?)
Seed time and harvest: [poems]. Printed Edinburgh: Tragara Press. 1978. [35] pp.
    A limited ed. of 110 copies printed by hand. OXB

FISH, Wallace Wilfrid Blair-, (Blair) *see* **BLAIR-FISH, Wallace Wilfrid**, (Blair)

FISHER, Arthur Stanley Theodore (1906– . b. Hoima, Uganda. Educated at Christ Church, Oxford. Taught in Darjeeling, India, 1929–31, at Bryanston School, Dorset, 1931–34, and at Little Missenden Abbey School, Buckinghamshire, 1935–36. Assistant Master and Chaplain, Leeds Grammar School, 1937–43, De Aston School, Market Rasen, 1943–46, Magdalen College School, Oxford, 1946–60. Rector of Westwell, West Oxfordshire, 1961–74. Historian, novelist, poet, and writer on religious and educational topics. Of Wolvercote, Oxford)
The comet, and earlier poems. Frederick Muller Ltd. 1948. 59 pp. OXB
Selected poems. Oxford: Author. 1978. [vi], 65 pp.
    Printed in facism. of author's calligraphic hand. OXB

FISHER, G.R.
Verse and worse. Ilfracombe: Arthur H. Stockwell Ltd. 1965. 24 pp.   OXB

FISHER, Philip John (1883–1961. Educated at Evesham and Cheltenham Grammar Schools. Trained for the Methodist ministry at Hartley College, Manchester, being ordained in 1905. Poet of the First World War. Chaplain to the Forces, 1915–19, serving in France and Flanders chiefly with 55th Division. Circuit Minister in several places in England, retiring in 1950)
Songs of desire and of divine love: [poems]. Epworth Press. 1950. 56 pp.

OXB

FISHER, Roy (1930– . b. Handsworth, Birmingham. Educated at Handsworth Grammar School and Birmingham University. Held various teaching posts in schools and colleges, 1953–63. Head of English & Drama, Bordesley College of Education, Birmingham, 1963–71. Appointed to Department of American Studies, Keele University. Associated with the American poets of the Black Mountain group in the 1950s. A pianist with jazz groups from 1946)
Collected poems, 1968. Fulcrum Press. 1969. 80 pp.   MPL
Poems 1955–1980. Oxford University Press. 1980. xii, 193 pp.   OXB
Wonders of obligation. Drawings [by] John Furnival. Bretenoux, France: Braad Press. [1979]. [21] pp. il.
     A limited ed. of 450 numbered copies of which numbers 1–26 have been signed by the author.   OXB

FITZPATRICK, James A.
Poems and sonnets. Ilfracombe: Arthur H. Stockwell, Ltd. 1946. 31 pp.

OXB

FITZROY, Olivia (1921–69. b. Christchurch, Hampshire, daughter of Captain the Hon. R.O. FitzRoy, later Viscount Daventry. Served in the Women's Royal Naval Service as a flight direction officer, stationed at Yeovilton and later in Ceylon. Married Sir Geoffrey Bates in 1957. Wrote the official history of the VIII King's Royal Irish Hussars)
Selected poems. [Privately printed]. [1970?]. [65] pp. il. por.   CWR
see also   23

FLAHERTY, P.J. (Gunner, Royal Artillery. Served with the Eighth Army in the Western Desert) *see*   46, 63

FLEMHOOD, Betty (Of Carmarthenshire) *see*   74, 75

FLEMING, Filippa
A clew to the Americas: being the narrative of what befell two who sailing westward left the white cliffs behind. Brighton: Fetherstons. 1945. 48 pp.   OXB

FLETCHER, Elaine Mary
The journey of life: [*poems*]. Printed Regency Press. [1972]. 39 pp.   OXB

FLETCHER, Iain *see* **FLETCHER, Ian**

FLETCHER, Ian (1920–   . b. London. Educated at Dulwich College, Goldsmiths' College, London, and Reading University. Served with Royal Army Ordnance Corps and Ministry of Information in the Middle East, 1942–46. Children's Librarian at Lewisham, 1946–55. Poet, playwright, literary critic and biographer. Appointed Reader in English Literature at Reading University in 1966, later Professor. Co-editor of the anthology *Return to Oasis*, 1980)
Orisons, picaresque and metaphysical: [*poems*]; [by] Iain Fletcher. Editions Poetry London. 1947. 74 pp.   OXB
see also   28, 63, 82

FLUDE, Kathleen M.
The road to the moon, and other poems. Ilfracombe: Arthur H. Stockwell, Ltd. 1946. 16 pp.   OXB

FLYING OFFICER X, pseud. *see* **BATES, Herbert Ernest**, (Flying Officer X, pseud.)

FOLDER, Reg
"Poetical personal points". Ilfracombe: Arthur H. Stockwell, Ltd. [1949]. 20 pp.   OXB

FOOTE, Catherine A.   *see*   16

FOOTTIT, Keith (1922–44. b. Naini Tal, India. Educated at Wellington College. Awarded an Exhibition to Brasenose College, Oxford, but instead joined the Royal Air Force. Trained in the United States. Killed when his aircraft was shot down over Magdeburg on 21 January 1944)
The end of the day: poems; by Keith Foottit and Andrew Tod. Edited, with an introduction by Michael Meyer. Fortune Press. [1948]. 51 pp. por.
      Not joint authorship.   OXB
see also   20, 76

FORBES, Henry Maurice
Way-of-the-world songs: [*poems*]. Quality Press Ltd. 1945. 70 pp.   OXB

FORBES, Henry N. (Padre to the Royal Air Force)
The cross in the cup: [*poems*]. Fortune Press. [1949]. 48 pp.   OXB
The new gods rising: [*poems*]. Oxford: Shakespeare Head Press. 1941. viii, 53 pp.   OXB

Trumpets and the new moon: [*poems*]. Fortune Press. 1946. 40 pp.

'To the memory of F.J.N.F., Captain, Bombay Sappers and Miners, killed in action in North Africa, January 3, 1942'. BPL

Wheat by the wine press: [*poems*]. British Authors' Press. 1945. 31 pp. OXB

see also 22

FORD, B.A. (Served in South-East Asia Command) *see* 35

FORD, Connie M. (1912– . Lived in South East London until 1941, thereafter chiefly in the East Midlands. A civil servant for over twenty years)

The crimson wing: a book of political verse. Nottingham: Trentside Publications. 1977. 47 pp. OXB

Veterinary ballads, and other poems. Printed Nottingham: Clearpoint Press Ltd. [1973]. [iv], 39 pp.

Title from cover. OXB

FORESTER, Maurice A.P.

Light and shade: poems; by J.W. Murray and Maurice A.P. Forester. Ilfracombe: Arthur H. Stockwell, Ltd. 1946. 32 pp.

Not joint authorship. No war poetry by Murray. OXB

FORGE, James William Lindus (1911– . Educated at King's College School, Wimbledon. Joined Army in 1940, serving with the Royal Corps of Signals in Egypt, India and Burma. Professional architect, and writer on the county of Surrey. Of Weybridge, Surrey) *see* 43

FORSYTH, James (1913– . b. Glasgow. Educated at Glasgow High School and Glasgow School of Art. Worked with the General Post Office Film Unit, 1937–40. Served in Scots Guards and 2nd Monmouthshire Regiment, 1940–46, as Captain and Battalion Adjutant. Writer for stage, film and television. Dramatist-in-Residence with Old Vic Company, London, 1946–48, and at Howard University, Washington, D.C., 1961–62. Director of Tufts University Programme in London, 1967–71. Founding member of Theatres Advisory Council. Of Haywards Heath, Sussex) *see* 25, 56

FORSYTH, Pamela, (Pamela, pseud.)

Out of the shadows, [*and other poems*]; by Pamela. Ilfracombe: Arthur H. Stockwell, Ltd. [1945]. 16 pp.

'Dedicated to her beloved grand-daughter, Pamela, aged nine years, killed on the road, March 23rd, 1944, and to the soldiers all over the world, and our heroines, prisoners of war'. OXB

A selection of verse; by "Pamela". Ilfracombe: Arthur H. Stockwell, Ltd. 1945. 18 pp. OXB

FOSTER, J. (Served in South-East Asia Command) *see* 35

FOSTER, Lilian
Poems for sweethearts and others. Ilfracombe: Arthur H. Stockwell, Ltd. [1944].
16 pp.   OXB

FOSTER, Norah
Hugh, [and other poems]. Abingdon-on-Thames: Abbey Press. 1968. [vi],
20 pp.   OXB

FOURIE, Mary
Zimbabwe tapestry, and other poems. Ilfracombe: Arthur H. Stockwell, Ltd.
[1963]. 44 pp.   OXB

FOURNIER, Robert
Exposition: poems I–XV. [Harrow Weald]: Raven Press. 1940. [24] pp.
    A limited ed. of 300 numbered copies.   OXB

FOWLER, Margaret (Of Essex)
Birds of Essex, and other verses. Printed Colchester: Benham & Co. Ltd. 1946.
15 pp.
    Reprinted from *The Essex Review*.   OXB

FOX, Ellen S.
Memory lane, and other poems. Ilfracombe: Arthur H. Stockwell, Ltd. 1949.
16 pp.   OXB

FOX, Oliver
Poems. Ilfracombe: Arthur H. Stockwell, Ltd. [1944]. 14 pp.   OXB

FOX, Roger (Educated at Oriel College, Oxford) *see* 55

FOXALL, Edgar (Worked in a factory office before he was fourteen, self-
educated afterwards. Of Wirral, Cheshire)
Poems. Fortune Press. [1946]. 28 pp.   IWM
Water-rat sonata, and other poems. Fortune Press. [1940]. 48 pp. por.   OXB

FRADD, Edith
Alone with you: a selection of verse. Ilfracombe: Arthur H. Stockwell, Ltd. [1942].
32 pp.   OXB

FRAMPTON, Raymond (1899– . b. Birmingham. Educated at King
Edward VI Grammar School and Birmingham University. Served in the Royal
Navy. Lecturer and schoolmaster. Of West Malvern, Herefordshire)
Poems, 1939–1960. Ilfracombe: Arthur H. Stockwell, Ltd. [1965]. 36 pp.
                                                                            OXB

FRANCIS, J.V. (Of Essex)   *see*   73

FRANCIS, Molly (b. Oxford. Served in Auxiliary Territorial Service) *see*   27

FRANCKE, Margaret, pseud.
  Poems; by "Margaret Francke". Ilfracombe: Arthur H. Stockwell, Ltd. [1942]. 16 pp.   OXB

FRANKAU, Gilbert (1884–1952. Educated at Eton College. Entered his father's business in 1904. Poet of the First World War. Commissioned in 9th East Surrey Regiment, October 1914, transferred to Royal Field Artillery, March 1915. Fought at Loos, Ypres and the Somme, invalided out with rank of Staff Captain, February 1918. Recommissioned in Royal Air Force Volunteer Reserve, August 1939, made Squadron Leader, 1940, and invalided out in 1941. Novelist and poet)
  Selected verses. Macdonald & Co. Ltd. 1943. 32 pp.
    'The author and the publishers have agreed to distribute their joint earnings between the benevolent funds of the Royal Regiment of Artillery and the Royal Air Force; to whose officers, non-commissioned officers and men these poems of two wars are most gratefully dedicated'.   OXB

FRANKAU, Ronald (1894?–1951. Younger brother of Gilbert Frankau. Educated at Eton College and the Guildhall School of Music. Spent some time in Canada, returning in 1914 to serve in the Army. After the war worked in concert parties, later forming his own. An entertainer of musical comedy, revue and radio, usually writing his own material. He first broadcast in 1927)
  Diverson: [poems]. Rhymed by Ronald Frankau. Pictured by Laurie Tayler. Raphael Tuck & Sons Ltd. [1942]. [27] pp. il., col. il.
      Loose-leaf binding.   OXB
  'He's a perfect little gentleman — the swine!' Pictured by Laurie Tayler. Raphael Tuck & Sons Ltd. [1942]. 16 pp. il.   BPL

FRASER, George Sutherland (1915–80. b. Glasgow. Educated at Aberdeen Grammar School and St Andrews University. Trained for journalism in Aberdeen before the war. Served in The Black Watch and Royal Army Service Corps, 1939–45, mainly in the Middle East, rising to rank of Warrant Officer 2. In Cairo he knew Keith Douglas, Lawrence Durrell and Bernard Spencer. Freelance journalist in London, 1946–59. British Cultural Attaché in Tokyo, 1950–51. Critic, reviewer and broadcaster, he taught English at Leicester University from 1959)
  The fatal landscape, and other poems. Poetry (London). [1941]. [iv], 19 pp. (PL pamphlets, 3).   OXB
  Home town elegy, [and other poems]. Editions Poetry London. [1944]. 44 pp.
                                                                                                                  OXB

Leaves without a tree: [*poems*]. Tokyo: Hokuseido Press. 1953. x, 71 pp.

OXB

The traveller has regrets, and other poems. Harvill Press; Editions Poetry London. 1948. viii, 96 pp.

MPL

see also   25, 29, 31, 33, 37, 39, 47, 56, 57, 63, 66, 76, 79, 82

FREEDMAN, Alan N. (Served in Royal Air Force in the Middle East and Europe. Posted to Air Attaché's Office at the British Embassies in Ankara and The Hague. Journalist in Bristol, Manchester and Fleet Street. Of Isleworth, Middlesex) *see* 39, 63

FREEGARD, Stella (b. London. Studied for stage at the Italia Conti School. Served with the London Ambulance Service during the early part of the war, later transferring to the Auxiliary Territorial Service)

Carried forward: [*poems*]. Printed Regency Press. [1977]. 32 pp.

OXB

FREEMAN, Gwendolen (1908– . b. Ealing, London Educated at Tiffin Girls School, Kingston-on-Thames, and Girton College, Cambridge. Publicity Officer with Ministry of Labour in the Midlands, 1941–45. Journalist on *Queen, Birmingham Post, Birmingham News* and *Spectator*)

Between two worlds: [*poems*]. Walton-on-Thames: Outposts Publications. 1978. 32 pp.

OXB

FREEMAN, Nancy (Of Tunbridge Wells, Kent)

The grandchild, and other verses. Printed Tunbridge Wells: Hepworth & Co. [1950]. 34 pp.

OXB

FREETH, A.E.

For us they go, and two other patriotic poems. Ilfracombe: Arthur H. Stockwell, Ltd. [1944]. 16 pp.

OXB

FREIXA, Rudolf Joseph (b. Yorkshire of a Spanish father and French mother. Studied the violin in Brussels and Paris. Violinist to Anna Pavlova for a time. Served in the Intelligence Corps)

The darkest path: [*poems*]. Chesterfield: Guild Press. 1952. 16 pp. (Guild poets).

BL

FRETTON, Ruby (Of Nottinghamshire) *see* 74

FREWIN, Leslie Ronald (1920– . Served in the Army. Novelist, historian, biographer, anthologist and writer on sport)

Battledress ballads: a volume of war-time verse. W.H. Allen & Co. Ltd. 1943. 28 pp.

IWM

FRIDJOHN, Harold M. (Served in the Middle East) *see* 39, 63

FRIEDLAENDER, V. Helen (Wrote novels and essays as well as verse. Reviewed poetry for *Country Life* and other periodicals)

Stand alone, [and other poems]. Fortune Press. [1949]. 48 pp.　　　　IWM
see also 41

FRIEDLICH, Phyllis (Of London) *see* 73

FROATS, Cecil S.
The British Commonwealth, and other poems. Solstice. 1979. 46 pp.　　　OXB

FROLIK, pseud. (Served in South-East Asia Command) *see* 35

FROST, Ernest (1918–　. b. Isleworth, Middlesex. Principal Lecturer in English at Gaddesdon College of Education, Hertfordshire, then at College of Education, Loughborough, Leicestershire. Novelist, poet and contributor to various journals. Of Canterbury, Kent) *see* 57

FRY, Christopher (1907–　. b. Bristol. Educated at Bedford Modern School. Actor at Bath, 1927, schoolmaster at Hazelwood School, Surrey, 1928–31, Director of Tunbridge Wells Repertory Players, 1932–35. Served in the Non-Combatant Corps, 1940–44. During the war directed at Arts Theatre, London, and at Oxford Repertory. Writer of verse plays and writer for radio, film and television. Recipient of Foyle Poetry Prize, 1951, and Queen's Gold Medal for Poetry, 1962) *see* 25

FULLER, Jean Overton (b. Iver Heath, Buckinghamshire. Educated at Brighton High School, Royal Academy of Dramatic Art, London University, and Academie Julien, Paris. During the war an examiner in postal censorship in London. Lecturer in Phonetics, 1951–52. Director of Fuller d'Arch Smith Ltd from 1969. Scholar, novelist, biographer and poet)

Carthage; and, The midnight sun. Villiers. 1966. 61 pp.　　　　　OXB
Tintagel. Frensham, Surrey: Sceptre Press. [1970]. [44] pp. il. (by the author).　　　　　BL

FULLER, Leonard John (1891–1973. Educated at Dulwich College and Royal Academy Schools. In the First World War served in France with 10th Battalion, Royal Fusiliers. Commissioned in East Surrey Regiment in 1915, transferring to Machine Gun Corps. Artist and portrait painter. Served in Home Guard, 1940–44. Lived in St Ives, Cornwall, where he was Principal of St Ives School of Painting)

Cornish pasty: a painter's adventures in a sister art: [poems]. With drawings by Marjorie Mostyn. [St Ives]: St Ives Printing & Publishing Co. [1956]. [41] pp. il.　　　　　OXB

FULLER, Roy (1912– . b. Oldham, Lancashire. Educated at Blackpool High School. Admitted a solicitor in 1934. Conscripted to the Royal Navy in 1941, he served in the Fleet Air Arm in East Africa. Commissioned in 1944. After the war became solicitor to a leading building society. Poet, novelist, literary critic and writer of children's books. Professor of Poetry, Oxford University, 1968–73; a Governor of the B.B.C., 1972–79; Member of the Arts Council, 1976–77; Member of the Library Advisory Council for England, 1977–79. Recipient of Queen's Gold Medal for Poetry, 1970, and Cholmondeley Award, 1980)

Collected poems, 1936–1961. Andre Deutsch. 1962. 248 pp. MPL

Counterparts: [poems]. Derek Verschoyle. 1954. 46 pp. OXB

Epitaphs and occasions: [poems]. John Lehmann. 1949. 60 pp. OXB

From the joke shop, [and other poems]. Andre Deutsch. 1975. 64 pp. MPL

The joke shop annexe: [poems]. Edinburgh: Tragara Press. 1975. [13] pp.

   A limited ed. of 115 copies printed by Alan Anderson. OXB

A lost season: [poems]. Hogarth Press. 1944. 60 pp. (New Hogarth library, XIV). BPL

The middle of a war, [and other poems]. Hogarth Press. [1942]. 48 pp. (New Hogarth library, VIII). BPL

An old war: [poems]. [Printed] Edinburgh: Tragara Press. 1974. [13] pp

   A limited ed. of ninety-five copies printed by Alan Anderson. BPL

Poems. Fortune Press. [1940]. 40 pp. OXB

The reign of sparrows: [poems]. London Magazine Editions. 1980. 69 pp.

   Dedicated to Alan Ross. OXB

[Selected poems]; [by] A. Alvarez, Roy Fuller, Anthony Thwaite. Harmondsworth, Middlesex: Penguin Books. 1970. 144 pp. (Penguin modern poets, 18).

   Not joint authorship. No war poetry by Alvarez or Thwaite.

Tiny tears, [and other poems]. Andre Deutsch. 1973. 92 pp. MPL

see also   2, 3, 4, 8, 10, 15, 18, 23, 25, 26, 33, 37, 45, 47, 48, 51, 56, 57, 58, 59, 69, 80, 82, 83, 87

FULLERTON, David (Of Renfrewshire)   *see*   37

FURNIVALL, C. Guy (Of Sussex ?)

Poems and verses. Printed Arundel: H. Mitchell Jacob. [1975]. [ii], 61 pp.

   Title from cover. OXB

FURSE, Jill (1915–44. Daughter of Sir Ralph Furse. Married the poet Laurence Whistler in 1939)

Jill Furse: her nature and her poems, 1915–1944. Chiswick Press. 1945. 63 pp. por.

   "Her nature" by Laurence Whistler. A limited ed. of 150 numbered copies printed for Laurence Whistler. OXB

FURSE, Sir Ralph (1887–1973). Educated at Eton College, and Balliol

College, Oxford. Assistant Private Secretary, Colonial Office, 1910–14. Served as a Major in the First World War, twice mentioned in despatches. Director of Recruitment, Colonial Service, 1931–48. Lived at Winkleigh, North Devon) *see* 6, 23, 80

G.C. *see* 23

G., E.R. *see* **LUCIAN**, pseud., (E.R.G.)

GABBOTT, Grace
Rustic ramblings: [*poems*]. Arcadian Press. [1970]. 53 pp.   OXB

GABRIEL, Frank (Of Caernarvon, North Wales)
"The hour has come", and other Christian verse. Ilfracombe: Arthur H. Stockwell, Ltd. 1944. [16] pp.
    'Dedicated to the ladies of the Caernarvon Y.M.C.A. Auxiliary'.   OXB

GALBRAITH, Winifred A. (Spent several years in China. Worked for an international organization in Geneva, 1946–52)
A poetical offering. Printed Ilfracombe: Arthur H. Stockwell, Ltd. [1968]. 44 pp.   OXB

GALE, Adrienne (Of Seascale, Cumberland)
The year: [*poems*]. Seascale: Author. 1942. 32 pp.   OXB

GALLATI, Mary (b. London. Educated at St John's College and Bedford Square College. Secretary, journalist, short story writer, novelist, broadcaster and writer on cookery)
"War shrapnel": [*poems*]. Ilfracombe: Arthur H. Stockwell, Ltd. 1947. 40 pp. por.   IWM

GALLIE, Brian D. (D.S.C. Captain, Royal Navy. Served in the Mediterranean) *see* 23, 63

GALLOWAY, Christian
Peace River, and other verse. Mitre Press. [1953]. 59 pp.   OXB

GALSWORTHY, Hubert J. (Lieutenant Commander, Royal Naval Volunteer Reserve. Commanding officer of a minesweeper)
Pad: [*poems*]; by Lieutenant-Commander J.A.B. Harrisson, D.S.C., R.N.V.R. and Lieutenant-Commander H.J. Galsworthy, R.N.V.R. Illustrations by M. Galsworthy. Foreword by Admiral Sir Arthur K. Waistell, K.C.B. Winchester: Warren & Son Ltd. [1944]. 55 pp. il.
    Sub-title on cover is *M/S nonsense verses*.   OXB
see also 23

GAMBLE, William (1888– . Writer on Irish literature, antiquities and archaeology)

Poems grave and gay. Ilfracombe: Arthur H. Stockwell, Ltd. 1946. 20 pp.
OXB

GANT, Roland (Served in a parachute regiment and worked on bomb disposal. Translator of Verlaine and other French poets. A director of the publishers William Heinemann Ltd)

Listen confides the wind: poems and fantasies. Fortune Press. 1947. 74 pp.   BL

GARDINER, Patrick (Officer in the Army, serving overseas) *see*   42

GARDINER, Rolf (1902–71. b. Fulham, London. Educated at Rugby School, Bedales School, and St John's College, Cambridge. Farmer and forester, chairman of companies and promoter of husbandry. Organized voluntary work camps, summer schools, festivals and international exchanges. Interested in rural industries and ecology. Lived at Fontmell Magna, Dorset)

Love and memory: a garland of poems, 1920–1960; made by Rolf Gardiner for his friends and members of the Springhead Ring and issued from Springhead, Fontmell Magna, Shaftesbury, Dorset. Printed Gillingham, Dorset: Blackmore Press. 1960. 67 pp.
OXB

GARDINER, Wrey (1901– . b. Plymouth, Devon. Educated at Oxford and in Paris bookshops. Founded the Grey Walls Press in 1940 and took over editorship of *Poetry Quarterly*. Editor of the anthology *This Living Stone*, 1941)

The gates of silence, [and other poems]. Drawings by Cecil Collins. Grey Walls Press. 1944. 80 pp. il.
OXB

Lament for strings, [and other poems]. Grey Walls. 1947. 70 pp.
OXB

Poems, 1948–1954. Tunbridge Wells: Peter Russell. 1955. 43 pp.

A limited ed. of 350 copies.
OXB

Questions for waking: selection of poems. Fortune Press. 1942. 32 pp.

Dedicated to Alex Comfort.
OXB

Sharp scorpions: poems. Billericay, Essex: Grey Walls Press. 1941. [xi], 73 pp.
OXB

see also   25

GARDNER, Charles W. (Of Guernsey, Channel Islands)

"Hymn of the besieged". Guernsey: Star Typ. 1945.

A broadside printed on Liberation Day, 8 May 1945.
IWM

GARDNER, Michael

The piper, and other poems. Williams & Norgate. 1947. 31 pp.   OXB

Poems of storm and calm. Printed Ditchling, Sussex: Ditchling Press. [1944]. [i], 23 pp.
BL

GARFITT, Roger (1944– . Educated at Oxford University where he was

President of Oxford University Poetry Society. Poet, literary critic and teacher of English. Editor of *Poetry Review* from 1978. Writer-in-Residence, Sunderland Polytechnic)

Caught on blue, [and other poems]. Oxford: Carcanet Press. 1970. 27 pp. OXB
West of elm: [poems]. Cheadle Hulme, Cheshire: Carcanet New Press. [1974]. 48 pp. OXB

GARIOCH, Robert, pseud. *see* **SUTHERLAND, Robert Garioch**, (Robert Garioch, pseud.)

GARLAND, B.D. (Served in the Middle East) *see* 63

GARMON, pseud. *see* **DAVIES, Idris**, (Garmon, pseud.)

GARNER, Katharine Minta (Of Nottinghamshire)
Calling all shipping: [poems]. Foreword by Vice-Admiral Sir William Agnew, K.C.V.O., C.B., D.S.O. Illustrations by Douglas Coyne, Rosemary Markham and Sydney Whaley. Newark:Byron Copying Office. 1954. 40 pp. il. OXB
Escape to childhood, [and other poems]. With a foreword by A.R. Bowen, D.F.C. Illustrations by Hugh Peebles and Douglas Coyne. Lincoln: Advance Publicity Service. 1954. 40 pp. il. BL
Poems of three shires and of the sea. With a foreword by Douglas P. Blatherwick, O.B.E. and illustrations by Douglas Coyne. Lincoln: Advance Publicity Service. 1953. 40 pp. il. OXB

GARRATT, John (A journalist)
The dancing beggars: poems. Illustrations and jacket design by Edward Wolfe. Fortune Press. [1946]. 24 pp. il. IWM

GARROD, Heathcote William (1878–1960. Educated at Hertford College, Oxford, and a Newdigate Prizewinner. Elected a Fellow of Merton College in 1901. Poet of the First World War. Served at Ministry of Munitions, 1915–18. Professor of Poetry, Oxford University, 1923–28. Prolific writer on English literature and the classics)
Epigrams: [poems]. Oxford: Basil Blackwell. 1946. 31 pp. OXB

GARWOOD, Anthony
Within a space: [poems]. Fortune Press. 1945. 32 pp. OXB

GASCOIGNE, Rita
The English weather, and other poems. Ilfracombe: Arthur H. Stockwell, Ltd. 1946. 16 pp. OXB

GASCOYNE, David (1916– . b. Harrow, Middlesex. Educated at Salisbury Cathedral Choir School, and Regent Street Polytechnic, London. Had published a novel and a volume of poems by the age of seventeen. Lived in France, 1937–39 and 1954–65. An actor during the war. Poet, playwright, novelist and literary critic. Recipient of an Atlantic Award, 1949. Of the Isle of Wight)

Collected poems. Edited with an introduction by Robin Skelton. Oxford University Press; Andre Deutsch. 1965. xviii, 163 pp.   MPL

Poems, 1937–1942. Editions Poetry London Ltd. 1943. [viii], 62 pp. col. il.   MPL

[Selected poems]; [by] David Gascoyne, W.S. Graham, Kathleen Raine. Harmondsworth, Middlesex: Penguin Books. 1970. 202 pp. (Penguin modern poets, 17).

    Not joint authorship. No war poetry by Graham or Raine.   MPL

A vagrant, and other poems. John Lehmann, 1950. 62 pp.   OXB

see also   15, 25, 26, 51, 52, 56, 57, 68, 76, 86

GAVED, Joan Arundel (Of Par, Cornwall) *see* 22

GAWSWORTH, John, pseud. *see* **ARMSTRONG, Terence Ian F.**, (John Gawsworth, pseud.)

GAYE, Phoebe Fenwick (1905– . b. Boston Spa, Yorkshire. Educated at Putney High School. Married F.L.S. Pickard. Of Saffron Walden, Essex)

Loweswater. Jonathan Cape. 1942. 37 pp.

    Written January–February, 1941.   IWM

GAZZARD, Roy A.J. (Served in H.M. Forces) *see* 74

GEE, Herbert Leslie (1901– . b. Bridlington, Yorkshire. Journalist and general writer. Of Bishopthorpe, Yorkshire)

Immortal few: the story of the Battle of Britain in verse. Epworth Press. 1943. 32 pp.

    Dedicated 'to the few on behalf of the many'.   OXB

GEE, Kenneth

32 poems. Fortune Press. [1942]. 47 pp.   OXB

GEERING, Ken (1925– . b. Horsted Keynes, Sussex. Educated at Hove Grammar School and Sussex University. Publisher and editor, formerly truck driver, land clearance and explosives contractor, hospital administrator and freelance journalist. Of Haywards Heath, Sussex) *see* 42

GELDER, Francis *see* 52, 79

GEMMELL, Constance Marjory Heddell

Through English windows: poems. Christopher Johnson. 1957. 88 pp.   OXB

Through Scottish windows: poems. Birmingham: Cornish Brothers Ltd. [1946].
64 pp.   OXB

Verses of variety: poems. Johnson Publications. 1964. 112 pp. por.   MPL

GENN, John Hawke- *see* **HAWKE-GENN, John**

GENTLE, Elvin (Of Middlesex) *see* 72, 75

GENTLEMAN, Catherine

To my mother, and other poems. Ilfracombe: Arthur H. Stockwell, Ltd. 1953.
48 pp.   OXB

GENTRY, R. (Served in Army Educational Corps) *see* 62

GEORGANO, A. de S.

Thoughts in words: [poems]. Ilfracombe: Arthur H. Stockwell, Ltd. 1977. 32 pp.
                                                                      OXB

GEORGE, Edwina E.

Hope, and other poems. Ilfracombe: Arthur H. Stockwell, Ltd. [1943]. 16 pp.
                                                                      OXB

GEORGE, G.A. St *see* **ST GEORGE, G.A.**

GEORGE, Richard A. (1919–   . Educated at Burnham Church of England
School. Studied for H.M. Customs & Excise. Joined Buckinghamshire
Yeomanry, Territorial Army. Called up in September 1939 as Gunner, Royal
Artillery. Served in France, India and Burma)

The living bough: [poems]. Mitre Press. [1957]. 24 pp.   OXB
see also 43

GERSHON, Karen (1923–   . b. Bielefeld, Germany. Came to England in
1938 with a children's transport from Germany, where both her parents later
died in concentration camps. Began writing poetry in English in 1950. Lived
with her four children in Jerusalem, 1969–73. Recipient of Arts Council Poetry
Award, *Jewish Chronicle* Book Prize, a grant from the President of Israel, all in
1967, and the Pioneer Women Poetry Award in 1968. Of St Austell, Cornwall)

Coming back from Babylon: 24 poems. Victor Gollancz Ltd. 1979. 55 pp.
(Gollancz poets).   OXB

Legacies and encounters: poems 1966–1971. Victor Gollancz Ltd. 1972. 48 pp.
                                                                      OXB

Selected poems. Victor Gollancz Ltd. 1966. 64 pp.   OXB
see also 86

GERVAIS, Terence White

Patrick freed, and other poems. Fortune Press. 1948. 96 pp.   BPL

GIBB, Iris (b. Lucknow, India, daughter of a serving army officer. Educated in Sussex. During the war served as a Light Rescue driver in Southwark, London. Of Henfield, Sussex)

Voice and verse: poems. Mitre Press. [1975]. 56 pp. OXB

GIBB, J.C.M. (Wing Commander, Royal Air Force) *see* 1, 25

GIBBINS, Margaret Celia (Contributor to women's magazines)

More poems for women. Mitre Press. 1965. 64 pp. MPL

GIBBON, Monk (1896– . b. Dublin. Educated at St Columba's College, Rathfarnham, and Keble College, Oxford. Poet of the First World War. Served as an officer in the Royal Army Service Corps in France, 1916–17, invalided out in 1918. Taught in Switzerland. A master at Oldfield School, Swanage, for ten years. Vice-President, Irish Academy of Letters, 1967. Of Sandycove, County Dublin)

This insubstantial pageant: [*poems*]. Phoenix House Ltd. 1951. 190 pp. OXB

GIBBONS, Charles Austin

Poems. Ilfracombe: Arthur H. Stockwell, Ltd. [1962]. 152 pp. por. MPL

GIBBS, Beatrice Ruth (1894– . b. Stoodley, Devon. Educated at St Margaret's School, Exeter, and Sherborne School for Girls. Married J.H.G. Gibbs. Co-Principal of Somerville School, St Leonards, Sussex. Short story writer, poet, journalist and writer of stories for children. Of Eastbourne)

The voices, and other poems. Hutchinson & Co. Ltd. 1949. 72 pp. OXB
see also 41, 84

GIBBS, Benjamin Richard (Writer on English literature) *see* 9, 84

GIBBS, Brian (Served on H92, Royal Navy. Of Lowestoft, Suffolk)

Michael: a little boy lost: poems. Illustrations by Hazel Gibbs. Lowestoft: [Author]. 1977. [40] pp. il.

A limited ed. of 100 numbered copies. OXB
That inward eye: poems and prose. Lowestoft: [Author]. 1979. [46] pp. il.

A limited ed. of 100 numbered copies. OXB

GIBSON, Douglas (1910– . b. Belmont, Surrey. Freelance journalist, poet and screenwriter. Contributed to over thirty anthologies and to many periodicals. Of Leigh-on-Sea, Essex)

"Song in storm", [*and other poems*]. Favil Press Ltd. [1941]. [6] pp. ("Resurgam" younger poets, 4).

Title from cover. BL
Thirty-three poems. With an introduction by Herbert Palmer. King Littlewood & King Ltd. [1943]. 31 pp. OXB

Winter journey, and other poems. Jonathan Cape. 1945. 95 pp.   IWM
see also   9, 22, 42, 52, 82

GIBSON, Peggy
Dream garden, and other poems. Ilfracombe: Arthur H. Stockwell, Ltd. [1943].
16 pp.   OXB

GIBSON, Ronald V. (Educated at Gonville & Caius College, Cambridge,
where he started a Liberal paper and became President of the Cambridge
Union. Joined staff of *The Times of India* in 1939, entering the Army in 1941.
Major, Army Educational Corps, he served with the Royal Indian Army
Service Corps until 1944. Co-editor of the anthology *Poems from India*,
1946)   *see*   43

GIBSON, Sydney
Reflections in rhyme. Ilfracombe: Arthur H. Stockwell, Ltd. 1946. 32 pp.
                                                                                  OXB

GIBSON, Wilfrid Wilson (1878–1962. b. Hexham, Northumberland, son of a
chemist. Educated at private schools. Moved to London in 1912, living above
Harold Monro's Poetry Bookshop. Poet of the First World War. Despite poor
eyesight he served in the Army Service Corps. Contributed to Sir Edward
Marsh's five volumes of *Georgian Poetry*, 1912–22. Lived in Weybridge, Surrey,
latterly)
The alert, [*and other poems*]. Oxford University Press. 1941. x, 42 pp.   IWM
Challenge, [*and other poems*]. Oxford University Press. 1942. xii, 42 pp.
   Dedicated to Laurence Binyon.   IWM
The outpost, [*and other poems*]. Oxford University Press. 1944. xiv, 90 pp.
                                                                            IWM
The searchlights, [*and other poems*]. Oxford University Press. 1943. viii, 92 pp.
                                                                            BPL
Solway Ford, and other poems: a selection made by Charles Williams. Faber &
Faber. 1945. 74 pp.   IWM
see also   9, 22, 38, 51, 80, 84

GIGGS, Barry
Between the lines: [*poems*]. Walton-on-Thames: Outposts Publications. 1973.
25 pp.   OXB

GILBERT, Margery Lyon
Songs my mother never taught me: [*poems*]. Walton-on-Thames: Outposts
Publications. 1974. 16 pp.   OXB

GILBEY, Jack (Educated at Stonyhurst College, and the Royal Military
College, Sandhurst. Served in France as a Captain with The Black Watch,
1914–18. Poet and general writer. Of Harlow, Essex)

Collected poems, 1935–1946. Burns Oates & Washbourne Ltd. 1946. 228 pp. por. OXB

'Come to Me all ye . . .', and other poems. Burns, Oates & Washbourne, Ltd. 1941. 48 pp. por. OXB

Haven, and other poems. Burns, Oates & Washbourne Ltd. 1941. 48 pp.
OXB

"In all the signs . . .", and other poems. Burns, Oates & Washbourne Ltd. 1944. 48 pp. por. OXB

Milestones, and other poems. Privately printed. 1943. 48 pp. por. OXB

Snowdrops at dusk, and other poems. Burns, Oates & Washbourne Ltd. 1945. 48 pp. il., por. OXB

GILCHRIST, Marjory

The London tree, [and other poems]. Walton-on-Thames: Outposts Publications. 1977. 40 pp. OXB

GILFILLAN, William

My heart reveals: poems. Ilfracombe: Arthur H. Stockwell, Ltd. [1944]. 45 pp.
OXB

GILL, Eric B. (Served in the Middle East) *see* 63

GILLILAND, Samuel W.

Masquerade of the pen, [and other poems]. Ilfracombe: Arthur H. Stockwell Ltd. 1978. 60 pp. OXB

GILLIVER, Alfred Joseph (1920– . b. London. Educated at St Dunstan's College, Catford. Worked in Civil Defence before entering the Royal Corps of Signals in 1940. Served in India Command, 1940–45) *see* 43

GILMAN, Edward Wilmot Francis (1876–1955. b. Shanghai, China. Educated at Bradfield College, and Brasenose College, Oxford. Entered Malayan Civil Service in 1899, holding a series of appointments. Hon. Secretary of Oxfordshire Branch of the Council for the Preservation of Rural England, 1934–47, member of Oxfordshire County Regional Planning Committee, 1939–47. Chief Warden, Air Raid Precautions, 1939–45. Lived at Islip latterly)

The wheat with the chaff: some translations and other verse. Islip, Oxon. : Ring Dove Press. [1943]. 24 pp. OXB

GIMSON, Clive (1919– . Educated at Uppingham School, and Clare College, Cambridge. Served in the Royal Artillery, 1939–46, awarded the M.C. in 1945. Held various teaching appointments including that of Headmaster, Blundell's School, 1971–80. Of Leiston, Suffolk) *see* 63

GINGELL, Broughton (1924–   . Educated at Oxford University. Served in
H.M. Forces. Worked for various publishing houses, Macmillan in New York
and London, 1953–57, and Longmans for the Far East, 1957–59. Director of
Longmans of Rhodesia from 1959)
    Human and all human: [*poems*]. Fortune Press. [1946]. 20 pp. por.   OXB
see also 49

GIRALDA, Michael
    Alan Brooke, and other poems. Hull: Dock Leaves Press. [1964]. [ii], 20 pp.
                       OXB
    Irish seed sporting lead: [*poems*]. Ilfracombe: Arthur H. Stockwell Ltd. 1973.
60 pp.   OXB
    Mediterranean seed, Atlantic fruit: poems. Southend-on-Sea: Citizen Publishing
Co. Ltd. [1964]. 36 pp.   BL

GIRDLESTONE, Magdalen (An Air Raid Warden in London)
    Poems of a London warden. Covenant Publishing Co., Ltd. 1942. 32 pp.
                       IWM

GITTINGS, Robert (1911–   . b. Portsmouth. Educated at St Edward's
School, Oxford, and Jesus College, Cambridge. Poet of the First World War.
Research Fellow and supervisor in history at Jesus College, 1933–40. B.B.C.
writer and producer, 1940–63. Held professorships at Vanderbilt University,
Tennessee, Boston University and Washington University. Poet, playwright,
literary critic, biographer and historian. Of East Dean, West Sussex)
    Collected poems. Heinemann. 1976. [x], 117 pp.   OXB
    Wentworth Place: poems. William Heinemann Ltd. 1950. viii, 75 pp.   OXB

GLADWYN, Margaret, pseud.
    Songs of England, and other poems; by "Margaret Gladwyn". Ilfracombe: Arthur
H. Stockwell, Ltd. [1942]. 24 pp.   OXB

The GLEANER, pseud. *see* **ROBERTS, Arthur**, (The Gleaner, pseud.)

GLOVER, Robin
    The Avon flows past, and other poems of war and peace, life and love, politics and sport.
Ilfracombe: Arthur H. Stockwell, Ltd. 1952. 72 pp.   OXB

GODFREY, Wilfred (Of Derby)
    The bard, [*and other poems*]. Derby: [Author]. 1956. 94 pp.
      'A private ed. of 400 copies' — author's handwritten note in copy seen.
                       OXB
    "The great divide". Derby: [Author]. 1972. 537 pp.   OXB
    The torch: poems. Printed Norwich: Jarrold & Sons Ltd. 1953. 100 pp.
      'A private ed. of 400 copies' — author's handwritten note in copy seen.
                       OXB

GOFFRON, E.A. (Of London) *see* 74

GOLDING, S.G.
Poems. Ilfracombe: Arthur H. Stockwell, Ltd. [1964]. 28 pp.   OXB

GOLDWYN, pseud. (1915–   . b. London. Moved to Leigh-on-Sea, Essex, at age of seventeen. Married a Southend man)
Thoughts in rhyme; by Goldwyn. Printed Regency Press. [1976]. 32 pp.
                                                                            OXB

GOMERSALL, Irvin (Radio Officer in the Merchant Navy. Had previously joined the Royal Air Force at the age of seventeen but was discharged on health grounds. Of Boston Spa, Yorkshire)
War memoirs in verse. Boston Spa: Author. [1945]. [12] pp.
     Title from cover. Proceeds in aid of Merchant Navy and Royal Air Force Benevolent Funds.   OXB

GOOD, Thomas (1901–70. b. Beeston, Nottinghamshire. Exempted from national service)
Out of circumstance: poems. Fortune Press. [1954]. 48 pp.   IWM
Overture: poems. Counterpoint; Oxford: Alden Press. 1946. 64 pp.   OXB
Selected poems. Edited by Michael Hamburger. St George's Press. 1973. xiv, 65 pp.
     A limited ed. of 250 numbered copies.   OXB

GOODBRAND, D.S. (Of Northern Ireland)
Mirage, and other poems. Manchester: John Sherratt & Son. 1946. 39 pp.
                                                                            MPL
Odin's mead: [poems]. Printed Altrincham: St Ann's Press. [1969]. 95 pp.
                                                                            OXB
see also 23

GOODMAN, John M.C.
Stray thoughts and memories in verse. Ilfracombe: Arthur H. Stockwell, Ltd. 1949. 16 pp.   OXB

GOODMAN, Richard (1911–   . Educated at Windsor, and New College, Oxford, where he edited *Oxford Poetry*. A schoolmaster and Workers Educational Association lecturer, he worked for a time with A.S. Neill. Lived in Paris before the war. Lieutenant, Royal Naval Volunteer Reserve. Of Sussex) *see* 14, 23

GOODRIDGE, Frank (Teacher of English and creative writing at Lancaster University)
The raw side, [and other poems]. Liskeard, Cornwall: Harry Chambers. 1978. 37 pp. (Peterloo poets).   OXB

GORDON, George (Served in H.M. Forces) *see* 49

GORDON, James
Epitaph for a squadron: [*poems*]. Ilfracombe: Arthur H. Stockwell Ltd. 1965.
viii, 55 pp. il. BPL

GORDON, Mary (Of Kingston)
Transparent web: [*poems*]. Arcadian Press. [1968]. 16 pp. OXB

GORDON, Pamela
Incidentally: a collection of poems. Arthur H. Stockwell, Ltd. [1940]. 64 pp.
OXB

GORDON, Rob
Bubbles: a miscellany of verse. Ilfracombe: Arthur H. Stockwell, Ltd. [1950].
32 pp. OXB

GORDON, Sheila Alice
Restoration, and other poems. Ilfracombe: Arthur H. Stockwell, Ltd. 1950.
16 pp. OXB

GORDON, William
Dunkirk; by Lilion Latham assisted by William Gordon. Printed Bexhill: F.J.
Parsons Ltd. [194-]. 7 pp.
Title from cover. BPL

GORELL, Lord *see* **BARNES, Ronald Gorell, Lord Gorell**

GOSLING, E.F. (Served in the Middle East) *see* 63

GOSS, John H. (Served in the Army)
A soldier's kit bag: poems. Fortune Press. [1941]. 56 pp. BPL

GOUDGE, Elizabeth (1900–84. b. Wells, Somerset. Daughter of Henry
Leighton Goudge, Regius Professor of Divinity, Oxford University. Educated at
Grassendale School and Reading University. Writer of novels, short stories,
plays, and books for children. Of Henley-on-Thames, Oxfordshire)
Songs and verses. Duckworth. 1947. 48 pp. BL

GOWLAND, A. Ray (Served in Air Raid Precautions) *see* 62

GRAHAM, John Wedderburn Barns- *see* **BARNS-GRAHAM, John
Wedderburn**

GRAHAM, Joyce Maxtone, (Jan Struther, pseud.) (1901–53. Née
Anstruther. Educated privately in London. Contributed poems, articles and

short stories to various magazines from 1917. Married twice, the second time to A.K. Placzek of Columbia University, United States. Author of best-selling wartime novel *Mrs Miniver*. Lived in Sussex) *see* 38

GRAHAM, Virginia (1910– . b. London, daughter of well-known lyricist Harry Graham. Educated at Notting Hill High School and privately. Married Antony Thesiger. Throughout the war she worked full time with the Women's Voluntary Service. A contributor to many periodicals including *Punch*, she was film critic for the *Spectator*, 1946–56)
   Consider the years 1938–1946: [*poems*]. Jonathan Cape. 1946. 96 pp.   BPL
see also 38

GRAHAM, W.G. (Served in the Middle East) *see* 39, 63

GRAHAM, William Sydney (1918– . b. Greenock, Renfrewshire. After training as an engineer in Glasgow he spent a year at Newbattle Abbey College. Received an Atlantic Award for Literature in 1947. Read his own verse on radio and television, and held poetry readings in the United States. Of Ayr)
   That ye inherit: [*poems*]. Printed Kilmarnock: Smith Brothers Ltd. [1968].
99 pp.   BL

GRAINGER, Elizabeth
   Con amore: a collection of poems. Ilfracombe: Arthur H. Stockwell Ltd. 1974.
31 pp.   OXB

GRAINGER, M. (Of County Durham) *see* 74

GRAINGER, Muriel (1905– . Educated at South Hampstead High School. Journalist and managing editor of a group of women's publications. Contributor to many anthologies and periodicals. Of Hampstead Garden Suburb, London)
   Music at midnight, [*and other poems*]. Fortune Press. [1950]. 32 pp.   OXB
   The stranded shell: [*poems*]. Walton-on-Thames: Outposts Publications. 1973.
20 pp.   OXB

GRANDFIELD, Denis Edward (1915– . Educated at Dumbarton House School, Swansea. Served in the Welsh Guards, being wounded at Arnhem)
   Gower poems. Hull: Guild Press. 1957. 39 pp.   OXB

GRANDIN, Reginald (In Jersey, Channel Islands, during the German occupation)
   Smiling through! Jersey, 1940–1945: [*poems*]. Printed St. Helier: *The Evening Post* Offices. [1946]. 141 pp. il.   IWM

GRANT, J.P. (Of Warwickshire) *see* 75

GRANT, John Cameron (1934– . b. Edinburgh. Educated at Buckhaven and Dalkeith High Schools and the Royal Scottish Academy of Music. Documentary film writer. Of Ponteland, Northumberland)

The keeper of the lodge, [and other poems]. Newcastle upon Tyne: Oriel Press Ltd. 1968. [viii], 82 pp.   OXB

Plough and coble: [poems]. Newcastle upon Tyne: Oriel Press Ltd. 1967. [xii], 119 pp.   OXB

The preacher on the moor: [poems]. Newcastle upon Tyne: Oriel Press. 1970. [xii], 105 pp.   OXB

GRANT, P.H.

A poem for every mood. Ilfracombe: Arthur H. Stockwell, Ltd. 1971. 60 pp.
                                                                                                                  OXB

GRANT, R.W. (Served in H.M. Forces) *see* 74

GRANT, V.C. (A Scotswoman) *see* 42

GRANTHAM, Alexandra Etheldreda (Writer on Chinese art and history. Poet of the First World War. Her son, Hugo Frederick Grantham, was killed at Gallipoli in 1915. Her grandson (?), Godfrey H. Grantham, an artist by profession, volunteered for the Royal Air Force Reserve in 1938. An Instructor Pilot Officer, he crashed fatally on 21 June 1942)

Godfrey Grantham: [poems]. Oxford: Joseph Vincent. 1942. 47 pp. il.   OXB

River roundels: [poems]. With six illustrations reproduced from pictures painted by Godfrey Grantham. Oxford: Joseph Vincent. 1943. 64 pp. il.   OXB

GRAVES, Charles (1892– . A journalist, he held posts in Leamington Spa and Glasgow and was drama critic for *The Scotsman*. Of Edinburgh)

Collected poems. Edinburgh: Ramsay Head Press. 1972. 176 pp.   OXB

Emblems of love and war: [poems]. Edinburgh: Ramsay Head Press. 1970. 56 pp.

Note in book states 'A limited cloth bound ed. of 150 copies has also been issued, each copy numbered and signed by the author' (Not seen)   OXB

GRAVES, Robert (1895–1985. b. Wimbledon, London. Educated at Charterhouse, and St John's College, Oxford. Major poet of the First World War. Served in France as a Captain with the Royal Welch Fusiliers. His autobiography *Goodbye To All That*, 1929, is a classic account of trench warfare. Professor of English Literature at Cairo University in 1926. Professor of Poetry, Oxford University, 1961–66. Poet, critic, historian and historical novelist, he made his home in Deya, Majorca, in 1929. Recipient of many literary prizes including gold medals for poetry. Over 130 of his books and MSS are on permanent exhibition at Lockwood Memorial Library, Buffalo, New York)

Collected poems (1914–1947). Cassell & Co. Ltd. 1948. xii, 240 pp.   OXB

Collected poems 1959. Cassell. 1959. [xviii], 320 pp.   OXB

Collected poems. New York: Doubleday & Co., Inc. 1961. 358 pp.   BL

Collected poems 1965. Cassell. 1965. [xx], 450 pp.   OXB

Collected poems, 1965. 2nd ed. Cassell. 1967. [xx], 450 pp.   OXB

Collected poems 1975. Cassell. 1975. [xxx], 592 pp.   OXB

The more deserving cases: eighteen old poems for reconsideration. [Marlborough]: Marlborough College Press. 1962. 36 pp. por. (by H.A. Freeth).

    A limited ed. of 750 numbered copies, 400 bound in full morocco leather and 350 in buckram cloth.   OXB

Poems, 1938–1945. Cassell & Co. Ltd. 1946. [viii], 40 pp.   IWM

Poems, 1938–1945. New York: Creative Age Press. [1946]. [x], 58 pp.   OXB

Poems selected by himself. Harmondsworth, Middlesex: Penguin Books. 1957. 208 pp. (Penguin poets, D39).   BL

Work in hand: [poems]; [by] Alan Hodge, Norman Cameron, Robert Graves. Hogarth Press. 1942. 64 pp.

    Not joint authorship.   BL

see also 15, 45

GRAY, Douglas (Educated at Batley Grammar School, London University and the Sorbonne. Lieutenant, Royal Army Medical Corps. Served in India) *see* 43

GRAY, G.H. (Of Hampshire?)

Occasional poems. Printed Andover: Chapel River Press. [1940]. 12 pp.

    Title from cover.   BL

Poems. Edward O. Beck Ltd. [1941]. 24 pp.   OXB

GRAY, John (Of London)   *see* 73

GRAY, K.R. (Captain, Royal Corps of Signals. Served in India)   *see* 43, 57

GREACEN, Robert (1920– . b. Londonderry. Educated at the Methodist College, Belfast, and Dublin University, where he studied social sciences. Worked in publishing and was assistant editor of *The Bell*. Poet, anthologist and broadcaster. Co-editor of the anthology *Lyra*, 1942. Of London)

A garland for Captain Fox: [poems]. Dublin: Gallery Press. 1975. 30 pp. (Gallery books, 20).

    A limited ed. of 700 copies, 180 of which are bound in cloth and signed by the author.   OXB

One recent evening: [poems]. Favil Press. 1944. [iv], 28 pp. (Resurgam books)   IWM

The undying day: [poems]. Falcon Press. 1948. 78 pp.   MPL

Young Mr. Gibbon: poems. Mornington, Meath: Profile Poetry. [1979]. 48 pp.   OXB

see also 21, 25, 29, 42, 52

GREATOREX, Clifford Willey (1896– . b. Worksop, Nottinghamshire. Educated at Worksop Secondary School and privately. Served in the First World War. Author and freelance journalist)   *see* 80

GREEN, Archibald Hylton (Served in Iraq, Syria and the Western Desert)
Conflicting conflicts: a selection of poems. Ilfracombe: Arthur H. Stockwell, Ltd.
1955. 16 pp.   OXB

GREEN, Edward Vaughan (–1944. Lieutenant, 1st Northamptonshire
Yeomanry. Killed in action in Holland after crossing the Wessem Canal on 14
November 1944)
Poems. [Brackley]: Old Brackleians' Society. [1949]. [16] pp. il., por. OXB

GREEN, Evelyn Fuller (A woman)
We have been told, and other poems. Ilfracombe: Arthur H. Stockwell, Ltd. 1953.
16 pp.   OXB

GREEN, Frederick Pratt (1903–   . b. Liverpool. Educated at Wallasey
Grammar School, and Rydal School, Colwyn Bay. A Methodist minister, he
retired to Norwich in 1969. Gained an international reputation as a writer of
hymns)
The old couple: poems new and selected. Stockport: Harry Chambers. 1976. 64 pp.
por. (Peterloo poets).   OXB
The skating parson, and other poems. Epworth Press. 1963. 69 pp. il.   OXB
This unlikely earth: poems 1946–1951. Aldington, Kent: Hand and Flower Press.
[1952]. 32 pp. (Poems in pamphlet, 1952, I).   OXB

GREEN, Henry J. (A young boy in the war)
First of the few: [poems]. Walton-on-Thames: Outposts Publications. 1977.
12 pp.   OXB

GREEN, Roger Lancelyn (1918–   . b. Norwich. Educated at Liverpool Col-
lege, and Merton College, Oxford. Part-time professional actor, 1942–45.
Deputy Librarian, Merton College, 1945–50. Held academic appointments at
Liverpool and St Andrews Universities. Poet, novelist and writer of children's
fiction. Edited the *Kipling Journal*, 1957–79)
The lost July, and other poems. Fortune Press. [1946]. 56 pp.   OXB

GREEN, Stuart (Educated at University College, Oxford) *see* 55

GREENE, Herbert (Brother of the novelist Graham Greene. Served with The
Suffolks in the First World War and with the Middlesex Yeomanry and Royal
Corps of Signals in the Second. In 1944 he commanded a unit attached to the
Yugo-Slav Balkan Mission. Of Plympton, Sussex)
Big Ben, and other verses. John Connell. [1960]. [vi], 80 pp.   BL
Big Ben, and other verses. 2nd ed. John Connell. 1961. [iv], 84 pp.   MPL
Wanted a lead, and other trifles. Printed Lewes: Farncombe & Co. Ltd. [1960].
48 pp.
    Poetry and prose. Dedicated to Winston Churchill. 'Profits from the sale of
this book will be handed to Lord Woolton's Fighting Fund'.   BL

GREENING, Michael Gillingham (Educated at St Paul's School, London. Corporal, Royal Engineers, serving in Norway and India. An active trade unionist) *see* 43

GREENWELL, Kenneth (–1942. Served in the Merchant Navy as Second Engineer on S.S. *Goulistan*. Lost with his ship on Convoy QP15 in November 1942)
Arctic convoy: a saga of the sea. With foreword by Rear-Admiral E.K. Boddam-Whetham. Printed Durham: Durham County Advertiser & General Printing Co. Ltd. 1943. 25 pp. por.   IWM
see also 23

GREEVES, Dorothy V.
Poems for our time. Chorley Wood, Herts.: C.T.U. [1941]. 16 pp.   OXB

GREGORY, Stanley (1891– . Of Monmouthshire ?)
Times and tides, and other poems. Printed Newport, Mon.: R.H. Johns Ltd. [1950]. 75 pp.   OXB

GRENFELL, Joyce (1910–79. b. London. Educated at Claremont, Esher, Surrey. Actress and writer. Radio critic for *The Observer*, 1936–39. Appeared in Herbert Farjeon's Reviews, 1939–42. Welfare Officer, Canadian Red Cross, 1941–43. Entertained troops in hospitals in Algiers, Malta, Sicily, Italy, Egypt, India and elsewhere. After the war appeared in films, on television and on stage in plays and concert shows, a much-loved entertainer who made many world-wide tours) *see* 41

GRETTON, Francis
A rattle of lamps: [poems]. Ilfracombe: Arthur H. Stockwell Ltd. 1973. 29 pp.
                                                                                      OXB

GRIEVE, Barbara
Who is God?, and other poems. Ilfracombe: Arthur H. Stockwell. [1942]. 48 pp.
                                                                                      OXB

GRIEVE, Christopher Murray, (Hugh MacDiarmid, pseud.) (1892–1978. b. Langholm, Dumfriesshire. Educated at Langholm Academy and Edinburgh University. Poet of the First World War. One of the founders of the Scottish Nationalist Party. Author, poet and journalist and a regular contributor to many British and foreign newspapers and magazines on literary, political and general topics. Founder of the Scottish Centre of the P.E.N. Club. President of the Poetry Society in 1976. Lived at Biggar, Lanarkshire)
The battle continues; by Hugh MacDiarmid. Edinburgh: Castle Wynd Printers Ltd. 1957. [viii], 107 pp.   OXB

A clyack-sheaf: [*poems*]; [by] Hugh MacDiarmid. Macgibbon & Kee. 1969. 57 pp. OXB

Collected poems of Hugh MacDiarmid (C.M. Grieve). Edinburgh: Oliver & Boyd. 1962. xiv, 498 pp. por. OXB

Collected poems of Hugh MacDiarmid. New York: Macmillan Co. 1962. xiv, 498 pp. BL

Collected poems of Hugh MacDiarmid. Revised ed. with enlarged glossary prepared by John C. Weston. New York: Macmillan Co. 1967. xxii, 498 pp. BL

Complete poems, 1920–1973; [by] Hugh MacDiarmid. Edited by Michael Grieve and W.R. Aitken. Martin Brian & O'Keeffe. 1978. 2 vols.
Cover-title is *The Complete Poems of Hugh MacDiarmid*. OXB

Poet at play, and other poems: being a selection of mainly vituperative poems; by Hugh MacDiarmid. Privately printed. [1965]. [14] pp.
Some poems in Scots dialect. A limited ed. of fifty-five numbered copies. OXB

The socialist poems of Hugh MacDiarmid. Edited by T.S. Law and Thurso Berwick. Routledge & Kegan Paul. 1978. xl, 106 pp. OXB
see also 30, 42, 64

GRIFFITH, Hubert Victor Nicoll- *see* **NICOLL-GRIFFITH, Hubert Victor**

GRIFFITH, Wyn (1890–1977. b. Glanwydden. Educated at Dolgellau Grammar School. Entered the Civil Service in 1909. Poet of the First World War, he fought on the Somme. Served as a Captain in the Royal Welch Fusiliers and on the General Staff, 1914–19. Awarded Croix de Guerre in 1918. Assistant Secretary, Inland Revenue, 1945–52, Chairman, Welsh Committee of Arts Council, 1949–56, Chairman, National Book League, 1957–58. One son was killed in action in 1942. Lived at Berkhamstead, Hertfordshire)
The barren tree, and other poems. Cardiff: Penmark Press Ltd. [1947]. 79 pp. OXB

see also 32

GRIFFITHS, Bryn (1933– . b. Swansea. Left school at age of fourteen, thereafter self-educated apart from one year at Coleg Harlech, 1961–62. Served in the Merchant Navy, 1951–60. A poet and dramatist, he worked as a welder, storeman, painter, labourer and salesman)
The dark convoys: sea poems. Solihull: Aquila Poetry. [1974]. 47 pp. OXB
The mask of pity, [*and other poems*]. Llandybie, Carmarthenshire: Christopher Davies Ltd. 1966. 46 pp. OXB

GRIFFITHS, Gertrude
Love's crown, and other poems. Ilfracombe: Arthur H. Stockwell Ltd. [1948]. 16 pp. OXB

GRIFFITHS, John A.
The countryside, and other poems. Ilfracombe: Arthur H. Stockwell, Ltd. [1942].
16 pp. OXB

GRIFFITHS, T.G. Longdon- *see* **LONGDON-GRIFFITHS, T.G.**

GRIFFITHS, Vivian (1934– . Educated at Coleg Harlech, University
College, Bangor, and University College, Swansea. Took a Diploma in
Education at Manchester University. Merchant seaman, 1950–58, and steel
erector, 1958–62. Lecturer, Cardiff College of Art, 1967–69. A teacher in
Swansea from 1969)
Sinews from salt, [*and other poems*]. Swansea: Christopher Davies. 1969. 47 pp.
OXB

GRIGSON, Geoffrey (1905–1985. b. Pelynt, Cornwall. Educated at St Edmund
Hall, Oxford. Poet, literary and art critic, journalist, writer on natural history
and travel and of non-fiction for children. Founder-editor of *New Verse*, 1933–39.
During the war worked as a monitor for the B.B.C. Of Swindon, Wiltshire)
The collected poems of Geoffrey Grigson, 1924–1962. Phoenix House Ltd. 1963.
268 pp. MPL
The Isles of Scilly, and other poems. Routledge. 1946. 45 pp. OXB
Several observations: thirty five poems. Cresset Press. [1940]. 54 pp. MPL
Under the cliff, and other poems. Routledge. 1943. 44 pp. IWM
see also 4, 69

GRIMES, C. (Sergeant. Served in South-East Asia Command) *see* 35

GRIMWADE, A.J. (Sub-Lieutenant, Royal Naval Volunteer Reserve) *see* 23

GRINDAL, R.F.W. (Aircraftman, Royal Air Force) *see* 1

GROOM, Gladys Laurence (–1948. Educated at Clifton and abroad. Poet,
critic and lecturer on English and French literature, she did considerable
Anglo-French Entente propaganda work after the First World War. Made her
home in Greece, where she was imprisoned for a few days in July 1942 by the
Italian invaders. Remained in Greece throughout the war, serving as a
voluntary worker with the International Red Cross. Married twice, to Arthur
Groom in 1913 and to Mavrikios Cordellis in 1943)
The magic country: poems. Castle Press. 1953. 64 pp. por. OXB

GROSCH, Alfred (1888– . b. St Pancras area of London. Volunteered for
the Army in the First World War) *see* 70, 71

GUINNESS, Bryan, Lord Moyne (1905– . b. London. Educated at Eton
College, and Christ Church, Oxford. Called to the Bar in 1930. Captain in

Royal Sussex Regiment, serving in Beirut and Damascus. Poet, novelist and playwright. A director of Arthur Guinness, Son & Co., 1949–79. Of Castleknock, County Dublin)

The clock: poems and a play. Portrait sketch by Augustus John. Dublin: Dolmen Press. [1973]. 88 pp. il., por.   OXB

Collected poems (1927–1955). William Heinemann Ltd. 1956. viii, 129 pp.
    OXB

Reflexions, [and other poems]. William Heinemann Ltd. 1947. [vi], 34 pp. il.
    OXB

GUNN, Thom (1929– . b. Gravesend, son of a journalist who became editor of the London *Evening Standard*. Educated at University College School, Hampstead, and Trinity College, Cambridge. Did two years national service in the Army, 1948–50. Lived in Paris in 1950, in Rome, 1953–54, and in California from 1954. Member of the English Department, University of California at Berkeley, 1958–66. Poetry reviewer for *Yale Review*, 1958–64. Recipient of several literary prizes and awards)

A geography, [and other poems]. Iowa City: Stone Wall Press. 1966. 32 pp. il.
    A limited ed. of 220 copies signed by the author.   OXB

Moly, [and other poems]; and, My sad captains, [and other poems]. New York: Farrar, Straus & Giroux. [1973]. [x], 91 pp.   OXB

My sad captains, and other poems. Faber & Faber. 1961. 51 pp.   OXB

My sad captains, and other poems. [New] ed. Faber & Faber. 1974. 51 pp.
    OXB

Selected poems; by Thom Gunn and Ted Hughes. Faber & Faber. 1962. 64 pp. (Faber paper covered editions).
    Not joint authorship. No war poetry by Hughes.   OXB

Selected poems, 1950–1975. Faber & Faber. 1979. x, 131 pp.   OXB

To the air: [poems]. Boston, Massachusetts: David R. Godine. [1974]. 24 pp. (First Godine poetry chapbook series, 6).   OXB

Touch, [and other poems]. Faber & Faber. 1967. 58 pp.   OXB

Touch, [and other poems]. [New] ed. Faber & Faber. 1974. 58 pp.   OXB
see also 30

GUNNELL, Peter Frederick
Poems, 1952–1954. Mitre Press. [1956]. 64 pp.   OXB

GURNETT, John J. (Lieutenant)
Visions and dreams: selected poems; by Lieut. Gurnett. Theosophical Publishing House. [1942]. 44 pp. por.   OXB

GUTTERIDGE, Bernard (1916–85. b. Southampton. Educated at Cranleigh School. Worked in advertising before the war. Joined the Army in 1939, a Major in the Royal Hampshire Regiment in 1940. Served in Combined Operations and with the 36th Division in Burma (with Alun Lewis), also

serving in Madagascar, Africa and India. A contributor to leading periodicals)
Old damson-face: poems 1934 to 1974. London Magazine Editions. 1975. 59 pp.
OXB

Traveller's eye: poems. Routledge. 1947. 64 pp.
    Dedicated to Amyas Northcote, killed in Burma 1944.   OXB
see also   25, 45, 59, 76

GWEN, pseud. *see* **DALY, Gwen,** (Gwen, pseud.)

GWYN, Peter
Poems of love and patriotism. Ilfracombe: Arthur H. Stockwell, Ltd. [1943].
24 pp.   OXB

GWYNN, Stephen (1864–1950. b. Dublin. Educated at St Columba's College, Rathfarnham, and Brasenose College, Oxford. Taught classics at various schools, 1887–96. Came to London in 1896 and began working as a journalist and writer. Returned to Ireland in 1904. Nationalist M.P. for Galway City, 1906–18. Poet of the First World War. Joined 7th Leinster Regiment as a Private in January 1915, becoming a Captain with 6th Connaught Rangers in July 1915. Served in France with 16th Irish Division, 1917–18. Lived in Dublin)
    Aftermath: [*poems*]. Dundalk: Dundalgan Press. 1946. [viii], 31 pp.   OXB
    Salute to valour: [*poems*]. Constable & Co. Ltd. 1941. [vi], 23 pp.   MPL
see also   38

GWYNNE, E.R.H. *see*   16

HACKER, Mary (b. London. Educated at London University. Novelist, poet and contributor to several periodicals. Married with two sons and a daughter. Of Harpenden, Hertfordshire) *see*   86

HADEN, John
    The first poetry of John Haden. Favil Press. 1942. [iv], 43 pp.   IWM

HADFIELD, Alan (1904– . b. Nottingham. Educated at Fitzwilliam College, Cambridge. Schoolmaster, portrait sculptor, potter and writer. Of Appledore, Devon)
Still "towards democracy". With a foreword by the Duke of Bedford, and a pendant of original verse. Harrogate: Northern Lights Press. [1943]. 24 pp.
(Nutshell notes on politics). (Northern Lights Press pamphlets, II).   OXB

HAFFENDEN, Alfred Henry
    99 stanzas European: a clarionesq, prefaced by remarks on God and war, tract fifteen.
C.W. Daniel Co. Ltd. 1941. 68 pp.   OXB

HAGGARD, Stephen (1911–43. b. New York, son of the British Consul-General, and a descendant of H. Rider Haggard. Educated at Haileybury School and Munich University. A notable theatre and film actor of great promise before the war. Staff Captain in the Devonshire Regiment and Intelligence Corps. Shot dead in mysterious circumstances on a train from Jerusalem to Cairo on 24 February 1943)

I'll go to bed at noon: a soldier's letters to his sons. Faber & Faber Ltd. 1944. 103 pp.

 Includes author's poems.   OXB

I'll go to bed at noon. Morley, Leeds: Morley-Baker. 1969. 103 pp.

 Letters and poems.   OXB

The unpublished poems of Stephen Haggard. With a preface by Christopher Hassall. Leeds: Salamander Press. 1945. 36 pp.

 A limited ed. of 350 copies.   BPL

see also 25, 33, 76

HAIGH, Mary Louise

Verses of valour, victory and vision. Ilfracombe: Arthur H. Stockwell, Ltd. [1942]. 16 pp.   OXB

HAILSHAM, Lord *see* **HOGG, Quintin, Lord Hailsham**

HAIME, Agnes Irvine Constance (1884– . b. Wandsworth, London. Educated at Battersea Secondary School and Southampton College. A schoolteacher)

Hope is the window: [poems]. P.R. Macmillan Ltd. [1960]. 80 pp. OXB

Reflections in verse. Richard Tilling. 1949. 72 pp.   OXB

HAINES, Gladys M. (b. Dorset, the family moving to the New Forest in 1923. Spent a great part of the war in London, working as a clerk in the War Office and experiencing the air raids. Of Ringwood, Hampshire)

Pines on the hill, and other poems. Hutchinson & Co., Ltd. [1947]. 36 pp.

                   MPL

HAINSWORTH, Ellen (Of Yorkshire) *see* 73, 74

HALDANE-DUNCAN, Alison

To a Queen, and other poems. Mitre Press. [1950]. 64 pp. por.

 'Dedicated to the immortal memory of Marie, Queen of Roumania and Princess of England'.   OXB

HALFORD, Henry John (Of Monmouthshire)

Selected poems. Mitre Press. [1946]. 40 pp.   OXB

see also 70, 73

HALL, A.F.
Sussex, glorious Sussex!, and other poems. Ilfracombe: Arthur H. Stockwell, Ltd.
1945. 32 pp.   OXB

HALL, Bertha Ann
Songs of fact and fancy: [poems]. Ilfracombe: Arthur H. Stockwell, Ltd. [1943].
24 pp.   OXB

HALL, Donald John (1903–   . b. Oxford. Educated at Shrewsbury School,
and Corpus Christi College. Cambridge. A solicitor, he served in the Foreign
Office during the war. Of Penrhyndeudraeth, Merioneth)
The phoenix-flower. Falcon Press. 1953. [viii], 222 pp.   IWM

HALL, Edward Theodore (1879–1962. Served in the King's Liverpool
Regiment Labour Corps during the First World War, when he saw the first
tanks going into action)
Poems. [Privately printed]. [196-]. [ii], 60 pp.   MPL

HALL, John Clive (1920–   . b. Ealing, London. Educated at Leighton Park
School, Reading, and Oriel College, Oxford. Employed as a social worker, on
the land and in publishing. Staff member of *Encounter* from 1955. Co-editor of
Keith Douglas's *Collected Poems*, 1966)
The burning hare, [and other poems]. Chatto & Windus; Hogarth Press. 1966.
50 pp. (Phoenix living poets).   OXB
A house of voices, [and other poems]. Chatto & Windus; Hogarth Press. 1973.
40 pp. (Phoenix living poets).   OXB
Selected poems; by John Hall, Keith Douglas, Norman Nicholson. John Bale &
Staples Ltd. 1943. 77 pp. (Modern reading library, 3).
      Not joint authorship.   BL
The summer dance, and other poems. John Lehmann. 1951. 64 pp.   OXB
see also   7, 25, 28, 38, 51, 52, 56

HALL, Pamela (Educated at Benenden School. First married to Lieutenant
F.C. Hall of the Rifle Brigade, who was killed fighting in North Africa. She later
became Mrs Holmes. Of West Hythe, Kent)   *see*   84

HALL, Richard (1903–   . Educated at Cambridge and London Universities.
Minister of the United Reformed Church at Haywards Heath, 1938–43, and at
Potters Bar and Brookmans Park, 1943–47. Held various other appointments,
becoming Moderator, General Assembly, 1976–77. Of Stowmarket, Suffolk)
Sronan, and other poems. Mitre Press. [1970]. 117 pp. por.   OXB

HALLAM, Robert Kay (1921–   . b. Glasgow. Ordinary Seaman in Dover
Gun-Boat Flotilla of Royal Navy, taken prisoner of war after boat was set on fire
and sunk. Spent some time in Stalag Luft III. Emigrated to Canada in 1949)

The scarecrow said, and other poems. Printed Villiers Publications Ltd. 1961.
80 pp. il., por.   OXB

HALLETT, F. (Of Middlesex) *see* 74

HALLETT, Olive E.
Topical tales, and other verses. Birmingham: Cornish Brothers Ltd. 1944. 20 pp.
OXB

HALLIDAY, R. *see* 23

HALLIWELL, Martin (Served in South-East Asia Command) *see* 35

HALSEY, Lewis (1917– . b. Lowestoft, Suffolk. Educated at Colchester
Royal Grammar School. Served in the Army, 1940–46, working on radar. A
chartered librarian and Fellow of the Library Association. Tutor/Librarian at
Salisbury College of Technology) *see* 25, 47

HAMBLETT, Charles (–1975. b. Newton, Lancashire. Educated in Vienna
and at the School of Arts & Crafts, Cambridge. Leading Aircraftman, Royal Air
Force. Editor of the anthology *I Burn for England*, 1966. Poet and playwright,
after the war becoming a journalist based in Hollywood, California)
The cactus harvest, and other poems. Fortune Press. 1946. 32 pp. por.   IWM
A letter to the living, and other poems. Putnam. [1960]. 32 pp.   OXB
see also 1, 25, 47, 65, 76

HAMBURGER, Michael (1924– . b. Berlin, Germany, coming to Britain in
1933. Educated at Westminster School, and Christ Church, Oxford. In the
Army, 1943–47, as an infantryman, then non-commissioned officer, then
Lieutenant, Royal Army Educational Corps. Served with the occupation forces
in Austria and Italy. Freelance writer, 1948–52. Held senior university posts in
Britain and United States. Married the poet Anne Beresford)
Flowering cactus: poems, 1942–49. Aldington, Kent: Hand and Flower Press.
1950. 69 pp.   IWM
In flashlight: poems. Leeds: Northern House. [1965]. 16 pp. (Northern House
pamphlet poets).   MPL
Later Hogarth; by Michael Hamburgher. Cope & Fenwick Ltd. 1945. [16] pp.
(William Tyndale series, 2).   OXB
Ownerless earth: new and selected poems. Cheadle, Cheshire: Carcanet Press.
1973. 160 pp.   OXB
see also 76

HAMBURGHER, Michael *see* **HAMBURGER, Michael**

HAMILTON, Ann (Married to Patrick Hamilton)
Poems. Mitre Press. [1946]. 32 pp.   OXB

HAMILTON, Sir George Rostrevor (1888–1967. Educated at Bradfield College, and Exeter College, Oxford. Poet of the First World War. Poet, writer and senior civil servant, a Special Commissioner of Income Tax from 1914)
Apollyon, and other poems of 1940. William Heinemann Ltd. 1941. viii, 45 pp.
                                                       IWM
Collected poems and epigrams. Heinemann. 1958. 356 pp.   MPL
Death in April, and other poems. Cambridge at the University Press. 1944. 46 pp.   IWM
The inner room: poems. William Heinemann Ltd. 1947. viii, 99 pp.   OXB
Selected poems and epigrams. William Heinemann Ltd. 1945. xiv, 152 pp.
                                                       IWM
The sober war, and other poems of 1939. William Heinemann Ltd. 1940. viii, 37 pp.   IWM
The trumpeter of Saint George: an engraving by Stephen Gooden A.R.A. with verses by G. Rostrevor Hamilton. George G. Harrap & Co. Ltd; Royal Society of Saint George. 1941. [11] pp. il.   OXB
see also   38, 42, 51, 80, 82, 84

HAMMOND, David   *see*   16

HAMMOND, Gilbert (Self-styled 'Yorkshire's Royal Rhymester'. Of Bradford)
Prosperity ahead! for Yorkshire: [*poems*]. Bradford: Author. [1945]. [20] pp.
   Title from cover.   OXB

HAMMOND, R.M.
The new British shell, and other poems. Arthur H. Stockwell, Ltd. [1941]. 12 pp.
                                                       OXB

HAMPSON, Norman (1922–   . b. Leyland, Lancashire. Educated at Manchester Grammar School, and University College, Oxford. Served in the Royal Navy as a Sub-Lieutenant on a corvette. Held university posts in Manchester and Newcastle upon Tyne, 1948–74. Appointed Professor of History, York University, 1974)   *see*   23, 25, 33, 45, 59, 76

HANKIN, John (Served in H.M. Forces)
The search, and other poems (1939–1946). Karachi: Ferozsons. [1950]. [iv], 63 pp.   IWM

HANLEY, Catherine C. Mary
"Ripples on the tide": [*poems*]. Ilfracombe: Arthur H. Stockwell, Ltd. 1952. 94 pp.   OXB

HANLON, John
Europe my confidante: [*poems*]. Outposts Publications. 1964. 20 pp.   OXB

HANMAN, Ada
From my window, and other poems. Ilfracombe: Arthur H. Stockwell, Ltd. [1944].
16 pp.   OXB

HANSON, G. (Of Yorkshire)   *see*   73

HANSSEN, Nora (Worked in the City of London)
Light after darkness: [*poems*]. Evesham: Arthur James. 1950. 77 pp.   OXB

HARBINSON, Robert, pseud. *see* **BRYANS, Robert Harbinson**, (Robert
Harbinson, pseud.)

HARBORD, John Bleasdale
Poems. Ilfracombe: Arthur H. Stockwell, Ltd. 1964. 40 pp.   OXB

HARDING, Edward Arthur (1925–46. Of Osterley, Middlesex. Educated at
Stowe School. Flight Lieutenant, Royal Air Force. Posted to Cambridge
University Air Squadron and subsequently trained in Canada. Killed in a night
flying accident on 25 April 1946)
A selection of writings and poems. [Osterley, Middlesex]: [Privately printed].
[1947]. 47 pp. por.
    For private circulation only. Cover bears initials E.A.H.   OXB

HARDING, Frank James William (Commissioned in the Army. Served in
Normandy and the Ardennes. Writer on Matthew Arnold)
War echoes over thirty years: [*poems*]. With extracts from letters of the late H.J.R.
Dunn. Ilfracombe: Arthur H. Stockwell Ltd. 1970. 92 pp.   OXB

HARDING, H.W.
The pendulum, [*and other poems*]. Williams & Norgate Ltd. 1949. 80 pp. por.
    IWM

HARDY, Henry Ernest, (Father Andrew) (1869–1946. A Roman Catholic
priest, member of the Society of the Divine Compassion. Parish priest in the
East End of London during the bombing raids)
The patch of blue, [*and other poems*]; by Father Andrew. A.R. Mowbray & Co.
Ltd. 1942. 80 pp. il.   OXB
Poems; by Father Andrew. Edited with an introduction by Hugh Collet. A.R.
Mowbray & Co. Ltd. 1950. xvi, 150 pp.   OXB
The tyranny; by Father Andrew. A.R. Mowbray & Co. Ltd. 1940. 32 pp.
    OXB

The ways of God, [and other poems]; by Father Andrew. A.R. Mowbray & Co. Ltd; New York: Morehouse-Gorham Co. 1946. 95 pp. il.   OXB

HARGRAVE, Ivan (Aircraftman, Royal Air Force)
The green fuse: [poems]. Frontispiece by Leonard Rosoman. Fortune Press [1940]. 48 pp. por.   OXB
There will be music: poems. Fortune Press. [1941]. 44 pp.   OXB
see also 1, 52

HARKER, G. (Signalman, Royal Corps of Signals. Served with the Eighth Army in the Western Desert) *see* 46

HARLEY, Gwen St. Clair
Union now; and, Winston Churchill: two poems. Ilfracombe: Arthur H. Stockwell, Ltd. [1949]. 16 pp.   OXB

HARPER, James (Served in the Army with the Military Police)
My autoverseography, 07–70: [poems]. Printed Regency Press. [1976]. 31 pp.   OXB

HARREY, Cyril
The golden chain: a sonnet sequence and other poems. Ilfracombe: Arthur H. Stockwell Ltd. 1944. 96 pp.   BPL

HARRIMAN, Jackie (A woman)
Garden of Eden, and other poems. Ilfracombe: Arthur H. Stockwell, Ltd. [1956]. 16 pp.   OXB

HARRIS, Daisy Myddelton
Here and hereafter: a selection of verse. Ilfracombe: Arthur H. Stockwell, Ltd. 1954. 32 pp.   OXB
Poems. Ilfracombe: Arthur H. Stockwell Ltd. [1968]. 75 pp.   OXB

HARRIS, Richard (1932–   . b. Limerick, Ireland. Educated at the Sacred Heart Jesuit College. Actor, trained at the London Academy of Dramatic Art. Made his stage debut in 1956, film debut in 1958)
I, in the membership of my days: poems. Michael Joseph. 1975. viii, 136 pp.   OXB

HARRIS, William Gregory (Clergyman, living at Combe Park, Bath, during the war)
Ballads of Bath, and other West-Country verses. Printed Bath: Mendip Press, Ltd. 1943. [x], 52 pp. por.   OXB

HARRISON, Elsie
True to life: [poems]. Ilfracombe: Arthur H. Stockwell. [1942]. 22 pp.   OXB

HARRISON, T.W. (Served in H.M. Forces) *see* 75

HARRISSON, John Anthony Bernard (D.S.C. Lieutenant Commander, Royal Naval Volunteer Reserve. Commanding Officer of a minesweeper)
Pad: [poems]; by Lieutenant-Commander J.A.B. Harrisson, D.S.C., R.N.V.R. and Lieutenant-Commander H.J. Galsworthy, R.N.V.R. Illustrations by M. Galsworthy. Foreword by Admiral Sir Arthur K. Waistell, K.C.B. Winchester: Warren & Son Ltd. [1944]. 55 pp. il.
    Sub-title on cover is *M/S nonsense verses*.   OXB
see also 23

HARRY, pseud.
Spare moments: [poems]; by Harry. Ilfracombe: Arthur H. Stockwell, Ltd. [1945]. 20 pp.   OXB

HARRY, R.C. Warlow- *see* **WARLOW-HARRY, R.C.**

HART, A. Graham (Member of the Institute of Journalists)
Walk I alone, [and other poems]. Mitre Press. [1947]. 48 pp.   OXB

HARTNOLL, Phyllis (1906– . b. London. Educated at St Hugh's College, Oxford. Lecturer, poet, publisher's reader. Writer on theatre, editor of *The Oxford Companion to the Theatre*. Of Lyme Regis, Dorset)
St. Luke: English poem on a sacred subject, 1947. Oxford: Basil Blackwell. 1947. 8 pp.   OXB
Winter war, and other poems. Epworth Press. 1968. 96 pp.   OXB

HARVEY, K.G. (Served with the Eighth Army) *see* 44

HARVEY, Marjorie G. (Served in the Women's Royal Air Force, working on radar)
Mimosa: poems. Bolton: Harwood Publishing Co. [1979]. 28 pp.   OXB

HARVEY, Thomas Edmund (1875–1955. b. Leeds, Yorkshire. Educated at Bootham School, York, Yorkshire College, Leeds, Christ Church, Oxford, and the Universities of Berlin and Paris. Assistant in British Museum, 1900–04, Warden of Toynbee Hall, 1906–11. Engaged in relief work in the war zone in France for the Society of Friends, 1914–20. Liberal M.P. for West Leeds, 1910–18, and for Dewsbury, 1923–24, Independent Progressive M.P. for Combined English Universities, 1937–45. Writer on Quakerism)
Songs in the night: [poems]. Malvern: Priory Press. 1942. 42 pp.   OXB

HARVEY, W.J. (Served in H.M. Forces. A member of Oxford University between 1944 and 1946)
Exile and return: poems 1943–1947. Fortune Press. [1949]. 46 pp.   IWM

The uncertain margin: [poems]. Fortune Press. [1946]. 40 pp.   IWM
see also 49

HARWOOD, Edmund
A clutch of words: [poems]. Walton-on-Thames: Outposts Publications. 1980.
12 pp.   OXB

HARWOOD, M.A. (Poet of the First World War)
Questing soul: poems, 1939–1961. Ilfracombe: Arthur H. Stockwell, Ltd. [1962].
32 pp.   OXB

HASKINS, Minnie Louise (1875–1957. Educated at Clarendon College, Clifton, and the London School of Economics. Taught in London and elsewhere, did some educational work in India and was supervisor of women's employment and industrial welfare in a factory. Poet of the First World War. A tutor at the London School of Economics until retirement in 1944. Novelist and poet)
Smoking flax: [poems]. Hodder & Stoughton. 1942. 124 pp.   MPL

HASSALL, Christopher (1912–63. Educated at Brighton College, and Wadham College, Oxford. An actor and lyricist before the war. Played Romeo in John Gielgud's production for Oxford University Dramatic Society in 1932. Served in the Royal Artillery and the Army Educational Corps, becoming a Staff Major at the War Office. Librettist, poet and biographer, he wrote musical plays and English versions of several operas. Biographer of Rupert Brooke, Stephen Haggard and Sir Edward Marsh. Hawthornden Prizewinner for *Penthesperon*, 1939. Lived in Canterbury, Kent)
Crisis: [poems]. William Heinemann Ltd. 1939. [54] pp.   OXB
S.O.S. . . 'Ludlow', [and other poems]. Jonathan Cape. 1940. 63 pp.   IWM
The slow night, and other poems 1940–1948. Title-page engraved by Joan Hassall.
Arthur Barker Ltd. [1949]. 64 pp.   BPL
Words by request: a selection of occasional pieces in verse and prose. Arthur Barker
Ltd. 1952. 94 pp.
     A limited ed. of 500 copies.   OXB
see also   21, 25, 47, 48, 76

HATT, L.J. (Leading Aircraftman, Royal Air Force. Served with the Eighth
Army) *see*   44

HAUSER, Frank Ivor (1922–   . b. Wales. Educated at Cardiff High School, and Christ Church, Oxford. Lieutenant, Royal Artillery, 1942–45, serving with the Eighth Army. Drama producer for the B.B.C., 1948–51. Director of Oxford Playhouse for sixteen years. Translated and produced the plays of Molière and Jules Romains. Freelance director) *see*   25, 44

HAWES, John (Of Northamptonshire ?)
Poems. Printed Kettering: Dalkeith Press Ltd. [1947]. 30 pp. il.
   Title from cover.   OXB

HAWES, William
The first instance: [*poems*]. Outposts Publications. 1966. 20 pp.   OXB

HAWKE-GENN, John (Served in H.M. Forces in North Africa) *see* 49

HAWKES, James R. (Of Essex) *see* 74, 75

HAWKINS, Desmond (1908– . b. Surrey. Novelist, critic, broadcaster, and
writer on Thomas Hardy. Farmed in Suffolk. Worked for B.B.C. West Region
as features producer, 1946, and Head of Programmes, 1955. Founded the
B.B.C. Natural History Unit in 1959, Controller of South & West Region,
1967–69. Of Blandford Forum, Dorset) *see* 25, 56, 76, 87

HAWKINS, J.B. (Corporal, Royal Army Medical Corps. Served in
India) *see* 43

HAWKINS, John (Of London) *see* 74

HAWKINS, Robert J. (Served in the Army, 1940–45)
Love, hope and despair: poems. Bournemouth: Apollo Press. [1975?]. ii, 24 pp.
                                              IWM

HAWKRIDGE, Margaret (Of Somerset) *see* 74

HAYCOCK, Myfanwy (Of Kensington, London)
More poems. Cardiff: Western Mail & Echo Ltd. 1945. 40 pp.   OXB
Poems. Cardiff: Western Mail & Echo Ltd. 1944. 40 pp.   OXB

HAYDON, Vernon
Poetical humour. Drawings by Raphael Nelson. John Crowther. [1943]. 32 pp.
il.   OXB

HAYMAN, Eric (Corporal. Served in South-East Asia Command) *see* 35

HAYNES, John (Spent early childhood at Albrighton, near Wolverhampton.
Did national service in the Royal Air Force. Read English at Southampton
University. Taught in Nigeria)
Sabon Gari: [*poems*]. London Magazine Editions. 1974. 51 pp.   OXB

HAYWARD, Maisie (Of London) *see* 74, 75

HAYWARD, Ruth
    Poems old and new. Ilfracombe: Arthur H. Stockwell Ltd. [1968]. 40 pp.
                                                                              OXB

HEAD, Adrian (1923– . Educated at the Royal Naval College, Dartmouth (invalided with polio), privately and at Magdalen College, Oxford. Called to the Bar in 1947, a circuit judge from 1972. Of Kings Lynn, Norfolk)
    The seven words; and, The civilian: two poems. Frederick Muller Ltd. 1946. 56 pp.
                                                                              BPL

HEALD, Rowland (Of Lancashire)   *see*   74

HEARD, George McP. (Experienced the London air raids)
    The nights of London (The blitz, 1940–41). Printed Brentford: H.R. Bohee & Son Ltd. [1944]. 12 pp.
        Title from cover.   OXB

HEATH-STUBBS, John (1918– . b. London. Educated at Bembridge School, Worcester College for the Blind, privately, and Queen's College, Oxford. A close friend of Sidney Keyes. Taught English at Hall School, Hampstead, 1944–45. Editorial assistant at the publishers Hutchinson, 1945–46. Gregory Fellow in Poetry, Leeds University, 1952–55. Held university appointments in Alexandria, Egypt, and Michigan, United States, 1955–61. Lecturer in English Literature, College of St Mark & St John, Chelsea, 1963–73. Awarded the Queen's Gold Medal for Poetry in 1973)
    The charity of the stars: [poems]. New York: William Sloane Associates, Inc. [1949]. xii, 110 pp.   BL
    The divided ways, [and other poems]. Routledge. 1946. 56 pp.   OXB
    Selected poems. Oxford University Press. 1965. xii, 144 pp.   OXB
    [Selected poems]; [by] John Heath-Stubbs, F.T. Prince, Stephen Spender. Harmondsworth, Middlesex: Penguin Books. 1972. 176 pp. (Penguin modern poets, 20).
        Not joint authorship.   MPL
see also   45, 57, 82

HEBDITCH, Wilfred Arthur (1908– . Educated at Selhurst Grammar School. A bank cashier, he served with the Auxiliary Fire Service until joining the Royal Air Force. A Squadron Leader, he spent some time in India) *see* 43

HEDLEY, Marjorie
    Selected poems 1956. Mitre Press. [1956]. 32 pp.   OXB

HELLINGS, Peter (A Welshman. Aircraftman 2, Royal Air Force. Served in the Middle East)

Firework music, [and other poems]. Fortune Press. [1950]. 70 pp.   IWM
see also   1, 25, 32, 33, 39, 63

HEMBLING, Robert E.
The mirror of life: [poems]. Ilfracombe: Arthur H. Stockwell Ltd. [1960]. 80 pp.
IWM

HENDERSON, Alexander (1910– . b. Romford, Essex. Educated at University College School and University College, London. Journalist, general writer and translator. Head of the British Information Office in Istanbul, 1940–44. Head of Balkans Section at the Ministry of Information, 1944–45. Chief Editor, United Nations Food & Agriculture Organization from 1953. Contributor to *Poetry Quarterly* and other periodicals)
The tunnelled fire: [poems]. Secker & Warburg. 1956. 71 pp.   OXB
see also   57

HENDERSON, Florence L. (Of Devonshire)   *see*   74

HENDERSON, Hamish (1919– . b. Blairgowrie, Perthshire. Educated at Blairgowrie High School, Dulwich College, and Downing College, Cambridge. Joined the Army in 1940, was commissioned in 1941 and posted to North Africa. An Intelligence Officer with the 1st South African Division at Alamein and with the 51st Highland Division in Libya, Tunisia and Sicily. On the Anzio beach-head with the 1st British Infantry Division. Recipient of the Somerset Maugham Award, 1949. Appointed to School of Scottish Studies, Edinburgh University, in 1951)
Elegies for the dead in Cyrenaica, for our own and the others. John Lehmann. 1948. 61 pp.   BPL
Elegies for the dead in Cyrenaica, for our own and the others. Edinburgh: EUSPB. [1977]. 69 pp.   OXB
see also   39, 45, 59, 63, 76

HENDERSON, Ivie Craik (Of Glasgow)   *see*   80

HENDERSON, John (1883–1965. Educated at Bancroft's School, Essex. Gazetted to King's Own Yorkshire Light Infantry in 1917. Served with 2/4th East Yorks in Bermuda, 1917–19. Manager and Secretary of Edinburgh Assurance Co., Ltd, 1927–43. Lived in Edinburgh)
Thorns and mary-lilies: [poems]. Edinburgh: William Blackwood & Sons Ltd. 1949. [x], 64 pp.   OXB

HENDRY, James Findlay (1912– . b. Glasgow. Educated at Glasgow University. Served in the Intelligence Corps. Scottish poet and leading theorist of the New Apocalypse movement, also novelist, short story writer, anthologist and writer on translation. After the war he worked in many parts of the world as a professional translator from five languages. Editor of *The Oxford Book of Scottish Verse*)

The bombed happiness, [and other poems]. Routledge. 1942. 40 pp.   IWM
The orchestral mountain: a symphonic elegy. Routledge. 1943. 56 pp.   OXB
see also   25, 33, 37, 42, 47, 56, 57, 65

HENFREY, George Patrick Basil
A wanderer's anthology: [poems]. Ilfracombe: Arthur H. Stockwell, Ltd. [1956]. 24 pp.   OXB

HENN, Thomas Rice (1901–74. Educated at Aldenham School, Hertfordshire, and St Catharine's College, Cambridge. Worked for Burmah Oil Co., 1923–25. Fellow of St Catharine's, 1926–69, working in the Faculty of English. Joined the Welch Regiment, commissioned in 1940, a Brigadier on the General Staff in 1945. Served in France and Italy. Writer on literary topics)

Shooting a bat, and other poems. Cambridge: Golden Head Press. 1964. [viii], 42 pp.   OXB

HENRI, Adrian (1932–   . b. Birkenhead, Cheshire. Educated at St Asaph Grammar School, North Wales, and King's College, Newcastle upon Tyne. Worked for ten seasons in a Rhyl fairground, later as a scenic artist, then a secondary school teacher. Taught in Manchester, then at Liverpool College of Art, 1961–67. Led the poetry/rock group Liverpool Scene, 1967–70, afterwards a freelance poet, painter, singer, songwriter and lecturer. President of Liverpool Academy of Arts from 1972)

Autobiography. Jonathan Cape. 1971. 46 pp.
    Covers the years 1932–64.   OXB

HENRY, Donald
The gift, and other poems. Ilfracombe: Arthur H. Stockwell, Ltd. [1943]. 16 pp.
    OXB

HENRY, J. (Signalman, Royal Corps of Signals. Served with the Eighth Army) *see*   44

HENRY, Patrick
Prisoners of war: a poem. Frensham, Surrey: Sceptre Press. [1970].
    A limited ed. of 100 numbered copies printed on a single sheet folded twice.
    BL

HEPBURN, Charles, pseud. *see* **JOHNSTON, Charles Hepburn**, (Charles Hepburn, pseud.)

HEPBURN, James (Served on coastal defence duty in the Orkneys)
My muse and I: [poems]. Ilfracombe: Arthur H. Stockwell, Ltd. [1959]. 32 pp.
    OXB

HEPPENSTALL, Rayner (1911–81. b. Huddersfield, Yorkshire. Educated at Leeds and Strasbourg Universities. A schoolmaster, 1934, freelance writer, 1935–39. Served in the Royal Artillery and the Royal Army Pay Corps, 1940–45. Novelist, dramatist, critic and French scholar. Worked as a producer for B.B.C. radio, 1945–67)

Poems, 1933–1945. Secker & Warburg. 1946. 100 pp.   OXB
see also   15, 42, 47, 76

HERBERT, Sir Alan Patrick (1890–1971. Educated at Winchester College, and New College, Oxford. Poet of the First World War. Served in Hawke Battalion, Royal Naval Division, 1914–17, at Gallipoli and in France, where he was wounded. Independent M.P. for Oxford University, 1935–50. Served with River Emergency Service on the Thames in London from 3 September 1939. Joined Naval Auxiliary Patrol in June 1940 as Petty Officer. Trustee of the National Maritime Museum, 1947–53. Writer of novels, musical plays and stage revues. Qualified as a barrister but never practiced)

A.T.I. 'There is no need for alarm'. Drawings by John Nicolson. Ornum Press Ltd. 1944. 32 pp. il.
   An alphabet of the war in verse.   BPL
Barbican regained. [1963]. [8] pp.   BL
Bring back the bells, [and other poems]. Methuen & Co. Ltd. 1943. 74 pp.
      BPL
'Full enjoyment', and other verses. Methuen & Co. Ltd. 1952. viii, 120 pp.
      OXB
Leave my old morale alone. New York: Doubleday & Co., Inc. 1948. [2], xxvi, 445 pp.
   Poetry and prose.   BL
'Less nonsense!', [and other poems]. Methuen & Co. Ltd. 1944. viii, 72 pp.
      BPL
Let us be gay. Methuen & Co. Ltd. 1941. 5 pp.
   'All proceeds accruing to both author and publisher will be handed over to one of the war funds'.   MPL
Let us be glum, [and other poems]. Methuen & Co. Ltd. 1941. xiv, 68 pp.
      MPL
Let us be glum, [and other poems]. 2nd ed. Methuen & Co. Ltd. 1941. xiv, 68 pp.
      BL
Light the lights: [poems]. Methuen & Co. Ltd. 1945. viii, 64 pp.   BPL
Siren song: [poems]. Methuen & Co. Ltd. 1940. x, 74 pp.   BPL
Siren song: [poems]. 3rd ed. Methuen & Co. Ltd. 1941. x, 74 pp.   CWR
   [No copy of 2nd ed. 1940 traced]
see also   23, 86

HERBERT, Wilfred
Poems. Ilfracombe: Arthur H. Stockwell, Ltd. [1942]. 16 pp.   OXB

HERBERTSON, Agnes Grozier (b. Oslo, Norway. Educated privately. Poet of the First World War. Novelist, short story writer, playwright, journalist and writer for children. Of Liskeard, Cornwall)

Here is my signature: poems. Hutchinson & Co., Ltd. [1947]. 91 pp.   IWM
Spitalfields: poems. Fortune Press. 1943. 48 pp.
    Dedicated 'to the wounded'.   IWM
This is the hour: poems. Fortune Press. [1942]. [ii], 30 pp.
    Dedicated to Winston Churchill.   IWM
see also 38

HERRIES, James William (1875– . Writer on Scotland)
Artists in cages, and other light and romantic verse. Edinburgh: Castle Wynd Printers Ltd. [1959]. [vi], 52 pp.   OXB

HERRING, Robert (1903–75. b. London. Educated at Clifton College, and King's College, Cambridge. Journalist, including film critic on *The Manchester Guardian*, 1928–38. Editor of *Life and Letters*, 1935–50)
Westward look: poems 1922–45. Glasgow: William Maclellan. [1946]. 43 pp. col. il. (Poetry Scotland series, 9).   IWM
see also 32

HERRY-PERRY, pseud.
First aid for first aiders, or, "What'll I do?": [poems]; by Herry-Perry and David York. Hutchinson & Co. Ltd. [1939]. viii, 60 pp. il.   IWM

HESELTINE, Nigel (1916– . b. London, of Irish parentage. Educated at Shrewsbury School, London University, and Trinity College, Dublin. Farmed in Ireland and Tanganyika. Worked for the United Nations Food & Agriculture Organization, mainly in Africa, 1950–65. Under-Secretary, National Development & Planning, Zambia, 1965–68. From 1968 Economic & Financial Adviser to the President of Madagascar)
The four-walled dream: poems. Fortune Press. [1941]. 53 pp.   IWM
see also 32

HESKETH, Phoebe (1909– . b. Preston, Lancashire. Educated in Southport and at Cheltenham Ladies' College. Journalist, scriptwriter and contributor to many periodicals. Worked on a northern newspaper. Awarded the Greenwood Prize of the Poetry Society, 1946. Her work was praised by Herbert Palmer and Siegfried Sassoon. Teacher of creative writing at Bolton School, 1976–78. Of Chorley, Lancashire)
Lean forward, spring!: poems. Sidgwick & Jackson. 1948. 103 pp.   MPL
see also 51

HEWINS, Elsie Vera (Of Warwickshire)   *see*   70, 71, 72, 73

HEWITT, J. (Served in H.M. Forces) *see* 75

HEWLETT, Audrey (Served in the Women's Land Army, East Sussex) *see* 50

HEYWOOD, Hugh (1896– . Educated at Haileybury School, and Trinity College, Cambridge. Served in the Manchester Regiment, 1914–17, being wounded and mentioned in despatches, and in the 74th Punjabis, Indian Army, 1917–23. Staff Captain, 1919–22. Ordained in 1928. Fellow and Dean of Gonville & Caius College, Cambridge, 1928–45. Writer on Christianity)
On a golden thread: [*poems*]. Printed Southwell, Nottinghamshire: Sydney Wood Ltd. 1960. [21] pp.   OXB

HIAWATHA, pseud.   *see*   **KIRKWOOD, Robert**, (Hiawatha, pseud.)

HICKFORD, Ralph
Hope from the heart: poems. Ilfracombe: Arthur H. Stockwell. [1943]. 40 pp.
                                                                              OXB

HICKS, John Searle (Major, Royal Marines)
Salvoes from a stone frigate: drawings and verses. Methuen & Co. Ltd. 1946. 48 pp. il.   IWM

HIER, James
The gift, and other poems. Ilfracombe: Arthur H. Stockwell, Ltd. [1945]. 16 pp.
                                                                              OXB

HIGGINS, Alexander George McLennan Pearce (Of Holywell Rectory, St Ives, Huntingdonshire)
Thirty-six sonnets. [St Ives], Huntingdonshire: Author. [1957]. [iv], 35 pp.
                                                                              OXB

HIGGINSON, Thomas Boyd
Juvenilia: [*poems*]. Mitre Press. [1960]. 31 pp.   MPL

HIGHAM, E.C. (Served in the Army. Of Ashford, Middlesex)
Middle East musings: [*poems*]. Ashford, Middlesex: Author. [1946]. 40 pp.
    Title from cover.   OXB

HILDGARD, R. (Served in the Western Desert) *see* 63

HILL, Brian (1896–1979. b. Hampstead, London. Educated at Merchant Taylors' School, and Wadham College, Oxford. Poet of the First World War. Served as Second-Lieutenant in the Durham Light Infantry. Worked as a chartered accountant, 1924–32, Assistant Publicity Manager, Gas Council,

1932–62. An air raid warden during the war. Novelist, poet and contributor to many periodicals)

Collected poems and translations. Southrepps, Norfolk: Warren House Press. 1974. 122 pp.   OXB

The sheltering tree, [and other poems]. Favil Press. 1945. 24 pp.   OXB

Take all colours: [poems]. Foreword by Clifford Bax. Favil Press. 1943. 24 pp.
                                                                                                                                     MPL

HILL, D.R. Oakley- *see* **OAKLEY-HILL, D.R.**

HILL, Geoffrey (1932–   . b. Bromsgrove, Worcestershire. Educated at Bromsgrove County High School, and Keble College, Oxford. Professor of English, Leeds University, then Fellow of Emmanuel College, Cambridge, from 1981. Recipient of many literary prizes)

For the unfallen: poems 1952–1958. Andre Deutsch. 1959. 59 pp.   OXB

King Log: [poems]. Andre Deutsch. 1968. 70 pp.   OXB

Preghiere: [poems]. Northern House Pamphlet Poets. 1964. [13] pp.

   Hand-set at the School of English, University of Leeds.   OXB

[Selected poems]; [by] Edwin Brock, Geoffrey Hill, Stevie Smith. Harmondsworth, Middlesex: Penguin Books. 1966. 128 pp. (Penguin modern poets, 8).

   Not joint authorship. No war poetry by Smith.   MPL

HILL, J.W.

The soul in splendour: [poems]. Ilfracombe: Arthur H. Stockwell Ltd. [1962]. 68 pp.   OXB

HILLAS, Joyce

They also serve. A. Brown & Sons, Ltd. [1944]. viii, 49 pp.

   'Proceeds from the sale of this book will be devoted to the benefit of the Red Cross and St. John's Organisation'.   IWM

HILLS, Janet (1919–56. Educated at Somerville College, Oxford. Joined the Women's Royal Naval Service, serving as an officer in Intelligence and Education departments. With the British Military Government in Berlin, 1945–46)

Fragments. Stroud: Harold, Margaret & Clare Hills. [1956]. [vi], 144 pp. por.

   Poetry and prose.   OXB

HINE, Beatrice Mary

The homward road, and other poems. Ilfracombe: Arthur H. Stockwell, Ltd. [1943]. 24 pp.   OXB

HOARE, Edward Godfrey (Poet of the First World War. Served as Lieutenant-Colonel, King's Own Royal Lancaster Regiment)

One hour together: [poems]. Frederick Muller Ltd. 1945. 80 pp.   OXB

HOBLEY, Leonard (1903– . A schoolmaster at Brighton, Sussex, 1929–63. Writer of history and geography school textbooks and of general non-fiction for children. Of Hove, Sussex)

Doubts and affirmations: [*poems*]. Walton-on-Thames: Outposts Publications. 1978. 48 pp.   OXB

HOBSBAUM, Philip (1932– . b. London, brought up in Bradford, Yorkshire. Educated at Bellevue Grammar School, Downing College, Cambridge, and Sheffield University. F.R. Leavis and William Empson were influential teachers. Lecturer in English at Queen's University, Belfast, 1962–66. Appointed Lecturer in English at Glasgow University in 1966, Reader in 1979. Poet and literary critic)

The place's fault, and other poems. Macmillan & Co. Ltd. 1964. x, 54 pp.
                                                                                    MPL

HODGE, Alan (1915–79. b. Scarborough, Yorkshire. Educated at Liverpool Collegiate School, and Oriel College, Oxford. Assistant Private Secretary to the Minister of Information, 1941–45. Journalist, historian and researcher. Editor of *History Today* from 1951)

Work in hand: [*poems*]; [by] Alan Hodge, Norman Cameron, Robert Graves. Hogarth Press. 1942. 64 pp.

   Not joint authorship.   BL

HODGES, Cyril, (Cyril Hughes, pseud.) (1915– . b. Cardiff. Small-scale industrial manufacturer in aeronautical engineering from 1948. Of Penarth, Glamorgan) *see* 19, 25

HODGKINSON, Margaret (Of Derbyshire. Writer on the Brontës, and playwright) *see* 70

HODGSON, Ethel, (Lakeland Parson's Daughter, pseud.) (Daughter of the Reverend John Hodgson, Vicar of Wasdale, 1892–1920)

Poems by a Lakeland parson's daughter. Ilfracombe: Arthur H. Stockwell, Ltd. [1953]. 32 pp.   OXB

HODGSON, Thomas Rahilley (1915–41. Wrote verse from the age of seventeen. Pilot Officer, Royal Air Force. Shot down and killed whilst flying on 17 May 1941)

This life, this death: [*poems*]. Routledge. 1942. 52 pp.   BPL
see also 1, 25, 76

HOFFMAN, John Kenneth Gibson (1913– . b. York. Educated at Ripon School and Cheltenham Training College. Had war service in the Middle East and the Mediterranean. Of Chesterfield, Derbyshire)

The immortal home: poems. Fortune Press. 1949. 56 pp.   OXB
The white radiance: poems. Fortune Press. 1948. 40 pp.
    Dedicated to Lady Margaret Sackville.   IWM

HOGG, Quintin, Lord Hailsham (1907–   . Educated at Eton College, and Christ Church, Oxford, where he was President of the Oxford Union Society in 1929. Barrister, Lincoln's Inn, 1932. Commissioned in The Rifle Brigade, September 1939, serving in the Western Desert, Egypt, Palestine and Syria. Held many important posts, including that of Lord High Chancellor of Great Britain. Writer on law and politics)
The devil's own song, and other verses. Hodder & Stoughton. 1968. [63] pp.
                                                                          IWM

see also 81

HOGHTON, Sir Anthony De   *see*   **DE HOGHTON, Sir Anthony**

HOLBROOK, David (1923–   . b. Norwich. Educated at Downing College, Cambridge. Tank troop officer, explosives and intelligence officer, East Riding of Yorkshire Yeomanry, serving in Europe, 1942–45. Assistant editor to Edgell Rickword on *Our Time* magazine, 1947–48. Assistant editor at Bureau of Current Affairs, 1948–51. Tutor in adult education and schoolteacher, 1951–61. Fellow of King's College, Cambridge, 1961–65. Writer-in-Residence, Dartington Hall, 1970–73. Poet, anthologist and writer of textbooks for children and student teachers)
Selected poems, 1961–1978. Anvil Press Poetry; Wildwood House. 1980. 143 pp.
                                                                          OXB

HOLDEN, Beatrice (Mrs Holden)
They're away: [poems]. Collins. 1945. 43 pp. il., col. il.   OXB

HOLDEN, Edward Arthur Ramsey
Twelve poems. Ilfracombe: Arthur H. Stockwell, Ltd. [1950]. 15 pp.   OXB

HOLDEN, Molly (1927–81. b. London. Her grandfather was the novelist Henry Gilbert. Educated at Commonweal Grammar School, Swindon, and King's College, London. Married Alan Holden, a schoolmaster. Poet, novelist and writer of children's fiction, she received an Arts Council Award in 1970 and a Cholmondeley Award in 1972. Lived at Bromsgrove, Worcestershire)
Air and chill earth: [poems]. Chatto & Windus; Hogarth Press. 1971. 72 pp.
(Phoenix living poets).   OXB

HOLDING, Cynthia Davril-   *see*   **DAVRIL-HOLDING, Cynthia**

HOLE, Edward Sidney (Served as a Fire Watcher)
Canonbury Watch: [poems]. Canonbury Square Fire Guard. 1943. [48] pp.
                                                                          IWM

Canonbury Watch farewell: [*poems*]; by E.S.H. [Privately printed]. [1945]. [32] pp
    Title from cover.   OXB

HOLE, W.G. (Poet of the First World War. Playwright as well as poet. Contributed to many periodicals)
John Englishman: an appreciation of the ordinary, practical-minded everyday Englishman, with something of an exposition of his views and character and of the part he and his kinsmen by blood and adoption have played and still are playing in the world to-day. Cambridge at the University Press. 1945. [vi], 82 pp.   OXB

HOLFORD, Ernest Roland
    Peasant songs and poems. Ilfracombe: Arthur H. Stockwell, Ltd. [1943]. 72 pp.
                                                                   OXB

HOLLAND, David Cuthbert Lyall (1915– . Educated at Eton College, and Trinity College, Cambridge. Served as Lieutenant in the Royal Sussex Regiment. Captured in France in 1940, held prisoner of war in Germany until 1945. Appointed to the House of Commons Library in 1946, its Librarian from 1967 to 1976) *see* 67

HOLLAND, Dick
    Some memories: [*poems*]. Ilfracombe: Arthur H. Stockwell, Ltd. [1944]. 16 pp.
                                                                     OXB

HOLLIS, Christopher (1902–77. Educated at Eton College, and Balliol College, Oxford. Toured abroad as a member of the Oxford Union Debating Society, 1924–25. Assistant master at Stonyhurst College, 1925–35. Engaged in economic research at Notre Dame University, Indiana, 1935–39. Served with the Royal Air Force during the war. Conservative M.P. for Devizes, Wiltshire, 1945–55. Chairman of the publishers Hollis & Carter) *see* 84

HOLLOWAY, Geoffrey (1918– . Library assistant with Shropshire County Council at Shrewsbury, 1935–39 and 1946. Social worker at Hatton Psychiatric Hospital, Warwick, 1946–48. Officer with Prisoner's Aid Society at Lincoln, 1950–51. Hospital porter at Lincoln Sanitorium, 1951–53. Mental health worker with Westmorland County Council at Kendal, 1953–74. Social worker with Cumbria County Council from 1974)
    All I can say: [*poems*]. Anvil Press; Rex Collings. 1978. 95 pp.   OXB
    Rhine jump, [*and other poems*]. London Magazine Editions. 1974. 51 pp.
    'To the memory of 225 Para Field Ambulance'.   OXB

HOLLOWAY, Mark (1917– . b. London. Educated at Bryanston School, and Trinity Hall, Cambridge. A conscientious objector. Poet and biographer) *see* 25, 52

HOLLOWAY, W.G. (Served in the Royal Artillery. His regiment was hammered in the First Battle of Alamein, returning to base at Almaza, Cairo) *see* 63

HOLME, Arthur
Modern poems. Ilfracombe: Arthur H. Stockwell, Ltd. 1946. 32 pp. OXB

HOLMES, Agnes Dorothy (Writer on Bristol and Bath. Of Shropshire)
Storm wrack, [and other poems]. Written and illustrated by A. Dorothy Holmes. Bath: Fyson & Co., Ltd. [1944]. 23 pp. il.
A limited ed. OXB
This lovely land, [and other poems]. Written and illustrated by A. Dorothy Holmes. Shrewsbury: Wilding & Son, Ltd. 1943. 47 pp. il. OXB
This lovely land, [and other poems]. 2nd ed. Shrewsbury: Wilding & Son, Ltd. 1943. 47 pp. il. (by the author). BL

HOLSTEIN, Peter A.
Life with Peter Holstein: [poems]. Ilfracombe: Arthur H. Stockwell Ltd. 1978. 16 pp. OXB

HOLT, Doris Margaret
Forty years on: [poems]. Mitre Press. [1952]. 32 pp. OXB

HOOLEY, Teresa (1888–1973. b. Risley Lodge, Derbyshire. Educated by private governess and at Howard College, Bedford. Poet of the First World War. Well known as a public speaker. Lived in Derby latterly)
Selected poems. Drawings by Freda Nichols. Jonathan Cape. 1947. 127 pp. il.
MPL
The singing heart: poems. Frederick Muller Ltd. 1944. 87 pp. IWM
Wintergreen: poems. Stoke-on-Trent: A.J. Chapple. 1959. 32 pp. BL

HOPE, Margaret, pseud. *see* **WICKSTEED, Margaret Hope**, (Margaret Hope, pseud.)

HOPEWELL, Peter
Broadway, and other poems. Ilfracombe: Arthur H. Stockwell, Ltd. [1944]. 16 pp. OXB

HOPKINS, Kenneth (1914– . b. Bournemouth. Educated at St Peter's School, Bournemouth. Served in the Army during the war. Literary editor of *Everybody's* magazine, 1949–54. Professor of English, Southern Illinois University from 1964. A prolific and versatile writer of poetry, biography, mystery novels, children's books and film scripts. Of Southrepps, Norfolk)

Collected poems, 1935–1965. Carbondale and Edwardsville: Southern Illinois University Press. [1965]. xvi, 232 pp.   OXB
   Love and Elizabeth: poems. Sylvan Press. 1944. 50 pp.
     A limited ed. of 1,200 copies.   IWM
   Miscellany poems. Grasshopper Press. 1946. [24] pp.   OXB
   Songs and sonnets, made in the time of the late wars and now newly imprinted. Grasshopper Press. 1947. 16 pp.
     A limited ed. of 250 copies.   OXB
see also   86

HOPKINSON, Joyce (Of Berkshire)   *see*   75

HOPKINSON, Peter R. (Served in North Africa)   *see*   63

HOPWOOD, Ronald Arthur (1868–1949. Educated at Cheam School. Poet of the First World War and writer on naval history. Specialized in gunnery, becoming an Admiral. Vice-President of Ordnance Committee, 1917–18. General Secretary of the Navy League, 1919–22. Lived in London latterly)
   The laws of the Navy, and other poems. John Murray. 1951. viii, 71 pp.   OXB

HORE-RUTHVEN, Hon. Patrick (Captain, Rifle Brigade. Fought in the Western Desert, becoming liaison officer to the small detachment of Frenchmen fighting in the Middle East. In the Syrian Campaign he was liaison officer to the 7th Australian Division. Eventually joined a Commando Unit operating in Tripolitania, where he was killed)
   Desert warrior: poems. 2nd ed. John Murray. 1944. 28 pp. por.
     1st ed. published under title *The Happy Warrior.*   BPL
   The happy warrior: poems. Angus & Robertson Ltd. 1943. [xii], 18 pp. por.
                                       BL

HORLE, Denis (Served in North Africa and Italy)
   A sword for Redonda: [poems]. Ilfracombe: Arthur H. Stockwell, Ltd. 1955. 16 pp.
     Dedicated to John Gawsworth.   OXB

HORNE, H.R. (Lieutenant, Sherwood Rangers. Captured in Crete in 1941, held prisoner of war in Germany until 1945)   *see*   67

HORNE, Margaret   *see*   22

HOROBIN, Sir Ian (1899–1976. b. Cambridge. Educated at Highgate School, and Sidney Sussex College, Cambridge. Served in the Royal Air Force as a Flight Lieutenant, 1918–19. Rejoined in 1939, rising to rank of Squadron

Leader before being captured in Java. Warden of Mansfield House University Settlement, 1923–61. Conservative M.P. for Oldham East, 1951–59).

Collected poems. With introductions by Sir John Betjeman and Laurens van der Post. Jameson Press. 1973. 183 pp.   MPL

HORSEBOX, pseud. *see* 23

HORSLEY, Terence (Served in Royal Naval Volunteer Reserve. Writer on fishing and other sports) *see* 61, 62

HORSTMANN, Lorna (Writer on spiritual healing)
The wheel. Mitre Press. [1950]. 22 pp.   OXB

HOTHERSALL, Elena D.
Poems. Ilfracombe: Arthur H. Stockwell Ltd. [1968]. 24 pp.   OXB

HOUSEHOLD, Horace West (1870–1954. b. King's Lynn, Norfolk. Educated at Shrewsbury School, and Christ Church, Oxford. Taught at Clifton College then became a Junior Inspector to the Board of Education, later Secretary for Education to Gloucester Council. Writer on sea power. Of Cheltenham, Gloucestershire)
An evening of mid-June, and other poems. Derby: Pilgrim Press Ltd. [1949]. 32 pp.   OXB

HOUSELANDER, Caryll (A woman. Writer on Roman Catholicism)
The flowering tree: [poems]. Sheed & Ward. 1945. 128 pp. il.   OXB
The flowering tree: [poems]. [Paperback] ed. Sheed & Ward. 1979. 128 pp.   OXB

HOUSTON, Libby (1941– . b. North London. Educated at Oxford University. A 'working poet', reading and talking about her work all over Britain, running poetry workshops, judging local poetry competitions, etc. A regular contributor to B.B.C. Schools Radio and poetry tutor for the Arvon Foundation, she established a poetry workshop in Bristol)
A stained glass raree show: [poems]. Allison & Busby Ltd. 1967. [ii], 56 pp. il. (by Malcolm Dean).   OXB

HOUSTON, Ursula
All Hallowe'en, and other verse. Ilfracombe: Arthur H. Stockwell, Ltd. [1945]. 20 pp.   OXB

HOWARD, Katherine
Poems for H.M. Forces, and a tribute to the Americans. Ilfracombe: Arthur H. Stockwell, Ltd. [1943]. 16 pp.   OXB

HOWARD, Margaret
Songs from a too late summer: [*poems*]. Walton-on-Thames: Outposts Publications. 1975. 40 pp.   OXB

HOWARD, Peter (1908–   . b. Maidenhead, Berkshire. Educated at Mill Hill School and Oxford University. His brother fought at Arnhem. Writer on Moral Re-armament, playwright and contributor to many periodicals. A Liveryman of the Worshipful Company of Wheelwrights. Of Sudbury, Suffolk)
Above the smoke and stir: [*poems*]. Grosvenor Books. 1975. [4], iv, 85 pp.
                                                                OXB

HOWARD, R.C.M. (Journalist on the *Sunday Chronicle* before the war. Served in the Royal Navy. A contributor to *Penguin New Writing*) *see* 23, 76

HOWARD, W.W.
Alpha and omega: [*poems*]. Ilfracombe: Arthur H. Stockwell, Ltd. 1961. 20 pp.
                                                                OXB

HOWARTH, Herbert (Worked for the British Information Office in Jerusalem. Writer on English literary topics) *see* 31

HOWE, Irene (Served in H.M. Forces) *see* 74

HOWE, Leslie (–1975. Bombardier, Royal Artillery, with the 7th Armoured Division, the original 'Desert Rats'. Returned to England in 1941 after being blinded. His sight was later partially restored) *see* 63

HOWELL, Thomas William (Served in India)
Mother India, and other poems. Ilfracombe: Arthur H. Stockwell, Ltd. 1951. 20 pp.   OXB

HOWES, Libby
Under the mushroom cloud: [*poems*]. Eastbourne: Downlander Publishing. 1980. 24 pp.   OXB

HOWLING, W.
The child who sat upon a stair, and other poems. Ilfracombe: Arthur H. Stockwell, Ltd. [1960]. 40 pp.   OXB

HOWORTH, Margaret *see* 78

HOWORTH, Muriel K. (b. Bishop Auckland, Durham. Educated at Canon Holland School, Royal Academy of Music, London, and in Paris and Vienna. Held wartime appointments in the Army Film Unit, the Ministry of Supply, the

Ministry of Information and the Royal Aircraft Establishment. Writer on the atom and nuclear energy. Of Eastbourne)
Poems and translations. Fortune Press. [1946]. 36 pp.　　　　　　　BPL

HOWROYD, Barbara (Third Officer, Women's Royal Naval Service. Served on H.M.S. *Nile*, Fleet Mail & Censor Office at Ras-el-Tin, 1943–46. Of Ilminster, Somerset) *see* 63

HUBBACK, Judith (1917– . b. London. Educated at Downe House, Newbury, Newnham College, Cambridge, and in Paris. Taught history at various schools. Married D.F. Hubback)
Islands and people, [and other poems]. Outposts Publications. 1964. 28 pp.
　　　　　　　OXB

HUDDLESTON, John D. (Served in H.M. Forces) *see* 75

HUDIS, Norman (1922– . b. Stepney, London. Served in the Royal Air Force, 1941–45, in the Middle East, including a brief time with a desert fighter squadron. Finally on the staff of *Air Force News* based at Middle East H.Q. Of Los Angeles, California) *see* 39, 63

HUDSON, Denis (Served in the Royal Navy as an Ordinary Seaman) *see* 38

HUGGINS, E.
Mixed verse. Ilfracombe: Arthur H. Stockwell, Ltd. [1962]. 63 pp.　　OXB

HUGGINS, M. Roper- *see* **ROPER-HUGGINS, M.**

HUGHES, Audrey (Of Somerset?)
Indeed to goodness! : a collection of childhood memories: [poems]. Printed Yeovil: Yeoprint. [1978]. 31 pp. il. (by Gagliardi).　　　　　　　OXB

HUGHES, Cyril, pseud. *see* **HODGES, Cyril**, (Cyril Hughes, pseud.)

HUGHES, Donald
Blitz bits, and other verse. Printed Bristol: Arrowsmith. 1941. 20 pp.　　OXB

HUGHES, Edward William
Poems. Ilfracombe: Arthur H. Stockwell, Ltd. 1943. 16 pp.　　　　　OXB

HUGHES, F.E. (Bombardier, Royal Artillery. Served with the Eighth Army in the Western Desert) *see* 46

HUGHES, Pennethorne (1907–67. b. Isle of Wight, son of a clergyman.

Educated at Hertford College, Oxford. Taught history at Oundle School, 1930–35. On B.B.C. staff, 1935–63, successively talks producer, head of programming for West of England, Director in Middle East, 1942–45, Director in New Delhi, 1945–47, then Head of Eastern Service. Finally in charge of Staff Training Department)

Thirty eight poems. Chosen and with a foreword by Geoffrey Grigson. Contributions from John Betjeman and John Arlott. John Baker. 1970. 61 pp.

MPL

HUGHES, Ted (1930– . b. Mytholmroyd, West Riding of Yorkshire. Educated at Mexborough Grammar School, and Pembroke College, Cambridge. Did two years national service before going up to Cambridge. Married American poet Sylvia Plath in 1956. Poet, playwright and writer of children's fiction. He worked as a rose gardener, a night-watchman, and a reader for Rank Brothers at Pinewood Film Studios. Winner of first prize, Guinness Poetry Awards, 1958, Guggenheim Fellowship, 1959–60, Somerset Maugham Award, 1960, and Hawthornden Prize, 1961. Appointed Poet Laureate in 1984 in succession to Sir John Betjeman)

The hawk in the rain, [and other poems]. Faber & Faber. 1957. 59 pp.   OXB
The hawk in the rain, [and other poems]. New York: Harper & Brothers. 1957. xii, 52 pp.   BL
The hawk in the rain, [and other poems]. Faber & Faber. 1968. 59 pp. (Faber paper covered editions).   OXB
Moortown: [poems]. Faber & Faber. 1979. 171 pp. il. (by Leonard Baskin).

OXB

HUGHES, W.R. (A Quaker)
The seeker, and other poems. Published by the author and obtainable from Friends' Book Centre. 1945. 63 pp.   IWM

HULL, Anthony
From a foreign shore: poems written in Mexico City, 1951–1954. Oxford: Scrivener Press. 1956. 60 pp.   OXB

HULTON, Paul (1918– . Educated at Kingswood School, and Worcester College, Oxford. Major in Army Educational Corps. Served four years in India and South-East Asia, much of the time as an artillery officer) *see* 43

HUMPAGE, Francis E.
Moon over Cairo, and other poems. Ilfracombe: Arthur H. Stockwell, Ltd. [1943]. 16 pp.   OXB

HUMPHREYS, Christmas (1901–83. b. London. Educated at Malvern College, and Trinity Hall, Cambridge. Called to the Bar in 1924, becoming a Q.C. in 1959. Held many important legal appointments, including that of circuit judge, 1968–76. Founding President of Buddhist Lodge, now the Buddhist Society)

Buddhist poems: a selection, 1920–1970. Goerge Allen & Unwin Ltd. 1971. 61 pp.
    Published for the Buddhist Society.   OXB
Poems of peace and war. Favil Press. 1941. [x], 53 pp.   BPL
Seagulls, and other poems. Favil Press. 1942. [vi], 40 pp.   IWM
Shadows, and other poems. Favil Press. 1945. 48 pp.   MPL
see also 84

HUMPHREYS, Emyr (1919– . b. Prestatyn, North Wales. Educated at University College, Aberystwyth, and University College, Bangor. A teacher in Wimbledon and Pwllheli, 1948–54. Producer for B.B.C. radio at Cardiff, 1955–58, and drama producer, B.B.C. television, 1958–62. Lecturer in drama at University College, Bangor, 1965–72. Novelist, winner of the Hawthornden Prize, 1959, and Welsh Arts Council Prize, 1972. Gregynog Arts Fellow, 1974–75) *see* 38

HUMPHRIES, C. (Served in H.M. Forces) *see* 75

HUNKIN, Gladys (Of St Ives, Cornwall)
Cornish crystal: poems. Fortune Press. [1952]. 64 pp.   OXB

HUNT, W.
Love's reminiscences, and other verse. Ilfracombe: Arthur H. Stockwell, Ltd. 1949. 24 pp.   OXB

HUNTER, Geoffrey (–1944. Educated at Winchester College and Oxford University. Flight Lieutenant, Royal Air Force. Killed in action over Germany in September 1944 and buried in Germany)
Twenty-six poems. Edited with a biographical introduction by Ralph Elwell-Sutton. Fortune Press. 1948. 60 pp. por.   OXB

HUNTER, R.J. (Assistant Ship's Barber, Royal Navy. Served on H.M. Motor Vessel *Rangitiki*) *see* 23

HUNTER, Robert (Served in South-East Asia Command) *see* 35

HURRY, Colin (Poet of the First World War)
Receding galaxy: a selection of verse, serious, light and flippant. Nicol Books. 1964. 57 pp.   OXB

HUSSEY, Effie Howie (Of West Lothian, Scotland)
Times and seasons: a book of verse. Ilfracombe: Arthur H. Stockwell, Ltd. 1954. 64 pp.   OXB

HUTCHESON, William James Fraser (1883– . b. Inverness. Served in the First World War with the 17th Highland Light Infantry. Of Milngavie, Dunbartonshire) *see* 42

HUTCHINSON, Erik (1916– . b. Nottingham. Educated privately. Novelist, playwright and journalist. Of Nottinghamshire) *see* 70, 71

HUTCHINSON, W.E. (Flying Officer, Royal Air Force. Served with the Eighth Army in Italy) *see* 44

HUTHWAITE, Pauline (Of Hawksworth, Nottinghamshire, and Grantham, Lincolnshire) *see* 21

HUTTON, Brian (A member of Oxford University between 1944 and 1946) *see* 54

HUTTON, T.B. (Served in H.M. Forces) *see* 49

HUXTABLE, Marjorie, (Simon Dare, pseud.) (1897– . b. Bristol. Educated at Mortimer House, Clifton. Novelist, and contributor to many newspapers and magazines)
These things he gave: poems; by Simon Dare. John Long Ltd. [1946]. 40 pp.
OXB

HYDE, W.F.M. (Signalman, Royal Corps of Signals. Served with the Eighth Army) *see* 44

HYLAND, Esther (Of Surrey) *see* 75

I.D.L. *see* **L., I.D.**

ILEY, Graeme (1931–50. Educated at Robert Richardson Grammar School, Ryhope, County Durham)
First awakening: the collected poems of Graeme Iley. Foreword by the Reverend James Duncan, O.B.E., M.A., Rector of Easington. Gateshead on Tyne: Northumberland Press Ltd. [1951]. 67 pp. por. OXB

ILIEW, Ilko
The bells' gentle thunder: poems. Poets' and Painters' Press. 1959. 93 pp. OXB

ILINSKA, Zofia (Lived in London during the war. Translated T.S. Eliot's *Murder in the Cathedral* into Polish)
Missing: eight poems. Glasgow: Polish Library. [1945]. 23 pp. OXB

INMAN, H.J. (Captain, Oxfordshire & Buckinghamshire Light Infantry)
A score of verses. Printed Buckenham's. [1945]. 33 pp. OXB

IREMONGER, Edmund (Spent fourteen years in the Army. Life President of the International Federation of Allied Ex-Servicemen. Awarded the Polish Freedom Cross and the Silver Medal of the City of Paris. Of Sussex)
With rhyme and reason: [poems]. Sidlesham, Sussex: Durley Press. 1980. 93 pp.
OXB

IREMONGER, Valentin (1918– . b. Dublin. Educated at the Christian Brothers School, Dublin, and the Abbey Theatre School of Acting, Dublin. Worked in Dublin with the Abbey Theatre, 1939–40, and the Gate Theatre, 1942–44. Won the AE Memorial Award in 1945 for the best literary work by an Irish writer under thirty-five. Entered the Irish Foreign Service in 1946. Ambassador to Sweden, Norway & Finland, 1964–68, Ambassador to India, 1968–73, and Ambassador to Luxembourg from 1973)
Horan's field, and other reservations: [poems]. Dublin: Dolmen Press. 1972. 80 pp.
OXB
Reservations: poems. Dublin: Envoy. 1950. 53 pp. OXB
Reservations: poems. Macmillan & Co. Ltd. 1950. 53 pp. OXB

IRVINE, John (Of Belfast)
Selected poems. [Belfast]: Arden Press. 1948. xiv, 124 pp. por. OXB
With no changed voice: poems. Belfast: William Mullan & Son; Dublin: Talbot Press Ltd. 1946. 52 pp. OXB

IRWIN, Dorcas W.
Flights of fancy: [poems]. Arthur H. Stockwell, Ltd. [1940]. 15 pp. OXB
Happy rhymes for the air raid shelter. Ilfracombe: Arthur H. Stockwell, Ltd. [1942]. 16 pp. OXB

IRWIN, Russell, pseud. *see* **RUSSELL, Peter,** (Russell Irwin, pseud.)

ISA, pseud.
Progressive poetry by the unknown poet Isa. Ilfracombe: Arthur H. Stockwell Ltd. 1972. 114 pp. OXB

ISAACS, Barbara M.
This England, and other poems. Ilfracombe: Arthur H. Stockwell, Ltd. 1946. 16 pp. OXB

IVESON, Stanley Eric (Radio Officer in the Merchant Navy)
The anchor is dropped: a booklet of verse. Ilfracombe: Arthur H. Stockwell, Ltd. 1947. 20 pp. OXB

J.F.T. *see* **T., J.F.**

J.G.M. *see* **M., J.G.**

J.P.C. *see* **C., J.P.**

JACK, Sheila Beryl (1918–   . Educated at Derby Diocesan Training College for Teachers. A remedial reading teacher. Member of Shropshire County Council and a school manager. Member of Wrockwardine Parish Council)
Another thirty-two poems. Ilfracombe: Arthur H. Stockwell, Ltd. 1974. 44 pp.
OXB

JACKSON, Ada (b. Warwickshire. E.V. Lucas named her 'the English Emily Dickinson' while in America she was called 'the Elizabeth Barrett Browning of our time'. Of Staffordshire)
Against the sun: [*poems*]. New York: Macmillan Co. 1940. xiv, 112 pp.   BL
Behold the Jew: the Greenwood Prize Poem for 1943. Poetry Society. [1943]. 20 pp.
     Reprinted from *The Poetry Review*, July–August 1943.   OXB
World in labour, [*and other poems*]. Birmingham: Cornish Brothers Ltd. 1942.
[viii], 48 pp.   IWM
see also   38, 41, 42

JACKSON, Edith W. (Of Lancashire)   *see*   74

JACKSON, Marion (Of Wakefield, Yorkshire)
Fragrant petals, [*and other poems*]. Ilfracombe: Arthur H. Stockwell, Ltd. 1978.
48 pp.   OXB

JACKSON, Norman (1923–   . b. Hull, Yorkshire. Educated at Hull College of Technology, Hull College of Arts & Crafts, Fircroft College, Birmingham, and Hull University. Worked in the building trade before winning scholarships to study painting and drawing. A painter, 1957–60, exhibiting at several galleries in the north of England. Awarded a Fulbright Scholarship and a lectureship at Iowa University, 1966–67. Gulbenkian Fellow in Poetry, Keele University, 1967–68, afterwards lecturer in creative writing)
Waking in the dark, [*and other poems*]. Beverley: Paston Press. 1980. 36 pp.
OXB

JACKSON, Winifred A. (Of Sussex?)
Dreams and realities: [*poems*]. Printed Eastbourne: O.C. Barley. [1940?]. 28 pp.
BPL

JAEL, pseud.   *see*   **WOODS, John L.**, (Jael, pseud.)

JAMES, David B.S.
Reflections and recollections (in verse). Ilfracombe: Arthur H. Stockwell, Ltd. [1943]. 62 pp. OXB

JAMES, Diana (Her work appeared in the *Spectator* when she was only fifteen and sixteen years of age. Married a farmer in Gloucestershire)
The tune of flutes: [*poems*]. Routledge. 1945. 44 pp. IWM
see also 41

JAMES, Edwin Stanley (Of Wales. Wrote poetry in the Welsh language)
Short measures: [*poems*]. Abingdon, Berks.: Abbey Press. [1949]. 55 pp.
OXB

JAMES, Flower (Of Worthing, Sussex)
Lest we forget: [*poems*]. Illustrations by Eileen Startup. Worthing: Privately published. [1956]. 40 pp. il. IWM

JAMES, J.D. (Served in H.M. Forces. A member of Oxford University between 1944 and 1946)
Early poems; by Raymond Chapman and J.D. James. Fortune Press. [1946]. 64 pp.
Not joint authorship. OXB
see also 49, 54

JAMES, Jessie
Harvest home: [*poems*]. Ilfracombe: Arthur H. Stockwell, Ltd. [1958]. 26 pp.
OXB

JAMES, Jonathan
Token, and other poems. Ilfracombe: Arthur H. Stockwell, Ltd. 1946. 56 pp.
OXB

JAMES, Joshua
Tarantell, and other poems. John Lane the Bodley Head. 1945. 45 pp. OXB

JAMES, Lynda M. (Of Glamorganshire) *see* 75

JAMES, Patrick
One aspect: [*poems*]. Ilfracombe: Arthur H. Stockwell, Ltd. [1955]. 16 pp.
OXB

JAMES, Thomas Irving (A novelist)
Stammerings, [*and other poems*]. Fortune Press. 1945. 32 pp. IWM
Tomorrow is mine, [*and other poems*]. Bath: Venturebooks Ltd. 1947. viii, 55 pp.
OXB

JAMES, Walter J.
Realism, rhyme and reason: verse. Ilfracombe: Arthur H. Stockwell, Ltd. 1945.
16 pp. OXB

JAMES, Sir William (1881–1973. Educated at Trinity College, Glenalmond.
Entered the Royal Navy, becoming Sub-Lieutenant in 1901 and Captain in
1918. Poet of the First World War. Chief-of-Staff, Atlantic Fleet, 1929–30. Held
other naval appointments, including Commander-in-Chief, Portsmouth,
1939–42, and Chief of Naval Information, 1943–44. Unionist M.P. for North
Portsmouth, 1943–45. President of Union Jack Services Clubs, 1955–64.
Deputy Lieutenant, County of Surrey, 1958–65. Writer on the British Navy.
Lived at Elie, Fife) *see* 23

JAMESON, Agnes
*Doggerel for the Forces, grave and gay, relative to the first phase of the war from its
declaration Sept. 3, 1939, to the evacuation of Dunkirk May 26, 1940 to June 5, 1940.*
Composed in honour of our fighters and defenders at home and abroad. William
Clowes & Sons, Ltd. 1940. 80 pp. OXB

JARMAIN, John (1910–44. b. Hatch End, Middlesex. Educated at
Shrewsbury School, and Queen's College, Cambridge. Tutor and writer.
Served with the 51st Highland Division from Alamein to Sicily, then in the
Normandy landings as an anti-tank gunner, attaining the rank of Major. Killed
by enemy mortar fire on 26 June 1944)
Poems. Collins. 1945. 64 pp. por. BPL
see also 17, 31, 51, 57, 63, 76

JARMAN, Wrenne (–1953. Great-granddaughter of the poet Robert
Millhouse, whose statue stands in Nottingham Castle. During the war she
worked on a lathe at the Hawker Aircraft factory at Kingston. Received into the
Roman Catholic Church in 1943. Editor of the *Kensington News*)
The breathless kingdom: poems. Fortune Press. 1948. 96 pp. IWM
Nymph in thy orisons: poems. Printed Llandeilo: St Albert's Press. 1960.
98 pp. por.
    A limited ed. of 250 numbered copies. OXB
Poems of Wrenne Jarman. With a foreword by Edmund Blunden. Hilary Press.
1970. 176 pp. por. OXB
see also 22, 52

JARRATT, Lita
The porcelain heart, and other poems. Ilfracombe: Arthur H. Stockwell, Ltd.
[1965]. 16 pp. OXB

JAST, Louis Stanley (1868–1944. b. Halifax, Yorkshire, of Polish parentage.
A professional librarian, he held public library appointments at Halifax,

Peterborough and Croydon before becoming Chief Librarian of Manchester. President of The Library Association in 1930. Author of several plays which were performed by the Unnamed Society in Manchester. Wrote various papers and pamphlets on literary and library topics)

   Poems and epigrams. Printed Keighley: Rydal Press. [1944]. vi, 90 pp. por.

     Title from cover. For private circulation.   MPL

JAY, E. (Of London) *see* 74

JEFFERSON, Gordon (Of Yorkshire)

   On trust: a selection of Yorkshire verse. Leeds: Yorkshire Dialect Society. 1955. 40 pp.

     Many verses in Yorkshire dialect.   MPL

JEFFERY, Colin (1942– . b. Caterham, Surrey. Educated at Clarks College, Croydon)

   Monument: [*poems*]. Walton-on-Thames: Outposts Publications. 1978. 12 pp.

                                    OXB

JENNETT, Sean (1912– . Education "more or less self-inflicted". Publisher, painter, advertising agent, photographer, and expert on typography and book design. His poems and short stories were published in Britain and the United States)

   Always Adam, [*and other poems*]. Faber & Faber. 1943. 64 pp.   IWM
   The cloth of flesh: [*poems*]. Faber & Faber. 1945. 61 pp.

     Typography by the author.   IWM
see also 37, 51, 57

JERROLD, Hebe (Served in the Timber Corps of the Women's Land Army) *see* 50

JESSE, Fryniwyd Tennyson(1888–1958. Daughter of the Reverend Eustace Tennyson d'Eyncourt Jesse, a nephew of Alfred, Lord Tennyson. She studied art at the Newlyn School in Cornwall, then in 1911 began a career as a journalist. Worked as a reporter in London for *The Times* and the *Daily Mail*. During the First World War she was one of the few women to report from the front. Worked also for the Ministry of Information, the National Relief Commission and the French Red Cross. A distinguished novelist and playwright, she married the playwright H.M. Harwood in 1918)

   The compass, and other poems. Printed William Hodge & Co., Ltd. 1951. [viii], 19 pp.

     A limited ed. of 250 numbered copies printed for private circulation.

                                      OXB

JOHN, A.I. (Served in South-East Asia Command) *see* 35

JOHN, Evan, pseud. *see* **SIMPSON, Evan John**, (Evan John, pseud.)

JOHN, Kristine Saint-, pseud. *see* **MAURER, Christine**, (Kristine Saint-John, pseud.)

JOHN, M.E. (Of Kent) *see* 74

JOHN, Monica (Of Kent) *see* 73

JOHN O' THE NORTH. pseud. *see* **BROWNE, Harry T.**, (John o' the North, pseud.)

JOHNSON, Albert Edward (Lived in Canada, England and America)
The crown and the laurel: [*poems*]. Oxford: George Ronald. 1953. [viii], 34 pp.
OXB

JOHNSON, Christoper S. (Of Staffordshire) *see* 74

JOHNSON, Elizabeth (Of Leicestershire) *see* 73

JOHNSON, Geoffrey (1893– . b. in the Black Country. Educated at Wolverhampton Grammar School and London University. A grammar school teacher. Published verse in most of the leading English, American and Canadian periodicals)
The heart of things, [*and other poems*]. Williams & Norgate. 1951. 53 pp.
OXB
The iron harvest: [*poems*]. Williams & Norgate, Ltd. 1950. 46 pp.   OXB
The magic stone: a collection of poems. Robert Hale Ltd. 1955. 47 pp.   OXB

JOHNSON, George Cambridge (Served as a telegraphist in the Royal Navy)
Flowing tide and slack water: [*poems*]. Mitre Press. 1961. 39 pp.   MPL

JOHNSON, H.A. (Served in the Royal Navy)
A handful of salt: [*poems*]. Ilfracombe: Arthur H. Stockwell, Ltd. [1948]. 24 pp.   OXB

JOHNSON, Michael (1928– . b. Harrow, Middlesex. Educated at New College, Oxford, St Mary's Hospital Medical School, London, and the Slade School. Physician and former ship's surgeon. Of Streatham, London)
For my rat, and other poems. Outposts Publications. 1966. 24 pp.   OXB

JOHNSON, Stowers (b. Brentwood, Essex. Educated at London University. Headmaster of Aveley School, Essex, 1939–68. Poet, art collector, writer on art and travel. Editor of *Anglo-Soviet Journal*, 1966–68. Honorary art curator at the National Liberal Club. Holder of various offices in the Poetry Society)

Branches green and branches black: fifty-one poems. Fortune Press. 1944. 48 pp.

OXB

London saga. Fortune Press. [1946]. [iv], 124 pp.
    Dedicated to 'the Rt. Hon. Winston S. Churchill, P.C., C.H.'.   IWM
Sonnets, they say—. Walpole Press. 1949. 40 pp.   OXB
When fountains fall: [poems]. Fortune Press. 1961. 78 pp.   MPL

JOHNSTON, Sir Charles Hepburn, (Charles Hepburn, pseud.) (1912– . b. London. Educated at Winchester College, and Balliol College, Oxford. Entered the Diplomatic Service in 1936. Held appointments in Tokyo, Cairo, Madrid, Bonn, Amman and Aden. High Commissioner of Australia, 1965–71. Poet and translator. A member of Lloyd's from 1962)
    Towards Mozambique, and other poems; [by] Charles Hepburn. Cresset Press. 1947. 45 pp.   BL
see also 40

JOHNSTON, J.W. (Minister of Townsend Street Presbyterian Church, Belfast. Chaplain to the Forces during the war)
    Poems of a parachute padre. Belfast: Quota Press [1943]. 76 pp. por.   BPL
    Poems of a parachute padre. [2nd ed.]. Belfast: Quota Press. [1943]. [ii], 76 pp. por.   BL
    Poems of a parachute padre. 3rd ed. Belfast: Quota Press. 1944. 76 pp. por.
    OXB
    Poems of a parachute padre. 4th ed. Belfast: Quota Press. 1945. 76 pp. por.
    IWM

JOHNSTONE, George Harcourt, Lord Derwent (1899–1949. Educated at Charterhouse, and Merton College, Oxford. Newdigate Prizeman in 1920. Honorary Attaché in Warsaw, Brussels, Madrid, Berne, 1923–40. Served in the Royal Air Force, 1942–44. President of Yorkshire Liberal Foundation. Lived at Scarborough) *see* 84

JOLLY, R.G. (Quartermaster-Sergeant. Served with the Eighth Army) *see* 44

JOLY, Robert (1924–45. b. Amoy, South China. Educated at Clifton College. Won a major scholarship to Peterhouse, Cambridge. Served with the Grenadier Guards in Normandy, Holland and Germany. Killed in action on 31 March 1945) *see* 20

JONES, A. (Leading Aircraftman, Royal Air Force. Served with the Eighth Army) *see* 44

JONES, Alan Pryce (Of Wales. Editor, anthologist and translator) *see* 32

JONES, Brian (1938– . Poet and radio playwright. A contributor to *London Magazine*, *Poetry Review* and other periodicals. A teacher in Canterbury, Kent)
  A family album: [poems]. Alan Ross. 1968. 48 pp. (London Magazine editions, 16).   OXB
  Poems. Alan Ross. 1966. 57 pp. (London Magazine editions, 8).   OXB
  Poems; and, A family album. London Magazine Editions. 1972. 93 pp.   OXB
  The Spitfire on the Northern Line, *[and other poems]*. Chatto & Windus. 1975. 32 pp. (Chatto poets for the young).   OXB

JONES, David Rhys Geraint (1922–44. b. Haverfordwest, Pembrokeshire. Educated at Cheltenham College, and Trinity Hall, Cambridge. Transferred from his Royal Armoured Corps unit to 159th Infantry Brigade H.Q. with rank of Lieutenant. Died of wounds in Normandy on 28 June 1944) *see* 20, 76

JONES, Denys L. (1917– . Educated at Exeter School. Went to sea before the war then spent six years in the Army. A contributor to *Penguin New Writing*) *see* 76

JONES, Derek Bourne- *see* **BOURNE-JONES, Derek**

JONES, Dorvil (Served in the Middle East) *see* 39, 63

JONES, Douglas H. (Sailed with the British Liberation Army, June 1944)
  Snow flowers: a booklet of verse. Ilfracombe: Arthur H. Stockwell, Ltd. [1944]. 32 pp.   OXB

JONES, Frederick Lloyd
  The blind child, and other poems. Ilfracombe: Arthur H. Stockwell, Ltd. 1954. 16 pp.   OXB

JONES, Glyn (1905– . b. Merthyr Tydfil, Glamorgan. Educated at St Paul's College, Cheltenham. Teacher of English in various parts of South Wales. Novelist, poet and short story writer. Of Cardiff)
  Selected poems of Glyn Jones. Llandysul: Gomer Press. 1975. 94 pp.   OXB

JONES, Gwen (Of Shoreham-by-Sea, Sussex. Served as an Air Raid Warden)
  Rhymes of those times, 1939–1945. Printed [Worthing]: Worthing and Littlehampton Gazettes, Ltd. [1946]. 39 pp. il.
    Title from cover.   OXB
  Rhymes of those times, 1939–1945. 2nd ed. Birmingham: Privately published. [194-]. 40 pp. il.
    Title from cover.   IWM
  The weapon of hate: a satire. Printed Brighton: S.P. Co., Ltd. [1944]. [4] pp. il.
    Title from cover.   BL
see also 75

JONES, Gwilym Richard (Playwright in the Welsh language) *see* 22

JONES, I.M., (John Jayne Westroppe, pseud.) (b. Stratford on Avon, son of the Rector of Tintern and New Church)
Here and there: now and then: [*poems*] *1937–1954*; by John Jayne Westroppe. Loughton, Essex: L. Forster-Jones. [1955]. [x], 111 pp.   OXB

JONES, Ivor Roberts- *see* **ROBERTS-JONES, Ivor**

JONES, John Allen (Served in the Royal Navy)
Deep sea murmurings: [*poems*]. Ilfracombe: Arthur H. Stockwell, Ltd. 1946. 23 pp.   OXB

JONES, Jonathan Morgan, pseud. *see* **DOCHERTY, John**, (Jonathan Morgan Jones, pseud.)

JONES, Sir Lawrence Evelyn (1885–1969. Educated at Eton College, and Balliol College, Oxford, where he was President of Oxford University Boat Club. Major in the Bedfordshire Yeomany in the First World War, awarded the M.C. Barrister-at-law, novelist and short story writer)
A la carte. With decorations by John Banting. Secker & Warburg. 1951. xiv, 162 pp. il.
A miscellany of poetry and prose, parodying the work of distinguished writers.   OXB
Stings and honey: [*poems*]. Rupert Hart-Davis. 1953. 93 pp.   MPL

JONES, Leonard Meyrick- *see* **MEYRICK-JONES, Leonard**

JONES, Maldwyn
Life's treasures: poems. Ilfracombe: Arthur H. Stockwell, Ltd. [1959]. 24 pp.
                    OXB

JONES, Melfin Williams (Of Cardiff)
These things remain: poems. Staples Press Ltd. 1946. 44 pp.   OXB

JONES, P.M. (Served in H.M. Forces) *see* 74

JONES, S. (Served in H.M. Forces) *see* 74

JONES, Thomas Harri *see* **JONES, Thomas Henry**

JONES, Thomas Henry (1921–65. b. Llanafan Fawr, Brecknockshire. Served in the Royal Navy throughout the war. Graduated in English from Aberystwyth. Taught in London, Portsmouth and at Newcastle University

College, New South Wales, Australia. Drowned in the Pacific at Newcastle in 1965)

The beast at the door, and other poems. Rupert Hart-Davis. 1963. 79 pp.
OXB

The collected poems of T. Harri Jones. Edited and with an introduction by Julian Croft and Don Dale-Jones. Llandysul: Gomer Press. 1977. xx, 267 pp. OXB

The enemy in the heart: poems 1946–1956. Rupert Hart-Davis. 1957. 80 pp.
OXB

JONES, W. Edgerton (Lance-Corporal. Served with the Eighth Army in the Western Desert and Italy) *see* 44, 46

JOYCE, Lionel

The higher — the Fuehrer: a pillory of parody.: [poems]. Sketches by Bois. Arts & Crafts Publishing Co. Ltd. [1940]. 36 pp. il.   OXB

JULIAN, Frederick Bennett (Writer on the psychological casualties of air raids and their first-aid treatment)

Ovid in Arcady, [and other poems]. Ilfracombe: Arthur H. Stockwell, Ltd. 1955. 48 pp.   OXB

K., pseud. (A British officer with the West African Forces. Served in South-East Asia Command) *see* 35

KAPPES, E.R., (Raymond Ross, pseud.) (b. Yorkshire. Called up in 1939, seeing active service in Egypt and Ethiopia)

Cousins in contrast: [poems]; [by] Raymond Ross and Christine A. Firman. Illustrations by John F. Williams. Printed Stockton-on-Tees: Edward Appleby Ltd. [1978]. [vi], 25 pp. il.

Not joint authorship. No war poetry by Firman.   OXB

KATZIN, Olga, (Sagittarius, pseud.) (1896– . b. London, of Russian stock. Educated privately. Married actor Hugh Miller in 1921. A journalist. Of London)

London watches: [poems]; by Sagittarius. Jonathan Cape. 1941. 31 pp. il.
IWM

Pipes of peace: [poems]; by Sagittarius. Jonathan Cape. 1949. 142 pp.   OXB

Quiver's choice: [poems]; by Sagittarius. Jonathan Cape. 1945. 296 pp. IWM

Sagittarius rhyming: [poems]; by Sagittarius. Jonathan Cape. 1940. 158 pp.
BPL

Strasbourg geese, and other verses; by Sagittarius. Jonathan Cape. 1953. 128 pp.
MPL

Targets: [poems]; by Sagittarius. Jonathan Cape. 1943. 120 pp.   IWM

see also 38

KAVANAGH, Patrick (1905–67. b. County Monaghan, Ireland. Educated at a local school which he left aged thirteen. A small farmer until 1939 when he went to live in Dublin. A freelance journalist during the war, he wrote a gossip column, 1942–44. Poet, film and television critic, and columnist for a farming newspaper)

Collected poems. Macgibbon & Kee. 1964. xvi, 202 pp.   OXB

Collected poems. Martin Brian & O'Keeffe. 1972. xvi, 202 pp.   OXB

Come dance with Kitty Stobling, and other poems. Longmans. 1960. [vi], 44 pp.   OXB

The complete poems of Patrick Kavanagh. Collected, arranged and edited by Peter Kavanagh. New York: Peter Kavanagh Hand Press. 1972. xvi, 391 pp.   BL

November haggard: uncollected prose and verse of Patrick Kavanagh. Selected, arranged and edited by Peter Kavanagh. New York: Peter Kavanagh Hand Press. [1971]. [vii], 229 pp. il., por., facsim.   BL

A soul for sale: poems. Macmillan & Co. Ltd. 1947. vi, 56 pp.   OXB

KAVANAGH, Patrick Joseph (1931–   . b. Worthing, Sussex. Educated at Douai School, Berkshire, Lycée Jaccard, Lausanne, and Merton College, Oxford. Worked for the British Council, 1957–59. Acted on stage, television and in films. Novelist, poet and journalist. Awarded Richard Hillary Memorial Prize, 1966, and *The Guardian* Fiction Prize, 1969. Of Cheltenham, Gloucestershire)

About time. Chatto & Windus; Hogarth Press. 1970.. 46 pp. (Phoenix living poets).   MPL

One and one: poems. Heinemann. 1959. 56 pp.   OXB

KAY, Constance

Songs of faith: poems. Ilfracombe: Arthur H. Stockwell, Ltd. [1960]. 20 pp.   OXB

KAY, Hester (Served in the Women's Auxiliary Air Force)

Love and the devil: [poems]. Mitre Press. [1967]. 38 pp.   BL

Poems, 1944–1954. Mitre Press. [1955]. 32 pp.   OXB

Shall vision perish?, and other poems. Mitre Press. [1957]. 32 pp.   OXB

KAYE, Barrington (1924–   . Novelist, poet, and writer on education and sociology. Lecturer in Education, 1951–54, and Social Research Fellow, University of the Gold Coast, 1956–62. Head, Department of Education, Redland College, Bristol, 1962–72 Chief Technical Adviser, United Nations Educational, Scientific & Cultural Organization, Paris, 1972–75. Head, Department of Education, Bristol Polytechnic, from 1976)

The song of my beloved, and other poems. Mitre Press. [1949]. 40 pp.   OXB

KAYE, Ian Eric (Served with the Army in Korea)
Pick and shovel poems. Ilfracombe: Arthur H. Stockwell, Ltd. [1960]. [viii],
85 pp.   OXB

KEENE, Dennis (1934–   . b. London. Educated at St John's College, Oxford,
where he was literary editor of *Isis*)
Surviving: [*poems*]. Manchester: Carcanet New Press Ltd. 1980. 69 pp. OXB

KEITH, Andrew (Of Stroud, Gloucestershire)
Poems. King, Littlewood & King Ltd. [1945]. 56 pp.   BPL

KELLY, Editha (Née Melbourne. Of Maidstone, Kent)
Wind on the heath: a collection of poems. Fortune Press. 1949. 56 pp.   BL

KELLY, Michael (1912–   . b. Sheffield. Served in the Royal Navy, 1940–45)
Sea days and after: [*poems*]. Printed Leeds: Partridge Printers Ltd. 1952. 69 pp.
Dedicated to 'Stephen Gwynn of Dublin'.   IWM

KEMP, B.D. (Served in H.M. Forces) *see* 75

KEMP, William Albert George (Poet of the First World War. Served in the
Royal Army Medical Corps. Of Northwood, Middlesex)
Men like these: sonnets. With a foreword by Air Chief Marshal Lord Dowding.
Chapman & Hall Ltd. 1946. 80 pp.   BPL

KEMPSELL, L.
Poems. Ilfracombe: Arthur H. Stockwell Ltd. [1969]. 19 pp.   OXB

KENDALL, David (Ordinary Seaman, Royal Navy)
Poems of an ordinary seaman. Fortune Press. [1946]. 44 pp.   IWM

KENDALL, Guy (1876–1960. Educated at Eton College, and Magdalen
College, Oxford. Became Warden at the University Settlement, Ancoats,
Manchester, in 1901. Poet of the First World War. Assistant Master at
Charterhouse, 1902–16. Borough Councillor at Godalming, Surrey, 1908–12.
Headmaster of University College School, Hampstead, 1916–36. Writer on
religious topics)
The poet's flower, and other verses. Hull: Guild Press. 1958. 16 pp.   OXB

KENDRICK, Charles (Of London) *see* 75

KENDRICK, George (A young boy in the war)
Bicycle tyre in a tall tree: poems. Cheadle Hulme, Cheshire: Carcanet Press Ltd.
1974. 62 pp.   OXB

KENMARE, Dallas (–1973. b. Temple Balsall, Warwickshire. Began writing at an early age. Her first stories were published when she was about twelve and at fourteen she was writing full-length novels. Married at nineteen. Engaged in social work for many years, particularly maternity and child welfare. A talented musician, she wrote literary studies of Robert Browning and D.H. Lawrence. After the war lived for many years in Tangier, where she died)

Beyond the stars: [*poems*]. Cheltenham: Burrow's Press Ltd. 1944]. 23 pp.
OXB

The city of white stones, [*and other poems*]. Cheltenham: Ed. J. Burrow & Co. Ltd. [1965]. 63 pp.
OXB

Collected poems. Cheltenham: Burrow's Press Ltd. [1953]. xiv, 190 pp.   MPL

The crystal mountain, and other poems. Edward J. Burrow & Co. Ltd. [1944]. 39 pp.
OXB

Elegy for two voices, and other poems. Cheltenham: Burrow's Press Ltd. [1947]. 44 pp.
OXB

Four words, and other poems. Edward J. Burrow & Co. Ltd. [1940]. 47 pp.
OXB

Selected poems. Printed Oxford: Shakespeare Head Press and sold by Basil Blackwell. 1939. [xiv], 81 pp.
BL

KENYON, Rowland Lloyd

Might-have-beens, and other meanderings including the Battle of Britain and the Blitz: [*poems*]. Ilfracombe: Arthur H. Stockwell, Ltd. [1956]. 48 pp.   OXB

KER, Alan (1904–67. b. Wu-hu, China. Educated at Rugby School, and New College, Oxford. Taught classics at Rugby School. In 1931 appointed Fellow and Tutor of Brasenose College, Oxford. In 1939 employed at the Admiralty, becoming Private Secretary to the First Lord, A.V. Alexander. Later seconded to the War Office. After the war taught at Wellington School. In 1953 became a Fellow of Trinity College, Cambridge)

Poems, 1904–1967. Eton, Windsor: Shakespeare Head Press. 1968. [vi], 58 pp.
IWM

KERR, MacFee

Poems. Glasgow: William Maclellan. 1949. 58 pp.   OXB

KERR, Ronald D.M. (Of Clydebank, Scotland)

The Cademuir poems. Printed BCM/MCQZ. [1975]. [iv], 52 pp.   OXB

KEY, Doreen

Thoughts and dreams: [*poems*]. Ilfracombe: Arthur H. Stockwell Ltd. 1969. 24 pp.
OXB

KEY, Robert Ellis (Colonel, of Kensington, London, originally from Fulford.

He was writing verse as early as 1911)

Collected poems. A.E. Callam. 1953. 225 pp.   OXB

New selection of poems. War-time ed. Art Store. [1943]. 93 pp.   OXB

KEYES, Sidney (1922–43. b. Dartford, Kent. Educated at Tonbridge School, and Queen's College, Oxford. Wrote poetry while still at school. A close friend of John Heath-Stubbs. Entered the Army in April 1942, commissioned in Queen's Own Royal West Kent Regiment in September 1942. Taken prisoner during the last days of the Tunisian campaign and died in enemy hands 'of unknown causes' on 29 April 1943. Posthumously awarded the Hawthornden Prize)

The collected poems of Sidney Keyes. Edited with a memoir and notes by Michael Meyer. Routledge. 1945. xxiv, 124 pp. por.   BPL

The collected poems of Sidney Keyes. Edited with a memoir and notes by Michael Meyer. Preface by Herbert Read. New York: Henry Holt & Co. [1947]. xxviii, 124 pp.   OXB

The cruel solstice, [and other poems]. Routledge. 1943. 60 pp.   BPL

The iron laurel: [poems]. Routledge. 1942. 48 pp.   IWM

see also 3, 11, 15, 18, 20, 25, 26, 30, 31, 33, 37, 48, 51, 56, 57, 58, 59, 63, 68, 76, 82

KIDWELL, Roy (Served in H.M. Forces. Possibly Ray Kidwell, b. 1926, educated at Magdalen College, Oxford, served in the Royal Air Force, 1945–48) *see* 49

KILNER, Marjorie

Poems light and gay. Ilfracombe: Arthur H. Stockwell, Ltd. 1952. 24 pp.

      OXB

KINCAID, John (1909– . Educated at Hillhead High School, Glasgow. A teacher, contributor to various periodicals and writer for B.B.C. radio)

Measures for masses: [poems]. Glasgow: William Maclellan. 1944. 36 pp.

Published for the Clyde Group, formed 'to publish the works of artists in various mediums'.   IWM

Time of violence: [poems]. Glasgow: Scoop Books Ltd. 1945. 32 pp. (Modern Scots poets).   BL

KINDERSLEY, N.H. (Major, Royal Artillery. Captured in France in 1940, held prisoner of war in Germany until 1945) *see* 67

KING, Francis (1923– . b. Adelboden, Switzerland. Educated at Shrewsbury School, and Balliol College, Oxford. Worked on the land during the war. Joined the British Council in 1949, serving in Italy, Greece, Egypt, Finland and Japan. Retired in 1965 to become a full-time writer. Novelist, short story writer and poet. Chairman, Society of Authors, 1975–77, and President, English P.E.N. from 1978)

Rod of incantation: poems. Longmans, Green & Co. 1952. viii, 44 pp.   OXB
see also   19, 25, 52, 56, 76

KING, Lynn (Of Wiltshire)   *see*   74

KINGDON, Claude Drewitt (Reverend, of Whitstone Rectory, Holsworthy, Devon)

Catholic sermons in war and peace (in verse). Ilfracombe: Arthur H. Stockwell, Ltd. [1942]. 95 pp.   OXB

KINROSS, Charles

Love and no love: [poems]. Saint Catherine Press Ltd. 1954. x, 78 pp.   OXB

KIRBY, Harold Percival

Lucem demonstrat umbra: [poems]. Ilfracombe: Arthur H. Stockwell, Ltd. 1951. 16 pp.   OXB

KIRK, Brenda A.

Souvenir of thoughts: [poems]. Ilfracombe: Arthur H. Stockwell, Ltd. 1959. 24 pp.   OXB

KIRK, Kenneth (Of Yorkshire)   *see*   74

KIRKHAM, Winifred Jessie (Of Lancashire?)

Poems. Printed Lytham: "Standard" Printers. [1949]. 24 pp. por.
   Title from cover.   OXB
"Through the years": over one hundred poems. Printed Lytham: "Standard" Printers. [1954]. [72] pp. por.
   Title from cover.   OXB

KIRKUP, James (1918–   . b. South Shields, County Durham. Educated at South Shields High School and Durham University. Held academic appointments in Britain, Sweden, Spain, Japan, Malaya and the United States. Gregory Fellow in Poetry at Leeds University, 1950–52. Travel writer, poet, novelist, playwright, translator and broadcaster. Recipient of an Atlantic Award in Literature, 1950)

The descent into the cave, and other poems. Oxford University Press. 1957. viii, 109 pp.   OXB
Refusal to conform: last and first poems. Oxford University Press. 1963. xii, 121 pp.   OXB
The submerged village, and other poems. Oxford University Press. 1951. viii, 96 pp.   OXB
see also   18

KIRKWOOD, Robert, (Hiawatha, pseud.) (Of Ulster)
Lays of an Ulster paradise, and other poems; by "Hiawatha". Belfast: *Irish News*.
1960. 168 pp. il.   OXB

KIRTLAN, Patric (Of Trowbridge, Wiltshire)
Pan's music: [*poems*]. Fortune Press. 1955. 32 pp.   OXB

KITCHEN, Fred (Served in India with the 13th Battalion, Sherwood
Foresters, 1942–44)
Indian scenes (in verse). Ilfracombe: Arthur H. Stockwell, Ltd. 1947. 16 pp.
                                                                                                        OXB

KNIGHT, H.G. (Lance-Corporal. Served with the Eighth Army in the
Western Desert and Italy)   *see*   25, 44, 46

KNOWLES, Susanne (1911–   . b. York. Educated in Italy. Before becoming
a freelance writer she did secretarial work in the House of Commons, the Civil
Service and the printing industry. Served in London Auxiliary Ambulance
Service during the war. Anthologist and poet, contributor to many periodicals.
Of London)
Arpies and sirens: verse. Drawings by Iris Brooke. George G. Harrap & Co. Ltd.
1942. 48 pp. il.   OXB
Birth of Venus, and other poems. Macmillan & Co. Ltd. 1945. vi, 34 pp. IWM
see also   61

KNOX, Edmund Valpy, (Evoe) (1881–1971. Educated at Rugby School, and
Corpus Christi College, Oxford. Poet of the First World War. Served in the
Lincolnshire Regiment, 1914–19, being wounded at Passchendaele. A Fellow of
the Institute of Journalists. Editor of *Punch*, 1932–49. Lived in Hampstead,
London)
In my old days: [*poems*]. Printed Oxford: Holywell Press Ltd. [1974].
x, 66 pp. por., facsim.   OXB

KOFFMAN, Elsa (Associate of the London College of Music and the Royal
College of Music)
Come dream with me: [*poems*]. Printed Regency Press. [1972]. 48 pp.   OXB
Enchantment, [*and other poems*]. Edgeware: Jupiter Press. 1975. [viii], 54 pp.
                                                                                                        OXB

KOLBABEK, Ella
The world's my theme: [*poems*]. Ilfracombe: Arthur H. Stockwell, Ltd. 1958.
44 pp.   OXB

KONIGSBERG, Isidore (Staff-Sergeant. Served with the Eighth
Army) *see* 44

KOPS, Bernard (1926– . b. London. Educated to age of thirteen in various London schools. Worked as docker, salesman, chef, waiter, liftman and barrow boy before becoming a full-time writer. Novelist, poet and playwright. Resident dramatist at the Old Vic, 1959. Received an Arts Council Award for Literature in 1975)

For the record: [*poems*]. Secker & Warburg. 1971. 64 pp.   OXB

KORRAGH, pseud. *see* **SPENCE, D.**, (Korragh, pseud.)

KRAMER, Lotte (b. Germany. Came to England in July 1939 as a Jewish refugee child with a children's transport organized by the Quakers. Her parents, other relatives and friends were lost in the German death camps. During the war she was sent to work in a laundry. Started to write poetry in 1970, only feeling able to write about her childhood and the German Jewish experience after thirty years)

Scrolls: a poem. Drawing by Trevor Covey. Richmond, Surrey: Keepsake Press. 1979. 2 pp. il. (Keepsake poems, 38).

Title from cover. A limited ed. of 180 copies of which twelve are signed by the author and the artist.   OXB

KREMER, Zelma (A German Jewish wife)

Versatile verse. Pan Press Publications, Ltd. [1945]. [16] pp.   OXB

L., I.D.

The bright and the bitter, [*and other poems*]; by I.D.L. Ilfracombe: Arthur H. Stockwell, Ltd. [1943]. 16 pp.   OXB

L., R. (Of Hertfordshire?)

Memories for ever; by R.L. Printed Letchworth: Letchworth Printers Ltd. [1945]. 47 pp.

Poetry and prose.   OXB

LAING, Allan Macdonald (1887– . Educated at Brae Street Board School, Liverpool. Self-styled 'freelance versifier'. Anthologist and member of the Shaw Society. Lived in Liverpool)

Bank holiday on Parnassus: a litter of competitions, [*and other poems*]. George Allen & Unwin, Ltd. 1941. [xvi], 135 pp.   OXB

LAKE, Phyllis

A hornet in my hair: poems. Mitre Press. [1976]. 48 pp.   OXB

LAKELAND PARSON'S DAUGHTER, pseud. *see* **HODGSON, Ethel**, (Lakeland Parson's Daughter, pseud.)

LA MARE, Walter De *see* **DE LA MARE, Walter**

LAMBERT, Donald Page, (D. Page, pseud.) (Colonel in the Army)
The martyr, and other poems; by D. Page. Macmillan & Co. Ltd. 1944. vi, 33 pp.
OXB

LAMING, Hugh (Served in the Middle East and Greece) *see* 39, 63

LAMONT, Archie (Doctor of Philosophy. Writer on Scotland)
Patria deserta, [*and other poems*]. Edinburgh: Oliver & Boyd Ltd. 1943. 72 pp.
IWM

Selected poems. Edinburgh: Oliver & Boyd Ltd. [1944]. 46 pp.
Title from cover.
OXB

LAMONT, J.A.K. (Served in South-East Asia Command) *see* 35

LAMPSON, Godfrey Locker (1875–1946. Educated at Eton College, and Trinity College, Cambridge. Served in the Foreign Office and the Diplomatic Service. M.P. for Salisbury, 1910–18. Served in the Royal Wiltshire Yeomanry, 1914–15, A.D.C. 4th Corps, 1916. Parliamentary Private Secretary, 1917–18, Under-Secretary of State, 1923–29, and member of the British Delegation to the League of Nations, Geneva, 1928. Privy Councillor, 1928)
Love lyrics, and other melic numbers. Frederick Muller Ltd. 1943. [vi], 33 pp.
OXB

Mellow notes: [*poems*]. Frederick Muller Ltd. 1944. [viii], 35 pp.   OXB
Sun and shadow: collected love lyrics and other poems. Frederick Muller Ltd. 1945. 140 pp.   OXB
Sun and shadow: collected love lyrics and other poems. 2nd ed. Frederick Muller Ltd. 1946. 148 pp.   OXB

LAND, V.M. (Of Warwickshire) *see* 74

LANDON, Margaret
Invitation: a book of verse. Ilfracombe: Arthur H. Stockwell, Ltd. [1942]. 96 pp.
OXB

LANES, Barbara
September sky, and other poems. Ilfracombe: Arthur H. Stockwell, Ltd. 1950. 16 pp.   OXB

LANG-RIDGE, A. Harvey
Ballads of Blighty. Quality Press, Ltd. 1943. 47 pp.   IWM

LANGFORD, E.M. (Of Staffordshire) *see* 75

LANYARD, pseud. *see* **MORGAN, Guy**, (Lanyard, pseud.)

LANYON, Carla Lanyon (1906– . b. County Down, daughter of a flax broker. Her mother was the Irish poet Helen Lanyon. Married Brigadier Edward S. Hacker, M.C. Poet, lecturer, poetry reader and contributor to anthologies and magazines. Her poems have also been recorded. Lived in Wiltshire and in Surrey)

Flow and ebb: a selection of poems written between 1946–1956. Cambridge: Poetry Publications. 1956. [iv], 28 pp.   OXB

Salt harvest: the autobiography of an Englishman. Williams & Norgate. 1947. 20 pp.   OXB

Selected poems. Chesterfield: Guild Press. 1954. 16 pp. (Guild poets).   OXB

Trusty tree: poems. Mitre Press. 1963. 48 pp.   MPL

Uncompromising gladness, [and other poems]. Outposts Publications. 1968. 53 pp.   OXB

see also 41

LAPSLEY, D.M. (Of Lanarkshire)   *see* 74

LARR, Frederic Haighton (1924– . Educated at Marlborough College. Lieutenant, Royal Artillery (Field). A volunteer, he served in India) *see* 43

LAST, C. (Served in the Home Guard. Of Hertfordshire?)

Blood, sweat and tear(e)s: some "die-hard" ditties; by Stanley Phillips and C. Last. Printed St Albans: Gainsborough Press. 1944. 24 pp.

Not joint authorship.   IWM

LATHAM, Lilion (Of Bexhill, Sussex)

Dunkirk; by Lilion Latham assisted by William Gordon. Printed Bexhill: F.J. Parsons Ltd. [194-]. 7 pp.

Title from cover.   BPL

LAUGHTON, Freda (1907– . b. Bristol and educated there. Was married twice, to L.E.G. Laughton and to John Midgley. Lived in Northern Ireland)

A transitory house: poems. Jonathan Cape. 1945. 64 pp.   OXB

LAURENT, Livia (A refugee from Germany, she came to Britain in 1933. Interned in the Isle of Man at the outbreak of war. Translator from the German)

Poems. Favil Press. 1942. [iv], 40 pp.

Written during a year's internment in the Isle of Man.   IWM

LAWLER, L.K. (Former B.B.C. executive, of Henley-on-Thames, Oxfordshire. Served in the Middle East) *see* 39, 63

LAWRENCE, Margery (–1969. b. Shropshire. Educated privately at home and abroad, she published a book of poems at the age of sixteen. Attended art

schools in Birmingham, London and Paris. Poet of the First World War. Married Arthur E. Towle. Lived in Bloomsbury, a friend of Shane Leslie and Humbert Wolfe. Novelist and short story writer)
Fourteen to forty-eight: a diary in verse. Robert Hale Ltd. [1950]. 84 pp. por.
OXB

LAWRENCE, Paul
Light and shadow: poems. Canterbury: Bernard Wilson. 1958. 31 pp.   OXB

LAWRENCE, Ralph (Writer on Surrey)
Aftermath, and other poems. Fortune Press. 1948. [ii], 46 pp.   OXB
The millstream, and other poems. Macmillan & Co. Ltd. 1944. viii, 80 pp.
IWM

LAY, Elizabeth Stanton
The high road, and other poems. A.E. Callam. 1951. [viii], 31 pp.   OXB

LEA, Barbara (1903–45. b. Isle of Ely, née Pell. Married in 1924 and had five children. In 1939 she became Chairman of the Women's Land Army in Worcestershire and a member of the County War Agricultural Committee. Awarded the O.B.E. in 1944)
The urgent voice, and other poems. Fortune Press. 1948. 44 pp. por.   OXB

LEA, Margery (1905– . Educated at Elizabeth Gaskell College, Manchester. School teacher in Buckinghamshire and Manchester. Appointed lecturer at Elizabeth Gaskell College, then Inspector of Schools in Manchester. Her wartime duties included visiting Manchester evacuee children billetted in Shropshire. Lecturer on diet, health and nutrition. Of Shrewsbury, Shropshire)
Some holy-days — and home: [poems]. Walton-on-Thames: Outposts Publications. 1975. 40 pp.   OXB
These days: poetry and verse. Shrewsbury: Wilding & Sons, Ltd. [1969]. 62 pp.
OXB

LEASOR, James (1923– . b. Erith, Kent. Educated at City of London School, and Oriel College, Oxford. Journalist on *Kentish Times*, 1941–42. Served in the Army, 1942–46, in Burma, India and Malaya, becoming a Captain in the Royal Berkshire Regiment. Torpedoed on a troopship from Calcutta to Chittagong. Staff reporter on the *Daily Express*, 1948–55. Novelist, biographer, general writer and company director. Of Salisbury, Wiltshire) *see* 35

LEAVER, Derek J.
Come with me: verse. Ilfracombe: Arthur H. Stockwell, Ltd. [1944]. 24 pp.
OXB

LEDWARD, Patricia (1920– . Educated at St Paul's Girls School. Employed in Fleet Street during the blitz of 1940–41, later working as a nurse in an emergency hospital. Joined the Auxiliary Territorial Service, spending three years as a driver with an anti-aircraft unit. Poet, novelist and anthologist. Contributor to *Poetry Quarterly* and other periodicals. Co-editor of the anthology *Poems of This War by Younger Poets*, 1942)

"*Over the edge*": [*poems*]. Favil Press Ltd. [1940]. [6] pp. ("Resurgam" younger poets, 2).

Title from cover.   BL

see also   19, 25, 27, 33, 37, 52, 65, 76, 78, 87

LEE, Christopher (1913– . b. London. Educated at Latymer Upper School, Merton College, Oxford, and King's College, Cambridge. Worked for the Arts Council, the British Council and Glyndebourne Opera. Staff tutor at Cambridge University Board of Extra-Mural Studies from 1946)

Remember man: a poem. Fortune Press. [1942]. 52 pp.

'For Robert Charles, prisoner in Poland'.   BPL

The secret field: poems. Fortune Press. [1940]. 48 pp.   BPL

Under the sun: poems. Bodley Head. 1948. 63 pp.   MPL

LEE, J.M. (Served in H.M. Forces)   *see*   74

LEE, Joan

The dousing, and other poems. Ilfracombe: Arthur H. Stockwell, Ltd. 1951. 23 pp.   OXB

LEE, Joy Elizabeth

Memories, and other poems. Ilfracombe: Arthur H. Stockwell Ltd. 1976. 32 pp.   OXB

LEE, Laurie (1914– . b. Gloucestershire. Educated at Slad Village School and Stroud Central School. Before the war worked as a builder's labourer. Travelled around the Mediterranean, including Spain, 1935–39. Worked with the G.P.O. Film Unit, 1939–40, and Crown Film Unit, 1941–43. Publications editor with Ministry of Information, 1944–46. with Green Park Film Unit, 1946–7, and Writer-in-Chief, Festival of Britain, 1950–51. Leading popular author)

My many-coated man, [and other poems]. Andre Deutsch. 1955. [x], 29 pp.

Printed on one side of leaf only.   BL

[*Selected poems*]. Vista Books. 1960. 47 pp. (Pocket poets).   OXB

The sun my monument: [poems]. Chatto & Windus; Hogarth Press. 1944. 56 pp. (Phoenix living poets).   MPL

The sun my monument: [poems]. New York: Doubleday & Co., Inc. 1947. 58 pp.   OXB

see also   7, 25, 26, 28, 56, 76, 77

LEE, William
  Quintessence: [*poems*]. With a foreword by Lieut.-Col. W.L. Miron, O.B.E.
Nottingham: Bromley Press. 1949. [112] pp.
    'Dedicated to Lieut.-Col. R. Halford, M.C.'   OXB

LEES, Walter Kinnear Pyke- *see* **PYKE-LEES, Walter Kinnear**, (Peter
Leyland, pseud.)

LEFTWICH, Joseph (Poet of the First World War and a friend of Isaac
Rosenberg. Writer on Jews and Judaism)
  Years following after: poems. James Clarke & Co., Ltd. 1959. 157 pp. por.
                                                                            OXB

LEHMANN, John (1907–   . b. Bourne End, Buckinghamshire. Brother of
novelist Rosamund Lehmann and actress Beatrix Lehmann. Educated at Eton
College, and Trinity College, Cambridge. Partner and General Manager of the
Hogarth Press, 1936–46. Founder-editor of *New Writing* and *The London
Magazine*. Managing director of the publishing house John Lehmann Ltd. An
important and influential editor during the war years. Recipient of many
literary honours. Editor of the anthology *Poems from New Writing, 1936–1946*)
  The age of the dragon: poems 1930–1951. Longmans, Green & Co. 1951.
x, 138 pp.   BPL
  Collected poems, 1930–1963. Eyre & Spottiswoode. 1963. 128 pp.   OXB
  Forty poems. Hogarth Press. [1942]. 52 pp. (New Hogarth library, IX).

                                                                            IWM
  The sphere of glass, and other poems. Hogarth Press. 1944. 31 pp.   MPL
see also 3, 45, 76

LEHMANN, Pauline M.
  The collected poetry of Pauline M. Lehmann. Printed Regency Press. [1976]. 32 pp.
                                                                            OXB

LEIGH-FERMOR, Patrick (1915–   . b. London. Novelist, travel writer and
translator. Awarded Heinemann Foundation Prize for Literature, 1950,
Kemsley Prize, 1951, and Duff Cooper Prize, 1958. Elected to the Academy of
Athens in 1980. Of Mani, Southern Greece) *see* 57

LE MESSURIER, Ralph Huie (1898–   . b. St John's Newfoundland.
Educated at McGill University, Montreal, and Keble College, Oxford. Clerk in
Holy Orders. Lived at Mevagissey, Cornwall)
  The absent Christ, and other poems. With an introduction by Dame Sybil
Thorndike, O.B.E. New Vision Publications. 1942. 32 pp.   OXB

LENNOX, Helen Brown S.
  Swords into ploughshares: poems. Glasgow: Strickland Press. 1944. 39 pp. OXB

LESAR, Joan
Tomorrows came and went: [*poems*]. Ilfracombe: Arthur H. Stockwell Ltd. [1966]. 16 pp.   OXB

LESCOMBE, Marie
Red letters: verse. Ilfracombe: Arthur H. Stockwell, Ltd. [1945]. 126 pp.
                                                                          OXB

LESLIE, Lionel
Ladies from hell: poems. Fortune Press. 1943. 32 pp.   BPL

LESTER, R.B. (Served in the Middle East)   *see*   63

LEVENSON, Christopher (1934–   . b. London. During the war he was evacuated to Lancaster for three years. Educated at Downing College, Cambridge. Then a practising Quaker he refused national service, going before a conscientious objectors' tribunal. Did alternative service with the Friends Ambulance Unit. Edited the literary magazine *Delta* and the anthology *Poetry from Cambridge*, 1958. After Cambridge taught in Holland, West Germany and Canada)
Cairns, [*and other poems*]. Chatto & Windus; Hogarth Press. 1969. 63 pp. (Phoenix living poets).   OXB

LEVERTOFF, Denise   *see*   **LEVERTOV, Denise**

LEVERTOFF, Olga (1914–64. Daughter of Dr Paul Levertoff, an Anglican clergyman, by birth a Russian Jew. Sister of Denise Levertov)
Rage of days, [*and other poems*]. Hutchinson & Co., Ltd. [1947]. 72 pp. MPL

LEVERTOV, Denise (1923–   . b. Ilford, Essex. Her mother was Welsh and her father, Dr Paul Levertoff, an Anglican clergyman, by birth a Russian Jew. Educated privately and evacuated to Buckinghamshire. Served as a nurse in the war. Married American writer Mitchell Goodman in 1947, becoming an American citizen in 1955. Held university appointments in New York, New Jersey and Massachusetts. Poet, essayist, translator and short story writer. Winner of several literary awards)
Collected earlier poems, 1940–1960. New York: New Directions. 1979. x, 133 pp.
                                                                          OXB
The double image: [*poems*]; by Denise Levertoff. Cresset Press. 1946. 45 pp.
                                                                          OXB
The Jacob's ladder, [*and other poems*]. Jonathan Cape. 1965. [x], 84 pp. OXB
see also   78

LEVY, A.A. (Pilot Officer, Royal Air Force)   *see*   1, 25, 33

LEVY, Alban (A serving officer)
Nab Valley, [and other poems]. John Lane the Bodley Head. 1945. 47 pp.
IWM

LEVY, Juliette de Bairacli- *see* **DE BAIRACLI-LEVY, Juliette**

LEVY, Reginald (1914– . b. Spitalfields, London. Educated at elementary schools in the East End. An office worker before the war, he joined the Army in 1940, becoming a Sergeant in the Royal Army Pay Corps. Served in India) *see* 43, 57, 76

LEWIS, Alun (1915–44. b. Aberdare, Glamorgan, in a mining village, of Welsh mining stock. Educated at Cowbridge Grammar School, and University College, Aberystwyth. He was teaching before joining the Army in 1940 as a Sapper in the Royal Engineers. Commissioned in the infantry, going to India in 1942 as Lieutenant, South Wales Borderers. Accidentally killed with his own revolver on 5 March 1944 while serving on the Arakan front)
Ha! Ha! Among the trumpets: poems in transit. Foreword by Robert Graves. George Allen & Unwin Ltd. 1945. 76 pp. por. BPL
Ha! Ha! Among the trumpets: poems in transit. Foreword by Robert Graves. George Allen & Unwin Ltd. 1945. 76 pp. por.
A limited ed. of fifty numbered copies. BL
Raiders' dawn, and other poems. George Allen & Unwin Ltd. 1942. 94 pp. por. BPL
Selected poetry and prose. With a biographical introduction by Ian Hamilton. George Allen & Unwin Ltd. 1966. 215 pp. IWM
Two poems: Raiders' dawn; Song of innocence. Wood engraving: John Petts. Llanllechid, Caernarvonshire: Caseg Press. [1941]. il. (Caseg broadsheets, 1).
Printed at the Gomerian Press, Llandyssul, South Wales. OXB
see also 3, 7, 9, 15, 25, 26, 28, 30, 32, 33, 36, 37, 43, 45, 47, 51, 56, 57, 58, 59, 68, 76, 83, 87

LEWIS, Arthur (1855–)
A dream of Adolf Hitler. Bristol: John Wright & Sons Ltd; Simpkin Marshall Ltd. 1939. 15 pp.
'All profits arising from the sale of this booklet will be given to help non-Aryan refugees'. IWM

LEWIS, Cecil Day *see* **DAY LEWIS, Cecil**

LEWIS, Clive Staples (1898–1963. b. Belfast. Educated at Malvern College for one year, afterwards privately. Poet of the First World War. Served as Second Lieutenant in the Somerset Light Infantry, 1918–19. Fellow and Tutor of Magdalen College, Oxford, 1925–54. Professor of Medieval and Renaissance

English at Cambridge from 1954. Christian apologist, poet, critic, writer of science fiction and of novels for children. Recipient of many academic honours)

Poems. Edited by Walter Hooper. Geoffrey Bles. 1964. xvi, 142 pp.   OXB

Poems. Edited by Walter Hooper. New York: Harcourt Brace Jovanovich. 1977. xvi, 142 pp. (Harvest/HBJ books).   OXB

see also 51

LEWIS, Eiluned (–1979. b. Newtown, Montgomeryshire. Educated at Levana School, Wimbledon, and Westfield College, London. A journalist on editorial staff of *The Sunday Times*, 1931–36, and a regular contributor to *Country Life*. Awarded Book Guild Gold Medal, 1934. Married Scottish engineer Graeme Hendrey in 1937. Lived at Blechingley, Surrey)

Morning songs, and other poems. Macmillan & Co. Ltd. 1944. viii, 48 pp.
   IWM

see also 42, 48

LEWIS, Leonard A. (Of Somerset) *see* 72, 73, 74

LEWIS, Walter K. (Of Ramsgate, Kent) *see* 70, 71, 72, 73, 74, 75

LEYDEN, R.V. (1908– . b. Berlin. Studied geology at Goettingen, Heidelberg, Berlin and in Greece. Left Germany in 1933 on political grounds, becoming a naturalized Briton. Served as Lance Corporal, Auxiliary Force, in India) *see* 43

LEYLAND, Peter, pseud. *see* **PYKE-LEES, Walter Kinnear,** (Peter Leyland, pseud.)

LIDDELL, Robert (1908– . b. Tunbridge Wells, Kent. Educated at Haileybury School, and Corpus Christi College, Oxford. Lecturer at the Universities of Cairo and Alexandria, 1942–51. Appointed Assistant Professor of English, Cairo, 1951. Head of English Department, Athens University, 1963–68. Novelist, literary critic, translator and travel writer) *see* 40, 57

LILENSTEIN, L. (Warrant Officer. Served with the Eighth Army) *see* 44

LINDSAY, Jack (1900– . b. Melbourne, Australia, brother of novelist Philip Lindsay. Educated at Brisbane Grammar School and Queensland University. Settled in Essex. Served in the British Army, in Royal Corps of Signals, 1941–43, and as a scriptwriter at the War Office, 1943–45. Co-editor of the anthology *New Lyrical Ballads*, 1945. Poet, novelist, essayist, historian, biographer, art critic and editor. Of Halstead, Essex)

Into action: the battle of Dieppe: a poem. Andrew Dakers Ltd. 1942. 60 pp.
   MPL

Peace is our answer: poems, with further prefatory poems by Paul Eluard, Pablo Neruda, Louis Aragon, and a foreword by J.G. Crowther. Linocuts by Noel Counihan. Collets Holdings Ltd. [1950]. [39] pp. il.   BL

Second front: poems. Andrew Dakers Ltd. 1944. 49 pp.   IWM

see also   36, 42, 64, 76

LINDSAY, John Maurice (1918–   . b. Glasgow. Educated at Glasgow Academy and the Scottish National Academy of Music, where his studies were interrupted by the war. Served as a Captain in The Cameronians. Editor of *Poetry Scotland* and of the anthology *Sailing To-morrow's Seas*, 1944. Poet, journalist, broadcaster, novelist, critic and television executive. Director of Scottish Civic Trust, Glasgow, from 1967. Of Dumbarton)

Collected poems; by Maurice Lindsay. Edinburgh: Paul Harris Publishing. 1979. 128 pp.   OXB

The enemies of love: poems, 1941–1945; by Maurice Lindsay. Glasgow: William Maclellan. 1946. 50 pp. (Poetry Scotland series, 8).   IWM

The exiled heart: poems, 1941–1956; by Maurice Lindsay. Edited, with an introduction, by George Bruce. Robert Hale Ltd. 1957. 72 pp.   IWM

No crown for laughter: poems; by Maurice Lindsay. Fortune Press. 1943. 41 pp.

Dedicated to Henry Treece.   OXB

One later day, and other poems; by Maurice Lindsay. Brookside Press. 1964. 46 pp.

The first twenty-five copies of the ed. are numbered and signed by the author.   BL

Perhaps to-morrow, [and other poems]. Oxford: Shakespeare Head Press. 1941. 40 pp.   OXB

Predicament: thirteen poems. Oxford: Alden Press. 1942. 16 pp.   OXB

The run from life: more poems, 1942–1972; [by] Maurice Lindsay. Burford, Oxfordshire: Cygnet Press. 1975. vi, 40 pp.

A limited ed. of 125 numbered copies.   OXB

Selected poems, 1942–1972; [by] Maurice Lindsay. Robert Hale & Co. 1973. 64 pp.   OXB

see also   25, 33, 62, 65, 76

LINDSAY, Maurice   *see*   **LINDSAY, John Maurice**

LING, Ellen (Poet of the First World War)

A prayer for peace, and other poems. Ilfracombe: Arthur H. Stockwell, Ltd. 1947. 15 pp.   OXB

LING, Robert Edmund (Member of the Royal Society of Teachers, and Fellow of the Royal Geographical Society)

Rhyme and reason: [poems]. Printed Chingford: E.G. Ellis & Sons. [1955]. 51 pp.   OXB

LINSTEAD, Edward Philip Basil
Disorderly poems. Gerald Duckworth & Co. Ltd. 1950. 35 pp.   IWM

LISTER, George Leslie (Served in the Royal Artillery, mainly in Palestine. Local government further education adviser. Of Wolsingham, Weardale, County Durham)
Rhymes of a Weardale lad. Printed Durham: G. Bailes & Sons Ltd. [1969]. 32 pp. col. il. (by George Morgan).
    Title from cover.   OXB

LITCHFIELD, T.
Poems. Ilfracombe: Arthur H. Stockwell, Ltd. [1942]. 16 pp.   OXB

LITTLE, Ida
A way of living, [and other poems]. Ilfracombe: Arthur H. Stockwell, Ltd. [1965]. 16 pp.   OXB

LITTLE, Lawrence (1921– . b. London. Educated at Alleyn's School. Employed in the Office of Works before the war. Served with the Royal Corps of Signals in Africa. Novelist, poet and a contributor to leading periodicals) *see* 11, 12, 25, 33, 45, 76

LITTLE, Peter J. (Staff Sergeant in the Army) *see* 12, 47

LITVINOFF, Emanuel (1915– . b. Whitechapel, London, of Russo-Jewish parentage. Before the war he worked in tailoring, cabinet-making and the fur trade. Joined the Pioneer Corps early in the war as a Private, later commissioned. Served as a Major in the Royal West African Frontier Force, 1940–46. Journalist, novelist, poet, playwright, short story writer and broadcaster. Director of the Contemporary Jewish Library in London from 1958. Of Hertfordshire)
Conscripts: a symphonic declaration, [and other poems]. Favil Press Ltd. [1941]. [6] pp. ("Resurgam" younger poets, 6).
    Title from cover.   BL
A crown for Cain, [and other poems]. Falcon Press. 1948. 81 pp.   IWM
Notes for a survivor: [poems]. Newcastle on Tyne: Northern House. 1973. [23] pp.   OXB
The untried soldier, [and other poems]. Routledge. 1942. 40 pp.   IWM
see also 18, 19, 25, 29, 33, 38, 47, 49, 52, 57, 65, 76, 79

LLOYD, Oscar
A poor man singing: [poems]. George Gill & Sons. 1943. 24 pp.   OXB

LLOYD, William (B.A. Poet of the First World War)

Morn mist, and other poems. Ilfracombe: Arthur H. Stockwell, Ltd. [1960].
38 pp.   OXB

LOBO, Edmund (Of Dublin)
Clay speaks of the fire: poems, sonnets. Williams & Norgate, Ltd. [1946]. [vi],
58 pp.   OXB

LOCHHEAD, Marion (1902– . B. Wishaw, Lanarkshire. Educated at
Glasgow University. Freelance journalist, novelist, poet, historian and
biographer. Of Edinburgh) *see* 42

LOCKE, V.J. (Served in the Middle East with the 16th Infantry
Brigade) *see* 63

LOCKWOOD, Derek John
Farrago: [*poems*]. Dulwich Village: Outposts Publications. 1960. 12 pp.
                                                                      OXB

LOCKWOOD, John
Losing ground: [*poems*]. Walton-on-Thames: Outposts Publications. 1969.
12 pp.   OXB

LOCKYER, Henry
Communion, and other poems. Ilfracombe: Arthur H. Stockwell, Ltd. [1944].
16 pp.   OXB

LOFTING, Hugh (1886–1947. b. Maidenhead, Berkshire. Educated at Mount
St Mary's College, Chesterfield, London Polytechnic and Massachusetts
Institute of Technology. A prospector and surveyor in Canada, 1908, civil
engineer in West Africa with the Lagos Railway, 1910–11, with United
Railways of Havana, Cuba, 1912. Wounded during the First World War while
serving with the Irish Guards in France and Flanders. Settled in the United
States in 1919. Creator of the fictional character Doctor Dolittle)
Victory for the slain. Jonathan Cape. 1942. 40 pp.   MPL

LOGAN, Chris
The day moves, [*and other poems*]. Horsham, Sussex: Causeway Press. 1977.
26 pp.
     A limited ed. of 75 numbered copies.   OXB

LOGUE, Christopher (1926– . b. Portsmouth. Educated at Prior Park
College, Bath, and Portsmouth Grammar School. Joined the Army in 1944 as a
Private in The Black Watch. Spent two years in an Army prison before being
discharged with ignominy in 1948. Lived in France, 1951–56. Poet, dramatist,

song writer, journalist and writer of screen plays. Actor on stage and television. Of London)

Songs: [poems]. Hutchinson. 1959. 117 pp.   OXB

LONG, Eleanor Herdman

Sentimental verse. Printed Regency Press. [1972]. 32 pp.   OXB

LONG, William, (Peter Yates, pseud.) (1922– . Novelist and dramatist)

The expanding mirror, and other poems; by Peter Yates. Chatto & Windus. 1942. 32 pp.   OXB

The motionless dancer, and other poems; by Peter Yates. Chatto & Windus. 1943. 40 pp.   OXB

LONGDON-GRIFFITHS, T.G. (Sub-Lieutenant, Royal Naval Volunteer Reserve) *see* 23

LONGHURST, Norman (Sergeant. Served with the Eighth Army) *see* 25, 39, 44, 63

LONGRIGG, John (A member of Oxford University between 1944 and 1946) *see* 34

LOOKER, Samuel Joseph (1888–1965. b. North London but lived in Sussex, Staffordshire and Leicestershire. Poet of the First World War. Writer, lecturer, journalist and publisher's reader. Worked for Constable & Co. from 1923. Expert on Richard Jefferies and President of the Richard Jefferies Society from its foundation in 1950. Contributor on prose fiction to *The Cambridge Bibliography of English Literature*. Served on Staffordshire County Council, 1949–54)

Green branches: selected poems. Billericay: Grey Walls Press. 1941. 48 pp.   OXB

LORD, Douglas (Served on the south coast during the Battle of Britain. Invalided out. Editor and translator from the French) *see* 42

LORD, Raie

Shades from life, in verse. Ilfracombe: Arthur H. Stockwell, Ltd. 1949. 16 pp.   OXB

LOTT, S.F. (Corporal. Served with the Eighth Army) *see* 44

LOUCH, T.W. (Served in the Middle East) *see* 39, 63

LOVELACE, Thornton (Of Yorkshire?)

Wartime moods: being a collection of poems. Printed Richmond, Yorkshire: Dundas Press. [1941]. 42 pp.   OXB

LOVELESS, Henry Alger (Served as an ordnance officer)
Poems of an ordnance officer. Fortune Press. 1943. 64 pp.   IWM

LOWBURY, Edward (1913–   . b. London. Educated at St Paul's School, University College, Oxford, and the London Hospital. Newdigate Prizewinner, 1934. Graduated in medicine in 1939, specializing in pathology and bacteriology. Married the daughter of poet Andrew Young. During the war served as a medical officer in the Royal Army Medical Corps. After the war worked for the Medical Research Council. Poet and writer of children's fiction. Of Birmingham)
Crossing the line, [and other poems]. Hutchinson & Co., Ltd. [1946]. 76 pp.
MPL

LOWE, Larry (Of Lancashire) *see* 75

LOWE, Robert Leighton (Served with the Army in the Sudan and Libya. Seconded to the Royal Air Force with flying visits to South Africa and Rhodesia)
To eat the wind: poems. Fortune Press. 1946. 16 pp.   IWM

LOWSLEY, David
Combat, and other poems. Ilfracombe: Arthur H. Stockwell, Ltd. 1959. 28 pp.
OXB

LUCAS, Bette (Of Lancashire) *see* 74

LUCAS, Cecil F.
Thoughtful moments: a booklet of verse. Ilfracombe: Arthur H. Stockwell, Ltd. [1942]. 16 pp.   OXB

LUCAS, Frank Laurence (1894–1967. Educated at Rugby School, and Trinity College, Cambridge. Served in 7th Royal West Kent Regiment and the Intelligence Corps, being wounded in 1916. Fellow of King's College, Cambridge. Worked at the Foreign Office, 1939–45. Wrote novels, plays and many works of criticism)
From many times and lands: a volume of poems. Bodley Head. 1953. 318 pp.
MPL
see also 38, 42, 84

LUCAS, Hedley (1880–1971. b. Sale, Cheshire. Educated at Sale Township School and privately. Barrister-at-law of Gray's Inn. Hospital administrator, 1915–25. Master of Manchester Royal Exchange, 1925–42. Latterly lived in Worthing, Sussex)
Collected poems, 1933–1953. Altrincham: John Sherratt & Son. 1953. xxiv, 430 pp.   MPL

Homage to Cheshire: [*poems*]. 2nd ed. Printed Altrincham: Mackie & Co. Ltd. 1940. [viii], 41 pp.   OXB
Homage to Cheshire: [*poems*]. 3rd ed. Printed Altrincham: Guardian Press. 1941. [viii], 43 pp.   MPL
Homage to Cheshire: [*poems*]. 4th ed. Altrincham: John Sherratt & Son. 1949. vi, 249 pp.   MPL
Homage to Cheshire: [*poems*]. 5th ed. Altrincham: John Sherratt & Son. 1955. xviii, 248 pp. por.   MPL
Homage to Cheshire: [*poems*]. 6th ed. Independent Press Ltd. 1960. 307 pp. por.
                                                                         MPL
   [1st ed. 1939 is pre-war]
Later poems, 1954–1960. Independent Press Ltd. 1961. 287 pp. por.   OXB

LUCAS, Joseph Gerald
Words with a tramp, and other poems. Ilfracombe: Arthur H. Stockwell, Ltd. 1952. 24 pp.   OXB

LUCIAN, pseud., (E.R.G.)
All clear: some basic verse; by Lucian (E.R.G.). Birmingham: Cornish Brothers Ltd. [1944]. 16 pp.   OXB

LUCIO, pseud.   *see*   PHILLIPS, Gordon, (Lucio, pseud.)

LUSK, A.T. (Served in South-East Asia Command)   *see*   35

LUXFORD, Bertha Penelope
Poems. Arthur H. Stockwell Ltd. [1941]. 24 pp.   OXB

LUXTON, B.P. (b. Shipley, Yorkshire. Educated at Bradford Grammar School. A teacher, connected with the Yorkshire Dialect Society)
A pulse in the mind: a collection of poems in dialect and standard English. 2nd ed. Embsay, North Yorkshire: Moorland Publications. 1979. [v], 23 pp. por.
                                                                         OXB
   [No copy of 1st ed. 1978 traced]

LYDFORD, David P. (Served in H.M. Forces)   *see*   73, 75

LYNCH, George (Of Yorkshire)   *see*   73, 74

LYND, Sylvia (1888–1952. b. Hampstead, London, daughter of A.R. Dryhurst of Dublin. Educated at King Alfred School, the Slade School and the Academy of Dramatic Art. Married Irish essayist and critic Robert Lynd in 1909. Poet of the First World War. Member of Vie Heureuse Committee in 1923 and Book Society Committee in 1929. Novelist, poet and short story writer. Lived in London)

Collected poems. Macmillan. 1945. viii, 100 pp.   IWM
see also   6, 41, 51, 80, 84

LYNN-ALLEN, Esmond Harcourt (Captain, Gloucestershire Regiment. Captured in France in 1940, held prisoner of war in Germany until 1945. A countryman, writer on game and rough shooting) *see* 67

LYON, D.M.
The Atlantic Pact, and other poems. Ilfracombe: Arthur H. Stockwell, Ltd. 1949. 16 pp.   OXB

LYON, Lilian Bowes *see* **BOWES LYON, Lilian**

LYTH, John Christopher (Doctor. Lived in York during the war)
One more cairn, and many things beside: poems. Sketches by Richard Fisher. Printed Hexham: Courant Printing Works. 1954. [viii], 128 pp. il.   OXB

LYTH, Phyllis (Lived in York during the war) *see* 22

LYTTON, Eileen (Of Hertfordshire) *see* 75

M., A.
Hearts o'erflowing on various musings: [*poems*]; by A.M. Ilfracombe: Arthur H. Stockwell Ltd. 1958. 64 pp.   OXB
Thoughts in verse; by "A.M.". Ilfracombe: Arthur H. Stockwell, Ltd. 1945. 16 pp.   OXB

M.B.B. *see* **BOOTH, Madeleine Beatrice**, (M.B.B.)

M., J.G. (Served in South-East Asia Command) *see* 35

MacALLAN, Harry
Poems (February–September 1942). Richards Press Ltd. [1943]. 32 pp.
                                                                    OXB

MacARTHUR, Bessie Jane Bird (1889–   . b. Duns, Berwickshire, née Bisset. Educated at Charlotte Square Institution and St George's High School for Girls, Edinburgh. Studied music in Scotland, 1912. Married J.C.C. MacArthur, a border sheep farmer, in 1914 and had three sons and a daughter. Two of her sons were killed in the war. Writer of Scottish poems and Celtic plays. Lived in Edinburgh)
From Daer Water: poems in Scots and English. Dunfermline: H.T. Macpherson. 1962. 63 pp.   OXB
Last leave, [*and other poems*]. Oliver & Boyd Ltd. 1943. 12 pp.
   'For the other members of a Catalina aircraft shot down while protecting

the North African convoy, and for Alistair'. 'Any profits will be given to the R.A.F. Benevolent Fund'. BPL

MACBETH, George (1932– . b. Scotland. Educated at King Edward VII School, Sheffield, and New College, Oxford. Producer and editor with B.B.C. Talks Department, 1955–76. Poet, playwright, novelist and writer of children's fiction. Editor of the Fantasy Poets series from the Fantasy Press, Oxford. Recipient of the Sir Geoffrey Faber Memorial Award, 1964, and the Cholmondeley Award, 1977. Of Thurne, Norfolk)

Collected poems, 1958–1970. Macmillan. [1971]. 254 pp. OXB
The colour of blood: poems. Macmillan. 1967. [viii], 77 pp. OXB
The Hiroshima dream. Academy Editions. 1970. 21 pp. OXB
Lecture to the trainees, [and other poems]. Oxford: Fantasy Press. 1962. 27 pp. (Fantasy poets). OXB
Shrapnel: poems. Macmillan. 1973. [x], 70 pp. OXB
Typing a novel about the war. Knotting, Bedfordshire: Martin Booth. 1980. [6] pp. OXB
   A limited ed. of 125 numbered copies of which the first fifty are signed by the author.
A war quartet: [poems]. Macmillan. 1969. 78 pp. il. BPL

McCAIG, Norman (1910– . b. Edinburgh. Educated at the Royal High School and Edinburgh University. A schoolmaster 1932–67 and 1969–70. Served in the Army in the Non-Combatant Corps. Fellow in Creative Writing at Edinburgh University, 1967–69. Lecturer in English Studies at Stirling University, 1970–72, Reader in Poetry, 1972–77. Recipient of Royal Society of Literature Award, 1967, Cholmondeley Award, 1975, and several Scottish Arts Council Awards)

The inward eye: [poems]. Routledge. 1946. 60 pp. OXB
see also 33

McCALLUM, Neil (Served as a Lieutenant with the Eighth Army. Novelist and short story writer) *see* 11, 25, 56, 57

McCARTHY, John F. (Of Glamorganshire) *see* 75

McCAW, A. (Of Northumberland) *see* 75

MacCOLL, Dugald Sutherland (1859–1948. b. Glasgow. Educated at Glasgow Academy, University College, London, and Lincoln College, Oxford. Newdigate Prizeman, 1882. Keeper of the Tate Gallery, 1906–11, Keeper of the Wallace Collection, 1911–24. Member of the Royal Fine Arts Commission, 1925–29. Initiated the foundation of the National Arts Collections Fund. Art critic, water-colour artist, lecturer on art history. Poet of the First World War)

Poems. Oxford: Basil Blackwell. 1940. x, 139 pp. por. OXB

McCORKINDALE, Bill
The mirror and the maze: [*poems*]. Aberdeen: Rainbow Books. [1979]. 76 pp.
OXB

McCOY, Kenneth Norman
Of people and places: poems. Ilfracombe: Arthur H. Stockwell, Ltd. [1958].
16 pp. OXB

McCUBBIN, Nellie
Memories, and other poems. Ilfracombe: Arthur H. Stockwell, Ltd. [1945].
23 pp. OXB

MacDIARMID, Hugh, pseud. *see* **GRIEVE, Christopher Murray**, (Hugh
MacDiarmid, pseud.)

McDIARMID, M.P. (Corporal. Served with the Eighth Army) *see* 44

McDONALD, Anthony (Captain, The Rifle Brigade. Served in the Middle
East) *see* 25, 33

MACDONALD, Mary
Flowers in the crevices: [*poems*]. Egremont: Arcadian Agency. [1962]. 16 pp.
(Arcadian series). OXB

MacDONALD, Norman (1904– . Of Fife?)
The wave oracle: poems and songs. Printed Cupar, Fife: Innes Ltd. [1978]. vi,
61 pp. OXB

MACDONALD, Prudence (Of Maidstone, Kent)
No wasted hour, and other poems. Sidgwick & Jackson. 1945. vi, 32 pp. BPL

McDONALD, Robert
First poems. Ilfracombe: Arthur H. Stockwell, Ltd. [1942]. 19 pp. OXB

MACDONOGH, Patrick (1902– . Educated at Avoca School, Blackrock,
County Dublin, and Trinity College, Dublin. A regular contributor of verse and
reviews to *The Dublin Magazine*)
One landscape still, and other poems. Secker & Warburg. 1958. x, 70 pp.
MPL
Over the water, and other poems. Dublin: Orwell Press. 1943. 23 pp. OXB
see also 9

MACDOUGALL, C.A.R. (Of Bedford)
Poems in blue. Ilfracombe: Arthur H. Stockwell, Ltd. [1943]. 16 pp.
OXB

McEWAN, John
   Songs of sun and shadow: [*poems*]. Ilfracombe: Arthur H. Stockwell, Ltd. 1949.
14 pp.   OXB

McEWEN, Sir John Helias Finnie (1894–1962. Educated at Eton College,
and Trinity College, Cambridge. Poet of the First World War. Served as
Captain in 5th Queen's Own Cameron Highlanders and in the Royal Air Force,
when he was taken prisoner. Entered the Diplomatic Service in 1920.
Conservative M.P. for Berwick & Haddington, 1931–45. Parliamentary Under
Secretary of State for Scotland, 1939–40)
   There is a valley: [*poems*]. Printed Edinburgh: C.J. Cousland & Sons, Ltd.
1950. 106 pp.   OXB
see also   42, 84

McEWEN, Leslie Psaila
   A small bouquet: (poems). Ilfracombe: Arthur H. Stockwell, Ltd. 1949. 20 pp.
                                                                          OXB

McFADDEN, Roy (1921–   . b. Belfast. Educated at Regent House School,
Newtownards, Country Down, and Queen's University, Belfast. Co-editor of
Ulster Voices, 1941–42, and *Rann*, an Ulster poetry quarterly, 1948–53. In
practice as a lawyer)
   Flowers for a lady, [*and other poems*]. Routledge. [1945]. 64 pp.   MPL
   The heart's townland, [*and other poems*]. Routledge. 1947. 57 pp.   OXB
   A poem: Russian summer. Dublin: Gayfield. 1941. [6] pp. il. (by Leslie Owen
Baxter).
      Title from cover.   OXB
   Swords and ploughshares: [*poems*]. Routledge. 1943. 32 pp.   OXB
   A watching brief: [*poems*]. Belfast: Blackstaff Press. [1979]. [vi], 50 pp.
                                                                          OXB
see also   25, 28, 29

McGEOCH, Andrew Jackson (1900–   . b. Glasgow. Educated at Kelvinside
Academy, Larchfield School and Mill Hill School. Joint managing director of
family engineering business until 1962)
   The alighting leaf: [*poems*]. Putnam. [1960]. 32 pp.   OXB
   Annus mirabilis, and other poems. William Heinemann Ltd. 1949. vi, 45 pp.
                                                                          OXB

MacGILL, Robert C.S. (Lieutenant, 7th Queen's Own Hussars, Captured in
Libya on 21 November 1941, held prisoner of war in Germany until
1945)   *see*   5, 67

MacGREGOR, George M. (Of Lanarkshire ?)
   Occasional verses. Compiled and edited with introduction and notes by James

K. Scobbie. Illustrations by Richard Y. Marshall. Printed [Motherwell]: Motherwell Times Ltd. [1978]. 112 pp. il., por.   OXB

McGUIRE, P.B. (Private. Served with the Eighth Army)   *see*   44

McHALE, A. (Of Lanarkshire)   *see*   74

McHALE, Edward (Served in the Middle East)   *see*   39, 63

McHARRIE, Dennis (Wing Commander, Royal Air Force. Posted to 38 Bomber Squadron in the Middle East as a Flight Lieutenant, moving to Barce near Benghazi. Of Blackpool)   *see*   63

McINTYRE, Cameron Alexander (Served in the London Scottish)
— *if it's only goodbye:* [*poems*]. Ipswich: Hadden, Best & Co., Ltd. 1969. vi, 42 pp.   OXB

MACINTYRE, Christian
When the gods laugh: [*poems*]. Balerno: Celandine Publishing Co. 1942. 43 pp.
                                                                       OXB

McINTYRE, L.M.
Petals in the wind: [poems]. Ilfracombe: Arthur H. Stockwell Ltd. 1979. 23 pp.
                                                                       OXB

MACK, Ernest (Served in H.M. Forces. Taken prisoner of war)
Luana Coral, and other poems. Ilfracombe: Arthur H. Stockwell, Ltd. 1945. 16 pp.   OXB

MACKAY, Agnes Ethel (Spent 1940–44 in German-occupied France, working on the land. Writer on French literature)
The secret country: poems. Fortune Press. 1947. 52 pp.   OXB

McKAY, Kathleen Jessie (Of Southampton)
Pause and ponder: poems. Ilfracombe: Arthur H. Stockwell, Ltd. 1955. 16 pp.
                                                                       OXB

MACKAY, Robert John (Of Embo, Dornoch, Sutherland)
Poetical musings. Embo, Dornoch: Author. 1940. 93 pp.
   Cover-title is *Poetical Musings (frae Bonnie Scotland).*   BL
Recent poems. Printed Aberdeen: Press & Journal Office. 1942. 24 pp.   BL
Scotland, my native land, and other poems. Printed Aberdeen: Press & Journal Office. 1943. 26 pp. por.   BL

MACKAY, Robert Ogilvie
Light verse and lyrics. Ilfracombe: Arthur H. Stockwell, Ltd. [1963]. 54 pp.
OXB

McKEE, O.B.
Poems. Ilfracombe: Arthur H. Stockwell, Ltd. 1962. 124 pp.   OXB

MACKERETH, James Allan (1871–   . b. Ambleside, Westmorland.
Educated at St Bees School. Poet of the First World War. Lived at Bingley,
Yorkshire)
Song of the young and old men, in years of world-wide suspicion, fear, and folly, [*and
other poems*]. Printed Bradford: Country Press. [1940]. [11] pp.   OXB
This greatness, [*and other poems*]. Printed Bradford: Country Press. [1940].
24 pp.   OXB

MACKIE, Albert David (1904–   . b. Edinburgh. Educated at Edinburgh
University. Journalist and writer on Scotland. Editor of *Edinburgh Evening
Dispatch*, 1946–54, Scottish news editor of *Picture Post*, 1955, and feature writer
for the *Scottish Daily Express*, 1956–65. Also worked as a journalist in Kingston,
Jamaica. Of Edinburgh)
*The book of Macnib: one hundred and sixteen of his choicest effusions over the past twenty
years*: [*poems*]; [by Albert D. Mackie]. Edinburgh: Castle Wynd Printers Ltd.
[1957]. 64 pp. il.   OXB

MACKINNON, J. (Served in H.M. Forces) *see* 74

MACKWORTH, Cecily (b. Llantilio, Monmouthshire. In Paris in June 1940.
Wandered through France for two months before returning to England via
Lisbon. Married the Marquis de Chabannes la Palice. Novelist, poet, critic,
literary biographer and journalist. Middle East correspondent for *Paris Presse*,
1947–48, features writer for *L'Information*, 1954, and Paris correspondent for
Twentieth Century, 1957–61) *see* 42

MACLAUGHLIN, I. *see* 22

MACLEAN, Alasdair (1926–   . Reviewer for *Times Literary Supplement*. Of
Ardnamurchan, Argyllshire)
Waking the dead, [*and other poems*]. Victor Gollancz Ltd. 1976. 80 pp. (Gollancz
poets).   OXB

MacLEAN, Jack (Took part in the D-Day landings)
The wheel of life, and other poems. Ilfracombe: Arthur H. Stockwell, Ltd. [1955].
20 pp.   OXB

MACLEAN, Sorley (1911– . b. Scottish Highlands. Educated at Edinburgh University. Poet writing in Gaelic. Of the Isle of Skye)

Poems to Eimhir: poems from Dain do Eimhir, translated from Gaelic by Ian Crichton Smith. Victor Gollancz Ltd. 1971. 64 pp. OXB

Poems to Eimhir: poems from Dain do Eimhir, translated from Gaelic by Ian Crichton Smith. Newcastle on Tyne: Northern House. [1971]. 64 pp. (Northern House pamphlet poets). OXB

Spring tide and neap tide: selected poems 1932–72. Glasgow: Canongate. 1977. x, 182 pp.

Parallel English and Gaelic texts. OXB
see also 63

McLENNAN, John (Of Renfrewshire) *see* 74

MACLEOD, Joseph Todd Gordon, (Adam Drinan, pseud.) (1903– . b. Middlesex. Educated at Rugby School, and Balliol College, Oxford. Called to the Bar in 1928. Was a private tutor, book reviewer, actor, producer and lecturer on theatre history. Directed Festival Theatre Repertory, Cambridge, 1933–36. Newsreader and commentator with the B.B.C., 1938–45. Managing director of Scottish National Film Studios, 1946–47. Of Florence, Italy)

The cove: a sequence of poems; by Adam Drinan. Printed St John's Wood: French & Son. 1940. [iv], 34 pp. OXB

The men of the rocks: [poems]; by Adam Drinan. Fortune Press. [1942]. 36 pp. BPL

Women of the happy island: [poems]; [by] Adam Drinan. Glasgow: William Maclellan. 1944. 43 pp. col. il. (By William Crosbie). (Poetry Scotland series). OXB

McLOUGHLIN, Patrick J. (An Ulsterman living in County Down)

Thoughts in print: [poems]. Goodmayes, Essex: Spearman Publishers. [1943]. 28 pp. OXB

MACLURE, James Drummond (1920–43. b. Finchley, London. Educated at Highgate School. Mobilized as a Territorial in the London Scottish in 1939. Volunteered for the Scottish Commando. Commissioned in 1st Battalion, Royal Scots. Served in India then became liaison officer to the 4th Brigade in Burma. Killed in action on night of 5–6 April 1943)

"Thoughts": [poems]. Newport, Mon.: R.H. Johns Ltd. 1946. 46 pp. por.

Privately printed for 'Jamie's many friends'. IWM
see also 20

McMILLAN, Ettie (Of Selkirkshire ?)
Thoughts through the years, 1939–1943: [*poems*]. Printed Galashiels: A. Walker & Son Ltd. [1943]. 23 pp.   OXB

MACMILLAN, Malcolm Kenneth (1913–78. Educated at Edinburgh University, becoming a journalist. Served as a Private in the infantry, 1939–40. Labour M.P. for the Western Isles, 1935–70. Chairman of the Scottish Parliamentary Labour Party, 1945–51. Lived in Stornaway and Glasgow)
The heart is highland: [*poems*]. Edinburgh: Moray Press. [1947]. 44 pp.

IWM

McMURDO, Fergus William Hamilton, (John Talifer, pseud.) (1911–50. Served as a Captain in the Royal Army Medical Corps. A survivor of Dunkirk, later a Regimental Medical Officer in the Middle East. After the war a doctor in general practice in Addlestone, Surrey)
Phoenix, and other poems, 1943 to 1950. [Addlestone]: Anchor Publishing Co. 1951. 56 pp.
    A limited ed. of seventy-five copies printed on hand-made paper at the Ditchling Press, Sussex.   OXB

McMURTRIE, Duncan Gilbert Scott (–1944. Educated at Winchester College and Cambridge University. Lieutenant, Scots Guards. Served in North Africa. Died of wounds received at Anzio in February 1944)
The diary of a heart: [*poems*]. Printed Oxford: University Press. 1951. 35 pp. por.   OXB

MACNAB, Roy (1923–   . b. Durban, South Africa. Educated at Hilton College, Natal, and Jesus College, Oxford. Served as a naval officer during the war. Cultural Attaché at the South African High Commission in London, 1955–59. Councillor of Cultural & Press Affairs, South African Embassy in Paris, 1959–67. Director of the South Africa Foundation in London from 1968)
The man of grass, and other poems. Saint Catherine Press Ltd. 1960. [x], 54 pp.

OXB

Testament of a South African: [*poems*]. Fortune Press. 1947. 32 pp.
    'Dedicated to the memory of Harry Francis Barker, killed in action in Italy on 12th June 1944'.   OXB
see also 49

MACNAUGHTON-SMITH, Michael (1923–44. Educated at City of London School, and St John's College, Oxford. Served in Royal Air Force Bomber Command. Killed returning from a raid on Wesseling on 22 June 1944) *see* 20

MacNEICE, Louis (1907–63. b. Belfast, son of a bishop. Educated at Marlborough College, and Merton College, Oxford. A university lecturer in classics and Greek before the war. At Cornell University, United States, at start of war. Returned to England to work at the B.B.C. as feature writer and producer, 1941–49. Director of the British Institute, Athens, 1950. Critic, dramatist and one of the leading poets of the 1930s)

Collected poems, 1925–1948. Faber & Faber Ltd. 1949. 310 pp. MPL
The collected poems of Louis MacNeice. Edited by E.R. Dodds. Faber & Faber. 1966. xviii, 575 pp. MPL
The collected poems of Louis MacNeice. Edited by E.R. Dodds. [New] ed. Faber & Faber. 1979. xviii, 575 pp. OXB
Eighty-five poems. Selected by the author. Faber & Faber. 1959. 128 pp. MPL
Holes in the sky: poems 1944–1947. Faber & Faber Ltd. 1948. 72 pp. OXB
The last ditch: [*poems*]. Dublin: Cuala Press. 1940. [viii], 35 pp.
　A limited ed. of 450 copies, twenty-five signed by the author and numbered one to twenty-five. BPL
Plant and phantom: poems. Faber & Faber Ltd. 1941. 86 pp. OXB
Poems, 1925–1940. New York: Random House. [1940]. xiv, 326 pp.
　OXB
Springboard: poems, 1941–1944. Faber & Faber. 1944. 55 pp. IWM
Visitations: [*poems*]. Faber & Faber. 1957. 60 pp. OXB
see also　4, 10, 15, 17, 25, 26, 37, 45, 56, 57, 76, 77, 83, 85, 86

McNICHOL, Vera Ernst
Reflections of sunshine: [*poems*]. Ilfracombe: Arthur H. Stockwell, Ltd. [1955]. 64 pp. OXB

MacPHAIL, Ian Shaw (Served in the Royal Air Force. Writer on music) *see* 62

McPHERSON, J. (Of Edinburgh) *see* 74

MACROBERT, J. (Of Renfrewshire) *see* 74

McWILLIAM, G.E.B. (A woman. Of North London)
Poems. [Privately printed]. 1955. 55 pp. BPL

MAGRAW, John Edward (Of Lancashire ?)
A fifth and final sonnet bouquet. Printed Wigan: J. Starr & Sons, Ltd. [1943]. 24 pp.
　'The whole of the purchase price to be given to the Royal Albert Edward Infirmary'. OXB
A fourth bouquet of English sonnets. Printed Wigan: James Starr & Sons, Ltd. [1942]. 24 pp.
　'For Red Cross funds'. OXB

A seventh bouquet of English sonnets. Printed Wigan: James Starr & Sons, Ltd. [1944]. 23 pp. OXB

Still another bouquet of English sonnets. Printed Wigan: James Starr & Sons, Ltd. [1942]. [ii], 28 pp. OXB

MAHON, Derek (1941– . b. Belfast. Educated at Belfast Institute, and Trinity College, Dublin. After graduating spent two years in Canada and America, working in a variety of jobs. Returned to Ireland in 1967, teaching English at Belfast High School, then lecturing at The Language Centre of Ireland in Dublin. Poet, reviewer and contributor to *Vogue* magazine. Founding editor of *Ariel*. Poet-in-Residence at Emerson College, Boston. Massachusetts, 1976–77, and at the New University of Ulster, Coleraine, 1977–79. Recipient of the Eric Gregory Award for Poetry in 1965)

Night-crossing: [poems]. Oxford University Press. 1968. [x], 38 pp. OXB
Poems, 1962–1978. Oxford University Press. 1979. [x], 117 pp. OXB
The snow party, [and other poems]. Oxford University Press. 1975. [viii], 38 pp. OXB

MAIDEN, Sydney *see* 84

MAIR, Mary (Poet of the First World War. Of Epsom, Surrey)
The small voice, [and other poems]. Fortune Press. 1945. 23 pp. OXB

MAIR-SCHUBERT, Gladys
How to keep the peace, and five other poems. Ilfracombe: Arthur H. Stockwell, Ltd. 1948. 13 pp. OXB

MALCOLM, George, Lord Malcolm (1903–76. Educated at Eton College, and the Royal Military College, Sandhurst. Joined the Argyll & Sutherland Highlanders in 1923, becoming Lieutenant-Colonel in 1943. Served in India, Egypt, Palestine and with Combined Operations in the Middle East and Central Pacific. Commanded 8th Battalion in Austria, 1945–46, retiring in 1947. Hereditary Chief of the Clan Malcolm, organizer of tattoos and clan gatherings) *see* 38, 39, 63

MALLALIEU, Herbert B. (1914– . b. New Jersey, United States, but resident in England since childhood. Educated at Wells, Somerset. Commissioned in Royal Artillery, serving 1940–46, taking part in the Sicily landing and the Italian campaign and subsequently stationed in Greece and Austria. A journalist on London and provincial newspapers. Associate editor of *Twentieth Century* and a contributor of poetry to leading periodicals)

Letter in wartime, and other poems. Fortune Press. [1940]. 44 pp. BPL
see also 6, 25, 33; 37, 45, 49, 59, 76

MALLONE, Ronald Stephen (1916– . b. Lewisham, London. Educated at

Addey and Stanhope School and London University. Journalist and lecturer on English literature. Editor of the *Christian Party News Letter*, 1941–45)

Blood and sweat and tears: a selection of poems written between November 18th, 1940, May 31st, 1942. With an introduction by Vera Brittain. New Vision Publications. 1942. 42 pp. (War poets series). IWM

Whose victory?: (selected poems, 1940–1945). Christian Party. 1945. 49 pp.
OXB

MALTHOUSE, J.
On patrol. Arthur H. Stockwell Ltd. [1940]. 11 pp. OXB

MANDER, John (1932– . Educated at Eton College, and Trinity College, Cambridge. Assistant literary editor of *New Statesman* from 1960, associate editor of *Encounter* from 1963. Writer on Anglo-German relations)
Elegiacs: [poems]. Printed Hatfield: Stellar Press. 1972. [x], 59 pp.
A limited ed. of 100 numbered copies signed by the author. OXB

MANFRED, Robert, pseud. *see* MARX, Erica, (Robert Manfred, pseud.)

MANIFOLD, John Streeter (1915– . b. Melbourne, Australia. Educated at Geelong Grammar School, and Jesus College, Cambridge. Worked for a publishing house in Germany before the war. Lieutenant in the Intelligence Corps, serving in West Africa alongside the Forces Françaises Combattantes in 1940, in the Middle East and in France. Poet and writer on music and theatre)
Nightmares and sunhorses: [poems]. Melbourne: *Overland*. [1961]. 48 pp.
OXB
Op. 8: poems 1961–69. St Lucia, Queensland: University of Queensland Press. 1971. [x], 45 pp. OXB
Selected verse. Dennis Dobson. 1948. 90 pp. OXB
see also 17, 25, 33, 36, 42, 47, 64, 76, 83

MANIZALES, Sheila
Ode to beauty, [and other poems]. Mitre Press. [1968]. 38 pp. OXB

MANN, Arthur (Of Ripley ?)
Lathkill Dale, Boston Stump (St. Botolph's), and other poems. Foreword by R. Pursglove. Printed Ripley: Ripley Printing Society Ltd. [1949]. viii, 69 pp. il.
OXB

MANN, George
The two generations: [poems]. Ilfracombe: Arthur H. Stockwell, Ltd. [1945]. 16 pp. OXB

MANNIN, Ethel (1900–84. b. London and educated at a local council school. In 1918 she became associate editor of *The Pelican*, a theatrical newspaper. A

prolific novelist, biographer and travel writer, she joined the Independent Labour Party in 1932. Married twice, to J.A. Porteous in 1920 and to Reginald Reynolds in 1938. Throughout the war she lived and worked in London. Of Teignmouth, Devon) *see* 80

MANNING, Hugo (Lance-Corporal, Intelligence Corps. Served in North Africa, where he was wounded. Jewish poet, a friend of the American playwright Arthur Miller. Of Hampstead, London)
Buenos Aires. Buenos Aires: Francisco A. Colombo. 1942. 23 pp.
    A limited ed. of 200 copies.   OXB
The crown and the fable: a poetic sequence. Chelsea: Gaberbocchus Press Ltd. 1950. 31 pp.   OXB
Smile, Ichabod: a war poem. Printed Plaistow: Curwen Press. 1944. 8 pp.
    A limited ed. of 100 copies.   BL
see also 13

MANNING, Jean C.
Minor minutes: a book of verse. Ilfracombe: Arthur H. Stockwell, Ltd. [1942]. 24 pp.   OXB

MANNING, Olivia (1915–80. b. Portsmouth, daughter of a Royal Navy Commander. Educated at private schools. Married Reginald Donald Smith in 1939. Press officer at United States Embassy in Cairo in 1942. Press assistant with Public Information Office in Jerusalem, 1943–44, and with British Council, Jerusalem, 1944–45. Novelist, short story writer and general writer. Reviewer of novels for the *Spectator* and *The Sunday Times*. Lived in London) *see* 40

MANNING, S.R.
Friendship, and other poems. Ilfracombe: Arthur H. Stockwell, Ltd. 1946. 15 pp.   OXB

MANSELL, L.R.
Of feeling and fancy: (a selection of verse). Ilfracombe: Arthur H. Stockwell, Ltd. [1942]. 16 pp.   OXB

MANSER, P.W. (Of London) *see* 74

MANWARING, Randle (1912– . Educated privately. Served in the Royal Air Force, 1940–46. Wing Commander commanding the Royal Air Force Regiment in Burma, 1945. Worked in insurance, becoming a company director. Diocesan reader in the Anglican Church)
Crossroads of the year (Songs of the four seasons): [poems]. White Lion Publishers Ltd. 1975. [x], 46 pp. il.   OXB

Posies once mine: poems. Fortune Press. [1954]. 64 pp.   IWM
Satires and salvation: [poems]. Mitre Press. [1960]. 79 pp.   MPL

MANZIE, Charles (Of Angus, Scotland) *see* 74

MARCHANT, Doreen
The collected poems of Doreen Marchant. Printed Regency Press. [1976]. 24 pp.
                                                                          OXB

MARCUS, pseud. (Served in South-East Asia Command) *see* 35

MARE, Walter De La *see* **DE LA MARE, Walter**

MARGHERITTA, B.C.
A book of verse. Halcyon Press. [1956]. 32 pp.
    Title from cover.   OXB
A book of verse. Vol. II. Cambridge: Poetry Publications. 1956. [iv], 28 pp.
                                                                          OXB

MARK, Albert R.
The world at war, and other poems. Ilfracombe: Arthur H. Stockwell, Ltd [1942].
16 pp.   OXB

MARKS, Stanford (Of London) *see* 74

MARLER, George (Chief Petty Officer, Royal Navy) *see* 23

MARRIOTT, P.H. (Sergeant. Served with the Eighth Army) *see* 44

MARRON, Os *see* 2

MARSDEN, A.W. (Served with the infantry in the Middle East) *see* 39, 63

MARSH, J.H.
Day by day: a collection of poems. Ilfracombe: Arthur H. Stockwell Ltd. 1975.
196 pp.   OXB

MARSHALL D.J. (Served in the Royal Air Force)
'Griff' on the Gremlin: [poems]; by D.J. Marshall and F.V.G. Royce. Illustrated
by Len Kirley. Pilot Press Ltd. 1943. 64 pp. il.   OXB

MARSHALL, Irene (Of Yorkshire) *see* 75

MARSHALL, T. (Served in H.M. Forces) *see* 73

MARSTON, Geoffrey C.
"A Hong Kong diary". [Author]. 1970.
A broadside.   IWM

MARTIN, pseud. *see* **MARTIN, Suzanna**, (Martin, pseud.)

MARTIN, David (1918–   . b. Hungary. Educated in Germany. Subsequently worked in Holland on the reclamation of the Zuider Zee, travelled to Hungary then spent a year on a kibbutz in Israel. Took part in the Spanish Civil War as a first-aid man on the Republican side. Settled in London in 1938. Worked for the *Daily Express* and later for the European Service of the B.B.C. Literary editor of *Reynolds News*, 1945–47, then *Daily Express* correspondent in India. Editor of the anthology *Rhyme and Reason*, 1944. Emigrated to Australia in 1949)
Battlefields and girls: poems. Glasgow: William Maclellan. 1942. 34 pp.
    'Royalties will aid soldiers of democracy who fought in Spain, now in French concentration camps'.   OXB
From life: selected poems. With a foreword by Dame Mary Gilmore. Sydney: Current Book Distributors. 1953. 32 pp.   BL
    The gift: poems 1959–1965. Brisbane: Jacaranda Press. 1966. 58 pp.   OXB
    Poems of David Martin, 1938–1958. Sydney: Edwards & Shaw. [1959]. 109 pp.
                                                                                OXB
see also   36, 64

MARTIN, James Sackville- *see* **SACKVILLE-MARTIN, James**

MARTIN, Michael (Served in the Middle East)   *see*   63

MARTIN, P.J. (Served in South-East Asia Command. Of Bracknell, Berkshire)   *see* 35

MARTIN, Raymond George
The duty of Bess, and other poems. Ilfracombe: Arthur H. Stockwell, Ltd. 1952. 40 pp.   OXB

MARTIN, Suzanna, (Martin, pseud.)
One way through life: [poems]; by Martin. Ilfracombe: Arthur H. Stockwell, Ltd. [1953]. 31 pp.   OXB
Pearls of thought: [poems]. Ilfracombe: Arthur H. Stockwell, Ltd. 1950. 16 pp.
                                                                                OXB

MARTINEAU, Gerard Durani (Officer with Royal Sussex Regiment, 1915–23, and with Royal Army Ordnance Corps from 1939 until invalided out in 1941. Writer on cricket. Of Kilve, Somerset)
Rhyme the rudder, swung by a service man: verses of our age for lovers of plain speech. British Authors' Press. [1944]. 93 pp.   OXB
see also   38

MARTLEW, George
> *The grotto, and other poems.* Ilfracombe: Arthur H. Stockwell, Ltd. 1953. 16 pp.
> OXB
> *Liberty!, and other poems.* Ilfracombe: Arthur H. Stockwell, Ltd. [1952]. 15 pp.
> OXB

MARTYN, Eva E.
> *For you!, and other poems.* Ilfracombe: Arthur H. Stockwell, Ltd. 1947. 32 pp.
> OXB

MARX, Erica, (Robert Manfred, pseud.) (1909–67. b. Streatham, London, daughter of a banker. Educated at various schools in England, Wales and France, and King's College, London. Commandant, Women's Home Defence, Surrey, 1941–43. Founded the Hand and Flower Press to assist novice poets, publishing the Poems in Pamphlet paperback series. On the board of management of The Poetry Book Society, 1953–57. Lived in Kent)
> *Escape from anger:* [*poems*]; by Robert Manfred. Aldington, Kent: Hand and Flower Press. 1951. 325–356 pp. (Poems in pamphlet, 1951, XI).　　　BL
> *Some poems: a small selection written between 1930 and 1953.* Ashford, Kent: Hand and Flower Press. [1955]. 47 pp.　　　OXB

MASEFIELD, John (1878–1967. b. Ledbury, Herefordshire. Educated at King's School, Warwick, and on the *Conway* where he learned seamanship. Spent many years adventuring by sea and land, chiefly in America. Poet of the First World War. Served with the Red Cross in France and the Dardanelles. Prolific writer of poetry, plays, novels, essays, criticism and short stories. Became Poet Laureate in 1930 in succession to Robert Bridges. Lived at Abingdon, Berkshire)
> *A generation risen:* [*poems*]. [Illustrated by] Edward Seago. Collins. [1942]. 72 pp. il.　　　IWM
> *Land workers.* William Heinemann Ltd. 1942. [iv], 12 pp.　　　BPL
> *Poems.* Complete ed. with recent poems. New York: Macmillan Co. 1966. xxii, 685 pp. por.　　　BL
> *Shopping in Oxford.* [Privately printed]. [1948]. [21] pp.　　　OXB
> *Some verses to some Germans.* William Heinemann Ltd. 1939. [iv], 10 pp.
> OXB
see also 38

MASON, Charles (Commissioned in the Army, stationed in Somalia)
> *Dusty days:* [*poems*]. Fortune Press. [1944]. 21 pp.　　　IWM

MASON, Evelyn (Of London)　*see*　74

MASON, G.J. (Served in H.M. Forces)　*see*　75

MASON, Kenneth　*see*　23

MASON, Stanley
    A necklace of words: poems as beads on the string of the years. Walton-on-Thames: Outposts Publications. 1975. [iv], 44 pp.   OXB

MASTERS, Laura
    Our heritage: poems. Pioneer Productions. [1980?]. [9] pp.
       Title from cover.   OXB

MATHIAS, Roland (1915– . b. Talybont-on-Usk, Breconshire. Educated at Caterham School, and Jesus College, Oxford. Headmaster at Pembroke Dock Grammar School, 1948–58, at Herbert Strutt School, Belper, Derbyshire, 1958–64, and at King Edward's Five Ways School, Birmingham, 1964–69. Editor of *The Anglo-Welsh Review.* Chairman, Literature Committee, Welsh Arts Council, from 1976. Of Brecon)
    Break in harvest, and other poems. Routledge. 1946. 57 pp.   OXB
    Days enduring, and other poems. Ilfracombe: Arthur H. Stockwell, Ltd. [1943]. 64 pp.   OXB
see also 32

MATHIESON, Robert
    Your finest hour, and other poems. Ilfracombe: Arthur H. Stockwell, Ltd. [1944]. 32 pp.   OXB

MATTHEWMAN, Sydney (b. Leeds, Yorkshire. Educated at Leeds University. Literary editor and agent. Editor of *Yorkshire Poetry*, 1921–24, associate editor of *The Decachord*, 1923–29, and editor of *The Bookmart*, 1946–47)
    Christmas: poems. Drawings by Albert Wainwright. Comyns Ltd. 1946. 21 pp. il.   OXB

MATTHEWS, Geoffrey (1920– . b. London. Educated at Kingswood School, Bath, and Corpus Christi College, Oxford. Served in the Royal Corps of Signals from May 1940. After the war became a university lecturer) *see* 36, 42, 76

MATTHEWS, Mary (Of London)
    "Our local", and other poems of London. Printed Clapham Park: Battley Brothers Ltd. [1950]. 8 pp.   OXB

MATTHEWS, Noel *see* 79

MATTHEWS, Winifred (Of Monmouthshire) *see* 71, 75

MATTHIAS, Ivan D.
    The common things: verse. Ilfracombe: Arthur H. Stockwell, Ltd. [1943]. 48 pp.   OXB

MAUNY, Erik de *see* **DE MAUNY, Erik**

MAURER, Christine, (Kristine Saint-John, pseud.) (Translator from the French. Of London)
Lament for a new age: [*poems*]; by Kristine Saint-John. Pre-publication Press. 1979. 41 pp.   OXB

MAWDSLEY, Norman (1921– . b. Clifton, Bristol. Educated at Clifton College, and Oriel College, Oxford. Editor of the anthology *Poetry from Oxford, Michaelmas, 1946—Trinity, 1948*. Held academic appointments in Oxford, Edinburgh and St Andrews. Professor of History at Brandon University, Manitoba, Canada, from 1970. Historian and writer on academic and legal dress)
Night pieces: [*poems*]. Fortune Press. 1948. 32 pp.   OXB

MAY, Derek J. *see* 16

MAYNARD, Theodore (1890–1956. b. Southern India, of English missionary parents. Intended to study for the Unitarian ministry but instead became a Catholic, spending seven months in the Dominican novitiate. Poet of the First World War. Worked in the Ministry of Munitions. Settled in the United States in 1920, eventually becoming an American citizen. Poet, critic, biographer, historian and writer on Roman Catholicism)
Collected poems. Introduction by Alfred Noyes. New York: Macmillan Co. 1946. xviii, 222 pp.   BL

MAYO, Frances *see* 36, 76

MAYOR, Beatrice (b. London. Educated in Paris. Poet of the First World War. Married R.G. Mayor. Poet, novelist, and writer of plays for children)
Voices from the crowd: [*poems*]. Fortune Press. [1943]. 75 pp.   BPL

MEADE, Walter
Verses out of pattern. Frederick Muller Ltd. 1944. 63 pp.   BPL

MEAKING, Evelyn *see* 16

MEARS, Norah G.
Intimations and avowals: [*poems*]. Edinburgh: Moray Press. 1944. viii, 36 pp.
                                                                        OXB

MEARS, W. (A clergyman)
Nature studies, and other verse. Ilfracombe: Arthur H. Stockwell, Ltd. [1943]. 200 pp.   OXB

MEDDEMMEN, J.G., pseud. *see* **BARKER, J.G.**, (J.G. Meddemmen, pseud.)

MEDRINGTON, Henry Noel Trevor (1923–44. b. Southport, Lancashire. Educated at Radley College, and Queen's College, Cambridge. Commissioned as Flying Officer in the Royal Air Force in March 1944. Missing over Munich after his thirtieth flight, 17–18 December 1944)   *see*   20

MEE, R.A. (Of Cheshire)   *see*   74

MEIKLE, Ian Ormiston (1920–44. b. Upminster, Essex. Educated at Wycliffe College. Won an open scholarship to St John's College, Cambridge. Served in the Royal Artillery in North Africa and Italy. Later transferred to 1st Air Landing Regiment, Royal Artillery. Killed in action at Arnhem on 21 September 1944)   *see*   20

MELDRUM, Elizabeth (Scottish. Of Pangbourne, Berkshire)
   Poems. Selected and arranged by James S. Wood. Aberdeen: G. & W. Fraser, Ltd. 1965. 58 pp. por.   OXB

MELHADO, Sydney L.
   My gate of vision: a booklet of verse. Arthur H. Stockwell, Ltd. [1940]. 11 pp.
                                                                              OXB

MELLOR, John
   The star, and other poems. Ilfracombe: Arthur H. Stockwell, Ltd. 1946. 32 pp.
                                                                              OXB

MELLOWS, Thomas Anthony (1920–44. b. Peterborough. Educated at Marlborough College, and King's College, Cambridge. Captain in the 27th Lancers. Served in the Middle East and as a member of the Special Force in Europe. Killed on 21 August 1944 after a parachute descent into enemy-occupied territory when he was fighting as an officer of the Maquisard forces at the defence of Mont-de-Marsan in the South of France. A roadside monument has been erected there in memory of himself and two comrades)
   The Battle of Blanco Creek, with other verses. Printed Sevenoaks: J. Salmon Ltd. 1946. [iv], 59 pp. col. il., por.   BPL
see also   20

MENAI, Huw, pseud. *see* **WILLIAMS, Hugh Menai**, (Huw Menai, pseud.)

MERCHANT, Thomas Frederick (Educated at Bristol University. Enlisted under age in the First World War and taken to Germany as a prisoner. A teacher)
   Poems. Printed John & Edward Bumpus Ltd. 1955. 60 pp. por.   OXB

MERITT, Sarah E. (Of Northern Ireland)

From the foot of the mountains: [*poems*]. Foreword by Professor Baxter of Queen's University, Belfast. Belfast: Quota Press. [1945]. 41 pp.   OXB

MERRILL, Walter R. (Of Warwickshire) *see* 75

MEYERSTEIN, Edward Harry William (1889–1952. b. Hampstead, London. Educated at Harrow School, and Magdalen College, Oxford. Poet of the First World War. Private in the Royal Dublin Fusiliers, 1914. Assistant in Department of Manuscripts, British Museum, 1913–18. Novelist, poet, playwright and biographer)

Azure: a narrative poem. Richards Press. 1944. 54 pp.   OXB
Division: a poem. Oxford: B.H. Blackwell, Ltd. 1946. [vi], 91 pp.   OXB
In time of war: poems. Richards Press. 1942. 39 pp.   BPL
Some poems. Selected and edited by Maurice Wollman. With an introduction by Nathaniel Micklem. Neville Spearman. 1960. 168 pp.   OXB
Three sonatas: [*poems*]. Printed Bath: J.G. Melluish & Son. 1948. 24 pp.
    A limited ed. of 150 numbered copies.   OXB
Verse letters to five friends. With a foreword and introduction by Rowland Watson. William Heinemann Ltd. 1954. xiv, 33 pp. il.   OXB
The visionary, and other poems. Richards Press. 1941. 54 pp.   OXB
see also 38, 42

MEYNELL, Sir Francis (1891–1975. Son of Wilfrid and Alice Meynell, and brother of Viola. Educated at Downside School, and Trinity College, Dublin. Book designer, poet and publisher, a director of Nonesuch Press Ltd. Wartime duties at the Board of Trade as Adviser on Consumer Needs, 1940. Director-General, Cement & Concrete Association, 1946–58. Lived at Lavenham, Suffolk)

Fifteen poems. Nonesuch Press Ltd; J.M. Dent & Sons Ltd. 1944. 24 pp.
                                                                  OXB
Poems and pieces, 1911 to 1961. Nonesuch Press. 1961. 59 pp.
    A limited ed. of 750 numbered copies.   OXB
Seventeen poems. Nonesuch Press Ltd; J.M. Dent & Sons Ltd. 1945. 25 pp.
    A reissue of the 1944 ed. on hand-made paper, bound in cloth, entitled *Fifteen Poems* and limited to 470 copies. This reissue is printed on mould-made paper and is paper-wrappered.   OXB

MEYNELL, Viola (1886–1956. b. Kensington, London. Daughter of Wilfrid and Alice Meynell, and sister of Francis. Married John Dallyn in 1922. Novelist and short story writer. Lived at Pulborough, Sussex) *see* 41

MEYRICK-JONES, Leonard (Of Cheltenham, Gloucestershire)
This for remembrance of Britain's brave, and other verse. Mitre Press. [1955]. 48 pp.
                                                                  OXB

MICHELL, K.W. (Lieutenant-Commander, Royal Navy)
Out pipes, [*and other poems*]. Printed Glasgow: Andrew Holmes & Co. Ltd.
[194-]. 39 pp.   IWM

MICHELL, Robert (Lieutenant-Commander, Royal Navy. Served on H.M.S.
Raleigh) *see* 23

MICHIE, James (1927– . b. London. Educated at Trinity College, Oxford. A
Latin scholar. Worked as an editor, and as a lecturer for London University. A
director of the publishers The Bodley Head)
Possible laughter: [*poems*]. Rupert Hart-Davis. 1959. 52 pp.   MPL

MICKLEM, Agatha Frances (1895–1961. Of Bedfordshire ?)
[*Poems*]. Printed Bedford: Sidney Press Ltd. 1961. [viii], 18 pp. por.
    Printed for private circulation.   OXB

MICKLEM, Nathaniel (1888–1976. Educated at Rugby School, and New
College, Oxford. Held professorships at Birmingham, 1921–27, and at
Kingston, Ontario, 1927–31. Principal of Mansfield College, Oxford, 1932–53.
President of the Liberal Party, 1957–58, and of Liberal International (British
Group), 1959–71. Patron of the World Liberal Union, 1973. Lived at
Abingdon, Oxfordshire)
A gallimaufry: [*poems*]. Nashville, Tennessee: Parthenon Press. 1954. 63 pp.
    Some poems in Latin.   IWM
The tree of life, and other verses. Oxford University Press. 1952. viii, 87 pp.
                                                                                                    MPL
see also 38

MIDDLETON, Christopher (1926– . b. Truro, Cornwall. Educated at
Oxford University. Formerly lecturer in German at King's College, London.
Appointed Professor of Germanic Languages & Literature, University of Texas,
Austin, 1965. Poet, librettist and translator. Awarded Geoffrey Faber Memorial
Prize for Poetry, 1963)
The lonely suppers of W.V. Balloon, [*and other poems*]. Cheadle Hulme, Cheshire:
Carcanet New Press. 1975. 103 pp.   OXB
Nocturne in Eden: poems. Fortune Press. [1945]. 48 pp.   OXB
Poems. Fortune Press. 1944. 40 pp.   OXB
Torse 3: poems 1949–1961. Longmans. 1962. [x], 82 pp.   OXB
Torse 3: poems 1949–1961. New York: Harcourt, Brace & World, Inc. 1962.
[x], 82 pp.   BL
see also 18, 54

MIDDLETON, Trevor H. (Leading Aircraftman, Royal Air Force) *see* 33,
61, 62

MIDGLEY, Graham (1923– . b. Bradford, Yorkshire. Educated at St Edmund Hall, Oxford. Served in the Army, 1942–46, as Lieutenant in the Royal Artillery. Lecturer in English literature at Bedford College, London, 1949–51. Fellow of St Edmund Hall, 1951, becoming Vice-Principal in 1978) *see* 55

MILES, Beryl (Served in the Women's Land Army. Writer on travel. Of Suffolk ?)
Poems of a land girl. 2nd ed. Printed Stowmarket: Newby. [1946]. 16 pp.
Title from cover. [No copy of 1st ed. 1945 traced]   OXB

MILES, Edgar (Of Bath, Somerset)
Winged thoughts for victory: [poems]; by Edgar and Helen Miles. Printed Bath: Harding & Curtis, Ltd. [1943]. [12] pp.
Title from cover. 'All profits for the City of Bath "Wings for Victory" week'.

MILES, Ernest (1909– . Of Shipley, Yorkshire)
No leafless land: poems. Fortune Press. [1948]. 56 pp.   OXB

MILES, Helen (Of Bath, Somerset)
Winged thoughts for victory: [poems]; by Edgar and Helen Miles. Printed Bath: Harding & Curtis, Ltd. [1943]. [12]pp.
Title from cover. 'All profits for the City of Bath "Wings for Victory" week'.   OXB

MILES, Laura
Wayside warblings: fifty poems. Mitre Press. [1948]. 58 pp.   OXB

MILLAR, P.S. (Lieutenant. Served with the Eighth Army) *see* 44

MILLAR, Robert (A member of Admiralty Delegations to Canada and the United States, 1942–44)
Musings in metre: [poems]. Johnson. 1967. 63 pp.   MPL

MILLARD, Geoffrey
Battlefields and cathedrals, and other poems. Walton-on-Thames: Outposts Publications. 1978. 48 pp.   OXB

MILLARD, J.H. (Served in the Royal Marines) *see* 23

MILLEN, Geoffrey Richard Lucas (1923–41. b. Oxford. Educated at the Dragon School and later at Wells Cathedral School, where he was head boy at the time of his death in January 1941 at the age of seventeen)
The poems of a youth. Oxford: Holywell Press. 1942. 16 pp.   OXB

MILLER, Lanette Bradford
Mid-day: [*poems*]. Walton-on-Thames: Outposts Publications. 1977. [iv],
52 pp.   OXB

MILLICAN, John
Morning without clouds, [*and other poems*]. Walton-on-Thames: Outposts
Publications. 1977. 24 pp.   OXB
Rivers in the desert: [*poems*]. Edited by Margaret George. Esher: Orchard Press.
1980. 32 pp.
    A limited ed. of 260 numbered copies signed by the author.   OXB

MILLIGAN, Spike *see* **MILLIGAN, Terence Alan P.S.**, (Spike Milligan)

MILLIGAN, Terence Alan P.S., (Spike Milligan) (1918–   . b. India, son of a
Royal Artillery Captain. Educated at the Convent of Jesus & Mary, Poona,
Brothers De La Salle, Rangoon, and South East London Polytechnic. Served in
the Army during the war. Comedy actor on stage and screen, and radio and
television personality. Writer of plays, scripts, and books for children)
Small dreams of a scorpion: poems; by Spike Milligan. With illustrations by Spike
and Laura Milligan. M. & J. Hobbs; Michael Joseph. 1972. 81 pp. il.

                                                      OXB
Values: poems; by Spike Milligan. Drawings by Rigby Graham. Leicester:
Offcut Press. 1969. [21] pp. il.   OXB

MILLS, Chloris Eusebia
Vignettes in verse. Ilfracombe: Arthur H. Stockwell, Ltd. [1942]. 16 pp.
                                                     OXB

MILLS, Janet Melanie Ailsa, (H.K. Challoner, pseud.) (1894–   . b. London.
Educated in Switzerland. A clerical worker at the War Office, 1914–17. Worked
in an antique shop for a time. Writer and journalist. Of Rye, Sussex)
Invocation, and other poems; [by] H.K. Challoner. [Rye]: [Author]. [1949]. [vi],
48 pp.   OXB

MILLWARD, Joseph (1922–   . b. Hackney, London. Educated at York
House School, Hampstead. Volunteered for the Army at eighteen, serving as a
Corporal in the Royal Warwickshire Regiment. Self-styled 'the soldier poet'.
Studied music. Co-director of the Lindley Puppet Theatre with his wife
Dorothy)
Ambrosia: the first poems by Joseph Millward. Nottingham: Arabesque
Publications. 1943. 14 pp. por.
    Title from cover.   BL
From the cathedral cloisters: an anthology of prose and verse. [Nottingham]:
Arabesque Publications. [1943]. 47 pp. il.   OXB
Poems. Nottingham: Arabesque Publications. 1942. [ii], 58 pp.   IWM

Poems. Nottingham: Arabesque Publications. [1943]. 14 pp. por. (Ambrosia series, I).

    Title from cover.   OXB

Poems for Dorothy. Lowestoft: Lindley Press. [1980]. [iv], 67 pp.   OXB

MILNE, Alan Alexander (1882–1956. Educated at Westminister School, and Trinity College, Cambridge, where he edited *Granta*. A freelance journalist, 1903–06. Editor of *Punch*, 1906–14. Poet of the First World War. Served as Lieutenant, Royal Warwickshire Regiment, and fought on the Somme. Writer of novels, plays and books for children, including *Winnie the Pooh*)

    Behind the lines: [poems]. Methuen & Co. Ltd. 1940. x, 102 pp.   OXB
see also 7

MILNE, Ewart (1903– . b. Dublin. Educated at Christ Church Cathedral Grammar School. Worked as a teacher, then a seaman, 1920–30. An ambulance driver with Medical Aid during the Spanish Civil War. Staff member of the magazine *Ireland Today*, 1937–40. Farmed in England, 1941–61. Book reviewer for *The Irish Press*. Of Bedford)

    Boding day: poems. Frederick Muller Ltd. 1947. 32 pp.   OXB

    Diamond cut diamond: selected poems. Bodley Head. 1950. 64 pp.   MPL

    Elegy for a lost submarine. [Burnham-on-Crouch]: Plow Poems. 1951. 4 pp.

           OXB

    A garland for the green: [poems]. Hutchinson. 1962. 96 pp.   MPL

    Jubilo: poems. Frederick Muller Ltd. 1944. vi, 50 pp.   OXB

    Letter from Ireland, [and other poems]. Dublin: Gayfield Press. 1940. x, 82 pp.

           OXB

    Listen Mangan: poems. Dublin: Sign of the Three Candles, Ltd. [1941]. [x], 104 pp.   OXB

    Time stopped: a poem-sequence with prose intermissions. Plow Poems. 1967. 165 pp.

           OXB
see also 42

MILNE, James Crawford (Of Arbroath, Angus)

    Abbey of Aberbrothic, [and other poems]. Arbroath: Herald Press. 1941. 22 pp. il., por.   OXB

    Silver wings: [poems]. Stirling: Eneas Mackay. 1943. 21 pp. por.   IWM

    Song of a poet, [and other poems]. Cover design and illustrations by Colin Gibson. Arbroath: Herald Press. 1975. 48 pp. il.   OXB

MILNER, Harry (1912– . b. Dublin, of English parentage. Joined the Royal Air Force and flew operational flights over Germany and occupied France. Later served in the South-East Asia theatre)

    Until Bengal: poems in war. Introduction by John Gawsworth. Calcutta: Susil Gupta. [194-]. 32 pp. por.

    A limited ed. of 250 copies.   BPL

MILNER, M.R. (Of Yorkshire) *see* 75

MILVILLE, H.
 Recent years: [*poems*]. Ilfracombe: Arthur H. Stockwell, Ltd. [1941]. 19 pp.
OXB

MINCHIN, Desmond P. (1923–44. Commissioned in the King's Own Scottish Borderers. Killed on active service at Haut du Bosq near Caen, Normandy, on 1 July 1944)
 Poems. Written between the ages of fourteen and twenty-one. Printed Edinburgh: R. & R. Clark Ltd. 1946. 48 pp. por.
OXB

MINSTER, Leo (English writer on literary and historical subjects) *see* 38

MITCHELL, Angela M. *see* 16

MITCHELL, John Edwin
 Songs of Malta, and other verse. Ilfracombe: Arthur H. Stockwell, Ltd. 1946. 16 pp.
OXB

MITCHELL, Robert Lindsay
 Sins and seasons: a booklet of verse. Ilfracombe: Arthur H. Stockwell, Ltd. [1954]. 16 pp.
OXB

MITCHELL, W.G. (Served in the Army at Dunkirk)
 Poems. Ilfracombe: Arthur H. Stockwell Ltd. [1969]. 40 pp.
OXB

MITCHELL, William Fraser (Of Yorkshire ?)
 A slim volume: poems. Huddersfield: Examiner Letterpress Department. 1960. 55 pp.
OXB

MITCHISON, Naomi (1897– . b. Edinburgh, daughter of J.S. Haldane. Educated at Dragon School, Oxford. Married G.R. Mitchison in 1916. Served on Argyll County Council for several periods between 1946 and 1965, on Highland & Island Advisory Panel, 1947–65, and Highlands & Islands Development Consultative Council, 1966–73. Tribal mother to the Bakgatla of Botswana from 1963. A feminist, socialist and prolific writer. Created a life peer in 1964 but preferring not to use the title. Of Carradale, Kintyre)
 The cleansing of the knife, and other poems. Edinburgh: Canongate. 1978. vi, 72 pp.
OXB

MOFFAT, Robert (Of East Kilbride, Lanarkshire)
 No prisoner of a dying world: poems. Glasgow: William Maclellan. 1963. 40 pp. il.
MPL

MOGG, R.P.L. (Warrant Officer, Royal Air Force. Shot down over Germany and taken prisoner early in the war)

For this alone, and other poems, Germany 1943. Printed in facsimile. Oxford: Basil Blackwell. 1944. [20] pp. col. il. (by Sgt J.W. Lambert).

Dedicated to James A.G. Deans, Sergeant Pilot, Royal Air Force.   OXB

Time to stand and stare: [*poems*]. Oxford: Basil Blackwell. 1945. 45 pp. por.

Written in German prisoner of war camps.   IWM

MOIR, J.G. (A member of Oxford University between 1944 and 1946) *see* 34

MOIR, L. (Of Surrey) *see* 74

MOLLISON, J.C.H. (1922– . Joined the Army in 1942. Sergeant, Intelligence Corps (Field Security). Served in India. Of Sevenoaks, Kent) *see* 43, 57

MOLONY, Francis Arthur (O.B.E. Lieutenant-Colonel)

Verses, chiefly relating to the present war. Printed Cambridge: John Arliss. [1940]. 12 pp.

Title from cover.   OXB

MONAHAN, James (1912– . Educated at Stonyhurst College, and Christ Church, Oxford. Critic and reporter for *The Manchester Guardian*, 1937–39. Attached to B.B.C. German Service, 1939–42. Served in Special Forces and No. 10 Commando, 1942–45. A Captain, mentioned in despatches. Administrator with the B.B.C. after the war. Appointed Director of the Royal Ballet School in 1977)

After battle: [*poems*]. Macmillan & Co. Ltd. 1948. vi, 46 pp.   BPL

Far from the land, and other poems. Macmillan & Co. Ltd. 1944. vi, 37 pp.

   BPL

see also 57

MONCRIEFF, Jean (Secretary, Women's Land Army Benevolent Fund) *see* 50

MONSON, William John (1873–1956. Of Bridgnorth, Shropshire)

"You takes your choice": [*poems*]. Printed T. Whittingham & Co., Ltd. [1944]. 68 pp.   OXB

MONTAGU, George, Lord Sandwich (1874–1962. Educated at Winchester College, and Magdalen College, Oxford. Conservative M.P. for South Huntingdonshire, 1900–06. Chairman, Central Prisoners of War Committee, 1917–18. Lord Lieutenant of Huntingdonshire, 1922–46. Held many other public appointments over the years. Lived at Hinchingbrooke, Huntingdon)

Flowers of fancy: [*poems*]. Saint Catherine Press Ltd. 1949. [vi], 95 pp.

OXB

Gleanings: [*poems*]. Saint Catherine Press Ltd. 1955. [viii], 32 pp. il.

OXB

MOODY, Betty
Wood of my dreams, [*and other poems*]. Arcadian Press. [194-]. 16 pp.   IWM

MOON, Marguerite L.
Memories, [*and other poems*]. Ilfracombe: Arthur H. Stockwell, Ltd. [1962].
16 pp.   OXB

MOOR, George
Beauty and richness: poems. Glasgow: William Maclellan. 1951. 46 pp.

OXB

MOORE, Harold William, (Holder Roome, pseud.) (Poet of the First World
War. Joined the 6th Battalion, Gloucester Regiment at the outbreak. Wounded
in Battle of the Somme, July 1916. Later commissioned in the Royal Artillery,
serving with the Essex Battery at Ypres, where he was again wounded)
I shot at a star: [*poems*]; [by] Holdar Roome. Mitre Press. [1966]. 126 pp.

OXB

see also   22

MOORE, John (Lieutenant Commander, Royal Naval Volunteer
Reserve) *see* 23

MOORE, Nicholas (1918–   . b. Cambridge, son of philosopher G.E. Moore.
Educated at Dragon School, Oxford, Leighton Park School, Reading, and
Universities of St Andrews and Cambridge. Associated for a time with the New
Apocalypse group of poets. Co-founder of the magazine *Seven* and editor of *Poetry
London*. Edited *New Poetry*, 1944–45. Anthologist of prose and poetry. Awarded
Patrons Prize, *Contemporary Poetry*, 1945, and Harriet Monroe Memorial Prize,
Poetry, Chicago, 1947)
A book for Priscilla: poems. Cambridge: Epsilon Pamphlets. 1941. [iv], 20 pp.
BPL

Buzzing around with a bee, and other poems. Poetry (London). [1943]. [iv], 20 pp.
(PL pamphlets, 4).   BPL

The cabaret, the dancer, the gentlemen: poems. Fortune Press. [1942]. 60 pp.

OXB

The glass tower, [*and other poems*]. Drawings by Lucian Freud. Editions Poetry
London. 1944. 128 pp. il., col. il.   IWM

The island and the cattle: poems. Fortune Press. [1941]. 64 pp.   BPL

Recollections of the gala: selected poems 1943/1948. Editions Poetry London. 1950.
79 pp.   OXB

A wish in season: poems. Fortune Press. [1941]. 36 pp.   OXB
see also   8, 9, 25, 29, 42, 52, 56, 65, 69, 78, 79

MOORE, Ralph Westwood (1906–53. Educated at Wolverhampton Grammar School, and Christ Church, Oxford. Taught at Rossall and Shrewsbury Schools. Head Master at Bristol Grammar School, 1938–42, and at Harrow School, 1942–53. Writer on Christianity and on the Romans in Britain)
Trophy for an unknown: [*poems*]. Oxford University Press. 1952. xiv, 76 pp.
                                                                          BPL

MOORE, Swinfen Bramley- *see* **BRAMLEY-MOORE, Swinfen**

MOREY, P.A.
Moments of meditation: [*poems*]. Ilfracombe: Arthur H. Stockwell, Ltd. 1949.
16 pp.   OXB

MORGAN, Charles (1894–1958. b. Kent. Went to sea as a midshipman in 1911 but resigned in 1913. Poet of the First World War. Rejoined the Royal Naval Division as a Lieutenant in 1914. Served at Antwerp, taken prisoner and interned in Holland. After repatriation went up to Oxford University. Joined editorial staff of *The Times* in 1921, also writing for *The Times Educational Supplement*. Novelist and playwright. Won the Femina Vie Heureuse Prize in 1930 and the James Tait Black Memorial Prize in 1940)
Ode to France. Macmillan & Co. Ltd. 1942. 8 pp.   IWM

MORGAN, Diana (1910–   . b. Cardiff. Educated at the Central School of Speech & Drama. Playwright and novelist. Received eight international awards for the filmscript *Hand in Hand*. Of London)
My sex, right or wrong: [*poems*]. Illustrated by Walter Trier. Methuen & Co. Ltd. 1947. x, 42 pp. il.   OXB

MORGAN, Edward Westropp- *see* **WESTROPP-MORGAN, Edward**

MORGAN, Guy, (Lanyard, pseud.) (Short story writer. Wrote on the Battle of the Atlantic)   *see*   23

MORICE, Peter (1911–42. b. East End of London in his father's parish. Educated at King's College, Taunton, and Pembroke College, Oxford. Joined the Royal Air Force in 1941, training in England and Canada as a navigator and attaining the rank of Flying Officer. Killed on an operational flight over Turin on the night of 20–21 November 1942)
Selected poems. Dublin: At the Sign of the Three Candles. 1948. [vi], 91 pp.
por.   OXB

MORNY, pseud.
War-piece, and other poems; by "Morny". Ilfracombe: Arthur H. Stockwell, Ltd.
[1945]. 15 pp.   OXB

MORIS, C.A. (Lieutenant. Served with the Eighth Army) *see* 44

MORRIS, N.T. (Trooper. Served with the Eighth Army) *see* 25, 44, 63, 82

MORRIS, Stephen (1937– . b. Birmingham. Educated at Moseley Art
School, University College, Cardiff, and Leicester University. An artist , he had
several one man exhibitions in Britain, the United States and Holland. Senior
Lecturer at the Faculty of Art, Wolverhampton Polytechnic, from 1972)
The kingfisher catcher, [and other poems]. Illus. John Sweet. Solihull: Aquila
Poetry. [1974]. 46 pp. il.   OXB
Too long at the circus, [and other poems]. Portree, Isle of Skye: Aquila. 1980.
48 pp.   OXB

MORRIS, William Edward (Lived in London during the war)
Mission, and other poems. Ilfracombe: Arthur H. Stockwell, Ltd. 1953. 20 pp.
                                                                             OXB

MORRISON, J.
Memories, and other poems. Ilfracombe: Arthur H. Stockwell, Ltd. 1954. 31 pp.
                                                                             OXB

MORRISON, John (Of Kent ?)
Poems for people. Printed Chatham: W. & J. Mackay & Co., Ltd. 1949. x,
198 pp.   BL

MORTON, Arthur Leslie (1903– . b. Hengrave, Suffolk. Educated at
Peterhouse, Cambridge. Became a socialist and communist after the First
World War. On the staff of *Daily Worker* in the 1930s. Recipient of a doctorate
from Rostock University, East Germany, in 1975. Of Clare, Suffolk)
Collected poems. Lawrence & Wishart. 1976. 91 pp.   OXB

MORTON, Ian (1917– . Educated at Steyning Grammar School, Sussex.
Bombardier, Royal Artillery (Field). Served in India, Ceylon and Burma, and
was wounded) *see* 43

MORTON, May (A schoolteacher, she retired in 1934. Of Ulster. Contributor
to literary magazines and to B.B.C. radio programmes in Northern Ireland)
Sung to the spinning wheel: [poems]. Belfast: Quota Press. 1953. 55 pp.   OXB

MOSDELL, Gerald William
Sounds and shadows: [poems]. Ilfracombe: Arthur H. Stockwell, Ltd. 1962.
36 pp.   OXB

MOULDING, A.H. (Of Gloucestershire) *see* 74

MOULDING, Peter M. (Served in the Middle East) *see* 63

MOULT, Thomas (–1974. b. Mellor, Derbyshire. Poet of the First World War. Engaged in Boys' Club work in London and Manchester. Had a special interest in Borstals and the prison system. Poet, critic, editor, novelist and lecturer. Editor of the anthology *The Best Poems of 1940–1943*. President of the Poetry Society. 1952–61. Chairman, editorial board of *Poetry Review*, 1952–62. Lived at Finchingfield, Essex) *see* 2, 42

MOUNSEY, Henry M.
The soul of things: a book of verse. Ilfracombe: Arthur H. Stockwell Ltd. [1942]. 24 pp.   OXB

MOUNTAIN, Julian, pseud. *see* **COWIE, Donald**, (Julian Mountain, pseud.)

MOWATT, Isabella Craig (b. Dundee. Emigrated to New Zealand on retirement)
Retrospect: a collection of poems. Edited and illustrated by Andrew D. Mowatt. Printed Motherwell: The Motherwell Times Ltd. [1976]. 80 pp. il., por.   OXB

MOWBRAY, A. Marian
Verse various. Ilfracombe: Arthur H. Stockwell, Ltd. [1947]. 40 pp. por.   OXB

MOYNE, Lord *see* **GUINNESS, Bryan, Lord Moyne**

MOYNIHAN, Martin John (1916– . Educated at Birkenhead School, and Magdalen College, Oxford. Appointed to the India Office in 1939. Joined the Indian Army in 1940, serving with Punjab Frontier Force Regiment on the North West frontier and in Burma. Awarded the M.C. After the war held diplomatic posts in India, Kuala Lumpur, Trinidad, Lesotho and the United States. Writer on administration, economics and philosophy)
South of Fort Hertz: a tale in rhyme. Mitre Press. 1956. 164 pp. mps (endpaper).   OXB
The strangers, and other poems. Sidgwick & Jackson. 1946. [vi], 40 pp.   IWM
see also 25, 33

MUIR, Edwin (1887–1959. b. Orkney. Educated at Kirkwall Grammar School. A clerk in various shipbuilding offices in Glasgow, he became a journalist, author and with his wife, Willa, a translator. Appointed Director, British

Institute, Rome, 1949. Warden of Newbattle Abbey College, Dalkeith, 1950–55. Norton Professor of Poetry at Harvard University, 1955–56)

Collected poems, 1921–1951. Faber & Faber. 1952. 196 pp.   OXB

Collected poems, 1921–1958. Faber & Faber. 1960. 310 pp. por.   OXB

Collected poems. [2nd ed.]. Faber & Faber. 1963 [i.e. 1964]. 310 pp.

    Previous ed. published 1960 as *Collected poems, 1921–1958*.   OXB

The labyrinth, [and other poems]. Faber & Faber. 1949. 61 pp.   OXB

The narrow place, [and other poems]. Faber & Faber Ltd. 1943. 50 pp.   OXB

Selected poems. With a preface by T.S. Eliot. Faber & Faber. 1965. 96 pp. (Faber paper covered editions).   OXB

The voyage, and other poems. Faber & Faber. 1946. 53 pp.   OXB

see also   38, 58, 82, 87

MUIR, Marianne (Of the Isle of Wight ?)

Verses from the West Wight. Ilfracombe: Arthur H. Stockwell, Ltd. [1945]. 16 pp.   OXB

MULLEN, George (Served in H.M. Forces) *see* 74

MULLIS, John H.

All this and the hills: fifty poems. Ilfracombe: Arthur H. Stockwell, Ltd. 1970. 72 pp.   OXB

MUMFORD, Nan

Silver lining, [and other poems]. Ilfracombe: Arthur H. Stockwell, Ltd. [1942] 20 pp.   OXB

Such days will pass: [poems]. Arthur H. Stockwell, Ltd. [1941]. 20 pp.   OXB

MUNBY, Alan Noel Latimer (1913–74. Educated at Clifton College, and King's College, Cambridge. In antiquarian book trade with Bernard Quaritch Ltd, 1933–37, and with Sotheby & Co., 1937–39 and 1945–47. Captain in Queen Victoria's Rifles, King's Royal Rifle Corps, 1939–45. Captured in France in 1940, held prisoner of war in Germany until 1945. Mentioned in despatches. Librarian of King's College, Cambridge from 1947 and a Fellow of the College. Held academic posts in bibliography. Appointed a trustee of British Museum, 1969, member of British Library Board, 1973, and President of Bibliographical Society, 1974) *see* 67

MUNDAY, Betty

The spirit of England, and other poems. Ilfracombe: Arthur H. Stockwell, Ltd. 1946. 16 pp.   OXB

MUNDY-CASTLE, Frances, (Peggy Whitehouse, pseud.) (1898– . b. Belfast. Poet of the First World War. Worked in the Ministry of Munitions and the Air Ministry. Novelist and poet) *see* 42

MUNNINGS, Sir Alfred (1878–1959. Educated at Framlingham College, Norwich School of Art and in France. Attached to Canadian Cavalry Brigade in France, 1917–18, as a war artist. First exhibited at the Royal Academy in 1898 then continually, becoming its President, 1944–49)
Ballads and poems: or, a rhyming succession of rhyming digression. Museum Press. 1957. 176 pp. il. (by the author). MPL

MURRAY, Drew *see* 16

MURRAY, Elisabeth Christie- *see* **CHRISTIE-MURRAY, Elisabeth**

MURRAY, N. Ross (Of Devonshire)
Verses grave and gay. With drawings by Harold Murray. Exmouth: Raleigh Press. [1947]. 44 pp. il.
    Cover-title is *Devon Gems*. OXB

MURRAY, Richard Hollins
Random thoughts in verse. Stockport: Cloister Press. [1952]. 116 pp. il.
MPL

MUSGRAVE, Victor (Served in the Middle East. A journalist. Wrote a biography of Lord Montgomery) *see* 63

MUSTOE, Winifred
The light left burning: [poems]. Dulwich Village: Outposts Publications. 1961. 16 pp. OXB

N., S. (Served in South-East Asia Command) *see* 35

NANCE, A. Morton
Triumphant St. George: a selection of verse. Ilfracombe: Arthur H. Stockwell, Ltd. [1942]. 33 pp. OXB

NAPIER, Priscilla, (Eve Stuart, pseud.) (1908–   . b. Oxford, daughter of Sir William Hayter. Educated at Downe House School, and Lady Margaret Hall Oxford. Married Trevylan Napier, a naval officer who died on active service as a destroyer captain in 1940. A writer, contributing to *Punch* and *Country Life*. A governor of Tavistock Grammar School. Of Market Harborough, Leicestershire)
Plymouth in war: a verse documentary. Printed Bury St. Edmunds: Denny Bros. [1978]. 127 pp.
    Title from cover. BPL

Sheet-anchor: [*poems*]; by Eve Stuart. Sidgwick & Jackson Ltd. 1944. [iv], 44 pp.

'Michael, the subject and inspiration of these poems, was a Naval Officer who died on duty, and of his duty, in the late summer of 1940. The author of the poems is his wife'.   IWM

NAPIER, Samuel (Of Northern Ireland) *see* 74

NAUMANN, Anthony (1921– . b. London, brought up in Surrey. Commissioned in 10th Battalion, Rifle Brigade. In 1942 went to Tunisia with Blade Force, a lightning strike group. Blinded and severely wounded in the arm during this operation)

Flame in the dark: poems. Collins. 1962. 53 pp.   MPL
If I may share, [*and other poems*]. Collins. 1964. 48 pp.   MPL

NAYLOR, George L. (Served in H.M. Forces) *see* 75

NEAL, Kenneth (Served in H.M. Forces) *see* 52, 76

NEEDLER, Arthur Percival

Songs by the way: [*poems*]. A. Brown & Sons, Ltd. [1940]. 54 pp.   OXB
Songs in the afternoon: [*poems*]. A. Brown & Sons, Ltd. 1952. 55 pp.

    OXB

NEGUS, J.E. (Served in H.M. Forces) *see* 75

NEILL, John C. (Served in the Royal Air Force. Of Shropshire ?)

Little bits of light and shade: [*poems*]. Printed Newport, Shropshire: Advertising Printing Works. 1945. 43 pp.   OXB

NEILL, W.C.H. (–1949. Of Dornoch, Sutherland)

Other verses. Printed Mexborough: Venables Ltd. [1945]. 23 pp.
   Title from cover.   OXB

NEVILL, J.W. (Served in South-East Asia Command) *see* 35

NEVILLE, Derek (1911– . b. London. Novelist and general writer, contributing to many periodicals. A member of Norwich Writers' Circle. Of Sheringham, Norfolk)

Poems: a second selection. Norwich: Author. [1943]. 32 pp.   OXB

NEVILLE, Elsa (Of Hampshire) *see* 74

NEVILLE, John R. (Of London) *see* 75

NEWBOLD, Francis (Army Private. Of Manchester)
The lost knight, [and other poems]. Dulwich Village: Outposts Publications. 1960. 16 pp.   OXB
see also   13

NEWEY, J.M.
Random thoughts: [poems]. Ilfracombe: Arthur H. Stockwell, Ltd. [1963]. 20 pp.   OXB

NEWGASS, Edgar (1887–   . b. London. Educated at Charterhouse, and Trinity College, Cambridge. Served in the ranks in the First World War, first in the Mounted Yeomanry then in Mechanical Transport. Writer on Bible history and hymnology. Lived in London)
Collected poems. A.E. Callam. 1961. [viii], 66 pp.   OXB
Collected poetry and verse, 1909–1972. Jameson Press. 1973. 128 pp.   MPL
England in peace and war: 'on earth peace': [poems]. Printed Millbrook Press Ltd. 1968. xii, 72 pp.   OXB
"On earth peace": poems and verse. BCM/MPXD. [1954]. 56 pp.   OXB
Pro patria: poems of freedom. Wyman & Sons, Ltd. [1940]. 56 pp.
      'Half the proceeds of this book go to the Royal National Life-Boat Institution'.   IWM
This precious stone. Steyning: D. & P. West. 1941. 28 pp.   OXB

NEWTON, Kathleen S. (Of Iona, Hebrides ?)
Iona verses. With decorations by Elizabeth Mary Watt. Edinburgh: George Stewart & Co. [1950]. [13] pp. il.   OXB
      Title from cover.

NEWTON, Muriel (Organizer for the Women's Voluntary Service in Dorset. Had two sons serving in the Forces. Journalist and short story writer)   *see*   38, 41

NICHOL, J. (Regimental Sergeant-Major. Served with the Eighth Army)
see   44

NICHOLAS, Thomas Evan (Poet, writer, lecturer and preacher. A writer in the Welsh language, his work has been translated into English)
The prison sonnets of T.E. Nicholas. Translated from the Welsh by Daniel Hughes, Dewi Emrys, Eric Davies, Will Ifan. Preface by Dr. Iorwerth Peate. W. Griffiths & Co. 1948. 91 pp.   OXB

NICHOLL, Theodore (1902–   . b. Llanelly, South Wales. Educated at King's School, Grantham, and Royal Grammar School, Worcester. Poet of the First World War. Served in Royal Air Force and with Ministry of Information. Novelist, poet, short story writer and freelance journalist)

The immortal ease: [poems]. Hutchinson & Co. Ltd. [1947]. 55 pp.
'Dedicated to Flight-Sergeant Ernest Payne and other comrades of flying personnel and ground staff'.   BPL

NICHOLLS, A.
Life, and other poems. Ilfracombe: Arthur H. Stockwell, Ltd. [1943]. 16 pp.
                                                                                              OXB

NICHOLS, George *see* 80

NICHOLS, John (Of Staffordshire)
In retrospect: a collection of poems. [Privately printed]. [1980]. 24 pp.   OXB

NICHOLS, Ross (Writer on myth and magic)
Prose chants and proems [sic]: [poems]. Fortune Press. [1942]. 56 pp.   OXB
Seasons at war: a cycle of rhythms: [poems]. Forge Press. 1947. 55 pp.
'Part of a war-time diary'.   IWM

NICHOLS, Wallace Bertram (1888– . b. Birmingham. Educated at Westminister School. Novelist, playwright and poet of the First World War. Lived at Newlyn, Cornwall)
Black Europe: twenty-six sonnets. Oxford: Shakespeare Head Press. 1939. 32 pp.
                                                                                              IWM

NICHOLSON, Ernest (Served abroad in the Forces. Of Berkshire ?)
Like pebbles forth: [poems]. Printed Abingdon: Burgess & Son Ltd. [1968]. 48 pp.
Sub-title on cover is *Selected verse*.   OXB

NICHOLSON, Hubert (1908– . b. Hull, Yorkshire. Journalist on newspapers in Hull, Bristol, Cheltenham and London before the war. With Reuters Ltd, 1945–67. Novelist, poet and essayist. Of Epsom, Surrey)
The mirage in the south, and other poems. William Heinemann Ltd. 1955. x, 49 pp.
                                                                                              IWM
New spring song: poems. Fortune Press. 1943. 40 pp.   BPL
see also 36, 64, 76

NICHOLSON, K.A. *Stalingrad, and poems of love.* Ilfracombe: Arthur H. Stockwell, Ltd. [1944]. 16 pp.   OXB

NICHOLSON, Mary (A member of the Royal Medico-Psychological Association. Writer of several novels)
Flowers from a country garden: [poems]. Ilfracombe: Arthur H. Stockwell, Ltd. 1950. 16 pp.   OXB

NICHOLSON, Norman (1914– . b. Millom, Cumberland. Educated at local schools. Became an established poet during the war. Lectured for the Workers Educational Association. Poet, novelist, anthologist and writer on Lake District topography. Received a Cholmondeley Award, 1967, and a Queen's Medal for Poetry, 1977. Of Millom)

Five rivers, [and other poems]. Faber & Faber. 1944. 86 pp.   IWM

Selected poems; by John Hall, Keith Douglas, Norman Nicholson. John Bale & Staples Ltd. 1943. 77 pp. (Modern reading library, 3).   BL

   Not joint authorship.

Selected poems. Faber & Faber. 1966. 64 pp. (Faber paper covered editions).

        OXB

see also   18, 25, 45, 52, 56, 58, 76, 87

NICHOLSON, Philip

Conflict and query: [poems]. Walton on Thames: Outposts Publications. 1970. 16 pp.   OXB

NICOLL-GRIFFITH, Hubert Victor (1888– . Educated in Hull, at Selwyn College, Cambridge, and Leeds Clergy School. An Anglican clergyman. Lived at Swanage, Dorset)

The rainbow: a volume of varied verse, being a selection of poems, sonnets, songs and rhymes. Ilfracombe: Arthur H. Stockwell Ltd. 1958. 128 pp. il.   OXB

NIXON, Daphne (Served in H.M. Forces)

In these five years: poems. Fortune Press. 1946. 32 pp.   IWM

see also   49

NIXON, James P. (Of Yorkshire)   *see*   74

NOAKES, Mary (Of Norfolk)

Selected variations: [poems]. Ilfracombe: Arthur H. Stockwell, Ltd. 1973. 16 pp.

        OXB

NOBLE, A.F. (Served in the Western Desert)   *see*   63

NOBLE, Peter (1917– . b. London, brought up in Clerkenwell. Journalist, actor and writer on films and film actors)

The city in the sun: twenty poems. Pendulum Publications. 1945. 24 pp.

        IWM

NOBODY OF ANY IMPORTANCE, pseud. (Of Manchester ?)

And now what?: a collection of topical rhymes and typical themes of the day; by nobody of any importance. With illustrations by K. Lamb. Manchester: Thomas Wyatt & Son Ltd. [1946]. 24 pp. il.

   Title from cover.   OXB

NOEL-BUXTON, Lord *see* **BUXTON, Rufus, Lord Noel-Buxton**

NOËL-PATON, Margaret Hamilton (1896– . b. Bombay, India. Granddaughter of the Scottish artist Sir Joseph Noël Paton. She spent the war years in rural Somerset. Former Secretary of the Y.W.C.A. in India and Ceylon. Writer of plays and verse. Of Edinburgh)
'Choose something like a star': 12 poems. Edinburgh: [Author]. 1972. 16 pp.

OXB

NORMAN, Barbara (1920–72. Daughter of Lord Norman who was Governor of the Bank of England. She married three times)
Selected poems, 1940–1972. Introduction by John Heath-Stubbs. Tuba Press. 1977. [xii], 113 pp. por.
    A limited ed. of 1,000 copies.   OXB

NORMAN, G.C. (Joined the Territorial Army in 1939. Served in France, Egypt, North Africa and Italy. Became a bank manager. Of Pyrford, Surrey) *see* 39, 63

NORMAN, Patricia (Spent the years 1940–44 in Malta when a child)
Seven to seventeen: [*poems*]. Ilfracombe: Arthur H. Stockwell, Ltd. 1956. 48 pp.

OXB

NORMANTON, John (1918– . b. Bradford, Yorkshire. Educated at Ikley Grammar School and Bradford Technical College. Poet, painter and textile trade worker. Of Ilkley)
Frail prelude: [*poems*]. Ilfracombe: Arthur H. Stockwell, Ltd. 1946. 64 pp.

OXB

NORRIS, Charles Gilman (A novelist)
Parnassian musings: [*poems*]. Ilfracombe: Arthur H. Stockwell, Ltd. [1949]. 84 pp.   OXB
Poems. Ilfracombe: Arthur H. Stockwell, Ltd. [1944]. 79 pp.   OXB

NORRIS, Leslie (1921– . b. Merthyr Tydfil, Glamorgan. Educated at Southampton University and City of Coventry College of Education. A friend of Alun Lewis. Joined the Royal Air Force in June 1940, invalided out in July 1941. Spent some time as an Air Raid Warden. Taught in Yeovil and Bath. Head Teacher, Aldingbourne School, Chichester, 1956–58. Principal Lecturer in English at the College of Education, Bognor Regis, 1958–73. Writer and contributor to many periodicals. Recipient of a Cholmondeley Prize for Poetry and a Welsh Arts Council Award)
Mountain polecats pheasants, and other elegies. Chatto & Windus; Hogarth Press. 1974. 48 pp. (Phoenix living poets).

OXB

Poems. Falcon Press. [1946]. 48 pp. (Resurgam books).   BL
see also   13, 79

NORRIS, Margaret S. (Of Belfast ?)
Listening in, [and other poems]. [Privately printed]. [1944]. 27 pp. il.   OXB

NORTON, A.W. (Lieutenant, Royal Naval Volunteer Reserve)
On land and sea: a booklet of verse. Ilfracombe: Arthur H. Stockwell, Ltd. [1945]. 24 pp.   OXB

NORTON, Hon. Eleanour (Poet of the First World War. Lived in London and at Stoke Poges, Buckinghamshire)
Beauty is deathless, and other poems. Printed John & Edward Bumpus Ltd. 1948. 42 pp.   OXB
see also   22

NOTTON, Betty
Steer straight, and other poems. Ilfracombe: Arthur H. Stockwell, Ltd. [1944]. 48 pp.   OXB

NOVLAN, Mary
Poems. Ilfracombe: Arthur H. Stockwell, Ltd. [1963]. 221 pp.   OXB

NOYCE, Wilfrid (1917–62. b. Simla, India. Educated at Charterhouse, and King's College, Cambridge. In 1939 he joined the Friends Ambulance Unit then in 1940 joined the Welsh Guards as a Private. Captain, King's Royal Rifle Corps, 1943–45, and Chief Instructor at the Aircrew Mountain Centre in Kashmir, 1944–45. A teacher at Malvern College, 1946–50, and at Charterhouse from 1950. A member of the 1953 British Everest Expedition. Retired from teaching in 1961 to write full-time. Writer on mountaineering and rock climbing)
Poems. Heinemann. 1960. 98 pp.   MPL

NOYES, Alfred (1880–1958. b. Staffordshire. Educated at Exeter College, Oxford, leaving without taking a degree. Married an American and travelled widely in the United States. Received many academic honours including a professorship of poetry at Princeton in 1914. Gave the Lowell lectures on 'The Sea in English Poetry'. Poet of the First World War. Temporarily attached to the Foreign Office, 1916–18. A prolific writer, he contributed to many periodicals. He wrote poetry, plays, essays and studies of William Morris and Voltaire)
Collected poems in one volume. John Murray. 1950. 415 pp.   OXB
Collected poems in one volume. 2nd ed. John Murray. 1963. [ii], 427 pp.   BL
If judgment comes: a poem. With drawings by John Alan Maxwell. New York: Frederick A. Stokes Co. 1941. [viii], 46 pp. il.   BPL

A letter to Lucian, and other poems. John Murray. 1956. x, 102 pp.   MPL
Shadows on the down, and other poems. Hutchinson & Co. Ltd. [1945]. 127 pp.
                                                                        IWM

NUGENT, J. (A Trooper with the 7th Armoured Brigade, taken prisoner at
Tobruk. Of Fleetwood, Lancashire)   *see*   63

OAKLEY, Ruth Anderson
Resurgence: [poems]. Mitre Press. [1961]. 69 pp.   MPL

OAKLEY-HILL, D.R. (Lieutenant-Colonel, 7th Ghurka Rifles. Captured in
Yugoslavia in 1941, held prisoner of war in Germany)   *see*   5

O'BRIEN, Gerry (Experienced the air raids on Merseyside)
Moon over the Mersey: [poems]. Ilfracombe: Arthur H. Stockwell Ltd. 1980.
28 pp.   OXB

O'BYRNE, Brendan (Served in North Africa)   *see*   63

O'CONNOR, Philip (1916–   . b. Leighton Buzzard, Bedfordshire. Educated
at convents in France, at an English public school and at Dorking High School.
Left school at age of sixteen and travelled in Greece, Italy, France and Holland
until the outbreak of war. Returned to London 'until the doodlebugs frightened
me away'. Edited his own magazine *Seven*, worked in a continental telephone
exchange and a library, then attended teachers' training college. Poet, prose
writer and scriptwriter)
Selected poems, 1936/1966. Jonathan Cape. 1968. 95 pp.   OXB

ODDESS, Olha (Probably Ukrainian-born but wrote in English)
Let there be light: [poems]. Chaika Publishing Ltd. 1973. 60 pp.   OXB

ODDY, G.S. (Of Ryde, Isle of Wight)
Sonnets in D minor. Ilfracombe: Arthur H. Stockwell, Ltd. [1944]. 59 pp.
                                                                        OXB
Sonnets in two keys. Mitre Press. [1954]. 72 pp.   OXB

ODGER, Samuel
The virgin's son, and other poems. Ilfracombe: Arthur H. Stockwell, Ltd. [1943].
24 pp.   OXB

O'DONNELL, P.A.T. (Educated at Keble College, Oxford. Of Cheltenham,
Gloucestershire)
Housewarming, and other poems. Fortune Press. 1960. 48 pp.   OXB

Moving day, and other poems (1939–1949). With drawings by the author. Fortune Press. [1951]. [iv], 42 pp. il.   **IWM**
see also   55

O'FARACHAIN, Roibeard *see* **FARREN, Robert**, (Roibeard O'Farachain)

OFFLEY, R.W. (Of London)   *see*   74

OGIER, Ruth J. (Of Guernsey, Channel Islands)
Poems on the German occupation of the Channel Isles. Ilfracombe: Arthur H. Stockwell, Ltd. 1946. 16 pp.
    'Dedicated to my sister, Priscilla, who was with me during those five years'.
    OXB

O'GRADY, Doris M.
Three women, and other poems. Ilfracombe: Arthur H. Stockwell, Ltd. 1956. 16 pp.   **OXB**

O'HARE, J.B. (Of North Wales ?)
A balled of Britain. Printed Colwyn Bay: Leigh & Williams Ltd. [1942]. [ii], 25 pp.   **OXB**

O'HARE, John (1910–   . b. London. Educated at a grammar school. Served in the Army for a time)
The return, [and other poems]. Aldington, Kent: Hand and Flower Press. [1951]. 293–324 pp. (Poems in pamphlet, 1951, X).   **BL**

O'HORAN, Padraig (b. Dublin. Educated at Christian Brothers schools in Dublin, Dublin College of Modern Irish, and Edgehill Theological College, Belfast. Vicar of Priddy, Somerset. Founder-member of the Irish Genealogical Research Society)
The proud and lovely: poems. Fortune Press. 1946. 64 pp.   **OXB**
Roadways of the heart: [poems]. Fortune Press. 1943. 44 pp.   **OXB**

OILB–117–2, pseud.
"War time nonsense": [poems]; by OILB–117–2. Ilfracombe: Arthur H. Stockwell, Ltd. [1945]. 16 pp.   **OXB**

OLIVE, H.B.
"It all depends on us!", and other verse. Ilfracombe: Arthur H. Stockwell, Ltd. 1946. 20 pp.   **OXB**

OLIVIER, Francis, pseud.
Exploits of the war, and other poems; by "Francis Olivier". Ilfracombe: Arthur H. Stockwell, Ltd. [1945]. 16 pp.   **OXB**

OMAND, Don (Served in Air Raid Precautions)

Tin hat memories: rhymes of the A.R.P. With a foreword by Naomi Jacob. W.H. Allen & Co., Ltd. 1943. 28 pp. OXB

O'NIONS, Beryl (A young girl in the war)

The vision, and other poems. Ilfracombe: Arthur H. Stockwell, Ltd. [1942]. 16 pp. OXB

O'QUIGLEY, James (Irish)

The priest, and other poems. Dublin: James Duffy & Co., Ltd. 1959. 48 pp. por. OXB

ORMEROD, Richard Caton (1915–81. Educated at Winchester College, and New College, Oxford. Entered the India Office in 1938. War service with the 7th Light Cavalry, Indian Army, 1941–45. Saw active service in Imphal and Burma, where he was wounded. Assistant Private Secretary to the Secretary of State for India & Burma, 1945–46, Principal, Burma Office, 1946. Held diplomatic appointments in Bombay, Wellington and Calcutta. Consul-General in Marseilles, 1967–71)

Ferns in the waste, [and other poems]. Macmillan & Co. Ltd. 1943. vi, 37 pp. IWM

ORMSBY, Frank (1947–   . b. County Fermanagh. Educated at St Michael's College, Enniskillen, and Queen's University, Belfast. Brought up in rural Ulster. Editor of *The Honest Ulsterman* magazine. Teacher of English at Royal Belfast Academical Institution. Won a Gregory Award for Poetry in 1974)

A store of candles: [poems]. Oxford University Press. 1977. viii, 54 pp. OXB

ORMSBY, Iërne (Of Thurgoland, Yorkshire)

A thrush sings, and other verses. British Authors' Press. 1950. [vi], 41 pp. BL

ORMSBY, M.L. (Irish)

Moods and places: [poems]. Dundalk: Dundalgan Press. 1946. [ii], 50 pp. il. OXB

OSBORN, Sir Frederic James (1885–1978. b. London. Estate Manager, Welwyn Garden City, 1919–36. Director, Murphy Radio Ltd, 1936–60. Served in Air Raid Precautions during the war. Member of New Towns Committee, 1946. President, Town & Country Planning Association. Writer on town planning and new towns)

Can man plan?, and other verses. George G. Harrap & Co. Ltd. 1959. 143 pp. OXB

OSBORNE, Albert
  Poems from life. Ilfracombe: Arthur H. Stockwell, Ltd. 1961. 44 pp.   OXB

O'SULLIVAN, Seumas, pseud. *see* **STARKEY, James Sullivan**, (Seumas O'Sullivan, pseud.)

OUGHTON, Maurice (–1941. Leading Aircraftman, Royal Air Force. Killed in action on 23 July 1941)
  Out of the oblivion: poems. Fortune Press. [1942]. 40 pp.   OXB

OULD, Hermon (1885–1951. b. London. Dramatist, poet, critic and general writer. General Secretary of International P.E.N. Club)
  To one who sang: a book of songs: [*poems*]. Tring: The Porch. 1942. 32 pp.
    OXB

OWEN, Bernard
  Cry for the moon: [*poems*]. Haverfordwest: Cromlech Press. [1954]. 20 pp.
    OXB

OWEN, Harold W. (Corporal)   *see*   36

OWEN, Patrick Tudor-   *see* **TUDOR-OWEN, Patrick**

OWEN, Rosemary (b. Wales. Of Swansea ?)
  Our world: poems. Printed Swansea: W. Walters & Son, Ltd. [1977]. [24] pp.
    Title from cover.   OXB

OWEN, Thomas Baden Powell (Sergeant, Royal Army Service Corps. Served in India from 1942)   *see*   43

OXENHAM, John, pseud. *see* **DUNKERLEY, William Arthur**, (John Oxenham, pseud.)

P., E.D. (Served in South-East Asia Command)   *see*   35

PAGE, D., pseud. *see* **LAMBERT, Donald Page**, (D. Page, pseud.)

PAGE, H.V.S. (Sergeant. Served with the Eighth Army. Of Liverpool)   *see*   25, 44

PAINTER, George Duncan (1914–   . b. Birmingham. Educated at King Edward's School, Birmingham, and Trinity College, Cambridge. Appointed assistant lecturer in Latin, Liverpool University, 1937. On staff of British Museum Department of Printed Books, 1954–74. Writer on French literature.

Winner of the Duff Cooper Memorial Prize and the James Tait Black Memorial Prize. Of Hove, Sussex)

The road to Sinodun: a winter and summer monodrama: [poems]. Rupert Hart-Davis. 1951. 77 pp.   OXB

PALFREY, John Herbert W.
Winged victory, [and other poems]. Ilfracombe: Arthur H. Stockwell, Ltd. 1950. 16 pp.   OXB

PALMER, Herbert (1880–1961. b. Market Rasen, Lincolnshire. Educated at Woodhouse Grove School, Birmingham University, and Bonn University, Germany. Poet of the First World War, a schoolmaster and private tutor until 1921 when he became a full-time writer. Awarded a Civil List pension in 1932 for his 'distinction as a poet'. Editor of *The Greenwood Anthology of New Verse*, 1948. Lived in St Albans, Hertfordshire)

The gallows-cross: a book of songs and verses for the times. J.M. Dent & Sons Ltd. 1940. viii, 24 pp.   BPL

A sword in the desert: a book of poems and verses for the present times. George G. Harrap & Co. Ltd. 1946. 95 pp.   BPL
see also   7, 9, 42, 84

PALMER, R. Rutherford
The voice of the workers: a booklet of verse. Ilfracombe: Arthur H. Stockwell, Ltd. [1944]. 28 pp.   OXB

PALMER, Ronald Frederick (Of Menai Bridge, Anglesey)
Military moments: some modern barrack room ballads. [Ilfracombe]: Arthur H. Stockwell, Ltd. [1951]. 40 pp.
    'Fifty per cent of all royalties will be donated to Service charities'.

                                                                                                        OXB

PAMELA, pseud.   *see*   **FORSYTH, Pamela**, (Pamela, pseud.)

PAPASIAN, John (Served in the Middle East)
Mediterranean poems. Illustrated by the author. Printed Cairo: Paul Barbey's Printers. [194-]. [75] pp. il.   IWM
see also   63

PARADOX, A. (Of Glasgow)   *see*   74

PARK, John (Of Lanarkshire)   *see*   74, 75

PARKER, Arthur C.
Lincolnshire, and other poems. Ilfracombe: Arthur H. Stockwell, Ltd. [1943]. 23 pp.   OXB

PARKER, Barrett (1908– . b. Orange, New Jersey. Educated at Harvard University. Served in England during the war. Managing editor of *US Army Talks*, 1943–44. With the United States Foreign Service, 1947–70, serving in London, Teheran and Ottawa. Lecturer in English at the American University, Washington, D.C., 1970–73. Poet, biographer, historian and writer on foreign relations)

Other poems. Nicholson & Watson. 1946. 39 pp. OXB

Selected poems, 1944–1974. Printed Wells: St Andrew's Press. [1974]. xii, 53 pp.
A limited ed. of 100 copies. OXB

A Yank in England, [*and other poems*]. Fortune Press. 1944. 40 pp. il. OXB

PARKS, Mavis Beth

Facts and fancies (in verse). Ilfracombe: Arthur H. Stockwell, Ltd. 1953. 16 pp. OXB

PARLOUR, Pauline Margaret

The highland warriors, and other poems. [Chard, Somerset]: [Avon Books]. [1963]. 18 pp. OXB

PARNELL, F.J.

First fruits: poems. Fortune Press. 1956. 52 pp. OXB

PARROTT, Thomas (Of Bracknell, Berkshire)

Thoughts in verse and line. Bracknell, Berks.: Author. [1978]. [vi], 116 pp. OXB

PARRY, G. (Of Cheshire) *see* 75

PARSONS, Clive Russell- *see* **RUSSELL-PARSONS, Clive**

PARSONS, Dorothy (Qualified as a doctor, one of the most distinguished medical students of her year at Edinburgh University. Worked as a doctor in the slums of Leith, Midlothian, and in China. Later won distinction in the field of cancer research. Poet of the First World War)

Collected poems of Dorothy Parsons. With a foreword by the Rev. Canon Adam Fox, D.D., formerly Professor of Poetry, Oxford University. Abingdon: Abbey Press. 1964. xii, 266 pp. MPL

PARSONS, Geoffrey (Aircraftman, Royal Air Force) *see* 1, 25

PARVIN, Brian

Pebbles in my pocket: [poems]. Dulwich Village: Outposts Publications. 1956. 12 pp. OXB

PATERSON, Evangeline (b. Limvady, Northern Ireland, brought up in

Dublin. Married a professor of geography, living in Cambridge, St Andrews, Leicester and South Africa. A prizewinner in national poetry competitions)

Whitelight, [and other poems]. Oxford: Mid-Day Publications Ltd. [1978]. [28] pp. (Old Fire Station poets, 3).　　　　　　　　　　　　　OXB

PATON, Margaret Hamilton Noël *see* **NOËL-PATON, Margaret Hamilton**

PATTERSON, Richard Ferrar (1888– . b. Holywood, Ireland. Educated at Oundle School and Cambridge University. On the editorial staff of publishers Blackie & Sons. General editor of the Scottish Text Society from 1924. Writer on English literature. Lived at Dumbarton)

Mein Rant: a summary in light verse of "Mein Kampf". Illustrated by W. Heath Robinson. Blackie & Son Ltd. 1940. x, 70 pp. il.　　　　　　　　　BPL

PATTON, Elsie Rankin (Of Northern Ireland)

Salome speaks, and other poems. Belfast: James M. Laird. 1957. 56 pp.　　OXB

PAUKER, John (Translator from the Hungarian) *see* 25

PAUL, Leslie (1905– . b. Dublin. Educated at a London central school. Entered Fleet Street at the age of seventeen. Founded The Woodcraft Folk, a youth organization, when twenty. Headed a delegation on cooperation to the Soviet Union in 1931. Tutor to Workers Educational Association and London County Council, 1933–40. Called up in 1941. Served with the Army Educational Corps in the Middle East, Staff Tutor at Mount Carmel College. Held a variety of official appointments after the war. Of Hereford)

Exile, and other poems. Caravel Press. 1951. 39 pp. il. (by Guy Worsdell).
　　A limited ed. of 200 numbered copies.　　　　　　　　　　　OXB

PAYNE, Robert (1911–83. b. Saltash, Cornwall. Educated at St Paul's School then studied to become a naval architect at Greenwich. Read pure science at Cape Town University. Reported the Spanish Civil War from the Loyalist side for a British newspaper. Devoted his life to writing and travel. Journalist, biographer, editor, poet, linguist, translator and novelist)

The granite island, and other poems. Jonathan Cape. 1945. 47 pp.　　　BPL
The rose tree, [and other poems]. New York: Dodd Mead. 1947. [x], 157 pp.

　　　　　　　　　　　　　　　　　　　　　　　　　　　　　　BL
Songs: [poems]. William Heinemann Ltd. 1948. [viii], 125 pp.　　　OXB

PEACE, John F.C.

Onward — ever onward: [poems]. Ilfracombe: Arthur H. Stockwell Ltd. 1979. 32 pp.　　　　　　　　　　　　　　　　　　　　　　　　　OXB

PEACHEY, Marjorie Doris

The running tide: [poems]. Mitre Press. [1965]. 66 pp.　　　　　　OXB

PEAKE, Mervyn (1911–68. b. Tuling, China, son of a missionary doctor. Educated at Tientsin Grammar School, Eltham College, Croydon School of Art and the Royal Academy Schools. Sapper in a Bomb Disposal Group, Royal Engineers, invalided out in 1943. Sent to work for the Ministry of Information as a war artist. Moved into a studio in Chelsea before end of war, in time to experience the flying bombs. Poet, novelist, playwright and illustrator. Settled in the Channel Islands)

The glassblowers, [and other poems]. Eyre & Spottiswoode. 1950. viii, 40 pp. il.
OXB

Peake's progress: selected writings and drawings of Mervyn Peake. Edited by Maeve Gilmore. With an introduction by John Watney. Allen Lane. 1978. 576 pp.
OXB

A reverie of bone, and other poems. Drawings by the author. Bertram Rota. 1967. [viii], 33 pp. il.
OXB

The rhyme of the flying bomb. With 22 illustrations by the author. J.M. Dent & Sons Ltd. 1962. [iv], 43 pp. il.
MPL

The rhyme of the flying bomb. With 22 illustrations by the author. Gerrards Cross: Colin Smythe Ltd. 1973. [iv], 43 pp. il.
OXB

Selected poems. Faber & Faber. 1972. 46 pp.
MPL

Selected poems. Faber & Faber. 1975. 46 pp. (Faber paperbacks).
OXB

Shapes and sounds: [poems]. Chatto & Windus. 1941. viii, 24 pp.
OXB

Shapes and sounds: [poems]. Preface by Maeve Gilmore. Village Press. 1974. 40 pp.
OXB

see also   15, 25, 38, 47, 56, 57

PEARCE, Frank

Our way of life, and other poems. Ilfracombe: Arthur H. Stockwell, Ltd. 1952. 16 pp.
OXB

PEARCE, L.H. (Served in H.M. Forces)   *see*   74, 75

PEARSE, Geoff (Served in the Middle East)   *see*   63

PEARSE, Henrietta S.

The land of verse, [and other poems]. Ilfracombe: Arthur H. Stockwell, Ltd. [1942]. 48 pp.
OXB

PEARSON, J.E. (Lieutenant in the Army. Captured in France in 1940, held prisoner of war in Germany until 1945)   *see*   67

PEARSON, Rosemary   *see*   78

PECK, Allene (Of Birmingham. Married Charles A. Peck)

Retrospect, and other poems. H. Wise & Co. Ltd. [1945]. 20 pp.
BPL

PECK, Charles A. (Of Birmingham. Married to Allene Peck)
Venture in verse; by Charles and Allene Peck. Birmingham: Authors. [1946]. [12] pp.
 Not joint authorship. Contains no war poetry by Allene Peck. Title from cover. OXB

PEGGE, Cecil Denis (1902– . Taught in Engineering Department, Cambridge University, 1940–51. General Secretary, Cambridge University Educational Film Council, 1946–55. Researcher on Film and Simulacrics, Institute of Experimental Physchology, Oxford, 1960–61. Novelist, poet and screenwriter)
The flying bird, and other poems. Glasgow: William Maclellan. 1955. 64 pp.
 OXB

PELHAM, C. Malory
Verses of simplicity. Printed Bristol: J.W. Arrowsmith Ltd. 1942. 54 pp.
 A privately printed ed. of 150 signed and numbered copies. OXB

PELLOW, J.D.C. (A civil servant)
Selected poems; [by] George Every, J.D.C. Pellow, S.L. Bethell. Staples Press Ltd. [1945]. 77 pp.
 Not joint authorship. No war poetry by Every. BL

PELLOW, Jean
Blue grey and gold: [*poems*]. Ilfracombe: Arthur H. Stockwell, Ltd. [1942]. 36 pp. OXB

PENDLEBURY, Bevis John (1898– . b. Handsworth, Birmingham. Educated at Birmingham University. Taught English at Harrogate Grammar School, 1921–31, and at Douglas High School for Boys, Isle of Man, 1931–59. Literary critic and writer on the English language)
Simple ditties. Heath Cranton Ltd. 1944. 27 pp. OXB

PENDLETON, Lizzie
Rhymes and recitations. Ilfracombe: Arthur H. Stockwell, Ltd. [1947]. 144 pp.
 OXB

PEPPER, Roland Neville
Poems. Eton, Windsor: Shakespeare Head Press. 1958. [viii], 56 pp. MPL

PERRIN, John (Doctor in an East End of London hospital during the first two years of war, then a member of the Royal Air Force Volunteer Reserve) *see* 38

PERSSON, Jon (Served in the Army)

"Upheavaled strife (in verse) and life". Ilfracombe: Arthur H. Stockwell Ltd. 1970. 36 pp. OXB

PESKIN, C.F. (Of Iron Bridge, Shropshire)
Stanzas and ballads. Printed Shrewsbury: Shrewsbury Chronicle Ltd. [1948]. 17–48 pp.
    Title from cover. IWM
Stanzas and ballads. Printed Shrewsbury: Shrewsbury Chronicle Ltd. [1948]. 49–72 pp.
    Title from cover. IWM

PETCHER, William
Poetry: written in moments of weakness. Ilfracombe: Arthur H. Stockwell. [1946]. 24 pp. OXB

PETERS E. Curt (Served in the Royal Air Force. Of Chalfont St Giles, Buckinghamshire)
Between two worlds: poems. Billericay: Grey Walls Press. 1941. [x], 46 pp.
IWM
see also 61, 62, 78

PETERS, Eric (Served in H.M. Forces. Of West London)
The irreplaceable melody: poems. Fortune Press. 1944. 24 pp. IWM
see also 49

PETERS, Olwyn (Of Lancashire) *see* 74

PETHERAM, F. (Private. Served with the Eighth Army) *see* 25, 44

PETTS, Gertrude Ilett (Worked as a typist in wartime London)
Off and away: [*poems*]. Ilfracombe: Arthur H. Stockwell Ltd. 1973. 40 pp.
OXB

PETTY, William Henry (1921– . b. Bradford, Yorkshire. Educated at Bradford Grammar School, Peterhouse, Cambridge, and London University. Served with the Royal Artillery in India and Burma, 1941–45. Held various posts in educational administration, 1946–73. Appointed County Education Officer of Kent in 1973. Of Hollingbourne, near Maidstone, Kent)
Conquest, and other poems. Outposts Publications. 1967. 16 pp. OXB

PHILIPS, Austin (1875–1947. Educated at Malvern College. Entered the Post Office in 1893, working in various departments. Lent to the Post Master General's Department, Pietermaritzburg, South Africa, for special survey duties, 1902–03. Became Postmaster of Droitwich in 1905. Resigned to become a full-time writer. Engaged in clerical work with the Home Guard, 1940–41, in

Civil Defence, 1942, and Fire Guard Area Officer, 1943–45. Poet, novelist, short story writer and playwright)

The collected poems of Austin Philips. Seeley, Service & Co. Ltd. [1949]. xvi, 336 pp.   OXB

PHILLIPS, Aloysius Vincent

War sonnets, and others. Hodder & Stoughton Ltd. 1942. 32 pp.   BPL

PHILLIPS, Clifford William

The harp in the rainbow: a medley of verse. Foreword by Eamonn Andrews. Southend-on-Sea: Citizen Publishing Co. Ltd. [1964]. 64 pp.   OXB

PHILLIPS, Gordon, (Lucio, pseud.) (1890–1952. Member of editorial staff of *The Manchester Guardian*)   *see*   38

PHILLIPS, Hubert (1891–1964. Educated at Merton College, Oxford. Served in the Army, 1914–19, becoming Acting Lieutenant-Colonel, Essex Regiment, in 1918. Mentioned in despatches. Worked for the Liberal Party. On editorial staff of *News Chronicle*, 1930–54, principal leader writer, 1942–46. Writer on bridge and indoor games. President, National Bridge Association. Made numerous broadcasts on radio and television)

Selected verse. Cornleaf Press; Macgibbon & Kee. 1960. xvi, 150 pp.   OXB

PHILLIPS, John Fleetwood Stewart- *see* **STEWART-PHILLIPS, John Fleetwood**

PHILLIPS, Keith

Poems. Abingdon: Abbey Press. [1945]. [viii], 192 pp.   OXB

PHILLIPS, Leslie (Corporal, Royal Army Service Corps)   *see*   25, 33

PHILLIPS, Stanley (Served in the Home Guard. Of Hertfordshire ?)

Blood, sweat and tear(e)s: some "die-hard" ditties; by Stanley Phillips and C. Last. Printed St Albans: Gainsborough Press. 1944. 24 pp.

Not joint authorship.   IWM

PHILLIPS, William Henry (Of Devonshire)

War-time rhymes; and, Peace-time rhythms: a frail craft launched on a tempestuous sea. Printed [Torquay]: Devonshire Press. [1945]. 32 pp.

Cover-title is *Rhymes of War, Rhythms of Peace*.   OXB

PHILLPOTTS, Eden (1862–1960. b. Mount Aboo, India. Educated at Plymouth. Clerk in an insurance office, 1880–90. On coming to London studied for the stage but abandoned the idea, turning instead to literature. Poet of the First World War. Lived in Devon, the setting of much of his work. Novelist, playwright and poet)

Miniatures: [*poems*]. Watts & Co. 1942. vi, 50 pp.   OXB
see also   80

PHYSICK, Gordon O. (1918–   b. Malaya. Educated privately and at
Corpus Christi College, Oxford. Served with the Eighth Army in the Western
Desert. An artist, sculptor and designer. Of London)   *see*   39, 46, 63

PICKERING, M.H.
Air poems, and others. Ilfracombe: Arthur H. Stockwell, Ltd. 1947. 15 pp.
                                                                       OXB

PICKIN, J.E.
Summer leaves: [*poems*]. Ilfracombe: Arthur H. Stockwell Ltd. [1941]. 24 pp.
                                                                       OXB

PICKTHALL, Edith (1893–   . Educated at a private school in Birkenhead,
Cheshire. Worked in a Liverpool office then trained as a maternity nurse and
midwife. Spent the war years in the village of Mylor, near Falmouth, Cornwall,
acting as an emergency midwife. Of Mold, North Wales)
The choice is mine: [*poems*]. Walton-on-Thames: Outposts Publications. 1969.
12 pp.   OXB
The quest for peace, [*and other poems*]. Outposts Publications. 1963. 12 pp.
                                                                       OXB

PIDDUCK, Garson (Winner of prizes for poetry at the St Albans Festival)
We pause to weep: [*poems*]. Walton-on-Thames: Outposts Publications. [1968].
12 pp.   OXB

PIERCE, Richard
Soundings: [*poems*]. Chard, Somerset: Avon Books. [1964]. 12 pp. por.
   Title from cover.   OXB

PIGGOTT, Percy J. (Of Derbyshire)   *see*   71

PIGGOT, Stuart (1910–   . Educated at Churchers College, Petersfield,
and St John's College, Oxford. Served in the ranks, 1939–41, then as
Lieutenant-Colonel, Intelligence Corps, in charge of military air photograph
interpretation in South-East Asia. Professor of Prehistoric Archaeology at
Edinburgh University, 1946–77. Writer on ancient history and archaeology. Of
Wantage, Oxfordshire)
Fire among the ruins (1942–1945): [*poems*]. Oxford University Press. 1948.
48 pp.   IWM
see also   43

PIKE, Frank (Served in the Western Desert) *see* 63

PIM, Moore (Poet of the First World War. Of Hove, Sussex)
A cure for cant: a satire on the atomic bomb. Galashiels: John McQueen & Son, Ltd. 1946. 24 pp. OXB

PINE, Edward (Writer on Westminster Abbey Choir School)
Last things, and other poems. Bushey: Kit-Cat Press. 1962. [19] pp. OXB

PINKNEY, J.E.
The glory of Stalingrad, and other poems. Middlesbrough: Hood & Co. Ltd. [1943]. 23 pp.
    Dedicated to the people of Russia. OXB

PINTO, Vivian de Sola (1895–1969. Educated at University College School and Christ Church, Oxford. Poet of the First World War. Served in the Royal Welch Fusiliers, 1915–19. University lecturer in English, 1922–26. Professor of English at Southampton University, 1926–38. Served in Intelligence Corps and Royal Engineers, 1940–42. Professor of English at Nottingham University, 1938–61. Writer on English literature)
This is my England, and other poems. Williams & Norgate Ltd. 1941. 47 pp.
    BPL

PIPE, Florence
Poems. Arthur H. Stockwell Ltd. [1940]. 12 pp. OXB

PITTAWAY, Thomas (1887–   . b. Old Hill, Staffordshire. Educated at Halesowen Grammar School, King Edward VI Grammar School, Stourbridge, and Worcester College, Oxford. Trained for the Church of England ministry at Wycliffe Hall, Oxford. Appointed Rector of Rodden Frome, Somerset, in 1931)
The miser's house, and other poems. Frome: Author. 1940. viii, 72 pp. OXB

PITTER, Ruth (1897–   . b. Ilford, Essex. Educated at Coburn School for Girls, Bow, East London. A painter for Walberswick Peasant Pottery Co. in Suffolk, 1918–30. Won the Hawthornden Prize in 1936, the Heinemann Foundation Award in 1954 and the Queen's Medal for Poetry in 1955. Created a Companion of Literature in 1974. Of Long Crendon, near Aylesbury, Buckinghamshire)
The bridge: poems 1939–1944. Cresset Press. 1945. 60 pp. IWM
End of drought, [and other poems]. Barrie & Jenkins. 1975. [viii], 47 pp.
    OXB
The ermine: poems, 1942–1952. Cresset Press. 1953. [vi], 62 pp. OXB
Poems, 1926–1966. Cresset Press. 1968. xvi, 280 pp. OXB
The rude potato: [poems]. Illustrated by Roger Furse. Cresset Press. 1941. viii, 56 pp. il. OXB

Urania, [and other poems]. Cresset Press. 1950. x, 178 pp.   OXB
see also   21, 41

PLATT, Mavis
Air cadets, and other poems. Ilfracombe: Arthur H. Stockwell, Ltd. [1943].
16 pp.   OXB

PLATTEN, Barbara (Of Norfolk)   *see*   73

PLOMER, William (1903–73. b. Pietersburg, South Africa. Educated at
Rugby School. Before the war a farmer in the Stormberg, South Africa, and a
trader in Zululand. Lived in Japan for two years. Travelled in Europe, settling
in Greece for a time. Served at the Admiralty, 1940–45. Poet, novelist, short
story writer and biographer. Received the Queen's Gold Medal for Poetry,
1963. President of the Poetry Society, 1968–71)
A choice of ballads. Jonathan Cape. 1960. 48 pp.
Made from his *Collected Poems* as a Christmas present, and printed in a
limited ed. of 350 numbered copies signed by the author.   OXB
Collected poems. Jonathan Cape. 1960. 225 pp.   MPL
Collected poems. Jonathan Cape. 1973. 303 pp.
Differs from the 1960 ed. in that poems are arranged in chronological order
rather than in categories.   OXB
The Dorking thigh, and other satires: [poems]. Jonathan Cape. 1945. 31 pp.
                                                                   OXB
In a bombed house: 1941: an elegy in memory of Anthony Butts. [Curwen Press].
1942. [4] pp.   OXB
Title from cover. Printed for private circulation.
see also   42, 76

PLUMBE, Wilfred John (Served in East Africa)
African poems, and others. Windsor: Savile Press. 1951. [viii], 29 pp.   OXB

PLUNKETT, Edward John Moreton Drax, Lord Dunsany (1878–1957.
Educated at Eton College, and the Royal Military College, Sandhurst. Served
in Boer War with the Coldstream Guards and in the First World War as a
Captain in the Royal Inniskilling Fusiliers, being wounded in 1916. Byron
Professor of English Literature at Athens University, 1940–41. Novelist, poet
and playwright)
A journey; by Lord Dunsany. Macdonald & Co. Ltd. [1943]. 95 pp.
A limited ed. of 250 numbered copies initialled by the author.   BPL
To awaken Pegasus, and other poems; by Lord Dunsany. Oxford: George Ronald.
1949. 80 pp.   MPL
Wandering songs: [poems]; by Lord Dunsany. Hutchinson & Co. Ltd. [1943].
88 pp.   BPL
War poems; by Lord Dunsany. Hutchinson & Co. Ltd. [1941]. 102 pp. BPL

The year; by Lord Dunsany. Jarrolds Publishers Ltd. 1946. 187 pp.   OXB
see also   6, 38, 42, 80, 84

POLLEN, A.N.H.
An exile's musings: verse. Ilfracombe: Arthur H. Stockwell, Ltd. 1946. 16 pp.
                                                                                OXB

POLWIN, Isabella Frances
Poems. Ilfracombe: Arthur H. Stockwell, Ltd. [1944]. 32 pp. il.   OXB

POMFRET, Joan (1913– . b. Darwen, Lancashire. Educated at Darwen Grammar School, and The Park School, Preston. Married Douglas C. Townsend. Deputy Chairman of Lancashire Authors' Association. Of Great Harwood, near Blackburn)
The Admiralty regrets . . . and other poems. Printed Preston: Guardian Press. [1941]. 16 pp.   MPL
     Published in aid of the Merchant Navy Comforts Service.
Coastal Command: poems. Printed Preston: Guardian Press. [1942]. 16 pp.
                                                                                MPL
Merchant Navy man, and other poems. With foreword by Godfrey Winn. Printed Preston: Guardian Press. [1947]. 16 pp.
     All proceeds in aid of the Merchant Navy Comforts Service.   BL
Rhymes of the war. Printed Manchester: Withy Grove Press, Ltd. [1940]. 31 pp.
     Published on behalf of the *Daily Dispatch* and *Evening Chronicle* War Relief Fund.   MPL
Second Officer, [and other poems]. With a foreword by the Dowager Lady Lloyd. Printed Preston: Guardian Press. [1944]. 16 pp.
     All proceeds in aid of the Merchant Navy Comforts Service.   MPL
see also   70

PONTREMOLI, A. (Served with the Middle East Forces in the Western Desert)
England, and other poems. Ilfracombe: Arthur H. Stockwell, Ltd. 1945. 16 pp.
                                                                                OXB

POOLE, Robert John
For Hecuba!: [poems]. Ilfracombe: Arthur H. Stockwell Ltd. 1975. 32 pp.
                                                                                OXB

POOLMAN, Kenneth (Educated at Cambridge University. Served in the Royal Navy. Writer on naval ships)   *see*   53

POPHAM, Hugh (1920– . Educated at Cambridge University, after which he went straight into the Royal Navy, becoming a Fleet Air Arm pilot on

H.M.S. *Illustrious*. Novelist, poet and military historian. Of Yeovil, Somerset)
   Against the lightning: poems. John Lane the Bodley Head. 1944. 55 pp.

                                                             IWM

  The journey and the dream: poems. John Lane the Bodley Head. 1945. 44 pp.

                                                             IWM

see also   1, 23, 25

PORTER, E.G. (Gunner, Royal Artillery. Served with the Eighth Army)
see 44

PORTER, Herbert
Selected poems. Fortune Press. 1944. 80 pp.   OXB

PORTER, John (Sergeant. Served with the Eighth Army) *see* 44

PORTER, Peter (1929– . b. Brisbane, Australia. Educated at Church of England Grammar School, Brisbane, and Toowoomba Grammar School. Worked as a journalist in Brisbane before coming to London in 1951. Clerk, bookseller and advertising writer before becoming a full-time writer in 1968. Poet, reviewer, journalist and broadcaster)
  Living in a calm country: [poems]. Oxford University Press. 1975. [viii], 60 pp.

                                                             OXB

  Once bitten, twice bitten: poems. Northwood, Middlesex: Scorpion Press. 1961. 57 pp.   OXB

  Preaching to the converted, [and other poems]. Oxford University Press. 1972. [x], 61 pp.   OXB

  [Selected poems]; [by] Kingsley Amis, Dom Moraes, Peter Porter. Harmondsworth, Middlesex: Penguin Books. 1962. 128 pp. (Penguin modern poets, 3).

     Not joint authorship. No war poetry by Amis or Moraes.   MPL
see also 30

PORTER, Roy (1921– . b. Godley, Cheshire. Educated at King's School, Macclesfield, Merton College, Oxford, and St Stephen's House, Oxford. Fellow, Chaplain and Tutor of Oriel College and university lecturer in theology, 1949–62. Appointed Professor of Theology, Exeter University in 1962, Canon of Chichester Cathedral from 1965. Contributed poetry to *The Times Literary Supplement*)
  World in the heart: poems. Fortune Press. 1944. 32 pp.   IWM

PORTEUS, Hugh Gordon (Aircraftman, Royal Air Force) *see* 1, 25, 40

POSNER, A.E.V. (Served in H.M. Forces) *see* 74

POTTER, Alex (1891– . b. Norwich. Served as an infantry officer in the First World War, being twice wounded. On the editorial staff of the *Continental*

Daily Mail for twenty-eight years. Interned in Saint-Denis camp for four years) *see* 76

POTTS, Paul (1911– . b. Datchet, Berkshire. Educated at Stonyhurst College, and Mary College, Turin. A Canadian citizen. Served with the 12th Commando in the war and with the Israeli Army in the first war of independence. Book reviewer for the *Sunday Telegraph*. Of London)
A ballad for Britain on May Day. Preface, Jack Lindsay, cover, Douglas Glass. Modern Literature Ltd. 1945. 16 pp. OXB
Instead of a sonnet, [and other poems]. Editions Poetry London. 1944. viii, 45 pp. facsim. (Ballad books, 2). BL
Instead of a sonnet, [and other poems]. The 1944 ed. with ten new poems. Tuba Press. 1978. [xii], 64 pp. OXB
see also 42

POULSON, Florence Ethel
Poems, prose and thoughts. Ilfracombe: Arthur H. Stockwell, Ltd. 1947 72 pp. OXB

POULTER, William M.
Dream girl, and other poems. Ilfracombe: Arthur H. Stockwell, Ltd. 1951. 20 pp. OXB

POVEY, Anne
Poems for days of stress and strain. Ilfracombe: Arthur H. Stockwell, Ltd. [1943]. 20 pp. OXB

POWELL, A.E.
As I linger by life's wayside: [poems]. Ilfracombe: Arthur H. Stockwell, Ltd. [1942]. 16 pp. OXB

POWELL, Enoch (1912– . Educated at King Edward's School, Birmingham, and Trinity College, Cambridge. Fellow of Trinity College, then Professor of Greek, Sydney University, New South Wales, before the war. Joined the Royal Warwickshire Regiment, rising from Private to Brigadier on the General Staff. Served in Egypt and India. Conservative M.P., 1950–74, Minister of Health, 1960–63. Ulster Unionist M.P. for South Down from 1974. Classicist, poet, translator, historian and political writer)
Dancer's end; and, The wedding gift: two books of poems. Falcon Press. 1951. 103 pp. por. OXB
see also 76

POWELL, H. (Served in H.M. Forces) *see* 74

POWELL, Roger (1936– . b. Worcestershire. A wartime childhood was spent in Cornwall. Educated at Liskeard Grammar School. Did national service in the Far East)

Winter berries: [*poems*]. Regency Press. [1973]. 32 pp. OXB

POWER, Norman Sandiford (1916–   . b. London. Educated at Worcester College and Ripon Hall, Oxford. Canon and Vicar of Ladywood, Birmingham)

Ends of verse. Introduction by Ruth Pitter. Mowbrays. 1971. 91 pp.

OXB

POWER, Violet

A woman's war poems. Walton-on-Thames: Outposts Publications. 1975. 24 pp.

BPL

POWERSCOURT, Lady *see* **WINGFIELD, Sheila, Lady Powerscourt**

POWIS, Sybil

Upland and valley, [*and other poems*]. Shrewsbury: Wilding & Son Ltd. 1941. 27 pp. OXB

POWLEY, Edward Barzillai (1887–1968. b. Narborough, Norfolk. Educated at King Edward VII Grammar School, King's Lynn, and King's College, London. Poet of the First World War. Served in the Royal Navy, 1914–18, with the Grand Fleet, the Dover Patrol and at the Admiralty. Taught at grammar schools in Lancaster, Caistor and Crosby. Held many public appointments)

Poems — 1914–1950. Frederick Muller, Ltd. 1950. x, 67 pp.

A limited ed. of 510 copies signed by the author. OXB

PRAEGER, Rosamond (1867–1954. b. Holywood, County Down. Educated in Holywood and London. Studied art at the Slade School, receiving a silver medal for drawing. Returned to Ireland to practice as a professional artist, illustrator and sculptor. Published fifteen children's picture books. Appointed M.B.E. in 1939)

Old fashioned verses and sketches. Dundalk: Dundalgan Press. 1947. [viii], 63 pp. il., col. il.

Printed on one side of leaf only. OXB

PRATT, Alan *see* **PRATT, Thomas Alan**

PRATT, Art

"Bally rot": versified reminiscences, many topical, all diabolical. Ilfracombe: Arthur H. Stockwell, Ltd. 1948. 96 pp. OXB

PRATT, Arthur Joseph (b. Norfolk, afterwards living in Sussex)

Poems, containing lyrics of nature, religion, romance, history, philosophy, humour and

tributes to revered friends. Collected and arranged by Louise M. Webb. Printed Hove: Eagle Press. [1960]. [vi], 257 pp.

Cover-title is *A Reverie in Verse*.　　　　　　　　　　　　　　　　OXB

PRATT, Thomas Alan (A chartered accountant. Member of the Poetry Society, the International Poetry Society and the Middle England Poets. Of Leicester)

Lobster potted people: [*poems*]; by Alan Pratt. Sutton Coldfield; MEPS Publications. [1979]. [iii], 21 pp.　　　　　　　　　　　　　　　　　OXB

PRENTICE, Maud

The glorious few, and other poems. Ilfracombe: Arthur H. Stockwell, Ltd. [1942]. 14 pp.　　　　　　　　　　　　　　　　　　　　　　　　　　　　OXB

PRESLAND, John, pseud. *see* **SKELTON, Gladys**, (John Presland, pseud.)

PRESS, John (1920–　. b. Norwich. Educated at King Edward VI School, Norwich, and Corpus Christi College, Cambridge. Served in the Royal Artillery, 1940–45. Held British Council posts in Athens, Salonika, Madras, Colombo, Birmingham, Cambridge, London, Paris and Oxford. Poet and writer on English literature)

Guy Fawkes night, and other poems. Oxford University Press. 1959. xii, 68 pp.

　　　　　　　　　　　　　　　　　　　　　　　　　　　　　　　OXB

Uncertainties, and other poems. Oxford University Press. 1956. viii, 103 pp.

　　　　　　　　　　　　　　　　　　　　　　　　　　　　　　　MPL

PREWETT, Frank (1893–1962. b. Ontario, Canada. Educated at Christ Church, Oxford. Poet of the First World War. Remained in Britain, serving as a Staff Officer. In World War II he joined a bomb disposal squad in Birmingham and was later employed in operational research at Fighter Command H.Q. Sent as adviser to Supreme Command in South-East Asia)

The collected poems of Frank Prewett. Cassell. 1964. viii, 63 pp. por.　　OXB

PRICE, Annie Rebecca

Quiet benison: [*poems*]. Ilfracombe: Arthur H. Stockwell, Ltd. [1942]. 16 pp.

　　　　　　　　　　　　　　　　　　　　　　　　　　　　　　　OXB

PRICE, Dorothy (Of Sussex?)

Friendship, and other poems. Printed Hove: Hove Shirley Press Ltd. 1962. 24 pp.

　　　　　　　　　　　　　　　　　　　　　　　　　　　　　　　OXB

The lighthouse, and other poems. Ilfracombe: Arthur H. Stockwell, Ltd. [1944]. 16 pp. il.　　　　　　　　　　　　　　　　　　　　　　　　　　OXB

PRICE, Nancy (1880–1970. Educated at Malvern Wells, Worcestershire. A distinguished actress, she began her stage career in 1889, playing more than 400

parts in all. Married Colonel Charles Raymond Maude in 1907. Produced eighty-seven plays. Appointed Honorary Director, People's National Theatre, 1933. Writer on nature and the countryside. Lived at High Salvington, Sussex)
  Hurdy-gurdy, [*and other poems*]. Frederick Muller Ltd. 1944. 47 pp.　　IWM

PRICHARD, John (Leading Writer, Royal Navy) *see* 25, 33, 47

PRIDE, R. (Flight Sergeant, Royal Air Force. Served with the Eighth Army) *see* 25, 44

PRINCE, Dorothy A.L. (Of Hertfordshire) *see* 71

PRINCE, Frank Templeton (1912– . b. Kimberley, South Africa. Educated at Christian Brothers College, Kimberley, and Balliol College, Oxford. Visiting Fellow at Princeton University, 1935–36. Captain, Intelligence Corps, 1940–46, serving in North Africa and elsewhere. Appointed lecturer in English literature at Southampton University in 1950, becoming Professor of English in 1957. Professor of English, University of the West Indies, 1975–78)
  Collected poems. Anvil Press; Menard Press. 1979. 206 pp.　　OXB
  The doors of stone: poems 1938–1962. Rupert Hart-Davis. 1963. 128 pp.　MPL
  [*Selected poems*]; [by] John Heath-Stubbs, F.T. Prince, Stephen Spender. Harmondsworth, Middlesex: Penguin Books. 1972. 176 pp. (Penguin modern poets, 20).
    Not joint authorship.　　MPL
  Soldiers bathing, and other poems. Fortune Press. 1954. 48 pp.　　IWM
  see also 15, 25, 33, 37, 45, 57, 59, 63, 76, 82

PRINCE, Hetty
  Laugh, love and live: [*poems*]. Ilfracombe: Arthur H. Stockwell Ltd. 1978. 80 pp.　　OXB

PRINT, S.G. (Served in H.M. Forces) *see* 74

PRITCHARD, Glenys M. (b. Anglesey. Became a student nurse at St Catherine's Hospital, Birkenhead in 1940, qualifying in 1943. Lived at Abergele, North Wales, as a nursing sister for many years. A novelist)
  Conway Castle, (and other poems). Printed Regency Press. [1975]. 32 pp.
　　OXB
  Wild buds: [*poems*]. Printed Regency Press Ltd. [1975]. 32 pp.
    Printed as the prize in the New Poets–1975 competition sponsored by Regency Press.　　OXB

PRIVATE A, pseud. (Of Norfolk ?)
  Twenty-five poems; by a Private. Printed Norwich: Caxton Press. [1941]. [16] pp.
    Title from cover.　　OXB

PROCTER, Ida (Writer on British art) *see* 84

PROCTOR, Joyce (Of Northumberland) *see* 74

PROKOSCH, Frederic (1908– . b. Madison, Wisconsin. Educated at schools in Wisconsin, Texas, Munich and Austria, Yale University, and King's College, Cambridge. Taught English at Yale, 1932–34. Cultural Attaché, American Legation in Sweden, 1943–45. Visiting lecturer at Rome University, 1950–51. Novelist, poet and expert on Chaucerian MSS. Of Grasse, South of France)

    Chosen poems. Chatto & Windus. 1945. [viii], 72 pp.

      Dedicated to Lady Cunard.   IWM

    Death at sea: poems. Chatto & Windus. 1940. [x], 54 pp.   BL

see also 38, 69

PROSSER, Glyn J. (Served in the Royal Air Force in India, Burma and Hong Kong)

    For the joy of doing: [poems]. Ilfracombe: Arthur H. Stockwell Ltd. [1968]. 24 pp.   OXB

see also 35

PROSSER, Kenneth (Educated at Oxford University)

    Poems, 1939–1954. Ilfracombe: Arthur H. Stockwell, Ltd. [1956]. 84 pp.

                                          OXB

PROUD, George Thomas

    Wheels within wheels: poems. Ilfracombe: Arthur H. Stockwell Ltd. [1956]. 32 pp.   OXB

PUDNEY, John (1909–77. b. Langley, Buckinghamshire, son of a farmer. Educated at Gresham's School, Holt, fellow-pupil of W.H. Auden. Producer and writer on B.B.C. staff, 1934–37. *News Chronicle* correspondent, 1937–41. Squadron Leader, Royal Air Force, 1941–45, seving in Intelligence and travelling widely on special assignments to Ireland, North and South America, Africa, Middle East, Malta, Greece and Yugoslavia. Co-editor of the anthology *Air Force Poetry*, 1944. Stood as Labour candidate for Sevenoaks in 1945. Book critic, *Daily Express*, 1947–48, literary editor, *News Review*, 1948–50. Director of the publishers Putnams, 1953–63. Poet, dramatist and fiction writer)

    Almanack of hope: sonnets. With drawings by John Nash. John Lane the Bodley Head. 1944. 32 pp. il.   OXB

    Beyond this disregard: poems. John Lane the Bodley Head. 1943. 32 pp.

                                          BPL

    Collected poems. Putnam. 1957. 176 pp.   IWM

    Dispersal point, and other air poems. John Lane the Bodley Head. 1942. 32 pp.   BPL

Dispersal point, and other air poems. John Lane the Bodley Head. 1942. 32 pp.
One of fifteen numbered copies printed on mould-made paper and signed by the author. BL

Flight above cloud, [and other poems]. New York: Harper & Brothers. [1944]. x, 54 pp. BL

For Johnny: poems of World War Two. Revised ed. Shepheard-Walwyn. 1976. 40 pp.
1st ed. published in 1957 by Putnam as *Collected Poems*. BPL

Selected poems. John Lane the Bodley Head. 1946. 48 pp. OXB

Selected poems. With decorations by Harold Jones. Published for The British Publishers Guild by The Bodley Head. 1947. [viii], 88 pp. il. (Guild books, 238). BL

South of forty: poems. John Lane the Bodley Head. 1943. 32 pp. BPL

Spill out: poems and ballads. J.M. Dent & Sons Ltd. 1967. viii, 55 pp.
OXB

Ten summers: poems (1933–1943). John Lane in the Bodley Head. 1944. 112 pp.
IWM

see also 1, 10, 11, 15, 17, 23, 25, 30, 31, 33, 36, 51, 59, 63, 64, 76, 77, 82

PUGH, John Geoffrey (Of Temple Guiting, Gloucestershire)

Poems. Printed Knight (Printers) Ltd. 1962. [ii], 72 pp.
A limited ed. of 250 numbered copies published by the author for private circulation. ·OXB

PURCELL, Nele

Drifts of time: a booklet of verse. Arthur H. Stockwell, Ltd. [1940]. 16 pp.
OXB

PURCELL-BURET, Theobald (1879–1974. Educated at Victoria College, Jersey. Entered the Merchant Service in 1916, awarded the D.S.C. in 1917. Commodore, Royal Mail Fleet, 1939–42)

The wanderer, and other poems. Printed [Dublin]: [R.T. White, Ltd]. [1952]. 97 pp. OXB

PURCHAS, Saint John

Poems and verse for you. Ilfracombe: Arthur H. Stockwell, Ltd. 1973. 125 pp.
OXB

PUTT, Samuel Gorley (1913– . Educated at Torquay Grammar School, Christ's College, Cambridge, and Yale University. Worked in B.B.C. Talks Department, 1936–38. At Queen's University, Belfast, 1939–40. Lieutenant Commander, Royal Naval Volunteer Reserve, 1940–46. After the war held a variety of academic posts. Fellow of Christ's College, Cambridge, from 1972. Literary critic, writer on Henry James)

Coastline: [poems]. Hugh Evelyn. 1959. 40 pp. IWM

PUXLEY, Peggy
Reasons in rhyme. Ilfracombe: Arthur H. Stockwell, Ltd. 1946. 48 pp.

OXB

PYATT, Henry Robert (1870–1945. b. Oxford. Educated at Harrow School, and Hertford College, Oxford. Taught at Fettes College and Carrington House, Edinburgh)
Wings, and other poems. Privately printed Edinburgh: R. & R. Clark, Ltd. 1949. 96 pp.

OXB

PYBUS, Rodney (1916– . Feature writer and literary editor of *The Journal*, Newcastle upon Tyne, 1962–64. Writer and producer for Tyne Tees Television, 1964–76. Lecturer in English at Macquarie University, Sydney, Australia, 1976–79. Literature Officer for Cumbria from 1979. Of Ambleside and Ulverston)
In memoriam Milena, [*and other poems*]. Chatto & Windus; Hogarth Press. 1973. 48 pp. (Phoenix living poets).

OXB

PYKE-LEES, Walter Kinnear, (Peter Leyland, pseud.) (1909–78. Educated at Liverpool College, and Wadham College, Oxford. Worked for London County Council, 1933–37. Assistant Secretary of General Medical Council, 1937–51. Seconded to H.M. Treasury, 1940–45. Registrar, General Medical Council, 1951–70. Council member of the Britain-Burma Society)
The naked mountain, [*and other poems*]; by Peter Leyland. William Heinemann Ltd. 1951. xx, 83 pp.

BL

QUADLING, B.W.J.G.
Heroines all!: verse written to the glory of all the British women engaged in the last war. Ilfracombe: Arthur H. Stockwell, Ltd. 1946. 36 pp. il.

OXB

QUARRELL, John (1935– . b. Stepney, London. Evacuated to Surrey at the age of eight)
Fifteen poems. East London Arts Magazine Society. 1965. [vi], 18 pp. il. (Firstprint).

OXB

QUENBY, David C.
Yesterday's prisoner, [*and other poems*]. Ilfracombe: Arthur H. Stockwell, Ltd. 1973. 46 pp.

QUIET WOMAN, pseud. (Of Kent)
A democrat's chapbook: a chronicle of some of the events of the present war, up to the entry of America, December 1941: with reflections; by a quite woman. John Lane the Bodley Head. 1942. 104 pp.

OXB

QUINN, Mick G. (Enlisted in the King's Own Royal Regiment. Served in

Egypt and India, then in North Africa with the Royal Armoured Corps. Of Bolton, Lancashire) *see* 63

R.L. *see* **L., R.**

R.W.F.W. *see* **W., R.W.F.**

RADCLIFFE, D.M. (Petty Officer Canteen Manager, Royal Navy) *see* 23

RADFORD, J.N. (Served in H.M. Forces) *see* 74

RADFORD, Maitland (1884–1945? Served as a doctor in the Royal Army Medical Corps in the First World War. Held various Medical Officer of Health posts in the London area)
Poems; by Maitland Radford. With a memoir by some of his friends. George Allen & Unwin Ltd. 1945. 46 pp. por.
    A limited ed. of 500 numbered copies.   OXB

RAIKES, David (1924–45. b. Blechingley, Surrey. Educated at Radley College, and Trinity College, Oxford. In the crew which won the Oxford Senior Eights in 1942. Served in the Royal Air Force as a bomber pilot in the Middle East and Italy. Reported missing from operations over the Po Valley on 21 April 1945)
The poems of David Raikes. With an introduction by Charles Wrinch. Oxford: Fantasy Press. 1954. viii, 122 pp. por.   BL
see also 20, 76

RAIKES, Iris M. (Of Suffolk ?)
Hark forrard!: poems. Illustrated by the author. Printed Beccles: William Clowes & Sons Ltd. [1939]. 36 pp. il.   OXB

RAINE, Kathleen (1908–. b. London of north-country parents, her mother a Scot. Spent several years of her childhood in Northumberland during the First World War. Educated at the County High School, Ilford, and Girton College, Cambridge, where she read natural sciences. Married Charles Madge, later divorced. Research Fellow of Girton College, 1955–61. Recipient of Bollingen Fellowship and Arts Council Prize for Poetry)
The collected poems of Kathleen Raine. Hamish Hamilton. 1956. xvi, 175 pp.
                                             OXB
Living in time: poems. Editions Poetry London. 1946. vi, 38 pp.   MPL
Selected poems. New York: Weekend Press. 1952. [vi], 21 pp.
    A limited ed. of 250 numbered copies of which 200 are for sale.   OXB
Stone and flower: poems 1935–43. With drawings by Barbara Hepworth. Nicholson & Watson. 1943. 68 pp. il., col. il.   MPL
see also 15, 56, 57

RAMPTON, Philip
Plain reflections: [*poems*]. Walton-on-Thames: Outposts Publications. 1974
12 pp.   OXB

RAMSAY, Allen Beville (1872–1955. Educated at Eton College, and King's
College, Cambridge. Taught at Eton, 1895–1925. Master of Magdalene
College, Cambridge, 1925–47. Vice-Chancellor of Cambridge University,
1929–31. A Latin scholar)
Flos malvae, [*and other poems*]. Cambridge at the University Press. 1946. [iv],
110 pp.
     Poems in English, Latin and Greek.   OXB

RAMSEY, Fred (b. Tantobie, County Durham. Started work as a miner at the
age of fourteen. In 1937 joined the Royal Navy Spanish Patrol taking
Republican refugees to Marseilles. A survivor of H.M.S. *Hyperion* in 1940 and of
H.M.S. *Imperial* in 1941)
The way I see it: [*poems*]. Whitley Bay: Strong Words. [1980]. 18 pp. il. (Strong
Words booklets).   OXB

RAMSEY, Georgina M. (Of County Fermanagh)
Lyrics of Fermanagh, and other verses. Printed [Enniskillen]: [William Trimble].
[1955]. 34 pp.   OXB

RAMSEY, Thomas Weston (1892–1952. b. London. Educated at Dulwich
College and London University. Taught modern languages for a time then
entered the family firm of wire workers in Clerkenwell. Served in the Middle
East. President of the Poetry Society, 1948–52)
Endymion to silver, [*and other poems*]. English Universities Press Ltd. [1944].
112 pp.   MPL
see also   42, 51, 63, 76

RANDALL, Celia (Of Holywood, County Down)
The leaping flame, [*and other poems*]. Manchester: Poetry Lovers' Fellowship.
1949. xvi, 68 pp. (Modern poets series, VI)   OXB

RANGER, Nora Adeline
Life is what you make it, and other poems. Ilfracombe: Arthur H. Stockwell Ltd.
1976. 32 pp.   OXB

RATA, A.A. (Served in the Army)
1939 — and how: a selection of verse. Arthur H. Stockwell Ltd. [1940]. 63 pp.
                                                                                       OXB

RATCLIFFE, Dorothy Una (1894–1967. b. Preston Park, Sussex. Educated
privately and in Weimar and Paris. Married three times. Lived in the Yorkshire

dales following her first marriage. Poet of the First World War. Lady Mayoress of Leeds in 1914. President of the Yorkshire Dialect Society and a contributor to many newspapers and magazines. A relative by marriage of the 1st Lord Brotherton, she gave his library to Leeds University, adding liberal endownments from his large fortune. Poet, playwright and general writer)

Over hill over dale: [poems]. Illustrations by Fred Lawson. Bodley Head. 1956. 109 pp. il. OXB

Under t'hawthorn: Yorkshire dialect lyrics. Decorations by Fred Lawson. Frederick Muller Ltd. 1946. 80 pp. il. OXB

Until that dawn: lyrics. University of London Press Ltd. 1949. [viii], 57 pp. il. (by Astrid Walford). OXB

Up dale: [poems]. Illustrated by Fred Lawson. Thomas Nelson & Sons Ltd. 1952. x, 110 pp. por.

In Yorkshire dialect. OXB

Yorkshire lyrics. Selected by Wilfrid J. Halliday. Thomas Nelson & Sons Ltd. 1960. xii, 176 pp. col. por.

Published for the Yorkshire Dialect Society. OXB

RATHBONE, E.
Current events: [poems]. Ilfracombe: Arthur H. Stockwell, Ltd. [1942]. 16 pp.
OXB

RATHBONE, Irene (b. Liverpool. Educated privately. Cousin of Eleanor Rathbone, M.P., and of Basil Rathbone the actor. She was much in contact with exiled European writers. Novelist) *see* 42

RATHBONE, James Parkhill
Wild corn: [poems]. Ilfracombe: Arthur H. Stockwell, Ltd. [1943]. 24 pp.
OXB

RATHKEY, William Arthur (Librettist)
German elegy. Peter Beavan. 1968. [iv], 31 pp.

A limited ed. of 200 copies. OXB

A questionnaire for God: [poems]. Printed Cambridge: Rampant Lions Press. 1978. [viii], 51 pp. OXB

Twenty five poems. Cock Robin Press. [1976]. [viii], 19 pp.

A limited ed. of 100 numbered copies. OXB

RATTENBURY, Arnold (1921– . b. Hankow, China, son of a missionary. Educated at St John's College, Cambridge. Served in the Army, 1940–44. Editor of *Our Time* and *Theatre Today*, 1944–49. Freelance journalist and designer. Editor of books on theatre and cinema)
Second causes: [poems]. Chatto & Windus; Hogarth Press. 1969. 48 pp. (Phoenix living poets). OXB
see also 36, 76

RAWLINGS, A.C. (Captain, The Buffs. Captured in France in 1940, held prisoner of war in Germany until 1945) *see* 67

RAYMOND, Ernest (1888–1974. Educated at St Paul's School, Durham University and Chichester Theological College. Taught at schools in Eastbourne and Bath, 1908–12. Ordained in 1914 but resigned holy orders in 1923. Attached to 10th Manchester Regiment, 1915–17, and 9th Worcester Regiment, 1917–19. Served in Gallipoli, Egypt, France, Mesopotamia, Persia and Russia. Best-selling novelist. Awarded Book Guild Gold Medal in 1936 for *We the Accused*) *see* 84

RAYNE, Sebastian *see* 25

READ, David Haxton Carswell (1910– . b. Cupar, Fife. Educated at Daniel Stewart's College, Edinburgh, Edinburgh University and in Montpellier, Strasbourg, Paris and Marburg. Ordained a minister of the Church of Scotland in 1936. Chaplain to the Forces, 1939–45. Captured at St Valery on 12 June 1940 when serving with the Royal Army Service Corps, held prisoner of war in Germany until 1945. Mentioned in despatches. Chaplain to the Queen in Scotland, 1952–55. Minister of Madison Avenue Presbyterian Church, New York City from 1956) *see* 5

READ, Sir Herbert (1893–1968. b. Kirbymoorside, Yorkshire. Educated at Crossley's School, Halifax, and Leeds University. Major poet of the First World War. A Captain in the Green Howards, he fought in France and Belgium, 1915–18. Awarded the M.C. and D.S.O. and mentioned in despatches. Poet and art critic, holder of many distinguished art appointments. A director of the publishers Routledge & Kegan Paul, Ltd. Author of numerous works on art, literature and politics. One of the leaders of philosophical anarchism)

    Collected poems. Faber & Faber. 1946. 201 pp.   OXB
    Collected poems. New ed. Faber & Faber. 1953. 203 pp.   MPL
    Collected poems [New] ed. Faber & Faber. 1966. 286 pp.   OXB
    Thirty-five poems. Faber & Faber. 1940. 80 pp.   BPL
    A world within a war. Hampden Press. 1943. 12 pp.
        A limited ed. of fifty numbered copies.   OXB
    A world within a war: poems. Faber & Faber. 1944. 50 pp.   BPL
see also 2, 25, 30, 42, 51, 56

READ, L. (Served in H.M. Forces) *see* 75

READ, Sylvia (Trained for the stage at the Royal Academy of Dramatic Art. During the war gave performances of poetry and music for the Forces all over the country. While still in her teens she took part in the first 'poetry in pubs' experiment. Co-founder and editor of *Here and Now*, 1940–49. Married actor William Fry. Worked for B.B.C. radio and television, Thames Television, Arts

Theatre, Albery Theatre and The Round House. Leading actress and scriptwriter, Theatre Roundabout Ltd, London, from 1964) *see* 19, 25, 42, 52

READE, Derek B. (1915– . Served in West Africa as a Lieutenant in the South Staffordshire Regiment and the Sierra Leone Regiment. A businessman of Tettenhall, Staffordshire) *see* 24, 61, 76

REDKNAP, Ellen Edith Hannah, (Ellen Edith Hannah Collins, pseud.) (1906– . Began work as a shorthand typist in 1924, working at Heston Airport. On staff of *Picture Post* then *Lilliput*, 1932–40. Bronze medallist, Twickenham & Richmond Music Festival, 1964 and 1965. Of Isleworth, Middlesex)
Poems for all seasons; by Ellen E.H. Collins. Southend-on-Sea: Citizen Publishing Co. Ltd. [1961]. 12 pp. OXB

REED, Henry (1914– . b. Birmingham. Educated at King Edward VI School and Birmingham University. A freelance writer before the war. Taught for a year before Army call-up in 1941. Released in 1942 to work at the Foreign Office for the duration of the war. Poet, radio dramatist, critic and translator. Held academic appointments at University of Washington, Seattle, 1964–67)
Lessons of the war: [poems]. New York: Chilmark Press. 1970. 37 pp. (Clover Hill editions).
A limited ed. of 530 copies, 110 copies numbered I–CX and signed by the author and 420 copies numbered 1–420. BL
A map of Verona: poems. Jonathan Cape. 1946. 59 pp. IWM
see also 3, 15, 17, 25, 30, 33, 37, 57, 58, 59, 76, 77, 82, 85, 86

REED, T.G. (Of Yorkshire) *see* 71, 72

REEDY, William Curran (1892–1970. Poet of the First World War. Able Seaman, Royal Navy. Served in the cruiser *Southampton* as a gunnery writer. Printer and author, he joined staff of *The Times* in 1907, retiring in 1957 as Late London Printer)
London garland: [poems]. Fortune Press. [1942]. 64 pp. OXB
Spindrift and spunyarn: [poems]. Fortune Press. [1942]. 64 pp. OXB

REEVE, Rea
You and me, and other poems. Ilfracombe: Arthur H. Stockwell, Ltd. [1943]. 16 pp. OXB

REEVES, James (1909–78. Educated at Stowe School and Cambridge University. Schoolmaster and lecturer in teacher training colleges, 1933–52. Freelance author, editor and broadcaster from 1952. Lived in Lewes, East Sussex)

Collected poems, 1929–1959. Heinemann. 1960. 191 pp. por.   OXB
Collected poems, 1929–1974. Heinemann. 1974. xii, 180 pp.   OXB
Selected poems. Allison & Busby Ltd. 1967. [ii], 56 pp.   OXB
Subsong: [poems]. Heinemann. 1969. viii, 54 pp.   OXB

REGAN, J. (Of London)   *see*   73

REID, Alexander (1914–   . Novelist and playwright)
Steps to a viewpoint: [poems]. Andrew Dakers Ltd. 1947. 48 pp.   MPL

REID, Herbert (M.C. A clergyman. Of Gourock, Renfrewshire)
The big adventure, and other verses in Scots. Glasgow: Distributed for the author by
John Smith & Son, Ltd. 1946. 75 pp. il., por.   BL
Rhyme-raivelins. Glasgow: Distributed for the author by John Smith & Son,
Ltd. 1944. 68 pp. il., por.   OXB

REILLY, Dion (Of Irish stock, originally from County Cavan. Worked as a
journalist in France)   *see*   42

REITZENSTEIN, Josefine Marie L., Baroness (A German national who
protested against the teaching of racial and other hatreds to German youth. She
escaped to Britain just before the Nazis took power)
For to-morrow: [poems]. Favil Press. 1945. 20 pp.   OXB

RENDALL, D. (Served in H.M. Forces)   *see*   73

RENDELL, J.M.
Time to dream: [poems]. Ilfracombe: Arthur H. Stockwell Ltd. [1968]. 40 pp.
OXB

RENDLE, Alfred Bernard (Associate of Royal College of Science. Writer on
gravitation)
The call of the stars, and other poems. Ilfracombe: Arthur H. Stockwell, Ltd. 1954.
23 pp.   OXB

RENNELL OF RODD, Lord *see* **RODD, James Rennell, Lord Rennell**

REYNOLDS, D.W. (b. South Africa. Taken prisoner at El Alamein and held
for over three years)
From this mire, [and other poems]. Sidgwick & Jackson. 1946. 45 pp.   IWM

REYNOLDS, Myles (Commissioned in the Army)
The spinning mirror: [poems]. Fortune Press. [1945]. 20 pp. por.   IWM

REYNOLDS, Reginald (1905–58. A Quaker. Spent some time in India where he was a friend and supporter of Mahatma Gandhi. A passionate advocate of Indian independence and a tireless worker in the cause of racial tolerance. A pacifist, he protested strongly against the British nuclear tests in the Pacific, 1957. A regular contributor to *New Stateman*. Married novelist Ethel Mannin)

Og and other ogres: [poems]. Drawings by Quentin Crisp. Preface by Laurence Housman. George Allen & Unwin Ltd. 1946. 75 pp. il.   OXB

see also 6

RHODES, Margaret Elizabeth (1915– . b. Colwyn Bay, North Wales. Educated at Somerville College, Oxford. Married Mark M. Plummer in 1939. Freelance writer, an expert on French cuisine. Of Catel, Guernsey)

Pole-star, and other poems. Hutchinson & Co., Ltd. [1946]. 59 pp.   OXB

RHYS, Augustine

How shall we remember them?, and other verses. Bognor Regis: John Crowther. [1945]. 36 pp.   OXB

RHYS, Ernest (1859–1946. b. London but spent much of his youth in Carmarthen. Became a mining engineer then abandoned it for a writing career. Anglo-Welsh editor and poet, perhaps best known as editor of the Everyman Library of classics. Poet of the First World War. Vice-President, Honourable Society of Cymmrodorion. Council member of the P.E.N. Club) *see* 48

RHYS, Keidrych (1915– . b. Llandeilo, Carmarthenshire. Educated at Llandovery Grammar School. Started career as a journalist. In 1937 founded the magazine *Wales* for Welshmen writing in English. Married the poet Lynette Roberts in 1939. Served in the London Welsh Regiment with an anti-aircraft unit near Dover during the Battle of Britain and later at Scapa. Became a war correspondent, 1944–45. Editor of the anthologies *Poems from the Forces*, 1941, *More Poems from the Forces*, 1943, and *Modern Welsh Poetry*, 1944. After the war a journalist in London. Established the Druid Press)

The van pool, and other poems. Routledge. 1942. 38 pp.   BPL

see also 11, 25, 33, 37, 47, 76

RICHARDS, Florence (Of Cornwall) *see* 74

RICHARDS, Margaret Ethel

Tributes to our fighters, and other verse. Ilfracombe: Arthur H. Stockwell, Ltd. [1943]. 15 pp.   OXB

RICHARDSON, Anthony (1899– . b. London. Educated at Marlborough College and Manchester University. Flight Lieutenant, Royal Air Force, serving in Bomber Command. Novelist and general writer)

Because of these: verses of the Royal Air Force. Hodder & Stoughton. 1942. 62 pp.
                                                                                    IWM

Full cycle, [and other poems]. Hodder & Stoughton. 1946. 64 pp.
'Dedicated to the memory of my comrades who gave their lives in the service of Bomber Command; especially those of No. 107 Squadron and No. 105 Squadron of No. 2 Group, Royal Air Force'.   BPL

These — our children: more verses of the Royal Air Force. George G. Harrap & Co. Ltd. 1943. 62 pp.   BPL
see also   1, 25

RICHARDSON, Iliffe

Ever green: a book of verse. Ilfracombe: Arthur H. Stockwell, Ltd. [1944]. 24 pp.
'Dedicated to my dear father and all other prisoners of war'.   OXB

RICHARDSON, Justin (1899–1975. b. Cape Town, South Africa. Educated at King Edward VII School, Durban, and Bishop's Stortford School. Joined the Army in 1919. A furniture manufacturer. Commander, Royal Naval Volunteer Reserve, 1940–45. Lived at Oxshott, Surrey)

The phoney phleet: [poems]. Illustrated by J.S. Hicks. Frederick Muller Ltd. 1946. [viii], 155 pp. il.   OXB
see also   23

RICHARDSON, M.   *see*   36

RICHBELL, Florence E.

Wings!, [and other poems]. Ilfracombe: Arthur H. Stockwell, Ltd. [1943]. 16 pp.
'Dedicated to all who fly, in memory of one who died'.   OXB

RICHEY, Margaret Fitzgerald (1883–1974. b. County Tyrone. Educated at Bedford College, London. German scholar and translator. Reader in German at Royal Holloway College, London. Latterly lived in Angus, Scotland)

Herzelroyde in paradise, and other poems. Oxford: Basil Blackwell, 1953. 28 pp.
                                                                                    OXB

RICHMOND, Oliffe Leigh (1881–1977. Educated at Eton College, and King's College, Cambridge. Fellow of King's College, 1905–14. Professor of Latin at University College of South Wales & Monmouthshire, 1914–19. Served as Captain in Intelligence Corps at the War Office and at Italian H.Q., 1916–19. Later became Professor of Humanity at Edinburgh University. Latterly lived near Reading, Berkshire)

Rawalpindi, and other verses in war-time (August, 1939 to December, 1940). Cambridge: W. Heffer & Sons Ltd. 1941. [x], 30 pp.   BPL

Song of freedom, and other verses in war-time (March to December 1941). Thomas Nelson & Sons Ltd. 1942. 72 pp.   BPL

Thames symphony. Illustrated by Roland Pym. Macdonald. 1947. 48 pp. il.
MPL
see also 38

RICKARD, Muriel J.
Winter sunshine: a booklet of verse (illustrated). Ilfracombe: Arthur H. Stockwell,
Ltd. 1945. 32 pp. il. OXB

RICKARD, Stephen (1917– . b. Surrey. Educated at an art school, winning
a scholarship to the Royal Academy Schools. Joined the Army in 1940, going to
India in 1942 as Captain, Royal Indian Army Service Corps) *see* 43

RIDER, Janet O.
Poems. Ilfracombe: Arthur H. Stockwell, Ltd. [1941]. 16 pp. OXB

RIDGE, A. Harvey Lang- *see* **LANG-RIDGE, A. Harvey**

RIDGWAY, Sydney (Of Cheshire ?)
First poems. Printed Stockport: Old Time Press. [1942]. 35 pp. MPL

RIDLER, Anne (1912– . b. Rugby, daughter of the poet H.C. Bradby who
was a housemaster at Rugby School. Educated at Downe House School, King's
College, London, and in Florence and Rome. Spent five years with the
publishers Faber & Faber Ltd, working as an editorial assistant and as
secretary to T.S. Eliot. Married Vivian Ridler, Printer to Oxford University, in
1938. Poet, librettist and anthologist, she wrote two verse plays. Of Oxford)
A dream observed, and other poems. Poetry (London). [1941]. [vi], 22 pp. (PL
pamphlets, 2). OXB
The nine bright shiners: [poems]. Faber & Faber. 1943. 64 pp. MPL
see also 4, 17, 25, 29, 56, 69, 76

RIDLER, Walter James Fisher (1922– . b. Shanghai, China, where he lived
until the age of eleven. Educated at Canford School, Dorset. Joined the Royal
Air Force in 1942. Served in India as a Flying Officer) *see* 43

RIDYARD, Walter
Poems. With a foreword by Frank H. Cumbers. Epworth Press. 1950. 36 pp.
OXB

RIGG, A.E. Walton (Private. Served with the British Expeditionary Force and
the Middle Eastern Forces, 1939–43)
Was it all in vain?: [poems]. Ilfracombe: Arthur H. Stockwell, Ltd. [1943].
16 pp. OXB

RIMINGTON, John (1918–77. b. Gibraltar into a naval family. Served with the Royal Army Service Corps in the desert, driving a tank transporter. Captured by the Germans but only briefly. Became a director of Brunnings Advertising) *see* 39, 63

RITCHIE, E. (Lieutenant, Parachute Regiment. Captured at Arnhem in 1944) *see* 67

RIVIERE, Michael Valentine B. (1919– . b. Norwich. Educated at Magdalen College, Oxford, where he contributed to the *Oxford Magazine*. Served in the Sherwood Rangers, taken prisoner in the Crete campaign in June 1941. Escaped twice from prison camps and was finally sent to Colditz Castle)
    The poetical works of Michael Riviere. Favil Press. 1956. 25 pp.
      Cover-title is *Poems*.   OXB
see also   45, 67, 76

RIVINGTON, Arabella (Of North West London)
    Poems. Printed John Roberts Press Ltd. 1973. [84] pp.
      A limited ed. of eighty copies privately printed.   OXB

ROBBINS, Alan (Of Surrey) *see* 74

ROBBINS, Harold Northway
    Leaves of life: [*poems*]. Watts & Co. 1953. [viii], 80 pp.   OXB

ROBERT THE RHYMER, pseud. *see* **WILLIAMS, Alan Moray**, (Robert the Rhymer, pseud.)

ROBERTS, Arthur, (The Gleaner, pseud.) (Of Blechingley, Surrey)
    Search for peaceful fields: being gleanings from a gift in thought, bestowed from time to time and herein faithfully set down for his true ladye Margaret. Printed Gloucester: John Bellows Ltd. [1947]. 57 pp.   OXB

ROBERTS, Cecil (1892–1976. Educated at Mundella Grammar School. Literary editor of *Liverpool Post*, 1915–18. Poet of the First World War. Naval correspondent and correspondent with the British Army on the western front and with the allied armies in the march to the Rhine. Editor of *Nottingham Journal*, 1920–25. Parliamentary Liberal candidate for Nottingham East in 1922. Member of the British Mission to the United States, 1940–46. Novelist and playwright)
    A man arose. Hodder & Stoughton. 1941. 15 pp. por.   IWM
    Selected poems, 1910—1960. Preface by Lord Birkett. Hutchinson. 1960. 151 pp.
                                                 OXB

ROBERTS, Leslie Gordon (Sub-Lieutenant, Royal Naval Volunteer Reserve) *see* 23

ROBERTS, Lynette (b. South America. Married Keidrych Rhys in 1939. Lived at Laugharne, Carmarthenshire)

    Gods with stainless ears: a heroic poem. Faber & Faber. 1951. 67 pp.   OXB

    Poems. Faber & Faber. 1944. 54 pp.   OXB

see also   25, 56

ROBERTS, Michael, pseud. *see* **ROBERTS, William Edward**, (Michael Roberts, pseud.)

ROBERTS, Peter (Flight Lieutenant, Royal Air Force. Navigator of a Halifax bomber shot down off the Norwegian coast during the attack on the *Tirpitz* and the *Prinz Eugen*. Prisoner of war in Germany after posted as missing)

    Take-of at dusk, and other poems. With a foreword by Ian Hay. Frederick Muller Ltd. 1944. 34 pp.   BPL

ROBERTS, R.M. (Served in the Western Desert) *see* 63

ROBERTS, William Edward, (Michael Roberts, pseud.) (1902–48. b Bournemouth. Educated at King's College, London, and Trinity College Cambridge. Taught physics at the Royal Grammer School, Newcastle upon Tyne, then became senior mathematics master at Mercers' School, London. In 1941 went to a war job in the European Services of the B.B.C. Towards the end of the war was appointed Principal of St Mark & St John College, Chelsea. Literary critic and anthologist. Edited *New Signatures* and *New Country*)

    Collected poems; [by] Michael Roberts. With an introductory memoir by Janet Roberts. Faber & Faber. 1958. 226 pp.   MPL

see also   23, 56

ROBERTS-JONES, Ivor (1913– . Educated at Oswestry Grammar School, Worksop College, Goldsmiths' College Art School and the Royal Academy Schools. Served with the Royal Artillery, 1939–46, seeing active service in Arakan and Burma. Teacher of sculpture at Goldsmiths' College, 1946–68. A sculptor whose work is in many public and private hands. Of Halesworth, Suffolk) *see* 43, 57

ROBERTSON, John Henry, (John Connell, pseud.) (1909–65. Educated at Loretto School, and Balliol College, Oxford. Joined the London Scottish, Territorial Army, in 1939. Commissioned in the Royal Artillery, serving in the Middle East and India. Chief Military Press Censor, India, 1944. A journalist, leader-writer for *The Evening News*, London, 1945–59. Deputy Mayor of St Pancras, 1951–52) *see* 43

ROBERTSON, Martin (1911– . Educated at The Leys School and Trinity College, Cambridge. Assistant Keeper, British Museum, 1936–48, released for war service 1940–46. Yates Professor of Art & Archaeology, London

University, 1948–61. Lincoln Professor of Classical Archaelogy & Art, Oxford University, 1961–78. Writer on the art of Ancient Greece. Of Cambridge)

Crooked connections: [poems]. Walton-on-Thames: Outposts Publications. 1970. 40 pp.   OXB

> *For Rachel, with eight shorter poems.* Abingdon: [Author]. 1972. 16 pp.
> A limited ed. of 250 copies printed at the Castlelaw Press, Scotland.

                                                                                OXB

A hot bath at bedtime: poems 1933–77. Oxford: Robert Dugdale. 1977. xxii, 122 pp.   OXB

ROBILLIARD, Adele

Odds and ends: (in verse). Ilfracombe: Arthur H. Stockwell, Ltd. 1946. 23 pp.
                                                                                OXB

ROBINS, Frederick William

A book of verse. Printed Bournemouth: Richmond Hill Printing Works, Ltd. [1948]. 76 pp.   OXB

From mood to mood: [poems]. Printed Cheltenham: Built-Leonard. [1943]. [28] pp.   OXB

From time to time: [poems]. Printed Cheltenham: Built-Leonard. [1941]. [28] pp.   OXB

ROBINS, Patricia (1921–   . Commissioned in the Women's Royal Air Force. Novelist and writer of children's fiction. Of East Grinstead, Sussex)

Seven days leave. Hutchinson & Co. Ltd. [1943]. 48 pp. por.

'A little novel in verse'.   IWM

ROBINSON, A.E. (Lived in New Zealand in the 1940s)

Poems. James Clarke & Co. Ltd. [1959]. [iv], 50 pp.   BL

ROBINSON, Charles (b. Australia. Educated at Melbourne Grammar School. Served as a stretcher bearer in the desert. After the war represented QUANTAS in London, then set up his own travel agency. Of Caterham, Surrey) *see* 63

ROBINSON, E.

O friend o' mine!, and other poems. Ilfracombe: Arthur H. Stockwell, Ltd. 1945. 16 pp.   OXB

ROBINSON, H.L. (Served in South-East Asia Command) *see* 35

ROBINSON, L.W. (Served in South-East Asia Command) *see* 35

ROBINSON, Philip (Writer on Spain)

A Charlie's rhymes. Fortune Press. [1949]. 24 pp.   BL

Collected poems. Fortune Press. [1965]. 160 pp.   OXB
Poems. Fortune Press. [1941]. 32 pp.   OXB
Poems (second sequence). Fortune Press. [1942]. 28 pp.   OXB
Ruins: miscellaneous poems. Fortune Press. 1959. 48 pp.   MPL

ROBSON, W.C. Attwood (Retired Commander, Royal Navy)
The gallant sailor: sea verses. Alex Moring, Ltd. [1948]. 58 pp.   IWM

ROCKETT, Brenda (Of London)   *see*   74

RODD, James Rennell, Lord Rennell (1858–1941). Educated at Haileybury
School, and Balliol College, Oxford. Newdigate Prizewinner in 1880. Entered
the Diplomatic Service in 1883. Held posts in Berlin, Athens, Rome, Paris,
Zanzibar, Cairo and Sweden. Ambassador to Italy, 1908–19. Poet of the First
World War. Conservative M.P. for St Marlyebone, 1928–32. British delegate to
the League of Nations, 1921 and 1923. Held other appointments on
international bodies)
War poems, with some others; by Lord Rennell of Rodd. Edward Arnold & Co.
1940. 32 pp.   IWM

RODGERS, Elizabeth
In our time: a selection of verse. Ilfracombe: Arthur H. Stockwell, Ltd. [1945].
16 pp.   OXB

RODGERS, William Robert (1909–69. b. Belfast. Educated at Queen's University, Belfast. Minister of Loughgall Presbyterian Church, County Armagh,
1934–46. Producer and scriptwriter for the B.B.C., 1946–52. Latterly lived in
Colchester, Essex)
Awake!, and other poems. Secker & Warburg. 1941. 70 pp.   IWM
Collected poems. With an introductory memoir by Dan Davin. Oxford University Press. 1971. xxvi, 149 pp.   MPL
Europa and the bull, and other poems. Secker & Warburg. 1952. 94 pp.   MPL
see also   3, 15, 28, 37, 51, 56

ROGERS, John (Sergeant-Navigator, Royal Air Force)
Poems of an airman. Ilfracombe: Arthur H. Stockwell, Ltd. [1944]. 31 pp.
                                                                   BPL

ROGERS, K.G.
England, and other poems. Ilfracombe: Arthur H. Stockwell Ltd. [1943]. 24 pp.
                                                                   OXB

ROGERS, Louis D.
Dreaming: verse. Ilfracombe: Arthur H. Stockwell, Ltd. 1946. 16 pp.   OXB

ROGERSON, James (Of Lancashire) *see* 75

ROLING, Ronald Frederick Benjamin (1919– . b. Gillingham, Kent. Employed before the war as a civilian at the Royal Navy Armament Depot, Chatham. Signalman, Royal Corps of Signals. Served in India) *see* 43

ROLL, C.H.W.
The return of Mrs. Brown, and other rhymes. Ilfracombe: Arthur H. Stockwell, Ltd. [1950]. 28 pp.   OXB

ROLLING, Gwen M.
Poems. Ilfracombe: Arthur H. Stockwell, Ltd. [1961]. 84 pp.   OXB

ROME, Moyra Wilding (Of Lancashire) *see* 72, 73

ROMER, Harold George (Of Worthing, Sussex)
The bells of Ouseley, [and other poems]. Ilfracombe: Arthur H. Stockwell Ltd. 1976. 39 pp.   OXB
Varied verse. Ilfracombe: Arthur H. Stockwell Ltd. 1970. 68 pp.   OXB

ROOK, Alan (1909– . b. Ruddington, Nottinghamshire. Educated at Uppingham School, Magdalen College, Oxford, and in France and Germany. Commissioned in 7th Battalion, Sherwood Foresters. Served with the Royal Artillery at Dunkirk. After a Staff course in 1941 promoted Deputy Adjutant General in 1942. Invalided out after service with the 6th Anti-Aircraft Division. Became managing director of a wine merchants in Nottingham. Poet, literary critic and writer on wine. Editor of the magazine *Kingdom Come* with Henry Treece)
Soldiers, this solitude: [poems]. Routledge. 1942. 43 pp.   BPL
These are my comrades: poems. Routledge. 1943. 39 pp.
'For Clive Calvert Johnstone-Wilson, Lieutenant, Royal Army Service Corps, Aide-de-Camp'.   BPL
We who are fortunate: [poems]. Routledge. 1945. 59 pp.   BPL
see also   2, 11, 14, 15, 25, 28, 33, 47, 51, 52, 56, 57, 66, 68, 76, 79, 82

ROOKE, Alfred R. (Of Lancashire ?)
The folded rose, [and other poems]. Printed Liverpool: Daily Post Printers. 1947. 54 pp. il.   OXB

ROOME, Holdar, pseud. *see* **MOORE, Harold**, (Holdar Roome, pseud.)

ROOTHAM, Jasper (1910–   . b. Cambridge. Educated at Tonbridge School, and St John's College, Cambridge. Entered the Civil Service in 1933. Private Secretary to the Prime Minister, 1938–39. Joined the Army in 1940, serving in the Middle East, the Balkans and Germany. Mentioned in despatches, demobilized as a Colonel. Joined the Bank of England staff in 1946, becoming Assistant to the Governor. Of Hexham, Northumberland)

Selected poems, 1928–1980. Weybrook Press. 1980. [viii], 56 pp.   OXB

Verses, 1928–1972. Cambridge: Rampant Lions Press. [1972]. [x], 66 pp.
   A limited ed. of 500 copies.   OXB

ROPER-HUGGINS, M.

Life's ceaseless waves: verse. Ilfracombe: Arthur H. Stockwell, Ltd. 1946. 32 pp. por.

   'In memory of Lieutenant L.W. Roper-Huggins, Somerset Light Infantry, killed in Normandy, 1944'.   OXB

ROPES, John (O.B.E. Lieutenant-Colonel in the Royal Artillery. Served in the Middle East, becoming Brigadier at G.H.Q. Cairo) *see* 31, 63

ROSCOE, Theodora (Educated in England and Dresden, Germany. Hon. Secretary of the Society of Women Journalists. Married E. Cecil Roscoe. Co-editor of the anthology *Poems by Contemporary Women*, 1944. Interested in painting as well as poetry. Of Chalfont St Peter, Buckinghamshire)

From the Chilterns: poems old and new. With a foreword by Arundell Esdaile. Ickenham: Ruislip Press. [1946]. 62 pp.   OXB

The martinet: poems. Ickenham: Ruislip Press. 1940. 24 pp.   OXB

St. Albans, and other poems. Eton: Alden & Blackwell Ltd; Eton College. 1953. 32 pp.   OXB

see also 41

ROSE, Charles (Served in the Royal Air Force. Of London)

Early verse of Charles Rose. [Author]. 1970. xii, 258 pp.   OXB

ROSE, Margaret (Of Surrey) *see* 74

ROSE, William (–1941. Lieutenant, Royal Navy. Killed on board H.M.S. *Cossack* in October 1941)

Poems. Ilfracombe: Arthur H. Stockwell Ltd. [1941]. 16 pp.   OXB

Spring deferred. E.M.E. Rose. 1945. [iv], 65 pp. por.
   Poems and essays.   OXB

ROSS, A.J.M. (Squadron Leader, Observer Corps)

Odd odes of the Observer Corps. Uxbridge: Perry & Routleff, Ltd. [194-]. 25 pp. il.

   'Proceeds of sale will be handed over to the Observer Corps Benevolent Fund'.   IWM

ROSS, Alan (1921– . b. Calcutta, India. Educated at Haileybury School, and St John's College, Oxford. Played against Cambridge in cricket and squash.

Joined the Royal Navy in 1942, serving as a seaman in the Arctic and the North Sea. Assistant Staff Officer, Intelligence, with 16th Destroyer Flotilla in 1944. On staff of Flag Officer, Western Germany, 1946. Employed by the British Council, 1946–50, then journalist with *The Observer*, 1950–71. Editor of *London Magazine*. Managing director of London Magazine Editions, formerly Alan Ross Publications, from 1961)

African negatives: [*poems*]. Eyre & Spottiswoode. 1962. 63 pp.   OXB
The derelict day: poems in Germany. John Lehmann. 1947. vi, 74 pp.   OXB
North from Sicily: poems in Italy 1961–64. Eyre & Spottiswoode. 1965. 63 pp.   OXB
Open sea: [*poems*]. London Magazine Editions. 1975. 63 pp.   BPL
Poems, 1942–67. Eyre & Spottiswoode. 1967. 208 pp.   MPL
Something of the sea: poems 1942–1952. Derek Verschoyle. 1954. 66 pp.   BPL
Summer thunder. Oxford: Shakespeare Head Press. 1941. 16 pp.   OXB
The Taj express: poems 1967–73. London Magazine Editions. 1973. 75 pp.   OXB
To whom it may concern: poems 1952–57. Hamish Hamilton. 1958. x, 84 pp.   OXB
Tropical ice: [*poems*]. Covent Garden Press Ltd. 1972. 31 pp. (Covent Garden poetry, 5).

A limited ed. of 600 copies of which 100 have been numbered and signed by the author.   OXB
see also   10, 23, 25, 42, 45, 57, 59, 76

ROSS, Chloris Heaton (Of Chesham, Buckinghamshire)
A flat in Bloomsbury, [*and other poems*]. Favil Press. 1945. [iii], 21 pp.   OXB
One of the few: [*poems*]. Favil Press. 1943. [iv], 20 pp.
'Dedicated to Sergeant-Pilot David Ross, 'one of the few', who was missing, presumed killed, on the night of 18th–19th September 1940'.   OXB

ROSS, J.C. (Of Warwickshire)   *see*   74

ROSS, Peter Mabyn
The old story, and other poems. Ilfracombe: Arthur H. Stockwell, Ltd. 1950. 16 pp.   OXB

ROSS, Raymond, pseud. *see* **KAPPES, E.R.**, (Raymond Ross, pseud.)

ROSSITER, D. (Private. Served with the Eighth Army)   *see*   44

ROTHERY, Christopher (Of Derbyshire ?)
Reflections through a glass darkly: poems. [Derby]: [Bergenway]. [1978]. 21 pp.   OXB

ROW, Arthur (Fellow of the Royal Society of Arts. A Vice-President of the Poetry Society. Of Hereford)
The blitzkrieg. [Privately printed]. [1944]. 8 pp.
    Dedicated to the Royal Air Force.   OXB
"The voice of England", [*and other poems*]. [Privately printed]. 1941. 23 pp.
    Title from cover.   OXB
see also 21

ROWE, Joyce (A descendant of the eighteenth century Poet Laureate Nicholas Rowe. Writer of poems, plays and radio scripts. Worked for the Overseas Service of the B.B.C.)
She died alive: [*poems*]. Foreword by Clifford Bax. Favil Press. 1945. 24 pp.
                                              OXB
see also 36, 42

ROWE, W.G. (Served in H.M. Forces)   *see* 74

ROWLAND, Henry F.
Lonely spring, and other verse. Ilfracombe: Arthur H. Stockwell, Ltd. [1944]. 32 pp.   OXB

ROWLEY, John W. (Of Staffordshire ?)
Poems. Printed Stoke-on-Trent: James Heap Ltd. [1946]. 48 pp.   OXB

ROWSE, Alfred Leslie (1903– . b. St. Austell, Cornwall. Educated at elementary and grammar schools in St Austell, and at Christ Church, Oxford. Fellow of All Souls College, Oxford, 1925–74. Holder of many academic appointments. Poet, historian and Elizabethan scholar. President of the Shakespeare Club, Stratford-upon-Avon, 1970–71)
Poems chiefly Cornish. Faber & Faber. 1944. 78 pp.   MPL
Poems of a decade, 1931–1941. Faber & Faber Ltd. 1941. 111 pp.
    Dedicated to David Cecil.   IWM
Poems of deliverance. Faber & Faber. 1946. 94 pp.
    'To the men who have returned from the war; in memory of those who did not come back'.   BPL
Strange encounter, [*and other poems*]. Jonathan Cape. 1972. 54 pp.   MPL
see also 38, 80

ROWSON, R.P. (Served in South-East Asia Command)   *see* 35

ROYAL, John
Factory without, [*and other poems*]. Ilfracombe: Arthur H. Stockwell, Ltd. [1944]. 31 pp.   OXB

ROYCE, F.V.G. (Served in the Royal Air Force)
'Griff' on the Gremlin: [*poems*]; by D.J. Marshall and F.V.G. Royce. Illustrated by Len Kirley. Pilot Press Ltd. 1943. 64 pp. il.   OXB

ROYDS, Thomas Fletcher (1880– . b. Haughton Rectory, Staffordshire. Educated at Marlborough College, and Worcester College, Oxford. Trained for the ministry at Wells Theological College. Poet of the First World War. Vicar Prebendary, Lichfield Cathedral. Lived at Chebsey Vicarage, Stafford, and later in Stone, Staffordshire. Writer on Virgil)
   My fifty versing years: [poems]. Favil Press. 1959. 44 pp.   BL

RUDLAND, Ernest Marston (1875– . b. Birmingham. Educated at King Edward's School. Poet of the First World War. A chartered accountant. Lived at Moseley, Birmingham)
   Further ballads of old Birmingham, with sincere greetings, Xmas, 1949. Moseley: [Author]. 1949. 13 pp.
      Title from cover.   BPL
   Further ballads of old Birmingham. [Birmingham]: City of Birmingham School of Printing. 1950. 31 pp.   BL

RUNDLE, Laura Emma
   Beyond compare: (a collection of poems). Ilfracombe: Arthur H. Stockwell, Ltd. [1956]. 24 pp.   OXB

RUSSELL, Arthur Wolseley (1908– . Educated at Canterbury University, New Zealand. Worked for the B.B.C. in London as a radio journalist and producer, 1935–64. Editor of *Asian Affairs*, 1970–72. Of Arundel, Sussex)
   Ice on the live rail: poems. Lowestoft: Scorpion Press. 1962. [iii], 21 pp. OXB
   In idleness of air, [and other poems]. Northwood, Middlesex: Scorpion Press. 1960. [ii], 22 pp.
      150 copies bound in boards and numbered, numbers 1 to 25 signed by the author. Remainder in wrappers and are unnumbered.   OXB

RUSSELL, Henry T., (Theodosius, pseud.) (Of Shiplake-on-Thames, Oxfordshire)
   Strife within: [poems]; by Theodosius. Printed Bennet Bros. [1940]. [vi], 38 pp.   OXB

RUSSELL, J.M. (Commissioned in 1944, serving with the 1st Battalion, Royal Scots Fusiliers, in Burma and India from January 1945 to March 1946)
   The grinning face, and other poems. Routledge. 1947. 96 pp.   BPL

RUSSELL, Midgley
   The sword of excellency, and other poems. Mitre Press. [1971]. 96 pp.   OXB

RUSSELL, P.W.R. (Lieutenant. Served with the Eighth Army in the Western Desert) *see* 46

RUSSELL, Peter, (Russell Irwin, pseud.) (1921– . b. Bristol. Educated at

Malvern College and London University. Served in the airborne artillery and the Indian Army, 1939–46. Owner of the Pound Press, 1951–56, and the Gallery Bookshop, 1959–63. Lecturer in Berlin and Venice, 1964–70. Poet-in-Residence at Victoria University, British Columbia, 1973–74, and at Purdue University, Indiana, 1976–77. Teaching Fellow, Imperial Iranian Academy of Philosophy, Teheran, 1977–79. Writer on Ezra Pound)

Omens and elegies. Aldington, Kent: Hand and Flower Press. [1951]. 231–260 pp. (Poems in pamphlet, 1951, VIII). BL

Picnic to the moon: poems; by Russell Irwin. Fortune Press. 1944. 96 pp.

BPL

see also 49

RUSSELL-PARSONS, Clive (Of Derbyshire ?)

Poems of war and peace, 1939–1949. Printed Chesterfield: Thomas Brayshaw Ltd. [1950]. 28 pp. IWM

RUTHVEN, Patrick Hore- *see* **HORE-RUTHVEN, Patrick**

RYE, Anthony (1904–75. b. Hampstead, London. Educated at Westminister School. An artist and writer, he worked for the lithographers Emery Walker Ltd, 1927–33. Served in the National Fire Service. Protége of Edmund Blunden. A keen amateur naturalist, he lived at Selbourne, Hampshire. Writer on Gilbert White and Selbourne)

To a modern hero, [*and other poems*]. Gainsborough. 1957. viii, 31 pp.

A limited ed. of 250 numbered copies printed at the Dolmen Press, Dublin.

OXB

RYOTT, Estelle

Wings over England, and other poems. Ilfracombe: Arthur H. Stockwell, Ltd. [1941]. 232 pp. OXB

S.E.S. *see* **S., S.E.**

S.N. *see* **N., S.**

S., S.E.

Poems; by S.E.S. Fortune Press. 1955. 68 pp. OXB

SABIN, N. (Served in H.M. Forces) *see* 74

SACKVILLE-MARTIN, James (Of Leigh, Lancashire)

From Hellas to Limerick: [*poems*]. Ilfracombe: Arthur H. Stockwell, Ltd. 1949. 64 pp. OXB

The garnered sheaf: a book of verse. Ilfracombe: Arthur H. Stockwell, Ltd. [1945]. 112 pp. OXB

SACKVILLE-WEST, Hon. Victoria (Vita) (1892–1962. b. Knole, Sevenoaks, Kent, daughter of the 3rd Baron Sackville. Educated at home. In 1913 married Sir Harold Nicolson, diplomat, author and critic. Lived at Sissinghurst Castle, Kent. Poet and novelist, she was an intimate friend of Virginia Woolf. Won the Hawthornden Prize in 1926. During the war she was on the Kent Committee of the Women's Land Army, still writing, and tending the magnificent garden she had planted at Sissinghurst. Awarded a Veitch memorial medal by the Royal Horticultural Society)

The garden. Michael Joseph Ltd. 1946. 135 pp.   OXB

Selected poems. Hogarth Press. 1941. 78 pp. (New Hogarth library, IV).

MPL

see also   8, 21, 38, 42

SADDINGTON, Stanley J. (Of Leicestershire)   *see*   73

SAGITTARIUS, pseud.   *see*   **KATZIN, Olga**, (Sagittarius, pseud.)

ST GEORGE, George A.

With lyre and saxophone: [poems]. Illustrated by Banbery. Bombay: Thacker & Co. Ltd. 1943. [6], viii, 95 pp. il., col. il.   IWM

SAINT-JOHN, Kristine, pseud.   *see*   **MAURER, Christine**, (Kristine Saint-John, pseud.)

ST. JOHN, Patricia Mary (1919–   . Trained as a nurse at St Thomas's Hospital, 1942–46. A missionary nurse in Morocco from 1949. Biographer, writer on Church of England foreign missions and of books for children. Of Canley, Coventry)

Verses. With illustrations by Ruth Scales. Children's Special Service Mission. 1953. [iv], 92 pp. il.   OXB

SALE, Stephen (Of Wokingham, Berkshire)

Verses — 1916 to 1961. Printed Shenval Press. 1962. 84 pp.   OXB

SALMON, K.M. (Served in the Women's Royal Navy Service)   *see*   23

SAMPSON, Ashley (1900–   . Fellow of the Royal Society of Literature)

From the ashes: poems. Williams & Norgate Ltd. 1942. 30 pp.   BPL

SAMSON, Alf (Served in the Middle East)   *see*   63

SAMUEL, Cecil Cadifor (Of North Wales)

The thinker, and other poems. Printed Bala: Bala Press. [1968]. 48 pp.

OXB

SANDERS, C. Rufane
Shadows and substance: [*poems*]. Ilfracombe: Arthur H. Stockwell, Ltd. 1946.
32 pp.   OXB

SANDERS, Peter A. (Captain in the Royal Army Ordnance Corps, appointed
Inspecting Ordnance Officer. Posted to the Western Desert in March 1941. Of
Godalming, Surrey) *see* 63

SANDERSON, Charles Reginald (Flight Lieutenant, Royal Air Force)
Contrast: poems. Fortune Press. 1944. 23 pp.   BPL
Prelude: poems. Fortune Press. 1960. 120 pp.   MPL
To what end is the dawn?: [*poems*]. Cambridge: W. Heffer & Sons Ltd. 1942. [iv],
40 pp.   OXB
see also 1, 25, 49

SANDFORD, Greer (Served in the Royal Air Force)
Brother to Icarus: poems. Belfast: Quota Press. [1948]. 26 pp.   OXB

SANDWICH, Lord *see* **MONTAGU, George, Lord Sandwich**

SANGUINETTI, Leopold P. (b. Malta)
The Calpean sonnets. Ilfracombe: Arthur H. Stockwell, Ltd. 1957. [vi], 76 pp.
                                                                                                OXB

SANSOM, Clive (1910– . Poet, critic, novelist and schoolmaster. Writer on
speech and drama, adjudicator and lecturer on verse-speaking. Supervisor of
Speech Education, Tasmania, 1950–65)
In the midst of death: poems. Privately printed. 1940. 30 pp.   OXB
The unfailing spring: [*poems*]. Favil Press. 1943. [vi], 18 pp. (Resurgam
library).   OXB
The witnesses, and other poems. Methuen & Co. Ltd. 1956. x, 106 pp.   MPL
see also 52, 80

SARGEANT, Charles
The seed and the flower: [*poems*]. Mitre Press. [1967]. 100 pp.   OXB

SARGESON, A.J.
Lyrics of a lifetime: [*poems*]. Ilfracombe: Arthur H. Stockwell, Ltd. [1941].
24 pp. por.   OXB

SASSOON, Siegfried (1886–1967. b. Kent. Educated at Marlborough
College, and Clare College, Cambridge. Major poet of the First World War.
Enlisted in 1914 with the Sussex Yeomanry. Served in the trenches as a Captain
in the Royal Welch Fusiliers. While convalescing at Craiglockhart Hospital he

met Wilfred Owen and greatly influenced Owen's poetry. Awarded the M.C. Poet and novelist, he became a pacifist after his war experiences. Converted to Roman Catholicism in 1957. Winner of the Hawthornden Prize in 1929 and a gold medal for poetry in 1957. Latterly lived at Heytesbury, Wiltshire)

Collected poems. Faber & Faber Ltd. 1947. xvi, 269 pp. OXB

Collected poems, 1908–1956. Faber & Faber Ltd. 1961. xx, 317 pp. OXB

Common chords: [poems]. [Stanford Dingley]: Mill House Press. 1950. [vi], 20 pp.

A limited ed. of 107 copies on hand-made paper, of which seven are on white parchment. OXB

Rhymed ruminations: [poems]. Faber & Faber Ltd. 1940. 52 pp.

Dedicated to Edmund Blunden. OXB

Selected poems. Faber & Faber. 1968. 93 pp. (Faber paper covered editions). OXB

Sequences: [poems]. Faber & Faber. 1956. x, 68 pp. OXB

see also 6, 9

SAUNDERS, Patricia M.

Arena: poems. Hutchinson & Co. Ltd. [1948]. 46 pp. OXB

SAUTER, Rudolf (1895–1977. Educated at Harrow School. Artist, painter and writer. Fellow of International P.E.N. Of Stroud, Gloucestershire)

"The soothing wind": a tribute to V.S. [Vida Sauter]: [poems]. Stroud: Stroud Typewriting & Duplicating Services. 1969. [i], 47 pp. il., col. il.

A limited ed. of 500 copies. OXB

SAVAGE, Derek Stanley (1917–   . b. Harlow, Essex. Educated at Hertford Grammar School, and Latymer School, London. A conscientious objector in the war. Worked as a clerk for some years before becoming a freelance writer and literary critic, contributing to many periodicals. Of Pentewan, Cornwall)

A time to mourn: (poems 1934–1943). Routledge. 1943. 32 pp. (Routledge new poets, 12). OXB

see also 25

SAVAGE, Michael (Squadron Leader, Royal Air Force) *see* 25, 52, 61, 62

SAVAGE, Patrick (1916–   . Educated at Westminster School, and Christ Church, Oxford. Served in the South Staffordshire Regiment, held prisoner of war from 1941 to 1945, mostly at Eichstatt Camp) *see* 24, 61, 76

SAVILL, E.M.

Collected poems. Mitre Press. [1948]. 110 pp. OXB

SAVILL, Francis E.W. (Of London) *see* 74

SAVILLE, Kenneth (Served in South-East Asia Command) *see* 35

SAWDON, M.L. (Of Herefordshire) *see* 75

SAYER, Jasper (Served in the Middle East. Novelist) *see* 39, 63

SAYERS, Dorothy Leigh (1893–1957. b. Oxford. Educated at Somerville College, Oxford. Married Captain Atherton Fleming in 1926. Author of detective novels, works on Dante, also plays and books on religious topics. Originator of the fictional detective Lord Peter Wimsey)
Aeneas at the court of Dido. [Privately printed]. 1945. [6] pp. OXB
see also 7, 76

SCAIFE, Christopher Henry Oldham (1900– . In the First World War tried unsuccessfully to join the Army at the age of fourteen. Educated at St John's College, Oxford. President of the Oxford Union, Newdigate Prizewinner in 1923. Lived in Egypt pre-war, working in the English Department at Cairo University. In 1940 volunteered for active service with the Libyan/Arab Force. Evacuated from Tobruk as a casualty in June 1941. Became a Major on the military establishment of the Ministry of Information, Middle East. In 1945 appointed Adviser to the Ministry of Education, Iraq. Later Professor of English at the American University of Beirut. Retired to Arezzo, Italy)
In middle age: 30 poems. Oxford: Basil Blackwell. 1953. 49 pp. OXB
see also 39, 63

SCAMMELL, William (1939– . b. Hythe, Hampshire. Educated at Bristol University)
Yes and no, [and other poems]. Liskeard: Harry Chambers. 1979. 55 pp. (Peterloo poets). OXB

SCANNELL, Vernon (1922– . b. Spilsby, Lincolnshire. Educated at Queen's Park School, Aylesbury, and Leeds University. Won the Northern Universities Boxing Championships at three weights. Served in the Gordon Highlanders with the 51st Highland Division from Alamein to Tunis, in the invasion of Sicily and in Normandy, where he was wounded. After the war held various jobs including teaching at Hazelwood Preparatory School, 1955–62. Poet, critic, novelist and broadcaster, he was awarded a Civil List pension in 1981 for services to literature)
Company of women: [poems]. Farnham, Surrey: Sceptre Press. [1971]. [20] pp.
　　A limited ed. of 150 numbered copies, with numbers 1–50 signed by the author. Printed on one side of leaf only, some leaves left blank. OXB
Epithets of war: poems 1965–69. Eyre & Spottiswoode. 1969. 59 pp. OXB
Graves and resurrections: poems. Fortune Press. 1948. 44 pp. BL
The loving game: poems. Robson Books. 1975. 47 pp. OXB

The masks of love, [and other poems]. Putnam. 1960. 31 pp. OXB
Mastering the craft, [and other poems]. Pergamon Press. 1970. vi, 36 pp.
(Pergamon English library. Poets today). MPL
New and collected poems, 1950–1980. Robson Books. 1980. 206 pp. OXB
Selected poems. Allison & Busby. 1971. [vi], 90 pp. OXB
Walking wounded: poems 1962–65. Eyre & Spottiswoode. 1965. 63 pp. OXB
The winter man: new poems. Allison & Busby. 1973. [vi], 58 pp. MPL
see also 76, 87

SCARFE, Francis (1911– . b. South Shields, County Durham. Educated at
Durham University, Fitzwilliam House, Cambridge, and in Paris. University
lecturer before the war. In Royal Army Ordnance Corps and Royal Army
Educational Corps, 1941–46. Served in the Orkneys and Faroes, reaching rank
of Lieutenant-Colonel in 1945. Returned to university teaching. Director of the
British Institute in Paris, 1959–78. Professor of French, London University,
1965–78. Novelist and literary critic)
Forty poems and ballads. Fortune Press. [1941]. 64 pp. BPL
Inscapes: poems. Fortune Press. 1940. 64 pp. por. BPL
see also 4, 15, 25, 28, 29, 33, 36, 56, 64, 65, 69, 76, 80, 82

SCHAVERIEN, D.A. (Served in South-East Asia Command) *see* 35

SCHIFF, Charles (Jewish medical practitioner)
A book of poems. Edgware, Middlesex: Keats Publishing House. 1973. [vi],
125 pp. OXB
see also 38

SCHUBERT, Gladys Mair- *see* **MAIR-SCHUBERT, Gladys**

SCOTT, Barbara Montagu (Novelist)
You and your ships, and other verse. Hutchinson & Co., Ltd. [1945]. 48 pp.
 IWM

SCOTT, Constance M.M. (Of Chatham, Kent)
June and a posy from Kent: [poems]. Chatham: Parrett & Neves, Ltd. 1941.
32 pp. OXB
Kent calling "blossom-time": [poems]. Chatham: Parrett & Neves Ltd. 1943.
31 pp. BL
Thoughts we can share: [poems]. Chatham: Parrett & Neves, Ltd. 1940. 32 pp.
 OXB
Woven on a Kentish loom: [poems]. Chatham: Parrett & Neves, Ltd. 1942. 32 pp.
 BL

SCOTT, David (1947–)
Days out: [poems]. [Hitchin, Herts.] : Mandeville Press. 1978. [16] pp.

A limited ed. of 250 copies of which thirty-five have been signed by the author.   OXB

SCOTT, Hardiman (1920–   . Educated at a grammar school and privately. Journalist, becoming a freelance broadcaster in 1948. Joined the B.B.C. staff in 1950, appointed Chief Assistant to the Director General in 1975. Of Colchester, Essex)
Adam and Eve and us: poems. Decorations by Betty Dougherty. Sylvan Press. 1946. 64 pp. il.
A limited ed. of 1,200 copies.   OXB
see also   25

SCOTT, May (Of the Scottish Highlands)
A collection of highland verse. Printed Perth: Danscot Print Ltd. [1977]. [66] pp.
Title from cover.   OXB

SCOTT, Paul (1920–78. b. London. Educated at Winchmore Hill Collegiate School. In accountancy before the war. Served with The Buffs, 1940–46, mainly in India and Malaya. Company Secretary, Falcon & Grey Walls Press, 1946–50. A director of literary agents David Higham Associates Ltd, 1950–60, resigning to become a full-time writer. Novelist and writer of television and radio plays. Won the Booker McConnell Prize in 1977 for *Staying On*)   *see*   12, 52, 62, 76

SCOTT, R. Brian (Served in the Army. Killed in Tunisia at the age of twenty-one)   *see*   31

SCOTT, Tom (1918–   . b. Glasgow. Educated at Edinburgh University. A Sergeant in the Royal Army Pay Corps, he served in the Middle East. One of the writers of the New Apocalypse movement. Freelance writer, editor of the Pergamon Press Scottish Literature series. Received an Atlantic Award in 1950. Of Edinburgh)
At the shrine o the unkent sodger: a poem for recitation. Preston: Akros Publications. [1968]. 22 pp.
In Scots dialect.   IWM
see also   25, 33, 47, 56, 65

SCOTT-ADIE, Catherine
Poems. Cambridge: Golden Head Press. 1965. 52 pp.   MPL

SCOVELL, Edith Joy (1907–   . b. Sheffield, daughter of Canon F.G. Scovell. Educated at Casterton School, Westmorland, and Somerville College, Oxford. Married Charles Elton, Fellow of Corpus Christi College, Oxford, in 1937. Of Oxford)
The midsummer meadow, and other poems. Routledge. 1946. 47 pp.   IWM

The river steamer, and other poems. Cresset Press. 1956. x, 52 pp.   OXB

Shadows of chrysanthemums, and other poems. Routledge. 1944. 44 pp.   IWM

see also   15

SCRAGG, Jean M.

The gentle heart: [poems]. Ilfracombe: Arthur H. Stockwell, Ltd. 1962. 44 pp.

OXB

SCRIMGEOUR, Adela Vernon (Of Richmond, Surrey)

Consider the lily, [and other poems]. [Richmond, Surrey]: [Author]. [1957]. 18 pp.

Title from cover.   OXB

SCUPHAM, Peter (1933–   . b. Liverpool. Lived in Cambridgeshire as a child during the war. Educated at Cambridge University. Founder and co-editor of the Mandeville Press, poetry publishers. Teacher, appointed to St Christopher's School, Letchworth, Hertfordshire, in 1961. Of Hitchin, Hertfordshire)

The snowing globe, [and other poems]. Manchester: E.J. Morten. 1972. 51 pp. il. (Peterloo poets).   OXB

Summer palaces: [poems]. Oxford University Press. 1980. viii, 55 pp.   OXB

SCURFIELD, George (Second-Lieutenant, Royal Artillery. Served in the Middle East. One of the leading spirits behind the Cambridge wartime magazine *Cambridge Front.* Novelist and writer on cookery. Of Folkestone, Kent)

The song of a red turtle: poems. Poetry (London). [1943]. [iv], 20 pp. (PL pamphlets, 1).   IWM

see also   25, 33, 47

SEAGER, Joan M.

Green leaves, [and other poems]. Ilfracombe: Arthur H. Stockwell, Ltd. [1943]. 16 pp.   OXB

SEGAL, J. (Sergeant. Served with the Eighth Army)   *see*   25, 44

SELBY, Mary A.

If I were blind, and other poems. Ilfracombe: Arthur H. Stockwell, Ltd. 1945. 16 pp.   OXB

SELBY-BOOTHROYD, C.B. (Army Captain. Captured in France in 1940, held prisoner of war in Germany until 1945)   *see*   67

SELF, David Michael (Writer on English literary topics)

Credere aude (Dare to believe): [poems]. Dulwich: Outposts Publications. 1962. 12 pp.   MPL

SERGEANT, Howard (1914– . b. Hull, Yorkshire. Educated at Hull Grammar School and Hull College of Commerce. Held various accountancy jobs, 1935–63. Travelling accountant with the Air Ministry, 1941–48, teacher at technical colleges, 1963–78. Writing Fellow, Queen Mary's College, Basingstoke, 1978–79. Recipient of Dorothy Tutin Award and Henry Shore Award, 1980. Founder-editor of *Outposts* quarterly poetry magazine and Outposts Publications. Poet, critic, anthologist and lecturer. Editor of the anthologies *An Anthology of Contemporary Northern Poetry*, 1947, *For Those Who Are Alive*, 1946, *Poetry of the 1940s*, 1970, and *These Years*, 1950. Of Walton-on-Thames, Surrey)

The headlands: [poems]. Putnam & Co. Ltd; Britannicus Liber Ltd. 1953. 56 pp.   OXB

The leavening air: [poems]. Fortune Press. 1946. 32 pp.   OXB

see also 2, 25 76

SERRAILLIER, Ian (1912– . b. London. Educated at Brighton College, and St Edmund Hall, Oxford. Held various teaching posts in public and grammar schools. Writer of fiction and non-fiction for children. From 1950 general editor of the New Windmill series published by Heinemann Educational Books. Of Chichester, Sussex)

The weaver birds, [and other poems]. Macmillan & Co. Ltd. 1944. viii, 84 pp.
    OXB

see also 28, 29, 52, 76

SETON-SMITH, D. (Sergeant. Served with the Eighth Army in the Western Desert) *see* 46

SEVERS, Kenneth (Grew up in the North Riding of Yorkshire. Became a journalist then read English at Leeds University. Lectured to the Forces in Cairo and Jerusalem. Appointed to a lectureship at Durham University)

A place of being, [and other poems]. Gerrards Cross, Buckinghamshire: Colin Smythe. 1975. [iv], 67 pp.   OXB

SEYMOUR, William Kean (1887–1975. Educated at Lawrence School, London. Poet of the First World War. Served in the Royal Naval Air Service and the Royal Air Force, 1917–18. Poet, novelist, playwright and journalist. A Vice-President of the Poetry Society. Conducted writer's craft courses at Moor Park College, Farnham, from 1962. Awarded Philippines Presidential Gold Medal for Poetry, 1968. Lived at Alresford, Hampshire)

Collected poems. Robert Hale Ltd. 1946. 257 pp.   MPL

SHANKS, Doris
The fairy glen, and other poems. Ilfracombe: Arthur H. Stockwell, Ltd. 1947. 20 pp.   OXB

SHANKS, Edward (1892–1953. Educated at Merchant Taylors' School, and Trinity College, Cambridge. Editor of *Granta*, 1912–13. Poet of the First World War. Second-Lieutenant, 8th South Lancashires, 1914, invalided out in 1915. Worked at the War Office, 1915–18. The first winner of the Hawthornden Prize in 1919. Assistant editor of *London Mercury*, 1919–22. Chief leader-writer of the *Evening Standard*, 1923–35)

The few. Printed Manchester: Withy Grove Press Ltd. [1948]. 32 pp.

Reprinted from the *Daily Sketch* of September 25, 27 and 28, 1944. Bound with Sir Arthur Bryant's prose work *The Battle of Britain*.   BL

For the birthday of a housewife (January 23rd, 1946). Dropmore Press, Ltd. 1946. [4] pp.

Title from cover. A limited ed. of 100 signed and numbered copies.

OXB

The great miracle, written in recollection of May–June, 1940. Printed Manchester: Withy Grove Press Ltd. [1948]. 31 pp.

Reprinted from the *Daily Sketch* of Thursday and Friday, June 3 and 4, 1943. Bound with Sir Arthur Bryant's prose work *The Summer of Dunkirk*.

BL

The man from Flanders, and other poems. Printed St. Clements Press Ltd. 1940. xxviii pp.

A limited ed. of 250 copies printed for private circulation.   OXB

The night watch for England, and other poems. Macmillan & Co. Ltd. 1942. viii, 51 pp.   BPL

Poems, 1939–1952. Macmillan & Co Ltd. 1954. xii, 107 pp.   MPL

see also   8, 84

SHANNON, Sheila (1913–   . b. London. Lived and worked in London throughout the war. Married writer Patric Dickinson in 1946. Poetry editor of *Spectator* for some years. Worked with W.J. Turner on publication of the Britain in Pictures series and the anthologies New Excursions into English Poetry. Of Rye, Sussex)

The lightning-struck tower, [and other poems]. Frederick Muller Ltd. 1947. 64 pp.

MPL

see also   68

SHARLAND, B.W.

Poems of peace and war. Ilfracombe: Arthur H. Stockwell, Ltd. 1945. 32 pp.

OXB

Tens to teens and have beens: [poems]. Ilfracombe: Arthur H. Stockwell, Ltd. [1947]. 24 pp. il.   OXB

SHARLAND, Malcolm Noel (–1944. Captain, Royal Engineers. Died of wounds on 19 July 1944 while serving with the First Army in Italy)

War poems on Italy. Published privately. 1946. 16 pp. por.   BPL

SHARPE, Margaret (Of Suffolk)   *see*   74

SHARROCK, Roger (1919–   . b. Robin Hood's Bay, Yorkshire. Educated at Queen Elizabeth's School, Wakefield, and St John's College, Oxford. Served with King's Own Yorkshire Light Infantry, 1939–41, and National Buildings Record, 1942–44. Assistant master at Rugby School, 1944–46. Held academic appointments at Southampton and Durham. Professor of English Language & Literature at King's College, London, 1968–81. Writer on English literature)
   Songs and comments: [*poems*]. Fortune Press. [1945]. 32 pp.   IWM

SHAW, D. Whitfield
   The Battle of Britain, and other poems. Ilfracombe: Arthur H. Stockwell, Ltd. [1944]. 16 pp.   OXB

SHAW, Duncan (1892–   . b. Edinburgh. Educated at Edinburgh Academy, Crewkerne Grammar School and the Slade School of Art. Held first class diplomas in drawing, painting and perspective. Served in the First World War, 1914–20, as a Major in the Army. Author and journalist)
   Tristesse, and other poems. Everybody's Books. [1945]. 62 pp.   OXB
see also   42

SHAW, G. (Of Staffordshire)   *see*   75

SHAW, Julia May (A spiritual healer)
   Friendship poems. Ilfracombe: Arthur H. Stockwell, Ltd. [1942]. 23 pp.
   'Dedicated to my son, Reginald Shaw, aged 26 (September, 1941 — reported missing, since located at Stalag VIII B) First Wireless Operator and drafted to a bomber squadron'.   OXB

SHAW, Robert (1933–   .)
   Causes, [*and other poems*]. Nottingham: Byron Press. 1972. 46 pp.   OXB

SHELDON, Gerard R.B.
   Remember Arnhem, and other poems. Fortune Press. 1949. [ii], 34 pp.   IWM
   A time for singing: [*poems*]. Ilfracombe: Arthur H. Stockwell, Ltd. [1943]. 16 pp.   OXB

SHELLEY, Avarne (Her youngest son died of wounds at Tobruk)
   Love in a mist, and other poems. Ilfracombe: Arthur H. Stockwell, Ltd. 1951. 15 pp.   OXB

SHELLEY, Hugh Bartholomew (Captain, Intelligence Corps. Served in India and Burma. Translator from the French)   *see*   43

SHERRARD, Guendolen
Fragments: collected poems. Ilfracombe: Arthur H. Stockwell, Ltd. 1980. 56 pp.
OXB

The holocaust: poems (to the children of England; that they may be spared). British Authors' Press. [1944]. 31 pp.　　　　OXB

SHEWARD, Cleon, pseud.
Modern poems; by "Cleon Sheward". Ilfracombe: Arthur H. Stockwell, Ltd. [1942]. 47 pp.　　　　OXB

SHILCOCK, Frederick Henry (Of The Three Tuns Inn, Walsall Road, Lichfield, Staffordshire)
Poems by a Lichfield innkeeper. Ilfracombe: Arthur H. Stockwell, Ltd. 1950. 32 pp.　　　　OXB

SHORT, John (1911– . b. Westmorland. Educated at Balliol College, Oxford. Served in the Army during the war. Career spent in adult education)
The oak and the ash, [and other poems]. J.M. Dent & Sons Ltd. 1947. 88 pp.
MPL
see also　42

SHORTER, P.E. (Of Yorkshire)　*see*　75

SHORTHOSE, William Townsend (Lieutenant-Colonel, South Staffordshire Regiment. Served with the British Army on the Rhine)
Pied hiker: a book of short poems. Stoke-on-Trent: Hughes & Harber, Ltd. 1943. [vi], 60 pp.　　　　OXB

SHORTO, Harry Leonard (1919– . Educated at the Royal Masonic School, and St John's College, Cambridge. Went straight into the Army from university in 1939. Captain, Intelligence Corps, serving with the Royal Artillery in Ceylon, India and Burma. Expert on the Mon language)　*see*　43

SHOYER, K.E. (Of Hampshire)　*see*　74

SHREWSBURY, Francis Henry Cheverton (Of Jesus College, Cambridge)
The scapegoat: poems. Printed Cambridge: Foister & Jagg. 1943. 16 pp.
OXB

SHUCKBURGH, Richard (Served in the Army)　*see*　24

SHUTTLEWORTH, Roberta (Of Guildford, Surrey)
In many moods: poems. Williams & Norgate Ltd. 1942. 48 pp.　　　　OXB
see also　21

SIBLY, John (1920– . b. Stonehouse, Gloucestershire. Educated at Cambridge University. Novelist and poet. Of Halesowen, West Midlands)
The death of William Rufus, [*and other poems*]. Fortune Press. 1949. 40 pp.
BPL

SIDDALL, Anne Elizabeth
The Maid of the Mersey, and other poems. Rockliff Publishing Corporation Ltd. 1945. [ii], 42 pp. OXB

SIDGWICK, J.B. (Lieutenant, Royal Artillery) *see* 25, 33, 47, 80

SILKIN, Jon (1930– . b. London. Evacuated to Wales during the war. Educated at Dulwich College and Leeds University. Did national service teaching in the Royal Army Educational Corps. Spent six years as a manual labourer and two years teaching English to foreign students. Founded *Stand* magazine in 1952. Held academic appointments in the United States, Israel and Australia. Co-founder and co-editor of publishers Northern House, Newcastle upon Tyne, 1964. Made several poetry-reading tours of the United States)
The psalms with their spoils: [*poems*]. Routledge & Kegan Paul. 1980. viii, 74 pp.
OXB
The two freedoms, [*and other poems*]. Chatto & Windus. 1958. 48 pp. OXB

SIM, Helen M.R. (Of Aberdeenshire) *see* 74

SIMMONDS, A.E. (Corporal. Served with the Eighth Army) *see* 25, 44

SIMMONS, James (1933– . b. Londonderry, Northern Ireland. Educated at Foyle College, Londonderry, Campbell College, Belfast, and Leeds University. Taught at Friends School, Lisburn, Northern Ireland, and Ahmadu University, Nigeria. In 1968 appointed to the Faculty of English at the New University of Ulster, Coleraine. Editor of *Poetry and Audience*, Leeds, 1957–58. Recipient of a Gregory Award for Poetry)
In the wilderness, and other poems. Bodley Head. 1969. 56 pp. MPL
Judy Garland and the cold war, [*and other poems*]. Belfast: Blackstaff Press. [1976]. [iv], 59 pp. OXB
No land is waste, Dr Eliot: [*poems*]. Richmond, Surrey: Keepsake Press. [1972]. [ii], 24 pp.
A limited ed. of 300 copies of which thirty copies are numbered and signed by the author. OXB
The selected James Simmons. Edited by Edna Longley. Belfast: Blackstaff Press. 1978. [viii], 102 pp. OXB
West Strand visions, [*and other poems*]. Belfast: Blackstaff Press. [1974]. 72 pp.
OXB

SIMMS, Colin (1939– . Member of Yorkshire Poets Association, Tyneside Poets, York Poetry Society, and Poets Conference, London. Naturalist poet. Of Kirbymoorside, Yorkshire)
Pomes and other fruit: [*poems*]. Sheffield: Headland Publications. 1971. 16 pp.
OXB

SIMPSON, B. (Of Rutland) *see* 73

SIMPSON, Charles Hunting (Educated at Pembroke College, Cambridge)
White cirrus: a collection of verse. Ilfracombe: Arthur H. Stockwell, Ltd. [1962]. [viii], 43 pp. OXB
White cirrus: a collection of verse. 2nd ed. Ilfracombe: Arthur H. Stockwell Ltd. [1963]. [vi], 42 pp. OXB

SIMPSON, D.L. (Sub-Lieutenant, Royal Naval Volunteer Reserve. Served on H.M.S. *Lady Rosemary*) *see* 23

SIMPSON, Evan John, (Evan John, pseud.) (Served in Cairo. Dramatist, biographer and general writer) *see* 66

SIMPSON, F. Vivienne (Served in the Women's Royal Air Force)
Let me walk with you, and other short poems. Largs: J. & R. Simpson, Ltd. 1942. [16] pp.
    Proceeds in aid of the Royal Air Force Benevolent Fund. OXB

SIMPSON, Harold (1909–55. Playwright)
Nazty nursery rhymes. Drawn by Bert Thomas. Andrew Dakers Ltd. 1940. [38] pp. il. OXB

SIMS, George (1923– . Writer of mystery and crime novels. Dealer in rare books and MSS since 1948 as G.F. Sims (Rare Books) of Hurst, Berkshire. Compiled catalogues of the Baron Corvo and the Llewelyn Powys MSS)
Poems. Fortune Press. 1944. 24 pp. OXB

SINCLAIR, A. (Served with the Eighth Army) *see* 25, 44

SINCLAIR, Karen A.
Poems. Ilfracombe: Arthur H. Stockwell, Ltd. [1944]. [16] pp. OXB

SINGER, Burns (1928–64. b. New York, brought to Scotland as a young child. Evacuated to Maud, Aberdeenshire, at the beginning of the war. Remained an American citizen)
The collected poems of Burns Singer. Edited and with an introduction by W.A.S. Keir. Preface by Hugh MacDiarmid. Secker & Warburg. 1970. xlviii, 240 pp.
OXB

Selected poems. Edited by Anne Cluysenaar. Manchester: Carcanet New Press
Ltd. 1977. xxiv, 122 pp. OXB

Still and all: poems. Secker & Warburg. 1957. 95 pp. OXB

SINGER, John (English, working in Scotland. A 'leftist' poet)
The fury of the living: poems. Glasgow: William Maclellan. 1942. 58 pp.
MPL

Storm and monument: second poems. Glasgow: William Maclellan. 1947. 49 pp.
IWM

see also 65

SINGLETON, Frank (1909–78. b. Bolton, Lancashire. Educated at Bolton
School, and Emmanuel College, Cambridge. Edited *Granta* and *Cambridge
Review* and was President of the Cambridge Union in 1937. Journalist with
Spectator, 1937, and with B.B.C. Overseas News Service, 1940. Novelist and
general writer. A director of Tillotsons Newspapers Ltd. Lived at Bolton)
The reluctant warrior, 1938–1945: [poems]. Bolton: Moor Platt Press. 1966.
29 pp. il. BL

see also 84

SINGLETON, Thomas
The penny poems. Ilfracombe: Arthur H. Stockwell, Ltd. 1950. 16 pp. OXB

SINKINSON, Walter Nugent (Of Yorkshire)
The Battle of Britain, and other poems. Printed Wakefield: West Yorkshire
Printing Co. Ltd. [1946]. [34] pp. BL

Quintet: (poems). With a preface by Clifford Bax. Printed Mirfield: Leslie
Brook. [1956]. 46 pp. OXB

SISSON, Charles Hubert (1914– . b. Bristol. Educated at Bristol
University, a postgraduate student in Berlin, Freiburg and Paris, 1934–36.
Entered the Ministry of Labour in 1936. Served in the Army Intelligence Corps,
1942–45, mainly in India. After the war held a variety of Civil Service
appointments, becoming Assistant Under Secretary of State at the Department
of Employment & Productivity in 1968, retiring in 1973. Of Langport,
Somerset)
In the Trojan ditch: collected poems and translations. Cheadle Hulme, Cheshire:
Carcanet Press. 1974. 228 pp. OXB

Numbers: [poems]. Methuen & Co Ltd. 1965. 63 pp. OXB

Poems. Fairwarp, Sussex: Peter Russell. 1959. 30 pp. OXB

SITWELL, Dame Edith (1887–1964. b. Scarborough, Yorkshire, sister of
Osbert and Sacheverell. Educated privately. Poet of the First World War.
Co-editor of *Wheels*, 1916–21, an annual anthology in revolt against the popular
poetry of the time. Author, editor, poet and friend of poets. Received honorary

degrees from Leeds, Durham, Oxford, Sheffield and Hull. Vice-President of Royal Society of Literature in 1958. Co-editor of the anthology *Poems of Our Time, 1900–1960*, 1959)

    The canticle of the rose: poems: 1917–1949. New York: Vanguard Press, Inc. [1949]. xxxviii, 290 pp.   OXB

    The canticle of the rose: selected poems, 1920–1947. Macmillan & Co. Ltd. 1949. x, 274 pp.   MPL

    Collected poems. Macmillan & Co. Ltd. 1957. xlvi, 445 pp.   OXB

    The collected poems of Edith Sitwell. New York: Vanguard Press. [1954]. [2], 1, 442 pp.   OXB

    Green song, and other poems. Macmillan & Co. Ltd. 1944. viii, 36 pp.
                                                IWM

    Selected poems. Harmondsworth, Middlesex: Penguin Books. 1952. xl, 134 pp. (Penguin poets, D16).   BL

    [*Selected poems*]. Vista Books. 1960. 48 pp. (Pocket poets).   OXB

    Selected poems of Edith Sitwell. Chosen with an introduction by John Lehmann. Macmillan. 1965. 150 pp. (Papermacs).   OXB

    The shadow of Cain. John Lehmann. 1947. 21 pp.   OXB

    The song of the cold, [and other poems]. Macmillan & Co. Ltd. 1945. viii, 116 pp.
                                              MPL

    The song of the cold, [and other poems]. New York: Vanguard Press, Inc. [1948]. 113 pp.   OXB

    Street songs: [poems]. Macmillan & Co. Ltd. 1942. viii, 35 pp.   MPL
see also   3, 15, 26, 30, 48, 58, 76, 82, 83

SKELTON, Gladys, (John Presland, pseud.) (1889–1975. b. Melbourne, Australia. Educated at Queen's College, London, and Girton College, Cambridge. Director of Y.M.C.A. Employment Bureau for Disabled Soldiers, 1919, lecturer at London University, 1920–27. A lecturer for the League of Nations Union. Member of the Council of British Societies for Relief Abroad, 1942–45. Novelist)

    Selected poems of John Presland. Linden Press. 1961. 139 pp.   MPL

SKELTON, Robin (1925– . b. Easington, Yorkshire. Educated at Pocklington Grammar School, Christ's College, Cambridge, and Leeds University. Served in the Royal Air Force, 1944–47. Taught English at Manchester University, 1951–63. Professor of English at Victoria University, British Columbia, from 1966. Founder-member of the Peterloo Group of poets and painters in Manchester, 1957–60. Poet and critic. Editor of the anthology *Poetry of the Forties*, 1968)

    The dark window: poems. Oxford University Press. 1962. viii, 96 pp.
                                              OXB

    The hunting dark: [poems]. Andre Deutsch. 1971. 80 pp.   MPL

SKELTON, Thomas (Served in the Western Desert)   *see*   63

SKINN, Richard West- *see* **WEST-SKINN, Richard**

SKINNER, Martyn (1906– . Educated at public schools and Magdalen College, Oxford, which he left without taking a degree. A farmer during the war. His *Letters to Malaya* were written during the war to a friend in the Malayan Civil Service and were eventually addressed to a Japanese prison camp. Vol. II was awarded the Hawthornden Prize in 1943. Of Taunton, Somerset)
Letters to Malaya; written from England to Alexander Nowell M.C.S. of Ipoh. Putnam. 1941. 63 pp.   IWM
Letters to Malaya, III and IV; written from England to Alexander Nowell M.C.S. of Ipoh. Putnam. 1943. 94 pp.   IWM
Letters to Malaya, V; written from England to Alexander Nowell M.C.S. of Ipoh. Putnam. 1947. 78 pp.   IWM
[Vol. II of this work not seen. Missing in all libraries visited]
see also 76

SLATER, Dora Helen Agnes, (Elizabeth Alexander, pseud.)
Joy and woe: [poems]; by Elizabeth Alexander. Printed Regency Press. [1976]. 36 pp.   OXB

SLATER, Eliot (1904– . Educated at Leighton Park School, Cambridge University, and St Geoge's Hospital, London. Medical Officer at Maudsley Hospital, 1931–39. Clinical Director at Sutton Emergency Hospital, 1939–45. Held other important medical appointments. Member of the Royal Commission on Capital Punishment, 1949. Writer on psychiatry. Editor of *British Journal of Psychiatry*, 1961–72)
The ebbless sea: poems (1922–1962). Outposts Publications. 1968. 43 pp.
OXB

SLATOR, J.W. (Of Leicestershire?)
Memories of Beacon Rock, Leicestershire: [poems]. Mitre Press. [1944]. 32 pp.
OXB

SMALE, Joseph
Topical poems. Ilfracombe: Arthur H. Stockwell. 1952. 14 pp.   OXB

SMEWIN, Fred (Able-Bodied Seaman, Royal Navy) *see* 23, 33

SMITH, Barbara E.
The homeland, and other poems. Ilfracombe: Arthur H. Stockwell, Ltd. [1943]. 16 pp.   OXB

SMITH, Basil K. Sundius- *see* **SUNDIUS-SMITH, Basil K.**

SMITH, C. Busby, pseud. *see* **SMITH, John**, (C. Busby Smith, pseud.)

SMITH, D. Seton- *see* **SETON-SMITH, D.**

SMITH, David Lea
The conference, and shorter poems. Ilfracombe: Arthur H. Stockwell Ltd. 1971.
19 pp.   OXB

SMITH, Dorothy A.
Dover Castle, and other poems. Ilfracombe: Arthur H. Stockwell, Ltd. 1962.
16 pp. il.   OXB

SMITH, Edna (Of Lancashire) *see* 73

SMITH, Elwyn (Of Cheshire?)
Dream stuff: [poems]. Printed Stockport: F. Boor. [1941]. [ii], 87 pp.   MPL
Poems. Printed Stockport: F. Boor. [1942]. [iv], 40 pp.   MPL

SMITH, F.Z. (Lieutenant. Served with the Eighth Army in the Western
Desert) *see* 46

SMITH, Florence Margaret (Stevie) (1902–71. b. Hull, Yorkshire but lived at
Palmers Green, North London, from age of three. Educated at Palmers Green
High School and North London Collegiate School. Worked as a secretary for
publishers Nevil Pearson and Sir Frank Newnes until 1953. Poet and novelist
known for her distinctive line drawings. Occasional writer and broadcaster for
the B.B.C. Often read her own poems with comments, sometimes singing them
to her own music based largely on Gregorian chants and hymn tunes. Served on
the Arts Council literary panel. Received Cholmondeley Award, 1966, and
Queen's Gold Medal for Poetry, 1969)
The collected poems of Stevie Smith. Allen Lane. [1975]. 591 pp. il. (by the
author).   OXB
Mother, what is man?: poems and drawings; by Stevie Smith. Jonathan Cape.
1942. 80 pp. il.   OXB
Not waving but drowning: poems; [by] Stevie Smith. Andre Deutsch. 1957.
76 pp. il. (by the author).   OXB
Selected poems; by Stevie Smith. Longmans. 1962. viii, 120 pp. il. (by the
author).   OXB
Two in one: Selected poems, and The frog prince, and other poems; by Stevie Smith.
Longmans. 1971. xvi, 318 pp. il. (by the author).   OXB

SMITH, G.E. (Aircraftman 2, Royal Air Force) *see* 33

SMITH, Gerald
Quiet evening, [and other poems]. Mitre Press. [1946]. 40 pp.   OXB

SMITH, Helen Ericson
Love and dreams: verse. Ilfracombe: Arthur H. Stockwell, Ltd. [1944]. 19 pp.
OXB

SMITH, Horace Arthur
Rhyme and reason: 52 verses intended to be understood not only by Horace Arthur Smith. Fortune Press. 1955. 68 pp. OXB

SMITH, Iain Crichton (1928– . b. Isle of Lewis, Outer Hebrides. Educated at Aberdeen University. Sergeant in the Army Educational Corps, 1950–52. Secondary school teacher at Clydebank, 1953–55, and at Oban High School, 1955–77. Poet, novelist, short story writer and dramatist, writing in both English and Gaelic)
Hamlet in autumn: [*poems*]. Loanhead, Midlothian: M. Macdonald. 1972. 61 pp. (Lines review editions, 2). OXB
Love poems and elegies. Victor Gollancz Ltd. 1972. 110 pp. OXB

SMITH, James E. (Served in H.M. Forces) *see* 74

SMITH, John, (C. Busby Smith, pseud.) (1924– . b. High Wycombe, Buckinghamshire. Educated at St James's School, Gerrards Cross. Managing director of literary agents Christy & Moore, Ltd. Poet, playwright, literary critic and writer of children's fiction. Editor of *Poetry Review*, 1962–65. Received Adam International Poetry Prize, 1953. Of Gerrards Cross, Buckinghamshire)
The birth of Venus: poems. Hutchinson. [1954]. [x], 41 pp. MPL
Gates of beauty and death: poems; by C. Busby Smith. Fortune Press. 1948. 68 pp.
OXB

SMITH, Joseph
Buds unfolding, and other poems. Ilfracombe: Arthur H. Stockwell, Ltd. 1952. 16 pp. OXB

SMITH, Lilian Sinclair (Of Lancashire?)
Poems. Printed Liverpool: C. Tinling & Co., Ltd. 1940. 64 pp.
Printed for private circulation. OXB

SMITH, Lily, (Wanderer, pseud.)
Holiday ramblings: [*poems*]; by "Wanderer". Ilfracombe: Arthur H. Stockwell, Ltd. [1953]. 16 pp. OXB

SMITH, Margery (1916– . Worked as a clerk in Nottingham, 1939, and as a guide at Newstead Abbey, Nottinghamshire. Co-founder of Nottingham Poetry Society during the war. Served in the Auxiliary Territorial Service, 1942–46. A teacher, she taught in Rumania, 1937, and in Iraq, 1950–53. Council member of the Poetry Society, 1965–68. Of Horsham, Sussex)

In our time: [*poems*]. Favil Press. 1941, [vi]. 42 pp.   OXB

Still in my hand: [*poems*]. Outposts Publications. 1964. 24 pp.   OXB
see also   52

SMITH,   Michael   MacNaughton- *see* **MACNAUGHTON-SMITH, Michael**

SMITH, N. Lister (Of Scotland)
Colinton Dell, and other poems. Arthur H. Stockwell Ltd. [1940]. 16 pp.
                                                                        OXB

SMITH, Norman Harry Charles (1919–   . b. London. Educated at Birmingham University. Volunteered for service in India in 1941. Lieutenant, Royal Indian Army Service Corps, serving as a Station Transport Officer) *see* 43

SMITH, Robert (Commissioned in the Royal Artillery)   *see*   60, 61

SMITH, Robert Buchanan
The third darkness, [*and other poems*]. Walton-on-Thames: Outposts Publications. 1980. 32 pp.   OXB

SMITH, Stevie   *see*   **SMITH, Florence Margaret** (Stevie)

SMITH, Sydney
A collection of poems. Ilfracombe: Arthur H. Stockwell, Ltd. 1954. 22 pp.
                                                                        OXB

SMITH, Sydney Goodsir (1915–75. b. Wellington, New Zealand. Studied medicine at Edinburgh University and history at Oriel College, Oxford. Worked for the War Office, teaching English to the Polish Army in Scotland. Joined the British Council's Edinburgh office in 1945. Poet, novelist and short story writer. Worked as a freelance journalist and broadcaster. Recipient of several literary awards)
Collected poems, 1941–1975. With an introduction by Hugh McDiarmid [sic]. John Calder. 1975. xvi, 269 pp. por. (Scottish library).
        In Scots dialect.   OXB
The deevil's waltz: [*poems*]. Illustrations by Denis Peploe. [Glasgow]: William Maclellan. 1946. 60 pp. il. (Poetry Scotland series, 7).
        In Scots dialect, with a glossary.   OXB
Figs and thistles: [*poems*]. Edinburgh: Oliver & Boyd. 1959. viii, 79 pp.
        In Scots dialect.   OXB
Selected poems. Oliver & Boyd. 1947. 24 pp.. (Saltire modern poets).
        In Scots dialect.   OXB

Skail wind: poems. Edinburgh: Chalmers Press. 1941. 67 pp.
    In Scots dialect.   OXB

SMITHIES, Alan (Served in North Africa. Of Exeter, Devon) *see* 63

SMITHIES, Arnold (Served in the Middle East) *see* 39, 63

SMITHIES, Catherine (Served in the Middle East) *see* 39, 63

SNAITH, J.W. (Of Staffordshire) *see* 73

SNAITH, Stanley (1903–76. b. Kendal, Westmorland. Educated at Kendal and privately. A professional librarian, he held senior public library posts in Kendal, Kingston-upon-Thames and Islington. Local Secretary, Ministry of Information, 1940–42. Served in the Royal Artillery, 1942–46, in heavy anti-aircraft batteries. Borough Librarian, Bethnal Green, 1950–65. Poet, novelist and general writer. Wrote numerous papers and pamphlets on antiquarian topics. Latterly lived at Swanage, Dorset)
    The common festival: [poems]. Denver: Alan Swallow. 1950. 24 pp. (Key poets, 5).
        Printed by the Blackmore Press, Gillingham, Dorset.   BL
    The flowering thorn: poems. Chingford Hatch, Essex: [Author]. 1946. 12 pp.
        A limited ed. of twenty-five numbered copies printed for private circulation.   BL
    The inn of night, [and other poems]. J.M. Dent & Sons Ltd. 1947. 88 pp.
                          MPL
    Stormy harvest: poems of peace and war. J. M. Dent & Sons Ltd. 1944. 40 pp.
                          MPL
see also 2, 51, 82

SNELGAR, J.M. (Lieutenant, Royal Naval Volunteer Reserve) *see* 23

SNELL, Shirley F. (Of Lincolnshire) *see* 75

SNOWDEN, A. (Served in H.M. Forces) *see* 74

SOMERLED, Ian (Of Elgin, Moray. Served in the desert)
    Arrows of hope: poems. Ilfracombe: Arthur H. Stockwell, Ltd. [1956]. 36 pp.
                          OXB

SOMERSET, Raglan (1885–1956. Educated at Bath College, and Queen's College, Cambridge. Called to the Bar in 1911. Recorder of Oswestry, Shropshire, 1933–37. Commissioned in the Royal Army Service Corps, transferred to Intelligence Department, War Office. Barrister, journalist, translator and literary critic. Lived in Monmouthshire and London)

The chieftains ground: (verses and translations grave and gay). Usk, Monmouthshire: Four Ash Press. 1953. [viii], 37 pp.

    Title from cover.   OXB

Twilight, and other verses. Fortune Press. 1948. 64 pp.   OXB

SOMERVILLE, William (1918–).

    Poetical works: Part I Prelude; [Part] II Twelve poems. Ilfracombe: Arthur H. Stockwell, Ltd. 1954–55. 2 vols in 1.   OXB

    Poetical works. Ilfracombe: Arthur H. Stockwell Ltd. 1955. 15 pp.   BL

SOPER, B. McKenny (Sergeant, Royal Air Force)   *see*   1

SOURBUTTS, Leonard

    Beginnings in gladness: poems. Fortune Press. [1965]. 64 pp.   OXB

SOUTAR, William (1898–1943. b. Perth. Educated at Perth Academy and Edinburgh University. Poet of the First World War. Joined the Royal Navy in 1916, serving on the lower deck in a variety of ships. Demobilized in 1919. Graduated with honours in English from Edinburgh in 1923. Paralysed from a spinal disease in 1929 and bedridden for the rest of his life)

    But the earth abideth: a verse-sequence. Andrew Dakers Ltd. 1943. 62 pp.

                                                  OXB

    Collected poems. Edited with an introductory essay by Hugh MacDiarmid. Andrew Dakers Ltd. 1948. 525 pp. por.

    Some poems in Scots dialect.   OXB

    The expectant silence: poems. Andrew Dakers Ltd. 1944. 64 pp.   IWM

    In the time of tyrants: poems. With an introductory note on pacifist faith and necessity. Perth: [Author]. 1939. 72 pp.

    A limited ed. of 100 copies numbered and signed by the author.   BL

    Poems in Scots and English. Selected by W.R. Aitken. Oliver & Boyd. 1961. 128 pp.   OXB

    Poems in Scots and English. Selected by W.R. Aitken. Edinburgh: Scottish Academic Press. 1975. 128 pp.   OXB

see also   7, 8, 9, 30, 48, 51

SOUTHGATE, Leslie Charles (Leading Aircraftman, Royal Air Force. Served east of the Brahmaputra for three years)   *see*   43

SOWDEN, Lewis (1905–74. b. Manchester. Educated at Witwatersrand University, South Africa. Reporter on the *Rand Daily Mail* and the *Sunday Times*, Johannesburg. Became literary editor of *Rand Daily Mail* in 1935. Drama critic, assistant editor and literary critic, 1945–66. Freelance writer in Europe, 1946–50. Settled in Israel)

    The charmed fabric: poems. Fortune Press. 1943. 56 pp.   OXB

    Poems with flute. Robert Hale Ltd. 1955. 68 pp.   OXB

SPALDING, Helen (1920–   . b. London. Educated at Wyggeston Grammar School, Leicester, and Central School of Speech Training & Dramatic Art, London. Worked in the press section, Ministry of Economic Warfare)

What images return: [poems]. Methuen & Co. Ltd. 1947. 44 pp.   OXB
see also   38, 42

SPALDING, Henry Norman (1877–1953. b. Blackheath. Educated at Eastbourne College, New College, Oxford, and in France and Switzerland. Civil servant in the Admiralty, 1901–09. Called to the Bar in 1906. Contested Sussex North as a Liberal candidate in 1910. Poet of the First World War. Served in the Admiralty and the Ministry of Munitions, 1915–18. Provided a Workers Educational Centre in Reading, Berkshire, and gave Oxford University a wild life sanctuary on the Cherwell)

In praise of life: [poems]. Oxford: Basil Blackwell. 1952. x, 290 pp.   MPL

SPARKS, A. (Of London)   *see*   74

SPENCE, D., (Korragh, pseud.) (Of Berkshire?)
Richmond rhymes, and other verses; by Korragh. Printed Abingdon-on-Thames: Abbey Press. 1941. 40 pp.

'Dedicated, without permission, to Lieutenant-Colonel B.V. Ramsden and the officers of the I.T.C., The Green Howards'.   OXB

SPENCE, Dermot Chesson
One man's war: variations on a theme with bayonets: [poems]. Abingdon: Abbey Press. [1940]. [iv], 25 pp.   BL

SPENCE, Philip
Struwwelhitler: a Nazi story book by Doktor Schrecklichheit: a parody on the original Struwwelpeter; [by] Philip and Robert Spence. The Daily Sketch and Sunday Graphic Ltd. [1941]. 26 pp. col. il.
Title from cover. Printed on one side of leaf only.   BPL

SPENCE, Robert
Struwwelhitler: a Nazi story book by Doktor Schrecklichheit: a parody on the original Struwwelpeter; [by] Philip and Robert Spence. The Daily Sketch and Sunday Graphic Ltd. [1941]. 26 pp. col. il.
Title from cover. Printed on one side of leaf only.   BPL

SPENCER, Bernard (1909–63. Educated at Marlborough College, and Corpus Christi College, Oxford. Worked as a schoolmaster, an advertising copywriter and in films. Lectured for the British Council in Greece, Egypt, Italy and Spain. Appointed to Fuad I University, Cairo).
Aegean islands, and other poems. Editions Poetry London. 1946. 47 pp.   OXB
Collected poems. Alan Ross Ltd. 1965. [vi], 96 pp.   MPL

With luck lasting: poems. Hodder & Stoughton. 1963. [57] pp.   MPL
see also   3, 31, 40, 57

SPENCER, N. (Mrs Spencer)
The gunner, and other poems. Ilfracombe: Arthur H. Stockwell, Ltd. [1942].
16 pp.   OXB

SPENCER, Philip S.-G. (1922–43. Lived in Burnley, Lancashire. Educated at
St John's College, Oxford. Volunteered for the Royal Air Force in February
1942 and was posted abroad six months later. Died on 25 November 1943 from
injuries received in an air crash in Cape Province, South Africa)
African crocus, and other poems. Fortune Press. 1954. 32 pp.   IWM

SPENCER, R. St E. (Served in South-East Asia Command) *see* 35

SPENCER, William F. (Served in H.M. Forces) *see* 74

SPENDER, Mary Doreen (A schoolmistress, Past President of London Head
Teachers Association. In charge of evacuees to South Wales. Aunt of Richard
Spender, the young poet who was killed in North Africa with the Parachute
Regiment) *see* 41

SPENDER, Richard (1921–43. b. Hereford. Educated at King Edward VI
School, Stratford upon Avon. Won a scholarship but enlisted instead of going
up to Oxford in 1940. Second-Lieutenant, London Irish Regiment, transferred
to 2nd Battalion, Parachute Regiment. Killed in action on 28 March 1943 while
leading his men against German machine-gun positions near Bizerta, Tunisia)
The collected poems of Richard Spender. Sidgwick & Jackson. 1944. viii,
77 pp. por.   BPL
Laughing blood: [poems]. Sidgwick & Jackson. [1942]. 64 pp.   BPL
Parachute Battalion: last poems from England and Tunisia. Sidgwick & Jackson
Ltd. 1943. 30 pp.   BPL
see also   9, 57, 76, 80

SPENDER, Sir Stephen (1909–   . b. London. Educated at University College
School and University College, Oxford. Eminent poet, editor and critic
belonging to the circle of left-wing poets of the 1930s. Served in the Spanish
Civil War. Fireman in the National Fire Service in London, 1941–44. Later
worked in the Foreign Office. Co-editor of *Horizon* magazine, 1939–41, and of
Encounter, 1953–67. Held senior academic appointments, many in the United
States. Professor of English at University College, London, from 1970.
Recipient of many literary honours)
Collected poems, 1928–1953. Faber & Faber. 1955. 211 pp.   OXB
The edge of being: [poems]. Faber & Faber. 1949. 57 pp.   MPL
The edge of being: poems. New York: Random House. [1949]. 57 pp.   OXB

The generous days, [and other poems]. Boston, Mass.: David R. Godine. 1969. [vi], 21 pp.

A limited ed. of 250 copies, fifty copies bound by hand and signed by the author.   OXB

The generous days: [poems]. Faber & Faber. 1971. 47 pp.   BL

Inscriptions: [poems]. Poetry Book Society Ltd. [1958]. [3] pp.

A limited ed. of 1,100 copies, the first of a series of holograph poems.

OXB

Ruins and visions: poems. Faber & Faber Ltd. 1942. 84 pp.   BPL

Selected poems. Faber & Faber. 1965. 80 pp. (Faber paper covered editions).

MPL

[Selected poems]; [by] John Heath-Stubbs, F.T. Prince, Stephen Spender. Harmondsworth, Middlesex: Penguin Books. 1972. 176 pp. (Penguin modern poets, 20).

Not joint authorship.   MPL

see also 4, 7, 8, 10, 15, 18, 25, 26, 38, 45, 48, 51, 56, 57, 68, 76, 82, 83, 87

SPERO, Leopold (1887–   . b. London. Educated at City of London School, and Sidney Sussex College, Cambridge. Qualified as a solicitor. Novelist, poet and journalist, he founded *Children's Digest*)

Stalingrad: a ballad. Press Contacts Ltd. [1943]. [6] pp.

First impression limited to 250 copies.   OXB

SPIEGAL, Pamela

Youthful poems. Ilfracombe: Arthur H. Stockwell, Ltd. 1947. 16 pp. il.

OXB

SPINK, Sylvia M. (Of Kent)   *see*   71

SPIRES, Joyce O. (Of Northamptonshire)   *see*   74

SQUIB, Daniel (Served in South-East Asia Command)   *see*   35

SQUIRE, Sir John Collings (1884–1958. b. Plymouth, Devon. Educated at Blundell's School, and St John's College, Cambridge. Poet of the First World War, unfit for active service because of poor eyesight. Journalist with *New Statesman* and *London Mercury*, 1913–34. A governor of the Old Vic, 1922–26. Chairman of the English Association, 1926–29. Poet, critic, anthologist and editor)

Collected poems. With a preface by John Betjeman. Macmillan & Co Ltd. 1959. xviii, 242 pp. por.   MPL

Poems of two wars. Hutchinson & Co. Ltd. 1940. 46 pp.   BPL

Selected poems. Oliver Moxon. 1948. [viii], 148 pp. por.   OXB

The symbol: (on the statue of Coeur de Lion outside Westminster Hall, bombed and his sword bent). 1940. il.

A broadside. OXB
see also 42, 84

STAFFORD, Sarah (Taught English to Belgian children. Of West London) *see* 9, 19, 25

STAFFORD-CLARK, David (1916– . Educated at Felsted School, London University and Guy's Hospital. Served in the Royal Air Force Volunteer Reserve as a medical parachutist, mentioned twice in despatches. Had three years post-graduate training in psychiatry. Held many important medical appointments. Medical adviser and director for a number of television and radio medical programmes. Author of books on psychology and psychiatry)
Autumn shadow, and other poems. Oxford: Shakespeare Head Press. 1941. 62 pp.
MPL
Sound in the sky, and other poems. Oxford: Basil Blackwell. 1944. 32 pp.
IWM

STAINTHORP, Sidney (Volunteered for the Army in January 1940. Trained in the Royal Armoured Corps. Went to the Middle East as a Sergeant and commissioned there. In the Intelligence Corps, Benghazi) *see* 63

STALLARD, Mrs Arthur *see* **STALLARD, Constance Louisa**

STALLARD, Constance Louisa (Novelist and playwright)
Feeble folk; by Mrs Arthur Stallard. Printed Brighton: Brighton Herald Ltd. 1946. 28 pp. OXB

STALLWORTHY, Jon (1935– . b. London. Educated at Dragon School, Oxford, Rugby School, and Magdalen College, Oxford. Newdigate Prizewinner, 1958. Served in the Royal West African Frontier Force pre-Oxford. Joined staff of Oxford University Press in 1959. Visiting Fellow at All Souls College for a sabbatical year, 1971–72)
The apple barrel: selected poems, 1955–63. Oxford University Press. 1974. [viii], 64 pp. OXB
Out of bounds, [and other poems]. Oxford University Press. 1963. x, 62 pp.
OXB
Root and branch: [poems]. Chatto & Windus; Hogarth Press. 1969. 63 pp. (Phoenix living poets). OXB
Root and branch: [poems]. Paperback ed. Chatto & Windus; Hogarth Press. 1976. 63 pp. (Phoenix living poets). OXB

STANFORD, Derek (1918– . b. Lampton, Middlesex. Educated at Latymer Upper School with John Bayliss and Terence Tiller. After studying law worked on the land at Cambridge. Served in the Army in a non-combatant corps,

1940–45. Lecturer and literary critic after the war. Fiction reviewer for *The Scotsman* and poetry critic for *Books and Bookmen*. Co-editor of *Forum*)
    Music for statues: [*poems*]. Routledge & Kegan Paul Ltd. 1948. 64 pp.   OXB
    A romantic miscellany: [*poems*]; by John Bayliss and Derek Stanford. Fortune Press. 1946. 63 pp.   BPL
        Not joint authorship.
see also   25, 76

STANFORD, Gladys M.
    Small fry, and other verses. Bognor Regis: New Horizon. [1980]. [viii], 89 pp.
                                              OXB

STANLEY, Christopher (Served in the Middle East) *see* 63

STANNARD, Mavis Joy
    Twenty poems. Ilfracombe: Arthur H. Stockwell, Ltd. 1950. 27 pp.   OXB

STARK, M. (A Scotswoman. Trainer in the Women's Land Army Timber Corps) *see* 42

STARK, Robert
    Errantes hederae: a companion to 'Fashions and fancies': [*poems*]. Oxford: H.G. Dixey. 1948. [ii], 26 pp.
        A limited ed. of eighty numbered copies hand-printed by H.G. Dixey.
                                              OXB

STARKEY, James Sullivan, (Seumas O'Sullivan, pseud.) (1879–1958). Member of the Irish Academy of Letters. Poet of the First World War. Edited *The Dublin Magazine*. Winner of Gregory Medal, 1957. Lived in Dublin)
    Collected poems; by Seumas O'Sullivan. Dublin: Orwell Press. 1940. 227 pp.
        A limited ed. of 300 copies.   MPL
    Dublin poems; by Seumas O'Sullivan. New York: Creative Age Press, Inc. [1946]. xvi, 176 pp.   BL
see also 21

STATHIS, George (Lived in London during the 1940s)
    Your thoughts, your dreams: [*poems*]. Vema Press. 1946. 38 pp.   OXB

STEEGMAN, Philip (Lieutenant, Royal Navy, formerly an Ordinary Seaman) *see* 84

STEELE, A.A. (Served with the Royal Air Force in India and South-East Asia) *see* 35

STEELE, J.
  Beside the guns: poems. Ilfracombe: Arthur H. Stockwell Ltd. [1941]. 16 pp.
  OXB

STEEN, Shiela (b. India, of Irish origins. Worked in Fleet Street)
  The honeysuckle hedge: [*poems*]. Oxford University Press. 1943. [2], vi, 48 pp.
  IWM
  see also 42

STEPHANIDES, Theodore (1896– . b. Bombay, of Greek parentage. Educated in India, Greece and France. Qualified as a doctor in 1929. During the First World War served in the Greek Artillery on the Macedonian front, 1917–18. Served in the Royal Army Medical Corps in the Western Desert, Greece, Crete and Sicily, 1940–45. Assistant radiologist at Lambeth Hospital, 1946–61. Of Kilburn, London)
  Cities of the mind: [*poems*]. Fortune Press. [1969]. 98 pp.   BL
  The golden face, [*and other poems*]. Fortune Press. [1965]. 96 pp.   OXB
  Worlds in a crucible: [*poems*]. Mitre Press. [1973]. 92 pp.   OXB
  see also   39, 63

STEPHENSON, G.R.
  Sunrise to sunset: poems. Ilfracombe: Arthur H. Stockwell, Ltd. [1944]. 16 pp.
  OXB

STEPHENSON, W. Palmer
  Autumn fires: [*poems*]. Ilfracombe: Arthur H. Stockwell, Ltd 1980. 24 pp.
  OXB

STEPHINSON, John R. (Of County Durham)   *see*   75

STERN, J.P. (Educated at Cambridge University. Served as air-gunner in the Royal Air Force)   *see*   53

STEUART, Douglas Stuart Spens (Poet of the First World War. Fellow of the Royal Meteorological Society. Of North West London)
  The world of tomorrow, and other anti-war poems. Glasgow: William Maclellan. 1948. 32 pp.   OXB

STEVENS, F. (Served in H.M. Forces)   *see*   74

STEVENSON, James Patrick (Chaplain to the Forces. Served with the Eighth Army)   *see*   44

STEVENSON, Patric (Corporal, Royal Air Force)
  Flowing water, [*and other poems*]. Resurgam Books. 1945. 48 pp.   IWM

STEWART, Alexander Ritchie

Poems. Fortune Press. 1947. 36 pp.. il., por.

'Dedicated to Alastair Ian Stewart (son of the late Alastair Mackichan Stewart, Flight-Lieutenant)'. IWM

STEWART, Anne

Afterthoughts: [poems]. Spearman Publishers. [1940]. 21 pp. BPL
Silver wings, [and other poems]. BCM/Spearman Publishers. [1942]. 23 pp.
OXB

STEWART, Desmond (1924– . Educated at Haileybury School, and Trinity College, Oxford. Assistant Professor of English at Baghdad University, 1948–56. Inspector of English in Islamic schools in Beirut, 1956–58. Writer of fiction and non-fiction with a Middle Eastern background)

The besieged city, [and other poems]. Fortune Press. [1946]. 76 pp. IWM
The forest, and other poems. Ilfracombe: Arthur H. Stockwell, Ltd. [1942].
16 pp. OXB

STEWART, Gervase (1920–41. Educated at St Catharine's College, Cambridge, where he edited *Granta* and was Chairman of Debates at the Union. Joined the Fleet Air Arm in 1940, was commissioned as Sub-Lieutenant and became a pilot. Killed in action on 25 November 1941)

No weed death: poems. With a foreword by Henry Treece. Fortune Press. [1942]. 44 pp. por. OXB
see also 1, 23, 25, 76, 83

STEWART, Louise Findlay (The first Scotswoman to fly over the Alps as a passenger. Elected Honorary Member of the Caledonian United Service Club in recognition of her war service, especially in connection with the Navy League. A member of the Society of Women Journalists. Writer and lecturer on Poland and writer of children's stories)

Sea and sky: war poems. Foreword by Sir George A. Waters. Printed Glasgow: William Reid & Sons. [1948]. [vi], 14 pp.

Dedicated to Winston Churchill. Title from cover. OXB
see also 41, 80

STEWART, Samuel R. (Of Dunbartonshire) *see* 74

STEWART, W.F.M. (1918– . b. Crieff, Perthshire. Educated at Morrison's Academy and Edinburgh University. Served as a Gunner in the Royal Artillery, later commissioned) *see* 11, 45

STEWART-PHILLIPS, John Fleetwood (1917– . Educated at Brighton College, and Worcester College, Oxford. A rugby and football blue. Served with

1st Battalion, Argyll & Sutherland Highlanders in North Africa and Crete. Captured in Crete on 1 June 1941, held prisoner of war in Germany until 1945. Entered the Diplomatic Service, holding posts in Sudan, Libya, Amman, Cyprus, Southern Yemen and Jordan. Of Horsham, Sussex) *see* 5, 67

STOBART, E.M. *see* 80

STOCKS, J.B. (Served with the Royal Air Force in the Middle East) *see* 25, 33

STOKES, Arthur Meredith (Of Linby, Nottinghamshire)
Poems. [Westerham]: Westerham Press Ltd. 1957. 45 pp.   BL
Poems of the countryside. Southend-on-Sea: Citizen Publishing Co. Ltd. [1963]. 44 pp.   OXB

STOKES, Stanley (1890–   . b. Exeter, Devon. Educated at Hele School, Exeter, and Shebbear College, North Devon. Contributor to many periodicals. Of Exeter)
Chime of fancy: poems. G. T. Foulis & Co. Ltd. [1951]. 48 pp.   BPL
Where oxen lay: Christmas poems. G.T. Foulis & Co., Ltd. [1948]. 32 pp.
                                                                          OXB

STOPES, Marie Carmichael (1880–1958. b. Dorking, Surrey. Educated at London University, and St George's, Edinburgh. Became the first female science lecturer at Manchester in 1904. Fellow in Palaeontology at University College, London. Poet of the First World War. The pioneer advocate of contraception, she founded the world's first birth control clinic in North London in 1921 with her second husband, Humphrey Verdon Roe, the aircraft manufacturer)
Instead of tears. Little Bookham, Surrey: Count Potocki of Montalk. 1942. [9] pp.
  A limited ed. of 300 numbered copies printed on handmade paper. 'In memoriam for officers and men who went down with H.M.S. *Cossack*'.
                                                                          OXB
Instead of tears. De La More Press. [1948]. [28] pp.
  'In memoriam for officers and men who went down with H.M.S. *Cossack*'.
                                                                          OXB
Joy and verity, other poems and a poetic drama. Hogarth Press. 1952. 128 pp.
                                                                          OXB
Wartime harvest: poems. With a preface by the Lord Alfred Douglas and a letter by George Bernard Shaw. Alexander Moring Ltd. 1944. 92 pp.   BPL
Wartime harvest: poems. With a preface by the Lord Alfred Douglas and a letter by George Bernard Shaw. 2nd ed. Alexander Moring Ltd. 1945. 96 pp.
                                                                          IWM
We burn: selected poems. With portrait frontispiece and twelve full page

illustrations by Gregorio Prieto. Alex Moring Ltd. 1950. [ii], 100 pp. il., por.
BL

see also   23, 41

STOREY, E. (Served in North Africa with the Northumberland
Fusiliers) *see*   63, 74

STOREY, Edward (1930– . Isle of Ely, Cambridgeshire. Educated at an
elementary school. Worked as a clerk and a salesman. Did national service in
the Royal Air Force. Arts Organizer, Peterborough Education Authority,
1959–64. Registrar and tutor, Peterborough College of Adult Education,
1964–69. Became a full-time writer in 1969)
   North bank night, [and other poems]. Chatto & Windus; Hogarth Press. 1969.
46 pp. (Phoenix living poets).   MPL

STORRIE, William
   Broken wings of song: a book of verse. Ilfracombe: Arthur H. Stockwell. [1942].
20 pp.   OXB

STOTT, H.W. (Of Bedfordshire) *see*   74

STRACHAN, James
   Autumn leaves: [poems]. James Clarke & Co., Ltd. 1954. 64 pp.   OXB

STRACHAN, Walter John (1903– . b. Hull, Yorkshire, Educated at Hymes
College and Cambridge University. General editor of the Methuen Twentieth
Century French Texts. Art critic and translator from the French. Of Bishop's
Stortford, Hertfordshire)
   Moments of time: poems. Sylvan Press. 1947. 55 pp.   IWM
   Poems. Engravings by Charles Marq. Christopher Hewett. [1976]. [73] pp. il.
   A limited ed. of 200 numbered copies printed by Christopher Skelton at
Skelton's Press, Wellingborough, Northamptonshire.   OXB

STRAND, H. (Served in H.M. Forces) *see*   75

STRAYNGE, Michael
   Hey, diddle diddle!: [poems]. Dedicated to the man in the moon. Fortune Press.
1945. [ii], 58 pp. col. il.   IWM

STRICK, John (1918–44. Eldest son of Major-General John Arkwright Strick.
Commissioned in the London Irish Rifles. Served in the Near East and took
part in the invasion of Sicily, being wounded three times during the campaign.
Killed on the Anzio beachhead on 18 February 1944)
   Poems. With a memoir by Harold Nicolson. Percival Marshall. 1948. [vi],
74 pp. por.   OXB

STRICKLAND, Dorothy
 Poems. Ilfracombe: Arthur H. Stockwell, Ltd. [1942]. 16 pp.   OXB

STRINGER, Dorothy
 Make me a mandrake: [poems]. Dulwich Village: Outposts Publications. 1957.
12 pp.   OXB

STRONG, Leonard Alfred George (1896–1958. b. Plympton, Devon.
Educated at Brighton College, and Wadham College, Oxford. Poet of the First
World War, exempted from military service because of a spinal complaint.
Assistant master at Summerfields Preparatory School, Oxford, for twelve years.
Novelist, poet and journalist. Visiting tutor at the Central School of Speech &
Drama. A director of publishers Methuen & Co. Ltd)
 The body's imperfection: the collected poems of L.A.G. Strong. Methuen & Co Ltd.
1957. 164 pp.   OXB

STROUD, Elizabeth
 The collected poetry of Elizabeth Stroud. Printed Regency Press. [1976]. 32 pp.
   OXB

STRUTHER, Jan, pseud. *see* **GRAHAM, Joyce Maxtone**, (Jan Struther,
pseud.)

STUART, Eve, pseud. *see* **NAPIER, Priscilla**, (Eve Stuart, pseud.)

STUART, Patricia Villiers- *see* **VILLIERS-STUART, Patricia**

STUBBS, John Heath- *see* **HEATH-STUBBS, John**

STYLES, Doreen (Educated at St Anne's College, Oxford) *see* 55

STYRING, Harold Knights (Writer on the Styring family)
 Moods, meditations and music: [poems]. Printed Sheffield: Hartley & Son Ltd.
1951. [ii], 68 pp.
  Printed on one side of leaf only.   OXB

STYRING, William, pseud. *see* **WATSON, William Styring**, (William
Styring, pseud.)

SULLY, J. (Corporal. Served with the Eighth Army) *see* 25,44

SULLY, Hal *see* **SUMMERS, Henry Forbes** (Hal)

SUMMERS, Henry Forbes (Hal) (1911– . b. Bradford, Yorkshire. Educated
at Fettes College, Edinburgh, and Trinity College, Oxford. Entered the Civil

Service in 1935. Principal in Ministry of Health, 1940, he joined Ministry of Housing & Local Government in 1951. Under-Secretary, Department of the Environment, 1955–71. Secretary of the Local Government Commission for England, 1961–66. Of Tunbridge Wells, Kent)

Hinterland, [and other poems]; by Hal Summers. J.M. Dent & Sons Ltd. 1947. 59 pp.   MPL

Smoke after flame: poems; by Hal Summers. J.M. Dent & Sons Ltd. 1944. 56 pp.   MPL

see also   51

SUMSION, Peter

Twelve poems. Printed Acme Press. [1951]. [8] pp.

   Title from cover.   OXB

SUNDIUS-SMITH, Basil K.

Sonnets of yesterday and to-day. Hove: Combridges. 1941. 27 pp.   BPL

SUTHERLAND, Robert Garioch, (Robert Garioch, pseud.) (1909–81. b.
Edinburgh. Educated at the Royal High School and Edinburgh University. Conscripted in 1941. A schoolmaster, he worked in the London area, 1946–59, then returned to Edinburgh. Writer-in-Residence, Edinburgh University, 1971–73)

The big music, and other poems; [by] Robert Garioch. Thurso: Caithness Books. [1971]. 54 pp. por. (Modern Scottish poets, 6).   BL

Chuckies on the cairn: poems in Scots and English; by Robert Garioch. Hayes, Kent: Chalmers Press. 1949. [iii], 16 pp.   BL

Collected poems; [by] Robert Garioch. Loanhead, Midlothian: Macdonald Publishers. [1977]. xiv, 208 pp.

   Some poems in Scots dialect.   OXB

Collected poems; [by] Robert Garioch. Paperback [ed.]. Manchester: Carcanet New Press Ltd; Loanhead: Macdonald Publishers. 1980. xiv, 208 pp.

   Some poems in Scots dialect.   OXB

Doktor Faust in Rose Street, [and other poems]; by Robert Garioch. Loanhead, Midlothian: M. Macdonald. 1973. 71 pp. (Lines review editions, 3).

   Some poems in Scots dialect.   BL

Selected poems; by Robert Garioch. With an introduction by Sydney Goodsir Smith. Edinburgh: M. Macdonald. 1966. 104 pp.   OXB

SUTTON, B. (Served in H.M. Forces) *see*   74

SUTTON, Beryl

Think on these things, [and other poems]. Ilfracombe: Arthur H. Stockwell, Ltd. 1946. 40 pp.   OXB

SUTTON, Lawrence
Peace — and war: [*poems*]. Walton-on-Thames: Outposts Publications. 1975.
24 pp.   OXB
A walk through time: [*poems*]. Walton-on-Thames: Outposts Publications.
1975. 24 pp.   OXB

SUTTON, Pamela
Treasures in verse. Ilfracombe: Arthur H. Stockwell, Ltd. 1953. 32 pp.   OXB

SWABEY, Maurice
Beethoven, and other poems. Cambridge: P.R. Macmillan. [1957]. viii, 54 pp.
(Poetry publications).   OXB

SWAIN, Geoffrey (Related to Sir Henry Newbolt)
Miscellaneous poems. With foreword by The Very Revd. The Dean of Exeter.
Printed Exeter: A. Wheaton & Co., Ltd. [1957]. 64 pp.   OXB
Sonnets and other poems. Bristol: Rankin Brothers Ltd. [1951]. 52 pp.   BL

SWAINE, Gordon (1920–   . b. Malaya. Educated at Blundell's School, and
Jesus College, Oxford. Captain, 22nd Light Anti-Aircraft Regiment, Royal
Artillery. Served in North Africa and Italy. After the war worked in publishing
and advertising) *see*   25, 33, 76

SWANNEY, William (Of Viggie, North Ronaldsay, Orkney Islands)
Island musings: [*poems*]. Ilfracombe: Arthur H. Stockwell, Ltd. 1954. 32 pp.
                                                                      OXB

SWEETING, F.M. (Regimental Sergeant-Major, Royal Engineers. Spent the
war at G.H.Q. India) *see*   46

SWIFT, Eric (Of Leicestershire?)
No nursery: poems 1941. Printed Leicester: Blackfriars Press Ltd. [1941]. [ii],
41 pp.   OXB

SWINBANK, Leonard (1915–   . b. Manchester. Spent his early life in the
Settle area of the Yorkshire dales. Served in the Army in India)
Around lakes/dales, and collective verse. Printed Grange-over-Sands: J.
Wadsworth Ltd. [1974]. 65 pp.
    Distributed by E.J. Morten, bookseller, Didsbury, Manchester.   OXB

SWINGLER, Randall (1909–67. Son of the Rector of Cranbrook, Kent.
Educated at Winchester College, and New College, Oxford. A schoolmaster for
some years then became a freelance writer. Reviewer, poet, librettist and
literary editor of the *Daily Worker*. Founder-editor of the magazine *Our Time*.
Called up in 1941, becoming Signaller, then Corporal in the 56th Divisional

Signals. Served in the Middle East and Italy, twice winning the M.M. Lived in Essex latterly)

The years of anger: [poems]. With drawings by James Boswell. Meridian Books Ltd. [1946]. 55 pp. il. (Garrick poets, 1).   IWM
see also   36, 64

SWINY, C.W. (Corporal, Royal Air Force)   *see*   1, 25

SYDDALL, H. (Served in H.M. Forces)   *see*   75

SYLVESTER, Philip. pseud.   *see*   **WORNER, Philip**, (Philip Sylvester, pseud.)

SYMES, Devina (Of Dorset)

Here — at Lulworth, [and other poems]. Printed Weymouth: Sherren & Son Ltd. [1975]. [30] pp. il., por.

Sub-title on cover is *A cascade of poems*.   OXB

SYMES, Gordon Pemberton (1917–   . b. Shropshire. Educated at Worcester College, Oxford. Joined the Army in 1939, first in the infantry then as a Lieutenant in the Intelligence Corps. Served in France, India and the United States. Journalist then writer and editor for various business organizations)

Whither shall I wander?: a sheaf of six poems. Hammersmith: Keepsake Limited Editions. 1959. 11 pp.

A limited ed. of 150 copies.   BL
see also   43, 76

SYMINGTON, S.P. (Captain, Leicestershire Regiment. Captured in Norway in 1940, held prisoner of war in Germany until 1945)   *see*   67

SYMONS, Julian (1912–   . b. London. A company secretary before the war. Editor of the magazine *Twentieth Century Verse*, 1937–39. Served in the Royal Armoured Corps from 1942 until invalided out in 1944. A freelance writer from 1947. Crime novelist, biographer, historian and book reviewer. *Sunday Times* reviewer from 1958. Chairman, Crime Writers Association, 1958–59. Editor of *An Anthology of War Poetry*, 1942)

The second man: poems. Routledge. 1943. 48 pp.

'For Roy Fuller'.   BPL
see also   4, 25, 33, 37, 56, 59, 69, 76, 82

T., A.

Montgomery: or, Legio Octavia in Monte Africano; by A.T. Printed Knapp, Drewett & Sons Ltd. 1943. 27 pp.   OXB

T., A.C.   *see*   **TARBAT, Alan Cecil.** (A.C.T.)

T.B. *see* **B., T.**

T., J.F. (Served on H.M. Transport D.9, Royal Navy) *see* 23

TAILBY, Gwenda M.
The little mouse, and other poems. Ilfracombe: Arthur H. Stockwell, Ltd. [1945]. 15 pp.   OXB

TALBOT, Ethel *see* 84

TALIFER, John, pseud. *see* **McMURDO, Fergus William Hamilton**, (John Talifer, pseud.)

TAMBIMUTTU, M.J. (1915–83. Sinhalese poet and entrepreneurial editor, friend and mentor of many first rank poets. Founded the publishers Poetry London in 1939. In London throughout the war, frequenting pubs in the West End area named 'Fitzrovia' and attracting a wide circle of friends from the world of literature and art, many on leave from the Forces. Editor of the anthology *Poetry in Wartime*, 1942. Founder and organizer of the Indian Arts Council in London)
Out of this war: a poem. Fortune Press. [1941]. 24 pp. por.   BPL
see also 25, 29, 52

TARBAT, Alan Cecil, (A.C.T.) (Served in South-East Asia Command)
The ballad of Buchenwald. Printed Cardiff: Western Mail & Echo Ltd. [1946]. 11 pp.   OXB
England. Begun at Glastonbury, late autumn, 1941. Printed Bristol: J.W. Arrowsmith Ltd. 1942. [8] pp.   OXB
Michaelmas Eve. Winchester: Warren & Son Ltd. [1943]. [6] pp.   BL
Six months of war: [poems]. With a foreword by Sydney Carroll. Printed Bristol: Arrowsmith. 1940. 39 pp.   BPL
see also 35

TATHAM, Silvia
Collected poems. Cambridge: Poetry Publications. [1957]. [iv], 32 pp.   OXB

TATTERSALL, Malcolm Hamilton (Of Bexhill and East Dean, Sussex)
The harp in the green window: [poems]. Fairwarp, Sussex: Peter Russell. 1959 68 pp.   OXB
More poems and translations. Printed Eastbourne: Waynford Press Ltd. [1950]. [180] pp.   BL

TAYLOR, Cecil John (Artist and poet of Seil Island, Oban)
New poems. Seil Island, Oban: Highland Arts Studios. [1975]. 16 pp. por.
                                                                                   OXB

TAYLOR, George (1931–)
Terminus, [*and other poems*]. Ilfracombe: Arthur H. Stockwell Ltd. 1974. 67 pp.
OXB

TAYLOR, George Albert (1914– . b. St Leonards, Sussex. Worked in local government before the war. Joined the Royal Air Force in 1941, serving as a Sergeant in India from 1943. In educational administration after the war)
Jacob's ladder: [*poems*]. Ilfracombe: Arthur H. Stockwell, Ltd. [1942]. 46 pp.
OXB
see also 43, 76

TAYLOR, Ivy (Of Surrey) *see* 70, 71

TAYLOR, Leonard (1900– . b. London. Poet of the First World War. Writer on aircraft and flying. Editor of *Air Review*, 1935–39, *Air Reserve Gazette*, 1939, and *Synopsis*, 1944–46)
The trackless way: poems. Air League of the British Empire. [1941]. 32 pp. il.
IWM
Wings of youth: poems. Rolls House Publishing Co. Ltd. 1957. 112 pp.
OXB

TAYLOR, Phyllis Mary (1906– . b. Gainsborough, Lincolnshire. Educated at King Edward VI Girls' Grammar School, Louth, Sheffield Training College and London University Institute of Education. A school teacher from 1929 to 1965. Served in the Auxiliary Territorial Service, 1939–45. Taught in Canada post-war including three years in the Arctic Circle. Of Byfield, Northamptonshire)
Cherry petals, and other poems. Walton-on-Thames: Outposts Publications. 1974. 28 pp.
OXB

TAYLOR, R.N.
Poems of the past and future. Ilfracombe: Arthur H. Stockwell, Ltd. 1947. 16 pp.
OXB

TAYLOR, Rex (1921– . b. Brindle, Lancashire. Educated at Wheelton and Silverdale Elementary Schools. A civil engineer. Writer on Irish topics)
Poems. Hutchinson. 1959. 77 pp.
MPL

TAYLOR, W.A. (Of Kent) *see* 74

TEICHMAN, Dennis Patrick (Major, 4th Battalion, Wiltshire Regiment)
These I have written: some verses. [Privately printed]. 1944. 23 pp.
OXB

TEMPEST, Peter (Translator from the Russian)
First poems. Lawrence & Wishart. 1957. 48 pp.
OXB

TEMPLE, John (1942–   )
The ridge: [poems]. Ferry Press. 1973. 32 pp.
 A limited ed. of 400 copies of which twenty-six lettered A–Z are signed and contain an additional holograph poem.   MPL

TEMPLE, Margaret F.
Promise of peace, and other poems. Ilfracombe: Arthur H. Stockwell, Ltd. [1943]. 16 pp.   OXB

TENNANT, John (Wounded at Tobruk in June 1942, becoming a prisoner of war)
Verses. [Privately printed]. [1963]. [32] pp.   IWM

TESSIMOND, Arthur Seymour John (1902–62. b. Birkenhead, Cheshire. Educated at Charterhouse and Liverpool University. Worked as a schoolmaster and a bookseller. From 1928 an advertising copywriter in London. Rejected as medically unfit for war service)
Morning meeting: poems. Introduced by Hubert Nicholson. Autolycus Publications. [1980]. 64 pp. por., facsim.   OXB

THEOBALD, Albert Edward (b. Lincoln)
Old vacant chair, and other poems. Ilfracombe: Arthur H. Stockwell, Ltd. 1954. 24 pp.   OXB

THEODOSIUS, pseud. *see* **RUSSELL, Henry T.**, (Theodosius, pseud).

THIRTY-FIVE ANONYMOUS ODES. Fortune Press. 1944. 32 pp.
                                                                    OXB

THOMAS, Denis (Served in South-East Asia Command) *see* 35

THOMAS, Dylan (1914–53. b. Swansea. Educated at Swansea Grammar School. Worked for a time as a reporter on the *South Wales Evening Post*. Established as a poet before the war. Rejected for military service on medical grounds. Poet, story writer and broadcaster. Wrote propoganda film scripts during the war. Died while on a visit to the United States)
Collected poems, 1934–1952. J.M. Dent & Sons Ltd. 1942. xiv, 178 pp. por.
                                                                    BL
Collected poems, 1934–1952. Dent. 1966. xvi, 172 pp. (Everyman's library).
                                                                    MPL
Deaths and entrances: poems. J.M. Dent & Sons Ltd. 1946. 66 pp.   OXB
Miscellany three: poems and stories. Dent. 1978. [vi], 119 pp. (Everyman's library). (Everyman paperbacks).   BL
Miscellany two: A visit to Grandpa's, and other stories and poems. J.M. Dent & Sons Ltd. 1966. vi, 117 pp. (Aldine paperbacks).   OXB

Miscellany two: A visit to Grandpa's, and other stories and poems. Hardbound ed. J.M. Dent & Sons Ltd. 1973. vi, 117 pp.   OXB

New poems. Norfolk, Connecticut: New Directions. [1943]. [30] pp. (The poets of the year).   OXB

The poems. Edited with an introduction and notes by Daniel Jones. J.M. Dent & Sons Ltd. 1971. xx, 291 pp.   MPL

The poems. Edited with an introduction and notes by Daniel Jones. Revised ed. J.M. Dent & Sons Ltd. 1974. xx, 291 pp.   MPL

The poems. Edited with an introduction by Daniel Jones. New paperback ed. J.M. Dent & Sons Ltd. 1978. xx, 291 pp.   OXB

The poems of Dylan Thomas. Edited with an introduction by Daniel Jones. New York: New Directions Publishing Corporation. 1971. xx, 291 pp. (New directions books).   OXB

Poesie, con testo a fronte. Traduzione introduzione e note di Roberto Sanesi. Parma: Guanda. 1962. 211 pp. (Collezione Fenice).

   Parallel English and Italian texts.   OXB

[*Selected poems*]; [by] Andrew Young [and] Dylan Thomas. Longmans. 1967. [iv], 28 pp. il. (Longmans poetry library).

   Not joint authorship. No war poetry by Young.   OXB

Selected poems. Edited with an introduction and notes by Walford Davies. J.M. Dent & Sons Ltd. 1974. viii, 136 pp.   OXB

Selected writings of Dylan Thomas. Introduction by John L. Sweeney. New York: James Laughlin. [1946]. xxiv, 184 pp. por. (New directions books).   OXB

Twenty-six poems. J.M. Dent & Sons Ltd. [1949]. 78 pp.

   A limited ed. of 150 copies, ten copies on Japanese vellum, numbered I to X and 140 copies on hand-made paper, numbered 11 to 60, all signed by the author.   BL

see also   3, 15, 25, 26, 28, 30, 37, 56, 57, 58, 68, 76, 82, 83

THOMAS, Gilbert (1891–1978. Educated at Wyggeston School, Leicester, and The Leys School, Cambridge. On the editorial staff of publishers Chapman & Hall, 1910–14. Poet of the First World War, imprisoned as a pacifist. Editor of *The Venturer*, 1919–21. Author and journalist. Lived at Chilwell, Nottingham)

Collected poems. Newton Abbot: David & Charles; George Allen & Unwin Ltd. [1969]. 206 pp.   OXB

THOMAS, Howard J.

Everyday thoughts: [*poems*]. Bognor Regis: New Horizon. [1979]. [iv], 54 pp.
                              OXB

THOMAS, Lilian Bryne-   *see*   **BRYNE-THOMAS, Lilian**

THOMAS, P.A.A. (Lance-Corporal. Served with the Eighth Army in the Western Desert) *see*   46

THOMAS, Robert Dalzell Dillon (1922–44. Educated at Sherborne School, and Hertford College, Oxford. Served as a Lieutenant in the Grenadier Guards in Italy. Killed in action near Florence on the night of 2–3 August 1944)

The note-book of a Lieutenant in the Italian campaign. [Privately printed]. [1946]. [iv], 38 pp.

Poems, jottings and quotations. 'Profits of sale will be given to a war charity'. BPL

THOMAS, Ronald Stuart (1915– . b. Cardiff. Educated at the University of Wales, and St Michael's College, Llandaff. Ordained deacon in 1936, priest in 1937. Held various church appointments in Wales. Vicar of St Hywyn, Aberdaron, with St Mary, Bodferin, from 1967. Poet, literary critic, and writer of children's fiction)

An acre of land: [*poems*]. Newtown: Montgomeryshire Printing Co. Ltd. 1952. [ii], 38 pp. OXB

The bread of truth: [*poems*]. Rupert Hart-Davis. 1963. 48 pp. OXB

Pietà, [*and other poems*]. Rupert Hart-Davis. 1966. 45 pp. OXB

[*Selected poems*]; [by] Lawrence Durrell, Elizabeth Jennings, R.S. Thomas. Harmondsworth, Middlesex: Penguin Books. 1962. 128 pp. (Penguin modern poets, 1).

Not joint authorship. No war poetry by Durrell or Jennings. MPL

[*Selected poems*]. Longmans. [1969]. [ii], 30 pp. (Longmans' poetry library). OXB

Song at the year's turning: poems 1942–1954. With an introduction by John Betjeman. Rupert Hart-Davis. 1955. 115 pp. OXB

The stones of the field: [*poems*]. Carmarthen: Druid Press Ltd. 1946. 49 pp. OXB

THOMAS, Sir William Beach (1886–1957. Educated at Shrewsbury School, and Christ Church, Oxford. President of Oxford University Athletic Club. War correspondent for the *Daily Mail*. A regular contributor to *The Observer* and *Spectator*)

The poems of a countryman. Michael Joseph Ltd. 1945. 72 pp. OXB

THOMLINSON, W.J.

Scenes from the sidelines: [*poems*]. Ilfracombe: Arthur H. Stockwell, Ltd. [1969]. 95 pp. OXB

THOMPSON, Donald (Spent most of the war years on active service overseas)

Spring sacrifice: poems. John Lane the Bodley Head. 1945. 43 pp. BPL

THOMPSON, Edward (1886–1946. b. Cumberland. Educated at Kingswood School and Richmond College. An educational missionary at Bankura College,

Bengal, 1910–22. Poet of the First World War. Chaplain to the Forces serving in Mesopotamia, 1916–17, and Palestine, 1918. Awarded the M.C. and mentioned in despatches. Fellow of Oriel College, Oxford, and lecturer in Bengali. Novelist and poet, editor of the Augustan Books of Poetry)

New recessional, and other poems. Secker & Warburg. 1942. 40 pp.   OXB

100 poems. Oxford University Press. 1944. x, 110 pp.   OXB

see also   2, 7, 42, 51, 80

THOMPSON, Eric

"Empire King", and other poems. Ilfracombe: Arthur H. Stockwell, Ltd. [1944]. 31 pp.   OXB

THOMPSON, Frank (1920–44. b. Darjeeling, India, son of the First World War poet Edward Thompson. Educated at Winchester College, and New College, Oxford. Served in the Royal Artillery and on Special Duties. Major with G.H.Q. Liaison (Phantom) Regiment. Fought in the desert campaign and the Sicily landings. Parachuted into Serbia to help the Bulgarian Partisan Army. Captured and publicly executed on 10 June 1944) *see*   20, 57, 76

THOMPSON, James Alan (Joined the Royal Marines in October 1939. Held a commission, serving in Norway, Egypt, Ceylon, India and the Far East)

Military honours, [and other poems]. Fortune Press. 1946. 56 pp.   IWM

see also   49

THOMPSON, James Matthew (1878–1956. b. Iron Acton Rectory, Gloucestershire. Educated at Winchester College, and Christ Church, Oxford. Fellow of Magdalen College, 1904–38. Dean of Divinity, 1906–15. Temporary master at Eton College, 1917–19. Held various university appointments at Oxford and Cambridge. Writer on French history)

Collected verse, 1939–1946. Oxford: Basil Blackwell. 1947. viii, 175 pp.

MPL

My apologia; by J.M.T. Printed Oxford: Alden Press. 1940. 112 pp.

A limited ed. of 100 numbered copies printed for private circulation only.

OXB

THOMPSON, Motson (A clergyman of Ramsgate, Kent)

This is the life for me: [poems]. Ilfracombe: Arthur H. Stockwell Ltd. [1962]. 12 pp.   OXB

THOMS, Edward (Served in the Western Desert) *see*   63

THOMSON, David Cleghorn (1900–   . Scottish playwright, and writer on industrial management)

The hidden path: poems 1922–1942. With a drawing by Michael Ayrton. Glasgow: William Maclellan. 1943. 79 pp. il.   OXB

THOMSON, Elizabeth McLean (1900–77. b. Paisley into the McNair family of grocers. Educated at Paisley Grammar School and the School of Domestic Science in Glasgow)

Complete poems. Paisley: [Privately printed]. 1979. [iv], 64 pp.　　　OXB

THOMSON, Ella Wells

Of common things: [poems]. Mitre Press. [1956]. 29 pp.　　　OXB

THOMSON, Geddes

A spurious grace: [poems]. Walton-on-Thames: Outposts Publications. 1980. 28 pp.　　　OXB

THOMSON, Hilda Trevelyan-　*see*　**TREVELYAN-THOMSON, Hilda**

THOMSON, P. (Served in the Royal Air Force)

War-time thoughts and impressions: some poems. Ilfracombe: Arthur H. Stockwell, Ltd. [1944]. 16 pp.　　　OXB

THORNE, Ann D.H. (1927–45. Daughter of a judge. Died ten months after leaving school)

Thoughts and fancies: [poems]. Fortune Press. 1947. 20 pp. por.　　　OXB

THORNE, Robert Henry (1920–43. Joined the Royal Navy in 1941, commissioned in 1942, serving on H.M.S. *Harvester*. Reported missing, presumed killed, on 1 March 1943)

Poems. Bristol: J.W. Arrowsmith Ltd. 1944. 56 pp. por.　　　OXB

THORNTON, Katherine (A professional artist. Painted portraits, flowers and landscapes, exhibiting at the Royal Academy)

Poems for thine entertainment! Ilfracombe: Arthur H. Stockwell Ltd. [1943]. 64 pp.　　　OXB

Poems of charm and mirth. Ilfracombe: Arthur H. Stockwell, Ltd. [1942]. 40 pp.　　　OXB

THORNTON, P.A. (Of London)　*see*　74

THORPE, Henry John

The last trip, and other poems. Ilfracombe: Arthur H. Stockwell Ltd. 1956. 16 pp.　　　OXB

THURTLE, R.F. (Died during the war, probably before 1943)

War-time verse, and earlier poems. Bristol: Arrowsmith. 1942. 48 pp.　　　IWM

THWAITES, Michael (1915–70. b. Brisbane, Australia. Educated at Geelong Grammar School, and New College, Oxford. Newdigate Prizewinner and Rhodes Scholar for Victoria. Lieutenant, Royal Navy, 1939–45. Awarded

King's Medal for Poetry, 1940. Lecturer in English at Melbourne University, 1947–49. Commonwealth civil servant from 1950)

The Jervis Bay, and other poems. Putnam & Co. Ltd. [1943]. viii, 59 pp.

MPL

Poems of war and peace. Pinner, Middlesex: Grosvenor Books. 1970. [viii], 62 pp. OXB

see also 23

TILLER, Terence (1916–   . b. Truro, Cornwall. Educated at Latymer Upper School, and Jesus College, Cambridge, receiving the Chancellor's Medal for English Verse in 1936. Lecturer in English at King Fuad I University, Cairo, 1939–45. Writer-producer, B.B.C. Drama Department, 1946–76. Poet, playwright, freelance writer and broadcaster)

The inward animal: [poems]. Hogarth Press. 1943. 60 pp. (New Hogarth library, XII). MPL

Poems. Hogarth Press. 1941. 63 pp. (New Hogarth library, V). BL

Unarm, Eros: [poems]. Hogarth Press. 1947. 55 pp. (New Hogarth library, XVI). IWM

see also 3, 15, 25, 40, 56, 57, 76

TILLEY, Harold Hugh (1910–   . Educated at Halesowen Grammar School and Birmingham University. Joined the Royal Corps of Signals in 1940, transferring to the Army Educational Corps in 1941. Served in India. Teacher, lecturer, author and journalist) *see* 43, 76

TINDALL, Daisy (Of Aberdeenshire) *see* 74

TIPTON, David (1934–   . b. Birmingham. Did two years national service in Malaya. Taught English in Argentina and Peru, 1960–70. Poet, biographer and translator. Of Sheffield)

Millstone grit: [poems]. Cardiff: Second Aeon Publications. [1972]. 28 pp.

OXB

Poems in transit. Dulwich: Outposts Publications. 1960. 12 pp. MPL

TITTERTON, William Richard (1876–1963. As a young man he drifted from job to job, hoping to reach Fleet Street. A self-described tramp, he wandered through France and Germany. An artists' model in London and Paris, posing for Jacob Epstein. Poet of the First World War. Author and journalist working for several leading newspapers and magazines. Received into the Roman Catholic Church in 1931, shortly afterwards joining the staff of the *Universe*)

London pride, and poems for the Forces, families and friends. Douglas Organ. 1944. [ii], 58 pp. IWM

Poems for the Forces. T. Werner Laurie Ltd. 1943. [ii], 57 pp. BPL

TOD, Andrew (1922–43. b. Scotland. Educated at Wellington College, and Magdalene College, Cambridge. Commissioned in the Royal Scots Fusiliers. Accidentally killed during training on 24 November 1943)

The end of the day: poems; by Keith Foottit and Andrew Tod. Edited, with an introduction by Michael Meyer. Fortune Press. [1948]. 51 pp. por.

Not joint authorship.   OXB
see also   20, 53

TODD, Kenneth B. (Served overseas in H.M. Forces)

"A passing glance": Poems. Ilfracombe: Arthur H. Stockwell, td. 1946. 31 pp.
    OXB

TODD, Ruthven (1914–78. b. Edinburgh. Educated at Fettes College and Edinburgh College of Art. A sub-editor of *New Verse* in the 1930s. Farmed in the Western Isles of Scotland. Author, critic, poet and lecturer. Became an American citizen. Moved to Majorca, Spain)

The acreage of the heart: [*poems*]. Glasgow: William Maclellan. 1944. 32 pp. col. il. (by John Maxwell). (Poetry Scotland series).   OXB

Garland for the winter solstice: selected poems. J.M. Dent & Sons Ltd. 1961. 160 pp.   OXB

The planet in my hand: twelve poems. Printed Chiswick Press. 1944. vi, 18 pp.

A limited ed. of fifty copies privately printed for Mavis de Vere Cole and the author.   BL

The planet in my hand: poems. Grey Walls Press. 1946. 80 pp.   OXB

Ten poems. Printed Edinburgh: T. & A. Constable Ltd. 1940. [16] pp.

A limited ed. of 150 numbered copies.   BPL

Until now: poems. Fortune Press. 1942. 52 pp.   BPL
see also   4, 25, 56, 65, 69, 76, 85

TODHUNTER, John Reginald

Occasional verses. Birmingham: Cornish Brothers Ltd. [1950]. 16 pp.
    OXB

TOMALIN, Ruth (b. Piltown, County Kilkenny, Ireland. Educated at Chichester High School, and King's College, London. Served in the Women's Land Army, 1941–42. A staff reporter on various newspapers, 1942–65, freelance press reporter at London Law Courts from 1966. Novelist, poet, biographer, writer on natural history and writer of children's stories)

Threnody for dormice, and other poems. Fortune Press. 1947. 24 pp.   IWM

TONG, Raymond (1922– . b. Winchester. Educated at London University. Served as Aircraftman in the Royal Air Force. British Council representative in the United Kingdom and abroad in Argentina, Iraq, India and Kuwait. Worked for the Overseas Education Service in Nigeria and Uganda, 1949–61. Poet and anthologist)

Angry decade: poems (1940–1950). Fortune Press. [1951]. 46 pp.   OXB
Crossing the border: poems. Hodder & Stoughton. [1978]. 78 pp.   OXB
Requiem for the war dead, and other poems. Fortune Press. 1942. 16 pp.
   'To Herbert Read'.   BPL
To-day the sun, and other poems. Fortune Press. 1946. 24 pp.   OXB
see also   1, 25, 49

TONKINSON, Frank (Educated in Somerset. Became a journalist in Ipswich.
Served with the Royal Electrical & Mechanical Engineers. While taking part in
the Northern European campaign sent his own private but officially authorized
despatches to *The Star* newspaper, East Anglia)
   Life is what it makes you: [poems]. [Ipswich]: [Author]. [1974]. 36 pp. por.
                                                                      OXB

TOOSEY, Catherine Brewster (b. North of England. Lived in Canada for two
years, returning to England for the war. Published short stories, articles and
poems in British and American magazines. Won first prize in an American
poetry competition. Encouraged by Walter De La Mare and Richard Church,
turned entirely to verse. Lived in Guildford, Surrey)
   Colour symphony: poems. Billericay: Grey Walls Press. 1941. [vi], 29 pp.
                                                                      OXB
   Unity. [Guildford]: [Author]. [1962?]. iv, 62 pp. (New narrative poetry
series, VI).   MPL

TOPHAM, F.B. (Major, Royal Artillery. Captured in Greece in 1941, held
prisoner of war in Germany until 1945) *see*   67

TOVEY, J.R. (Of Yorkshire) *see*   73

TOWER, Christopher
   A distant fluting: poems and sonnets. Illustrations by Roland Pym. Weidenfeld &
Nicolson. [1977]. [iv], 800 pp. il.   OXB

TOWNSEND, Flora (Of Lincolnshire) *see*   74

TOWNSEND, John Rowe (1922–   . b. Leeds, Yorkshire. Educated at Leeds
Grammar School, and Emmanuel College, Cambridge. Served as Flight
Sergeant, Royal Air Force, in the Middle East and Italy, 1942–46. Went up to
Cambridge after the war. Journalist on *Manchester Guardian Weekly*, 1949–69.
Children's book editor of *The Guardian*, 1968–78. Writer of children's fiction and
critic of children's literature) *see*   76

TOWNSHEND, Frank
   Hell: [poems]. Halcyon Press. 1955. 125 pp.   OXB

TOYNBEE, Lawrence (Son of Professor Arnold Toynbee. Served in the Army) *see* 38

TRAPNELL, N.J. (Served in the Western Desert) *see* 63

TREADWELL, J.E. (Served in H.M. Forces) *see* 74

TREE, E.E. *see* 22

TREECE, Henry (1912–66. b. Wednesbury, Staffordshire. Educated at Wednesbury Grammar School and Birmingham University, where he was captain of boxing. A grammar school master before the war. Flight-Lieutenant, Royal Air Force. Served in Intelligence, 1941–46. A leader of the New Apocalypse movement. Co-editor of the anthology *Air Force Peotry*, 1944. Novelist, poet, writer of short stories and radio verse-dramas)

The black seasons: [*poems*]. Faber & Faber. 1945. 92 pp.   BPL
The haunted garden, [*and other poems*]. Faber & Faber. 1947. 94 pp.
                                                                               MPL
Invitation and warning, [*and other poems*]. Faber & Faber Ltd. 1942. 96 pp.
                                                                               MPL
38 poems. Fortune Press. [1940]. 32 pp.   OXB
see also 1, 11, 15, 25, 33, 42, 51, 56, 65, 76, 79, 82, 86

TREMAYNE, Sydney Durward (1912– . b. Ayr, within a short distance of Robert Burns's cottage at Alloway. Educated at Ayr Academy. A journalist, working successively on *Daily Mirror, Daily Herald* and *The Sun*)

For whom there is no spring, [*and other poems*]. Pendulum Publications. 1946. 24 pp. (Pendulum poets, 2).   BL
The hardest freedom, [*and other poems*]. Collins. 1951. 63 pp.   OXB
Selected and new poems. Chatto & Windus. 1973. 96 pp.   MPL
The swans of Berwick, [*and other poems*]. Chatto & Windus; Hogarth Press. 1962. 48 pp. (Phoenix living poets).   MPL
Time and the wind: [*poems*]. Collins. 1948. 64 pp.   OXB
see also 14, 82

TRENCH, Maxwell Chenevix *see* **CHENEVIX TRENCH, Maxwell**

TRENCH, Robert Power, Lord Ashtown (1897–1966. Educated at Eton College. Served in the First World War as Lieutenant, 3rd Battalion, Royal West Surrey Regiment. Lived in County Tipperary)

Poems; by Lord Ashtown. Printed [Dublin]: Dolmen Press Ltd. 1965. 56 pp. Privately printed in a limited ed. of 250 copies.   OXB

TRENEER, Anne (1891– . b. Gorran, Cornwall. Educated at St Austell

Grammar School, University College, Exeter, and Lady Margaret Hall, Oxford. Biographer of Sir Humphry Davy)

This world's bliss, [and other poems]. Birmingham: Cornish Brothers Ltd. 1942. [vi], 22 pp.   **OXB**

TRENWITH, John Ballantyne (Of Warwickshire?)

"Grim and gay": a selection of war-time verse. Printed Leamington Spa: Courier Press. [1945?]. [vi], 38 pp.   **IWM**

TREVELYAN, Robert Calverley (1872–1951. Son of Sir George Otto Trevelyan. Educated at Harrow School, and Trinity College, Cambridge. Poet, playwright and translator from Greek and Latin)

Aftermath: [poems]. Hogarth Press. 1941. 92 pp.   **OXB**

see also 2

TREVELYAN-THOMSON, Hilda (Of London)

Our finest hour, and other verses. Foreword by Sir Cyril Norwood. Printed Middlesbrough: Wm Appleyard & Sons Ltd. [1943]. 36 pp.   **BPL**

see also 75

TREVOR, Joan

The enchanted wood, and other poems. Ilfracombe: Arthur H. Stockwell, Ltd. 1961. 52 pp.   **OXB**

TRIBBLE, William James

The peerless life, and other poems. Ilfracombe: Arthur H. Stockwell, Ltd. [1954]. 192 pp.   **OXB**

TRIM, Douglas (Served with the Royal Air Force in the Middle East and India)

The reality of stars, [and other poems]. Walton-on-Thames: Outposts Publications. 1973. 28 pp.   **OXB**

TRIPP, John (1927– . b. Bargoed, Glamorgan. Educated at Whitchurch Senior School, Cardiff, and Morley College, London. B.B.C. news researcher and sub-editor, 1951–58. Press Officer at Indonesian Embassy, London, 1958–67. Appointed Information Officer at Central Office of Information in 1967. Poet and literary editor)

Collected poems, 1958–78. Swansea: Christopher Davies. 1978. 128 pp.

    OXB

The loss of ancestry, [and other poems]. Llandybie, Carmarthenshire: Christopher Davies. 1969. 57 pp.   **OXB**

The province of belief: selected poems, 1965–1970. Llandybie, Carmarthenshire: Christopher Davies. 1971. 65 pp.   **OXB**

TROTT, F.H.
Crossroads of courage: [*poems*]. [Glasgow]: [United Publishing Co.]. [1944]. 24 pp. (Scoop books). OXB

TROUT, E.K.
Music of meditation: [*poems*]. Arthur H. Stockwell, Ltd. [1940]. 16 pp.   OXB

TRUDGETT, Richard W. (Served in H.M. Forces)
In a time of assassins: [*poems*]. Fortune Press. [1945?]. 32 pp.   BPL
Lost soldier, lost town, and other poems. Fortune Press. 1945. 32 pp.   BPL
see also 49

TRUELOVE, Frederick
Recall and reflect: poems. Ilfracombe: Arthur H. Stockwell. 1974. 155 pp.   OXB

TUCKER, Norman (1894–   . b. Swansea. A journalist in Canada on *Toronto Evening Telegram*, 1917–21. Novelist, Welsh historian, and writer of radio plays for children. Of Colwyn Bay, North Wales)
Maple and oak: verses written in Canada and the old country. 2nd ed. Printed Colwyn Bay: James Craig & Co. 1953. 36 pp.
    Sub-title on cover is *A collection of verses*. [1st ed. published pre-war]
OXB
Verses. Llandudno: Llandudno Advertiser, Ltd. 1941. 4 pp.
    Title from cover.   BL
Verses. [Privately printed?]. [1952]. [8] pp.
    Title from cover.   OXB

TUCKETT, Derek Fothergill (b. Sussex. Educated at St Paul's School, West Kensington. Served in the Royal Air Force)
Mindstream: 12 selected poems. Leicester: Golden Eagle Press. [1969]. 16 pp. por. (Golden Eagle pocket gems).   OXB

TUDOR-OWEN, Patrick (Educated at St Paul's School. A journalist. Leading Aircraftman, Royal Air Force. Served in Burma where he edited *The Jungle Times* for the 14th Army and his Group)
Patterns and poems. Fortune Press. 1944. 47 pp.   OXB
see also 43

TUNNARD, Patricia M. (Of Lincolnshire) *see* 74

TURLEY, B.
"Came the call". Illustrated by Margot Guild. Dundee: Valentine & Sons, Ltd. [1942]. 10 pp. il.   OXB

TURNBULL, Dora Amy, (Patricia Wentworth, pseud.) (1878–1961. b.

Mussoorie, India, daughter of Lieutenant-General Sir Edmund Roche Elles. Educated at Blackheath High School and privately. Married Lieutenant-Colonel George Dillon, who died in 1906, then Lieutenant-Colonel George Oliver Turnbull. Writer of mystery fiction and creator of the fictional character Miss Silver. Lived at Camberley, Surrey)

Beneath the hunter's moon: poems; by Patricia Wentworth. Hodder & Stoughton Ltd. 1945. 128 pp.   OXB

The pool of dreams: poems; by Patricia Wentworth. 1953. 136 pp.   OXB

TURNER, Irene P. *see* 22

TURNER, Marie R. (Of London) *see* 75

TURNER, Marjorie Dalton (Novelist)
The forest, and other poems. Saint Catherine Press Ltd. 1953. x, 90 pp.

OXB

TURNER, Vic *see* 28

TURNER, Walter James (1889–1946. b. Melbourne, Australia. Educated at Scotch College, Melbourne, and in Munich and Vienna. Came to London at the age of seventeen. Travelled in South Africa, Germany, Austria and Italy, 1910–14. Poet of the First World War. Served as Lieutenant, Royal Garrison Artillery, 1916–18. Music critic for *New Statesman*, 1916–40, drama critic for *London Mercury*, 1919–23, literary editor for *Daily Herald*, 1920–23, then for *Spectator*. Poet, novelist and critic)

Fossils of a future time?: [*poems*]. Oxford University Press. 1946. xiv, 143 pp.

OXB

see also 15

TURTON, Godfrey Edmund (1901– . Member of editorial staff of *Truth*, 1937–54. Lexicographer, *Oxford Latin Dictionary*, Clarendon Press, 1954–71. Novelist and historian. Of Oxford)

Mainly truth: [*poems*]. Truth Publishing Co. Ltd. 1941. 54 pp.   OXB

Truth prevails: [*poems*]. Truth Publishing Co. Ltd. 1946. 80 pp.   OXB

TURVEY, H. (Served in H.M. Forces) *see* 75

TUSHONE, W., pseud. *see* **TUSON, William Frederick**, (W. Tushone, pseud.)

TUSON, William Frederick, (W. Tushone, pseud.)
Strange stories in verse: narrative poems; by W. Tushone. Southend-on-Sea: Citizen Publishing Co. Ltd. 1963. 120 pp.   OXB

TWELVE, Dr. I.Q., pseud. (Anon. poet of the First World War)
Fifty years on: [*poems*]; by Dr. I.Q. Twelve. Ilfracombe: Arthur H. Stockwell, Ltd. [1965]. 120 pp. il.   OXB

TWEMLOW, Reginald
Poems. Ilfracombe: Arthur H. Stockwell, Ltd. [1961]. 80 pp.   OXB

TWYSDEN, Sir Anthony Roger Duncan (1918–46. Educated at Eton College. Lieutenant, Royal Irish Fusiliers. Captured in France in 1940, held prisoner of war in Germany until 1945) *see* 67

ULOTH, Alexander Wilmot (Childhood spent in the Cotswolds and London. Served in the First World War as a doctor on the western front. In September 1939 he was called up from the Territorial Army Reserve)
A coat of many colours: [*poems*]. Regency Press. [1970]. 76 pp.   OXB

UNDERDOWN, Audrey (A young girl in the war)
"15 years!": a book of verse. Arthur H. Stockwell. [1941]. 20 pp. por.
                                                                          OXB

URQUHART, James
The yellow door, and other poems. Glasgow: William Maclellan. 1954. 79 pp.
                                                                          OXB

URWICK, Hilary
21 poems. Fortune Press. 1944. 30 pp.   IWM

V., pseud.
The holy war, with elegiac verses; by V. Ilfracombe: Arthur H. Stockwell. [1942]. 72 pp.   OXB

V.H.F. *see* **F., V.H.**

VALBER, Joy
Collection of poems, written in hospital. Ilfracombe: Arthur H. Stockwell, Ltd. [1942]. 16 pp.   OXB

VALLINS, George Henry (–1956. Educated at Beckenham County School, and King's College, London. Taught at Wreight's School, Faversham, Kent, 1917–19, and for many years at Selhurst Grammar School, Croydon. Anthologist and writer on English language)
Sincere flattery: parodies from 'Punch': [*poems*]. Epworth Press. 1954. 116 pp. il.
                                                                          OXB
see also 23

VALLON, Katharine de Jacobi Du *see* **DU VALLON, Katharine de Jacobi**

VAN DEN BOGAERDE, Derek, (Dirk Bogarde, pseud.) (1921– . Educated at University College School, and Allan Glen's School. Served in the Queen's Royal Regiment, 1940–46, in Europe and the Far East, and in Air Photographic Intelligence. Film actor from 1947. Novelist and autobiographer. Of Grasse, South of France) *see* 76

VANSITTART, Robert Gilbert, Lord Vansittart (1881–1957. Educated at Eton College. Entered the Diplomatic Service, holding posts in Paris, Teheran, Cairo and Stockholm. Poet of the First World War. Principal Private Secretary to the Prime Minister, 1928–30. Chief Diplomatic Adviser to the Foreign Secretary, 1938–41)
Green and grey: collected poems. Hutchinson & Co. Ltd. 1944. 216 pp.   IWM
[*Selected poems*]. Eyre & Spottiswoode. [1943]. 32 pp. (Augustan poets).
OXB

see also 7, 38, 42, 84

VAN WART, Reginald Bramley (Writer on British rule in India) *see* 80

VARCOE, J.M. (Of London) *see* 75

VARCOE, J. Mitford
London 1940, and other war verse; by Joan Mary and J. Mitford Varcoe. Houghton & Sons Ltd. 1945. 39 pp. il.   IWM

VARCOE, Joan Mary
London 1940, and other war verse; by Joan Mary and J. Mitford Varcoe. Houghton & Sons Ltd. 1945. 39 pp. il.   IWM

VAUGHAN-WILLIAMS, Miles *see* 52

VAUGHAN WILLIAMS, Ursula, (Ursula Wood) (1911– . b. Malta. Educated privately in England and Brussels. Married twice, in 1933 to Michael Forrester Wood who died in 1942, and in 1953 to the composer Ralph Vaughan Williams who died in 1958. Novelist, poet, biographer and librettist. Wrote libretti for the operas and choral works of twenty-two composers including Anthony Milner, Elizabeth Lutyens, Malcolm Williamson and Ralph Vaughan Williams. Of London)
Fall of leaf: [*poems*]; by Ursula Wood. Oxford: Basil Blackwell. 1943. viii, 30 pp.   OXB
No other choice: [*poems*]; by Ursula Wood. Oxford: Basil Blackwell. 1941. [viii], 47 pp.   OXB
see also 68

VAWSER, Moira O'Callaghan (Served in the Auxiliary Territorial Service) *see* 62

VENABLES, Florence Mary (Of Bognor Regis, Sussex)
Ode to England, and other poems. Printed Bognor Regis: Southern Post, Ltd. [1945]. [16] pp.   BL
    Songs of Sussex: [poems]. Printed Bognor Regis: *The Southern Post*. [1951]. 18 pp.
    Title from cover.   OXB

VENABLES, Roger (1911– . b. Varna, Bulgaria. Educated at Christ Church, Oxford. Served in the Army. Lecturer at Army College, Welbeck, 1946–52, and at College of Further Education, St Annes, Lancashire, 1956–76. Poet and biographer)
    Bari. Printed Lytham: Harris Printers Ltd. [1975]. 28 pp.   IWM
    A poet in two places: [poems]. Lytham: Harris Printers Ltd. [1975]. 20 pp.
    Title from cover.   IWM

VICKERS, Ambrose (Poetry medallist. Of Bootle, Liverpool)
    Poems for everybody, including, A new national anthem. Bootle, Liverpool: Author. [1953]. [ii], 97 pp.   OXB

VICKERS, Donovan (Of Surrey) *see* 75

VICKERS, Marion (Of Surrey) *see* 75

VICKERS, Ray (Of Brackley, Northamptonshire)
    Wood chippings, [and other poems]. Birmingham: Cornish Brothers Ltd. 1945. [vi], 65 pp.   OXB

VILLIERS-STUART, Patricia
    I the I, [and other poems]. Fortune Press. [1951]. 95 pp.   OXB

VINCENT, Stanley
    Poems of the present era. Ilfracombe: Arthur H. Stockwell, Ltd. [1941]. 20 pp.
    OXB

W., R.W.F. (Served in South-East Asia Command) *see* 35

WADDINGTON, Lily
    Passing thoughts: a booklet of verse. Ilfracombe: Arthur H. Stockwell, Ltd. 1945. 19 pp.   OXB

WADDINGTON-FEATHER, John (1933– . b. Keighley, Yorkshire. Educated at Keighley Grammar School and Leeds University. Commissioned in the Intelligence Corps gaining his 'wings' as a paratrooper. Schoolmaster at

Wakeman School, Shrewsbury. Ordained in the Anglican ministry in 1977. Poet, critic, playwright, historian and writer of fiction for children)

Of mills, moors and men: [poems]. Driffield: Ridings Publishing Co. 1966. 24 pp.

OXB

A selection of poems. Ilfracombe: Arthur H. Stockwell, Ltd. [1962]. 24 pp.

OXB

WAGNER, Geoffrey Atheling (1927– . Educated at Christ Church, Oxford, where he gained two blues. Served with the Welsh Guards in North Africa, Sicily and Italy and was wounded. Became a lecturer at Rochester University, New York State, in 1948. A keen painter, he exhibited in both England and America. Novelist)

The passionate climate: [poems]. Resurgam Books. 1945. 20 pp. (Resurgam poetry).

OXB

The singing blood, [and other poems]. [Prairie City, Illinois]: Decker Press. [1948]. 70 pp.

OXB

see also 13, 51, 76

WAIN, John (1925– . b. Stoke-on-Trent, Staffordshire. Educated at The High School, Newcastle under Lyme, and St John's College, Oxford. Lecturer in English literature at Reading University, 1947–55. Resigned to become a freelance author and critic. Recipient of the Somerset Maugham Award, 1960. Visiting Professor at Bristol, 1967, and at Centre Universitaire Expérimental, Vincennes, France, 1969. Professor of Poetry, Oxford University, 1973–78. Poet, critic, novelist and short story writer)

Mixed feelings: nineteen poems. Printed [Reading]: University of Reading. School of Art. 1951. 37 pp.

A limited ed. of 120 copies.

OXB

Poems, 1949–1979. Macmillan. 1980. [viii], 182 pp.

OXB

Weep before God: poems. Macmillan & Co Ltd. 1961. [viii], 48 pp.

MPL

A word carved on a sill: [poems]. Routledge & Kegan Paul. 1956. 54 pp.

OXB

see also 3, 17, 86

WAIN, John Leslie

Hidden life, and other poems. Dulwich: Outposts Publications. 1962. 20 pp.

MPL

WAINE, Harry (1891– . Playwright)

The quiet heart: a book of verse. Gateshead on Tyne: Northumberland Press Ltd. 1956. 128 pp.

OXB

WAINWRIGHT, Jeffrey (1944– . b. Stoke-on-Trent, Staffordshire. Educated at Leeds University. Worked as a teacher in England, Wales and America. Lecturer at Manchester Polytechnic)

Heart's desire, [and other poems]. Manchester: Carcanet. 1978. 56 pp. OXB

WAINWRIGHT, Margaret (1927– . b. Bradford, Yorkshire, daughter of a painter and decorator. Evacuated during the first year of war. Educated at St Hilda's College, Oxford, becoming a teacher, then an editor with an educational publisher. Married Derek Surtees, a trawlerman, in 1971. Of Dewsbury)
All the quiet people: [*poems*]. Walton-on-Thames: Outposts Publications. 1970. 12 pp.   OXB

WAKE, Hugh (Lieutenant, Royal Navy)   *see*   23

WALKER, Gladstone (Writer on eugenics and on pauperism. Of Tynemouth, Northumberland)
A book of verse. Tynemouth: Author. 1951. [ii], 81 pp.   OXB

WALKER, James (1911– . b. Ancoats, Manchester. Spent his childhood on the fairground. Educated at Ffestiniog County Intermediate School, North Wales. Served with the Royal Air Force in the Middle East, 1941–45. Poet, playwright, novelist, critic and broadcaster)
Against the sun: poems. Fortune Press. 1946. 64 pp.   OXB
see also   7, 49, 51, 57, 63, 76

WALKER, Janet
The small sunset, [*and other poems*]. Ilfracombe: Arthur H. Stockwell Ltd. 1971. 40 pp.   OXB

WALKER, Kathrine Sorley (Poet, ballet critic and biographer. Freelance writer and editor of *Dancing Times*, *The Stage* and other specialist periodicals. Ballet critic for *The Daily Telegraph* from 1962)
Beauty is built anew: a selection of poems. Glasgow: William Maclellan. [1949]. 36 pp.   OXB

WALKER, Norman Leslie (Served in North Africa)
Boots of sand, and other poems of the atomic age. Ilfracombe: Arthur H. Stockwell, Ltd. [1954]. 16 pp.   OXB

WALKER, R.N. (1917– . b. Stoke-on-Trent, Staffordshire. Joined the Royal Army Medical Corps in 1941, serving in the Middle East. Posted to Cairo in 1942, re-trained as cipher operator then sent to Persia, Iraq, India and Burma. Commissioned in India. In 1945 at H.Q. of British Army on the Rhine at Bad Oeyenhausen and Lubecke, then at Nuremberg for the trials. A teacher, headmaster of a large comprehensive school)   *see*   39, 63

WALKERDINE, Wilfred Ernest (1878– . b. Derby. Educated at Derby School, and Corpus Christi College, Cambridge. Poet of the First World War. Appointed Vicar of Shareshill, Wolverhampton in 1925)

Collected poems, 1900–1950. Newtown, Montgomeryshire Printing Co., Ltd.: [1952]. xvi, 79 pp.   OXB

WALKIN, Jimmy (Of Yorkshire ?)
  A selection of poems Printed Bradford: James John Hopkinson. [1977]. 29 pp.
    Title from cover.   OXB

WALLACE, A. (Served in H.M. Forces)   *see*   73

WALLACE, H.B.
  The land of broken hearts, and other poems. Ilfracombe: Arthur H. Stockwell, Ltd. [1950]. 16 pp.   OXB

WALLACE, L.J.   *see*   23

WALLER, J.S.
  Missing, and other poems. Ilfracombe: Arthur H. Stockwell, Ltd. [1943]. 16 pp.
    OXB

WALLER, Sir John (1917– . b. Oxford. Educated at Weymouth College, and Worcester College, Oxford. Served with the Royal Army Service Corps, 1940–46, in the Middle East from 1941. Founder-editor of *Kingdom Come*, first literary magazine of the war. Founder-member of the Salamander Society of poets in Cairo, 1942. Editor, Ministry of Information, Middle East, 1943–45. Chief Press Officer, British Embassy, Baghdad, 1945. News and features editor of *MIME*, Cairo, 1945–46. Awarded the Greenwood Prize of the Poetry Society in 1947. Co-editor of the anthologies *Middle East Anthology*, 1946, and *Return to Oasis*, 1980. Author, poet and journalist. Succeeded to baronetcy in 1954)
  The confessions of Peter Pan. Oxford: Holywell Press. 1941. [11] pp.
    A limited ed. of 307 numbered copies.   OXB
  Crusade: a collection of forty poems. New York: Macmillan Co. 1946. x, 51 pp. por.   OXB
  Fortunate Hamlet, [*and other poems*]. Fortune Press. [1941]. 52 pp.   IWM
  The kiss of stars: [poems]. William Heinemann Ltd. 1948. viii, 73 pp.
    MPL
  The merry ghosts: poems. Editions Poetry London. 1946. 55 pp. por.
    'Written on board ship or in various parts of the Middle East, June 1941–December 1943'.   IWM
  Spring legend, [*and other poems*]. Cairo, Egypt: Salamander Society. [1942]. XXIII pp.   OXB
see also   25, 31, 33, 39, 47, 49, 51, 52, 56, 63, 66, 76, 78, 82

WALLER, Robert (1913– . b. Manchester. Novelist, biographer and journalist)

The two natures, [and other poems]. Aldington, Kent: Hand and Flower Press. [1951]. 97–129 pp. (Poems in pamphlet, 1951, IV).   BL

WALLIS, Hazel (Of Portsmouth)
On wings of verse: [poems]. Ilfracombe: Arthur H. Stockwell, Ltd. [1945]. 47 pp.
   'Dedicated to Form IV, Milton Girls' School, Portsmouth, 1944'.
                                                    OXB

WALMSLEY, E.A. (Served in the Middle East)   *see*   39, 63

WALSH, R.D. (Leading Seaman, Royal Navy. of Argyllshire)
For England, and other poems. Ilfracombe: Arthur H. Stockwell, Ltd. [1943]. 24 pp.   OXB
see also   75

WALTER, Ethel (Writer for children. Of Bradford, Yorkshire)   *see*   22

WALTON, Alan Hull (1917–   . b. Newcastle upon Tyne. Educated at the Royal Grammar School and Durham University. Translator from the French and writer on Baudelaire. Of London)
Ballet-shoe, [and other poems]. Fortune Press. 1943. 52 pp. por.   OXB

WALTON, C.R. (Bombardier No. 1711129, Royal Artillery)
Idle rhymes of an ack-ack gunner. Ilfracombe: Arthur H. Stockwell, Ltd. [1942]. 20 pp.   OXB
Soldier rhymes. Ilfracombe: Arthur H. Stockwell, Ltd. [1943]. 16 pp.
                                                    OXB

WALTON, Peter
A crown for David: poems 1956–70. Walton-on-Thames: Outposts Publications. 1970. 12 pp.   MPL

WANDERER, pseud.   *see*   **SMITH, Lily**, (Wanderer, pseud.)

WARBURG, Joan (Schoolgirl poet of the First World War)
The secret spring, and other poems. Eton, Windsor: Shakespeare Head Press. 1958. 84 pp.   MPL

WARBURTON, Brenda (b. Croydon, Surrey. Graduated in philosophy at St Andrews University. After marriage lived in Australia for three years)
In contrast: [poems]. Regency Press. [1974]. 103 pp.   OXB
Local lives: [poems]. Regency Press. [1975]. 32 pp.   OXB

WARD, O.I. (A woman journalist. Wrote on archaeology and travel)   *see*   41

WARDELL, R. (Of Yorkshire) *see* 75

WARLOW-HARRY, R.C. (M.C. Major, Royal Artillery. Captured in Egypt in 1942, held prisoner of war in Germany until 1945) *see* 67

WARNER, Nevill
 Poems of love, peace and war. Ilfracombe: Arthur H. Stockwell, Ltd. 1946. 48 pp.
 BPL

WARNER, Rex (1905– . b. Birmingham. Educated at St George's School, Harpenden, and Wadham College, Oxford. Schoolmaster in Egypt and England, 1928–45. Worked for the Control Commision in Berlin, 1945. Director of the British Institute in Athens, 1945–47. Greek scholar, poet, essayist and novelist. Worked in films and broadcasting. Professor of English at Connecticut University, 1964–74. Of Wallingford, Berkshire)
 Poems and contradictions. Revised ed. John Lane the Bodley Head. 1945. 55 pp.
 Dedicated to Cecil Day Lewis. [1st ed. published in 1937] MPL

WARNER, Sylvia Townsend (1893–1978. b. Harrow, Middlesex, daughter of a housemaster at Harrow School. Educated privately. Poet of the First World War, when she worked in a munitions factory. Novelist, short story writer and poet, she spent several years as co-editor of the Oxford University Press ten-volume work *Tudor Church Music*. A close friend of Valentine Ackland and T.F. Powys. Received the Prix Menton in 1969. Lived at Maiden Newton, Dorset, latterly) *see* 42

WARNOCK, Geoffrey James (1923– . Educated at Winchester College, and New College, Oxford. Served as Captain in the Irish Guards, 1942–45. Holder of Visiting Fellowships at the universities of Illinois, Princeton and Wisconsin and of various academic appointments in Oxford, including Principal of Hertford College from 1971 and Vice-Chancellor from 1981. Writer on philosophy)
 Poems. Oxford: Basil Blackwell. 1955. iv, 36 pp. OXB

WARR, Bertram (1917–43. b. Toronto, Canada. Arrived in England in January 1939. Became a firewatcher in London and, briefly, an air raid warden. Joined the Royal Air Force in 1941. Killed in action on 3 April 1943 aboard a Halifax bomber during the first thousand-plane raid over Essen)
 Acknowledgment to life: the collected poems of Bertram Warr. Edited and with an introduction by Len Gasparini. Preface by Earle Birney. Toronto: Ryerson Press. [1970]. 92 pp. OXB
 "Yet a little onwards": [poems]. Favil Press Ltd. [1940]. [6] pp. ("Resurgam" younger poets, 3).
 Title from cover. BL
see also 10, 25, 52, 78

WARREN, Clarence Henry (1895–1966. Educated at Maidstone Grammar School, and Goldsmiths' College, London. Poet of the First World War. Served as a Private in the Army Ordnance Corps, 1916–19. Worked for the B.B.C., 1929–33. Author, broadcaster, reviewer, lecturer and writer on country life)

The thorn tree: poems. Oxford: Dolphin Book Co. Ltd. 1963. 49 pp.   MPL

WARREN, Ian (A barrister) *see* 81

WARREN, J.D.

Moments of memory: [poems]. Ilfracombe: Arthur H. Stockwell, Ltd. 1946. 15 pp.   OXB

WARRY, John (1916– . b. Ilford, Essex. Educated at Haileybury School, Queen's College, Cambridge, and London University. Army Sergeant, 1940–46, serving with the Intelligence Corps in the Middle East. Lecturer in English at Alexandria University, 1946–51. Education Officer with the Colonial Service in Cyprus, 1953–57. Lecturer in English, Libya University, 1957–61. Senior Lecturer at the Royal Military Academy, Sandhurst, from 1961. Writer on Greek aesthetics)

Sun and sand: verses of a soldier. Worcester: Littlebury & Co. Ltd. [1944]. 44 pp.   IWM

see also 63

WART, Reginald Bramley Van *see* **VAN WART, Reginald Bramley**

WATERS, Ivor (Of Chepstow, Monmouthshire. Writer on Chepstow)

Collected verse. Printed Chepstow: Moss Rose Press. 1977. xii, 112 pp.

OXB

WATERTON, B.J. (Petty Officer Radio Mechanic, Royal Navy) *see* 23

WATKINS, A.H. (Lieutenant, Home Guard)

Home Guard rhymes: the Home Guard in "di-verse" moods. Sketches by Lt.-Col. J.C.T. Willis, R.E. Practical Press Ltd. 1943. 54 pp. il.   IWM

WATKINS, F.O. (Bombardier, Royal Artillery. Served with the Eighth Army in the Western Desert) *see* 46

WATKINS, Owen (Served in H.M. Forces) *see* 75

WATKINS, Vernon (1906–67. b. Maestog. Glamorgan. Educated at Repton School, and Magdalene College, Cambridge. Worked for Lloyds Bank, 1925–66. Sergeant, Royal Air Force, 1941–46. Poet and lecturer. Calouste Gulbenkian Fellow in Poetry at University College, Swansea. Lived near Swansea)

Cypress and acacia: [*poems*]. Faber & Faber. 1959. 102 pp.   MPL
The lady with the unicorn, [*and other poems*]. Faber & Faber. 1948. 104 pp.
MPL
The lamp and the veil: poems. Faber & Faber Ltd. 1945. 61 pp.   OXB
Selected poems. Norfolk, Conn.: New Directions. 1948. [viii], 92 pp.   IWM
see also 1, 25, 33, 43, 56

WATSON, Francis (1907– . b. Leeds, Yorkshire. Educated at Giggleswick
School and Cambridge University. Lived in India from 1938 to 1946.
Biographer and novelist)
Poems in India. Keepsake Press. [1962]. 11 pp.
  Privately printed for the author's friends.   OXB

WATSON, Jay
Think this of me, [*and other poems*]. Ilfracombe: Arthur H. Stockwell, Ltd. 1959.
24 pp.   OXB

WATSON, Keith (Corporal, Royal Air Force. Worked in the Public Relations
Office, Bombay. Assistant editor of *The Journal of the Air Forces* and *The Royal
Indian Air Force Journal*) *see* 43

WATSON, Nigel (Trooper in the Hussars) *see* 25, 33

WATSON, William Styring, (William Styring, pseud.) (Of Bradford,
Yorkshire)
The poetical works of William Styring. Vol. 1. Printed Bradford: Watmoughs Ltd.
1946. x, 158 pp.   OXB
The poetical works of William Styring. Vol.1. [New ed.]. Printed Bradford:
Watmoughs Ltd. 1947. x, 158 pp.   BL

WATT, J.O.R.M. (Served in South-East Asia Command) *see* 35

WATTS, Doreen C. (Married Simon Armetage. Writer of children's short
stories) *see* 41

WATTS, Ethel M. (Possibly Ethel Maud Watts who was connected with the
Birmingham Roman Catholic diocese)
Meditations in verse. Mitre Press. [1973]. 72 pp.   OXB

WATTS, S.G. (Corporal. Served with the Eighth Army)
Twilight reveries: Calm; and, Conflict: [*poems*]. Printed Newport: A.T.W. James.
1945. 87 pp. por.   BPL
see also 44

WAVELL, Archibald Percival, Lord Wavell (1883–1950. b. Winchester.

Educated at Winchester College, Royal Military College, Sandhurst, and Staff College. Commissioned in The Black Watch in 1901. His long military career included service in the Boer War and the First World War. Wounded in 1916, he lost the sight of one eye. Military Attaché with the Russian Army in the Caucasus, 1916–17. With the Egyptian Expeditionary Force, 1917–20. Appointed General in 1940, Field Marshal in 1943. Commander-in-Chief in the Middle East, 1939–41, and in India, 1941–43. Supreme Commander in South-West Pacific, 1942. Viceroy and Governor-General of India, 1943–47. Recipient of many military and other honours. Compiler of the poetry anthology *Other Men's Flowers*, 1944, still in print and still most popular) *see* 43

WAY, Judith *see* 22

WEATHERBURN, C.E. (Of Staffordshire) *see* 74

WEAVER, James A.
The new world symphony, and other poems. Ilfracombe: Arthur H. Stockwell, Ltd. 1946. 32 pp.   OXB

WEAVING, Willoughby (Poet of the First World War. Lieutenant, Royal Irish Rifles. Served on the western front. Invalided home in 1915)
Purple testament, 'the purple testament of bleeding war': [*poems*]. Oxford: Basil Blackwell. 1941. 56 pp.   OXB

WEBB, Fallon (Of London) *see* 74

WEBB, J. Roderick *see* 2

WEBER, Frederick Parkes (1863–1962. Educated at Charterhouse and Cambridge University. Trained as a doctor at St Bartholomew's Hospital, London, and in Paris and Vienna. Fellow of the Royal Society of Physicians. Specialist in dermatology and rare diseases. Writer on medical topics)
Rhymes, verses and epigrams. Printed E.T. Heron & Co., Ltd. 1955. [iv], 20 pp.
                                         OXB

WEBER, John (Served in H.M. Forces) *see* 49

WEDD, Mary
Heirs of a morning: [*poems*]. Walton-on-Thames: Outposts Publications. 1972. 12 pp.   OXB

WEDGE, John (1912– . Educated at Roan School. Served with the Royal Navy in the North Sea and Atlantic as a telegraphist. Later commissioned as Lieutenant) *see* 23, 25, 33, 47, 76, 80

WEINSTEIN, A. (Of London) *see* 75

WEIR, Archibald Nigel Charles (1919–40. Son of the founder of the famous pre-war Oxford University Air Squadron. Educated at Winchester College, and Christ Church, Oxford. A fencing half-blue. Flying Officer, Royal Air Force, posted in May 1940 to a fighter squadron on the south coast. Took part in many patrols and engagements that summer, destroying three German aircraft on 8 August. Killed in action in November when his plane was shot down into the sea. Awarded the D.F.C.)
  Verses of a fighter pilot. Faber & Faber Ltd. 1941. 78 pp. por.   BPL
see also 76

WEIR, Susan (Novelist)
  Wicker basket leaves: [poems]. Ilfracombe: Arthur H. Stockwell, Ltd. [1961]. 23 pp.   OXB

WEISSBORT, Daniel (1935– . Educated at Queen's College, Cambridge, and the London School of Economics. A university teacher, he took a post at Iowa City, United States. Translator of poetry from Russian into English)
  In an emergency: [poems]. Oxford: Carcanet Press. 1972. 63 pp.   MPL
  The leaseholder, [and other poems]. Oxford: Carcanet Press. 1971. 30 pp.
    A limited ed. of 600 copies of which forty have been signed by the author.
                                                                        OXB

WELCH, Denton (1915–48. b. Shanghai, China. Educated at Repton School, and Goldsmiths' College School of Art, London. A talented artist, short story writer and poet. Severely injured in a road accident in 1935 from which he never fully recovered)
  Dumb instrument: poems and fragments. Edited with an introduction and notes by Jean-Louis Chevalier. Decorations by Denton Welch. Enitharmon Press. 1976. 61 pp. il.
    A limited ed. of 660 copies, the first sixty specially bound.   OXB
see also 76

WELLES, Winifred *see* **BURKE, Winifred**, (Winifred Welles), (Clare Cameron, pseud.)

WELLESLEY, Dorothy, Duchess of Wellington (1889–1956. b. Croughton, Cheshire, daughter of Robert Ashton. Educated privately. Travelled widely. Married the Hon. Gerald Wellesley, who became the 7th Duke of Wellington. Editor of the Hogarth Living Poets series, 1928–32. A contributor to various periodicals and anthologies)
  Desert wells, [and other poems]. Michael Joseph Ltd. 1946. 55 pp.   OXB
  Early light: the collected poems of Dorothy Wellesley. Rupert Hart-Davis. 1955. 255 pp.   OXB

Lost planet, and other poems. Hogarth Press. 1942. 52 pp. MPL
The poets, and other poems. Tunbridge Wells: H.W. Baldwin. 1943. 27 pp.
(Penns in the rocks series, 1).

A limited ed. of 300 numbered copies. OXB
Selected poems. Williams & Norgate. 1949. 159 pp. por. OXB
see also 80

WELLINGTON, Duchess of *see* **WELLESLEY, Dorothy, Duchess of Wellington**

WELLS, Gerry (Educated at Lancing College and Kesteven College of Education. Served in the same tank regiment as Keith Douglas in the France-Germany campaign)
Obie's war: poems. [Lincoln?]: Lincolnshire & Humberside Arts. [1975].
38 pp. (Paperback poets, 3). OXB

WELLS, John Carveth (1911–)
Songs in chains: a collection of poems. Jarrolds Publishers Ltd. [1946]. 40 pp.
OXB

WENTWORTH, Lady Judith Anne Dorothea (1885–1957. Married the 3rd Earl of Lytton. Author, artist and owner of Crabbet Park Arabian Stud. President of the Arab Horse Society. Lived at Crawley, Sussex)
Passing hours: [poems]. Oxford: George Ronald. [1952]. [ii], 62 pp.
OXB
War nonsense: poems. Unwin Brothers Ltd. 1943. 48 pp. OXB

WENTWORTH, Patricia, pseud. *see* **TURNBULL, Dora Amy**, (Patricia Wentworth, pseud.)

WERE, Mary Winter (b. Edgbaston, Warwickshire, a collateral descendant of Robert Southey. Educated privately. Married Arthur Henry Hughes. Their daughter served in the Auxiliary Territorial Service. Co-editor of the anthology *Poems by Contemporary Women*, 1943. Poet and journalist. Of Beckenham, Kent)
To-morrow: new poems. Sands & Co. Ltd. [1942]. 40 pp. OXB
The wounded bird: poems, 1944–1954. Tunbridge Wells: Courier Publishing Co.,
Ltd. [1955]. 72 pp. IWM
see also 41, 42

WEST, Paul (1930– . b. Eckington, Derbyshire. Educated at Birmingham University, Lincoln College, Oxford, and Columbia University, New York. Novelist and writer on English and American literature. Winner of the Aga Khan Prize for Fiction, 1974, and of a National Endowment for Humanities Award, 1973. Settled in Pennsylvania, becoming an American citizen)
The snow leopard, [and other poems]. Hutchinson. 1964. 63 pp. MPL

WEST, Victor (1919– . b. London. Served with the 1st Rangers, King's Royal Rifle Corps in Greece and Crete, where he was captured. As a prisoner of war he ran clandestine anti-Fascist meetings under the noses of Nazi guards)
The horses of Falaise: poems on the experiences of a fighting soldier in World War II. Introduction by Vernon Scannell. Salamander Imprint. 1975. 48 pp.   BPL
see also   63

WEST, Hon. Victoria (Vita) Sackville- *see*   **SACKVILLE-WEST, Hon. Victoria** (Vita)

WEST-SKINN, Richard (Bookseller. Of Lincolnshire)   *see*   75

WESTERN, Daphne
A trip to the Boche, and other poems. Ilfracombe: Arthur H. Stockwell, Ltd. 1949. 16 pp.   OXB

WESTON, John W. (Of Thornaby-on-Tees, Yorkshire)
Thirteen poems. Thornaby-on-Tees: Author. [1945]. [22] pp.
   Title from cover.   OXB

WESTREN, Jo
Harvests: [*poems*]. Walton-on-Thames: Outposts Publications. 1978. 44 pp.
     OXB

WESTROPP-MORGAN, Edward
Selected sonnets. Mitre Press. [1951]. 32 pp.   OXB

WESTROPPE, John Jayne, pseud. *see* **JONES, I.M.**, (John Jayne Westroppe, pseud.)

WESTWOOD, Ada
Poetry miscellany. Pembroke Dock: Dock Leaves Ltd. 1968. 20 pp.   OXB

WETTON, George (Served in H.M. Forces)   *see*   75

WHARTON, Lewis
Songs of to-day and yesteryear: [*poems*]. Fortune Press. 1959. 80 pp.   OXB

WHEATLEY, John (Of Scarborough, Yorkshire)
Shadows and reflections: forty poems. Fortune Press. [1949]. 32 pp.   OXB

WHERRY, Daphne (Served in the Women's Royal Naval Service. Worked at the Allied cryptographic centre, Bletchley Park)   *see*   23

WHISTLER, Laurence (1912– . Younger brother of artist Rex Whistler.

Educated at Stowe School, and Balliol College, Oxford, receiving the Chancellor's Essay Prize in 1934. Joined the Army in 1940, commissioned in The Rifle Brigade in 1941, becoming a Captain in 1943. Poet, biographer, designer and diamond-point engraver on glass. Writer on architecture and glass engraving. Awarded the first King's Gold Medal for Poetry in 1934, and an Atlantic Award for Literature in 1945. Of Marlborough, Wiltshire)

The burning glass. Printed Chiswick Press. [1941]. [8] pp.

    A limited ed. of fifty numbered and signed copies printed for Laurence Whistler, Siegfried Sassoon and Geoffrey Keynes.   OXB

In time of suspense, [and other poems]. William Heinemann Ltd. 1940. x, 89 pp.
    OXB

Ode to the sun, and other poems. William Heinemann Ltd. 1942. [vi], 56 pp.
    OXB

To celebrate her living: [poems]. Rupert Hart-Davis. 1967. 125 pp. por.
    OXB

The view from this window: poems. Hart-Davis. 1956. 68 pp.   MPL

The world's room: the collected poems of Laurence Whistler. With decorations by Rex Whistler. William Heinemann. 1949. xiv, 210 pp. il.   MPL

see also   25, 38, 47, 48, 52, 80, 82

WHITAKER, Harold (Private tutor and writer on cartography. Of Worcester)

Salus populi suprema lex: [poems]. Printed Worcester: Charles Dann. [1943]. [8] pp. il.

    Title from cover.   OXB

WHITBY, Charles (1864– . b. Yeovil, Somerset. Educated at Oakham School, Emmanuel College, Cambridge, and Guy's Hospital, London. Poet of the First World War. Lived in Bath, Somerset)

In Yeovil town: poems. Fortune Press. [1946]. 56 pp.   OXB

WHITE, Alan (1920–44. Lieutenant, Royal Artillery. Killed in action at Cassino, Italy, on 12 May 1944)

Garlands and ash: [poems]. Fortune Press. 1947. 70 pp. por.

    Bound with author's *Drawings*.   IWM

see also   60, 61, 62

WHITE, B.C. (Farmer and dowser)

Poems from the West Country. Ilfracombe: Arthur H. Stockwell Ltd. 1976. 103 pp. por.   OXB

WHITE, Elisabeth

The corridors of dawn, and other poems. Hutchinson & Co. Ltd. [1944]. 32 pp. por.   MPL

WHITE, Henry Cracroft
   Moon owl, [and other poems]. Ilfracombe: Arthur H. Stockwell, Ltd. [1960].
19 pp.   OXB
   The quiet ones, [and other poems]. Ilfracombe: Arthur Stockwell Ltd. [1958].
16 pp.   OXB

WHITE, Jon (1924– . b. Cardiff. Educated at St Catharine's College, Cambridge. During the war served in the Royal Navy and the Welsh Guards. Member of the Foreign Service, 1952–56. In 1967 appointed Associate Professor in English Literature at Texas University, El Paso. Poet, novelist and writer on Ancient Egypt)
   Dragon, and other poems. Fortune Press. 1943. 32 pp.   BPL

WHITE, Joyce
   Reflections, and other verse. Ilfracombe: Arthur H. Stockwell, Ltd. [1946]. 20 pp.
                                                         OXB

WHITE, Ken (Served in H.M. Forces in jungle warfare)   *see* 75

WHITE, Margery   *see* 22

WHITE, Terence Hanbury (1906–64. b. Bombay, India. Educated at Cheltenham College, and Queen's College, Cambridge. Taught at a preparatory school then at Stowe School until 1936. Writer of fiction and poetry. Lived in Ireland, 1939–46, and in the Channel Islands, 1946–64)
   A joy proposed: poems. With an introduction and afterword and notes by Kurth Sprague. Bertram Rota. [1980]. xiv, 73 pp.
     A limited ed. of 500 numbered copies.   OXB
   Verses. Alderney: Author. 1962. 43 pp. por.
     A limited ed. of 100 numbered copies printed at the Shenval Press.
                                                  OXB
see also 38

WHITEHEAD, John (1924– . Volunteered at age of eighteen for the Royal Artillery. Did his officer training in India. Gazetted to the 8th Mahratta Anti-Tank Regiment, with which he fought in the later stages of the Burma campaign)
   Emblems of more: poems. Fortune Press. 1945. 32 pp.   BPL
   Flash and outbreak: [poems]. Collins. 1946. 64 pp.   BPL
   Murmurs in the rose: poems. Fortune Press. 1951. 40 pp.   BL

WHITEHOUSE, John (Leading Seaman, Royal Navy. Served as a regular, 1921–45, on the destroyer H.M.S. *Watchman* during the war. Of Audenshaw, Manchester)   *see* 23

WHITEHOUSE, Peggy, pseud. *see* **MUNDY-CASTLE, Frances**, (Peggy Whitehouse, pseud.)

WHITELEY, Robert
"Careless livery": a selection of verse. Ilfracombe: Arthur H. Stockwell, Ltd. [1946]. 24 pp.   OXB
Rough torrent: ten poems. Ilfracombe: Arthur H. Stockwell, Ltd. [1945?]. 16 pp.   OXB

WHITLA, Eva
Our faith looks up to Thee: [poems]. Arthur H. Stockwell Ltd. [1941]. 16 pp.
                                                                                                          OXB

WHITTLESTONE, Maurice
Poems. Ilfracombe: Arthur H. Stockwell, Ltd. [1964]. 64 pp.   OXB

WHITTOCK, Mike *see* 36, 64

WICKER, James Bruce (Of Betchworth, Surrey)
Poems. Betchworth: Author. [1946]. 11 pp.
Title from cover.   OXB

WICKSTEED, Margaret Hope, (Margaret Hope, pseud.) (Historical novelist)
Outlook Hill, [and other poems]; by Margaret Hope. Edinburgh: M. Macdonald. [1965]. 56 pp.   OXB

WIDDOWS, Paul Frederic (1918–   . b. London. Educated at Repton School, and Hertford College, Oxford. Went straight into the Army from Oxford. Served in India for over four years as a Company Sergeant Major in the Intelligence Corps) *see* 43

WILBERFORCE, Robert (1887–   . Educated at Stonyhurst College, and Balliol College, Oxford. Served in War Trade Intelligence Department, 1915–16. Attaché, H.M. Legation to the Holy See, 1917–19. Called to the Bar in 1921. Member of British Delegation to the Geneva Disarmament Conference, 1932–33. Director of British Information Services in New York, retiring in 1952. Of Corston, Somerset)
Meditations in verse. Foreword by Alfred Noyes. Catholic Truth Society. [1950]. 36 pp. (C.T.S. booklets).   OXB

WILCOCK, Ronald B. (Corporal, Royal Army Service Corps. Served in India and South-East Asia. Textile operative, trade union worker and political lecturer) *see* 35, 43

WILCOX, Ronald (Warrant Officer, Royal Air Force) *see* 1, 25

WILD, John B.
"Poet's paradise", [*and other poems*]. Ilfracombe: Arthur H. Stockwell, Ltd. [1962]. 23 pp.   OXB

WILD, W.E. (Of Yorkshire) *see* 74

WILDGOSSE, Barbara (Sergeant, Auxiliary Territorial Service) *see* 27

WILKES, Arnold (b. Oxford. A banker)
The window box, [*and other poems*]. Southport: Angus Downie. 1955. [vi], 58 pp.   OXB

WILKIE, Robert Blair (Member of the Scottish Nationalist Movement)
Remembered radiance, [*and other poems*]. Edinburgh: M. Macdonald. 1956. 53 pp. por.   OXB

WILKINSON, Darrell (1919– . Educated at Epsom College, and St Thomas's Hospital, London. Qualified as a doctor in 1941. Surgeon-Lieutenant, Royal Navy, 1942–46. Worked for some time with the Commandos. Regularly parachuted into Greece to tend the partisans. A consultant dermatologist) *see* 31, 39, 63

WILKINSON, Dick *see* **WILKINSON, Peter Richard** (Dick)

WILKINSON, Gladys Doreena (1900– . b. Calverley, Yorkshire. Married Walter Wilkinson in 1923. Of Greengates, Bradford)
Poems of the north country. Clapham, North Yorkshire: Dalesman Books. 1980. 64 pp. il.   OXB

WILKINSON, N. (Private. Served with the Eighth Army) *see* 44

WILKINSON, Peter Richard (Dick)
Slates of opal: [*poems*]; by Dick Wilkinson. Mitre Press. [1961]. 83 pp.
OXB

WILKINSON, R.E.
Pheasant shooting, and other poems. Glasgow: Strickland Press. [1950?]. [vi], 129 pp.   OXB

WILLETTS, Ronald Frederick (1915– . b. Halesowen, Worcestershire. Educated at Birmingham University. Historian and classical Greek scholar. Appointed Professor of Greek, Birmingham University, 1970)

The Baths of Aphrodite, [and other poems]. Aberystwyth: Celtion Publishing Co. 1979. 45 pp. (Celtion poetry). OXB

WILLIAMS, Alan Moray, (Robert the Rhymer, pseud.) (1915– . b. Petersfield, Hampshire. Educated at King's College, Cambridge. Foreign correspondent for various British newspapers in Russia and Scandinavia. Based in Denmark from the mid-1950s)

Autumn in Copenhagen: poems. With ten drawings by Poul Hoyrup. Copenhagen: Scandinavian Features Service. 1963. 96 pp. il.

A limited ed. of 1,500 hand-printed copies of which 100 are numbered and signed by the author. OXB

Children of the century: ballads and poems. Frederick Muller Ltd. 1947. 96 pp. MPL

WILLIAMS, E. (Of Yorkshire) *see* 75

WILLIAMS, Eliot Crawshay- *see* **CRAWSHAY-WILLIAMS, Eliot**

WILLIAMS, F. Irene (Studied at the Slade School of Art, London. A member of Kent & Sussex Poetry Society. Poet and verse-playwright)

Moods of one's mind: [poems]. Stroud, Gloucestershire: Ian Hodgkins & Co. 1980. x, 140 pp.

A limited ed. of 125 numbered copies. OXB

WILLIAMS, Gwyn (1904– . b. Port Talbot, Glamorgan. Educated at University College, Aberystwyth, and Jesus College, Oxford. Taught English at Cairo University, 1935–42, and at Alexandria University, 1942–51, thus temporarily exiled during the war. Professor of English, Libya University, Benghazi, 1956–61. Professor of English Literature, Istanbul University, Turkey, 1961–69. Author of novels, poetry, travel books and translations from the Welsh) *see* 40

WILLIAMS, Hilda Katharine (In Jersey during the German occupation of the Channel Islands)

The primrose way: songs from a cage: [poems]. Printed Jersey: Bigwoods Ltd. 1946. 106 pp. OXB

WILLIAMS, Hugh Menai, (Huw Menai, pseud.) (b. Caernarvon, North Wales. Poet of the First World War. Moved to the Rhondda Valley, South Wales, working as a pit weigher. Became an active socialist)

The simple vision: poems; by Huw Menai. With a preface by John Cowper Powys. Chapman & Hall Ltd. 1945. 95 pp. IWM

see also 32

WILLIAMS, John Stuart (1920– . b. Mountain Ash, Glamorgan. Educated at Mountain Ash County School, and University College, Cardiff. Taught English at Whitchurch Grammar School, Glamorgan. Head of English & Drama Department, Cardiff College of Education, 1956–77. Appointed Head, Department of Communications, South Glamorgan Institute of Higher Education, in 1977. Writer on Alun Lewis)

Banna Strand: poems 1970–74. Llandysul: Gomer Press. 1975. 54 pp.   OXB

WILLIAMS, Miles Vaughan- *see* **VAUGHAN-WILLIAMS, Miles**

WILLIAMS, P.C. (Of Surrey) *see* 75

WILLIAMS, Philip Claxton
Selected poems. Ilfracombe: Arthur H. Stockwell, Ltd. 1948. 16 pp.   OXB

WILLIAMS, Phyllis (Of Surrey) *see* 74

WILLIAMS, Ses
Poems to amuse and annoy you. Ilfracombe: Arthur H. Stockwell, Ltd. [1960]. 16 pp.   OXB

WILLIAMS, T. Lovatt
The crescent moon, and other poems. Fortune Press. [1950]. 44 pp.   OXB
Noonday, and other poems. Shrewsbury: Wilding & Son Ltd. 1944. 34 pp.
    OXB

WILLIAMS, Tudor
Poems for to-day. Ilfracombe: Arthur H. Stockwell Ltd. [1942]. 16 pp. OXB

WILLIAMS, Ursula Vaughan *see* **VAUGHAN WILLIAMS, Ursula**, (Ursula Wood)

WILLIAMSON, Dennis (Educated at Oriel College, Oxford)
The modern Genilon, and other poems. Fortune Press. 1952. 50 pp.   OXB
see also 55

WILLY, Margaret (1919– . Educated at Beckenham County School for Girls, and Goldsmiths' College, London. A copywriter for various publishers and book wholesalers, 1936–42. Served in the Women's Land Army, 1942–46. A freelance writer and lecturer after the war. Appointed editor of the journal *English* in 1954. Writer on English literature and recipient of several literary awards. Of Reigate, Surrey)
The invisible sun: [poems]. Chaterson Ltd. 1946. viii, 39 pp.   IWM

WILMOTH, M. St J. (Lieutenant. Served with the Eighth Army in the Western Desert) *see* 46

WILSON, Cyril Bradlaugh (Gunner, Royal Artillery. Served with the Eighth Army at the siege of Tobruk. Won the Montgomery Poetry Prize in 1943. Of Finedon, Northamptonshire) *see* 39, 44, 63

WILSON, Frank (1921– . Writer on English literature)
An elegy for lovers, [and other poems]. Fortune Press. [1948]. 16 pp.   OXB

WILSON, Hilda Mary
The three-sighted, and other poems. Linden Press. 1961. 53 pp.   OXB

WILSON, Jacynth
The lonely, and other poems. Ilfracombe: Arthur H. Stockwell, Ltd. 1950. 16 pp.
OXB

WILSON, Jonathan (1924–44. b. Villefranche, France. Educated at Marlborough College. Served in North West Europe as a Lieutenant with the Scots Guards. Died of wounds received in the fighting near Venloo, Holland, on 20 November 1944)
Poems. Introduction by G.M. Young. Jonathan Cape. 1946. 55 pp. por.
IWM

Poems. Introduction by G.M. Young. [New] ed. with additional poems. Jonathan Cape. 1946. 55 pp. por.   OXB
see also 20

WILSON, Mary, Lady (b. Diss, Norfolk, daughter of the Reverend D. Baldwin, a Congregational minister. Brought up in East Anglia and began to write verse at the age of six. Married Harold Wilson, Labour Prime Minister, later created Lord Wilson of Rievaulx. Poet and anthologist. Of London and the Isles of Scilly)
New poems. Hutchinson. 1979. 71 pp.   OXB

WILSON, Mollie
"If I should die–": [*poems*]. Ilfracombe: Arthur H. Stockwell, Ltd. [1944]. 32 pp.   OXB

WILSON, Robert Noble Denison (1899– . b. Ireland. Served in the First World War as a Cadet in the Royal Artillery. A schoolmaster in the Cotswolds throughout the Second World War. Writer on fine art and of textbooks for children) *see* 42

WINCHESTER, Barry
Eighty four days: a rhyming appreciation and comment on the Battle of Britain. With a foreword by Air Chief Marshal Sir Keith Park. Horsted Keynes, Sussex: Selma Press. 1974. xxiv, 176 pp. il.

'Dedicated to Squadron Leader Geoffrey Wellum, D.F.C., Spitfire pilot'. Appended is a facsim. of an Air Ministry account *The Battle of Britain, August–October 1940*.   BPL

WINCHESTER, Clarence (1895–1981. b. London. Educated privately and at technical schools. Learned to fly, 1913–14. Poet of the First World War. Associated with aeronautics and the theatre at home and abroad. Journalist on various newspapers and periodicals, working with several groups of publishers)

A great rushing of wings, and other poems. [Bognor Regis]: John Crowther. 1944. 44 pp.   BPL
Signatures of God: selected poems of truth, beauty and love. Evesham: Arthur James Ltd. 1977. 64 pp.   OXB

WINCKWORTH, Peter

The way of war: [poems]. Dacre Press. [1939]. [32] pp. il.
'A meditation on the Stations of the Cross in time of war'.   IWM

WINGFIELD, Sheila, Lady Powerscourt (1906–73. b. Hampshire, daughter of Lieutenant-Colonel Claude Beddington. Educated at Roedean School. Taught herself Greek, French, Russian and English classics. Travelled widely in Europe, the Middle East, West Africa and the United States. Married the Hon. M. Wingfield, later the 9th Baron Powerscourt, in 1932)

Beat drum, beat heart. Cresset Press. 1946. 78 pp.   MPL
A cloud across the sun: [poems]. Cresset Press. 1949. 35 pp.   OXB
Her storms: selected poems, 1938–1977. With a preface by G.S. Fraser. Dublin: Dolmen Press; John Calder. [1977]. 128 pp.   MPL
A kite's dinner: poems 1938–1954. Cresset Press. 1954. viii, 152 pp.   MPL

WINTLE, Irene

Patchwork: verses. Hove: Hove Shirley Press Ltd. 1964. 55 pp.   OXB

WITHERBY, Diana (1915– . b. London. Educated at North Foreland Lodge, Broadstairs. Worked as a reader for *Horizon* magazine during the war. Married Sir Samuel Cooke, later a High Court Judge, in 1943. Short story writer and poet, published in many periodicals. Of Hampstead, London)

Collected poems. H.F. & G. Witherby Ltd. 1973. 79 pp.   OXB
Poems. Derek Verschoyle. 1954. 32 pp.   MPL
see also 45

WOLFE, Humbert (1885–1940. b. Milan, Italy. Educated at Bradford Grammar School, and Wadham College, Oxford. Entered the Civil Service in 1908. Poet of the First World War, an official in the Ministry of Munitions. Appointed Deputy Secretary, Ministry of Labour in 1938)

Kensington Gardens in war-time: [poems]. William Heinemann Ltd. 1940. viii, 40 pp.   BPL
see also 86

WOLFF, William (1902– . b. London. Fellow of the Institute of Chartered Accountants. Of New Malden, Surrey)
    Colours and windows: [*poems*]. Chaterson Ltd. 1951. vi, 56 pp.   OXB
    The watcher: poems. British Authors' Press. 1949. 55 pp.   OXB

WOOD, Ann Kirby (b. Sussex. Educated at Bedford High School)
    This other autumn: [*poems*]. Mitre Press. 1961. 40 pp.   MPL

WOOD, G.E.P. (Lieutenant, Royal Marines, Captured in Crete in 1941, held prisoner of war in Germany until 1945) *see* 67

WOOD, Mary I. (Of Yorkshire?)
    Song in the valley, and other poems. Printed Scarborough: Royal Printing Works. [1948]. [vi], 136 pp. por.   OXB

WOOD, Olive M. (Of Carlyle, Cumberland)
    Interlude: [*poems*]. Ilfracombe: Arthur H. Stockwell, Ltd. [1944]. 24 pp.
    OXB

WOOD, Ursula *see* **VAUGHAN WILLIAMS, Ursula**, (Ursula Wood)

WOOD, William Irving (Of Ottery St Mary, Devon)
    Mountain of beauty: [*poems*]. Dedicated to all service and ex-service personnel of World War II, 1939–45 (United Kingdom and America). Ilfracombe: Arthur H. Stockwell, Ltd. 1955. 32 pp.   OXB

WOODBERRY, Doris (Of Tiverton, Devon)
    Links of gold: [*poems*]. Tiverton, Devon: Author. 1975. 31 pp.   OXB
    Poems. Ilfracombe: Arthur H. Stockwell, Ltd. [1942]. 20 pp.   OXB

WOODCOCK, George (1912– . b. Winnipeg, Canada. Educated at Sir William Borlase's School, Marlow. Editor of the literary review *Now*, London, 1940–47. Freelance writer, 1947–54. Held academic appointments at Washington University, 1954–56, and at British Columbia University, 1956–63. Writer of plays and documentaries for Canadian television. Editor of *Canadian Literature* from 1959. Of Vancouver, Canada)
    The centre cannot hold: [*poems*]. Routledge. 1943. 44 pp.   OXB
    Selected poems of George Woodcock. Design and illustration by Pat Gangnon. Toronto: Clarke, Irwin & Co. Ltd. 1967. [viii], [76] pp. il.   OXB
    The white island: [*poems*]. Fortune Press. [1940]. 40 pp.   OXB
see also 25, 28, 56, 69

WOODESON, Keith K.
    Impassionata: [*poems*]. Ilfracombe: Arthur H. Stockwell Ltd. 1980. 84 pp.
    OXB

WOODHAM, G.S.B. (Of London) *see* 74

WOODHOUSE, Charles (Served in the Military Police. Of Haslemere, Surrey)
Genesis, [and other poems]. Mitre Press. [1963]. 104 pp.   OXB
The waters of Camelsdale, and other poems. Mitre Press. [1960]. 48 pp.   OXB
see also 61

WOODHOUSE, Peter (Served on H.M.S. *Lowestoft*, Royal Navy) *see* 23

WOODMAN, Simon
Unexpected fairyland, and other poems. Wilson & Whitworth Ltd. 1947. 20 pp.
                                                                        OXB

WOODS, John L., (Jael, pseud.) (Held captive by the Japanese in Changi Prison, Malaya)
Who laughs last: or, echoes from an internment camp. Printed Ipoh, [Malaya]: Caxton Press. [1949?]. [xii], 141 pp.
        Poems, prose and a play *South Lower*.   IWM

WOODS, T.R. (Warrant Officer, Royal Air Force) *see* 1

WORNER, Philip, (Philip Sylvester, pseud.) (1910– . b. Southampton. Educated at Southampton University and Oxford University. Actor with Tunbridge Repertory Co., 1936. Tutor at Worcester College of Education, 1949–70. Poet and dramatist. Of Worcester)
All dreaming gone: [poems]; by Philip Sylvester. Favil Press. 1941. 15 pp.
        Dedicated 'among others, to Peter Rich, Royal Air Force Bomber Command, twenty-one this year'.   OXB
Freedom is my fame: poems; by Philip Sylvester. Fortune Press. [1943]. 40 pp.
                                                                        BPL
Wrack: poems. Mitre Press. 1971. 41 pp.   OXB

WORNUM, Miriam (b. San Francisco, California, née Gerstle. Taken travelling by her parents from the age of four so received little formal education. Came to London in her early twenties. Married architect George Grey Wornum in 1923. During the war she ran an art school for the Forces in the Bishop's Palace at Chichester, also a club for refugees. Lectured and practised occupational therapy in 'shell-shock' hospitals. Returned to live in San Francisco on the death of her husband)
An embroidery, and other poems. Robert Hale Ltd. 1961. 63 pp.   OXB

WRIGHT, Daisie Irene
God's commission, and other poems. Ilfracombe: Arthur H. Stockwell, Ltd. [1945?]. 23 pp.   OXB

WRIGHT, David (1920–   . b. Johannesburg, South Africa. Educated at Northampton School for the Deaf, and Oriel College, Oxford. On staff of *The Sunday Times* in London, 1942–47. Recipient of an Atlantic Award in Literature, 1950, and a Guinness Poetry Award, 1958 and 1960. Gregory Fellow in Poetry at Leeds University, 1965–67. Poet, literary critic and writer on travel)

Metrical observations: [poems]. Manchester: Carcanet New Press Ltd. 1980. 41 pp.   OXB

Poems. Editions Poetry London. 1947. [vi], 34 pp.   OXB

To the gods the shades: new and collected poems. Manchester: Carcenet New Press. 1976. 152 pp.   OXB

WRIGHT, Ena (Educated at Sheffield University. Became a teacher)

These have I loved: [poems]. Mitre Press. 1956. 52 pp.   OXB

The world my oyster: [poems]. Mitre Press. [1958]. 62 pp.   OXB

WRIGHT, John (Served in the Royal Air Force)

Airman singing: poems. Sidgwick & Jackson Ltd. 1944. vi, 50 pp.   BPL

Beyond the trumpet: poems. Sidgwick & Jackson Ltd. 1948. vi, 58 pp.   OXB

WRIGHT, Richard B. (Able-Bodied Seaman. Attached to the Fleet Air Arm)   *see*   19, 23, 25, 33

WRIGHT, Tom (b. Glasgow. Served in the Army, 1943–47, in Europe, Burma, India and Japan. Poet, dramatist and creator of stained-glass windows. Of Edinburgh)   *see*   86

WYATT, Horace (1876–1954. Educated at Malvern College, and St Catharine's College, Cambridge. Head of Engineering at Seafield Park College, 1901–05. In 1909 organized a deputation to the Chancellor of the Exchequer to obtain consessions in the taxation of industrial motor vehicles. Poet of the First World War. Writer on motor transport)

Jersey in jail, 1940–45. Pictures by Edmund Blampied. Jersey: Ernest Huelin. [1945]. 93 pp. il.

Poetry and prose. 750 copies of the ed. are numbered and signed by author and artist.   OXB

WYATT, Isabel (1901–   . b. Wednesbury, Staffordshire. Educated at Birmingham University. Married Carl Wyatt. Novelist and poet. Of Minehead, Somerset)

Stars' roundelay: [poems]. Andrew Dakers Ltd. 1947. 80 pp.   OXB

WYATT, William E. (Served in South-East Asia Command. Of Shirley, Surrey)   *see*   35

WYE, Paul de   *see*   **DE WYE, Paul**

WYLLIE, Thomas Hunter Steen (1910–48. Educated at Oxford University, winning the Chancellor's Prize for Latin Verse in 1930. Served in the Royal Engineers, first as Private then Lieutenant)

Palinode, and other verses. Oxford: B.H. Blackwell Ltd. 1950. [iv], 33 pp.
  A limited ed. of 200 numbered copies.   IWM

WYSE, Elizabeth (1957–   . Lived and worked in France for several years)

Auschwitz: a long poem. Illustrated by Paul Peter Piech. Printed Willow Dene, Herts.: Taurus Press. [1974]. [15] pp. col. il.
  A limited ed. of 125 numbered copies.   OXB

YATES, L.J. (1918–   . A clerk before the war. Served in the Army with the British Expeditionary Force. At Dunkirk and later posted to the Middle East) *see* 76

YATES, Peter, pseud. *see* **LONG, William**, (Peter Yates, pseud.)

YEATES, Henry Bamsey (Of Frome, Somerset)

The new voice: poems and lyrics. Frome: Author. 1947. 22 pp.   OXB

YORK, David

First aid for first aiders, or "What'll I do?": [*poems*]; by Herry-Perry and David York. Hutchinson & Co. Ltd. [1939]. viii, 60 pp. il.   IWM

YOUNG, Andrew (Of Tunbridge Wells, Kent) *see* 38

YOUNG, Andrew (1885–1971. b. Elgin, Morayshire. Educated at the Royal High School, Edinburgh, and Edinburgh University. Worked for the Y.M.C.A. in France during the First World War. Vicar of Stonegate, Sussex, 1941–59, a Canon of Chichester Cathedral from 1948. Poet and writer of drama, essays and radio scripts. Interested in a wide range of scholarship, including theology, metaphysics and Gothic architecture. Lived at Arundel, Sussex)

Complete poems. Arranged and introduced by Leonard Clark. Secker & Warburg. 1974. 367 pp.   OXB

YOUNG, C.K. (Lance-Corporal, Royal Corps of Signals) *see* 25, 47

YOUNG, C.P.S. Denham- *see* **DENHAM-YOUNG, C.P.S.**

YOUNG, Douglas (1913–   . b. Tayport, Fife. Educated at Merchiston Castle School, St Andrews University, and New College, Oxford. Sent to prison for refusing war service except in an independent Scotland's army. Elected Chairman of the Scottish Nationalist Party in 1942. After the war became a Labour parliamentary candidate. Greek scholar and writer on Scotland and

Scottish affairs. Taught classics at the Universities of Aberdeen and St Andrews. Professor of Greek, North Carolina University, United States)

Autran blads: an outwale o verses. Glasgow: William Maclellan. 1943. 52 pp. (Poetry Scotland series).

    In Scots dialect.   **BL**

A braird o thristles: Scots poems. Pictish decorations by George Bain. Glasgow: William Maclellan. 1947. 56 pp. il. (Poetry Scotland series, 12).

    In Scots dialect.   **OXB**

Selected poems. Oliver & Boyd. 1950. 23 pp. (Saltire modern poets).

    Published for the Saltire Society.   **BL**

YOUNG, E.D. *see* 52

YOUNG, Edwin

The footprints in the snow, of Edwin Young: [poems]. Ilfracombe: Arthur H. Stockwell, Ltd. [1941]. 24 pp.   **OXB**

YOUNG, Francis Brett (1884–1954. b. Halesowen, Worcestershire. Educated at Epsom College and Birmingham University. Trained as a physician, becoming a ship's doctor for a time. Poet of the First World War. Major, Royal Army Medical Corps. Served in the East African campaign, eventually invalided home with fever and exhaustion. Novelist, winner of the James Tait Black Memorial Prize in 1927)

The island. William Heinemann Ltd. 1944. vi, 451 pp.   **MPL**

The island. William Heinemann Ltd. 1944. x, 451 pp.

    A limited ed. of 100 numbered copies signed by the author.   **BL**

The island. [New] ed. William Heinemann Ltd. 1955. xii, 451 pp.   **MPL**

YOUNG, Geoffrey Winthrop (1876–1958. Educated at Marlborough College, Trinity College, Cambridge, and Jena University, Geneva. Assistant master at Eton College, 1900–05, H.M. Inspector of Secondary Schools, 1905–13. Poet of the First World War. Special war correspondent in Belgium and France, 1914. Commanded Friends Ambulance Units in France and Italy. Severely wounded. Received British, French, Belgian and Italian decorations. Reader in Comparative Education at London University, 1932–41. Poet and mountaineer) *see* 84

YOUNGER, William Antony (1917– . b. Scotland. Educated at Canford School, and Christ Church, Oxford. Poet and crime novelist)

The dreaming falcons: poems. Hutchinson & Co. Ltd. [1944]. 40 pp.   **BPL**

YOUNGMAN, Bernard Robert (1908– . b. Beccles, Suffolk. Educated at Sir John Leman School and Borough Road College, Isleworth. Headmaster of Bushey Meads School, 1948–58, and of Hoveton County Secondary School,

1958–64. Chief examiner in religious knowledge at O level, Associated
Examining Board. Of Norwich)

Straws in the wind: an anthology. Letchworth: Letchworth Printers Ltd. 1944. x,
142 pp.

    Poems and miscellaneous prose.   OXB

YOUNGSTAR, Felix (Flying Officer, Royal Air Force) *see* 1, 25

YVETTE, pseud. (Served in the Women's Royal Naval Service) *see* 23

ZIOLKOWSKA, Adele *see* 16

ZODIAC, pseud. (Man between thirty and forty years old in 1944. Traveller,
linguist, actor and alpinist, he served in the Near East) *see* 42

Title Index

For filing purposes the definite or indefinite article at the beginning of a title is ignored.

A la carte, L.E. Jones

A.T.I. There is no need for alarm, A.P. Herbert

Abbey of Aberbrothie, J.C. Milne

About time, P.J. Kavanagh

Above the smoke and stir, P. Howard

The absent Christ, R.H. Le Messurier

Acknowledgment to life, B. Warr

An acre of land, R.S. Thomas

The acreage of the heart, R. Todd

Acrobat, A. Bertolla

Adam and Eve and us, H. Scott

The Admiralty regrets..., J. Pomfret

Aegean islands, B. Spencer

Aeneas at the court of Dido, D.L. Sayers

African crocus, P. S.-G. Spencer

African negatives, A. Ross

African poems, W.J. Plumbe

After battle, J. Monahan

After the bombing, E. Blunden

Aftermath, S. Gwynn

Aftermath, R. Lawrence

Aftermath, R.C. Trevelyan

Afterthoughts, A. Stewart

Against the lightning, H. Popham

Against the sun, A. Jackson

Against the sun, J. Walker

The age of the dragon, J. Lehmann

Air and chill earth, M. Holden

Air cadets, M. Platt

Air poems, M.H. Pickering

Airman singing, J. Wright

Alamein to Zem Zem, K. Douglas

Alan Brooke, M. Giralda

The alert, W.W. Gibson

Alice in Wunderground, M. Barsley

The alighting leaf, A.J. McGeoch

All are waiting, L. Fainlight

All clear, Lucian, pseud.

All dreaming gone, P. Worner

All Hallowe'en, U. Houston

All I can say, G. Holloway

All the quiet people, M. Wainwright

All this and the hills, J.H. Mullis

Almanack of hope, J. Pudney

Alone with you, E. Fradd

Alpha and omega, W.W. Howard

Always Adam, S. Jennett

Ambrosia, J. Millward

The anchor is dropped, S.E. Iveson

And now what?, Nobody of Any Importance, pseud.

Angry decade, R. Tong

Annus mirabilis, A.J. McGeoch

Another time, W.H. Auden

Apollyon, G.R. Hamilton

The apple barrel, J. Stallworthy

Arctic convoy, K. Greenwell

Arena, P.M. Saunders

Arias from a love opera, R. Conquest

Around lakes/dales, L. Swinbank

Arpies and sirens, S. Knowles

Arrows of hope, I. Somerled
Artists in cages, J.W. Herries
As I linger by life's wayside, A.E. Powell
Aspects in adolescence, R. Ayers
The aspirin eaters, A. Craig
Aston Clinton, B.S. Arthur
At the shrine o the unkent sodger, T. Scott
The Atlantic Pact, D.M. Lyon
Atropos, J. Buxton
An attitude of mind, J. Cassidy
Auschwitz, R. Duncan
Auschwitz, E. Wyse
An autobiography in poetry, Angelina, pseud.
Autolycus' pack, A. Esdaile
Autran blads, D. Young
Autumn fires, W.P. Stephenson
Autumn in Copenhagen, A.M. Williams
Autumn leaves, J. Strachan
Autumn shadow, D. Stafford-Clark
Ave vita!, S. Baumer
Aviator loquitur, I. Davie
The Avon flows past, R. Glover
Awake!, W.R. Rodgers
The axe in the wood, C. Dyment
Azure, E.H.W. Meyerstein

A ballad for Britain on May Day, P. Potts
A ballad of Britain, J.B. O'Hare
The ballad of Buchenwald, A.C. Tarbat
Ballads and poems, by A. Munnings
Ballads of Bath, W.G. Harris
Ballads of Bermondsey, L. Davison
Ballads of Blighty, A.H. Lang-Ridge
Ballet-shoe, A.H. Walton
Bally rot, A. Pratt
Bank holiday on Parnassus, A.M. Laing
Banna Strand, J.S. Williams
The banner of Mars, A.K. Campbell
Barbican regained, A.P. Herbert
The bard, W. Godfrey
Bari, R. Venables
Barrage, E. Crawshay-Williams
The barren tree, W. Griffith
The Baths of Aphrodite, R.F. Willetts
The battle continues, C.M. Grieve
The Battle of Blanco Creek, T.A. Mellows
The Battle of Britain, D.W. Shaw
The Battle of Britain, W.N. Sinkinson
Battle with the dark, A. Bury

Battledress ballads, L.R. Frewin
Battlefields and cathedrals, G. Millard
Battlefields and girls, D. Martin
Battles long ago, A.W. Felton
The beast at the door, T.H. Jones
Beat drum, beat heart, S. Wingfield
Beauty and richness, G. Moor
Beauty for ashes, D.L. Cobbett
Beauty is built anew, K.S. Walker
Beauty is deathless, E. Norton
Because no angels came, B. Alane
Because of these, A. Richardson
Beethoven, M. Swabey
The beggar's lute, P. Baker
Beginnings in gladness, L. Sourbutts
Behind the lines, A.A. Milne
Behold the Jew, A. Jackson
The bells' gentle thunder, I. Iliew
The bells of Ouseley, H.G. Romer
The bells of victory, B. Devey
Beneath the hunter's moon, D.A. Turnbull
Beside the guns, J. Steele
The besieged city, D. Stewart
Between the lines, B. Giggs
Between two worlds, G. Freeman
Between two worlds, E.C. Peters
Beyond compare, L.E. Rundle
Beyond the minotaur, P. Beattie
Beyond the stars, D. Kenmare
Beyond the trumpet, J. Wright
Beyond the veil, V.H. Bennett
Beyond these voices, T.M. Auld
Beyond this disregard, J. Pudney
Bicycle tyre in a tall tree, G. Kendrick
The big adventure, H. Reid
Big Ben, H. Greene
The big music, R.G. Sutherland
Birds of Essex, M. Fowler
Birth of Venus, S. Knowles
The birth of Venus, J. Smith
Black Europe, W.B. Nichols
The black seasons, H. Treece
Blackout, R.G. Buchanan
The blind child, F.L. Jones
Blitz bits, D. Hughes
The blitzkrieg, A. Row
Blood and sweat and tears, R.S. Mallone
Blood, sweat and tear(e)s, C. Last & S. Phillips

Blue and gold, M. Crosbie
Blue feather poems, J. Clee
Blue grey and gold, J. Pellow
Boatrace, D.G. Davies
Boding day, E. Milne
The body's imperfection, L.A.G. Strong
The bombed happiness, J.F. Hendry
Bones and ashes, P. Crean
A book for Priscilla, N. Moore
The book of Macnib, A.D. Mackie
The book of Thomas Rhymer, T.M. Auld
Boots of sand, N.L. Walker
Bow bells are silent, M.D. Anderson
A braird o thristles, A. Young
Branches green and branches black, S. Johnson
The bread of truth, R.S. Thomas
Bread rather than blossoms, D.J. Enright
Break in harvest, R. Mathias
The breathless kingdom, W. Jarman
Brides of reason, D. Davie
The bridge, R. Pitter
Brief candles, J. Bevan
Brief matchlight, A.V. Bowen
The bright and the bitter, I.D.L.
Bright November, K. Amis
Brim of day, J.R. Anderson
Bring back the bells, A.P. Herbert
Britain, her allies and the Axis, J.J. Emery
Britain, please answer me, H. Benjamin
The British Commonwealth, C.S. Froats
The British Empire, E.G. Coates
The British Empire at war, C. Clark
Broadway, P. Hopewell
The broken melody, H. Desmond
Broken wings, V.H. Bennett
Broken wings of song, W. Storrie
Brother to Icarus, G. Sandford
Brown phoenix, C. Dover
Bubbles, R. Gordon
Buddhist poems, C. Humphreys
Buds unfolding, J. Smith
Buenos Aires, H. Manning
Buried god, M. Baldwin
The buried stream, G. Faber
Burma victory, A.A. Donald
The burning-glass, W. De La Mare
The burning glass, L. Whistler
The burning hare, J.C. Hall
The burning of the leaves, L. Binyon

But the earth abideth, W. Soutar
Buzzing around with a bee, N. Moore
By contrast, R. Emsworth

The cabaret, the dancer, the gentlemen, N. Moore
The cactus harvest, C. Hamblett
The Cademuir poems, R.D.M. Kerr
Cairns, C. Levenson
The call of the stars, A.B. Rendle
Calling all shipping, K.M. Garner
The Calpean sonnets, L.P. Sanguinetti
Came the call, B. Turley
The camp site, G. Clark
Can man plan? F.J. Osborn
Canonbury Watch, E.S. Hole
Canonbury Watch farewell, E.S. Hole
The canticle of the rose, E. Sitwell
Careless livery, R. Whiteley
Carnival town, G. Bircham
Carried forward, S. Freegard
Carthage, J.O. Fuller
A case of samples, K. Amis
Casual acquaintance, M. Battcock
Catholic sermons in war and peace, C.D. Kingdon
Caught on blue, R. Garfitt
Causes, R. Shaw
Celts, S. Bell
The centre cannot hold, G. Woodcock
Chain, R. Ball
Challenge, W.W. Gibson
The charity of the stars, J. Heath-Stubbs
A Charlie's rhymes, P. Robinson
The charmed fabric, L. Sowden
Cherry petals, P.M. Taylor
Chiaroscuro, M. Battcock
The chieftains ground, R. Somerset
The child who sat upon a stair, W. Howling
Children of the century, A.M. Williams
Chime of fancy, S. Stokes
The choice is mine, E. Pickthall
A choice of ballads, W. Plomer
Choose something like a star, M.H. Noël-Paton
Christmas, S. Matthewman
Christmas carols and winter poems, V.I. Arlett
The Christmas child, D.G. Bridson
Chromatic airs, A.J. Bull

Chuckies on the cairn, R.G. Sutherland
Churchill's finest hour, H. Desmond
Cities of the mind, T. Stephanides
Cities, plains and people, L. Durrell
The city in the sun, P. Noble
The city of white stones, D. Kenmare
The civilian, A. Head
Clarion call, R. Archibald
Clausentum, J. Arlott
Clay speaks of the fire, E. Lobo
Clean fingers, Elizabeth Jane, pseud.
The cleansing of the knife, N. Mitchison
A clew to the Americas, F. Fleming
The clock, B. Guinness
The cloth of flesh, W. Jarman
A cloud across the sun, S. Wingfield
A clutch of words, E. Harwood
A clyack-sheaf, C.M. Grieve
The coast of Barbary, A. Beecham
Coastal Command, J. Pomfret
Coastline, S.G. Putt
Coat of many colours, T. Bouch
A coat of many colours, A.W. Uloth
Cobwebs, C.C.M. Cook
Coggin's Barrow, L.E. Bell
Cold storage, J. Ennis, pseud.
Colditz cameo, A. Campbell
Colinton Dell, N.L. Smith
Collected green fingers, R. Arkell
A collection of highland verse, M. Scott
Collection of poems written in hospital, J. Valber
The colour of blood, G. Macbeth
Colour symphony, C.B. Toosey
Colours and windows, W. Wolff
Combat, D. Lowsley
Come dance with Kitty Stobling, P. Kavanagh
Come dream with me, E. Koffman
Come to Me all ye. . ., J. Gilbey
Come with me, D.J. Leaver
The comet, A.S.T. Fisher
Coming back from Babylon, K. Gershon
Common chords, S. Sassoon
The common festival, S. Snaith
The common things, I.D. Matthias
Communion, H. Lockyer
Company of women, V. Scannell
The compass, F.T. Jesse
Con amore, E. Grainger

The conference, D.L. Smith
The confessions of Peter Pan, J. Waller
Conflict and query, P. Nicholson
Conflicting conflicts, A.H. Green
Conquest, W.H. Petty
Conscripts, E. Litvinoff
Consider the lily, A.V. Scrimgeour
Consider the years 1938–1946, V. Graham
Contrast, C.R. Sanderson
Conway Castle, G.M. Pritchard
Cornish crystal, G. Hunkin
Cornish pasty, L.J. Fuller
The corridors of dawn, E. White
Counterparts, R. Fuller
The countryside, P.R. Bishop
The countryside, J.A. Griffiths
Cousins in contrast, E.R. Kappes
The cove, J.T.G. Macleod
A cow from Jersey, D. Falcke
Credere aude, D.M. Self
The crescent moon, T.L. Williams
The crimson wing, C.M. Ford
Crisis, C. Hassall
Crooked connections, M. Robertson
The cross in the cup, H.N. Forbes
Crossing the border, R. Tong
Crossing the line, E. Lowbury
Crossroads of courage, F.H. Trott
Crossroads of the year, R. Manwaring
The crossways, J. Alden
The crown and the fable, H. Manning
The crown and the laurel, A.E. Johnson
A crown for Cain, E. Litvinoff
A crown for David, P. Walton
Crucified landscape, G. Blunt
The cruel solstice, S. Keyes
Crusade, J. Waller
Cry for the moon, B. Owen
The crystal mountain, D. Kenmare
A cure for cant, M. Pim
A cure for the blues, G. Davidson
Current events, E. Rathbone
The curving shore, A. Beresford
The cycle of the months, E. Archer, pseud.
Cypress and acacia, V. Watkins

D-Day, anon.
Dale's feet, M. Beadnell
Dancer's end, E. Powell

The dancing beggars, J. Garratt
Dare to believe, D.M. Self
The dark convoys, B. Griffiths
The dark window, R. Skelton
The darkest path, R.J. Freixa
Dawn music, P. Chadwick
The dawn of peace, C. Dodd
Dawn passage, M. Chenevix Trench
Day by day, J.H. Marsh
The day moves, C. Logan
The day's alarm, P. Dehn
Days enduring, R. Mathias
Days of grace, J. Dark
Days out, D. Scott
De Londres à Carthage, T.I.F. Armstrong
Death at sea, F. Prokosch
Death in April, G.R. Hamilton
The death of William Rufus, J. Sibly
Deaths and entrances, D. Thomas
December spring, J. Brooke
Deep sea murmurings, J.A. Jones
The deevil's waltz, S.G. Smith
The defeated, P.D. Cummins
A democrat's chapbook, Quiet Woman, pseud.
The derelict day, A. Ross
The descent into the cave, J. Kirkup
Desert warrior, P. Hore-Ruthven
Desert wells, D. Wellesley
Desert wind, T. Eastwood
Deux poèmes de la Tunisie, T.I.F. Armstrong
The devil's kitchen, T. Blackburn
The devil's own song, Q. Hogg
Diamond cut diamond, E. Milne
The diary of a heart, D.G.S. McMurtrie
Different like a zoo, O.Q. Berington
Different weather, A. Beecham
The disasters of war, R. Ellis
Disorderly poems, E.P.B. Linstead
Dispersal point, J. Pudney
A distant fluting, C. Tower
Diversion, R. Frankau
The divided ways, J. Heath-Stubbs
The divine caller, E.G. Clarke
Division, E.H.W. Meyerstein
Dockyard M.T., anon.
Dodging the lions and tigers, H. Clark
Doggerel for the Forces, grave and gay, A. Jameson

Doktor Faust in Rose Street, R.G. Sutherland
The doors of stone, F.T. Prince
The Dorking thigh, W. Plomer
The double image, D. Levertov
The double man, W.H. Auden
The doubtful crown, J.E. Caspall
Doubts and affirmations, L. Hobley
The dousing, J. Lee
Dover Castle, D.A. Smith
Dragon, J. White
Dragons' teeth, J. Bevan
Dream garden, P. Gibson
Dream girl, W.M. Poulter
A dream observed, A. Ridler
A dream of Adolf Hitler, A. Lewis
Dream stuff, E. Smith
Dreaming, L.D. Rogers
The dreaming falcons, W.A. Younger
Dreams and realities, W.A. Jackson
Drift, A.J. Bull
Drifting leaves, C. Dunker
Drifts of time, N. Purcell
Driving west, P. Beer
Dublin poems, J.S. Starkey
Dumb instrument, D. Welch
Dunkirk, W. Gordon & L. Latham
Dust of war, F. Bratton
Dusty days, J. Masefield
The duty of Bess, R.G. Martin

The early drowned, H. Corke
Early light, D. Wellesley
Earthquake at Delphi, A.B.M. Cadaxa
East and west, W.C. Dampier
The ebbless sea, E. Slater
Ebony, D. Emery
Echoes of war, H.M. Attfield
The edge of being, S. Spender
The Eighth Army epic, L. Burrows
Eighty four days, B. Winchester
Elegiacs, J. Mander
Elegies, W. Bell
Elegies for the dead in Cyrenaica, H. Henderson
Elegy for a lost submarine, E. Milne
An elegy for lovers, F. Wilson
Elegy for two voices, D. Kenmare
The elements of death, J. Brooke
Emblems of love and war, C. Graves

Emblems of more, J. Whitehead
An embroidery, M. Wornum
Empire King, E. Thompson
The empty spaces, S. Churchill
The enchanted wood, J. Trevor
Enchantment, E. Koffman
End of drought, R. Pitter
The end of the day, K. Foottit & A. Tod
Ends of verse, N.S. Power
Endymion to silver, T.W. Ramsey
The enemies of love, J.M. Lindsay
The enemy in the heart, T.H. Jones
England, A. Pontremoli
England, K.G. Rogers
England, A.C. Tarbat
England in peace and war, E. Newgass
The English weather, R. Gascoigne
Ephemerid, W.H. Charnock
Epigrams, H.W. Garrod
Epilogue, W.H. Charnock
Epitaph for a squadron, J. Gordon
Epitaphs and occasions, R. Fuller
Epithets of war, V. Scannell
The ermine, R. Pitter
Eros in dogma, G. Barker
Eros uncrowned, A. Bury
Errantes hederae, R. Stark
Escape and surrender, R.E.S. Bruce
Escape from anger, E. Marx
Escape to childhood, K.M. Garner
Essays in doggerel, R. Bridgeman
Ettrick verse, W. Addison
Europa and the bull, W.R. Rodgers
Europe my confidant, J. Hanlon
Evening in Stepney, L. Bowes Lyon
An evening of mid-June, H.W. Household
Ever green, I. Richardson
Everyday thoughts, H.J. Thomas
Everyday thoughts and versatile verses, G. Daly
Exile, L. Paul
Exile and return, W.J. Harvey
The exiled heart, J.M. Lindsay
An exile's musings, A.N.H. Pollen
The expanding mirror, W. Long
The expectant silence, W. Soutar
Experience of England, J. Atkins
Exploits of the war, F. Olivier, pseud.
Exposition, R. Fournier

F as in flight, J.R.A. Bailey
Fact and fantasy in verse, J.G. Cogdon
Factory without, J. Royal
Facts and fancies, M.B. Parks
The fairy glen, D. Shanks
Faith and fancy, N.M. Darby
Faith in freedom, T. Brearley
Fall of a tower, F. Berry
Fall of leaf, U. Vaughan Williams
Fallen leaves, G. Davidson
A family album, B. Jones
Far from the land, J. Monahan
Farewell, Aggie Weston, C. Causley
Farewell and welcome, R. Bottrall
Farrago, D.J. Lockwood
A fastidious taste, D. Dunker
The fatal assonance, A. Bates
The fatal landscape, G.S. Fraser
Feeble folk, C.L. Stallard
The fern on the rock, P. Dehn
Ferns in the waste, R.C. Ormerod
The few, E. Shanks
A few simple verses, W.H. Edwards
15 years!, A. Underdown
A fifth and final sonnet bouquet, J.E. Magraw
Fifty years on, I.Q. Twelve, pseud.
Figs and thistles, S.G. Smith
The filigree bridge, M. Battcock
Fire among the ruins, S. Piggott
Firework music, P. Hellings
First aid for first aiders, Herry-Perry, pseud.
   & D. York
First attempt, J. Begg
First awakening, G. Iley
First fruits, F.J. Parnell
The first instance, W. Hawes
The first-known, F. Bellerby
The first miscellany, D. Brook-Browne
First of the few, H.J. Green
Five rivers, N. Nicholson
Flak, E. Crawshay-Williams
Flame in the dark, A. Naumann
Flash and outbreak, J. Whitehead
A flat in Bloomsbury, C.H. Ross
Flight above cloud, J. Pudney
Flights of fancy, D.W. Irwin
Flos malvae, A.B. Ramsay
Flow and ebb, C.L. Lanyon

Flowering cactus, M. Hamburger
The flowering thorn, S. Snaith
The flowering tree, C. Houselander
Flowers by post, M.J. Becker
Flowers for a lady, R. McFadden
Flowers from a country garden, M. Nicholson
Flowers in the crevices, M. Macdonald
Flowers of fancy, G. Montagu
Flowing tide and slack water, G.C. Johnson
Flowing water, P. Stevenson
The flying bird, C.D. Pegge
Flying bombs, V.H.F.
The flying castle, M. Burn
The folded rose, A.R. Rooke
A fool of time, S.H. Edwards
The footprints in the snow, E. Young
For England, R.D. Walsh
For Hecuba!, R.J. Poole
For Johnny, J. Pudney
For my rat, M. Johnson
For Rachel, M. Robertson
For such a time as this, L.M. Barber
For the birthday of a housewife, E. Shanks
For the few, R. Duncan
For the joy of doing, G.J. Prosser
For the record, B. Kops
For the unfallen, G. Hill
For this alone, R.P.L. Mogg
For those who died, R. Beck
For to-morrow, J.M.L. Reitzenstein
For us they go, A.E. Freeth
For whom there is no spring, S.D. Tremayne
For you! E.E. Martyn
Forays, R. Conquest
The forest, D. Stewart
The forest, M.D. Turner
Forgive me, sire, N. Cameron
Fortunate Hamlet, J. Waller
Fortune's wild wheel, G. Borman
Forty years on, D.M. Holt
Forward to victory, S. Bramley-Moore
Fossils of a future time? W.J. Turner
Four and twenty, R.D. Birch
The four-walled dream, N. Heseltine
Four words, D. Kenmare
Fourteen to forty-eight, M. Lawrence
A fourth bouquet of English sonnets, J.E. Magraw
The fourth man, T. Blackburn
Fragments, J. Hills
Fragments, G. Sherrard
Fragrant petals, M. Jackson
Frail prelude, J. Normanton
France, A. Comfort
Freedom is my fame, P. Warner
Friendship, S.R. Manning
Friendship, D. Price
Friendship poems, J.M. Shaw
The frog prince, A. Barnsley
From a foreign shore, A. Hull
From Daer Water, B.J.B. MacArthur
From Hellas to Limerick, J. Sackville-Martin
From life, D. Martin
From many times and lands, F.L. Lucas
From mood to mood, F.W. Robins
From my heart to yours, N.G. Cheyne
From my window, A. Hanman
From the ashes, A. Sampson
From the Caribbean to England in verse, N. Cressall
From the cathedral cloisters, J. Millward
From the Chilterns, T. Roscoe
From the foot of the mountains, S.E. Meritt
From the joke shop, R. Fuller
From this mire, D.W. Reynolds
From time to time, F.W. Robins
Fugue for our time, D. Cooke
Full cycle, A. Richardson
Full enjoyment, A.P. Herbert
Fūrin, G. Dixey
Further ballads of old Birmingham, E.M. Rudland
The fury of the living, J. Singer

The gallant sailor, W.C.A. Robson
Gallery, J. Corbett
A gallimaufry, N. Micklem
The galloping centaur, F. Berry
The gallows-cross, H. Palmer
The garden, V. Sackville-West
Garden of Eden, J. Harriman
Garden of memories, G.M. Cutting
A garland for Captain Fox, R. Greacen
A garland for the green, E. Milne
Garland for the winter solstice, R. Todd
A garland of verse, A.K. Carson

Garlands and ash, A. White
The garnered sheaf, J. Sackville-Martin
The gate, C. Day Lewis
Gates of beauty and death, J. Smith
The gates of silence, W. Gardiner
Gathered from my years, J.W. Barns-Graham
The gathering storm, W. Empson
A generation risen, J. Masefield
The generous days, S. Spender
Genesis, C. Woodhouse
The gentle heart, J.M. Scragg
A geography, T. Gunn
German elegy, W.A. Rathkey
Gethsemane, G.M. Bender
The gift, D. Henry
The gift, J. Hier
The gift, D. Martin
The glass tower, N. Moore
The glassblowers, M. Peake
The gleam and the dark, A. Buist
Gleams Britain's day, H. Clifton
Gleanings, G. Montagu
Gleanings of the years, D. Corrie
Glimpses in the dark, G. Davidson
The glitter shops, the girls, H. Corby
The glorious few, M. Prentice
The glory of Stalingrad, J.E. Pinkney
Godfrey Grantham, A.E. Grantham
God's commission, D.I. Wright
Gods with stainless ears, L. Roberts
The golden chain, C. Harrey
The golden face, T. Stephanides
Golden gleams, F.E. Feilden
Golden orchids, H. Desmond
Gower poems, D.E. Grandfield
Grabberwocky and other flights of fancy, M. Barsley
The grandchild, N. Freeman
The granite island, R. Payne
The grass grows through, C.P. Billot
Graves and resurrections, V. Scannell
The great divide, W. Godfrey
The great miracle, E. Shanks
The great musician, W. Blathwayt
A great rushing of winds, C. Winchester
The greater war, F.E. Feilden
Green and grey, R.G. Vansittart
Green branches, S.J. Looker
Green fingers again, R. Arkell

The green fuse, I. Hargrave
The green heart, B. Chamberlain
Green leaves, J.M. Seager
Green song, E. Sitwell
Greenfield verses, C.F. Elias
Griff on the Gremlin, D.J. Marshall
Grim and gay, L. Anderson
Grim and gay, J.B. Trenwith
The grinning face, J.M. Russell
Groping poet, W.D. Dunkerley
The grotto, G. Martlew
Grown over with green-ness, D. Bolton
The gunner, N. Spencer
Guy Fawkes night, J. Press

Ha! Ha! Among the trumpets, A. Lewis
Half century's verse, M. Cornish
Hamlet in autumn, I.C. Smith
Hampdens going over, H. Corby
A handful of salt, H.A. Johnson
Happy rhymes for the air raid shelter, D.W. Irwin
The happy warrior, P. Hore-Ruthven
The hardest freedom, S.D. Tremayne
Hark forrard!, I.M. Raikes
The harp in the green window, M.H. Tattersall
The harp in the rainbow, C.W. Phillips
Harvest home, J. James
Harvest in hell, I. Davie
Harvests, J. Westren
The haunted garden, H. Treece
Haven, J. Gilbey
The hawk in the rain, T. Hughes
He's a perfect little gentleman — the swine!, R. Frankau
The headlands, H. Sergeant
The hearing heart, L. Clark
The heart is highland, M.K. Macmillan
The heart of things, G. Johnson
Heart's desire, J. Wainwright
Hearts o'erflowing on various musings, A.M.
Hearts of oak, G.M. Cutting
The heart's townland, R. McFadden
Heather mixture, W.J. Cowie
Heirs of a morning, M. Wedd
Hell, F. Townshend
Helpful and comforting poems, H. Collis

Her storms, S. Wingfield
Here and hereafter, D.M. Harris
Here and there: now and then, I.M. Jones
Here — at Lulworth, D. Symes
Here in the country's heart, G.M. Blacker
Here is my signature, A.G. Herbertson
Here no security, A. Buist
Here. Now. Always., E. Brock
Heroines all!, B.W.J.G. Quadling
Herzelroyde in paradise, M.F. Richey
Hey, diddle diddle!, M. Straynge
Hidden life, J.L. Wain
The hidden path, D.C. Thomson
The high and the lowly, L. Aske
The high road, E.S. Lay
The higher — the Fuehrer, L. Joyce
The highland warriors, P.M. Parlour
Hinterland, H.F. Summers
The Hiroshima dream, G. Macbeth
Hitler, in 1944, E.H. Blakeney
Hitler's war, R.H. Bowers
Holes in the sky, L. MacNeice
Holiday ramblings, L. Smith
The holocaust, G. Sherrard
The holy war, V., pseud.
Homage to Cheshire, H. Lucas
Home Guard rhymes, A.H. Watkins
Home town elegy, G.S. Fraser
The homeland, B.E. Smith
The homeward journey, L. Aaronson
The homeward road, B.M. Hine
The honeysuckle hedge, S. Steen
A Hong Kong diary, G.C. Marston
Hope, E.E. George
Hope from the heart, R. Hickford
Hope is the window, A.I.C. Haime
Hope's harvest, G. Borman
Horan's field, V. Iremonger
A hornet in my hair, P. Lake
The horses of Falaise, V. West
A hot bath at bedtime, M. Robertson
The hour has come, F. Gabriel
A house of voices, J.C. Hall
Housewarming, P.A.T. O'Donnell
How shall we remember them?, A. Rhys
How to keep the peace, G. Mair-Schubert
Hubble-bubble, B. Fergusson
Hugh, N. Foster
Human and all human, B. Gingell

*Humorous verse, written during the German
    occupation of Jersey*, F.T. Du Feu
The hunting dark, R. Skelton
The hunting of the hare, S. Bracher
Hurdy-gurdy, N. Price
Hymn of the besieged, C.W. Gardner
Hymns without faith, G. Dixey

I from my small corner, J. Bishop
I, in the membership of my days, R. Harris
I shot at a star, H.W. Moore
I the I, P. Villiers-Stuart
I'll go to bed at noon, S. Haggard
I wonder, P. Emeric
Ice on the live rail, A.W. Russell
Idle rhymes of an ack-ack gunner, C.R. Walton
The idyll, J.B. Bradfield
If I may share, A. Naumann
If I should die —, M. Wilson
If I were blind, M.A. Selby
— if it's only goodbye, C.A. McIntyre
If judgment comes, A. Noyes
If men should ask, L. Atkin
If pity departs, R. Atthill
Immortal diamond, J. Durnford
The immortal ease, T. Nicholl
Immortal few, H.L. Gee
The immortal home, J.K.G. Hoffman
Impassionata, K.K. Woodeson
In a bombed house, W. Plomer
In a time of assassins, R.W. Trudgett
In all the signs, J. Gilbey
In an emergency, D. Weissbort
In another room, P. Champkin
In circles, P.S. Allfrey
In contrast, B. Warburton
In flashlight, M. Hamburger
In heaven's view, M.D. Bishop
In idleness of air, A.W. Russell
In many moods, R. Shuttleworth
In memoriam Milena, R. Pybus
In memory of Dylan Thomas, R. Ball
In middle age, C.H.O. Scaife
In my old days, E.V. Knox
In our time, E. Rodgers
In our time, M. Smith
In praise of life, H.N. Spalding
In retrospect, J. Nichols
In shabby streets, C.A. Alington

In the fire, T. Blackburn
In the footsteps of the opium eater, J. Ashbrook
In the midst of death, C. Sansom
In the stopping train, D. Davie
In the time of tyrants, W. Soutar
In the tower's shadow, N.K. Cruickshank
In the Trojan ditch, C.H. Sisson
In the wilderness, J. Simmons
In these five years, D. Nixon
In this our day, J. Ashwin
In time of suspense, L. Whistler
In time of war, M. Browne
In time of war, E.H.W. Meyerstein
In Yeovil town, C. Whitby
The incarnation, D. Burton
Incidentally, P. Gordon
Indeed to goodness!, A. Hughes
Indian landscape, R.N. Currey
Indian scenes, F. Kitchen
Inferior verse, H.I. Bransom
Initial effort, E. Baker
The inn of night, S. Snaith
The inner harbour, F. Adcock
The inner room, G.R. Hamilton
The inner voice, R. Carroll
Inscapes, F. Scarfe
Inscriptions, S. Spender
Instead of a sonnet, P. Potts
Instead of tears, M.C. Stopes
Interlude, O.M. Wood
Intimations and avowals, N.G. Mears
Into action, J. Lindsay
Into Europe, T.I.F. Armstrong
Into the westering sun, A.W. Cunningham
Invisibility is the art of survival, E. Brock
The invisible sun, M. Willy
Invitation, M. Landon
Invitation and warning, H. Treece
Invocation, J.M.A. Mills
The inward animal, T. Tiller
Inward companion, W. De La Mare
The inward eye, N. McCaig
Iona verses, K.S. Newton
Irish seed sporting lead, M. Giralda
The iron harvest, G. Johnson
The iron laurel, S. Keyes
The irreplaceable melody, E. Peters
The island, F.B. Young
The island and the cattle, N. Moore

Island legacy, A.H. Body
Island musings, W. Swanney
Island thoughts, M. Davidson
Islands and people, J. Hubback
The Isles of Scilly, G. Grigson
It all depends on us!, H.B. Olive

Jackdaw, D. Burnett
The Jacob's ladder, D. Levertov
Jacob's ladder, G.A. Taylor
Jenny Pluck Pears, G. Cooke
Jersey in jail, 1940–45, H. Wyatt
The Jervis Bay, M. Thwaites
Jewels and dust, I. Davies
John Englishman, W.G. Hole
Johnny Alleluia, C. Causley
The joke shop annexe, R. Fuller
A Joseph coat, E. Dickinson
A journey, E.J.M.D. Plunkett
The journey and the dream, H. Popham
The journey of life, E.M. Fletcher
Journey of the years, P. Croome
Journey to the silverless island, I. Apthomas
Joy and verity, M.C. Stopes
Joy and woe, D.H.A. Slater
A joy proposed, T.H. White
Jubilo, E. Milne
Judy Garland and the cold war, J. Simmons
June and a posy from Kent, C.M.M. Scott
Just a few lines, A.W. Bird
Just like the resurrection, P. Beer
Juvenialia, T.B. Higginson

The kaleidoscope of years, F.E. Feilden
Kaleidoscope plus, R. Cobham
The keeper of the lodge, J.C. Grant
Kensington Gardens in war-time, H. Wolfe
Kent calling blossom-time, C.M.M. Scott
Kentish rhymes, J. Alden
Kindred points, H. Compton
King Log, G. Hill
The kingfisher catcher, S. Morris
The kiss of stars, J. Waller
A kite's dinner, S. Wingfield

The labyrinth, E. Muir
Ladies from hell, L. Leslie
The lady with the unicorn, V. Watkins
The lair, A. Beresford

Lament for a new age, C. Maurer
Lament for strings, W. Gardiner
The lamp, R. Church
The lamp and the veil, V. Watkins
The land of broken hearts, H.B. Wallace
The land of verse, H.S. Pearse
Land workers, J. Masefield
The last ditch, L. MacNeice
Last leave, B.J.B. MacArthur
The last load home, E.H. Blakeney
Last things, E. Pine
The last trip, H.J. Thorpe
Late harvest, G. Cockerill
Later Hogarth, M. Hamburger
Latest news, D. Craig
Lathkill Dale, A. Mann
Laugh, love and live, H. Prince
Laughing blood, R. Spender
The laws of the Navy, R.A. Hopwood
Lays of an Ulster paradise, R. Kirkwood
Lean forward, spring, P. Hesketh
The leaping flame, C. Randall
The leaseholder, D. Weissbort
Leave my old morale alone, A.P. Herbert
The leavening air, H. Sergeant
Leaves of life, H.N. Robbins
Leaves without a tree, G.S. Fraser
Lecture to the trainees, G. Macbeth
Legacies and encounters, K. Gershon
Legacy to love, T.I.F. Armstrong
Less nonsense!, A.P. Herbert
Lessons of the war, H. Reed
Lest we forget, F. James
Let me walk with you, F.V. Simpson
Let there be light, O. Oddess
Let us be gay, A.P. Herbert
Let us be glum, A.P. Herbert
Letter from Ireland, E. Milne
Letter in wartime, H.B. Mallalieu
A letter to Lucian, A. Noyes
A letter to the living, C. Hamblett
Letters to Malaya, M. Skinner
Levant, R. Cecil
Liberty!, G. Martlew
Libya, L. Challoner
Life, A. Nicholls
Life is sweet, M.B. Booth
Life is what it makes you, F. Tonkinson
Life is what you make it, N.A. Ranger

Life's ceaseless waves, M. Roper-Huggins
Life's treasures, M. Jones
A lifetime of dying, E. Bartlett
Light after darkness, N. Hanssen
Light and shade, A.H. Berry
Light and shade, A. Cartledge
Light and shade, M.A.P. Forester
Light and shadow, P. Lawrence
The light left burning, W. Mustoe
Light the lights, A.P. Herbert
Light verse and lyrics, R.O. Mackay
The lighthouse, D. Price
The lightning-struck tower, S. Shannon
Like pebbles forth, E. Nicholson
Limerick pastoral, T.E.B. Adderley
Lincolnshire, A.C. Parker
A Lincolnshire garland, E.S. Dudley
Lines on life and love, B. Cartland
Links of gold, D. Woodberry
The lions' mouths, A. Brownjohn
Listen confides the wind, R. Grant
Listen Mangan, E. Milne
Listening in, M.S. Norris
Little bits of light and shade, J.C. Neill
The little monkey, A. Andrews
The little mouse, G.M. Tailby
The living bough, R.A. George
Living in a calm country, P. Porter
Living in time, K. Raine
Lobster potted people, T.A. Pratt
Local lives, B. Warburton
London, D. Cowie
London allegiance, C. Campbell
London garland, W.C. Reedy
London 1940, J.M. & J. Mitford Varcoe
London pride, W. R. Titterton
London saga, S. Johnson
The London tree, M. Gilchrist
London watches, O. Katzin
Londoners, G. Ewart
The lonely, J. Wilson
Lonely spring, H.F. Rowland
The lonely suppers of W.V. Balloon, C. Middleton
The long way round, A. Ayling
Look towards the green, G. Daniells
Losing ground, J. Lockwood
The loss of ancestry, J. Tripp
The lost July, R.L. Green

The lost knight, F. Newbold
Lost planet, D. Wellesley
A lost season, R. Fuller
Lost soldier, lost town, R.W. Trudgett
Love and dreams, H.E. Smith
Love and Elizabeth, K. Hopkins
Love and memory, R. Gardiner
Love and no love, C. Kinross
Love and the devil, H. Kay
Love, hope and despair, R.J. Hawkins
Love in a mist, A. Shelley
Love lyrics, G.L. Lampson
Love poems and elegies, I.C. Smith
Love triumphant, G.A. Browning
Love's crown, G. Griffiths
Love's reminiscences, W. Hunt
The loving game, V. Scannell
Loweswater, P.F. Gaye
Lowland soldier, B. Fergusson
Luana Coral, E. Mack
Lucem demonstrat umbra, H.P. Kirby
Lyrics of a lifetime, A.J. Sargeson
Lyrics of Fermanagh, G.M. Ramsey
Lyrics of leisure, L. Court
Lyrics of love and death, A.V. Bowen
Lyrics of lovely Lincolnshire, E.S. Dudley

The magic apple tree, E. Feinstein
The magic country, G.L. Groom
The magic stone, G. Johnson
The Maid of the Mersey, A.E. Siddall
Mainly truth, G.E. Turton
Make me a mandrake, D. Stringer
Malta to-day, E.H. Blakeney
A man arose, C. Roberts
The man from Flanders, E. Shanks
The man of grass, R. Macnab
Man = ship = tank = gun = plane, N. Cunard
Many moods, A. Aylwin, pseud.
A map of Verona, H. Reed
Maple and oak, N. Tucker
Marching on, P.V. Bradshaw
Marching soldier, J. Cary
Marlow Hill, T.I.F. Armstrong
The martinet, T. Roscoe
The martyr, D.P. Lambert
The mask of pity, B. Griffiths
The masks of love, V. Scannell

Masquerade of the pen, S.W. Gilliland
Mastering the craft, V. Scannell
Measures for masses, J. Kincaid
Meditations, J. Dominick
Meditations in verse, C.E. Allen
Meditations in verse, E.M. Watts
Meditations in verse, R. Wilberforce
Mediterranean poems, J. Papasian
Mediterranean seed, Atlantic fruit, M. Giralda
Mein Rant, R.F. Patterson
Mellow notes, G.L. Lampson
Memories, J.E. Lee
Memories, N. McCubbin
Memories, M.L. Moon
Memories, J. Morrison
Memories for ever, R.L.
Memories of Beacon Rock, Leicestershire, J.W. Slator
Memory lane, E.S. Fox
Memory reverie, M. Dawne
Men like these, W.A.G. Kemp
The men of the rocks, J.T.G. Macleod
Merchant Navy man, J. Pomfret
Mere verses, K. Crossley
The merry ghosts, J. Waller
Messiah every Christmas, A. Field
Metrical observations, D. Wright
Mice and men, R. Bain
Michael, B. Gibbs
Michaelmas Eve, A.C. Tarbat
Micheldever, J.R. Ackerley
Mid-day, L.B. Miller
Middle East musings, E.C. Higham
The middle of a war, R. Fuller
Midland poems, E. Billingham
The midsummer meadow, E.J. Scovell
Might-have-beens, R.L. Kenyon
Milestones, J. Gilbey
Military honours, J.A. Thompson
Military moments, R.F. Palmer
The millenium, S. De Chair
Millstone grit, D. Tipton
The millstream, R. Lawrence
Mimosa, M.G. Harvey
The mind of man, T.I.F. Armstrong
Mindstream, D.F. Tuckett
Mingling, N.M. Fincher
Miniatures, E. Phillpotts
Minor minutes, J.C. Manning

Mirage, D.S. Goodbrand
The mirage in the south, H. Nicholson
The mirror and the maze, B. McCorkindale
The mirror of life, R.E. Hembling
Miscellany poems, K. Hopkins
Miscellany three, D. Thomas
Miscellany two, D. Thomas
The miser's house, T. Pittaway
Missing, Z. Ilinska
Missing, J.S. Waller
Mission, W.E. Morris
The mistress, J. Barton
Mixed feelings, J. Wain
A mixed grill of Chester poems, A.R. Brierley
Mixed grill verse, T.B. Cooper
Mixed verse, E. Huggins
The modern Genilon, D. Williamson
Modern poems, A. Holme
Modern poems, C. Sheward, pseud.
Moly, T. Gunn
Moments grim and gay, C. Brooke
Moments of meditation, P.A. Morey
Moments of memory, J.D. Warren
Moments of time, W.J. Strachan
Montgomery, A.T.
Monument, C. Jeffery
Moods and places, M.L. Ormsby
Moods, meditations and music, H.K. Styring
Moods of one's mind, F.I. Williams
The moods of the year, H.F. Buin
Moon in cirrus, L.E. Druce
Moon over Cairo, F.E. Humpage
Moon over the Mersey, G. O'Brien
Moon owl, H.C. White
Moortown, T. Hughes
The more deserving cases, R. Graves
More dream roads, D.C. Cuthbertson
More poems for women, M.C. Gibbins
More than time, P. Dickinson
More verses from Dorset, R.L. Cocks
More verses from Mourne, W.H. Crowe
More war-time musings, M. Berners
Morn mist, W. Lloyd
Morning meeting, A.S.J. Tessimond
Morning prayer, J.L. Dalton
Morning songs, E. Lewis
Morning without clouds, J. Millican
Mother India, T.W. Howell
Mother, what is man?, F.M. Smith

The motionless dancer, W. Long
Mountain of beauty, W.I. Wood
Mountains beneath the horizon, W. Bell
Mountains polecats pheasants, L. Norris
Moving day, P.A.T. O'Donnell
Mural ditties and Sime Road soliloquies, C.C. Brown
Murdock, F. Berry
Murmurs in the rose, J. Whitehead
Music at midnight, M. Grainger
Music for statues, D. Stanford
Music of meditation, E.K. Trout
Musings in metre, R. Millar
My apologia, J.M. Thompson
My autoverseography, 07—70, J. Harper
My country, 'tis of thee, G. Boshell
My dog Pip, Cocklake, pseud.
My fifty versing years, T.F. Royds
My gate of vision, S.L. Melhado
My heart reveals, W. Gilfillan
My heart's desire, J. Carson
My life of verse, O.E. Bridle
My many-coated man, L. Lee
My maritime moods, E.R.A.V. Bennett
My muse and I, J. Hepburn
My pen my sword, G. Boshell
My sad captains, T. Gunn
My sad Pharaohs, J. Bevan
My sex, right or wrong, D. Morgan
My tongue is my own, T. Fassam
Myself is all I have, M. Coleman
The mysterious universe, S.H. Bennett

Nab Valley, A. Levy
The naked mountain, W.K. Pyke-Lees
Napier verse, W. Addison
The narrow place, E. Muir
The nature of the moment, V. Ackland
Nature revealed, K. Dabb
Nature studies, W. Mears
Nasty nursery rhymes, H. Simpson
A necklace of words, S. Mason
New bats in old belfries, J. Betjeman
The new British shell, R.M. Hammond
The new gods rising, H.N. Forbes
New recessional, E. Thompson
New spring song, H. Nicholson
The new voice, H.B. Yeates
The new world symphony, J.A. Weaver

New year letter, W.H. Auden
Night-crossing, D. Mahon
Night flight, E. Boyd
The night loves us, L. Adeane
Night on the plain, A.R. Cookes
Night pieces, N. Mawdsley
The night watch for England, E. Shanks
Nightmares and sunhorses, J.S. Manifold
The nights of London, G.M. Heard
The nine bright shiners, A. Ridler
1939 — and how, A.A. Rata
99 stanzas European, A.H. Haffenden
No crown for laughter, J.M. Lindsay
No fool like an old fool, G. Ewart
No land is waste, Dr Eliot, J. Simmons
No leafless land, E. Miles
No nursery, E. Swift
No other choice, U. Vaughan Williams
No prisoner of a dying world, R. Moffat
No stronger than a flower, J. Braddock
No summer song, J. Brockway
No wasted hour, P. Macdonald
No weed death, G. Stewart
Nocturne in Eden, C. Middleton
Noonday, T.L. Williams
North bank night, E. Storey
North from Sicily, A. Ross
The north star, L. Binyon
Not all the suns, E.M. Cust
Not waving but drowning, F.M. Smith
Not yet the dodo, N. Coward
The note-book of a Lieutenant in the Italian campaign, R.D.D. Thomas
Notes for a survivor, E. Litvinoff
November haggard, P. Kavanagh
November spell, M. Coleman
Now and then, E.H. Blakeney
Now or never, B. Allwood
Numbers, C.H. Sisson
Nymph in thy orisons, W. Jarman

O friend o' mine, E. Robinson
O, sweet oasis, E.M. Banister
The oak and the ash, J. Short
Obie's war, G. Wells
Occasional poems, G.H. Gray
Occasional verses, G.M. MacGregor
Occasional verses, J.R. Todhunter
Odd odes of the Observer Corps, A.J.M. Ross

Oddments, M.G. Beresford
Odds and ends, A. Robilliard
Ode on Saint Crispin's Day, 1939–1979, R.H. Ellis
Ode to beauty, S. Manizales
Ode to England, F.M. Venables
Ode to France, C. Morgan
Ode to the sun, L. Whistler
Odin's mead, D.S. Goodbrand
Of a son, E.J. Dennis
Of common things, E.W. Thomson
Of feeling and fancy, L.R. Mansell
Of mills, moors and men, J. Waddington-Feather
Of people and places, K.N. McCoy
Of period and place, J. Arlott
Off and away, G.I. Petts
Off the prong, C.I. Capron
Og and other ogres, R. Reynolds
Oil of joy, D.L. Cobbett
The old couple, F.P. Green
Old damson-face, B. Gutteridge
Old fashioned verses and sketches, R. Praeger
Old movies, J. Cotton
The old story, P.M. Ross
Old vacant chair, A.E. Theobald
An old war, R. Fuller
Omens and elegies, P. Russell
On a golden thread, H. Heywood
On earth peace, E. Newgass
On land and sea, A.W. Norton
On patrol, J. Malthouse
On the far side, R.A.A. Dawes
On the wing, C.I. Capron
On trust, G. Jefferson
On wings of verse, H. Wallis
Once bitten, twice bitten, P. Porter
One and one, P.J. Kavanagh
One aspect, P. James
One day later, J.M. Lindsay
One hour together, E.G. Hoare
One landscape still, P. Macdonogh
One man's war, A.H. Bailey
One man's war, D.C. Spence
One more cairn, and many things beside, J.C. Lyth
One of the few, C.H. Ross
One recent evening, R. Greacen
One way through life, S. Martin

One year in October, M.P. Ferris
Onward — ever onward, J.F.C. Peace
Op. 8, J.S. Manifold
Open day and night, M. Burn
Open sea, A. Ross
Operation by night, G. Eades
Or something, S. Deas
Orcadian twilight, C.J. Donaldson
The orchestral mountain, J.F. Hendry
Orisons, picaresque and metaphysical, I. Fletcher
Our faith looks up to Thee, E. Whitla
Our finest hour, H. Trevelyan-Thomson
Our fresh springs, C.I. Capron
Our heritage, L. Masters
Our local, M. Matthews
Our way of life, F. Pearce
Our world, R. Owen
Ourselves a dream, G. Dixey
Out of Africa, T.I.F. Armstrong
Out of bounds, J. Stallworthy
Out of circumstance, T. Good
Out of Seir, E.M. Almedingen
Out of the muddle, G. Cox
Out of the oblivion, M. Oughton
Out of the shadows, P. Forsyth
Out of this war, M.J. Tambimuttu
Out pipes, K.W. Michell
Outlook Hill, M.H. Wicksteed
The outpost, W.W. Gibson
Over hill over dale, D.U. Ratcliffe
Over the edge, P. Ledward
Over the water, P. Macdonogh
Overture, T. Good
Ovid in Arcady, F.B. Julian
Ownerless earth, M. Hamburger

Pad, H.J. Galsworthy & J.A.B. Harrisson
Padstow lights, M. Cherrill
The pageant of man, A.M.P. Dawson
Pages from a biography, A. Feiner
The pain and the pleasure, D. Bourne-Jones
Palinode, T.H.S. Wyllie
The palisades of fear, R. Bottrall
Panorama, P. Dunphy
Pan's music, P. Kirtlan
Panta re, A. Feiner
Parachute Battalion, R. Spender
The park, J.M. Corbett

Parnassian musings, C.G. Norris
Particles of truth, E. Dunworth
Passer-by, A.C. Bell
A passing glance, K.B. Todd
Passing hours, J.A.D. Wentworth
Passing thoughts, L. Waddington
The passionate climate, G.A. Wagner
The patch of blue, H.E. Hardy
Patchwork, I. Wintle
Patria deserta, A. Lamont
Patrick freed, T.W. Gervais
Patterns and poems, P. Tudor-Owen
Pause and ponder, K.J. McKay
Peace — and war, L. Sutton
The peace bells, D.C. Bradley
Peace in our time, Alceste, pseud.
Peace is our answer, J. Lindsay
The peace of God, F. Dege
Peace River, C. Galloway
Pearls of thought, S. Martin
Peasant songs and poems, E.R. Holford
Pebbles in my pocket, B. Parvin
The peerless life, W.J. Tribble
Pendulum, M. Darby
The pendulum, H.W. Harding
The penny poems, T. Singleton
Pensées en Tunisie, T.I.F. Armstrong
Peregrine, F. Buchanan
Perhaps to-morrow, J.M. Lindsay
A perpetual motion machine, A. Bold
Personal poems, W. Buchan
Petals in the wind, L.M. McIntyre
Pheasant shooting, R.E. Wilkinson
Phoenix, F.W.H. McMurdo
The phoenix-flower, D.J. Hall
The phoney phleet, J. Richardson
Pick and shovel poems, I.E. Kaye
Picnic to the moon, P. Russell
Pictures in verse, M.S. Burnell
Pied hiker, W.T. Shorthose
Piers Prodigal, I. Davie
Pietà, R.S. Thomas
Pilgrimage, W.J.T. Collins
Pines on the hill, G.M. Haines
The piper, M. Gardner
Pipes of peace, O. Katzin
A place for Tritons, A. Ball
A place of being, K. Severs
The place's fault, P. Hobsbaum

Plain reflections, P. Rampton
Plain song, O. Davies
The plains of the sun, W.G. Archer
The planet in my hand, R. Todd
Plant and phantom, L. MacNeice
Plash Mill, F. Bellerby
Plough and coble, J.C. Grant
Plymouth in war, P. Napier
A poem for every mood, P.H. Grant
Poems and contradictions, R. Warner
Poems by a Lichfield innkeeper, F.H. Shilcock
Poems by a quasi-rebel, T.E.B. Adderley
Poems chiefly Cornish, A.L. Rowse
Poems for all seasons, E.E.H. Redknap
Poems for days of stress and strain, A. Povey
Poems for Dorothy, J. Millward
Poems for everybody, A. Vickers
Poems for H.M. Forces, K. Howard
Poems for our time, D.V. Greeves
Poems for people, J. Morrison
Poems for sweethearts and others, L. Foster
Poems for the Forces, W.R. Titterton
Poems for the people, N. Abraham
Poems for thine entertainment!, K. Thornton
Poems for to-day, T. Williams
Poems from Belmont, A.E. Dodd
Poems from hospital, B.C. Edwards
Poems from life, A. Osborne
Poems from Sherwood Forest, P. Clarke
Poems from the West Country, B.C. White
Poems grave and gay, W. Gamble
Poems in blue, C.A.R. Macdougall
Poems in India, F. Watson
Poems in Scots and English, W. Soutar
Poems in transit, D. Tipton
Poems in wartime, C. Day Lewis
Poems light and gay, M. Kilner
The poems of a countryman, W.B. Thomas
Poems of a decade, K. Etheridge
Poems of a decade, 1931–1941, A.L. Rowse
Poems of a land girl, B. Miles
Poems of a London warden, M. Girdlestone
Poems of a parachute padre, J.W. Johnston
The poems of a prisoner of war, C. Dick
The poems of a youth, G.R.L. Millen
Poems of an agnostic, A.C. Bell
Poems of an airman, J. Rogers
Poems of an ordinary seaman, D. Kendall
Poems of an ordnance officer, H.A. Loveless

Poems of change, I. Coates
Poems of charm and mirth, K. Thornton
Poems of deliverance, A.L. Rowse
Poems of every day, G.K. Davies
Poems of love and patriotism, P. Gwyn
Poems of love, peace and war, N. Warner
Poems of many years, E. Blunden
Poems of peace and war, C. Humphreys
Poems of peace and war, B.W. Sharland
Poems of praise, M.S. Fidler
Poems of purpose, W.H. Bartlett
Poems of quality, D.D.D. Crowe
Poems of storm and calm, M. Gardner
Poems of the countryside, A.M. Stokes
Poems of the north country, G.D. Wilkinson
Poems of the past and future, R.N. Taylor
Poems of the present era, S. Vincent
Poems of three shires and of the sea, K.M. Garner
Poems of two wars, J.C. Squire
Poems of two worlds, C.W. Cockerell
Poems of war and peace, M. Thwaites
Poems of war and peace, 1939–1949, C. Russell-Parsons
Poems of war-time Sussex, E.R. Coleman
Poems old and new, R. Hayward
Poems old and new, grave and gay, G. Asplen
Poems on several occasions, E.G.C. Beckwith
Poems on the German occupation of the Channel Islands, R.J. Ogier
Poems to amuse and annoy you, S. Williams
Poems to Eimhir, S. Maclean
Poems with flute, L. Sowden
Poet at play, C.M. Grieve
A poet in two places, R. Venables
Poetic justice, J.P.C.
Poetic miscellany, R. Davies
Poetic pilgrimage, D.J. Curling
Poetic potpourri, C.A. Birch
Poetic reflections of university life at Pembroke College, Cambridge, H. Cross
Poetical humour, V. Haydon
Poetical medley, H. Brownlee
Poetical musings, R.J. Mackay
A poetical offering, W.A. Galbraith
Poetical personal points, R. Folder
A poetical walk, G.S. Burns
The poets, D. Wellesley
The poet's flower, G. Kendall

The poet's hour, A.V. Bowen
Poet's paradise, J.B. Wild
Pole-star, M.E. Rhodes
Poloniae testamentum, E.M. Almedingen
Pomes and other fruit, C. Simms
The pool of dreams, D.A. Turnbull
A poor man singing, O. Lloyd
The porcelain heart, L. Jarratt
The portraits and the poses, E. Brock
Portsmouth ho!, V.H. Bennett
Posies once mine, R. Manwaring
Possible laughter, J. Michie
Postcards to Pulcinella, R. Duncan
Prairie summer, M.D. Bishop
A prayer for peace, E. Ling
The preacher on the moor, J.C. Grant
Preaching to the converted, P. Porter
Predicament, J.M. Lindsay
Preghiere, G. Hill
Preliminaries, M. Boulton
The prelude, R. Carroll
Prelude, A. Donald
Prelude, C.R. Sanderson
The price, R. England
The priest, J. O'Quigley
The primrose way, H.K. Williams
Prince of the clouds, R. Chapman
Prison sonnets, T.E. Nicholas
Prisoners of war, P. Henry
A private country, L. Durrell
Pro patria, E. Newgass
Progressive poetry, Isa, pseud.
The Prometheans, A. Craig
Promise of peace, M.F. Temple
Prose chants and proems, R. Nichols
Prosperity ahead! for Yorkshire, G. Hammond
The proud and lovely, P. O'Horan
The province of belief, J. Tripp
The psalms with their spoils, J. Silkin
Pulp in Bosnia, R.K. Brady
A pulse in the mind, B.P. Luxton
Purple testament, A.G. Bennett
Purple testament, W. Weaving

Quake, quake, quake, P. Dehn
Queen's shores, C. Curr
The quest for peace, E. Pickthall
Questing soul, M.A. Harwood
A questionnaire for God, W.A. Rathkey

Questions for waking, W. Gardiner
Quiet benison, A.R. Price
Quiet evening, G. Smith
The quiet heart, H. Waine
Quiet lutes and laughter, A. Caddick
The quiet ones, H.C. White
Quintessence, W. Lee
Quintet, W.N. Sinkinson
Quiver's choice, O. Katzin

Rage of days, O. Levertoff
Raiders' dawn, A. Lewis
The rainbow, H.V. Nicoll-Griffith
Random reveries, J. Claridge
Random rhymes, B.H. Binder
Random rhymes, R. Blunt
Random thoughts, J.M. Newey
Random thoughts in verse, R.H. Murray
A rattle of lamps, F. Gretton
The raw side, F. Goodridge
Rawalpindi, O.L. Richmond
Realism, rhyme and reason, W.J. James
The reality of stars, D. Trim
Reasons in rhyme, P. Puxley
Rebel's progress, T. Earley
Recall and reflect, F. Truelove
Receding galaxy, C. Hurry
Recent years, H. Milville
Recollections of the gala, N. Moore
Red letters, M. Lescombe
Reflections, A.W. Andrews
Reflections, J. White
Reflections and recollections, D.B.S. James
Reflections in rhyme, S. Gibson
Reflections in verse, A.I.C. Haime
Reflections of sunshine, V.E. McNichol
Reflections through a glass darkly, C. Rothery
Reflexions, B. Guinness
Refusal to conform, J. Kirkup
Regime already, Alter Ego, pseud.
The reign of sparrows, R. Fuller
Relève into Maquis, N. Cunard
The reluctant warrior, F. Singleton
Remember Arnhem, G.R.B. Sheldon
Remember man, C. Lee
Remembered radiance, R.B. Wilkie
Requiem for the living, C. Day Lewis
Requiem for the war dead, R. Tong
Reservations, V. Iremonger

Rest awhile, J. Canon
Restoration, S.A. Gordon
Resurgence, R.A. Oakley
Retrospect, I.C. Mowatt
Retrospect, A. Peck
The return, J. O'Hare
The return of Mrs. Brown, C.H.W. Roll
A reverie of bone, M. Peake
Reviresco, A. Buist
The revolutionary generation, R.L. Cargnelli
Rhine jump, G. Holloway
Rhyme and reason, R.E. Ling
Rhyme and reason, H.A. Smith
The rhyme of the flying bomb, M. Peake
Rhyme-raivelins, H. Reid
Rhyme the rudder, swung by a service man, G.D.
    Martineau
Rhymed ruminations, S. Sassoon
Rhymes and recitations, L. Pendleton
Rhymes for quiet times, G. Daly
The rhymes of a rambling rhymer, J. Crawford
Rhymes of a Weardale lad, G.L. Lister
Rhymes of the war, J. Pomfret
Rhymes of those times, 1939–1945, G. Jones
Richmond rhymes, D. Spence
The ridge, J. Temple
Rime, gentlemen, please, R. Farren
A ring of willows, E.W. Barker
Ripples on the tide, C.C.M. Hanley
River people, J. Downar
River roundels, A.E. Grantham
The river steamer, E.J. Scovell
Rivers in the desert, J. Millican
Road from Delavan, M. Browne
The road of time, F.C. Clarke
The road to Sinodun, G.D. Painter
The road to the moon, K.M. Flude
Roadways of the heart, P. O'Horan
Rod of incantation, F. King
A romantic miscellany, J. Bayliss & D.
    Stanford
Root and branch, J. Stallworthy
The rose tree, R. Payne
Rough torrent, R. Whiteley
A rough walk home, L. Bowes Lyon
The rude potato, R. Pitter
Ruins, P. Robinson
Ruins and visions, S. Spender
The run from life, J.M. Lindsay

The running tide, M.D. Peachey
Russian summer, R. McFadden
Rustic ramblings, G. Gabbott

S.O.S. . . 'Ludlow', C. Hassall
Sabon Gari, J. Haynes
Sagittarius rhyming, O. Katzin
St. Albans, T. Roscoe
St. Luke, P. Hartnoll
Salome speaks, E.R. Patton
Salt harvest, C.L. Lanyon
Salus populi suprema lex, H. Whitaker
Salute the Empire in poem and song, A.L.
    Draper
A salute to Britain in peace or war, G.G.
    Deighton
Salute to valour, S. Gwynn
Salvoes from a stone frigate, J.S. Hicks
The sand castle, C.C. Abbott
The sands are sinking on the desert waste, H.
    Desmond
Saraband and satyricon, G. Brennand
Satires and salvation, R. Manwaring
Scant harvest, P. Beacall
The scapegoat, F.H.C. Shrewsbury
The scarecrow said, R.K. Hallam
The scarlet flower, I. Bell
Scattered verses, L. Einstein
Scenes from life, D.M. Evans
Scenes from the sidelines, W.J. Thomlinson
The scenic route, F. Adcock
A score of verses, H.J. Inman
Scotland, my native land, R.J. Mackay
Scrolls, L. Kramer
Sea acres, A. Ball
Sea and sky, L.F. Stewart
Sea and sympathy, C.A. Birch
Sea days and after, M. Kelly
Sea talk, G. Bruce
Seagulls, C. Humphreys
The search, J. Hankin
Search for peaceful fields, A. Roberts
The search of Llanretny, M. Deschamps
The searchlights, W.W. Gibson
Seasons at war, R. Nichols
Second causes, A. Rattenbury
Second front, J. Lindsay
Second harvest, A. Feiner
The second man, J. Symons

Second Officer, J. Pomfret
The secret country, A.E. Mackay
The secret field, C. Lee
The secret river, A.C. Brown
The secret spring, J. Warburg
The seed and the flower, C. Sargeant
Seed time and harvest, A. Finlay
The seeker, H.H. Chilton
The seeker, W.R. Hughes
Selected poems on West Penwith, A.W. Andrews
Selected variations, M. Noakes
Selections from everyday verse, A.E. Banks
Sentimental verse, E.H. Long
September sky, B. Lanes
Sequences, S. Sassoon
Services wrendered, J.E. Broome
Seven days leave, P. Robins
Seven to seventeen, P. Norman
The seven words, A. Head
A seventh bouquet of English sonnets, J.E. Magraw
Several observations, G. Grigson
Shades from life, R. Lord
Shades of khaki, W. Clarke
The shadow of Cain, E. Sitwell
Shadows, C. Humphreys
Shadows and reflections, J. Wheatley
Shadows and substance, C.R. Sanders
Shadows of chrysanthemums, E.J. Scovell
Shadows — of mystic make-believe, L.D. Dwyer
Shadows on the down, A. Noyes
Shall vision perish?, H. Kay
Shapes and sounds, M. Peake
Sharp scorpions, W. Gardiner
She died alive, J. Rowe
Sheet-anchor, P. Napier
Shells by a stream, E. Blunden
The sheltering tree, B. Hill
The shining sword, C. Cunningham
The shires, D. Davie
Shooting a bat, T.R. Henn
Shopping in Oxford, J. Masefield
Short measures, E.S. James
Shrapnel, G. Macbeth
The shrapnel in the tree, T. Fassam
Sign of the pentagram, B. Burnett
The signal to engage, A. Comfort

Signatures of all things, L. Daiken
Signatures of God, C. Winchester
Silhouette, J. Clement
Silver lining, N. Mumford
Silver wings, J.C. Milne
Silver wings, A. Stewart
Simple ditties, B.J. Pendlebury
The simple vision, H.M. Williams
Sincere flattery, G.H. Vallins
Sinews from salt, V. Griffiths
The singing blood, G.A. Wagner
Singing down the years, M. Armour
The singing heart, T. Hooley
Singing in the fog, M.S. Birnie
Sins and seasons, R.L. Mitchell
Siren song, A.P. Herbert
Sirmio unvisited, J. Beighton
Six months of war, A.C. Tarbat
Skail wind, S.G. Smith
The skating parson, F.P. Green
Slates of opal, P.R. Wilkinson
Slick but not streamlined, J. Betjeman
A slim volume, W.F. Mitchell
The slow night, C. Hassall
Slowly into twilight, E. Alleyne
A small bouquet, L.P. McEwen
Small dreams of a scorpion, T.A.P.S. Milligan
Small fry, G.M. Stanford
The small sunset, J. Walker
The small voice, M. Mair
Smile, Ichabod, H. Manning
Smiling through! Jersey, 1940–1945. R. Grandin
Smoke, L. Bryne-Thomas
Smoke after flame, H.F. Summers
Smoking flax, M.L. Haskins
Snatches of verse, P. Daymond
Snow flowers, D.H. Jones
The snow leopard, P. West
The snow party, D. Mahon
Snowdrops at dusk, J. Gilbey
The snowing globe, P. Scupham
The sober war, G.R. Hamilton
Social impressions of an air gunner, R. Farley
Soldier rhymes, C.R. Walton
Soldiers bathing, F.T. Prince
A soldier's kit bag, J.H. Goss
Soldiers, this solitude, A. Rook
Soliloquy in summer, W.H. Bartlett

The solitary man, R. Church
The solitudes, R. Duncan
Solway Ford, W.W. Gibson
Some Boston ballads, A.M. Cook
Some holy-days — and home, M. Lea
Some memories, D. Holland
Some thoughts, A. Alston
Some verses to some Germans, J. Masefield
Some way for reason, M.J. Craig
Something of the sea, A. Ross
Song at the year's turning, R.S. Thomas
Song in storm, D. Gibson
Song in the valley, M.I. Wood
Song of a poet, J.C. Milne
The song of a red turtle, G. Scurfield
Song of freedom, J.M. Bird
Song of freedom, O.L. Richmond
The song of my beloved, B. Kaye
Song of Noel, J.B. Fell
The song of the cold, E. Sitwell
Song of the young and old men, J.A. Mackereth
Songs, C. Logue
Songs, R. Payne
Songs and comments, R. Sharrock
Songs and snatches, B.J. Benson
Songs and sonnets, made in the time of the late wars, K. Hopkins
Songs and verses, M.G.U. Aitkenhead
Songs and verses, E. Goudge
Songs before sunset, S. Barton
Songs by the way, A.P. Needler
Songs by the wayside, S. Barton
Songs for courage, K.Etheridge
Songs from a lake, R. Bates
Songs from a too late summer, M. Howard
Songs from the dales, F.F. Brook
Songs in chains, J.C. Wells
Songs in the afternoon, A.P. Needler
Songs in the night, T.E. Harvey
Songs my mother never taught me, M.L. Gilbert
Songs of desire and of divine love, P.J. Fisher
Songs of England, M. Gladwyn, pseud.
Songs of fact and fancy, B.A. Hall
Songs of faith, G.W. Briggs
Songs of faith, C. Kay
Songs of London, F.W. Abbott
Songs of Malta, J.E. Mitchell
Songs of spiritual conquest, A.B. De Bary
Songs of sun and shadow, J. McEwan

Songs of Sussex, F.M. Venables
Songs of to-day and yesteryear, L. Wharton
Songs out of Oriel, R.H. Bryans
Sonnets from Libyan Tripoli, G. Dixey
Sonnets from the Levant, G. Dixey
Sonnets from the Western Desert, G. Dixey
Sonnets in D Minor, G.S. Oddy
Sonnets in sand, G. Dixey
Sonnets in two keys, G.S. Oddy
Sonnets of yesterday and to-day, B.K. Sundius-Smith
Sonnets on the fens, C. Breed
Sonnets, they say —, S. Johnson
The soothing wind, R. Sauter
A soul for sale, P. Kavanagh
The soul in splendour, J.W. Hill
The soul of things, H.M. Mounsey
Sound in the sky, D. Stafford-Clark
Soundings, R. Pierce
Sounds and shadows, G.W. Mosdell
South of Fort Hertz, M.J. Moynihan
South of forty, J. Pudney
Souvenir of thoughts, B.A. Kirk
Spare moments, Harry, pseud.
Sparks from a wayside fire, I.O. Evans
The speech of phantoms, A. Caddick
The sphere of glass, J. Lehmann
Spill out, J. Pudney
Spindrift and spunyarn, W.C. Reedy
The spinning mirror, M. Reynolds
The spirit of England, B. Munday
Spitalfields, A.G. Herbertson
The Spitfire on the Northern Line, B. Jones
Spring, A. Easton
Spring deferred, W. Rose
Spring legend, J. Waller
Spring sacrifice, D. Thompson
Spring sowing, P. Constantine
Spring tide and neap tide, S. Maclean
Springboard, L. MacNeice
Springtime in Devon, G.E. Connor
A spurious grace, G. Thomson
Sronan, R. Hall
A stained glass raree show, L. Houston
Stalingrad, K.A. Nicholson
Stalingrad, L. Spero
Stammerings, T.I. James
Stand alone, V.H. Friedlaender
Stanzas and ballads, C.F. Peskin

The star, J. Mellor
Stars' roundelay, I. Wyatt
The Statue of Liberty, E.C. Finlason
Steer straight, B. Notton
Steps to a viewpoint, A. Reid
Still and all, B. Singer
Still another bouquet of English sonnets, J.E.
  Magraw
Still in my hand, M. Smith
Still more dream roads, D.C. Cuthbertson
Still towards democracy, A. Hadfield
Stings and honey, L.E. Jones
Stone and flower, K. Raine
Stone in the midst, P. Dickinson
The stones of the field, R.S. Thomas
A store of candles, F. Ormsby
The store of things, J. Burns
Storm, C.W. Elliott
Storm and monument, J. Singer
Storm wrack, A.D. Holmes
Stormy harvest, S. Snaith
The Strad, J. Cook
The stranded shell, M. Grainger
Strange days and yet we sing, G. Borman
Strange encounter, A.L. Rowse
Strange stories in verse, W.F. Tuson
Strange Tempe, M.M. Crosland
A stranger here, W. Burke
The strangers, M.J. Moynihan
Strasbourg geese, O. Katzin
Straws in the wind, B.R. Youngman
Stray thoughts and memories in verse, J.M.C.
  Goodman
Street songs, E. Sitwell
Strife within, H.T. Russell
Struwwelhitler, P. & R. Spence
The stuttering water, F. Bellerby
The submerged village, J. Kirkup
Subsong, J. Reeves
Success, G. Crowder
Such days will pass, N. Mumford
Such liberty, J. Buxton
The summer dance, J.C. Hall
Summer leaves, J.E. Pickin
Summer palaces, P. Scupham
Summer thunder, A. Ross
Sun and sand, J. Warry
Sun and shade, M. Cottingham
Sun and shadow, G.L. Lampson

The sun my monument, L. Lee
Sung to the spinning wheel, M. Morton
Sunrise to sunset, G.R. Stephenson
Sunshine and shadow, A. Cochrane
Sunshine and shadow, M.R. Davey
Sunshine and showers, A. Day
Sunshine rays, N. Dawson
Surviving, D. Keene
Survivor's leave, C. Causley
Sussex, glorious Sussex!, A.F. Hall
The swallow, P. Beames
The swans of Berwick, S.D. Tremayne
The swinging lantern, W.H. Bartlett
A sword for Redonda, D. Horle
A sword in the desert, H. Palmer
The sword of excellency, M. Russell
Swords and ploughshares, M.I.E. Dolphin
Swords and ploughshares, R. McFadden
Swords into ploughshares, H.B.S. Lennox
The symbol, J.C. Squire

The Taj express, A. Ross
Take all colours, B. Hill
Take-off at dusk, P. Roberts
Talking bronco, R. Campbell
The tallest tower, M. Buesnel
Tarantell, J. James
Targets, O. Katzin
Tatie bread, R.R. Clark
Tea-leaves, dust and ashes, H. Dewar
Ten summers, J. Pudney
Tens to teens and have beens, B.W.
  Sharland
Terminus, G. Taylor
Testament of a South African, R. Macnab
Thames symphony, O.L. Richmond
That inward eye, B. Gibbs
That ye inherit, W.S. Graham
Theatre poems and songs, E. Bond
There is a valley, J.H.F. McEwen
There will be music, I. Hargrave
These are my comrades, A. Rook
These days, M. Lea
These have I loved, E. Wright
These have I written, D.P. Teichman
These — our children, A. Richardson
These things he gave, M. Huxtable
These things remain, M.W. Jones

Theseus and the minotaur, P. Dickinson
They also serve, J. Hillas
They're away, B. Holden
Think on these things, B. Sutton
Think this of me, J. Watson
The thinker, C.C. Samuel
The third darkness, R.B. Smith
Thirty-nine preludes, L. Clark
This day is mine, K. de J. Du Vallon
This England, B.M. Isaacs
This fine day, A. Bold
This for remembrance of Britain's brave, L.
  Meyrick-Jones
This greatness, J.A. Mackereth
This insubstantial pageant, M. Gibbon
This is my England, V. de S. Pinto
This is my harvest, J.B. Bickle
This is the hour, A.G. Herbertson
This is the life for me, M. Thompson
This life, this death, T.R. Hodgson
This lovely land, A.D. Holmes
This other autumn, A.K. Wood
This other planet, R.N. Currey
This precious stone, E. Newgass
This tremendous lover, G. Downey
This unlikely earth, F.P. Green
This watering place, F. Buchanan
This world's bliss, A. Treneer
The thorn tree, C.H. Warren
Thorns and mary-lilies, J. Henderson
Thoughtful moments, C.F. Lucas
Thoughts, M.M. Brand
Thoughts, J.D. Maclure
Thoughts and dreams, D. Key
Thoughts and fancies, G.C. Beaton
Thoughts and fancies, A.D.H. Thorne
Thoughts and poems, M. Cullwick
Thoughts for quiet moments, Dalma, pseud.
Thoughts in print, P.J. McLoughlin
Thoughts in rhyme, Goldwyn, pseud.
Thoughts in verse, A.M.
Thoughts in verse and line, T. Parrott
Thoughts in words, A. de S. Georgano
Thoughts through the years, 1939–1943, E.
  McMillan
Thoughts we can share, C.M.M. Scott
The three-sighted, H.M. Wilson
Three sonatas, E.H.W. Meyerstein
Three women, D.M. O'Grady

Threnody for dormice, R. Tomalin
Threshold, C.A. Berry
Through English windows, C.M.H. Gemmell
Through half-closed eyes, D. Dunker
Through Scottish windows, C.M.H. Gemmell
Through the years, W.J. Kirkham
Through years of stress, W. Blathwayt
A thrush sings, I. Ormsby
Thy muse hath wings, G. Eades
Tides and fashions, W.W. Blair-Fish
Time, R. Cecil
Time and the wind, S.D. Tremayne
A time for singing, G.R.B. Sheldon
Time in a blue prison, H. Corby
Time of violence, J. Kincaid
Time stopped, E. Milne
Time to dream, J.M. Rendell
A time to mourn, D.S. Savage
A time to speak, G. Anderson
Time to stand and stare, R.P.L. Mogg
Times and seasons, E.H. Hussey
Times and tides, S. Gregory
Time's beauty, G. Clark
Tin hat memories, D. Omand
Tintagel, J.O. Fuller
Tiny tears, R. Fuller
Tiresias, R.N. Currey
To a modern hero, A. Rye
To a Queen, A. Haldane-Duncan
To awaken Pegasus, E.J.M.D. Plunkett
To celebrate her living, L. Whistler
To eat the wind, R.L. Lowe
To find the new, A. Bold
To my mother, C. Gentleman
To one who sang, H. Ould
To the air, T. Gunn
To the city, C.P. Billot
To the gods the shades, D. Wright
To what end is the dawn?, C.R. Sanderson
To-day the sun, R. Tong
Token, J. James
To-morrow, M.W. Were
Tomorrow is a revealing, L. Bowes Lyon
Tomorrow is mine, T.I. James
Tomorrows came and went, J. Lesar
To-night is on the mountain, B.W.
  Cave-Brown-Cave
Tonypandy, I. Davies
Too long at the circus, S. Morris

Topical poems, J. Smale
Topical tales, O.E. Hallett
The torch, W. Godfrey
Torse 3, C. Middleton
Touch, T. Gunn
Towards Mozambique, C.H. Johnston
The trackless way, L. Taylor
The tranquil flame, G. Borman
A transitory house, F. Laughton
Transparent web, M. Gordon
Trapped man, break out, C. Austin
The traveller has regrets, G.S. Fraser
Traveller's eye, B. Gutteridge
Travelling home, F. Cornford
Tread lightly here, M. Crew
Treasures in verse, P. Sutton
The tree of life, N. Micklem
Triad one, E. Berridge
Tributes to our fighters, M.E. Richards
A trip to the Boche, D. Western
Tristesse, D. Shaw
The triumph of beauty, C.R. Cammell
Triumphant St. George, A.M. Nance
Trophy for an unknown, R.W. Moore
Tropical ice, A. Ross
True intent, E.J. Dennis
True to life, E. Harrison
The trumpeter of Saint George, G.R. Hamilton
Trumpets and the new moon, H.N. Forbes
Trusty tree, C.L. Lanyon
Truth is a naked lady, J. Beecham
Truth prevails, G.E. Turton
The tune of flutes, D. James
The tunnelled fire, A. Henderson
'Tween ten and twenty, M.J. Beer
Twelve years, G. Faber
Twentieth-century psalter, R. Church
Twicers, M. Abbott
Twilight, R. Somerset
Twilight reveries, S.G. Watts
Two children, G. Ewart
The two freedoms, J. Silkin
The two generations, G. Mann
Two in one, F.M. Smith
The two natures, R. Waller
Typing a novel about the war, G. Macbeth
The tyranny, H.E. Hardy

Unarm, Eros, T. Tiller

The unborn, S.H. Edwards
The uncertain margin, W.J. Harvey
Uncertainties, J. Press
Uncompromising gladness, C.L. Lanyon
Under t'hawthorn, D.U. Ratcliffe
Under the cliff, G. Grigson
Under the mushroom cloud, L. Howes
Under the sun, C. Lee
The undying day, R. Greacen
Unexpected fairyland, S. Woodman
The unfailing spring, C. Sansom
The unfinished C.M.F. pot pourri, L. Burrows
Union now, G. St. C. Harley
Union Street, C. Causley
Unity, C.B. Toosey
The unreturning spring, J. Farrar
Until Bengal, H. Milner
Until now, R. Todd
Until that dawn, D.U. Ratcliffe
The untried soldier, E. Litvinoff
The unwanted statue, S. Churchill
Up dale, D.U. Ratcliffe
Upheavaled strife (in verse) and life, J. Persson
Upland and valley, S. Powis
The upright position, A. Dixon
Urania, R. Pitter
The urgent voice, B. Lea

V for victory, A. Edwards
A vagrant, D. Gascoyne
Vain words?, D. Bourne-Jones
Values, T.A.P.S. Milligan
The van pool, K. Rhys
Varied verse, H.G. Romer
Various verses, E. Dunstan-Crarey
A veil of darkness, V.H. Bennett
The ventriloquist's doll, K. Allott
Venture in verse, C.A. Peck
Venus in Libra, J. Bayliss
Versailles summer, E.W. Edmonds
Versatile verse, Z. Kremer
Verse and worse, G.R. Fisher
Verse by the way, M. Douglas
Verse letters to five friends, E.H.W.
   Meyerstein
Verse various, A.M. Mowbray
Verses, chiefly relating to the present war, F.A.
   Molony
Verses from Dorset, R.L. Cocks

Verses from the West Wight, M. Muir
Verses grave and gay, J.H. Bamfield
Verses grave and gay, N.R. Murray
Verses of a fighter pilot, A.N.C. Weir
Verses of simplicity, C.M. Pelham
Verses of valour, victory and vision, M.L. Haigh
Verses of variety, C.M.H. Gemmell
Verses out of pattern, W. Meade
Veterinary ballads, C.M. Ford
Victory and peace, M.A. Bennett
Victory for the slain, H. Lofting
Victory poems, F.E. Beales
A view from Ben More, D. Bolton
The view from this window, L. Whistler
Vignettes in verse, C.E. Mills
The virgin's son, S. Odger
The vision, B. O'Nions
The visionary, E.H.W. Meyerstein
Visions and dreams, J.J. Gurnett
Visitations, L. MacNeice
Voice and verse, I. Gibb
A voice from the past, A.L. Draper
The voice of England, A. Row
The voice of the workers, R.R. Palmer
The voice of to-morrow, H. Desmond
The voices, B.R. Gibbs
Voices from the crowd, B. Mayor
The voyage, E. Muir

Waking in the dark, N. Jackson
Waking the dead, A. Maclean
Walk I alone, A.G. Hart
A walk round the city and other groans, J. Docherty
A walk through time, L. Sutton
Walking wounded, V. Scannell
The wanderer, T. Purcell-Buret
A wanderer's anthology, G.P.B. Henfrey
Wandering songs, E.J.M.D. Plunkett
Wanderlust, E. Barron
Wanted a lead, H. Greene
War, J.A. Chapman
War echoes over thirty years, F.J.W. Harding
War in a cock's egg, M. Cox
War memoirs in verse, I. Gomersall
War nonsense, J.A.D. Wentworth
War-piece, Morny, pseud.
War poems, W.W. Baker

War poems, M. Du Deney
War poems, E.J.M.D. Plunkett
War poems, J.R. Rodd
War poems, grave and gay, W. Brocklehurst
The war poems of a patriot, C. Clark
War poems on Italy, M.N. Sharland
A war quartet, G. Macbeth
War rumours, R. Arkell
War shrapnel, M. Gallati
War songs of the Allies, C. Clark
War sonnets, A.V. Phillips
Warchild, B. Bibby
Wartime harvest, M.C. Stopes
Wartime moods, T. Lovelace
Wartime musings, M. Berners
War time nonsense, Oilb—117—2, pseud.
War-time rhymes, W.H. Phillips
War-time thoughts and impressions, P. Thomson
War-time verse, R.F. Thurtle
War time verses, A.F. Fenn
Was it all in vain?, A.E.W. Rigg
The watcher, W. Wolff
A watching brief, R. McFadden
Water-rat sonata, E. Foxall
The waters, D. Blakelock
The waters of Camelsdale, C. Woodhouse
The wave oracle, N. MacDonald
The way I see it, F. Ramsey
A way of living, I. Little
Way-of-the-world songs, H.M. Forbes
The way of war, P. Winckworth
The ways of God, H.E. Hardy
Wayside thoughts, J. Buswell
Wayside warblings, L. Miles
We burn, M.C. Stopes
We have been told, E.F. Green
We Kentish men, R.C. Faulkner
We pause to weep, G. Pidduck
We take it singing, A. Cashmore
We three, D.E. Boocock
We who are fortunate, A. Rook
The weapon of hate, G. Jones
The weaver birds, I. Serraillier
Weep before God, J. Wain
Welshman in Bloomsbury, T. Earley
Wentworth Place, R. Gittings
West African rhymes, W.W. Barnhill
West of elm, R. Garfitt

West Strand visions, J. Simmons
Westward, J. Buxton
Westward look, R. Herring
What images return, H. Spalding
Wheat by the wine-press, H.N. Forbes
The wheat with the chaff, E.W.F. Gilman
The wheel, L. Horstmann
The wheel of life, J. McLean
Wheels within wheels, G.T. Proud
When fountains fall, S. Johnson
When she cried on Friday, H. Elvin
When soft voices die, E. Christie-Murray
When the gods laugh, C. Macintyre
Where oxen lay, S. Stokes
White allegory, A. Andrews
White cirrus, C.H. Simpson
The white country, R. Fedden
The white island, G. Woodcock
The white knight, J. Bayliss
A white light from the sea, J. Donovan
The white radiance, J.K.G. Hoffman
Whitelight, E. Paterson
Whither shall I wander?, G.P. Symes
Who is God?, B. Grieve
Who laughs last, J.L. Woods
Whose victory?, R.S. Mallone
Wicker basket leaves, S. Weir
Wide horizons, W.A. Dunkerley
Wild buds, G.M. Pritchard
Wild corn, J.P. Rathbone
The wild uncharted country, D. Bolton
The wilderness speaks, N. Burtenshaw
The willow wreath, J. De Bairacli-Levy
Wind on the heath, E. Kelly
The window box, A. Wilkes
Winged thoughts for victory, E. & H. Miles
Winged victory, O.C. Chave
The winged victory, L. Einstein
Winged victory, J.H.W. Palfrey
Wings, H.R. Pyatt
Wings!, F.E. Richbell
Wings of the morning, R.G. Barnes
Wings of youth, L. Taylor
Wings over England, E. Ryott
Winston Churchill, G. St. C. Harley
Winter berries, R. Powell
Winter crop, A.J. Bull
A winter garland, M. Elder
Winter journey, D. Gibson

The winter man, V. Scannell
Winter solstice, G. Bullett
Winter sunshine, M.J. Rickard
Winter war, P. Hartnoll
Wintergreen, T. Hooley
Wise men from the west, A. Esdaile
A wish in season, N. Moore
With love from Judas, E. Brock
With luck lasting, B. Spencer
With lyre and saxophone, G.A. St George
With no changed voice, J. Irvine
With rhyme and reason, E. Iremonger
Within a space, A. Garwood
Within the thunder, H. Dewar
Witness the darkness, E.R. Alder
The witnesses, C. Sansom
A woman's war poems, V. Power
Women of the happy island, J.T.G. Macleod
Wonders of obligation, R. Fisher
Wood chippings, R. Vickers
Wood of my dreams, B. Moody
A word carved on a sill, J. Wain
Word over all, C. Day Lewis
Words and music, A.E. Dodd
Words by request, C. Hassall
Words with a tramp, J.G. Lucas
Work in hand, N. Cameron, R. Graves, A. Hodge
The world at war, A.R. Mark
The world I see, P. Dickinson
World in labour, A. Jackson
World in the heart, R. Porter
The world's my theme, E. Kolbabek
The world my oyster, E. Wright
The world of tomorrow, D.S.S. Steuart
A world stretching out, D. Everett
A world within a war, H. Read
Worlds in a crucible, T. Stephanides
The world's room, L. Whistler
The wounded bird, M.W. Were
Woven on a Kentish loom, C.M.M. Scott
Wrack, P. Worner
A wreath for the living, A. Comfort
Wye Valley verse, G.A. Edwards

A Yank in England, B. Parker
The year, A. Gale
The year, E.J.M.D. Plunkett
Years following after, J. Leftwich

The years of anger, R. Swingler
The years of the right hand, M. Ferrett
The yellow door, J. Urquhart
The yellow night, D. Allison
Yes and no, W. Scammell
Yesterday's prisoner, D.C. Quenby
Yet a little onwards, B. Warr
The yew wreath, J. De Bairacli-Levy
Yorkshire lyrics, D.U. Ratcliffe
You and me, R. Reeve

You and your ships, B.M. Scott
You takes your choice, W.J. Monson
The young men and the old, S. Cloete
Young Mr. Gibbon, R. Greacen
Your finest hour, R. Mathieson
Your thoughts, your dreams, G. Stathis
Youth in the skies, H. Asquith
Youthful poems, P. Spiegal

Zimbabwe tapestry, M. Fourie

War poets
of other English speaking nations

Key. AU, Australia; CA, Canada; NZ, New Zealand; SA, South Africa; US, United States of America; Z, Zimbabwe.

US	ADAMS, Leona V.	Z	BRETTELL, N. H.
US	AIKEN, Conrad	AU	BRIGGS, Ernest
AU	ALLAN, James Alexander	US	BRINNIN, John Malcolm
SA	ALMENDRO, Juan, pseud. (i.e.	CA	BROWN, Audrey Alexandra
	Denis Saunders)	US	BROWN, Harry
AU	ANDERSON, Val	AU	BROWNING, T. S.
US	APPLEMAN, Philip	AU	BUDDEE, Paul
US	AUSLANDER, Joseph	CA	BUNTLIN, Robert F.
AU	AUSTIN, Albert Gordon	US	BURKE, Jenie L.
CA	AYLEN, Elise	AU	BURKITT, H.
US	BACON, Leonard	US	BURLINGAME, Roger
AU	BAKER, C. W.	US	BURT, Struthers
AU	BAKER, Raymond	SA	BUTLER, Guy
US	BAYES, Ronald H.	US	BYRNE, Brooke
AU	BELL, Mary	AU	BYRNES, R. S.
AU	BELLAMY, Victoria M.	NZ	CAMPBELL, Alistair
US	BELOOF, Robert	AU	CAMPBELL, David
US	BENET, Stephen Vincent	AU	CATO, Nancy
US	BENET, William Rose	AU	CHINNERY, A. E. L.
CA	BENSON, Nathaniel A.	US	CHISHOLM, Hugh
AU	BEROS, Bert	US	CIARDI, John
US	BERQUIST, Anne E.	AU	CLARK, Louis H.
US	BERRYMAN, John	AU	CLARKE, Colin G.
US	BEUM, Robert	AU	CLARKE, Donovan
AU	BIGGS, Maurice	CA	CLARKE, George Herbert
CA	BIRNEY, Earle	AU	CLOUGH, Maurice
CA	BOAG, John H.	US	COFFIN, Robert P. Tristram
CA	BOURINOT, Arthur S.	CA	COHEN, Leonard
US	BOWMAN, Peter	CA	COLMAN, Mary Elizabeth
US	BRADBURY, Bianca	US	CONNELLY, Margaret Schaffer
AU	BRADSHAW, K. H.	US	CONVERSE, Florence

CA	CREED, G. L.	US	HOFFMAN, Daniel Gerard
NZ	CURNOW, Allen	US	HORGAN, Paul
NZ	DAVIN, Daniel Marcus	AU	HOSKING, Breffni
AU	DAWE, Bruce	US	HUBBELL, Lindley Williams
AU	DAWES, Allan W.	AU	HUGHES, W. S. Kent
US	DERLETH, August	US	HUMPHRIES, Rolfe
US	DEUTSCH, Babette	AU	INGAMELLS, John
US	DOOLITTLE, Hilda	AU	IRVIN, Eric
US	DORAN, Mark Van	US	JARRELL, Randall
CA	DOWHAN, S. J.	US	JEFFERS, Robinson
US	DUGAN, Alan	CA	JOHNSTON, George
NZ	DUGGAN, Eileen	US	JONES, Leila
US	DURYEE, Mary Ballard	NZ	JOSEPH, Michael Kennedy
AU	DUTTON, Geoffrey	US	JUSTEMA, William
US	EASTMAN, Max	AU	KELAHER, Tip
US	EBERHART, Richard	AU	KELLAWAY, Frank
US	EBRIGHT, Frederick	AU	KINMOUNT, Joan
US	ELFRETH, Emily Allen	US	KIRSTEIN, Lincoln
US	ENGLE, Paul	SA	KRIGE, Uys
AU	FERRIER, N. W.	US	LANGLAND, Joseph
CA	FEWSTER, Ernest	CA	LAWRENCE, Sarah
CA	FINCH, Robert	AU	LEASK, Maurice
AU	FINNIN, Mary	US	LEE, Lawrence
US	FLETCHER, John Gould	US	LEITCH, Mary Sinton
US	FOWLER, Gene	US	LEONARD, Elizabeth Jane
US	FRANCIS, Robert Churchill	CA	LE PAN, Douglas
US	FREEMAN, Arthur	US	LEWIS, James Franklin
US	FRIED, Michael	US	LOWELL, Robert
CA	FRISCH, Anthony	AU	LYLE, Garry
US	FROST, Frances	AU	MACCALLUM, Mungo B.
US	FROST, Robert	US	McGINLEY, Phyllis
AU	FRY, Edith M.	US	McGRATH, Thomas
AU	GALLAGHAN, Patrick	AU	MACKENZIE, Kenneth
AU	GARDNER, Arnold	US	MacLEISH, Archibald
AU	GIFFORD, Kenneth	AU	McMAHON, James
US	GILLMAN, Richard	AU	McNICOLL, David
US	GINSBERG, Louis	US	MAGEE, John Gillespie
US	GIUSEPPE, Neville	CA	MARSHALL, Tom
US	GREGORY, Horace	SA	MARTIN, Michael C.
AU	GRESHAM, Roald	AU	MAYMAN, Ted
US	GRIFFIN, Howard	US	MERTON, Thomas
SA	GULSTON, Charles	AU	MIDDELTON, Peter
US	HALL, Amanda Benjamin	CA	MIDDLETON, J. E.
US	HALL, Donald	US	MILLAY, Edna St Vincent
CA	HARRISON, Elizabeth	US	MILLER, Alice Duer
AU	HARTE, Russel	US	MILLS, Clark
CA	HAUGHEY, Seamus	AU	MOLL, Ernest George
AU	HENDERSON, J.A.	CA	MOODY, Irene H.
CA	HILL, Agnes Aston	US	MOORE, Marianne

AU	MOORE, Tom Inglis	SA	SLATER, Francis Carey
US	MOSS, Stanley	AU	SLESSOR, Kenneth
US	MOWRER, Paul Scott	AU	SMITH, H.E. Wesley
AU	MUDIE, Ian	AU	SMITH, W. Hart
AU	MULLALLY, John	US	SMITH, William Jay
AU	MUNRO, D. V.	US	SMYTHE, Daniel
CA	NASH, Arthur Charles	CA	SOUSTER, Raymond
US	NATHAN, Robert	US	STEVENS, Wallace
US	NEMEROV, Howard	AU	STEWART, T. L.
US	NORMAN, Charles	US	STOUTENBURG, Adrien
AU	OAKES, Russell J.	US	STRALEY, Daniel B.
AU	O'CONNELL, Frank	US	STRYK, Lucien
US	O'CONOR, Norreys Jephson	US	SWAIN, Raymond C.
CA	O'HEARN, Walter	US	TAGGART, Gordon H.
AU	O'LEARY, Shawn	US	TATE, Allen
CA	PAN, Douglas Le	AU	THIELE, Colin
US	PARKER, Dorothy	US	THOMPSON, Dunstan
US	PATCHEN, Kenneth	AU	THOMPSON, John
US	PATTERSON, Frances Taylor	US	THOMSON, Rosamond Dargan
US	PIERCE, Edith Lovejoy	US	TIERNEY, Harry, Jr
US	PORTER, M. A.	SA	TOWNLEY, Noel Francis
CA	PRATT, Edwin John	US	TUCKER, Charles Waller
AU	QUINN, John	AU	TURNER, Alexander
US	RHOADES, John Harsen	US	TUTTLE, Edith
CA	ROBERTS, Sir Charles George Douglas	AU	VALLIS, Val
		US	VAN DOREN, Mark
US	ROBERTS, Walter	AU	VEITCH, A. Scott
US	RODMAN, Selden	US	VIERECK, Peter
NZ	ROSE, Owen	NZ	WALL, Arnold
US	ROSEBERY, Margerite T.	AU	WANNAN, William
US	ROSKOLENKO, Harry	CA	WARR, J. B.
US	ROSTEN, Norman	AU	WATERS, R. A.
US	SANDBURG, Carl	CA	WATT, Frederick Balmer
US	SARTON, May	SA	WATT, Marjorie Campbell
SA	SAUNDERS, Denis, (Juan Almendro, pseud.)	US	WELLS, Eleanor
		CA	WHITE, Sir Thomas
US	SCHEVILL, James	AU	WHITFORD, E. H.
CA	SCOTT, Duncan Campbell	US	WILBUR, Richard
CA	SERVICE, Robert William	US	WILLIAMS, Oscar
US	SHAPIRO, Karl	AU	WILLIAMS, Vic
AU	SIMMONS, Elva	AU	WRIGHT, Judith
US	SIMPSON Louis